Lecture Notes in Artificial Intelligence   13031

Subseries of Lecture Notes in Computer Science

More information about this subseries at http://www.springer.com/series/1244

Duc Nghia Pham · Thanaruk Theeramunkong ·
Guido Governatori · Fenrong Liu (Eds.)

PRICAI 2021: Trends in Artificial Intelligence

18th Pacific Rim
International Conference on Artificial Intelligence, PRICAI 2021
Hanoi, Vietnam, November 8–12, 2021
Proceedings, Part I

Springer

Editors
Duc Nghia Pham
MIMOS Berhad
Kuala Lumpur, Malaysia

Guido Governatori 🄳
Data61
CSIRO
Brisbane, QLD, Australia

Thanaruk Theeramunkong
Sirindhorn International Institute of Science
and Technology
Thammasat University
Mueang Pathum Thani, Thailand

Fenrong Liu 🄳
Department of Philosophy
Tsinghua University
Beijing, China

ISSN 0302-9743   ISSN 1611-3349 (electronic)
Lecture Notes in Artificial Intelligence
ISBN 978-3-030-89187-9   ISBN 978-3-030-89188-6 (eBook)
https://doi.org/10.1007/978-3-030-89188-6

LNCS Sublibrary: SL7 – Artificial Intelligence

This Springer imprint is published by the registered company Springer Nature Switzerland AG
The registered company address is: Gewerbestrasse 11, 6330 Cham, Switzerland

Preface

These three-volume proceedings contain the papers presented at the 18th Pacific Rim International Conference on Artificial Intelligence (PRICAI 2021) held virtually during November 8–12, 2021, in Hanoi, Vietnam.

PRICAI, which was inaugurated in Tokyo in 1990, started out as a biennial international conference concentrating on artificial intelligence (AI) theories, technologies, and applications in the areas of social and economic importance for Pacific Rim countries. It provides a common forum for researchers and practitioners in various branches of AI to exchange new ideas and share experience and expertise. Since then, the conference has grown, both in participation and scope, to be a premier international AI event for all major Pacific Rim nations as well as countries from all around the world. In 2018, the PRICAI Steering Committee decided to hold PRICAI on an annual basis starting from 2019.

This year, we received an overwhelming number of 382 submissions to both the Main track (365 submissions) and the Industry special track (17 submissions). This number was impressive considering that for the first time PRICAI was being held virtually during a global pandemic situation. All submissions were reviewed and evaluated with the same highest quality standard through a double-blind review process. Each paper received at least two reviews, in most cases three, and in some cases up to four. During the review process, discussions among the Program Committee (PC) members in charge were carried out before recommendations were made, and when necessary, additional reviews were sourced. Finally, the conference and program co-chairs read the reviews and comments and made a final calibration for differences among individual reviewer scores in light of the overall decisions. The entire Program Committee (including PC members, external reviewers, and co-chairs) expended tremendous effort to ensure fairness and consistency in the paper selection process. Eventually, we accepted 92 regular papers and 28 short papers for oral presentation. This gives a regular paper acceptance rate of 24.08% and an overall acceptance rate of 31.41%.

The technical program consisted of three tutorials and the main conference program. The three tutorials covered hot topics in AI from "Collaborative Learning and Optimization" and "Mechanism Design Powered by Social Interactions" to "Towards Hyperdemocary: AI-enabled Crowd Consensus Making and Its Real-World Societal Experiments". All regular and short papers were orally presented over four days in parallel and in topical program sessions. We were honored to have keynote presentations by four distinguished researchers in the field of AI whose contributions have crossed discipline boundaries: Mohammad Bennamoun (University of Western Australia, Australia), Johan van Benthem (University of Amsterdam, The Netherlands; Stanford University, USA; and Tsinghua University, China), Virginia Dignum (Umeå University, Sweden), and Yutaka Matsuo (University of Tokyo, Japan). We were grateful to them for sharing their insights on their latest research with us.

The success of PRICAI 2021 would not be possible without the effort and support of numerous people from all over the world. First, we would like to thank the authors, PC members, and external reviewers for their time and efforts spent in making PRICAI 2021 a successful and enjoyable conference. We are also thankful to various fellow members of the conference committee, without whose support and hard work PRICAI 2021 could not have been successful:

– Advisory Board: Hideyuki Nakashima, Abdul Sattar, and Dickson Lukose
– Industry Chair: Shiyou Qian
– Local/Virtual Organizing Chairs: Sankalp Khanna and Adila Alfa Krisnadhi
– Tutorial Chair: Guandong Xu
– Web and Publicity Chair: Md Khaled Ben Islam
– Workshop Chair: Dengji Zhao

We gratefully acknowledge the organizational support of several institutions including Data61/CSIRO (Australia), Tsinghua University (China), MIMOS Berhad (Malaysia), Thammasat University (Thailand), and Griffith University (Australia).

Finally, we thank Springer, Ronan Nugent (Editorial Director, Computer Science Proceedings), and Anna Kramer (Assistant Editor, Computer Science Proceedings) for their assistance in publishing the PRICAI 2021 proceedings as three volumes of its Lecture Notes in Artificial Intelligence series.

November 2021

Duc Nghia Pham
Thanaruk Theeramunkong
Guido Governatori
Fenrong Liu

Organization

PRICAI Steering Committee

Steering Committee

Quan Bai	University of Tasmania, Australia
Tru Hoang Cao	The University of Texas Health Science Center at Houston, USA
Xin Geng	Southeast University, China
Guido Governatori	Data61, CSIRO, Australia
Takayuki Ito	Nagoya Institute of Technology, Japan
Byeong-Ho Kang	University of Tasmania, Australia
M. G. M. Khan	University of the South Pacific, Fiji
Sankalp Khanna	Australian e-Health Research Centre, CSIRO, Australia
Dickson Lukose	Monash University, Australia
Hideyuki Nakashima	Sapporo City University, Japan
Abhaya Nayak	Macquarie University, Australia
Seong Bae Park	Kyung Hee University, South Korea
Duc Nghia Pham	MIMOS Berhad, Malaysia
Abdul Sattar	Griffith University, Australia
Alok Sharma	RIKEN, Japan, and University of the South Pacific, Fiji
Thanaruk Theeramunkong	Thammasat University, Thailand
Zhi-Hua Zhou	Nanjing University, China

Honorary Members

Randy Goebel	University of Alberta, Canada
Tu-Bao Ho	Japan Advanced Institute of Science and Technology, Japan
Mitsuru Ishizuka	University of Tokyo, Japan
Hiroshi Motoda	Osaka University, Japan
Geoff Webb	Monash University, Australia
Albert Yeap	Auckland University of Technology, New Zealand
Byoung-Tak Zhang	Seoul National University, South Korea
Chengqi Zhang	University of Technology Sydney, Australia

Conference Organizing Committee

General Chairs

Guido Governatori	Data61, CSIRO, Australia
Fenrong Liu	Tsinghua University, China

Program Chairs

Duc Nghia Pham   MIMOS Berhad, Malaysia
Thanaruk Theeramunkong   Thammasat University, Thailand

Local/Virtual Organizing Chairs

Sankalp Khanna   Australian e-Health Research Centre, CSIRO, Australia
Adila Alfa Krisnadhi   University of Indonesia, Indonesia

Workshop Chair

Dengji Zhao   ShanghaiTech University, China

Tutorial Chair

Guandong Xu   University of Technology Sydney, Australia

Industry Chair

Shiyou Qian   Shanghai Jiao Tong University, China

Web and Publicity Chair

Md Khaled Ben Islam   Griffith University, Australia

Advisory Board

Hideyuki Nakashima   Sapporo City University, Japan
Abdul Sattar   Griffith University, Australia
Dickson Lukose   Monash University, Australia

Program Committee

Eriko Aiba   The University of Electro-Communications, Japan
Patricia Anthony   Lincoln University, New Zealand
Chutiporn Anutariya   Asian Institute of Technology, Thailand
Mohammad Arshi Saloot   MIMOS Berhad, Malaysia
Yun Bai   University of Western Sydney, Australia
Chutima Beokhaimook   Rangsit University, Thailand
Ateet Bhalla   Independent Technology Consultant, India
Chih How Bong   Universiti Malaysia Sarawak, Malaysia
Poonpong Boonbrahm   Walailak University, Thailand
Aida Brankovic   Australian e-Health Research Centre, CSIRO, Australia
Xiongcai Cai   University of New South Wales, Australia
Tru Cao   University of Texas Health Science Center at Houston, USA
Hutchatai Chanlekha   Kasetsart University, Thailand
Sapa Chanyachatchawan   National Electronics and Computer Technology Center, Thailand
Siqi Chen   Tianjin University, China

Songcan Chen	Nanjing University of Aeronautics and Astronautics, China
Wu Chen	Southwest University, China
Yingke Chen	Sichuan University, China
Wai Khuen Cheng	Universiti Tunku Abdul Rahman, Malaysia
Boonthida Chiraratanasopha	Yala Rajabhat University, Thailand
Phatthanaphong Chomphuwiset	Mahasarakham University, Thailand
Dan Corbett	Optimodal Technologies, USA
Célia Da Costa Pereira	Université Côte d'Azur, France
Jirapun Daengdej	Assumption University, Thailand
Hoa Khanh Dam	University of Wollongong, Australia
Xuan-Hong Dang	IBM Watson Research, USA
Abdollah Dehzangi	Rutgers University, USA
Sang Dinh	Hanoi University of Science and Technology, Vietnam
Clare Dixon	University of Manchester, UK
Shyamala Doraisamy	University Putra Malaysia, Malaysia
Nuttanart Facundes	King Mongkut's University of Technology Thonburi, Thailand
Eduardo Fermé	Universidade da Madeira, Portugal
Somchart Fugkeaw	Thammasat University, Thailand
Katsuhide Fujita	Tokyo University of Agriculture and Technology, Japan
Naoki Fukuta	Shizuoka University, Japan
Marcus Gallagher	University of Queensland, Australia
Dragan Gamberger	Rudjer Boskovic Institute, Croatia
Wei Gao	Nanjing University, China
Xiaoying Gao	Victoria University of Wellington, New Zealand
Xin Geng	Southeast University, China
Manolis Gergatsoulis	Ionian University, Greece
Guido Governatori	Data61, CSIRO, Australia
Alban Grastien	Australian National University, Australia
Charles Gretton	Australian National University, Australia
Fikret Gurgen	Bogazici University, Turkey
Peter Haddawy	Mahidol University, Thailand
Choochart Haruechaiyasak	National Electronics and Computer Technology Center, Thailand
Hamed Hassanzadeh	Australian e-Health Research Centre, CSIRO, Australia
Tessai Hayama	Nagaoka University of Technology, Japan
Juhua Hu	University of Washington, USA
Xiaodi Huang	Charles Sturt University, Australia
Van Nam Huynh	Japan Advanced Institute of Science and Technology, Japan
Norisma Idris	University of Malaya, Malaysia
Mitsuru Ikeda	Japan Advanced Institute of Science and Technology, Japan

Masashi Inoue	Tohoku Institute of Technology, Japan
Takayuki Ito	Kyoto University, Japan
Sanjay Jain	National University of Singapore, Singapore
Guifei Jiang	Nankai University, China
Yichuan Jiang	Southeast University, China
Nattagit Jiteurtragool	Digital Government Development Agency, Thailand
Hideaki Kanai	Japan Advanced Institute of Science and Technology, Japan
Ryo Kanamori	Nagoya University, Japan
Natsuda Kaothanthong	Thammasat University, Thailand
Jessada Karnjana	National Electronics and Computer Technology Center, Thailand
C. Maria Keet	University of Cape Town, South Africa
Gabriele Kern-Isberner	Technische Universitaet Dortmund, Germany
Sankalp Khanna	Australian e-Health Research Centre, CSIRO, Australia
Nichnan Kittiphattanabawon	Walailak University, Thailand
Frank Klawonn	Ostfalia University, Germany
Sébastien Konieczny	CRIL-CNRS, France
Krit Kosawat	National Electronics and Computer Technology Center, Thailand
Alfred Krzywicki	University of New South Wales, Australia
Kun Kuang	Zhejiang University, China
Young-Bin Kwon	Chung-Ang University, South Korea
Weng Kin Lai	Tunku Abdul Rahman University College, Malaysia
Ho-Pun Lam	Data61, CSIRO, Australia
Nasith Laosen	Phuket Rajabhat University, Thailand
Vincent CS Lee	Monash University, Australia
Roberto Legaspi	KDDI Research Inc., Japan
Gang Li	Deakin University, Australia
Guangliang Li	Ocean University of China, China
Tianrui Li	Southwest Jiaotong University, China
Chanjuan Liu	Dalian University of Technology, China
Fenrong Liu	Tsinghua University, China
Michael Maher	Reasoning Research Institute, Australia
Xinjun Mao	National University of Defense Technology, China
Eric Martin	University of New South Wales, Australia
Maria Vanina Martinez	Instituto de Ciencias de la Computación, Argentina
Sanparith Marukatat	National Electronics and Computer Technology Center, Thailand
Michael Mayo	University of Waikato, New Zealand
Brendan McCane	University of Otago, New Zealand
Riichiro Mizoguchi	Japan Advanced Institute of Science and Technology, Japan
Nor Liyana Mohd Shuib	University of Malaya, Malaysia
M. A. Hakim Newton	Griffith University, Australia

Hung Duy Nguyen	Thammasat University, Thailand
Phi Le Nguyen	Hanoi University of Science and Technology, Vietnam
Kouzou Ohara	Aoyama Gakuin University, Japan
Francesco Olivieri	Griffith University, Australia
Mehmet Orgun	Macquarie University, Australia
Noriko Otani	Tokyo City University, Japan
Maurice Pagnucco	University of New South Wales, Australia
Laurent Perrussel	IRIT - Universite de Toulouse, France
Bernhard Pfahringer	University of Waikato, New Zealand
Duc Nghia Pham	MIMOS Berhad, Malaysia
Jantima Polpinij	Mahasarakham University, Thailand
Thadpong Pongthawornkamol	Kasikorn Business-Technology Group, Thailand
Yuhua Qian	Shanxi University, China
Joel Quinqueton	LIRMM, France
Teeradaj Racharak	Japan Advanced Institute of Science and Technology, Japan
Fenghui Ren	University of Wollongong, Australia
Mark Reynolds	University of Western Australia, Australia
Jandson S. Ribeiro	University of Koblenz-Landau, Germany
Kazumi Saito	University of Shizuoka, Japan
Chiaki Sakama	Wakayama University, Japan
Ken Satoh	National Institute of Informatics and Sokendai, Japan
Abdul Sattar	Griffith University, Australia
Nicolas Schwind	National Institute of Advanced Industrial Science and Technology, Japan
Nazha Selmaoui-Folcher	University of New Caledonia, France
Lin Shang	Nanjing University, China
Alok Sharma	RIKEN, Japan
Chenwei Shi	Tsinghua University, China
Zhenwei Shi	Beihang University, China
Mikifumi Shikida	Kochi University of Technology, Japan
Soo-Yong Shin	Sungkyunkwan University, South Korea
Yanfeng Shu	CSIRO, Australia
Tony Smith	University of Waikato, New Zealand
Chattrakul Sombattheera	Mahasarakham University, Thailand
Insu Song	James Cook University, Australia
Safeeullah Soomro	Virginia State University, USA
Tasanawan Soonklang	Silpakorn University, Thailand
Markus Stumptner	University of South Australia, Australia
Merlin Teodosia Suarez	De La Salle University, Philippines
Xin Sun	Catholic University of Lublin, Poland
Boontawee Suntisrivaraporn	DTAC, Thailand
Thepchai Supnithi	National Electronics and Computer Technology Center, Thailand
David Taniar	Monash University, Australia

Thanaruk Theeramunkong	Thammasat University, Thailand
Michael Thielscher	University of New South Wales, Australia
Satoshi Tojo	Japan Advanced Institute of Science and Technology, Japan
Shikui Tu	Shanghai Jiao Tong University, China
Miroslav Velev	Aries Design Automation, USA
Muriel Visani	Hanoi University of Science and Technology, Vietnam and La Rochelle University, France
Toby Walsh	University of New South Wales, Australia
Xiao Wang	Beijing University of Posts and Telecommunications, China
Paul Weng	Shanghai Jiao Tong University, China
Peter Whigham	University of Otago, New Zealand
Wayne Wobcke	University of New South Wales, Australia
Sartra Wongthanavasu	Khon Kaen University, Thailand
Brendon J. Woodford	University of Otago, New Zealand
Kaibo Xie	University of Amsterdam, The Netherlands
Ming Xu	Xi'an Jiaotong-Liverpool University, China
Shuxiang Xu	University of Tasmania, Australia
Hui Xue	Southeast University, China
Ming Yang	Nanjing Normal University, China
Roland Yap	National University of Singapore, Singapore
Kenichi Yoshida	University of Tsukuba, Japan
Takaya Yuizono	Japan Advanced Institute of Science and Technology, Japan
Chengqi Zhang	University of Technology Sydney, Australia
Du Zhang	California State University, USA
Min-Ling Zhang	Southeast University, China
Shichao Zhang	Central South University, China
Wen Zhang	Beijing University of Technology, China
Yu Zhang	Southern University of Science and Technology, China
Zhao Zhang	Hefei University of Technology, China
Zili Zhang	Deakin University, Australia
Yanchang Zhao	Data61, CSIRO, Australia
Shuigeng Zhou	Fudan University, China
Xingquan Zhu	Florida Atlantic University, USA

Additional Reviewers

Aitchison, Matthew
Akhtar, Naveed
Algar, Shannon
Almeida, Yuri
Boudou, Joseph
Burie, Jean-Christophe
Chandra, Abel

Cheng, Charibeth
Damigos, Matthew
Dong, Huanfang
Du Preez-Wilkinson, Nathaniel
Effendy, Suhendry
Eng, Bah Tee
Feng, Xuening

Fu, Keren
Gao, Yi
Geng, Chuanxing
Habault, Guillaume
Hang, Jun-Yi
He, Zhengqi
Hoang, Anh
Huynh, Du
Inventado, Paul Salvador
Jan, Zohaib
Jannai, Tokotoko
Jia, Binbin
Jiang, Zhaohui
Kalogeros, Eleftherios
Karim, Abdul
Kumar, Shiu
Lai, Yong
Laosen, Kanjana
Lee, Nung Kion
Lee, Zhiyi
Li, Weikai
Liang, Yanyan
Liu, Jiexi
Liu, Xiaxue
Liu, Yanli
Luke, Jing Yuan
Mahdi, Ghulam
Mayer, Wolfgang
Mendonça, Fábio
Ming, Zuheng
Mittelmann, Munyque
Nguyen, Duy Hung
Nguyen, Hong-Huy
Nguyen, Mau Toan
Nguyen, Minh Hieu
Nguyen, Minh Le
Nguyen, Trung Thanh
Nikafshan Rad, Hima
Okubo, Yoshiaki
Ong, Ethel
Ostertag, Cécilia

Phiboonbanakit, Thananut
Phua, Yin Jun
Pongpinigpinyo, Sunee
Preto, Sandro
Qian, Junqi
Qiao, Yukai
Riahi, Vahid
Rodrigues, Pedro
Rosenberg, Manou
Sa-Ngamuang, Chaitawat
Scherrer, Romane
Selway, Matt
Sharma, Ronesh
Song, Ge
Su Yin, Myat
Subash, Aditya
Tan, Hongwei
Tang, Jiahua
Teh, Chee Siong
Tettamanzi, Andrea
Tian, Qing
Tran, Vu
Vo, Duc Vinh
Wang, Deng-Bao
Wang, Kaixiang
Wang, Shuwen
Wang, Yuchen
Wang, Yunyun
Wilhelm, Marco
Wu, Linze
Xiangru, Yu
Xing, Guanyu
Xue, Hao
Yan, Wenzhu
Yang, Wanqi
Yang, Yikun
Yi, Huang
Yin, Ze
Yu, Guanbao
Zhang, Jianyi
Zhang, Jiaqiang

Contents – Part I

Data Mining and Knowledge Discovery

Evolutionary Computation/Optimisation

Knowledge Representation and Reasoning

Contents – Part II

Neural Networks and Deep Learning

Contents – Part III

AI Foundations/Decision Theory

Designing Bounded Min-Knapsack Bandits Algorithm for Sustainable Demand Response

Akansha Singh[1], P. Meghana Reddy[1], Shweta Jain[1(✉)], and Sujit Gujar[2]

[1] Indian Institute of Technology, Ropar, India
{2017csb1065,2017csb1094,shwetajain}@iitrpr.ac.in
[2] International Institute of Information Technology, Hyderabad, India
sujit.gujar@iiit.ac.in

Abstract. Recent trends focus on incentivizing consumers to reduce their demand consumption during peak hours for sustainable demand response. To minimize the loss, the distributor companies should target the right set of consumers and demand the right amount of electricity reductions. Almost all the existing algorithms focus on demanding single unit reductions from the selected consumers and thus have limited practical applicability. Even for single unit reductions, none of the work provides a polynomial time constant approximation factor algorithm to minimize the loss to the distributor company. This paper proposes a novel bounded integer min-knapsack algorithm (MinKPDR) and shows that the algorithm, while allowing for multiple unit reduction, also optimizes the loss to the distributor company within a factor of two (multiplicative) and a problem dependant additive constant. The loss is a function of the cost of buying the electricity from the market, costs incurred by the consumers, and compliance probabilities of the consumers. When the compliance probabilities of the consumers are not known, the problem can be formulated as a combinatorial multi-armed bandit (CMAB) problem. Existing CMAB algorithms fail to work in this setting due to the non-monotonicity of a reward function and time varying optimal sets. We propose a novel algorithm (Twin-MinKPDR-CB) to learn these compliance probabilities efficiently. Twin-MinKPDR-CB works for non-monotone reward functions, bounded min-knapsack constraints, and time-varying optimal sets. We theoretically show that Twin-MinKPDR-CB achieves sub-linear regret of $O(\log T)$ with T being the number of rounds for which demand response is run.

1 Introduction

A *Smart Grid* is an electricity network that enables power exchange between the source of electricity generation and its users. One of the major problems that the smart grid faces is a high peak load to average load ratio. Thus, a robust

---

A. Singh and P. M. Reddy—contributed equally.

© Springer Nature Switzerland AG 2021
D. N. Pham et al. (Eds.): PRICAI 2021, LNAI 13031, pp. 3–17, 2021.
https://doi.org/10.1007/978-3-030-89188-6_1

grid requires a lot more safety measures to handle this high ratio. Instead, the best solution would be to shift part of peak load to off-peak hours. Towards this, one can make the smart grid learn human behavior intelligibly and use it to implement informed decisions about the production/consumption of electricity via a *demand response program (DR)*. The demand response makes users more capable of monitoring and accessing ways to handle shortfall or excess electricity and time-varying grid conditions leading to efficient use of the resources and reducing the cost of infrastructure which in turn helps sustainability. There are many ways in which a distribution company (DC) can implement a demand response program. The popular one being introducing dynamic pricing by DC based on the supply shortage. The anticipation is that the consumers will shift their electricity loads to lower-priced – non-peaked hours whenever possible, thus reducing the peak demand. However, the consumers may not well understand such a scheme, leading to inefficiency in the system.

This paper considers a DR program where a DC asks the consumers to voluntarily optimize their electricity consumption by offering certain incentives [14,16,17,23] to a group of consumers. For a profitable DR, DC should select an optimal subset of consumers along with an allocation vector depicting the number of electricity unit reduction it is going to ask the selected consumers. The optimal subset and the allocation vector also depends on the shortage of electricity DC faces. Every consumer has a certain value associated with every unit (KWh) of electricity at that time and expects a compensation equivalent to this valuation for reducing the load. Additionally, each consumer has a limit to the amount of electricity it can reduce. Due to external stochastic factors such as climate change, uncertainty in renewable energy resources at consumers' end, or a sudden increase in workload, there is a certain probability with which the consumer can reduce the electricity. We refer to such probability as *compliance probability* (CP) and is typically unknown to the consumers. The DC's goal is thus to minimize (i) the expected loss, which is a function of the cost of buying the electricity from the market, which in turn depends upon unknown CPs, and (ii) the cost incurred for compensating the consumers via the demand-response program.

Typically, the costs due to shortage or surplus of electricity are quadratic in nature [15,23], thus leading to a quadratic optimization problem with integer constraints. A greedy optimal approach was proposed in [15] to solve the quadratic problem but does not consider the compensation cost to the consumers in the objective function. When these costs are added, the objective function is a non-monotone, supermodular function which in general is hard to optimize up to any approximate guarantees [23]. A greedy algorithm without any approximation guarantees was provided in [23]. Further, all the above approaches work towards solving single-unit reduction problem where each consumer is allowed to reduce only single unit of electricity at a given time. Almost no attempts have been made towards the multi-unit reduction problem except in [7] which proposed a mixed integer linear programming approach with no polynomial time optimal or approximate algorithm. By exploiting the heterogeneity in the consumer base, multiple units reduction provides more flexibility to the DC and ensures cost effective allocation. In this work, we introduce a novel transformation of the problem to the bounded min knapsack framework for demand response, MinKPDR and prove its equivalence up to an additional problem dependent constant factor. The bounded min-knapsack problem is a well studied problem with 2−approximate polynomial algorithms. Thus, MinKPDR framework not only helps us in obtaining polynomial time algorithm with approximate guarantees but also enables us an easy extension to multi-unit reduction case.

When CPs of the consumers are not known, they can be learnt using *combinatorial multi-armed bandits* (CMAB) algorithm by selecting different subsets of consumers at different rounds [14,15]. The existing combinatorial MAB (CMAB) literature [5] heavily relies on two assumptions: (i) The reward function is monotone in terms of the stochastic rewards (compliance probabilities in our case), and (ii) The optimal set is fixed over a period of time. The first assumption does not hold even for a single unit reduction case and since the amount of shortage of electricity varies over time, the optimal set changes every time thus violating the second assumption. Typically, if one has monotone reward functions, upper confidence bound (UCB) based algorithms work well in practice. Non-monotone reward function necessitates the design of a novel MAB algorithm. Towards this, we propose an ingenious combination of UCB and LCB (lower confidence bounds) to learn CPs in demand-response. Basically, we solve the problem twice, once with UCB in constraints and its twin problem – the same problem with LCB in constraints and opt for a solution better out of these two. We call the learning version of MinKPDR as Twin-MinKPDR-CB. We prove that Twin-MinKPDR-CB achieves sub-linear regret of $O(\log T)$ to learn CPs, with T being the number of rounds for which demand response is run. In summary, the following are our contributions.

- Transforming the optimization problem to a bounded integer min-knapsack problem and proving its equivalence up to an additional problem dependent constant factor.
- Proposing a novel combinatorial MAB algorithm Twin-MinKPDR-CB that solves TWIN problems every round to determine optimal set in the round and works with non-monotone reward function, along with the bounded min-knapsack constraints, and time varying optimal sets.
- Theoretically bounding the regret of Twin-MinKPDR-CB as $O(\log T)$, where T is the number of rounds for which the demand response is run.

2   Related Work

Popular demand response methods such as time-of-day tariff [2,12,21,22], real-time pricing [4], critical peak pricing [20,25], direct load control [11] and demand bidding [3] are generally too complex and are not well understood by the consumers. Instead of dynamic pricing for the electricity market, many works proposed different simpler and efficient incentive mechanisms to provide the offers to the consumers to incentivize them to reduce the electricity by their own [14–18,23]. The main challenge towards designing these mechanisms is to select the right subset of consumers and ask for the right amount of reductions from these consumers which is generally a hard problem. Optimal allocation of reductions units amongst the consumers is very important as it affects the efficiency of the proposed mechanism significantly. All the above works consider single unit reduction only and do not provide any polynomial time algorithm with good approximation guarantees that minimizes the loss to the distributor company. This paper provides a polynomial time algorithm for multi-unit reduction case with good approximation guarantees.

The most general works towards designing combinatorial MABs [5,6] assume the monotonicity on the reward function which fails to exist in our setting due to the quadratic nature of the loss function. The max-knapsack version [1] or the general concave reward function [24] seems to be a special version of our problem but in their framework, the concavity of the reward function and constraints are defined over a complete time period T, whereas in our case we have a non-monotone concave reward function each time. Hence these methods cannot be extended to the setting with time varying optimal sets. Further, in a typical CMAB framework, an arm is pulled only once at a given round whereas a multi-unit case requires pulling multiple instances of the arms at each round – we refer to it as *duplicating arms*. The closest work to duplicate arm setting considers a simple linear and monotone reward function [9].

Min-knapsack constraint problem further looks similar to assured accuracy bandit (AAB) framework [13] for a single unit case. AAB will lead to high regret in this setting because it aims to satisfy the constraint at each time which is not required in our setting. Further, the reward function in [13] was independent of stochastic parameters (CPs) as opposed to quadratic in our case. A general demand response model considered in [7] works with multi-unit reductions under the budget constraint on the number of consumers that can be selected at each round. However, a mixed integer linear programming (MILP) approach was proposed with no polynomial time optimal or approximate algorithm to solve the same.

3   Mathematical Model

There are $N = \{1, 2, \ldots, n\}$ consumers available for the demand response to whom a distributor company (DC) is distributing the electricity. Each consumer i has three quantities associated with them, k_i representing maximum units that the consumer i can reduce, c_i representing the compensation cost per unit reduction, and p_i denoting the probability of reducing one unit of electricity also known as compliance probability (CP). The DC asks the consumers to report their compensation cost c_i and maximum units of reduction k_i to participate in the demand response. If a consumer successfully reduces one electricity unit, he receives the offer of c_i per unit reduction. Thus, it is always beneficial for the consumer to reduce the electricity to the maximum units that he can. However, due to uncertainties at consumers' end such as failing to generate the expected electricity (renewable resources at consumers end), a consumer may not be able to reduce the required electricity units. This uncertainty is depicted by the quantity p_i which denotes the probability of reducing one unit of electricity.

There are two possibilities in which these uncertainties can be taken care of. One is to impose the penalties to the consumers in case they commit to reduce the consumption but they fail to reduce the committed reduction [16,17]. However, such penalties may disincentivize the consumers to participate in the demand response. Instead, we would like to design a demand response that subsumes these uncertainties in the optimization problem itself. Therefore, our goal is not only to select the consumers who have a lower cost of reducing the electricity but at the same time should also have a higher probability of reducing the electricity once committed for the demand response. Thus, apart from minimizing the costs, the demand response would minimize the variance to weed out the consumers with low CPs.

At each round t, a distributor company encounters a shortage of $\mathcal{E}_t \neq 0$ and the goal is to select an allocation vector of reduction units $\mathbf{x}_t = (x_{1,t}, x_{2,t}, \ldots, x_{n,t})$ where $x_{i,t}$ represents the amount of electricity units asked from a consumer i at time t to reduce. Let S_t and $|S_t|$ be the set and number of consumers who are asked to reduce at least one unit of electricity i.e. $S_t = \{i | x_{i,t} > 0\}$. At the round t, whatever shortage the distributor company faces, it would have to buy from the market and the cost of buying the electricity from the market leads to quadratic loss [13,15]. Even if a consumer i is asked to reduce $x_{i,t}$ units of electricity at time t, due to uncertainties involved, the actual units of electricity reduced will be a random variable. Let $X_{i,t}$ denote the actual units of electricity that consumer i reduces at time t. If the allocation vector at time t is $\mathbf{x}_t$, then the cost of buying the electricity from the market is proportional to: $M_t(\mathbf{x}_t) = \left(\sum_{i \in S_t} X_{i,t} - \mathcal{E}_t\right)^2$.

We assume that if the consumer i is asked to reduce $x_{i,t}$ units than he/she reduces each unit independently with probability p_i. Hence, $X_{i,t}$ is a binomial random variable with parameters $(x_{i,t}, p_i)$ such that $0 \leq x_{i,t} \leq k_i$. Let C represents the cost to buy the electricity from the market then the final expected loss $\mathbb{E}L(\mathbf{x}_t)$ at round t is given as the sum of the loss incurred due to buying electricity from the market and the expected compensation to the agents, i.e.

$$\mathbb{E}L(\mathbf{x}_t) = \mathbb{E}\left[CM_t(\mathbf{x}_t) + \sum_{i \in S_t} X_{i,t} c_i\right] = C\mathbb{E}M_t(\mathbf{x}_t) + \sum_{i \in S_t} p_i x_{i,t} c_i$$

$$= C\mathbb{E}\left[\left(\sum_{i \in S_t} Y_{i,t}\right)^2\right] + \sum_{i \in S_t} p_i x_{i,t} c_i = Cvar\left(\sum_{i \in S_t} Y_{i,t}\right) + C\left(\mathbb{E}\left[\sum_{i \in S_t} Y_{i,t}\right]\right)^2 + \sum_{i \in S_t} p_i x_{i,t} c_i$$

$$(Y_{i,t} = X_{i,t} - \mathcal{E}_t/|S_t|)$$

$$= C\left(\sum_{i \in S_t} x_{i,t} p_i - \mathcal{E}_t\right)^2 + C\sum_{i \in S_t} x_{i,t} p_i (1 - p_i) + \sum_{i \in S_t} x_{i,t} p_i c_i \qquad (1)$$

The goal is to select an allocation vector $\mathbf{x}_t$ so as to minimize $\mathbb{E}L(\mathbf{x}_t)$. Let c_{max} denote the maximum cost that any consumer incurs for a single unit of electricity i.e. $c_{max} = \max_i c_i$, we assume that the distributor company will always prefer to ask the consumers to reduce the electricity as opposed to buying from the electricity market i.e. $C \geq c_{max}$.

MinKPDR for Single Unit Reduction

For a better understanding of the novel transformation to the min-knapsack problem, let us first consider a simple setting with $k_i = 1\ \forall i$. The optimization problem becomes choosing a subset S_t to minimize $\mathbb{E}L(S_t)$ which is given as:

$$
C \left(\sum_{i \in S_t} p_i - \mathcal{E}_t \right)^2 + C \sum_{i \in S_t} p_i(1 - p_i) + \sum_{i \in S_t} p_i c_i \tag{2}
$$

Even though this problem is a significantly easier version of the original multi-unit version, it is still a minimization of a super-modular, non-monotone function [23]. It has been shown that it is impossible to approximate an arbitrary super-modular non-monotone function up to a constant factor [19]. A greedy algorithm achieving a local optimal solution was proposed in [23]. However, the global solution can be very far from the local optima. Further, their method could not be extended to the multi-unit case. By exploiting the assumption of $C \geq c_{max}$, we provide a novel framework by drawing an interesting relation from the min-knapsack problem for which a 2-approximate greedy algorithm exists [8]. With known CPs, our min-knapsack algorithm for demand response (MinKPDR) for single unit reduction works as follows. At round t, if $\sum_{i=1}^{n} p_i \leq \mathcal{E}_t$ then return $S_t = N$ otherwise return S_t by solving the following:

$$
\min_{S_t} \sum_{i \in S_t} \{Cp_i(1 - p_i) + p_i c_i\} \quad \text{s.t.} \quad \sum_{i \in S_t} p_i \geq \mathcal{E}_t \tag{3}
$$

3.1   Approximation Ratio of MinKPDR

We now prove that there is no significant difference in solving the minimum knapsack problem as oppose to the original problem. This is an interesting result because it proves that the seemingly hard problem can be converted to a well known problem for which greedy algorithms with a good approximate ratio exists such as 2-approximate algorithm proposed in [8].

Let us denote ε_t^* and ε_t as the difference between shortage of electricity and the total reduction by the consumers from the optimal set S_t^* to Eq. (2) and optimal set $\tilde{S}_t$ to Eq. (3) respectively i.e. $\varepsilon_t^* = \mathcal{E}_t - \sum_{i \in S_t^*} p_i$ and $\varepsilon_t = \mathcal{E}_t - \sum_{i \in \tilde{S}_t} p_i$. We begin with following bounds on ε_t^* and ε_t.

Lemma 1. *If $\tilde{S}_t \neq N$ then $-1 < \varepsilon_t < 0$.*

Proof. If $\varepsilon_t < -1$, then MinKPDR algorithm can drop at least one consumer from $\tilde{S}_t$ and can strictly reduce the objective function in Eq. (3).

Lemma 2. *If $\varepsilon_t^* > 0$ then either $\varepsilon_t^* < 1$ or $S_t^* = N$.*

Proof. If $\varepsilon_t^* > 1$ and $S_t^* \neq N$ then $\exists k \notin S_t^*$, thus:

$$\mathbb{EL}(S_t^*) - \mathbb{EL}(S_t^* \cup \{k\}) = C\varepsilon_t^{*2} - C(p_k - \varepsilon_t^*)^2 - Cp_k(1 - p_k) - cp_k$$
$$= -Cp_k^2 + 2C\varepsilon_t^* p_k - Cp_k + Cp_k^2 - c_k p_k > 0$$
$$(c \leq C, \varepsilon_t^* > 1)$$

Leading to the contradiction that S_t^* is the optimal set.

Theorem 1. *Let $\tilde{S}_t$ be the selected set from solving Eq. (3) and S_t^* be the optimal set from solving Eq. (2). Then $\mathbb{EL}(\tilde{S}_t) \leq \mathbb{EL}(S_t^*) + 4C + 1$.*

Proof. Let $g(\tilde{S}_t)$ represent the objective function value of Eq. (3). If $\varepsilon_t^* \leq 0$ then $g(\tilde{S}_t) \leq g(S_t^*)$. When $\varepsilon_t^* > 0$ and $S_t^* \neq N$ then let $S_{new} = S_t^* \cup S_{ext}$ be the set such that $\sum_{i \in S_{new}} p_i \geq \mathcal{E}_t$ and S_{ext} includes minimum number of such consumers. If such a set is not possible, $S_{new} = N$. From Lemma 2, $\varepsilon_t^* < 1$ and thus $\sum_{i \in S_{ext}} p_i \leq 2$. The reason is we are at max one unit short and we cannot overshoot much since $p_i < 1 \ \forall i$. $g(S_{new}) - g(S_t^*) = C\sum_{i \in S_{ext}} p_i(1 - p_i) + \sum_{i \in S_{ext}} p_i c_i \leq 4C$. Further, if $\sum_{i \in S_t^*} p_i < \mathcal{E}_t$ and $S_t^* = N$, then $g(S_t^*) = g(\tilde{S}_t)$. Thus, $g(\tilde{S}_t) \leq g(S_t^*) + 4C$. We now have following two cases:

Case 1: $\tilde{S}_t \neq N$: From Lemma 1, $\mathbb{EL}(\tilde{S}_t) = g(\tilde{S}_t) + \varepsilon_t^2 \leq g(S_t^*) + 4C + 1 \leq \mathbb{EL}(S_t^*) + 4C + 1$.

Case 2: $\tilde{S}_t = N$: In this case, $\varepsilon_t < \varepsilon_t^*$. Thus, $\mathbb{EL}(\tilde{S}_t) = g(N) + \varepsilon_t^2 \leq g(S_t^*) + 4C + \varepsilon_t^{*2} \leq \mathbb{EL}(S_t^*) + 4C$.

Note: If the selected set S_t is $\alpha-$approx solution to Eq. (3), then $\mathbb{EL}(S_t) \leq g(S_t) + 1 \leq \alpha g(\tilde{S}_t) + 1 \leq \alpha(g(S_t^*) + 4C + 1) + 1$.

MinKPDR for Multi-unit Reduction

For multi-unit case, at each round t, the algorithm outputs $\mathbf{x}_t = \{x_{1,t}, \ldots, x_{n,t}\}$ so as to minimize:

$$C\left(\sum_{i \in S_t} x_{i,t} p_i - \mathcal{E}_t\right)^2 + C\sum_{i \in S_t} x_{i,t} p_i(1 - p_i) + \sum_{i \in S_t} x_{i,t} p_i c_i \quad \text{s.t.} \ \ 0 \leq x_{i,t} \leq k_i$$

$$(4)$$

At any round t, if $\sum_{i=1}^n k_i p_i < \mathcal{E}_t$ then $\mathbf{x}_t = \{k_1, k_2, \ldots, k_n\}$ else solve the following:

$$\min_{\mathbf{x}_t} C\sum_{i \in S_t} x_{i,t} p_i(1 - p_i) + \sum_{i \in S_t} x_{i,t} p_i c_i \quad \text{s.t.} \ \ \sum_{i \in S_t} x_{i,t} p_i \geq \mathcal{E}_t \text{ and } 0 \leq x_{i,t} \leq k_i \ \forall i$$

$$(5)$$

This is the bounded min-knapsack problem where instead of one instance, k_i instances of the item i are available. Thus, any min-knapsack algorithm can be used to solve its bounded version with same approximation factor but maybe with an increased complexity. Further, the following theorem follows the exact same steps as the proof of Theorem 1.

Theorem 2. *Let $\tilde{\mathbf{x}}_t$ be the optimal allocation vector to Eq. (5) and $\mathbf{x}_t^*$ be the allocation vector to Eq. (4). Then $\mathbb{E}L(\tilde{\mathbf{x}}_t) \leq \mathbb{E}L(\mathbf{x}_t^*) + 4C + 1$.*

4 Multi-armed Bandit Setting for Unknown CPs

When the compliance probabilities of the consumers are not known, these have to be learnt over a period of time. The problem can be formulated as the combinatorial multi-armed bandit problem (CMAB), where at each round a subset of arms (consumers) need to be selected and the reward (amount of electricity reduced) from these arms are observed. We first note that the existing CMAB algorithms will not work in our setting due to the following reasons:

1. All the UCB based algorithms [5,6] assume monotonicity on stochastic parameters (CP) which is not the case here (Lemma 3)
2. The naive algorithms such as epsilon-greedy or Thompson sampling algorithm do not work with constraints.

Lemma 3. *The multi-unit loss function in Eq. (4) is not monotone in terms of compliance probabilities.*

Proof. This can be proved by using a counter example, let us take 2 agents with $p_1 = 0.6; x_{1,t} = 2; p_2 = 0.3; x_{2,t} = 0; E_t = 1; p_1' = 0.9; p_2' = 0.3; p_1'' = 0.3; p_2'' = 0.3$. For $C = 11, c_1 = 1$, we have, $\mathbb{E}_p(x_t) \leq \mathbb{E}_{p''}(x_t)$ and $\mathbb{E}_p(x_t) \leq \mathbb{E}_{p'}(x_t)$.

4.1 Regret Definition

Since finding the optimal allocation is hard, we define the regret at round t as the difference in the cost of the allocation vector $\mathbf{x}_t$ returned by our algorithm with unknown CPs and the cost of the allocation vector $\tilde{\mathbf{x}}_t$ obtained by MinKPDR with known CPs i.e. $\mathcal{R}_t(\mathbf{x}_t) = \mathbb{E}L(\mathbf{x}_t) - \mathbb{E}L(\tilde{\mathbf{x}}_t)$.

4.2 Proposed MAB Algorithm: Twin-MinKPDR-CB

Under monotonicity assumption, existing algorithms [5,6] use Upper confidence bound (UCB) based algorithm that work on the principle of optimism in the face of uncertainty. Twin-MinKPDR-CB (Algorithm 1) uses both UCB and lower confidence bound (LCB) to intelligently select the allocation vector. Let us denote $\hat{p}_{i,t}^+ = \hat{p}_{i,t} + \sqrt{\frac{2\ln t}{n_i(t)}}$ and $\hat{p}_{i,t}^- = \hat{p}_{i,t} - \sqrt{\frac{2\ln t}{n_i(t)}}$ as UCB and LCB on CPs respectively. Here, $\hat{p}_{i,t}$ is the estimated value of CP which denote the fraction of units of electricity reduced to the units of electricity reduction allotted to the consumer i till round t. And $n_i(t)$ denotes the number of units allocated to consumer i till round t. The algorithm starts with allocating the complete set at first round and initializing the bounds on $\hat{p}_{i,t}^+$ (with upper bound as 1) and $\hat{p}_{i,t}^-$ (with lower bound as 0). The following two twin problems are solved at round t:

Algorithm 1: Twin-MinKPDR-CB

Input: $\{c_1, c_2, ...c_n\}$, $\{k_1, k_2, ...k_n\}$, Number of Rounds T.
Output: Allocations in each round $\mathbf{x}_1, \mathbf{x}_2, ...\mathbf{x}_T$
1. $\mathbf{x}_1 = \{k_1, k_2, ...k_n\}$ Make offer of full amount of electricity they can reduce to get initial estimate of CPs. i.e $n_i(1) = k_i \; \forall i$.
2. **for** $t \leftarrow 2 : T$ **do**

    Observe the values of D_t and $X_{i,t-1}$ i.e actual amount reduced by i at $t-1$.

    Update $\hat{p}_i = \frac{\sum_{t'=1}^{t-1} X_{i,t'}}{n_i(t-1)}$, $\hat{p}_i^+ = \hat{p}_i + \sqrt{\frac{2\ln t}{n_i(t-1)}}$ and $\hat{p}_i^- = \hat{p}_i - \sqrt{\frac{2\ln t}{n_i(t-1)}}$.

    Solve for $\mathbf{x}_t^+$, $\mathbf{x}_t^-$ from (6) and (7) and substitute in (8) and (9) to obtain $\mathbb{EL}_{\hat{p}_t^+}(x_t^+)$ and $\mathbb{EL}_{\hat{p}_t^-}(x_t^-)$ respectively.

    if $\mathbb{EL}_{\hat{p}_t^+}(\mathbf{x}_t^+) < \mathbb{EL}_{\hat{p}_t^-}(\mathbf{x}_t^-)$ **then**

        $\mathbf{x}_t = \mathbf{x}_t^+$, $\tilde{p} = p_i^+$

    else

        $\mathbf{x}_t = \mathbf{x}_t^-$, $\tilde{p} = p_i^-$

$$\min_{\mathbf{x}_t^+} C \sum_{i \in S_t^+} x_{i,t}^+ \hat{p}_{i,t}^- (1 - \hat{p}_{i,t}^+) + \sum_{i \in S_t^+} x_{i,t}^+ \hat{p}_{i,t}^- c_i \;\; \text{s.t.} \sum_{i \in S_t^+} x_{i,t}^+ \hat{p}_{i,t}^+ \geq \mathcal{E}_t \quad (6)$$

$$\min_{\mathbf{x}_t^-} C \sum_{i \in S_t^-} x_{i,t}^- \hat{p}_{i,t}^- (1 - \hat{p}_{i,t}^+) + \sum_{i \in S_t^-} x_{i,t}^- \hat{p}_{i,t}^- c_i \;\; \text{s.t.} \sum_{i \in S_t^-} x_{i,t}^- \hat{p}_{i,t}^- \geq \mathcal{E}_t \quad (7)$$

Let $\mathbf{x}_t^+$ and $\mathbf{x}_t^-$ be the allocated vectors by solving Eqs. (6) and (7) respectively. The expected loss functions will be:

$$\mathbb{EL}_{\hat{p}_t^+}(x_t^+) = C \left(\sum_{i \in S_t^+} x_{i,t}^+ \hat{p}_i^+ - \mathcal{E}_t \right)^2 + C \sum_{i \in S_t^+} x_{i,t}^+ \hat{p}_i^- (1 - \hat{p}_i^+) + \sum_{i \in S_t^+} x_{i,t}^+ \hat{p}_i^- c_i \quad (8)$$

$$\mathbb{EL}_{\hat{p}_t^-}(x_t^-) = C \left(\sum_{i \in S_t^-} x_{i,t}^- \hat{p}_i^- - \mathcal{E}_t \right)^2 + C \sum_{i \in S_t^+} x_{i,t}^- \hat{p}_i^- (1 - \hat{p}_i^+) + \sum_{i \in S_t^+} x_{i,t}^- \hat{p}_i^- c_i \quad (9)$$

Let $\mathbb{EL}_{\tilde{p}}(\mathbf{x}_t)$ be the minimum loss from the above two equations i.e. $\mathbb{EL}_{\tilde{p}}(\mathbf{x}_t) = \min\{\mathbb{EL}_{\hat{p}_t^+}(\mathbf{x}_t^+), \mathbb{EL}_{\hat{p}_t^-}(\mathbf{x}_t^-)\}$ and $\tilde{p} = argmin_{\hat{p}_t^+, \hat{p}_t^-}\{\mathbb{EL}_{\hat{p}_t^+}(\mathbf{x}_t^+), \mathbb{EL}_{\hat{p}_t^-}(\mathbf{x}_t^-)\}$. Then, Twin-MinKPDR-CB simply returns $\mathbf{x}_t$.

4.3 Regret of Twin-MinKPDR-CB:

In order to bound the regret, we need two properties monotonicity and the bounded smoothness property that we prove next.

Lemma 4. *Let* $\mathbb{EL}_p(\mathbf{x}_t)$ *be the expected loss function of* $\mathbf{x}_t$ *with true CP vector* p. *Then,* $\mathbb{EL}_{\tilde{p}}(\mathbf{x}_t) \leq \mathbb{EL}_p(\mathbf{x}_t)$.

Proof. From Hoeffding's inequality, for each i, $\hat{p}_{i,t}^- \leq p_i \leq \hat{p}_{i,t}^+$ with probability $1 - 2t^{-2}$. Thus, $\forall i, \forall \mathbf{x}_t$, with probability $1 - 2nt^{-2}$, we have:

$$\sum_{i \in S_t} x_{i,t} \hat{p}_{i,t}^- - \mathcal{E}_t \leq \sum_{i \in S_t} x_{i,t} p_i - \mathcal{E}_t \leq \sum_i x_{i,t} \hat{p}_{i,t}^+ - \mathcal{E}_t$$

$$\sum_i x_{i,t} \hat{p}_{i,t}^-(1 - \hat{p}_{i,t}^+) \leq \sum_i x_{i,t} p_i (1 - p_i) \text{ and } \sum_i x_{i,t} \hat{p}_{i,t}^- c_i \leq \sum_i x_{i,t} p_i c_i$$

Thus, $\mathbb{EL}_{\tilde{p}}(x_t) \leq \mathbb{EL}_p(x_t)$.

Lemma 5. *Bounded Smoothness Property:* *Consider any two CP vectors* $p = \{p_1, p_2, \dots, p_n\}$ *and* $p' = \{p_1', p_2', \dots, p_n'\}$, *then* $|\mathbb{EL}_p(\mathbf{x}_t) - \mathbb{EL}_{p'}(\mathbf{x}_t)| \leq f(\delta)$ *if* $|p_i - p_i'| \leq \delta \; \forall i$ *where* f *is a strictly increasing and invertible function.*

Proof. Let $K = \sum_i k_i \geq \sum_{i \in S_t} k_i \geq \sum_{i \in S_t} x_{i,t}$ We have:

$$\left| \sum_{i \in S_t} x_{i,t} p_i c_i - \sum_{i \in S_t} x_{i,t} p_i' c_i \right| \leq \delta \sum_{i \in S_t} x_{i,t} c_i \leq KC\delta$$

$$\left| \sum_{i \in S_t} x_{i,t} p_i (1 - p_i) - \sum_{i \in S_t} x_{i,t} p_i' (1 - p_i') \right| \leq \sum_{i \in S_t} x_{i,t} |p_i - p_i'| (1 + |p_i + p_i'|) \leq 3K\delta$$

$$\left| \left(\sum_{i \in S_t} x_{i,t} p_i - \mathcal{E}_t \right)^2 - \left(\sum_{i \in S_t} x_{i,t} p_i' - \mathcal{E}_t \right)^2 \right|$$

$$\leq \left| \sum_{i \in S_t} x_{i,t} p_i + \sum_{i \in S_t} x_{i,t} p_i' \right| \left| \sum_{i \in S_t} x_{i,t} p_i - \sum_{i \in S_t} x_{i,t} p_i' \right| \leq 2K^2\delta$$

Thus,

$$|\mathbb{EL}_p(x) - \mathbb{EL}_{p'}(x)| \leq f(\delta) = (4CK + 2CK^2)\delta \tag{10}$$

Even when we have these two properties, the regret bound proof cannot follow the proof provided in [6] as the optimal set in our setting varies each time as opposed to a fixed optimal set. Another important difference is that the optimal as well as the selected set by the algorithm can be an empty set. We define an allocation $\mathbf{x}_t$ as suboptimal when $\mathbb{EL}(\mathbf{x}_t) > \mathbb{EL}(\tilde{\mathbf{x}}_t)$. Recall that $\tilde{\mathbf{x}}_t$ is the allocation vector obtained by MinKPDR with known CPs. Let $T_{i,t}$ be the number of times consumer i is allocated atleast one unit of electricity reduction till time t. We maintain the counters $N_{i,t} \leq T_{i,t}$ for all consumers in the following way. We initialize the $N_{i,1} = 1 \; \forall i$ after the first round since the allocation happens to all the consumers. At any round t if a suboptimal allocation is chosen, we increment $N_{i,t}$ of a consumer i by one where i is chosen such that $x_{i,t} > 0$ and $i = \arg\min_j \{N_{j,t} | x_{j,t} > 0\}$. If many such consumers exists, we pick one such random i. We now show that for each sub-optimal allocation (including no allocation), the counter of exactly one consumer is incremented everytime.

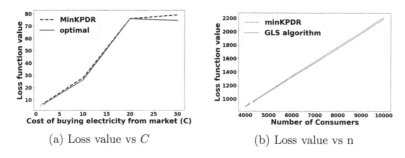

(a) Loss value vs C (b) Loss value vs n

Fig. 1. Loss comparison of MinKPDR

Lemma 6. *If* $\mathbf{x}_{i,t} = 0 \ \forall i$ *then* $\tilde{\mathbf{x}}_{i,t} = 0 \ \forall i$

Proof. $\mathbf{x}_{i,t} = 0 \ \forall i$ then $\mathbb{E}L_{\tilde{p}}(x_t) = C\mathcal{E}_t^2 \leq \mathbb{E}L_{\tilde{p}}(\tilde{\mathbf{x}}_t) \leq \mathbb{E}L_p(\tilde{\mathbf{x}}_t) \implies \tilde{\mathbf{x}}_{i,t} = 0 \ \forall i$. Here first inequality is due to the optimization problem solved by MinKPDR and second inequality is due to Lemma 4.

Now, let $\Delta = \min\{\mathbb{E}L_p(\mathbf{x}_t) - \mathbb{E}L_p(\tilde{\mathbf{x}}_t) | \mathbb{E}L_p(\mathbf{x}_t) > \mathbb{E}L_p(\tilde{\mathbf{x}}_t)\}$ and $l_t = \frac{8 \ln t}{(f^{-1}(\Delta))^2}$. Let $\mathcal{E}_{max} = \max_t\{\mathcal{E}_t\}$, then the maximum regret at any round t is upperbounded by $\mathcal{E}_{max}$ and the expected regret is bounded by: $\mathbb{E}[\sum_{i=1}^n N_{i,T}]C\mathcal{E}_{max}^2$.

Theorem 3. *The regret of the algorithm is bounded by* $\left(\frac{8 \ln T}{(f^{-1}(\Delta))^2} + \frac{\pi^2}{3} + 1\right)nC\mathcal{E}_{max}^2$

Proof. The following steps are similar to [6]:

$$\sum_{i=1}^n N_{i,T} - n(l_T + 1) = \sum_{n+1}^T \mathbb{I}(\mathbf{x}_t \neq \tilde{\mathbf{x}}_t) - nl_T \leq \sum_{t=n+1}^T \sum_{i=1}^n \mathbb{I}(\mathbf{x}_t \neq \tilde{\mathbf{x}}_t, N_{i,t} > N_{i,t-1}, N_{i,t-1} > l_T)$$

$$\leq \sum_{t=n+1}^T \sum_{i=1}^n \mathbb{I}(x_t \neq x_t^*, N_{i,t} > N_{i,t-1}, N_{i,t-1} > l_t) = \sum_{t=n+1}^T \mathbb{I}(\mathbf{x}_t \neq \tilde{\mathbf{x}}_t, \forall i : x_{i,t} > 0, T_{i,t-1} > l_t)$$

When $T_{i,t-1} > l_t \ \forall i$, from Hoeffding's bound we have:

$$\mathbb{P}\left(|\hat{p}_{i,t}^+ - p_i| > f^{-1}(\Delta)\right) \leq \mathbb{P}\left(|\hat{p}_{i,t}^+ - p_i| \geq 2\sqrt{\frac{2 \ln t}{T_{i,t-1}}}\right) \leq 2t^{-2}$$

$$\mathbb{P}\left(|\hat{p}_{i,t}^- - p_i| > f^{-1}(\Delta)\right) \leq \mathbb{P}\left(|\hat{p}_{i,t}^- - p_i| \geq 2\sqrt{\frac{2 \ln t}{T_{i,t-1}}}\right) \leq 2t^{-2}$$

Thus with probability $1 - 2nt^{-2}$, $\mathbb{E}L_p(\mathbf{x}_t) < \mathbb{E}L_{\tilde{p}}(\mathbf{x}_t) + \Delta \leq \mathbb{E}L_{\tilde{p}}(\tilde{\mathbf{x}}_t) + \Delta \leq \mathbb{E}L_p(\tilde{\mathbf{x}}_t) + \Delta$ Here, the first inequality comes from the Bounded smoothness property, second from the definition of $\mathbf{x}_t$, and third from Lemma 4. Thus, leading to the contradiction to the definition of Δ. Thus, the expected regret is bounded by $\left(n(l_T + 1) + \sum_{t=1}^T \frac{2n}{t^2}\right)C\mathcal{E}_{max}^2 \leq \left(\frac{8 \ln T}{(f^{-1}(\Delta))^2} + \frac{\pi^2}{3} + 1\right)nC\mathcal{E}_{max}^2$.

From Lemma 5, $f^{-1}(\Delta) \propto K^2$, thus leading $O(n^5)$ regret. This upper bound is attributed to the fact that although we are pulling several instances of arm i at one instance, we are incrementing the counter $N_{i,t}$ only once. However, we can see from the simulation section, the regret turns out to be quadratic in n.

5   Simulation Results

The goal of the simulation-based experiments is two-fold, (i) to study the efficacy of MinKPDR as compared to bruteforce and GLS in an offline setting, and (ii) Validate our theoretical results about regret. To compare our algorithms, we take two benchmark algorithms, first the brute force algorithm that considers all possible subsets (hence takes exponential time) and second, the GLS algorithm [23] having a time complexity of $O(n \log n)$, with n being the number of consumers. We use greedy algorithm [8] to obtain the solution of the minknapsack problem for both MinKPDR and Twin-MinKPDR-CB algorithms which has time complexity of $O(n \log n)$. Further, note that the GLS algorithm does not have any approximate guarantees and does not work in multi-unit reduction case.

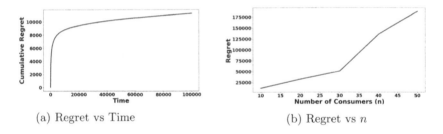

(a) Regret vs Time   (b) Regret vs n

Fig. 2. Regret comparison of Twin-MinKPDR-CB

Setting: For each consumer i, CPs p_i and compensation costs c_i both $\sim U[0, 1]$. The value of C is kept as 3 (except in Fig. (1a)) and for Figs. (1a, 2a) the value of n is fixed at 10. The maximum units of reduction k_i by any consumer i is generated randomly from 1 to 5. The demand shortage $\mathcal{E}_t \sim U[1, \frac{K}{4}]$ with K being sum of maximum reductions from all the consumers.

Comparison of MinKPDR for Offline Setting: Figure (1a) compares the worst-case loss function of MinKPDR and the optimal algorithm over 500 samples. As can be seen from the figure that the loss differences between the optimal one and MinKPDR are very close and always less than $4C + 1$. Further, MinKPDR algorithm performed 20 times faster as compared to the optimal algorithm which is implemented using mixed-integer linear programming solver Gurobi [10]. Figure (1b) compare the worst-case loss over 500 samples for the GLS and MinKPDR. Since GLS works only for a single unit, the figure is generated by implementing MinKPDR for single unit reduction case. It clearly shows the MinKPDR algorithm outperforming the GLS algorithm. Note that the GLS algorithm works only for single unit reduction with no approximation guarantees whereas MinKPDR works for multi-unit reduction with theoretical approximate guarantees.

Comparison of Twin-MinKPDR-CB for Online Setting: Figures (2a) and (2b) represent the average cumulative regret over 100 runs obtained by Twin-MinKPDR-CB versus the number of rounds and number of consumers respectively. Once the allocation vector is generated by Twin-MinKPDR-CB, the actual amount of electricity reduced by customer is generated as binomial random variable for every round. For Figure (2b), the cumulative regret is computed with respect to the solution obtained by solving the bounded min-knapsack problem for $T = 10^4$ rounds. We get logarithmic regret in terms of T and quadratic regret in terms of n.

6   Conclusion

The paper presented a novel min-knapsack framework that can be used to minimize the loss to the distributor company. Most of the existing work considered only single unit reduction, which does not fully optimize the distributor company's loss function. The proposed novel transformation to min-knapsack allowed an easy extension to multi-unit reduction. When unknown uncertainties are involved a novel combinatorial multiarmed bandit Twin-MinKPDR-CB algorithm is proposed that achieves sub-linear regret and works for non-monotone reward function, non-convex constraints, and time-varying optimal set. A combinatorial MAB algorithm for general non-monotone reward function is strongly required as these functions exist in many other settings such as resource allocation, influence maximization, etc. We believe that our novel Twin technique of combining UCB and LCB will be extremely beneficial for other settings involving such non-monotone reward functions with knapsack constraints.

References

1. Agrawal, S., Devanur, N.R.: Bandits with concave rewards and convex knapsacks. In: Proceedings of the Fifteenth ACM Conference on Economics and Computation, pp. 989–1006 (2014)
2. Akasiadis, C., et al.: Incentives for rescheduling residential electricity consumption to promote renewable energy usage. In: 2015 SAI Intelligent Systems Conference (IntelliSys), pp. 328–337, November 2015
3. Anderson, R., Fuloria, S.: On the security economics of electricity metering. In: Proceedings of the WEIS (2010)
4. Chao, H.: Competitive electricity markets with consumer subscription service in a smart grid. J. Regul. Econ. 1–26 (2012)
5. Chen, W., Hu, W., Li, F., Li, J., Liu, Y., Lu, P.: Combinatorial multi-armed bandit with general reward functions. Adv. Neural Inf. Process. Syst. **29**, 1659–1667 (2016)

6. Chen, W., Wang, Y., Yuan, Y.: Combinatorial multi-armed bandit: General framework and applications. In: International Conference on Machine Learning, pp. 151–159 (2013)
7. Chen, X., Nie, Y., Li, N.: Online residential demand response via contextual multi-armed bandits. arXiv preprint arXiv:2003.03627 (2020)
8. Csirik, J.: Heuristics for the 0–1 min-knapsack problem. Acta Cybernetica **10**(1–2), 15–20 (1991)
9. Gai, Y., Krishnamachari, B., Jain, R.: Combinatorial network optimization with unknown variables: multi-armed bandits with linear rewards and individual observations. IEEE/ACM Trans. Netw. **20**(5), 1466–1478 (2012)
10. Gurobi Optimization L: Gurobi optimizer reference manual (2021). http://www.gurobi.com
11. Hsu, Y.Y., Su, C.C.: Dispatch of direct load control using dynamic programming. IEEE Trans. Power Syst. **6**(3), 1056–1061 (1991)
12. Jain, S., Balakrishnan, N., Narahari, Y., Hussain, S.A., Voo, N.Y.: Constrained tâtonnement for fast and incentive compatible distributed demand management in smart grids. In: Proceedings of the Fourth International Conference on Future Energy Systems, pp. 125–136. ACM (2013)
13. Jain, S., Gujar, S., Bhat, S., Zoeter, O., Narahari, Y.: A quality assuring, cost optimal multi-armed bandit mechanism for expertsourcing. Artif. Intell. **254**, 44–63 (2018)
14. Jain, S., Narayanaswamy, B., Narahari, Y.: A multiarmed bandit incentive mechanism for crowdsourcing demand response in smart grids (2014)
15. Li, Y., Hu, Q., Li, N.: Learning and selecting the right customers for reliability: a multi-armed bandit approach (2018)
16. Ma, H., Parkes, D.C., Robu, V.: Generalizing demand response through reward bidding. In: Proceedings of the 16th Conference on Autonomous Agents and MultiAgent Systems, pp. 60–68. AAMAS 2017, International Foundation for Autonomous Agents and Multiagent Systems, Richland, SC (2017)
17. Ma, H., Robu, V., Li, N.L., Parkes, D.C.: Incentivizing reliability in demand-side response. In: the proceedings of The 25th International Joint Conference on Artificial Intelligence (IJCAI 2016), pp. 352–358 (2016)
18. Methenitis, G., Kaisers, M., La Poutré, H.: Forecast-based mechanisms for demand response. In: Proceedings of the 18th International Conference on Autonomous Agents and MultiAgent Systems, pp. 1600–1608. International Foundation for Autonomous Agents and Multiagent Systems (2019)
19. Mittal, S., Schulz, A.S.: An FPTAS for optimizing a class of low-rank functions over a polytope. Math. Program. **141**(1–2), 103–120 (2013)
20. Park, S., Jin, Y., Song, H., Yoon, Y.: Designing a critical peak pricing scheme for the profit maximization objective considering price responsiveness of customers. Energy **83**, 521–531 (2015)
21. Ramchurn, S., Vytelingum, P., Rogers, A., Jennings, N.: Agent-based control for decentralised demand side management in the smart grid. In: AAMAS, pp. 5–12, February 2011
22. Robu, V., Chalkiadakis, G., Kota, R., Rogers, A., Jennings, N.R.: Rewarding cooperative virtual power plant formation using scoring rules. Energy **117**, 19–28 (2016). https://doi.org/10.1016/j.energy.2016.10.077
23. Shweta, J., Sujit, G.: A multiarmed bandit based incentive mechanism for a subset selection of customers for demand response in smart grids. In: Proceedings of the AAAI Conference on Artificial Intelligence, vol. 34, pp. 2046–2053 (2020)

24. Xu, H., Liu, Y., Lau, W.C., Li, R.: Combinatorial multi-armed bandits with concave rewards and fairness constraints. In: Proceedings of the Twenty-Ninth International Joint Conference on Artificial Intelligence, pp. 2554–2560 (2020)
25. Zhang, Q., Wang, X., Fu, M.: Optimal implementation strategies for critical peak pricing. In: 2009 6th International Conference on the European Energy Market, pp. 1–6. IEEE (2009)

Designing Refund Bonus Schemes for Provision Point Mechanism in Civic Crowdfunding

Sankarshan Damle[1($\boxtimes$)] (ID), Moin Hussain Moti[2] (ID), Praphul Chandra[3], and Sujit Gujar[1] (ID)

[1] Machine Learning Lab, IIIT, Hyderabad, India
sankarshan.damle@research.iiit.ac.in, sujit.gujar@iiit.ac.in
[2] The Hong Kong University of Science and Technology (HKUST),
Hong Kong, China
mhmoti@cse.ust.hk
[3] KoineArth, Bangalore, India
praphulcs@koinearth.com

Abstract. Civic crowdfunding (CC) is a popular medium for raising funds for public projects from interested agents. With Blockchains gaining traction, we can implement CC reliably and transparently with smart contracts (SCs). The fundamental challenge in CC is free-riding. PPR, the proposal by Zubrickas [21] of giving refund bonus to the contributors when the project is not provisioned, has attractive properties. As observed by Chandra et al. [6], PPR incentivizes the agents to defer their contribution until the deadline, i.e., a race condition. For this, their proposal, PPS, considers temporal aspects of a contribution. However, PPS is computationally complex and expensive to implement as an SC. In this work, we identify essential properties a refund bonus scheme must satisfy to curb free-riding while avoiding the race condition. We prove Contribution Monotonicity and Time Monotonicity as sufficient conditions for this. We show that if a unique equilibrium is desirable, these conditions are also necessary. We propose three refund bonus schemes satisfying these conditions leading to three novel mechanisms for CC - PPRG, PPRE, and PPRP. We show that PPRG is the most cost-effective when deployed as an SC. We prove that under certain modest assumptions, in PPRG, the project is funded at equilibrium.

Keywords: Civic crowdfunding · Refund bonus schemes · Nash equilibrium

1 Introduction

Crowdfunding is the practice of raising funds for a project through voluntary contributions from a large pool of interested participants and is an active research

---

M. H. Moti—Work done while at IIIT, Hyderabad.

© Springer Nature Switzerland AG 2021
D. N. Pham et al. (Eds.): PRICAI 2021, LNAI 13031, pp. 18–32, 2021.
https://doi.org/10.1007/978-3-030-89188-6_2

area [2,3,7,15,18]. For *private* projects, specific reward schemes incentivize the participants to contribute towards crowdfunding. Using crowdfunding to raise funds for *public* (non-excludable) projects[1], however, introduces the free-riding problem. Observe that we cannot exclude non-contributing participants from enjoying the benefits of the public project. Thus, strategic participants, henceforth *agents*, may not contribute. If we can address this challenge, "civic" crowdfunding (CC), i.e., crowdfunding of public projects, can lead to greater democratic participation. It also contributes to citizens' empowerment by increasing their well-being by solving societal issues collectively. Thus, this paper focuses on solving the challenge of free-riding in CC.

With the advancement of the *blockchain* technology, *smart contracts* (SC) now allow for the deployment of such CC projects. A smart contract is a computer protocol intended to digitally facilitate, verify, or enforce the negotiation or performance of a contract [16]. Since a crowdfunding project as an SC is on a trusted, publicly distributed ledger, it is open and auditable. This property makes the agents' contributions and the execution of the payments transparent and anonymous. Besides, there is no need for any centralized, trusted third party, which reduces the cost of setting up the project. WeiFund [19] and Starbase [17] are examples of decentralized crowdfunding platforms on public blockchains like *Ethereum*.

Traditionally, a social planner uses the voluntary contribution mechanism with a provision point, *provision point mechanism* (PPM) [4]. The social planner sets up a target amount, namely the provision point. If the net contribution by the agents crosses this point, the social planner executes the project. We call this as *provisioning* of the project. Likewise, the project is said to be *under-provisioned*, if the net contribution does not exceed the provision point. In the case of under-provisioning, the planner returns the contributions. PPM has a long history of applications, but consists of several inefficient equilibria [4,14].

Zubrickas proposes *Provision Point mechanism with Refund* (PPR), which introduces an additional *refund bonus* to be paid to the contributing agents. This refund is paid along with each agent's contribution, in the case of under-provisioning of the project [21]. This incentive induces a simultaneous move game in PPR, in which the project is provisioned at equilibrium. Chandra et al. [6] observe that PPR may fail in online settings (e.g., Internet-based platforms [11,12]) since, in such a setting, an agent can observe the current amount of funds raised. Hence, in online settings, strategic agents in PPR would choose to defer their contributions until the end to check the possibility of free-riding and contribute only in anticipation of a refund bonus. Such deference leads to a scenario where every strategic agent competes for a refund bonus at the deadline. We refer to this scenario as a *race condition*. As the agents can observe the contributions' history in online settings, it induces a sequential game. Thus, we refer to such settings as *sequential settings*.

---

[1] For example, the crowdfunding of the Wooden Pedestrian Bridge in Rotterdam: https://www.archdaily.com/770488/the-luchtsingel-zus.

Provision Point Mechanism with Securities. (PPS) [6] introduces a class of mechanisms using complex prediction markets [1]. These markets incentivize an agent to contribute *as soon as it arrives*, thus avoiding the race condition. The challenge with the practical implementation of sophisticated mechanisms such as PPS is that as it uses complex prediction markets, it is difficult to explain to a layperson and computationally expensive to implement, primarily as an SC.

The introduction of the refund bonus is *vital* in these mechanisms as it incentivizes agents to contribute, thus avoiding free-riding. Consequently, we focus on provision point mechanisms with a refund bonus. Our primary goal is to abstract out conditions that *refund bonus schemes* should satisfy to avoid free-riding and the race condition. We believe that such a characterization would further make it easier to explore simpler and computationally efficient CC mechanisms.

Towards this, we introduce, *Contribution Monotonicity* (CM) and *Time Monotonicity* (TM). Contribution monotonicity states that an agent's refund should increase with an increase in its contribution. Further, time monotonicity states that an agent's refund should decrease if it delays its contribution. We prove these two conditions are *sufficient* to provision a public project via crowdfunding in a sequential setting at equilibrium and avoid the race condition (Theorem 1). We also prove that TM and *weak* CM are also *necessary*, under certain assumptions on equilibrium behavior (Theorem 2).

With these theoretical results on CM and TM, we propose three elegant refund bonus schemes that satisfy CM and TM. These schemes are straightforward to explain to a layperson and are computationally efficient to implement as an SC. With these three schemes, we design novel mechanisms for CC, namely *Provision Point mechanism with Refund through Geometric Progression* (PPRG); *Provision Point mechanism with Refund based on Exponential function* (PPRE), and *Provision Point mechanism with Refund based on Polynomial function* (PPRP). We analyze the cost-effectiveness of these mechanisms and PPS when deployed as SCs and show that PPRG is significantly more cost-effective, i.e., PPRG requires the least amount of capital to set up.

We omit proofs of some of the results presented in this paper. The formal proofs are available in the extended version [10].

2   Preliminaries

We focus on Civic Crowdfunding (CC) which involves provisioning of projects without coercion where agents arrive over time and *not* simultaneously, i.e., CC in a sequential setting. We assume that agents are aware of the history of contributions, i.e., the provision point and the total amount remaining towards the project's provision at any time. However, the agents have no information regarding the number of agents yet to arrive or the agents' sequence. Ours is the first attempt at providing a general theory for refund bonuses in CC to the best of our knowledge. Thus, we also assume that agents do not have any other information regarding the project. This information can be arbitrarily anything. E.g., an agent may deviate from its strategy if it knows about spiteful contributions and related corruption. Thus, unlike [8,9], every agent's belief is symmetric towards the project's provision [4,6,21].

2.1 Model

A social planner (SP) proposes crowdfunding a public project P on a web-based crowdfunding platform; we are dealing with sequential settings. SP seeks voluntary contributions towards it. The proposal specifies a target amount H necessary for the project to be provisioned, referred to as the *provision point*. It also specifies deadline (T) by which the funds need to be raised. If the target amount is not achieved by the deadline, the project is not provisioned, i.e., the project is under-provisioned. In the case of under-provisioning, the SP returns the contributions.

A set of agents $N = \{1, 2, \ldots, n\}$ are interested in the crowdfunding of P. An Agent $i \in N$ has value $\theta_i \geq 0$ if the project is provisioned. It arrives at time y_i to the project, observes its valuation (θ_i) for it *as well as* the net contribution till y_i. However, no agent has knowledge about any other agent's arrival or their contributions towards the project.

Agent i may decide to contribute $x_i \geq 0$ at time t_i, such that $y_i \leq t_i \leq T$, towards its provision. Let $\vartheta = \sum_{i=1}^{i=n} \theta_i$ be the total valuation, and $C = \sum_{i=1}^{i=n} x_i$ be the sum of the contributions for the project. We denote h^t as the amount that remains to be funded at time t.

A project is provisioned if $C \geq H$ and under-provisioned if $C < H$, at the end of deadline T. SP keeps a budget B aside to be distributed as a refund bonus among the contributors if the project is under-provisioned. This setup induces a game among the agents as the agents may now contribute to getting a fraction of the budget B in anticipation that the project may be under-provisioned.

Towards this, let $\sigma = (\sigma_1, \ldots, \sigma_n)$ be the vector of strategy profile of every agent where Agent i's strategy consists of the tuple $\sigma_i = (x_i, t_i)$, such that $x_i \in [0, \theta_i]$ is its voluntary contribution to the project at time $t_i \in [y_i, T]$. We use the subscript $-i$ to represent vectors without Agent i. The payoff for an Agent i with valuation θ_i for the project, when all the agents play the strategy profile σ is $\pi_i(\sigma; \theta_i)$. Note that, in this work, we assume that every agent only contributes once to the project. We justify this assumption while providing the strategies for the agents (Sect. 5). We leave it for future study to explore the effect of splitting of an agent's contribution to the project's provision and its payoff.

Let $\mathcal{I}_X$ be an indicator random variable that takes the value 1 if X is true and 0 otherwise. Further, let $R : \sigma \to \mathbf{R}^n$ denote the refund bonus scheme. Then the payoff structure for a provision point mechanism with a refund bonus scheme $R(\cdot)$ and budget B, for every Agent i contributing x_i and at time t_i, will be

$$\pi_i(\sigma; \theta_i) = \mathcal{I}_{C \geq H}(\theta_i - x_i) + \mathcal{I}_{C < H}(R_i(\sigma)), \tag{1}$$

where $R_i(\sigma)$ is the share of refund bonus for Agent i as per $R(\sigma)$ such that $R(\sigma) = (R_1(\sigma), \ldots, R_n(\sigma))$. We use $R(\cdot)$ to denote a refund bonus scheme and

$R_i(\cdot)$ to denote Agent i's share of the refund bonus as per $R(\cdot)$ whenever the inputs are obvious.

Important Game-Theoretic Definitions. We require the following definitions for the understanding of the results presented in this paper.

Definition 1 (Pure Strategy Nash Equilibrium (PSNE)). *A strategy profile $\sigma^* = (\sigma_1^*, \ldots, \sigma_n^*)$ is said to be a Pure Strategy Nash equilibrium (PSNE) if for every Agent i, it maximizes the payoff $\pi_i(\sigma^*; \theta_i)$ i.e., $\forall i \in N$,*

$$\pi_i(\sigma_i^*, \sigma_{-i}^*; \theta_i) \geq \pi_i(\sigma_i, \sigma_{-i}^*; \theta_i) \; \forall \sigma_i, \forall \theta_i.$$

The strategy profile for the Nash Equilibrium is helpful in a simultaneous move game. However, for sequential settings, where the agents can see the actions of the other agents, they may not find it best to follow the PSNE strategy. For this, we require a strategy profile that is the best response of every agent during the project, i.e., the best response for every sub-game induced during it. Such a strategy profile is said to be a *Sub-game Perfect Equilibrium.*

Definition 2 (Sub-game Perfect Equilibrium (SPE)). *A strategy profile $\sigma^* = (\sigma_1^*, \ldots, \sigma_n^*)$, with $\sigma_i^* = (x_i^*, t_i^*)$, is said to be a sub-game perfect equilibrium if for every Agent i, it maximizes the payoff $\pi_i(\upsilon_i^*, \sigma_{-i|H^{t_i^*}}^*; \theta_i)$ i.e. $\forall i \in N$,*

$$\pi_i(\sigma_i^*, \sigma_{-i|H^{t_i^*}}^*; \theta_i) \geq \pi_i(\sigma_i, \sigma_{-i|H^{t_i^*}}^*; \theta_i) \; \forall \sigma_i, \forall H^t, \forall \theta_i.$$

Here, H^t is the history of the game till time t, constituting the agents' arrivals and their contributions and $\sigma_{-i|H^{t_i^*}}^*$ indicates that the agents who arrive after t_i^* follow the strategy specified by σ_{-i}^*. Informally, at every stage of the game, it is Nash Equilibrium for each agent to follow the SPE strategy irrespective of what has happened.

In this work, we aim to derive deterministic strategies for the induced CC game. Non-deterministic strategies in our context will refer to equilibrium concepts like Bayesian Nash equilibrium (BNE). A layperson will be required to perform complex randomization to play such a strategy in practice. Besides, it will also need assurance over the correctness of its calculation. As a result, we focus on PSNE, a more robust and straightforward notion a layperson to play in practice. The choice of PSNE is also consistent with the CC literature.

3 Related Work

This paper focuses on the class of mechanisms that require the project to aggregate a minimum level, provision point, of funding before the SP can claim it. There is extensive literature on mechanism design for CC with provision point (see [6] and the references therein). Our work is most closely related to PPM, PPR, and PPS.

Provision Point Mechanism (PPM). PPM [4] is the simplest mechanism in this class where agents contribute voluntarily. Agents gain a positive payoff only when the project gets provisioned and a payoff of zero otherwise i.e., $R^{PPM}(\sigma) = ((0) \mid \forall i \in N)$. Then the payoff structure of PPM, for every Agent i, is,

$$\pi_i(\cdot) = \mathcal{I}_{C \geq H} \times (\theta_i - x_i)$$

where, $\pi_i(\cdot)$ and x_i are Agent i's payoff and contribution respectively. PPM has been shown to have multiple equilibria and also does not guarantee strictly positive payoff to the agents. It has led the mechanism to report under-provisioning of the project, i.e., the provision point not being reached.

Provision Point Mechanism With Refund (PPR). PPR [21] improves upon the limitations of PPM by offering refund bonuses to the agents in case the project does not get provisioned. This refund bonus scheme is directly proportional to agent's contribution and is given as $R_i^{PPR}(\sigma) = \left(\frac{x_i}{C}\right) B \; \forall i \in N$, where $B > 0$ is the total budget. Then the payoff structure of PPR, for every Agent i is,

$$\pi_i(\cdot) = \mathcal{I}_{C \geq H} \times (\theta_i - x_i) + \mathcal{I}_{C < H} \times R_i^{PPR}(\sigma).$$

In PPR, an agent does not know other agents' contributions. Thus, as shown in [6], PPR collapses to a one-shot simultaneous game where every agent delays its contribution till the deadline. This delay results in each agent attempting to contribute at the deadline, leading to a *race condition*, defined as follows.

Definition 3 (Race Condition). *A strategy profile $\sigma^* = (\sigma_1^*, \ldots, \sigma_n^*)$ is said to have a race condition if $\exists S \subseteq N$ with $|S| > 1$, for which $\forall i \in S$ the strategy $\sigma_i^* = (x_i^*, t)$, with x_i^* as the equilibrium contribution, is the PSNE of the induced game i.e., $\forall \sigma_i, \forall i \in S$,*

$$\pi_i(\sigma_i^*, \sigma_{-i}^*; \theta_i) \geq \pi_i(\sigma_i, \sigma_{-i}^*; \theta_i) \; where \; t \in [\bar{y}, T] \; s.t., \bar{y} = \max_{j \in S} y_j.$$

Here, $\sigma_i = (x_i^*, t_i) \; \forall t_i \in [y_i, T]$.

For PPR, $S = N$ and $t = T$, i.e., the strategy $\sigma_i^* = (x_i^*, T) \; \forall i \in N$ constitutes a set of PSNE of PPR in a sequential setting as the refund bonuses here are independent of time of contribution. Thus, agents have no incentive to contribute early. Such strategies lead to the project not getting provisioned in practice and are undesirable.

Provision Point Mechanism With Securities (PPS). PPS [6] addresses the shortcomings of PPR by offering early contributors higher refund than a late contributor for the same amount. The refund bonus of a contributor is determined using securities from a cost based complex prediction market [1] and is given as $R_i^{PPS}(\sigma) = (r_i^{t_i} - x_i) \; \forall i \in N$ where, t_i and $r_i^{t_i}$ are Agent i's time of contribution and the number of securities allocated to it, respectively. $r_i^{t_i}$ depends on the contribution x_i and the total number of securities issued in the market at the time contribution t_i denoted by q^{t_i}. Then the payoff structure of PPS, for every Agent i, can be expressed as,

$$\pi_i(\cdot) = \mathcal{I}_{C \geq H} \times (\theta_i - x_i) + \mathcal{I}_{C < H} \times R_i^{PPS}(\sigma)$$

To set up a complex prediction market in the context of CC, PPS requires a cost function (C_0) satisfying [6, CONDITIONS 1–4,6–7]. C_0 can either be based on the *logarithmic* [6, Eq. 3] or the *quadratic* scoring rule [6, Eq. 4].

PPS awards every contributing agent securities for the project not getting provisioned. These securities are dependent on the agent contribution, i.e., the greater the contribution, the higher the number of securities are allocated to the agent. Each of these securities pays out a unit amount if the project is not provisioned. However, setting up such a market and computing securities to be allotted is computationally expensive to implement as a smart contract. Hence, we want to look for more desirable refund bonus schemes.

4 Desirable Properties of Refund Bonus Schemes

Motivated by the theoretical guarantees of PPR and PPS, we look for CC mechanisms with refund bonus schemes in this paper. In this context, a *desirable* refund bonus scheme should not just restrict the set of strategies so that the project is provisioned at equilibrium, but should also incentivize *greater* and *early* contributions, to avoid the race condition, from all interested agents. A refund bonus scheme without these would fail in a sequential (web-based) setting, similar to PPR, and hence these are essential for a provision point mechanism's implementation online. We formalize these desirable properties as the following two *conditions* for a refund bonus scheme $R(\sigma)$ where $\sigma = ((x_i, t_i) \mid \forall i \in N)$ such that $x_i \in (0, H]$, $t_i \in [y_i, T]$ $\forall i \in N$ and with budget B.

Condition 1 (Contribution Monotonicity). *The refund must always increase with the increase in contribution so as to incentivize greater contribution i.e., $\forall i \in N$, $R_i(\sigma) \uparrow$ as $x_i \uparrow$. Further, if $R_i(\cdot)$ is a differential in x_i $\forall i$, then,*

$$\frac{\partial R_i(\sigma)}{\partial x_i} > 0 \ \forall t_i. \tag{2}$$

Note. If the strict inequality is replaced with $\geq$ in Eq. 2, we call it *"weak"* CM.

Condition 2 (Time Monotonicity). *The refund must always decrease with the increase in the duration of the project so as to incentivize early contribution i.e., $R(\sigma)$ must be a monotonically decreasing function with respect to time $t_i \in (0, T)$, $\forall x_i$, $\forall i \in N$ or*

$$R_i(\sigma) \downarrow \ as \ t_i \uparrow \ and \ \exists \ t_i < T, and \ \Delta t_i \ s.t.,$$
$$\frac{R_i\left((x_i, t_i + \Delta t_i), \sigma_{-i}\right) - R_i\left((x_i, t_i), \sigma_{-i}\right)}{\Delta t_i} < 0 \tag{3}$$

Note that, with Condition 2 we impose that $\nexists t \in [0, T]$ such that there is a race among the agents to contribute at t. We now analyze the consequence of such a refund bonus scheme on the game's characteristics induced by it.

4.1 Sufficiency of the Refund Bonus Scheme

We show that a refund bonus scheme satisfying Conditions 1 and 2, is sufficient to implement civic crowdfunding projects in sequential settings. For this, let G be the game induced by the refund bonus scheme $R(\cdot)$, for the payoff structure as given by Eq. 1. We require G to satisfy the following properties.

Property 1. *In G, the total contribution equals the provision point at equilibrium, i.e., $C = H$.*

Property 2. *G must avoid the race condition.*

Property 3. *G is a sequential game.*

Theorem 1. *Let G be the game induced by a refund bonus scheme $R(\cdot)$ for the payoff structure as given by Eq. 1, and with $\vartheta > H, 0 < B < \vartheta - H$. If $R(\cdot)$ satisfies Conditions 1 and 2, Properties 1, 2 and 3 hold.*

Proof Sketch.

1. Condition 1 $\implies$ Property 1. At equilibrium, $C < H$ can not hold as $\exists i \in N$ with $x_i < \theta_i$, at least, since $\vartheta > H$. Such an Agent i could obtain a higher refund bonus by marginally increasing its contribution since $R(\cdot)$ satisfies Condition 1 and $B > 0$. For $C > H$, any agent with a positive contribution could gain in payoff by marginally decreasing its contribution.
2. Condition 2 $\implies$ Properties 2 and 3. Every Agent i contributes as soon as it arrives, since $R(\cdot)$ satisfies Condition 2. This implies that, for the same contribution x_i and for any $\epsilon > 0$, we have $\pi_i(\cdot, y_i) > \pi_i(\cdot, y_i + \epsilon)$. Further, as the race condition is avoided, G results in a sequential game. □

4.2 Necessity of the Refund Bonus Schemes

Theorem 1 shows that Condition 1 is sufficient to satisfy Property 1 and Condition 2 is sufficient to satisfy Properties 2 and 3. With Theorem 2, we further prove that Condition 2 is necessary for Properties 2 and 3; while *weak* Condition 1 is necessary for Property 1. However, we remark that Theorem 2 does not characterize G completely. For the theorem to hold, *unlike* in the case of Theorem 1, we assume there exists a unique equilibrium defined by the strategy $(x_i^*, t_i^*), \forall i \in N$.

Theorem 2. *Let G be the game induced by a refund bonus scheme $R(\cdot)$ for the payoff structure as given by Eq. 1, and with $\vartheta > H, 0 < B < \vartheta - H$. If $R(\cdot)$ satisfies Properties 1, 2 and 3 and there is unique equilibrium, then "weak" Condition 1 and Condition 2 hold.*

Proof Sketch.

1. Property 1 $\implies$ weak Condition 1. Assume weak Condition 1 does not hold. This implies that $\exists i \in N$ for whom $R_i(x_i, \cdot) > R_i(x_i + \epsilon, \cdot)$ for some $\epsilon > 0$. Now consider a case, wlog, that the agent i is the last agent. Further, the project will be funded if agent i contributes $x_i + \epsilon$, i.e., where its funded payoff equals its unfunded payoff [21]. Since $R_i(x_i, \cdot) > R_i(x_i + \epsilon, \cdot)$, agent i will prefer to contribute x_i and at equilibrium, $C \neq H$. This is a contradiction as it is given that Property 1 holds.
2. Properties 2 and 3 $\implies$ Condition 2. Property 2 implies that G avoids the race condition. That is, $\nexists i \in N$ for whom $\pi_i(x_i, y_i) > \pi_i(x_i, y_i + \epsilon)$ for any $\epsilon > 0$ which in turn implies Condition 2. This is because, for the same x_i, π_i and R_i are both decreasing with respect to t_i. $\qquad\square$

Theorem 1 shows that a refund bonus scheme satisfying Conditions 1 and 2 avoids the race condition (Property 2) and induces a sequential game (Property 3). Thus, a mechanism deploying such a refund bonus scheme can be *implemented sequentially*, i.e., over web-based (or online) platforms. Additionally, refund bonus schemes should also be clear to explain to a layperson. Moreover, these should be computationally efficient and cost-effective when deployed as a smart contract. Through this generalized result on refund bonus schemes, we show the following proposition.

Proposition 1. *PPS satisfies Condition 1 and Condition 2.*

Proof. Since every cost function used in PPS for crowdfunding must satisfy $\frac{\partial(r_i^{t_i} - x_i)}{\partial x_i} > 0$, $\forall i$ [6, CONDITION-7], PPS satisfies Condition 1.

For Condition 2, observe that $\forall i$, from [6, Eq. 6]

$$(r_i^{t_i} - x_i) = C_0^{-1}(x_i + C_0(q^{t_i})) - q^{t_i} - x_i. \tag{4}$$

In Eq. 4, as $t_i \uparrow$, $q^{t_i} \uparrow$ as it is a monotonically non-decreasing function of t and thus R.H.S. of Eq. 4 decreases since R.H.S. of Eq. 4 is a monotonically decreasing function of q^{t_i} [6, Theorem 3 (Step 2)]. Thus, PPS also satisfies Condition 2. $\square$

Corollary 1. *PPS avoids the race condition and thus can be implemented sequentially.*

In the following subsection, we present three novel refund schemes satisfying Conditions 1 and 2 and the novel provision point mechanisms based on them.

4.3   Refund Bonus Schemes

Table 1 presents three novel refund schemes for an Agent i contributing x_i at time t_i as well as the mechanisms which deploy them. Note that we require all the refund bonus schemes to converge to a particular sum that can be precomputed. This convergence allows these schemes to be *budget balanced*. The

Table 1. Various Refund schemes satisfying Condition 1 and Condition 2 for an Agent i. Note that, in R^{PPRG} and R^{PPRP}, the subscript i denotes the order of the contribution.

Mechanism	Refund scheme	Parameters	Covergence of sum	Based on
PPRG	$R_i^{PPRG}(\cdot) = \left(\frac{x_i + a \times (1/\gamma)^{i-1}}{C+K_1} \right) B$	$a > 0, 1/\gamma < 1, K_1 = \frac{a\gamma}{\gamma-1}$	$\sum_{i=1}^{\infty} \left(x_i + a(1/\gamma)^{i-1} \right) = C + K_1$	Geometric Progression (GP)
PPRE	$R_i^{PPRE}(\cdot) = \left(\frac{x_i + K_2 e^{-t_i}}{C+K_2} \right) B$	$K_2 > 0$	$\sum_{i=1}^{\infty} (x_i) + \int_{t=t_i}^{\infty} (K_2 e^{-t} dt) \leq C + K_2$	Exponential Function (EF)
PPRP	$R_i^{PPRP}(\cdot) = \left(\frac{x_i + K_3 \times \frac{1}{i(i+1)}}{C+K_3} \right) B$	$K_3 > 0$	$\sum_{i=1}^{\infty} \left(x_i + K_3 \frac{1}{i(i+1)} \right) = C + K_3$	Polynomial Function (PF)

parameters a, γ, K_1, K_2, K_3 and B are mechanism parameters (for their respective mechanisms) which the SP is required to announce at the start. Additionally, the refund schemes presented deploy three mathematical functions: geometrical, exponential, and polynomial decay. $R^{PPRG}(\cdot)$ and $R^{PPRP}(\cdot)$ refunds the contributing agents based on the sequence of their arrivals (similar to PPS), while the refund scheme $R^{PPRE}(\cdot)$ refunds them based on their time of contribution.

Sufficiency Conditions. We now show that PPRG satisfies Conditions 1 and 2.

Claim 1 $R^{PPRG}(\sigma)$ *satisfies Condition 1* $\forall i \in N$.

Proof. Observe that $\forall i \in N$,

$$\frac{\partial R_i^{PPRG}(\sigma)}{\partial x_i} = \frac{B}{C+K_1} > 0 \; \forall t_i.$$

Therefore, $R^{PPRG}(\cdot)$ satisfies Condition 1 $\forall i$. □

Claim 2 $R^{PPRG}(\sigma)$ *satisfies Condition 2.*

Proof. For every Agent $i \in N$ arriving at time y_i, its share of the refund bonus given by $R^{PPRG}(\cdot)$ will only decrease from that point in time, since its position in the sequence of contributing agents can only go down, making it liable for a lesser share of the bonus, for the same contribution. Let $\tilde{t}_i$ be the position of the agent arriving at time y_i, when it contributes at time t_i. While $\tilde{t}_i$ will take discrete values corresponding to the position of the agents, for the purpose of differentiation, let $\tilde{t}_i \in \mathbf{R}$. Now, we can argue that at every epoch of time t_i, Agent $\tilde{t}_i$ will contribute to the project. With this, $R^{PPRG}(\cdot)$ can be written as,

$$R_i^{PPRG}(\sigma) = \left(\frac{x_i + a \times (1/\gamma)^{\tilde{t}_i - 1}}{C+K} \right) B.$$

Further observe that $\forall i \in N$,

$$\frac{\partial R_i^{PPRG}(\sigma)}{\partial \tilde{t}_i} = -\left(\frac{a \times (1/\gamma)^{\tilde{t}_i}}{C+K_1} \right) B < 0 \; \forall x_i.$$

Therefore, $R^{PPRG}(\cdot)$ satisfies Condition 2. □

We can similarly prove that R^{PPRE} and R^{PPRP} satisfy Conditions 1 and 2.

Table 2. Gas consumption comparison between PPS, PPRG, PPRE and PPRP for an agent. All values are in Gas units.

Operation	PPS		PPRG		PPRE		PPRP	
	Operations	Gas consumed	Operations	Gas consumed	Operations	Gas consumed	Operations	Gas consumed
ADD	2	6	2	6	2	6	2	6
SUB	2	6	0	0	0	0	0	0
MUL	2	10	2	10	2	10	3	15
DIV	2	10	1	5	1	5	2	10
EXP(x)	2	$10 + 10 \times (log(x))$	0	0	1	$10 + 10 \times (log(x))$	0	0
LOG(x)	2	$365 + 8 \times$ (bytes logged)	0	0	0	0	0	0
	Total gas: 407 (at least)		**Total gas: 21**		**Total gas: 31 (at least)**		**Total gas: 31**	

4.4   Gas Comparisons

As aforementioned, CC is now being deployed as smart contracts (SCs) over the Ethereum network. Thus, CC mechanisms deployed as SCs must be efficient, i.e., result in less *gas* consumption. Gas is a unit of fees that the Ethereum protocol charges per computational step executed in a contract or transaction. This fee prevents deliberate attacks and abuse on the Ethereum network [5].

We show a hypothetical cost comparison between PPS, PPRG, PPRE, and PPRP based on the Gas usage statistics from [5,20]. For the relevant operations, the cost in Gas units is: ADD: 3, SUB: 3, MUL: 5, DIV: 5, EXP(x): $10+10*log(x)$ and LOG(x): $365 + 8*$ size of x in bytes. Table 2 presents the comparison[2]. We remark that the only difference in the induced CC game will be the computation of the refund bonus for each contributing agent. This refund will depend on the underlying refund bonus scheme. Thus, we focus only on the gas cost because of the said schemes.

From Table 2, for every agent, PPRG takes 21 gas units, PPRP takes 31 gas units, PPRE takes at least 31 gas units, and PPS takes at least 407 gas units. When implemented on smart contracts, PPS is an expensive mechanism because of its logarithmic scoring rule for calculating payment rewards. PPRG, PPRP, and PPRE, on the other hand, use simpler operations and therefore have minimal operational costs.

Inference from Table 2. Note that the average gas price per unit varies. At the time of writing this paper, we have the average gas price $\approx$200 GWei, i.e., 2×10^{-7} ETH; and also 1 ETH $\approx$ 1162 USD. As a result, the cost incurred by a crowdfunding platform, assuming when $n = 100$, is (approximately) (i) PPS: 10 USD (at least); (ii) PPRG: 0.5 USD; (iii) PPRE: 0.72 USD (at least); and (iv) PPRP: 0.72 USD. Further, in December 2019, Kickstarter had 3524 active projects [12]. The data implies the total cost across the projects for (i) PPS: 35240 USD; and (ii) PPRG: 2537.28 USD. PPRG reduces the cost incurred by the platform by (at least) $\approx$14 times.

---

[2] We do not require any exponential calculation in PPRG – by storing the last GP term in a temporary variable.

5 PPRG

We now describe the mechanism *Provision Point mechanism with Refund through Geometric Progression* (PPRG), for crowdfunding a public project. PPRG incentivizes an interested agent to contribute as soon as it arrives at the crowdfunding platform. In PPRG, for the exact contribution of Agent i and Agent j, i.e., $x_i = x_j$, the one who contributed earlier obtains a higher share of the refund bonus. These differences in shares are allocated using an infinite geometric progression series (GP) with a common ratio of < 1.

Refund Bonus Scheme. The sum of an infinite GP with $a > 0$ as the first term and $0 < 1/\gamma < 1$ as the common ratio is: $K_1 = a \times \sum_{i=0}^{\infty}(1/\gamma)^i = \frac{a\gamma}{\gamma-1}$. With this, we propose a novel refund bonus scheme,

$$R_i^{PPRG}(\sigma) = p_i = \left(\frac{x_i + a \times (1/\gamma)^{i-1}}{C + K_1}\right) B \tag{5}$$

for every Agent $i \in N$, $B > 0$ as the total bonus budget allocated for the project by the SP and where $\sigma = ((x_i, t_i) \mid \forall i \in N)$. The values a and γ are mechanism parameters which the SP is required to announce at the start of the project.

Equilibrium Analysis of PPRG. The analysis follows from Theorem 1.

Theorem 3. *For PPRG, with the refund p_i as described by Eq. 5 $\forall i \in N$, satisfying $0 < B \leq \vartheta - H$ and with the payoff structure as given by Eq. 1, a set of strategies $\left\{(\sigma_i^* = (x_i^*, y_i)) : \text{ if } h^{y_i} = 0 \text{ then } x_i^* = 0 \text{ otherwise } x_i^* \leq \frac{\theta_i(H+K_1)-aB\times(1/\gamma)^{i-1}}{H+K_1+B}\right\} \forall i \in N$ are sub-game perfect equilibria, such that at equilibrium $C = H$. In this, x_i^* is the contribution towards the project, y_i is the arrival time to the project of Agent i, respectively.*

Proof. We prove the theorem with the following steps.

Step 1: Since $R^{PPRG}(\cdot)$ satisfies Condition 1 (Claim 1) and Condition 2 (Claim 2) and has a payoff structure as given by Eq. 1, from Theorem 1 we get the result that PPRG induces a sequential move game and thus, can be implemented in a sequential setting.

Step 2: From Claim 2, the best response for any agent is to contribute as soon as he arrives i.e., at time y_i.

Step 3: We assume that each agent is symmetric in its belief for the provision of the project. Moreover, from Theorem 1, agents know that the project will be provisioned at equilibrium. Therefore, for any agent, its equilibrium contribution becomes that x_i^* for which its provisioned payoff is *greater than or equal to* its not provisioned payoff. Now, with $C = H$ at equilibrium,

$$\theta_i - x_i^* \geq p_i = \left(\frac{x_i^* + a \times (1/\gamma)^{i-1}}{C + K_1}\right) B$$

$$\Rightarrow x_i^* \leq \frac{\theta_i(H + K_1) - aB \times (1/\gamma)^{i-1}}{H + K_1 + B}$$

Step 4: Summing over x_i^*, $\forall i$ we get,

$$B \leq \frac{(H + K_1)\vartheta - H^2 - HK_1}{H + K_1}.$$

as $\sum_{i \in N} x_i^* = H$. From the above equation, we get

$$0 < B \leq \frac{(H + K_1)\vartheta - H^2 - HK_1}{H + K_1} = \vartheta - H$$

as a sufficient condition for existence of Nash Equilibrium for PPRG.

Step 5: We can also show that the set of strategies are also sub-game perfect through backward induction and by observing specific scenarios [10, Theorem 2 (Step 5)].

Discussion. Observe that, as the refund bonus decreases with time (Claim 2), each agent in PPRG is better off contributing once instead of breaking up its contribution. This result follows as we assume that each agent's belief for the project's provision is symmetric and does not vary.

With Theorem 3, we identify a set of pure-SPE at which the project is provisioned. However, we do not claim that these are the only set of pure-SPE possible. We leave it for future work to explore other possible pure-SPE at which the project gets provisioned. Also, the equilibrium analysis of PPRE and PPRP is similar to Theorem 3.

Coalition-Proof. Along similar lines of the argument presented in [21, Sect. 4.2], we can show that the game induced in PPRG will be coalition-proof. This is because the equilibrium in the induced game follows the *aggregate concurrence principle* [13], i.e., at equilibrium, agents must agree on the choice of aggregate outcomes. As it immediately follows from this principle, the equilibria produced by PPRG (Theorem 3) are coalition-proof.

6   Conclusion

In this paper, we looked for provision point mechanisms for CC with refund bonus schemes. Towards it, we introduced Contribution Monotonicity and Time Monotonicity for refund bonus schemes in CC mechanisms. We proved that these two conditions are sufficient to implement provision point mechanisms with refund bonuses to possess an equilibrium that avoids free-riding and the race condition (Theorem 1). We then proposed three simple refund bonus schemes and design novel mechanisms that deploy them, namely, PPRG, PPRE, and PPRP. We showed that PPRG has much less cost when implemented as a smart contract over the Ethereum framework. We identified a set of sub-game perfect equilibria for PPRG in which it provisions the project at equilibrium (Theorem 3).

References

1. Abernethy, J., Chen, Y., Vaughan, J.W.: Efficient market making via convex optimization, and a connection to online learning. ACM Trans. Econ. Comput. **1**(2), 12 (2013)
2. Alaei, S., Malekian, A., Mostagir, M.: A dynamic model of crowdfunding. In: Proceedings of the 2016 ACM Conference on Economics and Computation, pp. 363–363. EC 2016, ACM, New York, NY, USA (2016). https://doi.org/10.1145/2940716.2940777
3. Arieli, I., Koren, M., Smorodinsky, R.: The crowdfunding game. In: Proceedings of the Web and Internet Economics - 13th International Conference, WINE 2017, 17–20 December 2017, Bangalore, India (2017)
4. Bagnoli, M., Lipman, B.L.: Provision of public goods: fully implementing the core through private contributions. Rev. Econ. Stud. **56**(4), 583–601 (1989)
5. Buterin, V.: Ethereum: a next-generation smart contract and decentralized application platform (2014). https://github.com/ethereum/wiki/wiki/%5BEnglish%5D-White-Paper
6. Chandra, P., Gujar, S., Narahari, Y.: Crowdfunding public projects with provision point: a prediction market approach. In: ECAI, pp. 778–786 (2016)
7. Chandra, P., Gujar, S., Narahari, Y.: Referral-embedded provision point mechanisms for crowdfunding of public projects. In: Larson, K., Winikoff, M., Das, S., Durfee, E.H. (eds.) Proceedings of the 16th Conference on Autonomous Agents and MultiAgent Systems, AAMAS 2017, 8–12 May 2017, São Paulo, Brazil, pp. 642–650. ACM (2017). http://dl.acm.org/citation.cfm?id=3091218
8. Damle, S., Moti, M.H., Chandra, P., Gujar, S.: Aggregating citizen preferences for public projects through civic crowdfunding. In: Proceedings of the 18th International Conference on Autonomous Agents and MultiAgent Systems (AAMAS 2019), pp. 1919–1921. International Foundation for Autonomous Agents and Multiagent Systems, Richland (2019)
9. Damle, S., Moti, M.H., Chandra, P., Gujar, S.: Civic crowdfunding for agents with negative valuations and agents with asymmetric beliefs. In: Kraus, S. (ed.) Proceedings of the Twenty-Eighth International Joint Conference on Artificial Intelligence, IJCAI 2019, 10–16 August 2019, Macao, China, pp. 208–214. ijcai.org (2019). https://doi.org/10.24963/ijcai.2019/30
10. Damle, S., Moti, M.H., Gujar, S., Chandra, P.: Designing refund bonus schemes for provision point mechanism in civic crowdfunding. CoRR abs/1810.11695 (2018). http://arxiv.org/abs/1810.11695
11. GoFundMe: Gofundme – Wikipedia, the free encyclopedia (2020). https://en.wikipedia.org/w/index.php?title=GoFundMe
12. Kickstarter: Kickstarter – Wikipedia, the free encyclopedia (2020). https://en.wikipedia.org/w/index.php?title=Kickstarter
13. Martimort, D., et al.: Aggregate representations of aggregate games (04 2010)
14. Schmidtz, D.: The limits of government (boulder) (1991)
15. Shen, W., Crandall, J.W., Yan, K., Lopes, C.V.: Information design in crowdfunding under thresholding policies. In: Proceedings of the 17th International Conference on Autonomous Agents and MultiAgent Systems, pp. 632–640. International Foundation for Autonomous Agents and Multiagent Systems (2018)
16. Smart Contract: Smart contract – Wikipedia, the free encyclopedia (2006). https://en.wikipedia.org/wiki/Smart_contract
17. Starbase: Starbase (2016). https://starbase.co/

18. Strausz, R.: A theory of crowdfunding: a mechanism design approach with demand uncertainty and moral hazard. Am. Econ. Rev. **107**(6), 1430–76 (2017)
19. WeiFund: Weifund - decentralised fundraising (2015). http://weifund.io/
20. Wood, G.: Ethereum: a secure decentralised generalised transaction ledger. Ethereum Project Yellow Paper **151**, 1–32 (2014)
21. Zubrickas, R.: The provision point mechanism with refund bonuses. J. Public Econ. **120**, 231–234 (2014)

Federated Learning for Non-IID Data: From Theory to Algorithm

Bojian Wei[1,2] , Jian Li[1(✉)] , Yong Liu[3] , and Weiping Wang[1]

[1] Institute of Information Engineering, Chinese Academy of Sciences, Beijing, China
{weibojian,lijian9026,wangweiping}@iie.ac.cn
[2] School of Cyber Security, University of Chinese Academy of Sciences,
Beijing, China
[3] Renmin University of China, Beijing, China
liuyonggsai@ruc.edu.cn

Abstract. Federated learning suffers from terrible generalization performance because the model fails to utilize global information over all clients when data is non-IID (not independently or identically distributed) partitioning. Meanwhile, the theoretical studies in this field are still insufficient. In this paper, we present an *excess risk* bound for federated learning on non-IID data, which measures the error between the model of federated learning and the optimal centralized model. Specifically, we present a novel error decomposition strategy, which decomposes the *excess risk* into three terms: *agnostic error*, *federated error*, and *approximation error*. By estimating the error terms, we find that Rademacher complexity and discrepancy distance are the keys to affecting the learning performance. Motivated by the theoretical findings, we propose `FedAvgR` to improve the performance via additional regularizers to lower the *excess risk*. Experimental results demonstrate the effectiveness of our algorithm and coincide with our theory.

Keywords: Federated learning · Non-IID · Excess risk bound

1 Introduction

Federated learning (FL) [25] is a new machine learning paradigm where a large number of clients collaboratively train a model under the coordination of a central server. Different from centralized learning (CL), in FL setting, the raw data of each client is stored locally, other clients and the central server have no access to it. Instead, the global model is updated by alternately performing local training and server aggregating. At present, FL still faces many problems [14], one severe problem in FL is that training data is usually non-IID among clients, and this leads to the decline of the model's effectiveness compared to CL.

Some studies [28,31,33] try to solve this problem by designing new optimization algorithms. `FedAvg` [25] is an efficient algorithm based on iterative model averaging, but it might be less accurate when dealing with non-IID data. `FedProx`

The original version of this chapter was revised: The second affiliation of the author Bojian Wei has been corrected as "School of Cyber Security, University of Chinese Academy of Sciences, Beijing, China". The correction to this chapter is available at https://doi.org/10.1007/978-3-030-89188-6_45

D. N. Pham et al. (Eds.): PRICAI 2021, LNAI 13031, pp. 33–48, 2021.
https://doi.org/10.1007/978-3-030-89188-6_3

[15] adds a proximal term to local objectives to constrain the gap between local models and the global model, but the convergence is slower. SCAFFOLD [9] controls variates to reduce the variance among local updates, while it increases communication costs. Using local momentum [38] instead of local SGD empirically improves the accuracy in heterogeneous settings, but such methods also require additional communication. FL with server momentum [35] performs better than many existing methods including SCAFFOLD without increasing communication costs, but such methods do not consider the specific non-IID setting. FedNova [34] was proposed to tackle objective inconsistency problem and it could be combined with some acceleration techniques [17], while it has not taken the distribution discrepancy into account. Another effective way is to apply clustering [5,30] to FL, where clients are divided into several groups based on their similarities, but the metric of clustering and the number of clusters needs to be determined in advance.

On the contrary, there are only a few generalization analysis [13,21] for FL under non-IID setting. Many works have analyzed federated optimization from the aspect of homogeneity [2,32] or heterogeneity [18,36], where some works focus on the convergence of federated stochastic algorithms [7] and have made progress in relaxing the assumptions [18]. Most theoretical works paid more attention to the optimization problem with convergence analysis [9,16] on non-IID data, some of which showed that the heterogeneity of data slows down the convergence. From the perspective of generalization, agnostic federated learning [26] provided a new point on FL, but the target is to optimize the worst case in the hypothesis, which often performs not well in practice, and it only focused on the generalization error of FL. Thus, there is still a lack of generalization analysis between FL and CL under the traditional framework, which may help to further improve the performance of FL under non-IID setting.

In this paper, we analyze the *excess risk* of FL on non-IID data, which measures the gap between FL and the optimal CL, and we give the corresponding *excess risk* bound. With proper error decompositions, the *excess risk* can be divided into *agnostic error*, *federated error*, and *approximation error*, then we further construct ingenious error decompositions to derive the upper bound of these errors by means of Rademacher complexity [1,27] and discrepancy distance [3,24,40]. Based on the theoretical analysis, we devise an effective algorithm, where we introduce three regularizers to ensure the performance of FL on non-IID data. Experimental results on the synthetic dataset and real-world datasets show that our proposed algorithm outperforms the previous methods and validates our theory.

The contributions of our work are summarized as follows:

- Theoretically, we give the *excess risk* bound between FL on non-IID data and CL for the first time and find out the factors that affect the accuracy decline. We give a reasonable explanation for the bound by decomposing the *excess risk* into three terms: *agnostic error*, *federated error* and *approximation error*, where each term has a detailed analysis with complete proof.

– Algorithmically, we propose a novel algorithm `FedAvgR` (Federated Averaging with Regularization) to improve the performance of FL on non-IID data, which is regularized by Rademacher complexity and discrepancy distance. Furthermore, we design a learning framework for a linear classifier with nonlinear feature mapping, where all the parameters will be updated automatically through back-propagation.

2 Preliminaries and Notations

There are some general notations used in this paper. Assume that there are K clients in a FL setting, where data on the k-th client is drawn i.i.d. from distribution ρ_k, data on different clients may not have the same distribution ($\rho_i \neq \rho_j$), and all clients participate in each round (cross-silo FL). The global distribution is assumed to be a mixture distribution of local distributions on all K clients: $\rho = \sum_{k=1}^{K} p_k \rho_k$, where p_k is the mixture weight ($\sum_{k=1}^{K} p_k = 1$). Actually, the mixture weight p_k is unknown, so an estimated weight $\widehat{p}_k$ will be applied in practice, which brings us the estimated global distribution $\widetilde{\rho} = \sum_{k=1}^{K} \widehat{p}_k \rho_k$.

In this paper, we focus on the multi-classification task. We denote the hypothesis space $\mathcal{H} = \{x \to f(x)\}$ consisting of labeling functions $f : \mathcal{X} \to \mathcal{Y}$, where $\mathcal{X} \subseteq \mathbb{R}^d$ represents the input space and $\mathcal{Y} \subseteq \mathbb{R}^C$ represents the label space, training samples (x^k, y^k) on the k-th client with size of n_k are i.i.d. drawn from $\rho_k(x, y)$. The labeling function f is formed as $f(x) = W^T \phi(x)$, where $W \in \mathbb{R}^{D \times C}$, $\phi(x) \in \mathbb{R}^D$ and $\phi(\cdot)$ is the feature mapping with learnable parameters φ.

Let $\ell(f(x), y)$ be the loss function, which is assumed to be upper bounded by M ($M > 0$), and $\mathcal{L} = \{\ell(f(x), y) | f \in \mathcal{H}\}$ be the family of loss functions on the hypothesis $\mathcal{H}$, the expected loss of FL on ρ can be described as

$$\mathcal{E}_\rho(f) = \sum_{k=1}^{K} p_k \mathcal{E}_{\rho_k}(f) = \sum_{k=1}^{K} p_k \int_{\mathcal{X} \times \mathcal{Y}} \ell(f(x), y) d\rho_k(x, y),$$

and the corresponding empirical loss is

$$\widehat{\mathcal{E}}_\rho(f) = \sum_{k=1}^{K} p_k \widehat{\mathcal{E}}_{\rho_k}(f) = \sum_{k=1}^{K} p_k \frac{1}{n_k} \sum_{i=1}^{n_k} \ell(f(x_i^k), y_i^k).$$

The empirical learner of FL on the estimated distribution $\widetilde{\rho}$ is denoted by $\widetilde{f}_{fl} = \arg\min_{f \in \mathcal{H}} \sum_{k=1}^{K} \widehat{p}_k \widehat{\mathcal{E}}_{\rho_k}(f)$, and we define the expected (optimal) learner in $\mathcal{H}$ as $f^* = \arg\min_{f \in \mathcal{H}} \mathcal{E}_\rho(f)$, which minimizes the expected loss on ρ.

The performance of a learning model is usually measured by the *excess risk*: $\mathcal{E}_\rho(\widetilde{f}_{fl}) - \mathcal{E}_\rho(f^*)$. Unlike the generalization error, *excess risk* represents the gap between an empirical model and the optimal model, which has not been considered recently in FL. In the following, we consider bounding this *excess risk*.

3 Generalization Analysis

In this section, we will derive the *excess risk* bound between FL and CL.

To this end, we decompose the *excess risk* into *agnostic error* A_1, *federated error* A_2, and *approximation error* A_3:

$$\mathcal{E}_\rho(\widetilde{f}_{fl}) - \mathcal{E}_\rho(f^*) \le \underbrace{\mathcal{E}_\rho(\widetilde{f}_{fl}) - \mathcal{E}_\rho(\widehat{f}_{fl})}_{A_1 :=} + \underbrace{\mathcal{E}_\rho(\widehat{f}_{fl}) - \mathcal{E}_\rho(\widehat{f}_{cl})}_{A_2 :=} + \underbrace{\mathcal{E}_\rho(\widehat{f}_{cl}) - \mathcal{E}_\rho(f^*)}_{A_3 :=},$$

$$(1)$$

where $\widehat{f}_{fl} = \arg\min_{f \in \mathcal{H}} \sum_{k=1}^{K} p_k \widehat{\mathcal{E}}_{\rho_k}(f)$ denotes the empirical learner on the unknown real distribution ρ and $\widehat{f}_{cl} = \arg\min_{f \in \mathcal{H}} \frac{1}{n} \sum_{i=1}^{n} \ell(f(\boldsymbol{x}_i), y_i)$ denotes the empirical learner of CL.

As mentioned above, $\widehat{p}_k \ne p_k$ results in the difference between $\widetilde{f}_{fl}$ and $\widehat{f}_{fl}$, which is caused by the agnostic nature of the mixture weight. And, in CL setting, model is trained directly on the samples $\{(\boldsymbol{x}_n, y_n), ..., (\boldsymbol{x}_n, y_n)\}$ i.i.d. drawn from $\rho(\boldsymbol{x}, y)$ with size of n ($n = \sum_{k=1}^{K} n_k$).

In (1), A_1 represents the difference of expected loss for FL between the estimated distribution and the real distribution, A_2 represents the difference of expected loss between FL and CL, and A_3 represents the approximation error of CL to the optimal solution.

3.1   Bounds of Three Error Terms

To measure the performance gap of a model on different distributed data, we introduce the discrepancy distance [24] as follows:

$$disc_L(Q_1, Q_2) = \sup_{f \in \mathcal{H}} |\mathcal{E}_{Q_1}(f) - \mathcal{E}_{Q_2}(f)|, \tag{2}$$

where Q_1 and Q_2 are two different distributions.

Using Rademacher complexity and discrepancy distance, we bound A_1, A_2, and A_3 as follows.

Theorem 1 (Agnostic Error Bound).   *Assume that $\ell(f(\boldsymbol{x}), y)$ is λ-Lipschitz equipped with the 2-norm, that is $|\ell(f(\boldsymbol{x}), y) - \ell(f(\boldsymbol{x}'), y')| \le \lambda \| f(\boldsymbol{x}) - f(\boldsymbol{x}')\|_2$, $B = \sup_{f = \boldsymbol{W}^T \phi(\boldsymbol{x}) \in \mathcal{H}} \| \boldsymbol{W}\|_*$, where $\| \cdot \|_*$ denotes the trace norm. With probability at least $1 - \delta$ ($\delta > 0$), we have:*

$$A_1 \le 2 disc_L(\widetilde{\rho}, \rho) + 4\sqrt{2}\lambda B \sum_{k=1}^{K} \frac{\widehat{p}_k}{n_k} \sqrt{C} \| \phi(\boldsymbol{X}^k)\|_F + 6M \sqrt{\frac{\mathcal{S}(\widehat{\boldsymbol{p}} \| \bar{\boldsymbol{n}}) \log(2/\delta)}{2n}},$$

where $\| \phi(\boldsymbol{X}^k)\|_F = \sqrt{\sum_{i=1}^{n_k} \langle \phi(\boldsymbol{x}_i^k), \phi(\boldsymbol{x}_i^k)\rangle}$, $\mathcal{S}(\widehat{\boldsymbol{p}} \| \bar{\boldsymbol{n}}) = \chi^2(\widehat{\boldsymbol{p}} \| \bar{\boldsymbol{n}}) + 1$, χ^2 denotes the chi-squared divergence, $\widehat{\boldsymbol{p}} = [\widehat{p}_1, ..., \widehat{p}_K]$, and $\bar{\boldsymbol{n}} = \frac{1}{n}[n_1, ..., n_K]$.

Proof. We first decompose A_1 into the following parts:

$$A_1 = \mathcal{E}_\rho(\widetilde{f}_{fl}) - \mathcal{E}_{\widetilde{\rho}}(\widetilde{f}_{fl}) + \underbrace{\mathcal{E}_{\widetilde{\rho}}(\widetilde{f}_{fl}) - \mathcal{E}_{\widetilde{\rho}}(\widehat{f}_{fl})}_{A_1' :=} + \mathcal{E}_{\widetilde{\rho}}(\widehat{f}_{fl}) - \mathcal{E}_\rho(\widehat{f}_{fl}),$$

$$(3)$$

According to 2, we know that $\mathcal{E}_\rho(\widetilde{f}_{fl}) - \mathcal{E}_{\widetilde{\rho}}(\widetilde{f}_{fl}) \leq disc_L(\rho, \widetilde{\rho})$ and $\mathcal{E}_{\widetilde{\rho}}(\widehat{f}_{fl}) - \mathcal{E}_\rho(\widehat{f}_{fl}) \leq disc_L(\widetilde{\rho}, \rho)$. Then, We further decompose A_1' as:

$$A_1' = \underbrace{\mathcal{E}_{\widetilde{\rho}}(\widetilde{f}_{fl}) - \widehat{\mathcal{E}}_{\widetilde{\rho}}(\widetilde{f}_{fl})}_{A_{11}:=} + \underbrace{\widehat{\mathcal{E}}_{\widetilde{\rho}}(\widetilde{f}_{fl}) - \widehat{\mathcal{E}}_{\widetilde{\rho}}(\widehat{f}_{fl})}_{A_{12}:=} + \underbrace{\widehat{\mathcal{E}}_{\widetilde{\rho}}(\widehat{f}_{fl}) - \mathcal{E}_{\widetilde{\rho}}(\widehat{f}_{fl})}_{A_{13}:=}.$$

where A_{11} and A_{13} represent the generalization errors of $\widetilde{f}_{fl}$ and $\widehat{f}_{fl}$, respectively, which can be bounded by weighted Rademacher complexity.

Definition 1 (Weighted Rademacher Complexity). *Let $\mathcal{H}$ be a hypothesis space of f defined over $\mathcal{X}$, $\mathcal{L}$ be the family of loss functions associated to $\mathcal{H}$, $\mathbf{n} = [n_1, ..., n_K]$ be the vector of sample sizes and $\mathbf{p} = [p_1, ..., p_K]$ be the mixture weight vector, the empirical weighted Rademacher complexity of $\mathcal{L}$ is*

$$\widehat{\mathcal{R}}(\mathcal{L}, \mathbf{p}) = \mathbb{E}_\epsilon \left[\sup_{f \in \mathcal{H}} \sum_{k=1}^K \frac{p_k}{n_k} \sum_{i=1}^{n_k} \epsilon_i^k l(f(\mathbf{x}_i^k), y_i^k) \right],$$

and the empirical weighted Rademacher complexity of $\mathcal{H}$ is

$$\widehat{\mathcal{R}}(\mathcal{H}, \mathbf{p}) = \mathbb{E}_\epsilon \left[\sup_{f \in \mathcal{H}} \sum_{k=1}^K \frac{p_k}{n_k} \sum_{i=1}^{n_k} \sum_{c=1}^C \epsilon_{ic}^k f_c(\mathbf{x}_i^k) \right],$$

where $f_c(\mathbf{x}_i^k)$ is the c-th value of $f(\mathbf{x}_i^k)$ corresponding to the C classes, ϵ_i^ks and ϵ_{ic}^ks are independent Rademacher variables, which are uniformly sampled from $\{-1, +1\}$, respectively.

For any sample $S = \{S_1, ...S_n\}$ drawn from ρ, define $\Phi(S)$ by $\Phi(S) = \sup_{f \in \mathcal{H}} (\mathcal{E}_{\widetilde{\rho}}(f) - \widehat{\mathcal{E}}_{\widetilde{\rho}}(f))$. According to [26], we have

$$\Phi(S) \leq 2\widehat{\mathcal{R}}(\mathcal{L}, \widehat{\mathbf{p}}) + 3M \sqrt{\frac{\chi^2(\widehat{\mathbf{p}} \| \bar{\mathbf{n}}) + 1}{2n} \log \frac{2}{\delta}}. \tag{4}$$

According to [8], it holds that $\widehat{\mathcal{R}}(\mathcal{L}, \widehat{\mathbf{p}}) \leq \sqrt{2}\lambda\widehat{\mathcal{R}}(\mathcal{H}, \widehat{\mathbf{p}})$ under the Lipschitz assumption. Applying Hölder's inequality, we have:

$$\widehat{\mathcal{R}}(\mathcal{H}, \widehat{\mathbf{p}}) = \mathbb{E}_\epsilon \left[\sup_{f \in \mathcal{H}} \sum_{k=1}^K \frac{\widehat{p}_k}{n_k} \langle \mathbf{W}_k, \mathbf{\Phi}_k \rangle \right] \leq \mathbb{E}_\epsilon \left[\sum_{k=1}^K \frac{\widehat{p}_k}{n_k} \sup_{f \in \mathcal{H}} \langle \mathbf{W}_k, \mathbf{\Phi}_k \rangle \right]$$

$$\leq \mathbb{E}_\epsilon \left[\sum_{k=1}^K \frac{\widehat{p}_k}{n_k} \sup_{f \in \mathcal{H}} \|\mathbf{W}_k\|_* \|\mathbf{\Phi}_k\|_F \right] \leq \mathbb{E}_\epsilon \left[\sum_{k=1}^K \frac{\widehat{p}_k}{n_k} B \|\mathbf{\Phi}_k\|_F \right] \tag{5}$$

$$= B \sum_{k=1}^K \frac{\widehat{p}_k}{n_k} \mathbb{E}_\epsilon [\|\mathbf{\Phi}_k\|_F] \leq B \sum_{k=1}^K \frac{\widehat{p}_k}{n_k} \sqrt{\mathbb{E}_\epsilon [\|\mathbf{\Phi}_k\|_F^2]}.$$

where $\boldsymbol{W}_k, \boldsymbol{\Phi}_k = [\sum_{i=1}^{n_k} \epsilon_{i1}^k \phi(\boldsymbol{x}_i^k), ..., \sum_{i=1}^{n_k} \epsilon_{iC}^k \phi(\boldsymbol{x}_i^k)] \in \mathbb{R}^{D \times C}$ and $\langle \boldsymbol{W}_k, \boldsymbol{\Phi}_k \rangle = $ $\mathrm{Tr}(\boldsymbol{W}_k^T \boldsymbol{\Phi}_k)$. $\mathbb{E}_\epsilon[\|\boldsymbol{\Phi}_k\|_F^2]$ can be further bounded as follows [10]:

$$
\mathbb{E}_\epsilon[\|\boldsymbol{\Phi}_k\|_F^2] \le \mathbb{E}_\epsilon \left[\sum_{c=1}^{C} \left\| \sum_{i=1}^{n_k} \epsilon_{ic}^k \phi(\boldsymbol{x}_i^k) \right\|_2^2 \right] \le \sum_{c=1}^{C} \mathbb{E}_\epsilon \left[\left\| \sum_{i=1}^{n_k} \epsilon_{ic}^k \phi(\boldsymbol{x}_i^k) \right\|_2^2 \right]
$$
$$
\le \sum_{c=1}^{C} \mathbb{E}_\epsilon \left[\sum_{i,j=1}^{n_k} \epsilon_{ic}^k \epsilon_{jc}^k \langle \phi(\boldsymbol{x}_i^k), \phi(\boldsymbol{x}_j^k) \rangle \right] = C \|\phi(\boldsymbol{X}^k)\|_F^2.
$$

(6)

Based on the definition of learners, $\widetilde{f}_{fl}$ minimizes the empirical loss on $(\boldsymbol{x}, y) \sim \widetilde{\rho}$, while $\widehat{f}_{fl}$ minimizes the empirical risk on $(\boldsymbol{x}, y) \sim \rho$, so it is obvious that $\widetilde{\mathcal{E}}_{\widetilde{\rho}}(\widetilde{f}_{fl}) \le \widehat{\mathcal{E}}_\rho(\widehat{f}_{fl})$. Therefore, the proof of Theorem 1 is completed.

A_1 (*agnostic error*) is mainly caused by the gap between the estimated distribution $\widetilde{\rho}$ and the real distribution ρ, because the underlying mixture weight p_k is unknown. $\mathcal{S}(\widehat{p}\|\bar{n})$ represents the distance between $\widehat{p}_k$ and the uniform mixture weight $\frac{n_k}{n}$, which gives a guidance on the choice of $\widehat{p}_k$.

Theorem 2 (Federated Error Bound). *Under the same assumptions as Theorem 1, with probability at least $1 - \delta(\delta > 0)$, we have:*

$$
A_2 \le \sum_{k=1}^{K} p_k \left(disc_L(\rho_k, \rho) + \frac{4\sqrt{2}\lambda B}{n_k} \sqrt{C} \|\phi(\boldsymbol{X}^k)\|_F \right) + \sum_{k=1}^{K} p_k \left(6M \sqrt{\frac{\log(2/\delta)}{2n_k}} \right).
$$

Proof. Note that $A_2 = \sum_{k=1}^{K} p_k [\underbrace{\mathcal{E}_{\rho_k}(\widehat{f}_{fl}) - \mathcal{E}_\rho(\widehat{f}_{cl})}_{A_2':=}]$, we decompose A_2' as:

$$
\underbrace{\mathcal{E}_{\rho_k}(\widehat{f}_{fl}) - \widehat{\mathcal{E}}_{\rho_k}(\widehat{f}_{fl})}_{A_{21}} + \underbrace{\widehat{\mathcal{E}}_{\rho_k}(\widehat{f}_{fl}) - \widehat{\mathcal{E}}_{\rho_k}(\widehat{f}_{cl})}_{A_{22}} + \underbrace{\widehat{\mathcal{E}}_{\rho_k}(\widehat{f}_{cl}) - \mathcal{E}_{\rho_k}(\widehat{f}_{cl})}_{A_{23}} + \underbrace{\mathcal{E}_{\rho_k}(\widehat{f}_{cl}) - \mathcal{E}_\rho(\widehat{f}_{cl})}_{A_{24}}.
$$

Substituting A_{22} into the equation of A_2, due to the definition of $\widehat{f}_{fl}$, we have $\sum_{k=1}^{K} p_k [\widehat{\mathcal{E}}_{\rho_k}(\widehat{f}_{fl}) - \widehat{\mathcal{E}}_{\rho_k}(\widehat{f}_{cl})] \le 0$. Similar to Theorem 1, the rest parts of A_2' can be bounded by Rademacher complexity [27] and discrepancy distance. Therefore, the proof is completed by bounding the four parts.

A_2 (*federated error*) is mainly caused by the FL setting. Samples on different clients are drawn from different distributions, which results in the discrepancy between ρ_k and ρ, where the CL model is directly trained on ρ.

Theorem 3 (Approximation Error Bound). *Under the same assumptions as Theorem 1, with probability $1 - \delta(\delta > 0)$, we have:*

$$
A_3 \le \frac{4\sqrt{2}\lambda B}{n} \sqrt{C} \|\phi(\boldsymbol{X})\|_F + 3M \sqrt{\frac{\log(2/\delta)}{2n}},
$$

where $\|\phi(\boldsymbol{X})\|_F = \sqrt{\sum_{i=1}^{n} \langle \phi(\boldsymbol{x}_i), \phi(\boldsymbol{x}_i) \rangle}$.

A_3 *(approximation error)* is a classic excess risk bound in CL setting, which represents the gap between an empirical learner and the optimal learner in $\mathcal{H}$.

Remark 1 (Proof Novelty). 1) The *excess risk* bound for FL on non-IID data can not be derived directly. To bridge $\widetilde{f}_{fl}$ to f^*, we decompose the *excess risk* into three error terms. 2) There is no available tool can be applied to bound A_1 and A_2 directly. Thus, we propose a two-stage error decomposition for A_1 and a novel decomposition for A_2 (See proofs for details).

3.2 Excess Risk Bound

The *excess risk* bound is obtained by combining the above bounds together.

Theorem 4 (Excess Risk Bound). *Under the same assumptions as Theorem 1, With probability at least $1 - \delta$ ($\delta > 0$), the excess risk bound of federated learning on non-IID data holds as follows:*

$$\mathcal{E}_\rho(\widehat{f}_{fl}) - \mathcal{E}_\rho(f^*) \leq \mathcal{O}\left(G_1 + G_2 + G_3\right), \tag{7}$$

where $G_1 = disc_L(\widetilde{\rho}, \rho) + \sum_{k=1}^{K} \frac{\widehat{p}_k B\sqrt{C}}{n_k} \|\phi(\boldsymbol{X}^k)\|_F + \sqrt{\frac{S(\widehat{p}\|\bar{n})}{n}}$, $G_2 = \frac{B\sqrt{C}}{n} \|\phi(\boldsymbol{X})\|_F +$

$\sqrt{\frac{1}{n}}$ *and* $G_3 = \sum_{k=1}^{K} p_k[disc_L(\rho_k, \rho) + \frac{B\sqrt{C}}{n_k} \|\phi(\boldsymbol{X}^k)\|_F + \sqrt{\frac{1}{n_k}}]$.

According to Theorem 4, to lower the *excess risk*, we need to reduce $disc_L(\rho_k, \rho)$, constrain $\|\boldsymbol{W}\|_*$ and $\|\phi(\boldsymbol{X}^k)\|_F$, and at the same time reduce $disc_L(\widetilde{\rho}, \rho)$.

In non-IID condition, samples on different clients are drawn from different distributions, so the gap between ρ_k and ρ certainly exists. Furthermore, p_k is unknown, how can we reduce $disc_L(\widetilde{\rho}, \rho)$? Actually, if we reduce $disc_L(\rho_k, \rho)$, the differences among local distributions will become smaller, that is, the degree of non-IID will be reduced. At this time, ρ_k is approximate to ρ, so $\widehat{p}_k$ has a small effect on $disc_L(\widetilde{\rho}, \rho)$, especially, when $\rho_k = \rho$, whatever value we choose for $\widehat{p}_k$, it's not going to make big difference to the global distribution. Therefore, we are able to lower the *excess risk* by reducing $disc_L(\rho_k, \rho)$, $\|\boldsymbol{W}\|_*$ and $\|\phi(\boldsymbol{X}^k)\|_F$.

On the other hand, when $\phi(\cdot)$ is upper bounded by κ^2 and $\widehat{p}_k$ is equal to p_k, if we can reduce $disc_L(\rho_k, \rho)$ to 0, then (7) will be $\mathcal{O}[(\kappa B\sqrt{C}+1)\sum_{k=1}^{K} \widehat{p}_k \sqrt{\frac{1}{n_k}}]$. In this case, if the number of samples is equal ($n_k = n/K$, $\forall k = 1, ..., K$), we have $\mathcal{O}(\kappa B\sqrt{KC/n})$, which is the convergence rate for the counterpart of distributed learning. Moreover, if we have only one client, we have $\mathcal{O}(\kappa B\sqrt{C/n})$, which is the convergence rate for the counterpart of centralized learning. Thus, our theory gives a more general framework that can be applied to FL as well as distributed learning [37] and CL, with the latter two being a special case of the former.

Remark 2 (Novelty). Few of the existing theoretical studies of FL are concerned with the excess risk. [26] analyzed federated learning under the agnostic framework, which aims to improve the performance under the worst condition, and this may not get the optimal solution. Also, they just give the generalization bound of agnostic federated learning. In this paper, we analyze the excess risk between federated learning model on non-IID data and the optimal centralized model under a more general framework and derive the excess risk bound, which may provide a new path for theoretical analysis of federated learning.

4   Algorithm

Motivated by the *excess risk* bound, we propose FedAvgR (Federated Averaging with Regularization) to improve the performance of FL on non-IID data.

Algorithm 1. FedAvgR. K clients are indexed by k, $\mathcal{B}$ is the local mini-batch size, E is the number of local epochs, η is the learning rate, $\boldsymbol{F}$ represents the objective function.

Server-Aggregate

1: initialize $\boldsymbol{W}_0$ and $\boldsymbol{\varphi}_0$
2: **for** $k = 1, ..., K$ **do**
3:     $\widehat{\rho}_k^\phi \leftarrow$ estimate the distribution of $\phi(\boldsymbol{x})$
4:     upload the parameters of $\widehat{\rho}_k^\phi$ to the server
5: **end for**
6: get the global distribution $\widehat{\rho}^\phi = \sum_{k=1}^{K} \widehat{p}_k \widehat{\rho}_k^\phi$
7: **for** each round $t = 1, 2, ...$ **do**
8:     **for** each client k **do**
9:         $\boldsymbol{W}_{t+1}^k, \boldsymbol{\varphi}_{t+1}^k, \widehat{\rho}_k^\phi \leftarrow$ Client-Update$(k, \boldsymbol{W}_t, \boldsymbol{\varphi}_t, \widehat{\rho}^\phi)$
10:    **end for**
11:    update the global distribution $\widehat{\rho}^\phi$
12:        $\boldsymbol{W}_{t+1} \leftarrow \sum_{k=1}^{K} \widehat{p}_k \boldsymbol{W}_{t+1}^k, \boldsymbol{\varphi}_{t+1} \leftarrow \sum_{k=1}^{K} \widehat{p}_k \boldsymbol{\varphi}_{t+1}^k$
13: **end for**

Client-Update$(k, \boldsymbol{W}_t, \boldsymbol{\varphi}_t, \widehat{\rho}^\phi)$

1: draw samples $Z_{\widehat{\rho}^\phi}$ from $\widehat{\rho}^\phi$
2: **for** epoch$= 1, ..., E$ **do**
3:     **for** $(\boldsymbol{x}, y) \in \mathcal{B}$ **do**
4:         calculate MMD$[\widehat{\rho}_k^\phi, \widehat{\rho}^\phi]$ by $(\boldsymbol{x}, y)$ and $Z_{\widehat{\rho}^\phi}$
5:         $\boldsymbol{F} = \frac{1}{\mathcal{B}} \sum_{(\boldsymbol{x},y) \in \mathcal{B}} \ell(f(\boldsymbol{x}), y) + \alpha \|\boldsymbol{W}\|_* + \beta \|\phi(\boldsymbol{X})\|_F + \gamma \text{MMD}[\widehat{\rho}_k^\phi, \widehat{\rho}^\phi]$
6:         $\boldsymbol{W}_{t+1}^k \leftarrow \boldsymbol{W}_t - \eta \nabla_{\boldsymbol{W}_t} \boldsymbol{F}, \boldsymbol{\varphi}_{t+1}^k \leftarrow \boldsymbol{\varphi}_t - \eta \nabla_{\boldsymbol{\varphi}_t} \boldsymbol{F}$
7:     **end for**
8:     $\widehat{\rho}_k^\phi \leftarrow$ estimate the distribution of $\phi(\boldsymbol{x})$
9: **end for**

4.1   Regularization

Based on Theorem 4, we can constrain $\|\boldsymbol{W}\|_*$, $\|\phi(\boldsymbol{X}^k)\|_F$, and $disc_L(\rho_k, \rho)$ by adding them to the objective function as regularizers [11,12].

Unlike $\|\boldsymbol{W}\|_*$ and $\|\phi(\boldsymbol{X}^k)\|_F$, the discrepancy distance $disc_L(\rho_k, \rho)$ is not an explicit variable-dependent term, so we need to find an approach to quantify it.

Another problem is that the local distribution ρ_k won't change during training, so we shall reduce the discrepancy after feature mapping. In other words, we can reduce $disc_L(\rho_k^\phi, \rho^\phi)$ instead of $disc_L(\rho_k, \rho)$, where ρ_k^ϕ and ρ^ϕ are respectively the local feature distribution on client k and global feature distribution.

We choose MMD (Maximum Mean Discrepancy) [4] to measure the distance between different distributions Q_1 and Q_2, which is formed as $\text{MMD}[Q_1, Q_2] = \sup_{f \in \mathcal{H}}(\mathbb{E}_{Q_1}[f(x)] - \mathbb{E}_{Q_2}[f(x)])$. Assume that $\mathcal{H}$ is a complete inner product space of f, then $\mathcal{H}$ can be termed a reproducing kernel Hilbert space when the continuous linear point evaluation mapping $f \to f(x)$ exists for all $x \in \mathcal{X}$. Thus, we can use inner product to represent $f(x)$: $f(x) = \langle f, \phi(x)\rangle_{\mathcal{H}}$, so it holds that $\text{MMD}[Q_1, Q_2] = \|\mathbb{E}_{Q_1}[\phi(x)], \mathbb{E}_{Q_2}[\phi(x')]\|_{\mathcal{H}}$, and the related expansion is:

$$\frac{1}{m^2}\sum_{i,j=1}^{m}\langle\phi(x_i),\phi(x_j)\rangle_{\mathcal{H}} + \frac{1}{n^2}\sum_{i,j=1}^{n}\langle\phi(x_i'),\phi(x_j')\rangle_{\mathcal{H}} - \frac{2}{mn}\sum_{i,j=1}^{m,n}\langle\phi(x_i),\phi(x_j')\rangle_{\mathcal{H}},$$

where m and n denotes the number of samples on Q_1 and Q_2, respectively.

Taking $\text{MMD}[\rho_k^\phi, \rho^\phi]$ as a regularizer with $\|W\|_*$ and $\|\phi(X^k)\|_F$, the objective function on the k-th client is

$$\min_{W,\varphi} \frac{1}{n_k}\sum_{i=1}^{n_k}\ell(f(x_i^k), y_i^k) + \alpha\|W\|_* + \beta\|\phi(X^k)\|_F + \gamma\text{MMD}[\rho_k^\phi, \rho^\phi].$$

4.2   Learning Framework

The procedure of `FedAvgR` is listed in Algorithm 1. First, the server sends the initial parameters to all clients, then we estimate the empirical local distribution $\widehat{\rho}_k^\phi$ and upload them to the server to get the empirical global distribution $\widehat{\rho}^\phi$. Next, at each communication round, each client updates the model parameters and reestimates $\widehat{\rho}_k^\phi$ locally. Then, the server aggregates local updates and renews $\widehat{\rho}^\phi$ based on $\widehat{\rho}_k^\phi$, which will be sent to all clients again [23].

In order to calculate $\text{MMD}[\rho_k^\phi, \rho^\phi]$ in client-update, we first drawn samples $Z_{\widehat{\rho}^\phi}$ from $\widehat{\rho}^\phi$, and then calculate $\text{MMD}[\rho_k^\phi, \rho^\phi]$ by $\phi(x^k)$ and $Z_{\widehat{\rho}^\phi}$. In server-aggregate, we choose $\widehat{p}_k = n_k/n$ to aggregate the updates, so that $\mathcal{S}(\widehat{p}\|\bar{n})$ can be minimized. Particularly, when $disc_L(\rho_k^\phi, \rho^\phi)$ is close to 0, the learning problem degenerates into the distributed learning, where n_k/n is widely used.

We design a learning framework (Fig. 1) for linear classifier to update all the parameters automatically through back-propagation, where $W^T\phi(x)$ can be treated as a fully-connected neural network with one hidden layer and we only need to initialize the parameters. Besides, we apply D feature mappings with different parameters to reduce variance. Moreover, this framework is generalizable, where $\phi(\cdot)$ can be replaced by neural network, kernel method [22], etc.

5   Experiment

In this section, we will introduce our experimental setup and conduct extensive experiments to demonstrate our theory and show the effectiveness of `FedAvgR`.

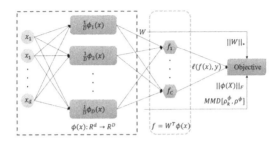

Fig. 1. Architecture of local learning framework

5.1   Experimental Setup

We evaluate our algorithm and make further analysis on some real-world datasets and the synthetic dataset. All the experiments are trained on a Linux_x86_64 server (CPU: Intel(R) Xeon(R) Silver 4214 (RAM: 196 GB)/GPU: NVIDIA GeForce RTX-2080ti).

The synthetic dataset in our experiment is generated related to the method in [16], where the number of samples n_k on client k follows a power law. We choose three binary-classification datasets (a1a, svmguide1 and splice) and six multi-classification datasets (vehicle, dna, pendigits, satimage, usps and MNIST) from LIBSVM [6]. We apply the partitioning method related to [25] to all these datasets to get non-IID data. We sort each dataset by the label and divide it into N/N_s shards of size N_s, where N is the total number of samples, then we assign each client 2 shards. The detailed information for the real-world datasets [6] is listed in Table 1, where the training sets and the test sets are officially splited except vehicle.

Table 1. Information of different datasets

Dataset	Class	Training size	Testing size	Features
a1a	2	1605	30956	123
svmguide1	2	3089	4000	4
splice	2	1000	2175	60
vehicle	4	500	446	18
dna	3	2000	1186	180
pendigits	10	7494	3498	16
satimage	6	4435	2000	36
usps	10	7291	2007	256
MNIST	10	60000	10000	28×28

In the following experiments, we use random Fourier feature to do the feature mapping. According to [29], random feature mapping can be formed as

$\sqrt{2}\cos(\boldsymbol{\omega}^T\boldsymbol{x}+b)$, where $\boldsymbol{\omega}$ is sampled from $\mathcal{N}(0,\sigma^2)$, σ is related to the corresponding Gaussian kernel, and b is uniformly sampled from $[0, 2\pi]$.

5.2   Analysis of `FedAvgR`

In this part, we will discuss the effects of different components on the performance of our algorithm. We set the feature dimension as 100, the minimum number of local samples as 100, and the number of clients as 10.

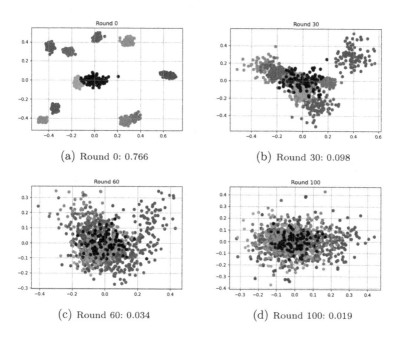

(a) Round 0: 0.766

(b) Round 30: 0.098

(c) Round 60: 0.034

(d) Round 100: 0.019

Fig. 2. Distributions Changes via Training: Black points are sampled from $\widehat{\rho}^\phi$, and others are sampled from $\widehat{\rho}_k^\phi$s, the corresponding discrepancy distance is labeled at the bottom of each figure.

Impact of $\mathbf{MMD}[\rho_k^\phi, \rho^\phi]$. $\mathrm{MMD}[\rho_k^\phi, \rho^\phi]$ is used to match local distributions to the global distribution, which is the key component to solve the non-IID problem. We run 100 rounds on the synthetic dataset with $(u, v) = (1, 1)$ and sample 100 points from each $\widehat{\rho}_k^\phi$ and $\widehat{\rho}^\phi$. To show its impact, we visualize the distributions changes via training process in Fig. 2, where all the points are transformed to 2D by PCA (Principal Component Analysis) and $disc_L(\rho_k^\phi, \rho^\phi)$ labeled in Fig. 2 is calculated by the distance among the centroids of each group of points. (a) shows the distributions after initializing by random feature, we find that there exists a certain distance between $\widehat{\rho}_k^\phi$ and $\widehat{\rho}^\phi$. (b) shows the distributions after 30 rounds training, and (c) shows the result after 60 rounds training, it is apparent that $disc_L(\widehat{\rho}_k^\phi, \widehat{\rho}^\phi)$ is getting smaller. (d) shows the distributions after 100 rounds, where the local distributions of all clients converge toward the global distribution, which can reduce the negative impact of non-IID, and this also demonstrate the effectiveness of `FedAvgR`.

Impacts of Different Regularizers. We conduct an experiment to analyze the three regularizers. We run 250 rounds on the synthetic dataset with $(u, v) = (0.5, 0.5)$ and some real-world datasets with non-iid partitioning. As shown in Table 2, `FedAvgR` mostly performs the best, and `FedAvgR` without regularization (equal to `FedAvg`) performs the worst. The performances are close when `FedAvgR` only contains $\|\boldsymbol{W}\|_*$ or $\|\phi(\boldsymbol{X}^k)\|_F$, because both of them are designed to limit the Rademacher complexity. The performance of `FedAvgR` only with $\mathrm{MMD}[\rho_k^\phi, \rho^\phi]$ is only second to `FedAvgR` with all three regularizers on most datasets, which exactly demonstrates our theory that when the gap between ρ_k and ρ becomes smaller, the performance of the model will be improved.

Table 2. Test accuracy of `FedAvgR` with different regualrizers

Dataset	No regularizer	$\|\boldsymbol{W}\|_*$	$\|\phi(\boldsymbol{X}^k)\|_F$	MMD	All regularizers
svmguide1	89.05	89.20	89.45	89.61	**90.70**
vehicle	77.12	77.17	77.17	77.46	**78.32**
dna	95.33	95.52	95.36	95.45	**95.70**
pendigits	95.70	95.71	95.74	**95.94**	95.90
usps	94.57	94.72	**94.82**	94.80	**94.82**
synthetic	95.82	96.07	96.06	96.12	**96.23**

5.3   Comparison with Other Methods

In this part, we compare `FedAvgR` with `OneShot` [39], `FedAvg` [25], `FedProx` [15] and `FL+HC` [5] on several LIBSVM datasets. The regularization parameters of `FedAvgR` are selected in $\alpha \in \{10^{-8}, 10^{-7}, ..., 10^{-4}\}$, $\beta \in \{10^{-6}, 10^{-5}, ..., 10^{-2}\}$, and $\gamma \in \{10^{-4}, 10^{-3}, ..., 10^{-1}\}$ through 3-folds cross-validation [19,20], the regularization parameters of `FedProx` are selected in $\{10^{-4}, 10^{-3}, ..., 10^{-1}\}$, and the number of clusters is set as 2 in `FL+HC`. The top-1 accuracy is used to evaluate the performance, and the communication round is set as 300 with 10 epochs on each client per round. We implement all the methods based on Pytorch and use Momentum as optimizer with 10 instances in a mini-batch for training. We run all the methods on each dataset 10 times with different random seeds, and we apply t-test to estimate the statistical significance.

Instead of partitioning the test samples to each client, we test all the algorithms with the entire test set of each dataset, because our target is to learn a global model that has the best generalized performance on the global distribution

ρ. OneShot aggregates local models when local trainings converge, FedAvg iteratively averages local models by n_k/n, FedProx adds the last-round's global model to local training as regularization based on FedAvg, and FL+HC uses hierarchical clustering to divide clients into several clusters and applies FedAvg separately.

According to the results in Table 3, FedAvgR shows the best performances on all datasets, which means that the use of three regularizers brings notable improvement coincides with our theoretical analysis. OneShot, FedAvg and FedProx do not consider or explicitly deal with the differences among local distributions, which limits the model's performance on non-IID data, while FedAvgR reduces the discrepancies between $\widehat{\rho}_k^{\phi}$s and $\widehat{\rho}^{\phi}$. FL+HC is a personalized method for scenarios where each client has its own test samples. In particular, when the number of clusters is 1, FL+HC is equal to FedAvg.

On most datasets, FedAvgR is significantly better than other methods with confidence at level 95%. However, on a1a and splice, the advantage of our algorithm is not significant. The reason is that the datasets are not balanced, where the number of training samples is far less than the number of test samples.

Table 3. Test Accuracy on Real-World Datasets. We run methods on each dataset 10 times, each with 300 rounds. We bold the numbers of the best method and underline the numbers of other methods which are not significantly worse than the best one.

Dataset	OneShot	FedAvg	FedProx	FL+HC	FedAvgR
a1a	76.86 ± 0.30	84.29 ± 0.06	84.27 ± 0.06	81.63 ± 0.94	**84.30 ± 0.06**
svmguide1	71.50 ± 4.21	90.95 ± 0.86	91.19 ± 0.84	85.66 ± 4.48	**91.77 ± 1.01**
splice	75.95 ± 4.56	90.37 ± 0.21	90.38 ± 0.20	85.12 ± 2.14	**90.40 ± 0.26**
vehicle	52.31 ± 4.36	78.61 ± 1.08	78.58 ± 1.06	62.24 ± 8.12	**78.82 ± 0.98**
dna	63.73 ± 1.02	95.23 ± 0.17	95.18 ± 0.21	92.09 ± 3.25	**95.59 ± 0.23**
pendigits	46.70 ± 2.32	94.87 ± 0.58	94.85 ± 0.59	86.81 ± 4.58	**95.12 ± 0.48**
satimage	73.07 ± 2.39	88.83 ± 0.41	88.46 ± 0.31	76.72 ± 2.96	**88.93 ± 0.39**
usps	56.83 ± 4.06	94.57 ± 0.15	94.53 ± 0.13	88.03 ± 3.62	**94.80 ± 0.19**
MNIST	68.80 ± 2.06	97.26 ± 0.09	97.24 ± 0.07	85.13 ± 2.23	**97.34 ± 0.06**

6   Conclusion

In this paper, we give an *excess risk* bound for federated learning on non-IID data through Rademacher complexity and discrepancy distance, analyzing the error between it and the optimal centralized learning model. Based on our theory, we propose FedAvgR to improve the performance of federated learning in non-IID setting, where three regularizers are added to achieve a sharper bound. Experiments show that our algorithm outperforms the previous methods. As the first work to analyze the *excess risk* under a more general framework, our work will provide a reference for the future study of generalization properties in federated learning with non-IID data. Besides, the proof techniques in this paper are helpful to the research of error analysis related to the distributed framework.

Acknowledgement. This work was supported in part by Excellent Talents Program of Institute of Information Engineering, CAS, Special Research Assistant Project of CAS (No. E0YY231114), Beijing Outstanding Young Scientist Program (No. BJJWZYJH01 2019100020098), National Natural Science Foundation of China (No. 62076234, No. 62106257) and Beijing Municipal Science and Technology Commission under Grant Z191100007119002.

References

1. Bartlett, P.L., Bousquet, O., Mendelson, S.: Localized rademacher complexities. In: COLT, vol. 2375, pp. 44–58 (2002)
2. Basu, D., Data, D., Karakus, C., Diggavi, S.N.: Qsparse-local-SGD: distributed SGD with quantization, sparsification and local computations. In: NeurIPS, pp. 14668–14679 (2019)
3. Ben-David, S., Blitzer, J., Crammer, K., Kulesza, A., Pereira, F., Vaughan, J.W.: A theory of learning from different domains. Mach. Learn. **79**(1-2), 151–175 (2010)
4. Borgwardt, K M., Gretton, A., Rasch, M.J., Kriegel, H., Schölkopf, B., Smola, A.J.: Integrating structured biological data by Kernel maximum mean discrepancy. In: Proceedings of the 14th International Conference on Intelligent Systems for Molecular Biology, pp. 49–57 (2006)
5. Briggs, C., Fan, Z., Andras, P.: Federated learning with hierarchical clustering of local updates to improve training on non-IID data. In: International Joint Conference on Neural Networks, IJCNN, pp. 1–9. IEEE (2020)
6. Chang, C.C., Lin, C.J.: LIBSVM: a library for support vector machines. ACM Trans. Intell. Syst. Technol. **2**, 27:1–27:27 (20)
7. Charles, Z., Konečný, J.: Convergence and accuracy trade-offs in federated learning and meta-learning. In: AISTATS, vol. 130, pp. 2575–2583 (2021)
8. Cortes, C., Kuznetsov, V., Mohri, M., Yang, S.: Structured prediction theory based on factor graph complexity. In: NIPS, pp. 2514–2522 (2016)
9. Karimireddy, S.P., Kale, S., Mohri, M., Reddi, S.J., Stich, S.U., Suresh, A.T.: SCAFFOLD: stochastic controlled averaging for federated learning. In: ICML, vol. 119, pp. 5132–5143 (2020)
10. Li, J., Liu, Y., Wang, W.: Automated spectral Kernel learning. In: AAAI, pp. 4618–4625 (2020)
11. Li, J., Liu, Y., Yin, R., Wang, W.: Approximate manifold regularization: Scalable algorithm and generalization analysis. In: IJCAI. pp. 2887–2893 (2019)
12. Li, J., Liu, Y., Yin, R., Wang, W.: Multi-class learning using unlabeled samples: theory and algorithm. In: IJCAI, pp. 2880–2886 (2019)
13. Li, J., Liu, Y., Yin, R., Zhang, H., Ding, L., Wang, W.: Multi-class learning: from theory to algorithm. In: NeurIPS, pp. 1593–1602 (2018)
14. Li, T., Sahu, A.K., Talwalkar, A., Smith, V.: Federated learning: challenges, methods, and future directions. IEEE Sig. Process. Mag. **37**(3), 50–60 (2020)
15. Li, T., Sahu, A.K., Zaheer, M., Sanjabi, M., Talwalkar, A., Smith, V.: Federated optimization in heterogeneous networks. In: MLSys (2020)
16. Li, X., Huang, K., Yang, W., Wang, S., Zhang, Z.: On the convergence of FedAvg on non-iid data. In: ICLR (2020)

17. Li, Z., Kovalev, D., Qian, X., Richtárik, P.: Acceleration for compressed gradient descent in distributed and federated optimization. In: ICML, vol. 119, pp. 5895–5904 (2020)
18. Lian, X., Zhang, C., Zhang, H., Hsieh, C., Zhang, W., Liu, J.: Can decentralized algorithms outperform centralized algorithms? A case study for decentralized parallel stochastic gradient descent. In: NeurIPS, pp. 5330–5340 (2017)
19. Liu, Y., Jiang, S., Liao, S.: Efficient approximation of cross-validation for kernel methods using Bouligand influence function. In: ICML, vol. 32, pp. 324–332 (2014)
20. Liu, Y., Liao, S., Jiang, S., Ding, L., Lin, H., Wang, W.: Fast cross-validation for kernel-based algorithms. IEEE Trans. Pattern Anal. Mach. Intell. **42**(5), 1083–1096 (2020)
21. Liu, Y., Liao, S., Lin, H., Yue, Y., Wang, W.: Generalization analysis for ranking using integral operator. In: AAAI, pp. 2273–2279 (2017)
22. Liu, Y., Liao, S., Lin, H., Yue, Y., Wang, W.: Infinite Kernel learning: generalization bounds and algorithms. In: AAAI, pp. 2280–2286 (2017)
23. Liu, Y., Liu, J., Wang, S.: Effective distributed learning with random features: improved bounds and algorithms. In: ICLR (2021)
24. Mansour, Y., Mohri, M., Rostamizadeh, A.: Domain adaptation: learning bounds and algorithms. In: COLT (2009)
25. McMahan, B., Moore, E., Ramage, D., Hampson, S., y Arcas, B.A.: Communication-efficient learning of deep networks from decentralized data. In: AISTATS, vol. 54, pp. 1273–1282 (2017)
26. Mohri, M., Sivek, G., Suresh, A.T.: Agnostic federated learning. In: ICML, vol. 97, pp. 4615–4625 (2019)
27. Mehryar, A.R.M., Talwalkar, A.: Foundations of Machine Learning. The MIT Press, Cambridge second edn. (2018)
28. Pustozerova, A., Rauber, A., Mayer, R.: Training effective neural networks on structured data with federated learning. In: AINA, vol. 226, pp. 394–406 (2021)
29. Rahimi, A., Recht, B.: Random features for large-scale Kernel machines. In: NIPS, pp. 1177–1184 (2007)
30. Sattler, F., Müller, K.R., Samek, W.: Clustered federated learning: model-agnostic distributed multitask optimization under privacy constraints. IEEE Trans. Neural Netw. Learn. Syst. **32**(8), 3710–3722 (2021)
31. Smith, V., Chiang, C., Sanjabi, M., Talwalkar, A.S.: Federated multi-task learning. In: NIPS, pp. 4424–4434 (2017)
32. Stich, S.U.: Local SGD converges fast and communicates little. In: ICLR (2019)
33. Wang, H., Yurochkin, M., Sun, Y., Papailiopoulos, D.S., Khazaeni, Y.: Federated learning with matched averaging. In: ICLR (2020)
34. Wang, J., Liu, Q., Liang, H., Joshi, G., Poor, H.V.: Tackling the objective inconsistency problem in heterogeneous federated optimization. In: NeurIPS (2020)
35. Wang, J., Tantia, V., Ballas, N., Rabbat, M.G.: SLOWMO: improving communication-efficient distributed SGD with slow momentum. In: ICLR (2020)
36. Wang, S., et al.: Adaptive federated learning in resource constrained edge computing systems. IEEE J. Sel. Areas Commun. **37**(6), 1205–1221 (2019)
37. Yin, R., Liu, Y., Lu, L., Wang, W., Meng, D.: Divide-and-conquer learning with nyström: optimal rate and algorithm. In: AAAI, pp. 6696–6703 (2020)
38. Yu, H., Jin, R., Yang, S.: On the linear speedup analysis of communication efficient momentum SGD for distributed non-convex optimization. In: ICML, vol. 97, pp. 7184–7193 (2019)

39. Zhang, Y., Duchi, J.C., Wainwright, M.J.: Divide and conquer kernel ridge regression: a distributed algorithm with minimax optimal rates. J. Mach. Learn. Res. **16**, 3299–3340 (2015)
40. Zhang, Y., Liu, T., Long, M., Jordan, M.I.: Bridging theory and algorithm for domain adaptation. In: ICML, vol. 97, pp. 7404–7413 (2019)

Fixed-Price Diffusion Mechanism Design

Tianyi Zhang[1,3,4], Dengji Zhao[1,2(✉)], Wen Zhang[1], and Xuming He[1,2]

[1] ShanghaiTech University, Shanghai, China
{zhangty,zhaodj,zhangwen,hexm}@shanghaitech.edu.cn
[2] Shanghai Engineering Research Center of Intelligent Vision and Imaging,
Shanghai, China
[3] Shanghai Institute of Microsystem and Information Technology,
Chinese Academy of Sciences, Shanghai, China
[4] University of Chinese Academy of Sciences, Beijing, China

Abstract. We consider a fixed-price mechanism design setting where a seller sells one item via a social network. Each buyer in the network has a valuation of the item independently derived from a given continuous distribution. Initially, the seller can only directly communicate with her neighbors and sells the item among them. In order to get a higher revenue, she needs more buyers to participate in the sale. One recent solution is to design dedicated mechanisms to incentivize buyers to invite their neighbors to join the sale, but they have relatively high time complexity and may evoke concern for privacy. We propose the very first fixed-price mechanism to achieve the same goal with less time complexity and better preservation of privacy. It improves the maximal expected revenue of the fixed-price mechanism without diffusion. Especially, when the valuation distribution is uniform on $[0, 1]$, it guarantees a lower bound of the improvement.

Keywords: Mechanism design · Fixed-price mechanism · Information diffusion · Social network

1 Introduction

Social networks, drawing support from popular platforms such as Facebook, Twitter etc., can facilitate the diffusion of sale information [11]. The diffusion of sale information promotes the sale and improves the seller's revenue. To that end, some desirable rules must be set up for participants to follow. Mechanism design aims to build up a set of rules so that the strategic behaviors of participants lead to the desirable results [19].

Therefore, how to design mechanisms on social networks to promote the sale has attracted much attention from researchers in economics, computer science and artificial intelligence [6].

There has been some recent work to tackle this issue [15,16,21–23]. They studied the well-known Vickrey-Clarke-Groves (VCG) mechanism [5,8,20] in the scenario of social networks and proposed new mechanisms with dedicated

© Springer Nature Switzerland AG 2021
D. N. Pham et al. (Eds.): PRICAI 2021, LNAI 13031, pp. 49–62, 2021.
https://doi.org/10.1007/978-3-030-89188-6_4

payment schemes to attract more buyers via social networks. However, these mechanisms have relatively high computational complexity and may evoke concern for privacy because they require all buyers to report their valuations of the items for sale.

Therefore, designing a faster mechanism of better preservation of privacy running on social networks is worth exploring. We noticed that fixed-price mechanisms are characterized by simplicity and preservation of privacy [1,3,7,9,12,13]. In a fixed-price mechanism for selling one item, a seller sets a fixed price for the item in advance and each buyer decides whether to buy it or not according to her valuation of the item. With such simplicity and preservation of privacy, fixed-price mechanisms have been the most applied trading rules for selling products in practice [17]. So, in this paper, we aim to design a fixed-price mechanism on social networks to attract more buyers. The goal is to promote the sale and improve the seller's revenue.

How to approximate the optimal revenue in fixed-price mechanisms has been investigated in the literature. Babaioff *et al.* [2] considered a dynamic auction model with fixed prices and showed that sequential posted-price mechanisms cannot guarantee a constant fraction of the optimal revenue that is achievable if the distribution is unknown to the seller. Chawla *et al.* [4] generalized the optimal single-parameter auction mechanism proposed by Myerson [18] to multi-parameter auction settings and proposed an approximately optimal sequential posted pricing mechanism. Alaei *et al.* [1] proved that the seller's revenue under fixed-price mechanisms can achieve at least $\frac{1}{e}$ of Myerson's optimal mechanism when valuation distributions are independent and non-identical. Jin *et al.* [12] provided a tight approximation ratio $\frac{1}{2.62}$ for the fixed-price mechanism compared with the optimal auction under single-item Bayesian mechanism design setting.

However, the above studies assumed that the number of participants remains a constant in the selling process. Obviously, more buyers will increase the chance of selling out the items and may increase the revenue of the seller. Actually, we will show in the later section that under the fixed-price setting there is an optimal expected revenue for a fixed number of buyers. Therefore, the seller is willing to attract more buyers to increase her revenue.

This paper considers designing a fixed-price mechanism to help the seller attract more buyers via a social network. We assume that the seller is located on the social network and initially she can only contact her neighbors. We want the seller's neighbors to help her attract more buyers. However, they would not do so without giving them a proper incentive (because they are competitors for the item). The goal of our mechanism is to design such an incentive for them.

To achieve the goal, we design a *fixed-price diffusion mechanism* (FPDM) for selling one item via social networks. It integrates the merits of both fixed-price mechanisms and social networks, and distinguishes itself with the following:

- Helping the seller to attract more buyers via social networks.
- Improving the maximal expected revenue of the fixed-price mechanism without diffusion, and guaranteeing a lower bound of the improvement for the seller when the valuation distribution is the uniform distribution on $[0, 1]$.
- Having less time complexity and better protection of privacy compared with the previous mechanisms [15, 16, 21–23].

The rest of the paper is structured as follows. Section 2 describes the model. Section 3 investigates the optimal price and the maximum revenue of the fixed-price mechanism without diffusion. Section 4 defines our fixed-price diffusion mechanism. Section 5 studies the properties of the proposed mechanism. We conclude in Sect. 6.

2   The Model

We consider a market where a seller sells one item via a social network denoted by a direct acyclic graph (DAG) $\langle V \cup \{s\}, E \rangle$, where the source node s represents the seller and the other nodes in the DAG represent the buyers. Each buyer $i \in V$ has a valuation $v_i \geq 0$ for the item. We assume that all the buyers' valuations are independently drawn from a continuous distribution with both cumulative distribution function (CDF) $F(x)$ and probability density function (PDF) $f(x)$ of a support set $[0, v_{max}]$ [19]. For each edge $(i, j) \in E$, j is called a neighbor of i and all neighbors of i is denoted by $n_i \subseteq V \setminus \{i\}$. Each $i \in V$ is not aware of others except her neighbors n_i.

Initially, the seller only knows her neighbors and invites them to participate in the sale. To improve the seller's revenue, each of the seller's neighbors is incentivized to invite her neighbors to participate in the sale. Again, each invitee makes further invitations, and so on. Finally, all the buyers in the network can join the sale.

Since our mechanism is expected not to require agents to report their valuations but to diffuse the sale information to their neighbors, we let n_i be the *type* of $i \in V$. Let $a = (n_1, \cdots, n_{|V|})$ be the type profile of all agents. Let $n_i' \subseteq n_i$ or $n_i' = nil$ be the *action* of i, where nil indicates that i is not informed or she does not want to participate in the sale. The tuple $a' = (n_1', \cdots, n_{|V|}')$ is the action profile of all agents. We also write $a' = (n_i', n_{-i}')$, where $n_{-i}' = (n_1', \cdots, n_{i-1}', n_{i+1}', \cdots, n_{|V|}')$ is the action profile of all agents except i.

Definition 1. *Given a type profile a, an action profile a' is feasible if for each agent $i \in V$, her action is not nil if and only if i is informed the sale information following the action profile of n_{-i}'.*

A feasible action profile indicates that a buyer cannot join the mechanism if she is not informed by anyone. If she is informed, she can further inform more buyers from her neighbors. Let $\mathcal{F}(a)$ be the set of all feasible action profiles of all agents under a type profile a.

Definition 2. *A mechanism consists of an allocation policy* $\pi = (\pi_i)_{i \in V}$ *and a payment policy* $p = (p_i)_{i \in V}$, *where* $\pi_i : \mathcal{F}(a) \to \{0, 1\}$ *and* $p_i : \mathcal{F}(a) \to \mathbb{R}$ *are the allocation and payment functions of buyer* i *respectively.*

The mechanism is defined only on feasible action profiles. Given a feasible action profile $a' \in \mathcal{F}(a)$, $\pi_i(a') = 1$ indicates that i receives the item whereas $\pi_i(a') = 0$ indicates that i does not. If $p_i(a') \geq 0$, then i pays $p_i(a')$ to the mechanism; otherwise i receives $|p_i(a')|$ from the mechanism.

We assume that each buyer will express her willingness to buy the item when her valuation is not lower than her payment.

Next, we introduce the related properties of the mechanism.

Definition 3. *An allocation policy* π *is feasible if for all* $a' \in \mathcal{F}(a)$,

- *for all* $i \in V$, *if her action is nil, then* $\pi_i(a') = 0$.
- $\sum_{i \in V} \pi_i(a') \leq 1$.

In the rest of the paper, only feasible allocations are considered.

Given a feasible action profile a' and a mechanism (π, p), the utility of i is defined as

$$u_i(a', (\pi, p)) - \pi_i(a') \cdot v_i - p_i(a').$$

A mechanism is individually rational if, for each buyer, her utility is always non-negative no matter how many neighbors she informs. That is, such a mechanism incentivizes all the buyers to participate in the sale.

Definition 4. *A mechanism* (π, p) *is individually rational (IR) if* $u_i(a', (\pi, p)) \geq 0$ *for all* $i \in V$, *for all* $a' \in \mathcal{F}(a)$.

In a standard mechanism design setting, a mechanism is incentive compatible if and only if for each buyer, reporting her truthful action is a dominant strategy [19]. In our setting, the action of each buyer is diffusing the sale information. Hence, diffusion incentive compatibility indicates that for each buyer, diffusing the sale information to all her neighbors is a dominant strategy.

Definition 5. *A mechanism* (π, p) *is diffusion incentive compatible (DIC) if* $u_i(a', (\pi, p)) \geq u_i(a'', (\pi, p))$ *for all* $i \in V$, *for all* $a', a'' \in \mathcal{F}(a)$ *such that* $n_i' = n_i$ *and for all* $j \neq i$, $n_j'' = n_j'$ *if there exists an invitation chain from the seller* s *to* j *following the action profile of* (n_i'', n_{-i}').

In this paper, we design a fixed-price diffusion mechanism that is IR and DIC. Besides, it improves the seller's maximal expected revenue and guarantees a lower bound of the revenue improvement for the seller when the valuation distribution is $U[0, 1]$.

3   Fixed-Price Mechanism Without Diffusion

In this part, we investigate the optimal fixed price to maximize the revenue under the fixed-price mechanism, which will be compared with the revenue of our diffusion mechanism.

Proposition 1. *Given the continuous valuation distribution $F(x)$, there exists an optimal fixed price p_0 to maximize the seller's expected revenue ER, and the maximum expected revenue ER_0 is an increasing function of $|n_s|$, where $|n_s|$ is the number of seller's neighbors.*

Proof. Since the valuations of all buyers on the item have the independent and identical distribution $F(x)$, the probability that a buyer's valuation $v_i < p$ equals $P(v_i < p) = F(p)$, and the probability that the seller's neighbors' valuations are less than p equals $F^{|n_s|}(p)$, which is also the probability that the item cannot be sold. So, the probability that the item can be sold is $(1 - F^{|n_s|}(p))$ with the seller's revenue being p. Thus we get the seller's expected revenue $ER = (1 - F^{|n_s|}(p)) \cdot p$, which is continuous on $[0, v_{max}]$. According to the Maximum Principle, ER attains its maximum at some point $p_0 \in [0, v_{max}]$. Since $F(p_0) \in [0, 1]$, the maximum expected revenue $ER_0 = (1 - F^{|n_s|}(p_0)) \cdot p_0$ increases with $|n_s|$.   □

Using the above optimal price p_0 which can be obtained by numerical methods (e.g. Newton's iteration), the fixed-price mechanism for continuous valuation distribution can be described as follows.

Fixed-price Mechanism without Diffusion

---

1. Compute the optimal price p_0.
2. The seller informs all her neighbors of p_0.
3. If there are buyers expressing to buy the item, the seller selects one among them (with random tie-breaking) to allocate the item and charges her p_0.
4. Otherwise, the seller keeps the item.

Proposition 2. *When the valuation has the uniform distribution $U[0,1]$, the optimal price p_0 and the maximum revenue ER_0 have analytic expressions as follows:*

$$p_0 = \left(\frac{1}{1 + |n_s|} \right)^{\frac{1}{|n_s|}}, \tag{1}$$

$$ER_0 = (1 - p_0^{|n_s|}) \cdot p_0. \tag{2}$$

The above expressions can be derived easily by solving the maximum point of the seller's expected revenue $ER = (1 - p^{|n_s|}) \cdot p$, where p is the fixed price of the item.

4   Fixed-Price Diffusion Mechanism

In the fixed-price mechanism discussed in the last section, the seller sells the item only among her neighbors at the optimal price and gets the maximal expected revenue. In this section, to further improve the revenue, a fixed-price diffusion mechanism is designed to increase the number of participants by incentivizing those aware of the sale to diffuse the information to all their neighbors.

We first give some definitions and notations defined on the DAG $\langle V, E \rangle$.

Definition 6. *For each buyer $i \in V$ such that her action is not nil, her depth denoted by d_i is defined as the length of the shortest path from the seller to i. The length of a path is the number of edges on it.*

Definition 7. *For any two buyers $i \neq j \in V$ such that their actions are not nil, we say i is j's critical node if all the paths starting from the seller to j pass through i. If $c_1, c_2, \cdots, c_t$ are all the critical nodes of i and their depths satisfy the condition $d_{c_1} \leq d_{c_2} \leq \cdots \leq d_{c_t}$, we call $C_i = \{c_1, c_2, \cdots, c_t\}$ the critical sequence of i.*

Let the branch $BR_i(1 \leq i \leq |n_s|)$ denote the set of the nodes having i as their critical node, k_i denote the cardinality of BR_i, and k_{-i} denote the number of all buyers except BR_i.

Given an action profile $a' \in \mathcal{F}(a)$, by the invitations described in Sect. 2, a DAG $\langle V', E' \rangle \subseteq \langle V, E \rangle$ is generated, where $V' \subseteq V$ is the set of agents participating in the sale.

Key points of our mechanism can be sketched as follows. First, when a buyer invites more neighbors, the other buyers' expected winning prices increase (so the buyer will have a higher chance to get the item). In order to further strengthen the incentive to invite neighbors, the winner shares some utility with her critical nodes. Second, the DAG generated by an action profile is transformed into a tree-shape graph where each branch is separated from the others. Third, the item is promoted firstly among the seller's neighbors and then sequentially among the branches of the tree-shape graph.

The proposed mechanism is formally described in the following.

Fixed-price Diffusion Mechanism (FPDM)

Given an action profile $a' \in \mathcal{F}(a)$, generate a DAG $\langle V', E' \rangle$.

- **Transformation:** Transform the DAG $\langle V', E' \rangle$ into a tree-shape graph TG using Algorithm 1.
- **Allocation:** Compute the fixed price p_0 for the seller's neighbors and inform them of the price.
  - If there are neighbors expressing to buy the item, among them select the buyer j with the most number of neighbors (with random tie-breaking) and let $\pi_j(a') = 1$.

- If all neighbors do not express to buy the item, then for $i = 1, 2, \cdots, |n_s| + l$ (assuming $k_1 \geq k_2 \geq \cdots \geq k_{|n_s|+l}$), do
    * set the fixed-price $p_i(a')$ to be either the maximum point of $(1 - F^{k-i}(p)) \cdot p$ for $k_{-i} \neq 0$ or $\frac{1}{2}$ for $k_{-i} = 0$.
    * inform the buyers in $BR_i \setminus n_s$ of the above price. If there are buyers expressing to buy the item, select one buyer j with the smallest depth and the most number of neighbors from them (with random tie-breaking) and let $\pi_j(a') = 1$.
- Otherwise, let s keep the item.
- **Payment:**
  - If there exists some buyer $j \in BR_i$ $(1 \leq i \leq |n_s| + l)$ such that $\pi_j(a') = 1$, then for each buyer $r \in V'$, the payment is:

$$
p_r(a') = \begin{cases} p_0 & \text{if } r = j \in n_s, \\ p_i(a') & \text{if } r = j \notin n_s, \\ -p_i(a') \cdot \alpha \cdot (\frac{1}{2})^{d_r} & \text{if } r \in C_j, \\ 0 & \text{else,} \end{cases}
$$

    where $\alpha \in (0, 1)$ is predefined and d_r is the depth of buyer r.
  - Otherwise, let $p_r(a') = 0$ for each $r \in V'$.

Algorithm 1. Transformation into a tree-shape graph TG from a DAG $\langle V', E' \rangle$

Input: The DAG $\langle V', E' \rangle$
Output: A TG $\langle s, BR_1, \cdots, BR_{|n_s|+l} \rangle$

1: Initialize A=ϕ;
2: **for** $i = 1, 2, \cdots, |n_s|$ **do**
3:　　Find out the branch BR_i;
4:　　Delete the set of edges (denoted by E_i) out from BR_i;
5:　　Set $E' = E' \setminus E_i$;
6: Set $A = V' \setminus \{BR_1, \cdots, BR_{|n_s|}\}$ and $l = |A|$ representing the cardinality of A;
7: **for** $j = 1, 2, \cdots, l$ **do**
8:　　Take a node q from A;
9:　　Set $A = A \setminus \{q\}$;
10:　　Draw an edge e_j from s to q;
11:　　Set $BR_{|n_s|+j} = \{q\}$ and $E' = E' \cup \{e_j\}$;
12: Set $TG = \langle s, BR_1, \cdots, BR_{|n_s|+l} \rangle$;
13: **return** TG

When the valuation distribution is the uniform distribution $U[0,1]$, $p_i(a')$ is computed by substituting $|n_s|$ in Formula (1) for k_{-i}, i.e.

$$p_i(a') = \left(\frac{1}{1+k_{-i}}\right)^{\frac{1}{k_{-i}}}. \tag{3}$$

We exemplify FPDM with the following example.

Example 1. Suppose buyers' valuations of the item are independently drawn from the distribution $U[0,1]$. The upper sub-figure in Fig. 1 is the DAG generated by a feasible action profile a'. The bottom sub-figure in Fig. 1 is the tree-shape graph transformed from the DAG, with s standing for the seller and the numbers $1,2,\cdots,10$ standing for the buyers. The set of the nodes having node 1 as their critical node is $\{4,5,6,10\}$. By deleting the edge from node 6 pointing to node 7, we get the first branch $BR_1 = \{1,4,5,6,10\}$. Similarly, we get $BR_2 = \{2,8\}$, $BR_3 = \{3\}$, $BR_4 = \{7\}$ and $BR_5 = \{9\}$.

Next, by Formula (3) and Formula (1), we get $p_1(a') = 0.699$, $p_2(a') = 0.760$, $p_3(a') = 0.774$, $p_4(a') = 0.774$, $p_5(a') = 0.774$ and $p_0 = 0.630$. The seller first tells the fixed price 0.630 to her neighbors $n_s = \{1,2,3\}$. According to their valuations (not revealed), all the neighbors do not express their willingness to buy the item. Next, the seller tells the fixed price 0.699 to all the buyers in $\{4,5,6,10\}$ and only buyer 5 and 10 express their willingness to buy the item. Since buyer 5 has the depth of 3 and buyer 10 has the depth of 4, the seller allocates the item to buyer 5 and buyer 5 pays the seller 0.699. It can be worked out that $C_5 = \{1\}$ and $d_1 = 1$. Let $\alpha = 0.1$. Then the payment of buyer 1 is $-p_1(a') \cdot \alpha \cdot (\frac{1}{2})^{d_1} = -0.03$. So the utility of buyer 1 is 0.03 and the utilities of others except both buyer 1 and winner 5 are 0. The seller's revenue is $0.699 - 0.03 = 0.669$.

5   Properties of FPDM

Now we consider the individual rationality, diffusion incentive compatibility, lower bound of the revenue improvement and time complexity of FPDM.

First, individual rationality means that each participant of the sale has non-negative utility.

Theorem 1. *The fixed-price diffusion mechanism is individually rational.*

Proof. Given an action profile $a' \in \mathcal{F}(a)$, generate a DAG $\langle V', E' \rangle$. We need to prove that, for all $i \in V'$, it holds that

$$u_i(a', (\pi^{FPDM}, p^{FPDM})) \geq 0.$$

Without loss of generality, we assume that $i \in BR_j$ $(1 \leq j \leq |n_s| + l)$. The i's utility has four possibilities.

- If $i \in n_s$ and $\pi_i(a') = 1$, then by the allocation of the mechanism, i's utility is higher than 0.

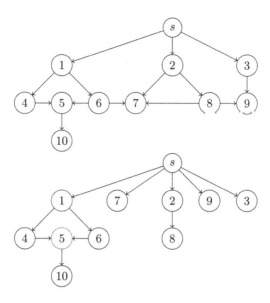

Fig. 1. Transformation from a DAG $\langle V', E' \rangle$ to a tree-shape graph

- If $i \in V' \setminus n_s$ and $\pi_i(a') = 1$, then by the allocation of the mechanism, i's utility is higher than 0.
- If $\pi_i(a') = 0$, $\pi_w(a') = 1$ ($w \in BR_j$) and $i \in C_w$, then i's utility is $p_j(a') \cdot \alpha \cdot (\frac{1}{2})^{d_i}$. Since $p_j(a') > 0$, $\alpha > 0$ and $d_i > 0$, it holds that $p_j(a') \cdot \alpha \cdot (\frac{1}{2})^{d_i} > 0$.
- Otherwise, i's payment and utility are both 0.

Therefore, we have $u_i(a', (\pi^{FPDM}, p^{FPDM})) \geq 0$ for all $i \in V'$. □

As for the diffusion incentive compatibility of the proposed mechanism, we only need to prove that, for each buyer, in stages of both transformation and selling (including allocation and payment), diffusing the information to all her neighbors is her dominant strategy (maximizing her utility), which means the mechanism incentivizes her to do so.

Theorem 2. *The fixed-price diffusion mechanism is diffusion incentive compatible.*

Proof. Given an action profile $a' \in \mathcal{F}(a)$, generate a DAG $\langle V', E' \rangle$. First, each buyer cannot utilize the transformation of the DAG to choose between her critical nodes and the branch she belongs to and further to decide her payment. So she has no incentive not to diffuse the information to all her neighbors. That is, diffusing the information to all her neighbors is her dominant strategy.

Next in the selling stage, when each buyer i's action is not *nil* ($i \in V'$), the buyer i must fall into one of the following categories.

1. The winner w, i.e. the buyer who receives the item;
2. The buyers in C_w, i.e. the critical nodes of the winner;
3. The others.

Next we prove the statement in every category. Without loss of generality, we assume the winner $w \in BR_j$ $(1 \le j \le |n_s| + l)$.

Category 1: If $w \in n_s$, diffusing the sale information to all her neighbors brings her the utility $u_w(a', (\pi^{FPDM}, p^{FPDM})) = v_w - p_0$. Since p_0 is only related to the number of seller's neighbors, her utility is independent of her diffusion. If $w \notin n_s$, the same diffusion brings her the utility $u_w(a', (\pi^{FPDM}, p^{FPDM})) = v_w - p_j(a')$, which is also independent of her diffusion.

Instead, whether $w \in n_s$ or not, not diffusing the information to all her neighbors either leads her to lose the item and thus to fall into **Category 3** with zero utility or makes her still be in **Category 1** and thus her utility does not change. In summary, not diffusing the information to all neighbors does not make her utility better off. So, diffusing the sale information to all her neighbors is her dominant strategy.

Category 2: In this case, diffusing the information to all her neighbors brings the buyer i the utility $u_i(a', (\pi^{FPDM}, p^{FPDM})) = p_j(a') \cdot \alpha \cdot (\frac{1}{2})^{d_i}$. Since $p_j(a')$, α and d_i are all independent of i's action, so is the i's utility.

Besides, if i does not diffuse the information to all her neighbors, by the allocation policy, she cannot become the winner. She either still stays in **Category 2** with her utility unchanged, or falls into **Category 3** with zero utility. So, not diffusing the information to all her neighbors does not improve her utility. That is, diffusing the sale information to all her neighbors is her dominant strategy.

Category 3: By FPDM, if i informs more neighbors, the chance increases that she gets into **Category 1** or **Category 2**, hence her revenue may be raised. If else, her revenue will remain to be zero. In other words, diffusing the sale information to all her neighbors is her dominant strategy.   □

According to Theorem 2, we can get $\langle V', E' \rangle = \langle V, E \rangle$. Next, we compare the seller's revenue under FPDM with that of without diffusion. The FPDM first sells the item among the seller's neighbors; if the sale fails, it sells among the branches. Therefore, the expected revenue of FPDM is greater than or equal to that of without diffusion. When the valuation distribution is specified, the improvement of the revenue can be computed. Taking into account the importance and tractability of the uniform distribution, we compute the revenue improvement under $U[0, 1]$. But precise computation requires enumerating all possible TGs, which has the time complexity of $O((|n_s| + l)^{|V|})$. To cope with this EXPTIME problem, we resort to the statistical analysis and statistically infer a lower bound of revenue improvement in Theorem 3. To that end, we introduce a lemma.

Lemma 1 (Larsen and Marx [14]). *Suppose population X has the Bernoulli distribution $B(1, p)$. Then the maximum likelihood estimate (MLE) for mean p is the sample mean.*

Using Lemma 1, we have the following theorem.

Theorem 3. *The seller's expected revenue of fixed-price diffusion mechanism ER_{FPDM} is greater than or equal to ER_0 defined in Sect. 3. Under the uniform* *valuation distribution $U[0,1]$, statistically, the revenue improvement has a lower bound*

$$\frac{1-\alpha}{4} \cdot \frac{1}{|n_s|} \cdot \left(1 - \left(\frac{1}{|V|}\right)^{\frac{1}{2 \cdot |n_s|}}\right),$$

where $|n_s|$ is the number of seller's neighbors, $|V|$ is the number of all buyers in the network and $\alpha \in (0,1)$ is the reward factor.

Proof. From Algorithm 1, there are $|n_s|+l$ branches in tree-shape graph TG. The numbers of buyers in branches $BR_1, \cdots, BR_{|n_s|+l}$ are denoted by $k_1, \cdots, k_{|n_s|+l}$ respectively. Then, given an action profile $a' \in \mathcal{F}(a)$, the seller's expected revenue under FPDM is:

$$ER_{FPDM} = ER_0 + \frac{1}{1+|n_s|} \cdot \{[1 - (p_1(a'))^{k_1-1}] \cdot p_1(a')$$

$$+ \sum_{i=2}^{b} (p_1(a'))^{k_1-1} \cdots (p_{i-1}(a'))^{k_{i-1}-1} \cdot (1 - (p_i(a'))^{k_i-1}) \tag{4}$$

$$\cdot p_i(a')\} \cdot (1 - \alpha).$$

Obviously, it holds that $ER_{FPDM} \geq ER_0$.

Next, we prove the second part of the statement. According to formula (4), we have

$$ER_{FPDM} \geq ER_0 + \left(\frac{1-\alpha}{1+|n_s|}\right) \cdot [1 - (p_1(a'))^{k_1-1}] \cdot p_1(a'),$$

which is equivalent to the following

$$ER_{FPDM} - ER_0 \geq \left(\frac{1-\alpha}{1+|n_s|}\right) \cdot [1 - (p_1(a'))^{k_1-1}] \cdot p_1(a'), \tag{5}$$

where $p_1(a') = \left(\frac{1}{1+k_{-1}}\right)^{\frac{1}{k_{-1}}}$ and $k_{-1} = |V| - 1 - k_1$. Next we estimate k_1 (the number of all buyers in BR_1).

Let $\hat{m} = V - n_s - \{s\}$ (denoting the set of the buyers on the DAG $\langle V, E \rangle$ except both the seller and her neighbors), $m = |\hat{m}|$ (denoting the cardinality of $\hat{m}$), and $\hat{i}$ ($i \in n_s$) denotes the group of the buyers connecting to i. To approximate k_1, we need to draw i.i.d. samples from a population. For any buyer j in $\hat{m}$, since we have no a prior knowledge about which group she belongs to, according to the Bayesian principle of indifference [10] we assume she uniformly falls into each group with the probability of $\frac{1}{|n_s|+l}$, which means the discrete uniform distribution serves as the population. Because the number k_1 of buyers in BR_1 has a binomial distribution, i.e. $k_1 \sim b\left(m, \frac{1}{|n_s|+l}\right)$, we have $k_1 = X_1 + X_2 + \cdots + X_m$ where $X_i \sim b\left(1, \frac{1}{|n_s|+l}\right)$. From Lemma 1, we know that the MLE of $\frac{1}{|n_s|+l}$ is $\frac{k_1}{m}$. So, an estimate of k_1 is $\overline{k}_1 = \frac{m}{|n_s|+\overline{l}}$, where $\overline{l}$ is an estimate of l. Next, we compute $\overline{l}$.

For the buyer j, the probability for her to belong to sole group is $\frac{1}{|n_s|} \cdot$ $\left(1 - \frac{1}{|n_s|}\right)^{|n_s|-1}$, denoted by q. So the probability for j to belong to at least two groups is $1 - q$. Therefore, the number l of the buyers belonging to at least two groups has a binomial distribution, i.e. $l \sim b(m, 1 - q)$. By the way similar to the deduction of $\overline{k}_1$, we can get $\overline{l} = m \cdot (1 - q)$. From both $\overline{k}_1 = \frac{m}{|n_s|+\overline{l}}$ and $\overline{l} = m \cdot (1 - q)$, we have $\overline{k}_1 = \frac{m}{|n_s|+m\cdot(1-q)}$. So we obtain the following expression of the lower bound of the revenue improvement

$$B = \left(\frac{1-\alpha}{1+|n_s|}\right) \cdot \left[1 - \left(\frac{1}{|V|-\overline{k}_1}\right)^{\frac{\overline{k}_1-1}{|V|-\overline{k}_1-1}}\right]$$

$$\cdot \left(\frac{1}{|V|-\overline{k}_1}\right)^{\frac{1}{|V|-\overline{k}_1-1}},$$

where $\overline{k}_1 = \frac{m}{|n_s|+m\cdot(1-q)}$, $m = |V| - |n_s| - 1$ and $q = \frac{1}{|n_s|} \cdot \left(1 - \frac{1}{|n_s|}\right)^{|n_s|-1}$.

Denote $1 - \left(\frac{1}{|V|-\overline{k}_1}\right)^{\frac{\overline{k}_1-1}{|V|-\overline{k}_1-1}}$ by A and $\left(\frac{1}{|V|-\overline{k}_1}\right)^{\frac{1}{|V|-\overline{k}_1-1}}$ by C. We further shrink A and C.

For A, from $q \geq \frac{1}{|n_s|} \cdot \left(1 - \frac{1}{|n_s|}\right)^{|n_s|}$ and $\left(1 - \frac{1}{|n_s|}\right)^{|n_s|} \geq (\frac{1}{2})^2 = \frac{1}{4}$ ($|n_s| \geq 2$), we have $1 - q \leq 1 - \frac{1}{4\cdot|n_s|}$ ($|n_s| \geq 2$). Therefore it holds that $\overline{k}_1 \geq 1 - \frac{2\cdot|n_s|}{|V|}$ ($|V| \geq 2$). Again it is easy to know that $\overline{k}_1 < \frac{m}{|n_s|}$. By tedious calculations, we have $\left(\frac{1}{|V|-\overline{k}_1}\right)^{\frac{\overline{k}_1-1}{|V|-\overline{k}_1-1}} \leq \left(\frac{1}{|V|}\right)^{\frac{1}{2\cdot|n_s|}}$. Therefore, we get $A \geq 1 - \left(\frac{1}{|V|}\right)^{\frac{1}{2\cdot|n_s|}}$.

For C, letting $x = |V| - \overline{k}_1 - 1 \geq 1$, we have $C = \left(\frac{1}{1+x}\right)^{\frac{1}{x}} \geq \frac{1}{2}$.

Combining the above estimates of A and C with the expression B, we have

$$B \geq \frac{1-\alpha}{1+|n_s|} \cdot \left(1 - \left(\frac{1}{|V|}\right)^{\frac{1}{2\cdot|n_s|}}\right) \cdot \frac{1}{2}$$

$$\geq \frac{1-\alpha}{4} \cdot \frac{1}{|n_s|} \cdot \left(1 - \left(\frac{1}{|V|}\right)^{\frac{1}{2\cdot|n_s|}}\right),$$

where $|n_s|$ is the number of seller's neighbors, $|V|$ is the number of all buyers in the network and $\alpha \in (0, 1)$ is the reward factor.   □

It is noticed that the lower bound increases with the number of all buyers in the network. That is, the more buyers participating in the sale, the higher the lower bound of revenue improvement. In addition, for some other simple valuation distributions, the computation of lower bound of revenue improvement can be performed similarly. For example, when PDF $f(x) = 2x(0 < x < 1)$ and CDF $F(x) = x^2(0 < x < 1)$, we obtain the same lower bound as for $U[0,1]$. But for more complicated distributions, the computation can be intractable.

The FPDM has lower time complexity than the previous work [15,16,21–23]. In what follows, taking the information diffusion mechanism (IDM) proposed by Li *et al.* [16] for example, we demonstrate this attribute of FPDM.

Theorem 4. *The fixed-price diffusion mechanism has lower time complexity than that of the IDM proposed by Li et al. [16].*

Proof. After the DAG $\langle V, E \rangle$ is constructed, the IDM proposed by Li *et al.* [16] repeatedly invokes Depth-First-Search (DFS) to compute the payments of all buyers, with the time complexity being $O(|V| \cdot (|V| + |E|))$. In contrast, our mechanism only needs the node numbers of all branches, which can be obtained by operating DFS only once. So, our mechanism has lower time complexity of $O(|V| + |E|)$. □

6 Conclusion

We designed the fixed-price diffusion mechanism (FPDM) for selling an item via a social network when buyers' valuation has a given continuous distribution. By incentivizing buyers to willingly propagate the sale information to all their neighbors, FPDM promotes the sale and improves the seller's maximal expected revenue of without diffusion. Especially, when the buyers' valuations of the item are uniform on $[0, 1]$, it guarantees a lower bound of the revenue improvement. In addition, not revealing the buyers' valuations, it has better preservation of their privacy and less time complexity than other existing diffusion mechanisms.

However, our mechanism utilizes the structure information of the social networks. As future work, it would be very interesting to try to hide the social network structure from the seller in mechanism design. To that end, a decentralized mechanism could be a promising choice.

References

1. Alaei, S., Hartline, J., Niazadeh, R., Pountourakis, E., Yuan, Y.: Optimal auctions vs. anonymous pricing. Games Econ. Behav. **118**, 494–510 (2019)
2. Babaioff, M., Blumrosen, L., Dughmi, S., Singer, Y.: Posting prices with unknown distributions. ACM Trans. Econ. Comput. (TEAC) **5**(2), 1–20 (2017)
3. Blumrosen, L., Holenstein, T.: Posted prices vs. negotiations: an asymptotic analysis. EC 10, 1386790–1386801 (2008)
4. Chawla, S., Hartline, J.D., Malec, D.L., Sivan, B.: Multi-parameter mechanism design and sequential posted pricing. In: Proceedings of the Forty-Second ACM Symposium on Theory of Computing, pp. 311–320 (2010)
5. Clarke, E.H.: Multipart pricing of public goods. Public Choice **11**(1), 17–33 (1971)
6. Domingos, P., Richardson, M.: Mining the network value of customers. In: Proceedings of the Seventh ACM SIGKDD International Conference on Knowledge Discovery and Data Mining, pp. 57–66 (2001)
7. Feldman, M., Gravin, N., Lucier, B.: Combinatorial auctions via posted prices. In: Proceedings of the Twenty-Sixth Annual ACM-SIAM Symposium on Discrete Algorithms, pp. 123–135. SIAM (2014)

8. Groves, T.: Incentives in teams. Econometrica: J. Econometric Soc. **41**, 617–631 (1973)
9. Hartline, J.D., Roughgarden, T.: Simple versus optimal mechanisms. In: Proceedings of the 10th ACM Conference on Electronic Commerce, pp. 225–234 (2009)
10. Hawthorne, J., Landes, J., Wallmann, C., Williamson, J.: The principal principle implies the principle of indifference. British J. Philos. Sci. **68**(1), 123–131 (2017)
11. Jackson, M.O.: The economics of social networks (2005)
12. Jin, Y., Lu, P., Qi, Q., Tang, Z.G., Xiao, T.: Tight approximation ratio of anonymous pricing. In: Proceedings of the 51st Annual ACM SIGACT Symposium on Theory of Computing, pp. 674–685 (2019)
13. Jin, Y., Lu, P., Tang, Z.G., Xiao, T.: Tight revenue gaps among simple mechanisms. In: Proceedings of the Thirtieth Annual ACM-SIAM Symposium on Discrete Algorithms, pp. 209–228. SIAM (2019)
14. Larsen, R.J., Marx, M.L.: An Introduction to Mathematical Statistics. Prentice Hall, Hoboken (2005)
15. Li, B., Hao, D., Zhao, D., Yokoo, M.: Diffusion and auction on graphs. In: Proceedings of the 28th International Joint Conference on Artificial Intelligence, pp. 435–441. AAAI Press (2019)
16. Li, B., Hao, D., Zhao, D., Zhou, T.: Mechanism design in social networks. In: Proceedings of the Thirty-First AAAI Conference on Artificial Intelligence, pp. 586–592 (2017)
17. Mathews, T.: The impact of discounting on an auction with a buyout option: a theoretical analysis motivated by Ebay's buy-it-now feature. J. Econ. **81**(1), 25–52 (2004)
18. Myerson, R.B.: Optimal auction design. Math. Oper. Res. **6**(1), 58–73 (1981)
19. Nisan, N., Roughgarden, T., Tardos, É., Vazirani, V.V. (eds.): Algorithmic Game Theory. Cambridge University Press, Cambridge (2007)
20. Vickrey, W.: Counterspeculation, auctions, and competitive sealed tenders. J. Financ. **16**(1), 8–37 (1961)
21. Zhang, W., Zhao, D., Chen, H.: Redistribution mechanism on networks, pp. 1620–1628. AAMAS 2020, International Foundation for Autonomous Agents and Multiagent Systems, Richland, SC (2020)
22. Zhang, W., Zhao, D., Zhang, Y.: Incentivize diffusion with fair rewards. In: ECAI 2020–24th European Conference on Artificial Intelligence. Frontiers in Artificial Intelligence and Applications, vol. 325, pp. 251–258. IOS Press (2020)
23. Zhao, D., Li, B., Xu, J., Hao, D., Jennings, N.R.: Selling multiple items via social networks. In: Proceedings of the 17th International Conference on Autonomous Agents and MultiAgent Systems, pp. 68–76 (2018)

Multiclass Classification Using Dilute Bandit Feedback

Gaurav Batra[✉][iD] and Naresh Manwani[iD]

Machine Learning Lab, KCIS, IIIT Hyderabad, Hyderabad, India
naresh.manwani@iiit.ac.in

Abstract. This paper introduces a new online learning framework for multiclass classification called *learning with diluted bandit feedback*. At every time step, the algorithm predicts a candidate label set instead of a single label for the observed example. It then receives a feedback from the environment whether the actual label lies in this candidate label set or not. This feedback is called "diluted bandit feedback". Learning in this setting is even more challenging than the bandit feedback setting, as there is more uncertainty in the supervision. We propose an algorithm for multiclass classification using dilute bandit feedback (MC-DBF), which uses the exploration-exploitation strategy to predict the candidate set in each trial. We show that the proposed algorithm achieves $\mathcal{O}(T^{1-\frac{1}{m+2}})$ mistake bound if candidate label set size (in each step) is m. We demonstrate the effectiveness of the proposed approach with extensive simulations.

Keywords: Multi-class classification · Online learning · Dilute bandit feedback

1 Introduction

In multi-class classification, the learning algorithm is given access to the examples and their actual class labels. The goal is to learn a classifier which given an example, correctly predicts its class label. This is called the full information setting. In the full information setting, online algorithms for multiclass classification are discussed in [6,7,13]. In many applications, we do not get labels for all the examples. Instead, we can only access whether the predicted label for an example is correct. This is called bandit feedback setting [10]. Bandit feedback-based learning is useful in several web-based applications, such as sponsored advertising on web pages and recommender systems as mentioned in [10].

In the linearly separable case, Kakade et al. [10] propose Banditron algorithm which can learn using bandit feedbacks. Banditron makes $\mathcal{O}(\sqrt{T})$[1] expected number of mistakes in the linearly separable case and $\mathcal{O}(T^{2/3})$ in the worst case. On the other hand Newtron [8] (based on the online Newton method) achieves $\mathcal{O}(\log T)$ regret bound in the best case and $\mathcal{O}(T^{2/3})$ regret in the worst case. Beygelzimer et al. [4] propose Second Order Banditron (SOBA) which achieves $\mathcal{O}(\sqrt{T})$ regret in the worst case.

---

[1] T is number of trials.

© Springer Nature Switzerland AG 2021
D. N. Pham et al. (Eds.): PRICAI 2021, LNAI 13031, pp. 63–75, 2021.
https://doi.org/10.1007/978-3-030-89188-6_5

Fig. 1. The three types of supervised learning settings are explained in this figure. (a) Full Information Setting: In this setting, the agent receives the correct label on prediction. (b) Bandit Feedback Setting: Here, the agent gets the information whether his prediction is accurate or not. (c) Partial Bandit Feedback Setting: In this setting, the agent predicts a set of labels and gets the feedback whether the correct label lies in the predicted set or not.

In the bandit feedback-based approaches, the algorithm predicts a single label and seeks the feedback whether the predicted label is correct. Here, we introduce a new learning framework called "learning under diluted bandit feedback". At every time step, when the algorithm observes a new example, it predicts a candidate label set instead of a single label. Now the algorithm seeks the oracle's feedback whether the actual label lies in this candidate label set or not. Note that learning in this setting is even more challenging than bandit feedback setting as there is another level of uncertainty in the supervision. That is, if the feedback says that the actual label lies in the predicted candidate label set, we still do not know which of the label in the candidate set is the true one. Using the example presented in Fig. 1, we can see the difference between bandit feedback and diluted bandit feedback.

Diluted bandit feedback-based learning can be useful in many applications. For example, consider the situation where a doctor is trying to diagnose a patient. Based on the patient's initial symptoms, she starts the treatment with some idea about possible diseases. Based on the treatment outcome, the doctor would know whether the actual disease was correctly diagnosed in the possible diseases guessed by the doctor. The result of the treatment here is diluted bandit feedback. It does not tell the exact disease but only indicates whether the actual disease lies in a possible set of diseases.

Another example would be that of advertising on web pages. The user first queries the system. Based on the query and user-specific information, the system makes a prediction as a set of advertisements. Finally, the user may either click on one of the ads or just ignore all of them. The action of the user clicking or ignoring the advertisements is the dilute bandit feedback. In the cases mentioned above, knowing the ground truth label beforehand may not always be possible.

Hence, this provides the motivation for coming up with the setting and the corresponding algorithm.

Note that diluted bandit feedbacks make the supervision weaker than bandit feedbacks. In this paper, we attempt the problem of learning multiclass classifier using diluted bandit feedbacks. To the best of our knowledge, this is the first work in this direction. Following are the key contributions in this paper·

1. We propose an algorithm which learns multiclass classifier using diluted bandit feedbacks.
2. We show that the proposed algorithm achieves sub-linear mistake bound of $\mathcal{O}(T^{1-(m+2)^{-1}})$, where m is the size of the subset predicted.
3. We experimentally show that the proposed approach learns efficient classifiers using diluted bandit feedbacks.

The main novelty of the MC-DBF algorithm is that it is able to train even under the dilute bandit feedback setting. The proposed algorithm MC-DBF achieves an error rate that is comparable to that of algorithms that receive bandit feedback (SOBA [4]) or full feedback (Perceptron [6]) during training.

2   Problem Setting: Diluted Bandit Feedback

We now formally describe the problem statement for our multi-class classification with diluted bandit feedback. The classification is done in a sequence of rounds. At each round t, the algorithm observes an instance $\mathbf{x}^t \in \mathbb{R}^d$. The algorithm predicts a set of labels $\tilde{Y}^t \subset \{1, \ldots, k\}$ such that $|\tilde{Y}^t| = m$. After predicting the set of labels, we observe the feedback $\mathbb{I}\{y^t \in \tilde{Y}^t\}$ where y^t is the true label corresponding to the input $\mathbf{x}^t$. $\mathbb{I}\{y^t \in \tilde{Y}^t\}$ is 1 if $y^t \in \tilde{Y}^t$ else 0. In this type of bandit feedback, the classifier receives the information if the predicted set contains the correct label or not. There are two possibilities of the value of m.

1. Case 1 ($m = 1$): Here, $\tilde{Y}^t = \tilde{y}^t$ and the feedback reduces to $\mathbb{I}\{y^t = \tilde{y}^t\}$ which is discussed in [2,9,10]. Thus, when $\mathbb{I}\{y^t = \tilde{y}^t\} = 1$, we know the true label. On the other hand, $\mathbb{I}\{y^t = \tilde{y}^t\} = 0$, the true label can be anything among $[k] \setminus \tilde{y}_t$.
2. Case 2 ($1 < m < k$): Here, the uncertainty is present in both possibilities of the feedback $\mathbb{I}\{y^t \in \tilde{Y}^t\}$. When $\mathbb{I}\{y^t \in \tilde{Y}^t\} = 1$, then the true label could be anything among the labels in the set $\tilde{Y}^t$. When $\mathbb{I}\{y^t \in \tilde{Y}^t\} = 0$, the true label lies in the set $[k] \setminus \tilde{Y}^t$. Thus, in both possibilities of the feedback, there is ambiguity about the true label. Hence the name **diluted bandit feedback**.

This paper is mainly concerned about Case 2, where $1 < m < k$ (diluted bandit feedback setting). The algorithm's final goal is to minimize the number of prediction mistake $\hat{M}$ as defined below.

$$\hat{M} := \sum_{t=1}^{T} \mathbb{I}\{y^t \notin \hat{Y}^t\} \tag{1}$$

To the best of our knowledge, this is first time diluted bandit feedback setting has been proposed.

Algorithm 1: MC-SLP: Multiclass Classification using Subset Label Prediction

---

Parameters: $\gamma \in (0,1.0)$;
Initialize $W^1 = 0 \in \mathbb{R}^{k \times d}$;
for $t= 1,\ldots,T$ **do**
    Receive $\mathbf{x}^t \in R^d$;
    Predict $\hat{Y}(\mathbf{x}^t, W^t)$ and receive feedback y^t;
    Define $U^t_{r,j} = x^t_j \left(\mathbb{I}\{r = y^t\} - \frac{1}{m}\mathbb{I}\{r \in \hat{Y}(\mathbf{x}^t, W^t)\} \right)$;
    Update: $W^{t+1} = W^t + \tilde{U}^t$;
end

---

3   Proposed Approach

The algorithm tries to learn a linear classifier parameterized by a weight matrix $W \in \mathbb{R}^{k \times d}$. To formulate the algorithm which learns using diluted bandit feedback, let us first look at a simple full information approach.

3.1   Multiclass Algorithm with Subset Label Prediction: A Full Information Approach

Consider the approach where the algorithm can predict a subset of labels. We first define *label set prediction function*.

Definition 1. Label Set Prediction Function $\hat{Y}(\mathbf{x}, W)$: *Given an example* $\mathbf{x}$ *and a weight matrix* $W \in \mathbb{R}^{k \times d}$, *we denote predicted label set of size* m *as* $\hat{Y}(\mathbf{x}, W)$. *We define* $\hat{Y}(\mathbf{x}, W) := \{a_1, \ldots, a_m\}$ *where*

$$a_i = \underset{j \in [k] \setminus \{a_1, \ldots, a_{i-1}\}}{\arg\max} (W\mathbf{x})_j.$$

Thus, $\hat{Y}(\mathbf{x}, W)$ predicts top m-labels based on m-largest values in the vector $W\mathbf{x}$. Then we observe the true label $y \in [k]$.[2] We use following variant of 0–1 loss to capture the discrepancy between the true label (y) and the predicted label set $\hat{Y}(\mathbf{x}, W)$.

$$L_{0-1} = \mathbb{I}\{y \notin \hat{Y}(\mathbf{x}, W)\} \tag{2}$$

But, this loss is not continuous. So, we use following average hinge loss as a surrogate loss function,

$$L_{avg}(W, (\mathbf{x}, y)) = [1 - (W\mathbf{x})_y + \frac{1}{m} \sum_{i \in \hat{Y}(\mathbf{x},W)} (W\mathbf{x})_i]_+ \tag{3}$$

where $[A]_+ = A$ if $A > 0$ else 0. It is easy to see that L_{avg} is upper bound to L_{0-1}.

---

[2] Note that this setting is exactly opposite to the partial label setting [3,5]. In the partial label setting, ground truth is a labelled subset, and the algorithm predicts a single label.

Lemma 1. L_{avg} *is an upper-bound on* $\mathbb{I}\{y \in \hat{Y}(\mathbf{x}, W)\}$, *that is* $L_{avg} \geq \mathbb{I}\{y \notin \hat{Y}(\mathbf{x}, W)\}$.

An online algorithm in this setting can be easily derived by using stochastic gradient descent on the loss L_{avg}. We call it MC-SLP (multiclass classification using subset label prediction). The algorithm works as follows. At trial t we observe example $\mathbf{x}^t$. We predict the label set $\hat{Y}(\mathbf{x}^t, W^t)$ using the existing parameters W^t. Then we observe the true label y^t. We update the parameters using stochastic gradient descent on the loss L_{avg} which results in the update equation $W^{t+1} = W^t + U^t$ where U^t is described as follows.

$$U_{r,j}^t = x_j^t \left(\mathbb{I}\{r = y_t\} - \frac{\mathbb{I}\{r \in \hat{Y}(\mathbf{x}^t, W^t)\}}{m} \right). \tag{4}$$

We repeat this process for T number of trials. The complete description of this approach is given in Algorithm 1. Note that MC-SLP is a full information type algorithm as we get access to the true label for each example. The following is true for MC-SLP (Algorithm 1).

Lemma 2. *Let* W^t *be the weight matrix in the beginning of trial t of MC-SLP and* U^t *be the update matrix in trial t by MC-SLP. Let* $\langle W^t, U^t \rangle = \sum_{r=1}^{k} \sum_{j=1}^{d} W_{r,j}^t U_{r,j}^t$ *(matrix inner product). Then,*

$$L_{avg}(W^t, (\mathbf{x}^t, y^t)) \geq \mathbb{I}\{y^t \notin \hat{Y}(\mathbf{x}^t, W^t)\} - \langle W^t, U^t \rangle$$

This lemma gives us a lower bound on the loss L_{avg} computed for example $\mathbf{x}^t$ at trial t. This is a useful result which we will need later.

3.2   MC-DBF: Multiclass Learning with Diluted Bandit Feedback

We now describe the algorithm for learning using diluted bandit feedback. Here, for each example $\mathbf{x}^t$, we do not receive the true label y^t. We instead receive the feedback whether y^t lies in the predicted label set $\tilde{Y}^t$ (i.e. $\mathbb{I}\{y^t \in \hat{Y}^t\}$). The algorithm works as follows.

At each iteration t, we receive $\mathbf{x}^t$ as input. We find $\hat{Y}(\mathbf{x}^t, W^t) = \{a_1, \ldots, a_m\}$ where

$$a_i = \operatorname*{arg\,max}_{j \in [k] \setminus \{a_1, \ldots, a_{i-1}\}} (W^t \mathbf{x}^t)_j.$$

We define probability distribution $\mathbb{P}$ on individual class labels as follows.

$$\mathbb{P}(r) = \frac{(1 - \gamma)}{m} \mathbb{I}\{r \in \hat{Y}(\mathbf{x}^t, W^t)\} + \frac{\gamma}{k}, \ \forall r \in [k] \tag{5}$$

Here, γ is the exploration parameter. Let $\mathbb{S}$ denote the set of all m size subsets of $\{1, \ldots, k\}$. We call them **superarms** of size m. Now, we define probability distribution Z on the set $\mathbb{S}$ as follows. For all $A = \{b_1, \ldots, b_m\} \in \mathbb{S}$, we define

$$Z(A) = \mathbb{P}(b_1)\mathbb{P}(b_2|b_1) \ldots \mathbb{P}(b_m|b_1, \ldots, b_{m-1}),$$

Algorithm 2: MC-DBF: Multiclass Classification Using Diluted Bandit Feedback

---

Parameters: $\gamma \in (0,1.0)$;
Initialize $W^1 = \mathbf{0}^{d \times k}$;
for $t = 1, \ldots, T$ **do**

> Receive $\mathbf{x}^t \in \mathbb{R}^d$;
> Find $\hat{Y}(\mathbf{x}^t, W^t)$;
> Define $\mathbb{P}(r) := \frac{(1-\gamma)}{m}\mathbb{I}\{r \in \hat{Y}(\mathbf{x}^t, W^t)\} + \frac{\gamma}{k}, \forall r \in [k]$;
> Define $Z(A) = \mathbb{P}(b_1)\mathbb{P}(b_2|b_1)\ldots\mathbb{P}(b_m|b_1,\ldots,b_{m-1}), \forall A = \{b_1,\ldots,b_m\} \in \mathbb{S}$;
> Randomly sample $\tilde{Y}^t$ according to Z;
> Predict $\tilde{Y}^t$ and receive feedback $\mathbb{I}\{y^t \in \tilde{Y}^t\}$;
> Compute $\forall r \in [K]$ and $\forall j \in [d]$;
> $\tilde{U}^t_{r,j} = x^t_j \left[\frac{\mathbb{I}\{y^t \in \tilde{Y}^t\}\mathbb{I}\{r \in \tilde{Y}^t\}}{Z(\tilde{Y}^t)\tau_1} - \tau_2 - \frac{\mathbb{I}\{r \in \hat{Y}(\mathbf{x}^t, W^t)\}}{m} \right]$;
> Update: $W^{t+1} = W^t + \tilde{U}^t$;

end

---

where $\mathbb{P}(b_i|b_1,\ldots,b_{i-1}) = \frac{\mathbb{P}(b_i)}{(1-\mathbb{P}(b_1) - \cdots - \mathbb{P}(b_{i-1}))}$. $Z(A)$ is the probability of choosing $b_1, b_2, \ldots, b_m$ from the set $[k]$ without replacement.[3]

We randomly sample $\tilde{Y}^t$ from Z and predict $\tilde{Y}^t$. We receive the diluted bandit feedback $\mathbb{I}\{y^t \in \tilde{Y}^t\}$. We update the weight matrix as $W^{t+1} = W^t + \tilde{U}^t$, where

$$\tilde{U}^t_{r,j} = x^t_j \left(\frac{\mathbb{I}\{y^t \in \tilde{Y}^t\}\mathbb{I}\{r \in \tilde{Y}^t\}}{Z(\tilde{Y}^t)\tau_1} - \frac{\mathbb{I}\{r \in \hat{Y}(\mathbf{x}^t, W^t)\}}{m} - \tau_2 \right) \quad (6)$$

where $\tau_1 = m^{k-2}P_{m-1}$ and $\tau_2 = \frac{m-1}{k-m}$. $\tilde{U}^t$ accesses y^t only through the indicator $\mathbb{I}\{y^t \in \tilde{Y}^t\}$. We will see that $\tilde{U}^t$ is an unbiased estimator of U^t as follows.

Lemma 3. *Consider $\tilde{U}^t$ defined in Eq. (6). Then, $\mathbb{E}_Z[\tilde{U}^t] = U^t$, where U^t is defined in Eq. (4).*

4   Mistake Bound Analysis of MC-DBF

In this section, we derive the expected mistake bound ($\mathbb{E}_Z[\hat{M}]$) for the proposed approach MC-DBF (Algorithm 2). To get the mistake bound, we first need to derive some intermediate results. We first derive an upper bound the expected value of the Frobenius norm of the update matrix $\tilde{U}^t$.

---

[3] We see that $\sum_A Z(A) = 1$ as follows.

$$\sum_A Z(A) = \sum_A \mathbb{P}(b_1)\ldots\mathbb{P}(b_m|b_1,\ldots,b_{m-1}) = \sum_{b_1}\mathbb{P}(b_1)\cdots\sum_{b_m}\frac{\mathbb{P}(b_m)}{(1-\mathbb{P}(b_1)\cdots-\mathbb{P}(b_{m-1}))}$$

But, $\sum_{b_i}\frac{\mathbb{P}(b_i)}{(1-\mathbb{P}(b_1)-\cdots-\mathbb{P}(b_{i-1}))} = 1$. Thus, $\sum_A Z(A) = 1$.

Lemma 4.

$$\mathbb{E}_Z[||\tilde{U}^t||_F^2] \le ||\mathbf{x}^t||_2^2 \Big[\frac{mk^m\,{}^kP_m}{\gamma^m\tau_1^2} - \frac{2m\tau_2}{\tau_1} - \frac{2}{\tau_1}$$

$$+ k[\tau_2^2 + \frac{1}{km} + \frac{2\tau_2}{k}]\Big] + \frac{2||\mathbf{x}^t||_2^2}{\tau_1}\mathbb{I}\{y^t \notin \hat{Y}(\mathbf{x}^t, W^t)\}$$

Now we derive the expected mistake bound $\mathbb{E}_Z[\hat{M}]$ using Theorem as follows.

Theorem 1. *Assume that for the sequence of examples,* $(\mathbf{x}^1, y^1), \ldots, (\mathbf{x}^t, y^t)$, *we have, for all* t, $\mathbf{x}^t \in \mathbb{R}^d$, $||\mathbf{x}^t|| \le 1$ *and* $y^t \in [k]$. *Let* W^* *be any matrix and let* R_T *be the cumulative average hinge loss of* W^* *defined as follows.*

$$R_T = \sum_{t=1}^{T} L_{avg}(W^*, (\mathbf{x}^t, y^t)).$$

Let D *be the complexity of* W^* *defined as below:* $D = 2||W^*||_F^2$. *Then the number of mistakes* $\hat{M}$ *made by the Algorithm 2 satisfies*

$$\mathbb{E}_Z[\hat{M}] \le R_T + \sqrt{\frac{\lambda_1 D R_T}{2}} + 3\max\left(\frac{\lambda_1 D}{2}, \sqrt{\frac{(\lambda_2 + 1)DT}{2}}\right)$$

$$+ \gamma T. \tag{7}$$

where $\hat{M} = \sum_{t=1}^{T} \mathbb{I}\{y^t \notin \hat{Y}(\mathbf{x}^t, W^t)\}$, $\lambda_1 = \frac{2}{\tau_1}$ *and*

$$\lambda_2 = \Big[\frac{mk^m\,{}^kP_m}{\gamma^m\tau_1^2} - \frac{2m\tau_2}{\tau_1} - \frac{2}{\tau_1} + k[\tau_2^2 + \frac{1}{km} + \frac{2\tau_2}{k}]\Big]$$

We will now analyze different cases and find out the mistake bound in those cases. Before going ahead, we state a new separability definition as follows.

Definition 2. Linear Separability: *A sequence of examples,* $(\mathbf{x}^1, y^1), \ldots,$ $(\mathbf{x}^T, y^T)$ *is linearly separable if there exists a matrix* $W^* \in \mathbb{R}^{k \times d}$ *such that*

$$(W^*\mathbf{x}^t)_{y^t} - (W^*\mathbf{x}^t)_i \ge 1, \ \forall i \ne y^t, \ \forall t \in [T].$$

Note that linear separability also implies $(W^*\mathbf{x}^t)_{y^t} - \frac{1}{m}\sum_{i \in \hat{Y}(\mathbf{x}, W^*)}(W^*\mathbf{x}^t)_i \ge 1, \forall t \in [T]$. Which implies $L_{avg}(W^*, (\mathbf{x}^t, y^t)) = 0, \ \forall t \in [T]$. Thus, when a sequence of examples $(\mathbf{x}^1, y^1), \ldots, (\mathbf{x}^T, y^T)$ is linearly separable with respect to a weight matrix W^*, then

$$R_T = \sum_{t=1}^{T} L_{avg}(W^*, (\mathbf{x}^t, y^t)) = 0.$$

Corollary 1. *Let* $(\mathbf{x}^1, y^1), \ldots, (\mathbf{x}^T, y^T)$ *be the sequence linearly separable examples presented to algorithm MC-DBF. Then MC-BDF achieves* $\mathcal{O}(T^{(1-\frac{1}{(m+2)})})$ *mistake bound on it.*

Corollary 2. *Moreover, if we consider* $R_T \leq \mathcal{O}(T^{(1-\frac{1}{(m+2)})})$, *by setting* $\gamma = \mathcal{O}((\frac{1}{T})^{\frac{1}{(m+2)}})$, *we get that* $\mathbb{E}_Z[\hat{M}] \leq \mathcal{O}(T^{(1-\frac{1}{(m+2)})})$.

Thus, we see that on increasing m, running time complexity of the algorithm also increases.

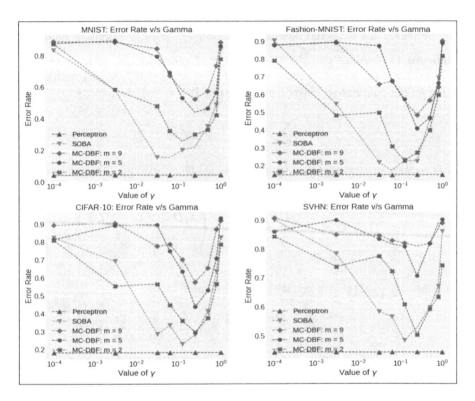

Fig. 2. Searching best value of γ: graphs show converged error rates for MC-DBF (with different values of m) and Second Order Banditron (SOBA) for varying values of γ. The γ values on the X-axis are on a log scale.

5   Experiments

In this section, we present experimental results of the proposed algorithm MC-DBF (Algorithm 2) and its comparison with other benchmark algorithms on various datasets.

5.1   Datasets Used and Preprocessing

We use CIFAR-10 [11], SVHN [14], MNIST [12] and Fashion-MNIST [16] datasets to show experimental results. We use VGG-16 [15] model that is pre-

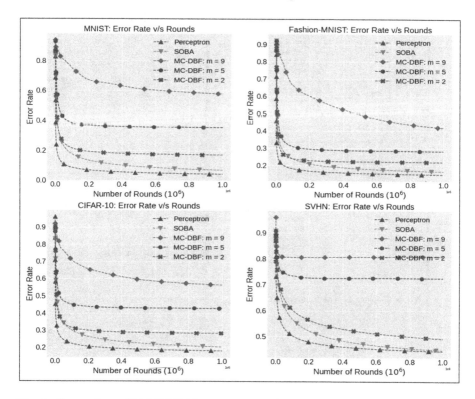

Fig. 3. Comparison of MC-DBF Algorithm using different values of m with Perceptron (benchmark algorithm with full information feedback) and Second Order Banditron (SOBA) (benchmark algorithm for bandit feedback).

trained on ImageNet dataset to extract the features. We use TensorFlow framework [1] on all the datasets mentioned above for feature extraction using VGG-16. All the experiments have been executed on a machine with Intel (R) Xeon(R) CPU @ 2.30 GHz with 12.72 Gb of RAM.

The images are passed through the VGG-16 network, and then relevant features are extracted from the last layer of VGG-16 network. The final dimension of the features extracted for each dataset is 512.

In addition to the datasets mentioned above, we also use a synthetic linearly separable dataset SYNSEP [10] for the purpose of comparison.

5.2   Benchmark Algorithms

We compare the proposed approach MC-DBF with Perceptron [6], which is an algorithm for full information setting, Second Order Banditron (SOBA) [4], which is a bandit feedback algorithm. We also compare with MC-SLP, which is a full information version of MC-DBF. We will use three types of values of m - (low, medium, high) in MC-DBF to observe the effect of variations in m.

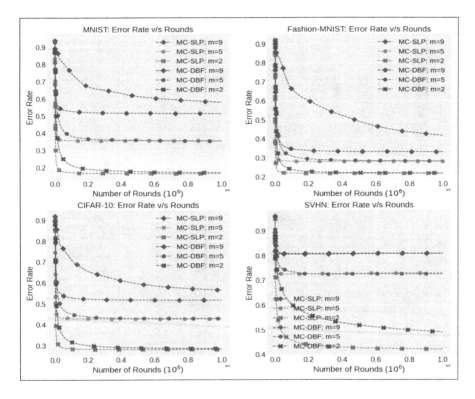

Fig. 4. Comparison of MC-DBF Algorithm with different values of m with MC-SLP

5.3   Experimental Setup and Performance Metric

We run each of the algorithms mentioned above for $1,000,000$ iterations for 10 independent runs for every dataset. In each iteration, we calculate the error rate (number of incorrectly classified samples averaged over the total number of rounds). For calculating the error rate we compare the ground truth label y_t, with the predicted label $\hat{y}^t = \arg\max_{j \in [k]} (W^t \mathbf{x}^t)_j$. The final plots have error rate averaged over the 10 independent trials.

5.4   Choosing Optimal Value of γ in MC-DBF

MC-DBF takes γ as a parameter. To choose the parameter's best values, we plot the trend of error rates for varying values of γ. We choose the value of γ for which the error rate value is minimized from these plots. While calculating the error rate, we compare the true label y_t with the predicted label $\hat{y}^t = \arg\max_{j \in [k]} (W^t \mathbf{x}^t)_j$. We use a similar process to get optimal values of hyper-parameters for the other benchmark algorithms.

Figure 2 shows the trend of the converged error rates with $\log(\gamma)$ on all the datasets for all the algorithms. The best values of γ for MCDBF for different

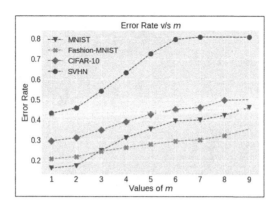

Fig. 5. Variation of the error rate of MC-DBF algorithm with different values of m.

Table 1. Optimal values of γ for different algorithms

SOBA		MC-DBF (m: low)	
Dataset	γ	Dataset	γ
MNIST	0.02	MNIST	0.12
Fashion-MNIST	0.1	Fashion-MNIST	0.12
CIFAR-10	0.3	CIFAR-10	0.28
SVHN	0.25	SVHN	0.31
MC-DBF (m: medium)		MC-DBF (m: high)	
Dataset	γ	Dataset	γ
MNIST	0.12	MNIST	0.25
Fashion-MNIST	0.2	Fashion-MNIST	0.3
CIFAR-10	0.25	CIFAR-10	0.3
SVHN	0.3	SVHN	0.5

datasets have been summarized in Table 1. All the final plots have been made using these optimal values.

5.5   Comparison of MC-BDF with Benchmarking Algorithms

Figure 3 presents the comparison results of our proposed algorithm (MC-DBF) using different values of m with Perceptron [6] (full information setting) and SOBA [4] (bandit feedback setting).

We observe that MC-DBF algorithm achieves higher error rate compared to the Banditron and Perceptron algorithms for $m \geq 2$. This happens because MC-DBF gets dilute bandit feedback. Also, increasing the value of m forces the bandit feedback to become more diluted, which results in further increase in the error rate as shown in Fig. 3.

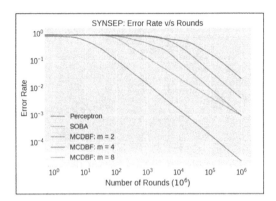

Fig. 6. Plot to show the variation of the error rate of MC-DBF algorithm with other benchmark algorithms on SYNSEP (linearly separable dataset)

Figure 4 show the comparison results of our proposed algorithm MC-DBF with MC-SLP (full information version of MC-DBF) for different values of m. We observe that MC-DBF converges to MC-SLP in all the datasets, which is expected as according to Lemma 3 ($E_Z[\tilde{U}] = U$).

Figure 6 shows the comparison of the various benchmark algorithms with our proposed algorithm (MC-DBF) using different values of m on the SYNSEP dataset, which is a linearly separable dataset. Both the axes have been plotted on a log scale. We observe that our proposed algorithm performs comparable to Second Order Banditron (SOBA), in the linearly separable case as well.

5.6   Effect of Changing Values of m

Figure 5 shows the trend of the error rate of MC-DBF versus m for all the datasets. We observe that the error rate increases on increasing m which is not surprising as increasing m implies feedback to the algorithm becomes increasing dilute leading to increasing error-rate for the same number of rounds and constant γ.

6   Conclusion

This paper proposed a multiclass classification algorithm that uses diluted bandit feedback for training, namely MC-BDF. We used the exploration-exploitation strategy to predict a subset of labels in each trial. We then update the matrix, using an unbiased estimator of the MC-SLP update matrix (full information version of MC-DBF). We also proved the upper bound for the expected number of mistakes made by our algorithm. We also experimentally compared MC-DBF with other benchmark algorithms for the full/bandit feedback settings on various datasets. The results show that our algorithm MC-DBF performs comparably to the benchmark algorithms, despite receiving lesser feedback on most of the datasets.

References

1. Abadi, M., et al.: TensorFlow: large-scale machine learning on heterogeneous systems (2015). http://tensorflow.org/, software available from tensorflow.org
2. Arora, M., Manwani, N.: Exact passive-aggressive algorithms for multiclass classification using bandit feedbacks. In: Proceedings of The 12th Asian Conference on Machine Learning, vol. 129, pp. 369 384, 18–20 November 2020, Bangkok, Thailand (2020)
3. Arora, M., Manwani, N.: Exact passive aggressive algorithm for multiclass classification using partial labels. In: 8th ACM IKDD CODS and 26th COMAD, pp. 38–46 (2021)
4. Beygelzimer, A., Orabona, F., Zhang, C.: Efficient online bandit multiclass learning with $\tilde{O}(\sqrt{T})$ regret. CoRR abs/1702.07958 (2017). http://arxiv.org/abs/1702.07958
5. Bhattacharjee, R., Manwani, N.: Online algorithms for multiclass classification using partial labels. In: Proceedings of the 24th Pacific-Asia Conference on Knowledge Discovery and Data Mining (PAKDD), pp. 249–260 (2020)
6. Crammer, K., Singer, Y.: Ultraconservative online algorithms for multiclass problems. J. Mach. Learn. Res. **3**(null), 951–991 (2003)
7. Fink, M., Shalev-Shwartz, S., Singer, Y., Ullman, S.: Online multiclass learning by interclass hypothesis sharing, pp. 313–320 (2006). https://doi.org/10.1145/1143844.1143884
8. Hazan, E., Kale, S.: NEWTRON: an efficient bandit algorithm for online multiclass prediction. In: Shawe-Taylor, J., Zemel, R., Bartlett, P., Pereira, F., Weinberger, K.Q. (eds.) Advances in Neural Information Processing Systems, vol. 24, pp. 891–899. Curran Associates, Inc. (2011). https://proceedings.neurips.cc/paper/2011/file/fde9264cf376fffe2ee4ddf4a988880d-Paper.pdf
9. Hazan, E., Kale, S.: NEWTRON: an efficient bandit algorithm for online multiclass prediction. In: Proceedings of the 24th International Conference on Neural Information Processing Systems, pp. 891–899 (2011)
10. Kakade, S.M., Shalev-Shwartz, S., Tewari, A.: Efficient bandit algorithms for online multiclass prediction. In: Proceedings of the 25th International Conference on Machine Learning, pp. 440–447. ICML 2008 (2008)
11. Krizhevsky, A., Hinton, G., et al.: Learning multiple layers of features from tiny images (2009)
12. LeCun, Y., Cortes, C., Burges, C.: MNIST handwritten digit database. ATT Labs [Online]. http://yann.lecun.com/exdb/mnist 2 (2010)
13. Matsushima, S., Shimizu, N., Yoshida, K., Ninomiya, T., Nakagawa, H.: Exact passive-aggressive algorithm for multiclass classification using support class. In: Proceedings of the SIAM International Conference on Data Mining, SDM 2010, Columbus, Ohio, USA, pp. 303–314 (2010)
14. Netzer, Y., Wang, T., Coates, A., Bissacco, A., Wu, B., Ng, A.: Reading digits in natural images with unsupervised feature learning. NIPS (01 2011)
15. Simonyan, K., Zisserman, A.: Very deep convolutional networks for large-scale image recognition. CoRR abs/1409.1556 (2014). http://arxiv.org/abs/1409.1556
16. Xiao, H., Rasul, K., Vollgraf, R.: Fashion-MNIST: a novel image dataset for benchmarking machine learning algorithms (2017)

A Study of Misinformation Games

Constantinos Varsos[1,2]([✉]), Giorgos Flouris[1], Marina Bitsaki[1],
and Michail Fasoulakis[1]

[1] Institute of Computer Science, Foundation for Research and Technology,
Vasilika Vouton 100, 70013 Heraklion, Greece
{varsosk,fgeo,mfasoul}@ics.forth.gr, bitsaki@tsl.gr
[2] Computer Science Department, University of Crete, Voutes University Campus,
70013 Heraklion, Greece

Abstract. A common assumption in game theory is that players have a
common and correct (albeit not always complete) knowledge with regards
to the abstract formulation of the game. However, in many real-world
situations it could be the case that (some of) the players are misinformed
with regards to the game that they play, essentially having an *incorrect*
understanding of the setting, without being aware of it. This would invalidate the common knowledge assumption. In this paper, we present a new
game-theoretic framework, called *misinformation games*, that provides
the formal machinery necessary to study this phenomenon, and present
some basic results regarding its properties.

Keywords: Misinformation in games · Natural misinformed
equilibrium · Price of misinformation · Normal-form games · Load
balancing games

1 Introduction

A fundamental issue in interacting situations is the way decisions are made by
the participants, a process captured by game theory, where typically is assumed
that the rules of interaction (i.e., the game definition) are common knowledge
among players (but see [5,11,19] for some exceptions). This may be unrealistic in
circumstances where *misinformation* may cause players to have different and/or
incorrect knowledge about the rules of interaction.

This can happen for various reasons. Specifically, such scenarios could occur
on purpose (e.g., by deceptive agents communicating wrong information), due
to random effects (e.g., noise in the communication channels, erroneous sensor
readings), by design (e.g., by the game designer in order to enforce a socially-
optimal behaviour), or due to environmental changes (e.g., the setting changes
without players' knowledge). Misinformation could play a prominent role in the
outcome of the game, without necessarily negative effects.

For this work the fourth author was supported by the Stavros Niarchos-FORTH postdoc
fellowship for the project ARCHERS.

© Springer Nature Switzerland AG 2021
D. N. Pham et al. (Eds.): PRICAI 2021, LNAI 13031, pp. 76–87, 2021.
https://doi.org/10.1007/978-3-030-89188-6_6

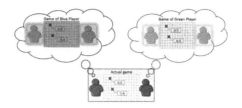

Fig. 1. Schematic representation of a misinformation game with 2 players.

As a more concrete example, consider the classical Prisoner's Dilemma (PD) game, where two suspects (the players) are being interrogated, having the option to betray the other (B), or stay silent (S). Each of them will get a penalty reduction if he/she betrays the other, but if they both remain silent, the police can only convict them for lesser charge and not for the principal crime; if they both betray, they will get a reduced penalty for the principal crime. Using classical game theory, this situation is modelled by payoff matrix presented in Table 1a, where the only Nash equilibrium is for both players to betray.

Now suppose that the cogent evidence with regards to the lesser charge has been obtained in an illegal manner, and thus cannot be used in court. As a result, players' actual payoffs are as shown in Table 1b; however, this is not disclosed to the suspects, who still believe that they play under Table 1a. This would lead players to betray, although, had they known the truth (Table 1b), they also had other options (Nash equilibria), e.g., to both stay silent. We will refer to this game as the *misinformed Prisoner's Dilemma (mPD)* in the rest of this paper.

Table 1. Payoff matrices for the PD and mPD

	S	B
S	$(-1, -1)$	$(-3, -1/2)$
B	$(-1/2, -3)$	$(-2, -2)$

(a) Payoffs (in PD); also, players' view (in mPD).

	S	B
S	$(0, 0)$	$(-3, -1/2)$
B	$(-1/2, -3)$	$(-2, -2)$

(b) Actual game (in mPD).

To study situations like mPD, we relax the classical assumption of game theory that agents know the correct information related to the abstract formulation of the game, and *admit the possibility that each player may have a different (and thus incorrect) perception about the game being played*, unknowingly to himself/herself or the other player(s). We call such games *misinformation games*. As shown in Fig. 1, the main defining characteristic of misinformation games is that agents are unwitting of their misinformation, and will play the game under the misconceived game definition that they have. This essentially means that the assumption of common knowledge is dropped as well.

Obviously, in such a setting, game theory dictates the *actual player behaviour* in his/her own view, which may be different from the behaviour regarding the actual game. On the other hand, *the payoffs received* by the players are the ones provisioned by the actual game, which may differ from the ones they assume.

This paper's main objective is to *introduce the formal machinery necessary to study misinformation games*. Specifically, the contributions of this paper consisted of: i) defining misinformation games and recasting basic game-theoretic concepts without the assumption of common and correct knowledge (Subsect. 3.1), ii) introducing a new metric, called the *Price of Misinformation (PoM)*, to quantify the effect of misinformation on the social welfare of players (Subsect. 3.2), and iii) applying our ideas to load balancing games (Sect. 4).

2   Related Work

Starting from the concept of games with misperceptions (see Chap. 12 in [19]) many studies model subjective knowledge of players with regards to game specifications, leading to the introduction of hypergames (HG) ([3,5,7,18,27,34] etc.) and games with unawareness (GwU) ([8,11,26,28,29] etc.), where players may be playing different games. Although we share motivation with these approaches, there are also some crucial distinctions. First, HG/GwU are behaviour-oriented (*what* the players will play), whereas misinformation games are outcome-oriented. Furthermore, HG focus on perceptional differences among players, and do not model the "actual game", hence, HG lack grounding to the reality of the modelled situation. In misinformation games we close this gap, modelling also the environment, and allowing differences to also occur between each player and the environment. Moreover, in GwU, though the "actual game" is used as the basis of the models, the analysis based on consistency criteria and belief hierarchies. In misinformation games we do not make such assumptions.

In [15] authors define the notion of games with awareness based on an extensive-form game; they agglomerate descriptions of reality, changes in players' awareness and players' subjective views. Also, they define a generalized Nash equilibrium that is similar with our equilibrium concept. Nevertheless, their analysis is behaviour-oriented. The work in [11] incorporates game and unawareness as interrelated objects, whereas in [8] awareness architectures are provided to study players' limited awareness of strategies. Further, in [33] authors focus on how unawareness affects incentives, whereas [30] provides a dynamic approach for extensive-form games with unawareness. Moreover, [23] proposed a model for games with uncertainty where players may have different awareness regarding a move of nature.

In [6,14] studied the case where one of the players knows the (mis)perceptions of the opponents. Also, in [32] the concept of subjective games is proposed, but without introducing any equilibrium concept. Another approach is given in [10] where an equilibrium concept is defined, but has a probabilistic dependence on the actual game specifications.

Initiated by Harsanyi [16] the concept of incomplete knowledge in games has attracted significant attention, mainly through the Bayesian games approach

([12,13,31,35], etc.), where a key assumption is that of common priors. Although this provides significant modeling advantages, it cannot address the situations considered by misinformation games, cases where knowledge is not common. Moreover, in Bayesian games, although agents are unsure as to their actual payoff, they are well-aware of that, and they do their best out of the uncertainty that they have. On the contrary, in misinformation games, the agents play according to their subjective game definition, without considering mitigation measures.

In particular, the mPD scenario (Table 1) cannot be captured by Bayesian games, as the players do not distinct the actual situation from the one provided to them. But even if a player suspects that the police are lying, has no clue as to what they are lying about. Therefore, he/she cannot form any probability distribution over an array of alternative plausible scenarios.

In [2,4,24] the case of uncommon priors was studied, but without addressing the scenario of private priors, which is the case considered in misinformation games. Additionally, the idea of agents understanding a different payoff matrix than the actual one has been considered in [1,20]. In these studies, the agents privately choose to modify their own objective payoffs (only), for personal reasons (i.e. bias). Here misinformation is restricted only to each agent's own payoffs, therefore our work can be viewed as a more general case of such settings.

3   Normal-Form Games

A *game in normal-form* is represented by a *payoff matrix* that defines the payoffs of all players for all possible combinations of pure strategies. Formally:

Definition 1. *A normal-form game G is a tuple $\langle N, S, P \rangle$, where:*

- *N is the set of the players,*
- *$S = S_1 \times \cdots \times S_{|N|}$, S_i is the set of pure strategies of player $i \in N$,*
- *$P = (P_1, \ldots, P_{|N|})$, $P_i \in \mathbb{R}^{|S_1| \times \cdots \times |S_{|N|}|}$ is the payoff matrix of player i.*

If player i randomly selects a pure strategy, then he/she plays a mixed strategy $\sigma_i = (\sigma_{i,1}, \ldots, \sigma_{i,|S_i|})$ which is a discrete probability distribution over S_i. Let the set of all possible mixed strategies σ_i be Σ_i. A strategy profile $\sigma = (\sigma_1, \ldots, \sigma_{|N|})$ is an $|N|$-tuple in $\Sigma = \Sigma_1 \times \ldots \times \Sigma_{|N|}$. We denote by σ_{-i} the $|N-1|$-tuple strategy profile of all other players except for player i in σ. The payoff function of player i is defined as: $f_i : \Sigma \to \mathbb{R}$, such that:

$$f_i(\sigma_i, \sigma_{-i}) = \sum_{k \in S_1} \cdots \sum_{j \in S_{|N|}} P_i(k, \ldots, j) \cdot \sigma_{1,k} \cdot \ldots \cdot \sigma_{|N|,j}, \qquad (1)$$

where $P_i(k, \ldots, j)$ is the payoff of player i in the pure strategy profile $(k, \ldots, j)$. In other words, $f_i(\sigma_i, \sigma_{-i})$ represents player's i expected payoff as a function of σ. The *Nash equilibrium* in a normal-form game is defined as follows:

Definition 2. *A strategy profile $\sigma^* = (\sigma_1^*, \ldots, \sigma_{|N|}^*)$ is a Nash equilibrium, iff, for any i and for any $\hat{\sigma}_i \in \Sigma_i$, $f_i(\sigma_i^*, \sigma_{-i}^*) \geq f_i(\hat{\sigma}_i, \sigma_{-i}^*)$.*

3.1   Misinformation in Normal-Form Games

Misinformation captures the concept that different players may have a specific, subjective, and thus different view of the game that they play.

Definition 3. *A* misinformation normal-form game *(or simply* misinformation game*) is a tuple* $mG = \langle G^0, G^1, \ldots, G^{|N|} \rangle$, *where all* G^i *are normal-form games and* G^0 *contains* $|N|$ *players.*

G^0 is called the *actual game* and represents the game that is actually being played, whereas G^i (for $i \in \{1, \ldots, |N|\}$) represents the game that player i thinks that is being played (called the *game of player i*). We make no assumptions as to the relation among G^0 and G^i, and allow all types of misinformation to occur. An interesting special class of misinformation games is the following:

Definition 4. *A misinformation game* $mG = \langle G^0, G^1, \ldots, G^{|N|} \rangle$ *is called* canonical *iff:*

- *For any i, G^0, G^i differ only in their payoffs.*
- *In any G^i, all players have an equal number of pure strategies.*

Although, non-canonical misinformation games may occur, e.g., when communication problems deprives a player from the option to use a viable strategy. However, we can transform any non-canonical misinformation game into an equivalent canonical game (in terms of strategic behaviour), using the process of *inflation* described as follows.

Let mG be a non-canonical misinformation game. To transform it into a canonical misinformation game with the same strategic behaviour, we compare G^0 with each G^i ($i > 0$). Then:

1. If G^i does not include a player of G^0, then we "inflate" G^i by adding this new player, with the same strategies as in G^0. We extend the elements of the payoff matrix of G^i to represent the payoffs of the new player, using any fixed constant value. Moreover, the current payoff matrix of G^i is increased by one dimension, by replicating the original payoff matrix as many times as needed (to accommodate the new player's strategies).
2. If G^i contains an imaginary player not included in G^0, then we add a new player in G^0, using the process described in #1 above. In addition, since Definition 3 requires that each player in G^0 is associated with a game in mG, we add a new game in mG, which is a replica of G^0.
3. If G^i does not contain a certain strategy which appears in G^0 (for a certain player), we add this new strategy, with payoffs small enough to be dominated by all other strategies.
4. If G^i contains an imaginary strategy that does not appear in G^0 (for a certain player), we inflate G^0 as in #3 above.

Repeating the above process a sufficient (finite) number of times, we derive a misinformation game that satisfies the first condition of Definition 4 and has the same strategic properties as the original. For the second condition, we inflate the games according to the largest dimension (number of strategies) of the largest game, as in #3 above. Therefore, we focus on canonical misinformation games.

The definition of misinformed strategies and strategy profiles is straightforward, once noticing that they refer to each player's own game:

Definition 5. *A misinformed strategy, $m\sigma_i$ of a player i is a strategy of i in the game G^i. We denote the set of all possible misinformed strategies of player i as Σ_i^i. A misinformed strategy profile of mG is an $|N|$-tuple of misinformed strategies $m\sigma = (m\sigma_1, \ldots, m\sigma_{|N|})$, where $m\sigma_i \in \Sigma_i^i$.*

As usual, we denote by $m\sigma_{-i}$ the $|N-1|$-tuple strategy profile of all other players except for player i in a misinformed strategy $m\sigma$. The payoff function f_i of player i under a given profile $m\sigma$ is determined by the payoff matrix of G^0, and is defined as $f_i : \Sigma_1^1 \times \cdots \times \Sigma_{|N|}^{|N|} \to \mathbb{R}$, such that:

$$f_i(m\sigma_i, m\sigma_{-i}) = \sum_{k \in S_1^1} \cdots \sum_{j \in S_{|N|}^{|N|}} P_i^0(k, \ldots, j) \cdot m\sigma_{1,k} \cdot \ldots \cdot m\sigma_{|N|,j},$$

where $P_i^0(k, \ldots, j)$ is the payoff of player i in the pure strategy profile $(k, \ldots, j)$ under the actual game G^0. Also, S_i^j denotes the set of pure strategies of player i in game G^j.

Observe that, although each player's strategic decisions are driven by the information in his/her own game (G^i), the received payoffs are totally dependent on the actual game G^0, that may differ than G^i. Further, the payoff function would be ill-defined if we consider non-canonical misinformation games.

Next, we define the solution concept of a misinformation game, where each player chooses a Nash strategy, neglecting what other players know or play:

Definition 6. *A misinformed strategy, $m\sigma_i$, of player i, is a misinformed equilibrium strategy, iff, it is a Nash equilibrium strategy for the game G^i. A misinformed strategy profile $m\sigma$ is called a natural misinformed equilibrium iff it consists of misinformed equilibrium strategies.*

In the following, we denote by nme_{mG} (or simply nme, when mG is obvious from the context) the set of natural misinformed equilibria of mG and by NE the set of Nash equilibria of G. Moreover, any natural misinformed equilibrium is consisted of Nash equilibrium strategy profiles, regarding G^is. The computation of a Nash equilibrium for each G^i is **PPAD**-complete [9]. Thus, the same holds for a natural misinformed equilibrium.

3.2   Price of Misinformation

Inspired by the seminal work of [17] that introduced the *Price of Anarchy (PoA)* metric we define a metric, called the *Price of Misinformation (PoM)* to measure the effect of misinformation compared to the social optimum. For that, we consider a social welfare function $SW(\sigma) = \sum_i f_i(\sigma)$, and denote by *opt* the socially optimal strategy profile, i.e., $opt = \arg\max_\sigma SW(\sigma)$. *PoM* is defined as follows:

Definition 7. *Given a misinformation game mG, the* Price of Misinformation *(PoM) is defined as:*

$$PoM = \frac{SW(opt)}{\min_{\sigma \in nme} SW(\sigma)} \tag{2}$$

Using the definition of *PoA* [17] and (2) we derive the following formula:

$$\frac{PoM}{PoA} = \frac{\min_{\sigma \in NE} SW(\sigma)}{\min_{\sigma \in nme} SW(\sigma)} \tag{3}$$

Observe that, if *PoM* < *PoA*, then misinformation has a beneficial effect on social welfare, as the players are inclined (due to their misinformation) to choose socially better strategies. On the other hand, if *PoM* > *PoA*, then misinformation leads to a worse outcome from the perspective of social welfare.

Moreover, misinformation is a powerful tool for mechanism design as shown in the following proposition.

Proposition 1. *For any normal-form game G and strategy profile σ there is a misinformation game* $mG = \langle G^0, G^1, \ldots, G^{|N|} \rangle$ *such that* $G^0 = G$ *and the only natural misinformed equilibrium of mG is σ.*

Proof. Let *G'* be a normal form game such that *σ* is the only Nash equilibrium (we can always construct such a game). Then $mG = \langle G, G', \ldots, G' \rangle$ is the desired misinformation game. □

Corollary 1. *For every normal-form game G there is a misinformation game* $mG = \langle G^0, G^1, \ldots, G^{|N|} \rangle$ *such that* $G^0 = G$ *and PoM = 1.*

The above results show that, given sufficient misinformation, anything is possible in terms of improving (or deteriorating) the social welfare.

4   Load Balancing Games

In this section, we apply our framework in load balancing games, as defined in [22], where tasks selfishly choose to be assigned to machines, so that no task has any incentive to deviate from its machine. Formally:

Definition 8. *A* load balancing game *(lbg) is a tuple* $G = \langle k, m, s, w \rangle$, *where* $k = \{1, \ldots, |k|\}$ *is the set of tasks, each associated with a weight* $w_j \geq 0$, *and* $m = \{1, \ldots, |m|\}$ *is the set of machines, each with speed* $s_i > 0$.

We consider the case where tasks play only pure strategies, thus, the *assignment* of tasks to machines is determined by a mapping $A : k \to m$ (note that each task is assigned to exactly one machine). The load of machine $i \in m$ under *A* is defined as $l_i = \sum_{j \in k : i = A(j)} w_j / s_i$. The cost of task *j* for choosing machine *i* is $c_j^i = l_i$. Furthermore, the social cost of assignment *A* is defined as $cost(A) = \max_{i \in m}(l_i)$, in other words the makespan under the assignment *A*. An assignment A^* is optimal if $cost(A^*) \leq cost(A)$ for all possible assignments *A*. An assignment *A* is a pure Nash equilibrium, if and only if, for any *j* and for any $\hat{i} \in m$, $c_j^{A(j)} \leq c_j^{\hat{i}}$, in other words for any alternative assignment of task *j* (say to machine $\hat{i}$) the cost is worse.

4.1   Misinformation in Load Balancing Games

Introducing misinformation in lbgs follows similar patterns as in Sect. 3.1:

Definition 9. *A misinformation lbg is a tuple* $mG = \langle G^0, G^1, \ldots, G^{|k|}\rangle$, *where all G^j are lbgs and G^0 contains $|k|$ tasks.*

Definition 10. *A misinformation lbg* $mG = \langle G^0, G^1, \ldots, G^{|k|}\rangle$ *is called* canonical, *if and only if, for any j, G^0, G^j differ only with regards to the weights of the tasks and the speeds of the machines.*

Like in the standard case, a misinformed assignment nmA is a mapping of tasks to machines $nmA : k \to m$, where any task j chooses a machine according to its game G^j. Given a specific misinformed assignment nmA, the *actual load of a machine i* is $l_i^0 = \sum_{j \in k : i = nmA(j)} w_j^0 / s_i^0$, whereas the *perceived load of a machine i for task h* is $l_i^h = \sum_{j \in k : i = nmA(j)} w_j^h / s_i^h$. The *actual cost* of task j for choosing machine i is $c_j^{i,0} = l_i^0$, whereas the *perceived cost* is $c_j^{i,j} = l_i^j$. Similarly, the actual social cost of mA is $cost(nmA) = \max_{i \in m}(l_i^0)$.

As with normal-form games, the tasks choose the Nash equilibrium assignments in their own game without regards to what other tasks do. Formally:

Definition 11. *A misinformed task assignment $nmA(j)$ of task j is a* pure misinformed equilibrium task assignment, *if and only if it is a pure Nash equilibrium assignment for game G^j. A misinformed assignment nmA is called a* pure natural misinformed equilibrium assignment *if and only if it consists of pure misinformed equilibrium task assignments.*

As each G^j is an lbg, the existence of a pure Nash equilibrium assignment in every G^j is warranted by the results of [21,22,25], hence a natural misinformed equilibrium assignment in misinformation lbgs always exists. Moreover, using complexity results for standard lbgs [22], we can show the following:

Proposition 2. *Consider a misinformation lbg mG with k tasks, such that each G^j has m identical machines. Then, the computational complexity of computing a natural misinformed equilibrium assignment in mG is $O(k^2 \log k)$.*

Proof. On identical machines we can transform any assignment A into a pure Nash equilibrium in time $O(k \log k)$ [22]. To find a natural misinformed equilibrium, we repeat this once for each G^j ($j > 0$), which requires $O(k^2 \log k)$ time.

4.2   Price of Misinformation in Load Balancing Games

PoM in misinformation lbgs (that aim at minimizing cost instead of maximizing payoff) is defined as follows:

$$PoM = \frac{\max_{A \in nmA} cost(A)}{cost(A^*)}, \tag{4}$$

where $cost(A)$ is the worst cost among the pure natural misinformed equilibria assignments nmA and $cost(A^*)$ is the cost of the optimal assignment in the actual game. The following example is illustrative of the concepts presented in this section:

Example 1. Suppose that there are two identical machines with speed $s = 1$ and four tasks with $w_1 = w_2 = 1$ and $w_3 = w_4 = 2$. The optimal assignment maps a task of weight 1 and a task of weight 2 to each of the machines ($A^* = (1, 2, 1, 2)$). The worst pure Nash equilibrium assignment is $A = (1, 1, 2, 2)$ with $cost(A) = 4$, Fig. 2-(b).

Now, consider the misinformation game mG in which tasks have different information on the weights. Let $w^1 = (w_1^1 = 6, w_2^1 = 1, w_3^1 = 2, w_4^1 = 2)$ be the weights in G^1 and $w^j = (w_1^j = 7, w_2^j = 1, w_3^j = 1, w_4^j = 1)$ in G^j, for $j = \{2, 3, 4\}$. The pure Nash equilibrium assignments in each game G^j are $A_1 = (1, 2, 2, 2)$ and $A_2 = (2, 1, 1, 1)$, thus the pure natural misinformed equilibrium assignments are all combinations aligned with i) task 1 is assigned to a different machine than tasks $\{2, 3, 4\}$ or ii) all tasks are assigned to the same machine. From the above, the worst natural misinformed equilibrium assignment is derived to be $nmA = (1, 1, 1, 1)$ (or $nmA = (2, 2, 2, 2)$) with $cost(nmA) = 6$, Fig. 2-(c-d). It is interesting that in this example $PoA = 4/3$ and $PoM = 2$ implying that misinformation worsens the behaviour of the game. □

(a)   (b)   (c)   (d)

Fig. 2. (a) optimal assignment, (b) worst Nash equilibrium allocation, (c–d) worst natural misinformed equilibrium allocation.

In terms of mechanism design, misinformation is equally strong and flexible for lbgs as for normal-form games. In particular, for any lbg G and assignment A, we can construct a misinformation lbg $mG = \langle G^0, G^1, \ldots, G^{|N|} \rangle$ such that $G^0 = G$ and the only pure natural misinformed equilibrium assignment of mG is A, as well as a misinformation lbg $mG = \langle G^0, G^1, \ldots, G^{|N|} \rangle$ such that $G^0 = G$ and $PoM = 1$.

Due to the special form of lbgs, we can prove various bounds regarding their cost and PoM, based on the task weights and machine speeds. Propositions 3, 4, 5 show some such results:

Proposition 3. *Consider a canonical misinformation lbg $mG = \langle G^0, G^1, \ldots, G^{|k|} \rangle$, such that $G^0 = \langle k, m, s, w \rangle$ and $s_i > 0$ for all i. Then, for any assignment nme, $cost(nme) \leq \sum_{j=1}^{k} w_j / \min_i s_i$.*

Proof. The worst possible assignment nmA^* (from the social cost perspective) is to assign all tasks to the slowest machine, with $cost(nmA^*) = \sum_{j=1}^{k} w_j / \min_i s_i$. Misinformation can achieve this effect, so the result follows.   □

Proposition 4. *Consider a misinformation lbg* $mG = \langle G^0, G^1, \ldots, G^{|k|} \rangle$, *such that* G^0 *has m identical machines and finite task weights. Then, the Price of Misinformation is* $PoM \leq m$.

Proof. An optimal assignment $cost(A^*)$ cannot be smaller than the average load over all machines (i.e., $(\sum_{j \in [k]} w_j)/m$). Also, the worst scenario is that all tasks are assigned into one machine, with cost $(\sum_{j \in [k]} w_j)$. Then, using Eq. (4), we conclude.   □

Next, we consider the case of uniformly related machines, i.e., the case where the cost (processing time) of a job j of weight w_j on machine i with speed s_i is w_j/s_i. We can show the following:

Proposition 5. *Consider a misinformation lbg* $mG = \langle G^0, G^1, \ldots, G^{|k|} \rangle$, *such that* $G^0 = \langle k, m, s, w \rangle$ *with m uniformly related machines and finite task weights. Then, the Price of Misinformation is*

$$PoM \leq k \cdot \frac{S}{s} \cdot O\left(\frac{\log m}{\log \log m}\right), \qquad (5)$$

where s is the slowest speed and S is the fastest speed.

Proof. Since there is the case that all tasks be assigned to the slowest machine we have that $cost(nmA) \leq \sum_{i=1}^{k} w_i/s \leq k \cdot M/s$, where M is the largest weight. Also, we have that $PoM = PoA \cdot \frac{\max_{A \in nmA} Cost(A)}{\max_{B \in NE} Cost(B)}$ with A be the worst natural misinformed equilibrium assignment, B the worst Nash equilibrium assignment and NE the set of Nash equilibria assignments. Furthermore, we have that $\max_{B \in NE} Cost(B) \geq M/S$. Finally, by Chap. 20 of [22] we have that $PoA \leq O\left(\frac{\log m}{\log \log m}\right)$.   □

5   Synopsis and Future Work

This paper is motivated by the idea that misinformation is a fact of life in most multi-player interactions, and thus having the formal machinery to analyse misinformation can help understand many real-world phenomena. Towards this aim, we introduce a novel game-theoretic framework, called *misinformation games*.

We argue that the concept of misinformation games has the potential to explain various phenomena, and raises several interesting problems to be studied from different perspectives. From the designer's perspective, we can consider questions like the sensitivity of the game against misinformation, or the identification of ways to exploit the misinformation as a means to improve social welfare (through PoM). From the players' perspective, one could study how the players will revise their game definition following the realisation that it is wrong, or the question of how to protect them from deceptive efforts. Finally, from the more general perspective, it makes sense to study various forms of equilibria, as well as the effect of different misinformation patterns on the game's outcome.

References

1. Acar, E., Meir, R.: Distance-based equilibria in normal-form games. In: The 34th AAAI Conference on Artificial Intelligence, AAAI 2020, The 32nd Innovative Applications of Artificial Intelligence Conference, IAAI 2020, The 10th AAAI Symposium on Educational Advances in Artificial Intelligence, EAAI 2020, pp. 1750–1757. AAAI Press (2020)
2. Antos, D., Pfeffer, A.: Representing Bayesian games without a common prior. In: 9th International Conference on Autonomous Agents and Multiagent Systems, AAMAS 2010, pp. 1457–1458. IFAAMAS (2010)
3. Bakker, C., Bhattacharya, A., Chatterjee, S., Vrabie, D.L.: Metagames and hypergames for deception-robust control. ACM Trans. Cyber-Phys. Syst. 5(3), 25 (2021)
4. Banks, D., Gallego, V., Naveiro, R., Ríos Insua, D.: Adversarial risk analysis: an overview. WIREs Comput. Stat., e1530 (2020). https://doi.org/10.1002/wics.1530
5. Bennett, P.G.: Hypergames: developing a model of conflict. Futures 12(6), 489–507 (1980)
6. Chaib-Draa, B.: Hypergame analysis in multiagent environments. In: Proceedings of the AAAI Spring Symposium, pp. 147–149 (2001)
7. Cho, J.-H., Zhu, M., Singh, M.: Modeling and analysis of deception games based on hypergame theory. In: Al-Shaer, E., Wei, J., Hamlen, K.W., Wang, C. (eds.) Autonomous Cyber Deception, pp. 49–74. Springer, Cham (2019). https://doi.org/10.1007/978-3-030-02110-8_4
8. Copic, J., Galeotti, A.: Awareness as an equilibrium notion: normal-form games (2006)
9. Daskalakis, C., Goldberg, P.W., Papadimitriou, C.H.: The complexity of computing a Nash equilibrium. SIAM J. Comput. 39(1), 195–259 (2009)
10. Esponda, I., Pouzo, D.: Berk-Nash equilibrium: a framework for modeling agents with misspecified models. Econometrica 84(3), 1093–1130 (2016)
11. Feinberg, Y.: Games with unawareness. B.E. J. Theor. Econ. 21, 433–488 (2020)
12. Gairing, M., Monien, B., Tiemann, K.: Selfish routing with incomplete information. Theor. Comput. Syst. 42(1), 91–130 (2008)
13. Gao, J.: Uncertain bimatrix game with applications. Fuzzy Optim. Decis. Making 12(1), 65–78 (2013). https://doi.org/10.1007/s10700-012-9145-6
14. Gharesifard, B., Cortés, J.: Stealthy strategies for deception in hypergames with asymmetric information. In: 2011 50th IEEE Conference on Decision and Control and European Control Conference, pp. 5762–5767 (2011)
15. Halpern, J.Y., Rêgo, L.C.: Extensive games with possibly unaware players. Math. Soc. Sci. 70, 42–58 (2014)
16. Harsanyi, J.C.: Games with incomplete information played by "Bayesian" players, I–III part I. The basic model. In: Management Science, vol. 14, no. 3, pp. 159–182 (1967)
17. Koutsoupias, E., Papadimitriou, C.: Worst-case equilibria. In: Proceedings of the 16th Annual Conference on Theoretical Aspects of Computer Science (STACS), pp. 404–413 (1999)

18. Kovach, N.S., Gibson, A.S., Lamont, G.B.: Hypergame theory: a model for conflict, misperception, and deception. Game Theor. **2015**, 20 (2015)
19. Luce, R.D., Raiffa, H.: Games and Decisions: Introduction and Critical Survey. Wiley, New York (1957)
20. Meir, R., Parkes, D.C.: Playing the wrong game: smoothness bounds for congestion games with behavioral biases. SIGMETRICS Perf. Eval. Rev. **43**(3), 67–70 (2015)
21. Nash, J.F.: Non-cooperative games. Ann. Math. **54**(2), 286–295 (1951)
22. Suzuki, M., Vetta, A.: How many freemasons are there? The consensus voting mechanism in metric spaces. In: Harks, T., Klimm, M. (eds.) SAGT 2020. LNCS, vol. 12283, pp. 322–336. Springer, Cham (2020). https://doi.org/10.1007/978-3-030-57980-7_21
23. Ozbay, E.Y.: Unawareness and strategic announcements in games with uncertainty. In: Proceedings of the 11th Conference on Theoretical Aspects of Rationality and Knowledge, pp. 231–238 (2007)
24. Roponen, J., Ríos Insua, D., Salo, A.: Adversarial risk analysis under partial information. Eur. J. Oper. Res. **287**(1), 306–316 (2020)
25. Rosenthal, R.W.: A class of games possessing pure-strategy Nash equilibria. Int. J. Game Theor. **2**, 65–67 (1973). https://doi.org/10.1007/BF01737559
26. Sasaki, Y.: Generalized Nash equilibrium with stable belief hierarchies in static games with unawareness. Ann. Oper. Res. **256**(2), 271–284 (2017)
27. Sasaki, Y., Kijima, K.: Hypergames and Bayesian games: a theoretical comparison of the models of games with incomplete information. J. Syst. Sci. Complexity **25**(4), 720–735 (2012)
28. Schipper, B.C.: Unawareness - a gentle introduction to both the literature and the special issue. Math. Soc. Sci. **70**, 1–9 (2014)
29. Schipper, B.C.: Self-confirming games: Unawareness, discovery, and equilibrium. In: TARK (2017)
30. Schipper, B.C.: Discovery and Equilibrium in Games with Unawareness. University Library of Munich, Germany, MPRA Paper (2018)
31. Székely, G.J., Rizzo, M.L.: The uncertainty principle of game theory. Am. Math. Mon. **114**(8), 688–702 (2007)
32. Teneketzis, D., Castañón, D.: Informational aspects of a class of subjective games of incomplete information: static case. J. Optim. Theor. Appl. **54**, 413–422 (1983)
33. von Thadden, E.-L., Zhao, X.: Multi-task agency with unawareness. Theor. Decis. **77**(2), 197–222 (2013). https://doi.org/10.1007/s11238-013-9397-9
34. Vane, R., Lehner, P.: Using hypergames to increase planned payoff and reduce risk. Auton. Agent. Multi-Agent Syst. **5**(3), 365–380 (2002)
35. Zamir, S.: Bayesian games: games with incomplete information. In: Meyers, R. (eds.) Encyclopedia of Complexity and Systems Science. Springer, New York (2009). https://doi.org/10.1007/978-0-387-30440-3_29

Influence-Driven Explanations for Bayesian Network Classifiers

Emanuele Albini[1][(✉)], Antonio Rago[1], Pietro Baroni[2], and Francesca Toni[1]

[1] Department of Computing, Imperial College London, London, UK
{emanuele,antonio,ft}@imperial.ac.uk
[2] Dip.to di Ingegneria dell'Informazione, Università degli Studi di Brescia,
Brescia, Italy
pietro.baroni@unibs.it

Abstract. We propose a novel approach to building *influence-driven explanations* (IDXs) for (discrete) Bayesian network classifiers (BCs). IDXs feature two main advantages wrt other commonly adopted explanation methods First, IDXs may be generated using the (causal) influences between *intermediate*, in addition to merely input and output, variables *within BCs*, thus providing a *deep*, rather than shallow, account of the BCs' behaviour. Second, IDXs are generated according to a configurable set of properties, specifying which influences between variables count towards explanations. Our approach is thus *flexible* and can be tailored to the requirements of particular contexts or users. Leveraging on this flexibility, we propose novel IDX instances as well as IDX instances capturing existing approaches. We demonstrate IDXs' capability to explain various forms of BCs, and assess the advantages of our proposed IDX instances with both theoretical and empirical analyses.

1 Introduction

The need for explainability has been one of the fastest growing concerns in AI of late, driven by academia, industry and governments. In response, a multitude of explanation methods have been proposed, with diverse strengths and weaknesses.

We focus on explaining the outputs of (discrete) Bayesian classifiers (BCs) of various kinds. BCs are a prominent method for classification (see [4] for an overview), popular e.g. in medical diagnosis [15,17,25], owing, in particular, to their ability to naturally extract causal influences between variables of interest.

Several bespoke explanation methods for BCs are already available in the literature, including *counterfactual* [1], *minimum cardinality* and *prime implicant* [23] explanations. Further, model-agnostic *attribution methods*, e.g. the popular *LIME* [21] and *SHAP* [16], can be deployed to explain BCs. However, these (bespoke or model-agnostic) explanation methods for BCs are predominantly *shallow*, by focusing on how inputs influence outputs, neglecting the causal influences between intermediate variables in BCs. Furthermore, most explanation methods are *rigid* wrt the users, in the sense that they are based on a single,

D. N. Pham et al. (Eds.): PRICAI 2021, LNAI 13031, pp. 88–100, 2021.
https://doi.org/10.1007/978-3-030-89188-6_7

hardwired, notion of explanation. This sort of one-size-fits-all approach may not be appropriate in all contexts: different users may need different forms of explanation and the same user may be interested in exploring alternative explanations.

To overcome these limitations, we propose the novel formalism of *influence-driven explanations* (IDXs), able to support a principled construction of various forms of explanations for a variety of BCs. The two main ingredients of IDXs are *influences* and *explanation kits*. Influences provide insights into the causal relations between variables *within BCs*, thus enabling the possibility of deep explanations, consisting of influence paths where influences are labelled with *influence types*. An explanation kit consists, of a set of influence types, each associated with a Boolean *property* specifying the condition an influence has to meet to be labelled with that type. By using different influences for the same BC and/or different explanation kits for the same BC and set of influences, a user can thus configure explanations and adjust them to different needs. Specifically, we propose four concrete instances of our general IDX approach: two amount to novel notions of deep explanations, whereas the other two are shallow, corresponding to LIME and SHAP. We evaluate the proposed instances theoretically, in particular as regards satisfaction of a desirable principle of *dialectical monotonicity*. We also conduct extensive empirical evaluation of our IDX instances.[1]

2   Related Work

There are a multitude of methods in the literature for providing explanations (e.g. see the recent surveys [6,9,26]). Many are *model-agnostic*, including: *attribution* methods such as LIME [21] and SHAP [16], which assign each feature an *attribution value* indicating its contribution towards a prediction; and methods relying upon symbolic representations, either to define explanations directly (e.g. *anchors* [22]), or to define logic-based counterparts of the underlying models from which explanations are drawn (e.g. [12,13]). Due to their model-agnosticism, all these methods restrict explanations to "correlations" between *inputs* and *outputs* and make implicit assumptions constraining the explanation [2,14]. Instead, our focus on a specific model (BCs) allows us to define *model-aware* explanations providing a deeper representation of how BCs are functioning via (selected) influences between input, output and (if present) *intermediate* model components.

Regarding BCs, [23] define *minimum cardinality* and *prime implicant* explanations to ascertain pertinent features based on a complete set of classifications, i.e. a decision function representing the BC [24]. These explanations are defined for binary variables only and again explain outputs in terms of inputs. The *counterfactual explanations* of [1] may include also intermediate model's components, but they are rigidly based on a single, hardwired notion of explanation, whereas we present a flexible method for tailoring explanations to different settings. Other works related to explaining BCs include explanation trees for causal Bayesian networks [19] and studies linking causality and explanation [10,11]. Differently from these works, influences included in our explanations represent

---

[1] An extended version (with proofs) is available at https://arxiv.org/abs/2012.05773.

causal behaviour *in the BC* rather than *in the world*. Finally, [27] use support graphs as explanations showing the interplay between variables (as we do) in Bayesian networks, but (differently from us) commit to a specific influence type.

3 Bayesian Network Classifiers and Influences

We first define (discrete) BCs and their *decision functions*:

Definition 1. *A BC is a tuple* $\langle \mathcal{O}, \mathcal{C}, \mathcal{V}, \mathcal{D}, \mathcal{A} \rangle$ *such that:*

- $\mathcal{O}$ *is a (finite) set of* observations;
- $\mathcal{C}$ *is a (finite) set of* classifications; *we call* $\mathcal{X} = \mathcal{O} \cup \mathcal{C}$ *the set of* variables;
- $\mathcal{V}$ *is a set of sets such that for any* $x \in \mathcal{X}$ *there is a unique* $V \in \mathcal{V}$ *associated to* x, *called* values of x *($\mathcal{V}(x)$ for short);*
- $\mathcal{D} \subseteq \mathcal{X} \times \mathcal{X}$ *is a set of* conditional dependencies *such that* $\langle \mathcal{X}, \mathcal{D} \rangle$ *is an acyclic directed graph (we refer to this as the underlying* Bayesian network*); for any* $x \in \mathcal{X}$, $\mathcal{D}(x) = \{y \in \mathcal{X} | (y, x) \in \mathcal{D}\}$ *are the* parents *of* x;
- *For each* $x \in \mathcal{X}$, *each* $x_i \in \mathcal{V}(x)$ *is equipped with a* prior probability $P(x_i) \in [0, 1]$ *where* $\sum_{x_i \in \mathcal{V}(x)} P(x_i) = 1$;
- *For each* $x \in \mathcal{X}$, *each* $x_i \in \mathcal{V}(x)$ *is equipped with a set of* conditional probabilities *where if* $\mathcal{D}(x) = \{y, \ldots, z\}$, *for every* $y_m, \ldots, z_n \in \mathcal{V}(y) \times \ldots \times \mathcal{V}(z)$, *we have* $P(x_i | y_m, \ldots, z_n)$, *again with* $\sum_{x_i \in \mathcal{V}(x)} P(x_i | y_m, \ldots, z_n) = 1$;
- $\mathcal{A}$ *is the set of all possible* input assignments: *any* $a \in \mathcal{A}$ *is a (possibly partial) mapping* $a : \mathcal{X} \mapsto \bigcup_{x \in \mathcal{X}} \mathcal{V}(x)$ *such that, for every* $x \in \mathcal{O}$, a *assigns a value* $a(x) \in \mathcal{V}(x)$ *to* x, *and for every* $x \in \mathcal{X}$, *for every* $x_i \in \mathcal{V}(x)$, $P(x_i | a)$ *is the posterior probability of the value of* x *being* x_i, *given* a.[2]

Then, the decision function *(of the BC) is* $\sigma : \mathcal{A} \times \mathcal{X} \mapsto \bigcup_{x \in \mathcal{X}} \mathcal{V}(x)$ *where, for any* $a \in \mathcal{A}$ *and any* $x \in \mathcal{X}$, $\sigma(a, x) = argmax_{x_i \in \mathcal{V}(x)} P(x_i | a)$.[3]

We consider various concrete BCs, all special cases of Definition 1 satisfying, in addition, an *independence property* among the parents of each variable. For all these BCs, the *conditional probabilities* can be defined, for each $x \in \mathcal{X}, x_i \in \mathcal{V}(x)$, $y \in \mathcal{D}(x), y_m \in \mathcal{V}(y)$, as $P(x_i | y_m)$ with $\sum_{x_i \in \mathcal{V}(x)} P(x_i | y_m) = 1$. For single-label classification we use Naive Bayes Classifiers (NBCs), with $\mathcal{C} = \{c\}$ and $\mathcal{D} = \{(c, x) | x \in \mathcal{O}\}$. For multi-label classification we use a variant of the Bayesian network-based Chain Classifier (BCC) [7] in which leaves of the network are observations, the other variables classifications, and every classification c is estimated with an NBC where the children of c are inputs. In the remainder, unless specified otherwise, we assume as given a generic BC $\langle \mathcal{O}, \mathcal{C}, \mathcal{V}, \mathcal{D}, \mathcal{A} \rangle$ satisfying independence.

---

[2] Posterior probabilities may be estimated from prior and conditional probabilities. Note that, if $a(x) = x_i$, then we assume $P(x_i | a) = 1$ and, $\forall x_j \in \mathcal{V}(x) \setminus \{x_i\}$, $P(x_j | a) = 0$.

[3] Note that if $a(x) = x_i$ then $\sigma(a, x) = x_i$.

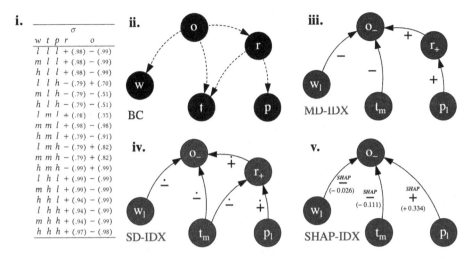

Fig. 1. (i) Decision function (with posterior probabilities explicitly indicated) and (ii) Bayesian network for the play-outside BC, with conditional dependencies as dashed arrows. (iii–v) Corresponding MD-IDX, SD-IDX and SHAP-IDX (shown as graphs, with influences given by edges labelled with their type) for input *low wind* (w_l), *medium temperature* (t_m), and *low pressure* (p_l) and output *not play outside* (o_-) (for the SHAP-IDX we also show the attribution values).

For illustration, consider the *play-outside* BCC in Fig. 1i–ii, in which classifications *play outside* and *raining* are determined from observations *wind*, *temperature* and *pressure*. Here, $\mathcal{C} = \{o, r\}$, $\mathcal{O} = \{w, t, p\}$ and $\mathcal{D}$ is as in Fig. 1ii. Then, let $\mathcal{V}$ be such that $\mathcal{V}(w) = \mathcal{V}(t) = \{low, medium, high\}$, $\mathcal{V}(p) = \{low, high\}$ and $\mathcal{V}(r) = \mathcal{V}(o) = \{-, +\}$, i.e. w and t are categorical while p, r and o are binary. Figure 1i gives the posterior probabilities and decision function by the BCC. Given our focus on *explaining* BCs, we ignore how they are obtained.

Our method for generating explanations relies on modelling how the variables within a BC *influence* one another. For this, we use two alternative sets of influences. First, similarly to [1], we use *deep influences*, defined as the (acyclic) relation $\mathcal{I}_d = \{(x, c) \in \mathcal{X} \times \mathcal{C} | (c, x) \in \mathcal{D}\}$. Second, we use *input-output influences*, defined as the (acyclic) relation $\mathcal{I}_{io} = \mathcal{O} \times \mathcal{C}_o$, where $\mathcal{C}_o \subseteq \mathcal{C}$ are designated outputs. Obviously, $\mathcal{I}_{io}$ ignore the inner structure of BCs. Note that deep influences indicate the direction of the inferences in determining classifications' values, neglecting dependencies between observations as considered in the BCs of [8].

For illustration, in Fig. 1i–ii, $\mathcal{I}_d = \{(w, o), (t, o), (r, o), (t, r), (p, r)\}$ and $\mathcal{I}_{io} = \{(w, o), (t, o), (p, o)\}$ for $\mathcal{C}_o = \{o\}$, while $\mathcal{I}_{io} = \{(w, r), (t, r), (p, r), (w, o), (t, o), (p, o)\}$ for $\mathcal{C}_o = \{o, r\}$. Note that in the former $\mathcal{I}_{io}$ case, r is neglected, while in the latter, the influence (w, r) is extracted even though *wind* cannot influence *raining* in this BC, highlighting that using $\mathcal{I}_{io}$, instead of $\mathcal{I}_d$, may have drawbacks for non-naive BCs, except when the notions coincide, i.e. when $\mathcal{D} = \mathcal{C}_o \times \mathcal{O}$.

4   Influence-Driven Explanations

Our explanations are drawn from (deep or input-output) influences by categorising (some of) them as being of different *types*, depending on the satisfaction of *properties*. The choice of types and properties is captured in *explanation kits*:

Definition 2. *Given influences $\mathcal{I}$, an* explanation kit *for $\mathcal{I}$is a finite set of pairs $\{\langle t_1, \pi_1 \rangle, \ldots \langle t_n, \pi_n \rangle\}$ with $\pi_i : \mathcal{I} \times \mathcal{A} \rightarrow \{true, false\}$, for $i \in \{1, \ldots, n\}$: we say that t_i is an* influence type *characterised by* influence property *π_i, and that π_i is* satisfied *for $(x, y) \in \mathcal{I}$ and $a \in \mathcal{A}$ iff $\pi_i((x, y), a) = true$.*

We will focus on explanation kits $\{\langle t_1, \pi_1 \rangle, \langle t_2, \pi_2 \rangle\}$ with two *mutually exclusive* "dialectical" influence types, of "attack" (t_1) and "support" (t_2): intuitively an influence (x, y) is of type attack (support) if x is a "reason" against (for, resp.) y; mutual exclusion is guaranteed for t_1 and t_2 iff $\pi_i((x, y), a) = true$ implies $\pi_j((x, y), a) = false$ (for $i, j = 1, 2, i \neq j$). We will show that these influence types may be characterised by different influence properties, leading to explanations which can all be deemed "dialectical", while differing in other respects.

In general, explanations are obtained from explanation kits as follows:

Definition 3. *Given influences $\mathcal{I}$ and explanation kit $EK = \{\langle t_1, \pi_1 \rangle, \ldots \langle t_n, \pi_n \rangle\}$ for $\mathcal{I}$, an* influence-driven explanation *(IDX) drawn from EK for explanandum $e \in \mathcal{C}$ with input assignment $a \in \mathcal{A}$ is a tuple $\langle \mathcal{X}_r, \mathcal{I}_{t_1}, \ldots, \mathcal{I}_{t_n} \rangle$ with:*

- $\mathcal{X}_r \subseteq \mathcal{X}$ *such that $e \in \mathcal{X}_r$ (we call $\mathcal{X}_r$ the set of* relevant variables*);*
- $\mathcal{I}_{t_1}, \ldots \mathcal{I}_{t_n} \subseteq \mathcal{I} \cap (\mathcal{X}_r \times \mathcal{X}_r)$ *such that for any $i \in \{1 \ldots n\}$, for every $(x, y) \in \mathcal{I}_{t_i}$, $\pi_i((x, y), a) = true$;*
- $\forall x \in \mathcal{X}_r$ *there is a sequence $x_1, \ldots, x_k, k \geq 1$, such that $x_1 = x, x_k = e$, and $\forall 1 \leq i < k$ $(x_i, x_{i+1}) \in \mathcal{I}_{t_1} \cup \ldots \cup \mathcal{I}_{t_n}$.*

An IDX thus consists of a set of *relevant variables* ($\mathcal{X}_r$), including the explanandum, connected to one another by influences satisfying the influence properties specified in the explanation kit. Several choices of $\mathcal{X}_r$ may be possible and useful: in the remainder we will restrict attention to *maximal IDXs*, i.e. IDXs with $\subseteq$-maximal $\mathcal{X}_r$ satisfying the conditions set in the second and third bullets of Definition 3. These may be deemed to convey in full the workings of the underlying BC, shaped by the chosen explanation kit. We leave the study of non-maximal IDXs to future work. Note that maximal IDXs, for mutually exclusive influence types, are guaranteed to be unique for a given explanandum and input assignment, due to the "connectedness" requirement in the third bullet of Definition 3.

We will define four instances of our notion of IDX: the first two use $\mathcal{I}_d$, whereas the others use $\mathcal{I}_{io}$. In doing so, we will make use of the following notion.

Definition 4. *Given influences $\mathcal{I}$, a variable $x \in \mathcal{X}$ and an input $a \in \mathcal{A}$, the* modified input *$a'_{x_k} \in \mathcal{A}$ by $x_k \in \mathcal{V}(x)$ is such that, for any $z \in \mathcal{X}$: $a'_{x_k}(z) = x_k$ if $z = x$, and $a'_{x_k}(z) = a(z)$ otherwise.*

A modified input thus assigns a desired value (x_k) to a specified variable (x), keeping the preexisting input assignments unchanged. For example, if $a \in \mathcal{A}$ amounts to *low wind*, *medium temperature* and *low pressure* in the running example, then $a'_{w_h} \in \mathcal{A}$ refers to *high wind*, *medium temperature* and *low pressure*.

4.1   Monotonically Dialectical IDXs

Our first IDX instance draws inspiration from work in bipolar argumentation [3] to define an instance of the explanation kit notion so as to fulfil a form of *dialectical monotonicity*: intuitively, this requires that attacks (supports) have a negative (positive, resp.) effect on influenced variables. Concretely, we require that an influencer is an attacker (a supporter) if its assigned value minimises (maximises, resp.) the posterior probability of the influencee's current value.

Definition 5. *An explanation kit* $\{\langle t_1, \pi_1 \rangle, \langle t_2, \pi_2 \rangle\}$ *for* $\mathcal{I}_d$ *is* monotonically dialectical *iff* $t_1 = -$ *(called* monotonic attack*),* $t_2 = +$ *(monotonic support)* *and for any* $(x, y) \in \mathcal{I}_d$, $a \in \mathcal{A}$, *the influence properties* $\pi_1 = \pi_-$, $\pi_2 = \pi_+$ *are defined as:*

- $\pi_-((x,y),a) = true$ *iff* $\forall x_k \in V(x) \setminus \{\sigma(a,x)\}$ $P(\sigma(a,y)|a) < P(\sigma(a,y)|a'_{x_k})$;
- $\pi_+((x,y),a) = true$ *iff* $\forall x_k \in V(x) \setminus \{\sigma(a,x)\}$ $P(\sigma(a,y)|a) > P(\sigma(a,y)|a'_{x_k})$.

A monotonically dialectical IDX (MD-IDX) *(for given explanandum and input assignment) is an IDX drawn from a monotonically dialectical explanation kit.*

For illustration, consider the MD-IDX in Fig. 1iii (for explanandum o and input assignment a such that $a(w) = l$, $a(t) = m$, $a(p) = l$): here, for example, p_l monotonically supports r_+ because $\sigma(a,r) = +$, $P(\sigma(a,r)|a) = 0.94$ whereas for a' such that $a'(p) = h$ (the only other possible value for p), $P(\sigma(a,r)|a') = 0.01$.

   Even though dialectical monotonicity is a natural property, it is a strong requirement that may lead to very few influences, if any, in MD-IDXs. For contexts where this is undesirable, we introduce a weaker form of IDX next.

4.2   Stochastically Dialectical IDXs

Our second IDX instance relaxes the requirement of dialectical monotonicity while still imposing that attacks/supports have a negative/positive, resp., effect on their targets. Concretely, an influencer is an attacker (a supporter) if the posterior probability of the influencee's current value is lower (higher, resp.) than the average of those resulting from the influencer's other values, weighted by their prior probabilities (with all other influencers' values unchanged). Formally:

Definition 6. *An explanation kit* $\{\langle t_1, \pi_1 \rangle, \langle t_2, \pi_2 \rangle\}$ *for* $\mathcal{I}_d$ *is* stochastically dialectical *iff* $t_1 = \dot{-}$ *(called* stochastic attack*),* $t_2 = \dot{+}$ *(stochastic support)* *and for any* $(x, y) \in \mathcal{I}_d$, $a \in \mathcal{A}$, *the influence properties* $\pi_1 = \pi_{\dot{-}}$, $\pi_2 = \pi_{\dot{+}}$ *are defined as:*

- $\pi_{\underline{\cdot}}((x,y),a) = \textit{true iff } P(\sigma(a,y)|a) < \dfrac{\sum\limits_{x_k \in \mathcal{V}(x) \setminus \{\sigma(a,x)\}} \left[P(x_k) \cdot P(\sigma(a,y)|a'_{x_k}) \right]}{\sum\limits_{x_k \in \mathcal{V}(x) \setminus \{\sigma(a,x)\}} P(x_k)};$

- $\pi_{\underline{\cdot}+}((x,y),a) = \textit{true iff } P(\sigma(a,y)|a) > \dfrac{\sum\limits_{x_k \in \mathcal{V}(x) \setminus \{\sigma(a,x)\}} \left[P(x_k) \cdot P(\sigma(a,y)|a'_{x_k}) \right]}{\sum\limits_{x_k \in \mathcal{V}(x) \setminus \{\sigma(a,x)\}} P(x_k)}.$

A stochastically dialectical IDX (SD-IDX) (for given explanandum and input assignment) is an IDX drawn from a stochastically dialectical explanation kit.

For illustration, Fig. 1iv gives the SD-IDX for our running example (using uniform prior probabilities on the domains $\mathcal{V}(w)$, $\mathcal{V}(t)$, and $\mathcal{V}(p)$ and $P(r_+) = .67$, $P(o_+) = 0.22$). Note that this SD-IDX extends the MD-IDX in Fig. 1iii by including the negative (stochastic) effect which t_m has on r_+.

SD-IDXs are *stochastic* in that they take into account the prior probabilities of the possible changes of the influencers. This implies that attacks and supports in SD-IDXs will not be empty except in special cases.

4.3 Attribution Method Based Dialectical IDXs

We further show the versatility of the notion of IDX by instantiating it to integrate attribution methods, notably LIME and SHAP. For our purposes, attribution methods can be thought of as mappings $\alpha : \mathcal{O} \times \mathcal{A} \times \mathcal{C}_o \mapsto \mathbb{R}$, basically assigning real values to input-output influences, given input assignments. These values represent the importance of input features towards outputs, and are computed differently by different attribution methods (we will use α_{LIME} and α_{SHAP}, omitting the computation details). To reflect attribution methods' focus on input-output variables, these instances are defined in terms of $\mathcal{I}_{io}$, as follows:

Definition 7. *Given an attribution method α, an α-explanation kit $\{\langle t_1, \pi_1 \rangle,$ $\langle t_2, \pi_2 \rangle\}$ for $\mathcal{I}_{io}$ is such that $t_1 = \overset{\alpha}{-}$ (α-attack), $t_2 = \overset{\alpha}{+}$ (α-support) and for any $(x,y) \in \mathcal{I}_{io}$, $a \in \mathcal{A}$, the influence properties $\pi_1 = \pi_{\underset{-}{\alpha}}$ and $\pi_2 = \pi_{\underset{+}{\alpha}}$, are defined as:*

- $\pi_{\underset{-}{\alpha}}((x,y),a) = \textit{true iff } \alpha(x,a,y) < 0;$
- $\pi_{\underset{+}{\alpha}}((x,y),a) = \textit{true iff } \alpha(x,a,y) > 0.$

An α-IDX is an IDX drawn from an α-explanation kit.

LIME- and SHAP-explanation kits are instances of α-explanation kits for choices, resp., of $\alpha = \alpha_{LIME}$ and $\alpha = \alpha_{SHAP}$. Then, *LIME-IDXs* and *SHAP-IDXs* are drawn, resp., from LIME- and SHAP-explanation kits. For illustration, Fig. 1v shows a SHAP-IDX for our running example. Here, the restriction to input-output influences implies that the intermediate variable *raining* is not considered in the IDX. Thus, IDXs based on attribution methods are suitable only when the users prefer explanations with a simpler structure. However, in real world applications such as medical diagnosis, where BCs are particularly prevalent, the inclusion of intermediate information could be beneficial: we will illustrate this in Sect. 5.2.

5   Evaluation

We evaluate IDXs theoretically (by showing how different IDX instances relate and how they differ in satisfying a desirable *principle of dialectical monotonicity*) and empirically (for several BCs/datasets). Proofs are omitted for lack of space.

5.1   Theoretical Analysis

Our first two results show the relation/equivalence between MD- and SD-IDXs.[4]

Proposition 1. *Given MD-IDX* $\langle \mathcal{X}_r, \mathcal{I}_-, \mathcal{I}_+ \rangle$ *and SD-IDX* $\langle \mathcal{X}_r', \mathcal{I}_{\dot{-}}, \mathcal{I}_{\dot{+}} \rangle$, *both for* $e \in \mathcal{X}_r \cap \mathcal{X}_r'$ *and* $a \in \mathcal{A}$, *it holds that* $\mathcal{X}_r \subseteq \mathcal{X}_r'$, $\mathcal{I}_- \subseteq \mathcal{I}_{\dot{-}}$ *and* $\mathcal{I}_+ \subseteq \mathcal{I}_{\dot{+}}$.

Thus, an MD-IDX, for given explanandum/input assignment, is always (element-wise) a subset of the SD-IDX for the same explanandum/input assignment.

When all variables are binary, MD-IDXs and SD-IDXs are equivalent:

Proposition 2. *Given MD-IDX* $\langle \mathcal{X}_r, \mathcal{I}_-, \mathcal{I}_+ \rangle$ *and SD-IDX* $\langle \mathcal{X}_r', \mathcal{I}_{\dot{-}}, \mathcal{I}_{\dot{+}} \rangle$, *both for explanandum* $e \in \mathcal{X}_r \cap \mathcal{X}_r'$ *and input assignment* $a \in \mathcal{A}$, *if, for all* $x \in \mathcal{X}_r' \setminus \{e\}$, $|\mathcal{V}(x)| = 2$, *then* $\mathcal{X}_r = \mathcal{X}_r'$, $\mathcal{I}_- = \mathcal{I}_{\dot{-}}$ *and* $\mathcal{I}_+ = \mathcal{I}_{\dot{+}}$.

In general, as discussed in Sect. 4.1, MD-IDXs may be much smaller (element-wise) than SD-IDXs, due to the strong requirements imposed by the principle of *dialectical monotonicity*, defined formally as follows, for generic dialectical IDXs:

Principle 1. *An explanation kit* $\{\langle a, \pi_a \rangle, \langle s, \pi_s \rangle\}$[5] *for* $\mathcal{I}$ *satisfies dialectical monotonicity iff for any IDX* $\langle \mathcal{X}_r, \mathcal{I}_a, \mathcal{I}_s \rangle$ *drawn from the kit (for any explanandum* $e \in \mathcal{X}_r$, *input assignment* $a \in \mathcal{A}$), *it holds that, for any* $(x, y) \in \mathcal{I}_a \cup \mathcal{I}_s$, *if* $a' \in \mathcal{A}$ *is such that* $\sigma(a', x) \neq \sigma(a, x)$ *and* $\sigma(a', z) = \sigma(a, z) \ \forall z \in \mathcal{X} \setminus \{x\}$ *such that* $(z, y) \in \mathcal{I}$, *then:*

- *if* $(x, y) \in \mathcal{I}_a$ *then* $P(\sigma(a, y)|a') > P(\sigma(a, y)|a)$;
- *if* $(x, y) \in \mathcal{I}_s$ *then* $P(\sigma(a, y)|a') < P(\sigma(a, y)|a)$.

Monotonically dialectical explanation kits satisfy this principle by design, while it is worth noting that this does not hold for the other explanations kits:

Proposition 3. *Monotonically dialectical explanation kits satisfy dialectical monotonicity; stochastically dialectical, LIME and SHAP explanation kits do not.*

---

[4] From now on the subscript *io* and *d* of influences for instantiated IDXs will be left implicit, as it is univocally determined by the IDX instance being considered.

[5] Here a and s are some form of attack and support, resp., depending on the specific explanation kit; e.g. for *stochastically* dialectical explanation kits $a = \dot{-}$ and $s = \dot{+}$.

5.2 Empirical Analysis

For an empirical comparison of the proposed IDX instances, we used several datasets/Bayesian networks (see Table 1),[6] for each of which we deployed an NBC (for single-label classification dataset) or a BCC (for multi-label classification datasets and non-shallow Bayesian networks). Two illustrative IDXs for the same input assignment and explanandum (amounting to the output computed by a model built from the *Child* dataset) are shown in Fig. 2. Note that the MD-IDX provides a deeper account of the influences within the BC than the SHAP-IDX, while also being selective on observations included in the explanations (with two observations playing no role in the MD-IDX), to better reflect the inner workings (Bayesian network) of the model.

Table 1. Characteristics of datasets/BCs used in the empirical analysis. (†) NBC (Naive BC) or BCC (Bayesian Chain Classifier); (‡) **B**inary or **C**ategorical; (§) accuracy and macro F1 score on the test set, averaged for multi-label settings.

Dataset	BC†	Size	Variables		Types‡		Performance§	
			$|\mathcal{O}|$	$|\mathcal{C}|$	$\mathcal{O}$	$\mathcal{C}$	Accuracy	F1
Votes	NBC	435	16	1	B	B	90.8%	0.90
German	NBC	750	20	1	C	B	76.4%	0.72
COMPAS	NBC	6951	12	1	C	B	70.5%	0.71
Emotions	BCC	593	72	6	C	B	80.2%	0.70
Asia	BCC	4	2	6	B	B	100%	1.00
Child	BCC	1080	7	13	C	C	80.6%	0.66

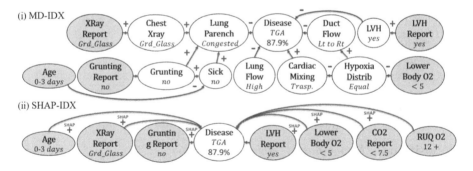

Fig. 2. Example MD-IDX (i) and SHAP-IDX (ii), in graphical form, for explanandum *Disease* for the *Child* BCC (predicting value *TGA* for *Disease* with posterior probability 87.9%). Each node represents a variable with the assigned/estimated value in italics. Grey/white nodes indicate, resp., observations/classifications. +/⁺̄ᴴᴬᴾ and −/⁻̄ᴴᴬᴾ indicate, resp., supports (green arrows) and attacks (red arrows). (Color figure online)

---

[6] *Votes/German*: ML Repo [28]; *COMPAS*: ProRepublica Data Store [20]; *Emotions*: Multi-Label Classification Dataset Repo [18]; *Asia/Child*: Bayesian Net Repo [5].

Table 2. Average percentages of influences that are part of IDXs (on the left, with types as shown and where, for types t, t', $\mathcal{I}^C_{t\,t'} = \{(x,y) \in \mathcal{I}_t \cup \mathcal{I}_{t'} | x, y \in \mathcal{C}\}$) and (on the right) of influences in IDXs violating dialectical monotonicity (all percentages are drawn from a sample of 25,000 influences for 250 data-points). Here, $\times$ indicates percentages that must be 0 due to the BC type. On the left, percentages may not sum to 100 as some influences may not be part of IDXs.

Dataset	% influences in explanations										% violating influences		
	SD-IDX			MD-IDX			LIME-IDX		SHAP-IDX		SD-IDX	LIME-IDX	SHAP-IDX
	$\mathcal{I}_+$	$\mathcal{I}_-$	$\mathcal{I}^C_{-+}$	$\mathcal{I}_+$	$\mathcal{I}_-$	$\mathcal{I}^C_{-+}$	$\mathcal{I}_{\text{LIME}+}$	$\mathcal{I}_{\text{LIME}-}$	$\mathcal{I}_{\text{SHAP}+}$	$\mathcal{I}_{\text{SHAP}-}$			
Votes	77.1	22.9	$\times$	77.1	22.9	$\times$	77.1	22.9	73.2	7.3	0.0	0.2	0.1
German	59.3	40.7	$\times$	29.6	22.0	$\times$	55.9	44.1	46.9	36.4	18.5	20.8	19.8
COMPAS	67.0	33.0	$\times$	45.4	20.3	$\times$	65.7	34.3	35.6	19.1	12.3	12.5	22.7
Emotions	56.9	24.0	1.1	10.3	5.4	1.1	60.6	39.4	56.8	10.3	12.0	11.9	8.9
Child	77.5	22.5	64.0	65.4	15.1	64.0	54.0	41.3	24.4	9.7	7.1	2.5	5.6
Asia	87.5	12.5	62.5	87.5	12.5	62.5	70.8	29.2	54.2	20.8	0.0	0.0	0.0

The comparison is carried out by analysing the computational viability of IDXs and two aspects linked to their effectiveness, i.e. the size of the produced explanations and the actual amount of violations of dialectical monotonicity.

Computational Cost. MD-IDXs and SD-IDXs can be computed efficiently, in linear time in the number of variables' values. Formally, let t_p be the time to compute a prediction and its associated posterior probabilities by the BC (in our experiments, t_p ranged from 3 μs for the simplest NBC to 40 ms for the most complex BCC).[7] The time complexity to compute whether an influence $(x,y) \in \mathcal{I}$ belongs to MD-/SD-IDXs, denoted as T_{1-IDX}, is a function of $|\mathcal{V}(x)|$ because determining membership of (x,y) in MD-/SD-IDXs requires checking how the posterior probability of y changes when changing x. Specifically: $T_{1-IDX}((x,y)) = \Theta\left(t_p \cdot [1 + |\mathcal{V}(x)| - 1]\right) = \Theta\left(t_p \cdot |\mathcal{V}(x)|\right)$. Then, assuming that the cost for checking the inequalities of Definitions 5 and 6 is negligible wrt the cost of a BC call, it turns out that the cost to compute a full MD-/SD-IDX, denoted as T_{IDX}, corresponds to iterating $T_{1-IDX}((x,y))$ over all variables $x \in \mathcal{X}$: $T_{IDX}(\mathcal{V}) = \Theta\left(t_p \cdot \sum_{x \in \mathcal{X}} |\mathcal{V}(x)|\right)$, showing linearity. Thus, MD-/SD-IDXs are competitive wrt attribution methods, which rely on costly sampling of the input space. For illustration, the time taken to generate MD-IDXs for the *Child* BC is at most $60 \cdot t_p$ while the time taken to generate LIME explanations with default parameters is $5000 \cdot t_p$.

Size of the Explanations. In order to understand *how many influences contribute to IDXs*, we calculated the percentage of influences (per type) in each of the instantiated IDXs from Sect. 4: the results are reported on the left in Table 2. We note that: **(1)** when non-naive BCs are used, MD- and SD-IDXs include influences between classifications (see $\mathcal{I}^C_{-+}$ and $\mathcal{I}^C_{-+}$ in Table 2), as a consequence of using $\mathcal{I}_d$ and thus being non-shallow; this suggests that our deep

---

[7] We used a machine with *Intel i9-9900X* at 3.5 GHz and 32 GB of RAM with no GPU acceleration. For BCCs, we did not use optimised production-ready code.

IDXs can provide better insights into models than shallow IDXs drawn from *input-output influences*; **(2)** SD- and LIME-IDXs tend to behave similarly, and MD-IDXs tend to include fewer influences than SD-IDXs (in line with Proposition 1); **(3)** in some settings, SHAP-IDXs fail to capture the majority of attacks captured by the other IDX instances (e.g. for *Votes* and *Emotions*).

Satisfaction of Dialectical Monotonicity. We calculated the percentage of influences in SD-/LIME-/SHAP-IDXs which do not satisfy *dialectical monotonicity*: the results are reported in Table 2 (right). We note that: **(1)** All three forms of IDXs may violate the principle for deep and shallow BCs; **(2)** SM-IDXs violate the principle significantly ($p < 0.05$) less for all NBCs, but the percentage of violations by SM-IDXs increases for BCCs, possibly due to SM-IDXs being non-shallow for BCCs (differently from LIME-/SHAP-IDXs, which are always shallow). Note that the violation of dialectical monotonicity may give rise to counter-intuitive results from a dialectical perspective. For illustration, consider the (shallow) SHAP-IDX in Fig. 2ii: one would expect that for values of *Age* for which this is no longer a supporter the diagnosis that *Disease* is *TGA* becomes less likely, but this is not so here. Instead, in the MD-IDX of Fig. 2i, *Age* is an attacker of the inner *Sick* and no misunderstandings may arise.

6   Conclusions

IDXs offer a new perspective on explanation for BCs and open numerous directions for future work, including investigating other instances and other principles, exploring IDXs for other AI methods, as well as conducting user studies to assess how best IDXs can be delivered to users.

Acknowledgement. This research was funded in part by J.P. Morgan and by the Royal Academy of Engineering under the Research Chairs and Senior Research Fellowships scheme. Any views or opinions expressed herein are solely those of the authors listed, and may differ from the views and opinions expressed by J.P. Morgan or its affiliates. This material is not a product of the Research Department of J.P. Morgan Securities LLC. This material should not be construed as an individual recommendation for any particular client and is not intended as a recommendation of particular securities, financial instruments or strategies for a particular client. This material does not constitute a solicitation or offer in any jurisdiction.

References

1. Albini, E., Rago, A., Baroni, P., Toni, F.: Relation-based counterfactual explanations for Bayesian network classifiers. In: Proceedings of the 29th International Joint Conference on Artificial Intelligence, IJCAI, pp. 451–457 (2020)
2. Barocas, S., Selbst, A.D., Raghavan, M.: The hidden assumptions behind counterfactual explanations and principal reasons. In: FAT* 2020: Proceedings of the 2020 Conference on Fairness, Accountability, and Transparency, pp. 80–89 (2020)

3. Baroni, P., Rago, A., Toni, F.: How many properties do we need for gradual argumentation? In: Proceedings of the 32nd AAAI Conference on Artificial Intelligence, pp. 1736–1743 (2018)
4. Bielza, C., Larrañaga, P.: Discrete Bayesian network classifiers: a survey. ACM Comput. Surv. **47**(1), 5:1–5:43 (2014)
5. BNlearn: Bayesian network repository - an R package for Bayesian network learning and inference (2020). https://www.bnlearn.com/bnrepository
6. Burkart, N., Huber, M.F.: A survey on the explainability of supervised machine learning. J. Artif. Intell. Res. **70**, 245–317 (2021)
7. Enrique Sucar, L., Bielza, C., Morales, E.F., Hernandez-Leal, P., Zaragoza, J.H., Larrañaga, P.: Multi-label classification with Bayesian network-based chain classifiers. Pattern Recogn. Lett. **41**, 14–22 (2014)
8. Friedman, N., Geiger, D., Goldszmidt, M.: Bayesian network classifiers. Mach. Learn. **29**(2–3), 131–163 (1997)
9. Guidotti, R., Monreale, A., Ruggieri, S., Turini, F., Giannotti, F., Pedreschi, D.: A survey of methods for explaining black box models. ACM Comput. Surv. **51**(5), 93:1–93:42 (2019)
10. Halpern, J.Y., Pearl, J.: Causes and explanations: a structural-model approach - Part II: explanations. In: Proceedings of the 17th International Joint Conference on Artificial Intelligence, IJCAI, pp. 27–34 (2001)
11. Halpern, J.Y., Pearl, J.: Causes and explanations: a structural-model approach: Part 1: causes. In: UAI 2001: Proceedings of the 17th Conference in Uncertainty in Artificial Intelligence, pp. 194–202 (2001)
12. Ignatiev, A., Narodytska, N., Marques-Silva, J.: Abduction-based explanations for machine learning models. In: Proceedings of the 33rd AAAI Conference on Artificial Intelligence, pp. 1511–1519 (2019)
13. Ignatiev, A., Narodytska, N., Marques-Silva, J.: On relating explanations and adversarial examples. In: Advances in Neural Information Processing Systems 32: Annual Conference on Neural Information Processing Systems 2019, NeurIPS 2019, pp. 15857–15867 (2019)
14. Kumar, I.E., Venkatasubramanian, S., Scheidegger, C., Friedler, S.A.: Problems with Shapley-value-based explanations as feature importance measures. Mach. Learn. Res. **119**, 5491–5500 (2020)
15. Lipovetsky, S.: Let the evidence speak - using Bayesian thinking in law, medicine, ecology and other areas. Technometrics **62**(1), 137–138 (2020)
16. Lundberg, S.M., Lee, S.: A unified approach to interpreting model predictions. In: Advances in Neural Information Processing Systems 30: Annual Conference on Neural Information Processing Systems 2017, pp. 4765–4774 (2017)
17. McLachlan, S., Dube, K., Hitman, G.A., Fenton, N.E., Kyrimi, E.: Bayesian networks in healthcare: distribution by medical condition. Artif. Intell. Med. **107**, 101912 (2020)
18. Moyano, J.M.: Multi-label classification dataset repository (2020). http://www.uco.es/kdis/mllresources/
19. Nielsen, U.H., Pellet, J., Elisseeff, A.: Explanation trees for causal Bayesian networks. In: UAI 2008, Proceedings of the 24th Conference in Uncertainty in Artificial Intelligence, pp. 427–434 (2008)
20. ProPublica Data Store: Compas recidivism risk score data and analysis (2016). https://www.propublica.org/datastore/dataset/compas-recidivism-risk-score-data-and-analysis

21. Ribeiro, M.T., Singh, S., Guestrin, C.: "Why should I trust you?": explaining the predictions of any classifier. In: Proceedings of the 22nd ACM SIGKDD International Conference on Knowledge Discovery and Data Mining, pp. 1135–1144 (2016)
22. Ribeiro, M.T., Singh, S., Guestrin, C.: Anchors: high-precision model-agnostic explanations. In: Proceedings of the 32nd AAAI Conference on Artificial Intelligence, pp. 1527–1535 (2018)
23. Shih, A., Choi, A., Darwiche, A.: A symbolic approach to explaining Bayesian network classifiers. In: Proceedings of the 27th International Joint Conference on Artificial Intelligence, IJCAI, pp. 5103–5111 (2018)
24. Shih, A., Choi, A., Darwiche, A.: Compiling Bayesian network classifiers into decision graphs. In: Proceedings of the 33rd AAAI Conference on Artificial Intelligence, pp. 7966–7974 (2019)
25. Stähli, P., Frenz, M., Jaeger, M.: Bayesian approach for a robust speed-of-sound reconstruction using pulse-echo ultrasound. IEEE Trans. Med. Imaging **40**(2), 457–467 (2021)
26. Stepin, I., Alonso, J.M., Catala, A., Pereira-Farina, M.: A survey of contrastive and counterfactual explanation generation methods for explainable artificial intelligence. IEEE Access **9**, 11974–12001 (2021)
27. Timmer, S.T., Meyer, J.-J.C., Prakken, H., Renooij, S., Verheij, B.: Explaining Bayesian networks using argumentation. In: Destercke, S., Denoeux, T. (eds.) ECSQARU 2015. LNCS (LNAI), vol. 9161, pp. 83–92. Springer, Cham (2015). https://doi.org/10.1007/978-3-319-20807-7_8
28. UCI Center for Machine Learning and Intelligent Systems: Machine Learning Repository (2020). https://archive.ics.uci.edu/ml/datasets.php

Public Project with Minimum Expected Release Delay

Guanhua Wang and Mingyu Guo[✉]

School of Computer Science, University of Adelaide, Adelaide, Australia
{guanhua.wang,mingyu.guo}@adelaide.edu.au

Abstract. We study the excludable public project model where the decision is binary (build or not build). In a classic excludable and binary public project model, an agent either consumes the project in its whole or is completely excluded. We study a setting where the mechanism can set different project release time for different agents, in the sense that high-paying agents can consume the project earlier than the low-paying agents. The mechanism design objective is to minimize the expected maximum release delay and the expected total release delay. We propose the single deadline mechanisms. We show that the optimal single deadline mechanism is asymptotically optimal for both objectives, regardless of the prior distributions. For small number of agents, we propose the sequential unanimous mechanisms by extending the largest unanimous mechanisms from Ohseto [8]. We propose an automated mechanism design approach via evolutionary computation to optimize within the sequential unanimous mechanisms.

Keywords: Automated mechanism design · Public project · Cost sharing

1 Introduction

The public project problem is a fundamental mechanism design model with many applications in multiagent systems. The public project problem involves multiple agents, who need to decide whether or not to build a public project. The project can be **nonexcludable** (*i.e.*, if the project is built, then every agent gets to consume the project, including the non-paying agents/free riders) or **excludable** (*i.e.*, the setting makes it possible to exclude some agents from consuming the project) [8]. A public project can be **indivisible/binary** or **divisible** [7]. A binary public project is either built or not built (*i.e.*, there is only one level of provision). In a divisible public project, there are multiple levels of provision (*i.e.*, build a project with adjustable quality).

In this paper, we study an excludable public project model that is "divisible" in a different sense. In the model, the level of provision is binary, but an agent's consumption is divisible. The mechanism specifies when an agent can start consuming the project. High-paying agents can consume the project earlier, and

© Springer Nature Switzerland AG 2021
D. N. Pham et al. (Eds.): PRICAI 2021, LNAI 13031, pp. 101–112, 2021.
https://doi.org/10.1007/978-3-030-89188-6_8

the free riders need to wait. The waiting time is also called an agent's **delay**. The delay is there to incentivize payments. The model was proposed by Guo *et al.* [6]. The authors studied the following mechanism design scenario. A group of agents come together to crowd-fund a piece of security information. No agent is able to afford the information by herself.[1] Based on the agents' valuations on the information, the mechanism decides whether or not to crowd-fund this piece of information (*i.e.*, purchase it from the security consulting firm that is selling this piece of information). If we are able to raise enough payments to cover the cost of the security information, then *ideally* we would like to share it to all agents, including the free riders, in order to maximizes the *overall protection of the community*. However, if all agents receive the information regardless of their payments, then no agents are incentivized to pay. To address this, the mechanism releases the information only to high-paying agents in the beginning and the non-paying/low-paying agents need to wait for a delayed release. The mechanism design goal is to minimize the delay as long as the delay is long enough to incentivize enough payments to cover the cost of the information. Guo *et al.* [6] proposed two design objectives. One is to minimize the *max-delay* (*i.e.*, the maximum waiting time of the agents) and the other is to minimize the *sum-delay* (*i.e.*, the total waiting time of the agents). The authors focused on *worst-case mechanism design* and proposed a mechanism that has a constant approximation ratio compared to the optimal mechanism. The authors also briefly touched upon *expected* delay. The authors used simulation to show that compared to their worst-case competitive mechanism, the *serial cost sharing mechanism* [7] has much lower expected *max-delay* and *sum-delay* under various distributions.

In this paper, we focus on minimizing the expected *max-delay* and the expected *sum-delay*. We propose a mechanism family called the **single deadline mechanisms**. For both objectives, under minor technical assumptions, we prove that there exists a single deadline mechanism that is *near optimal* when the number of agents is large, *regardless of the prior distribution*. Furthermore, when the number of agents approaches infinity, the optimal single deadline mechanism approaches optimality asymptotically. For small number of agents, the single deadline mechanism is not optimal. We extend the single deadline mechanisms to multiple deadline mechanisms. We also propose a genetic algorithm based automated mechanism design approach. We use a sequence of offers to represent a mechanism and we evolve the sequences. By simulating mechanisms using multiple distributions, we show that our genetic algorithm successfully identifies better performing mechanisms for small number of agents.

2   Related Research

Ohseto [8] characterized all strategy-proof and individually rational mechanisms for the binary public project model (both excludable and nonexcludable), under minor technical assumptions. Deb and Razzolini [2] further showed that on top of Ohseto's characterization, if we require *equal treatment of equals* (*i.e.*, if two

---

[1] Zero-day exploits are very expensive [4,5].

agents have the same type, then they should be treated the same), then the only strategy-proof and individually rational mechanisms are the *conservative equal cost mechanism* (nonexcludable) and the *serial cost sharing mechanism* (excludable), which were both proposed by Moulin [7]. It should be noted that Ohseto's characterization involves *exponential* number of parameters, so knowing the characterization does not mean it is easy to locate good mechanisms. Wang *et al.* [11] proposed a neural network based approach for optimizing within Ohseto's characterization family. The authors studied two objectives: maximizing the number of consumers and maximizing the social welfare. It should be noted that Ohseto's characterization does not apply to the model in this paper, as our model has an additional spin that is the release delay. In this paper, we propose a family of mechanisms called the sequential unanimous mechanisms, which is motivated by Ohseto's characterization. We apply a genetic algorithm for tuning the sequential unanimous mechanisms. Mechanism design via evolutionary computation [9] and mechanism design via other computational means (such as linear programming [1] and neural networks [3,10,11]) have long been shown to be effective for many design settings.

3   Model Description

There are n agents who decide whether or not to build a public project. The project is binary (build or not build) and nonrivalrous (the cost of the project does not depend on how many agents are consuming it). We normalize the project cost to 1. Agent i's type $v_i \in [0,1]$ represents her private valuation for the project. We use $\vec{v} = (v_1, v_2, \ldots, v_n)$ to denote the type profile. We assume that the v_i are drawn *i.i.d.* from a known prior distribution, where f is the probability density function. For technical reasons, we assume f is *positive* and *Lipschitz continuous* over [0,1].

We assume that the public project has value over a time period [0,1]. For example, the project could be a piece of security information that is discovered at time 0 and the corresponding exploit expires at time 1. We assume the setting allows the mechanism to specify each agent's release time for the project, so that some agents can consume the project earlier than the others. Given a type profile, a mechanism outcome consists of two vectors: $(t_1, t_2, \ldots, t_n)$ and $(p_1, p_2, \ldots, p_n)$. *I.e.*, agent i starts consuming the project at time $t_i \in [0,1]$ and pays $p_i \geq 0$. $t_i = 0$ means agent i gets to consume the public project right from the beginning and $t_i = 1$ means agent i does not get to consume the public project. We call t_i agent i's *release time*. We assume the agents' valuations over the time period is uniform. That is, agent i's valuation equals $v_i(1 - t_i)$, as she enjoys the time interval $[t_i, 1]$, which has length $1 - t_i$. Agent i's utility is then $v_i(1 - t_i) - p_i$. We impose the following mechanism design constraints:

- Strategy-proofness: We use t_i and p_i to denote agent i's release time and payment when she reports her true value v_i. We use t_i' and p_i' to denote agent i's release time and payment when she reports a false value v_i'. We should have

$$v_i(1 - t_i) - p_i \geq v_i(1 - t_i') - p_i'$$

- Individual rationality: $v_i(1 - t_i) - p_i \geq 0$
- Ex post budget balance:

If the project is not built, then no agent can consume the project and no agent pays. That is, we must have $t_i = 1$ and $p_i = 0$ for all i.

If the project is built, then the agents' total payment must cover exactly the project cost. That is, $\sum_i p_i = 1$.

Our aim is to design mechanisms that minimize the following design objectives:

- Expected *Max-Delay*: $E_{v_i \sim f}(\max\{t_1, t_2, \ldots, t_n\})$
- Expected *Sum-Delay*: $E_{v_i \sim f}(\sum_i t_i)$

4   Single Deadline Mechanisms

We first describe the *serial cost sharing mechanism (SCS)* proposed by Moulin [7]. Under SCS, an agent's release time is either 0 or 1.[2]

Let $\vec{v}$ be the type profile. We first define the following functions:

$$I(\vec{v}) = \begin{cases} 1 & \exists k \in \{1, 2, \ldots, n\}, k \leq |\{v_i | v_i \geq \frac{1}{k}\}| \\ 0 & \text{otherwise} \end{cases}$$

$I(\vec{v})$ equals 1 if and only if there exist at least k values among $\vec{v}$ that are at least $\frac{1}{k}$, where k is an integer from 1 to n.

$$K(\vec{v}) = \begin{cases} \max\{k | k \leq |\{v_i | v_i \geq \frac{1}{k}\}|, k \in \{1, 2, \ldots, n\}\} & I(\vec{v}) = 1 \\ 0 & I(\vec{v}) = 0 \end{cases}$$

Given $\vec{v}$, there could be multiple values for k, where there exist at least k values among $\vec{v}$ that are at least $\frac{1}{k}$. $K(\vec{v})$ is the largest value for k. If such a k value does not exist, then $K(\vec{v})$ is set to 0.

Definition 1 (Serial Cost Sharing Mechanism [7]). *Given $\vec{v}$, let $k = K(\vec{v})$.*

- *If $k > 0$, then agents with the highest k values are the consumers. The consumers pay $\frac{1}{k}$. The non-consumers do not pay.*
- *If $k = 0$, then there are no consumers and no agents pay.*

---

[2] Because the concept of release time does not exist in the classic binary excludable public project model.

Essentially, the serial cost sharing mechanism finds the largest k where k agents are willing to equally split the cost. If such a k exists, then we say *the cost share is successful* and these k agents are *joining the cost share*. If such a k does not exist, then we say *the cost share failed*.

Next we introduce a new mechanism family called the single deadline mechanisms.

Definition 2 (Single Deadline Mechanisms).
*A single deadline mechanism is characterized by one parameter $d \in [0, 1]$. d is called the mechanism's **deadline**. We use $M(d)$ to denote the single deadline mechanism with deadline d.*

*The time interval before the deadline $[0, d]$ is called the **non-free** part. The time interval after the deadline $[d, 1]$ is called the **free** part.*

We run the serial cost sharing mechanism on the non-free part as follows. For the non-free part, the agents' valuations are $d\vec{v} = (dv_1, \ldots, dv_n)$. Let $k = K(d\vec{v})$. Agents with the highest k values get to consume the non-free part, and each needs to pay $\frac{1}{k}$.

The free part is allocated to the agents for free. However, we cannot give out the free part if the public project is not built.

If we give out the free part if and only if $I(d\vec{v}) = 1$, then the mechanism is not strategy-proof, because the free parts change the agents' strategies.[3] Instead, we give agent i her free part if and only if $I(dv_{-i}) = 1$. That is, agent i gets her free part if and only if the other agents can successfully cost share the non-free part without i.

If an agent receives both the non-free part and the free part, then her release time is 0. If an agent only receives the free part, then her release time is d. If an agent does not receive either part, then her release time is 1. Lastly, if an agent only receives the non-free part, then her release time is $1 - d$, because such an agent's consumption interval should have length d (i.e., $[1 - d, 1]$).

Proposition 1. *The single deadline mechanisms are strategy-proof, individually rational, and ex post budget balanced.*

5 Max-Delay: Asymptotic Optimality

Theorem 1. *The optimal single deadline mechanism's expected max-delay approaches 0 when the number of agents approaches infinity.*

Proof. We consider a single deadline mechanism $M(d)$. Every agent's valuation is drawn *i.i.d.* from a distribution with PDF f. Let V_i be the random variable representing agent i's valuation. Since f is positive and Lipschitz continuous, we have that $\forall d, \exists k, P(dV_i \geq \frac{1}{k}) > 0$. That is, for any deadline d, there always exists an integer k, where the probability that an agent is willing to pay $\frac{1}{k}$ for the

---

[3] For example, an agent may over-report to turn an unsuccessful cost share into a successful cost share, in order to claim the free part.

non-free part is positive. Let $p = P(dV_i \geq \frac{1}{k})$. We define the following Bernoulli random variable:

$$B_i = \begin{cases} 1 & dV_i \geq \frac{1}{k} \\ 0 & \text{otherwise} \end{cases}$$

B_i equals 1 with probability p. It equals 1 if and only if agent i can afford $\frac{1}{k}$ for the non-free part. The total number of agents in $\vec{v}$ who can afford $\frac{1}{k}$ for the non-free part then follows a Binomial distribution $B(n, p)$. We use B to denote this Binomial variable. If $B \geq k + 1$, then every agent receives the free part, because agent i receives the free part if excluding herself, there are at least k agents who are willing to pay $\frac{1}{k}$ for the non-free part. The probability that the max-delay is higher than d is therefore bounded above by $P(B \leq k)$. According to Hoeffding's inequality, when $k < np$, $P(B \leq k) \leq e^{-2n\left(p-\frac{k}{n}\right)^2}$. We immediately have that when n approaches infinity, the probability that the max-delay is higher than d is approaching 0. Since d is arbitrary, we have that asymptotically, the single deadline mechanism's expected max-delay is approaching 0.

Next, we use an example to show that when $n = 500$, the optimal single deadline mechanism's expected max-delay is close to 0.01. We reuse all notation defined in the proof of Theorem 1. We make use of the Chernoff bound. When $k < np$, we have $P(B \leq k) \leq e^{-nD\left(\frac{k}{n}||p\right)}$, where $D(a||p) = a \ln \frac{a}{p} + (1-a) \ln \frac{1-a}{1-p}$.

When all agents receive the free part, the max-delay is at most d. Otherwise, the max-delay is at most 1. The expected max-delay is at most

$$P(B \leq k) + d(1 - P(B \leq k)) \leq P(B \leq k) + d$$

Example 1. Let us consider a case where $n = 500$. We set $d = 0.01$ and $k = 250$.

– f is the uniform distribution $U(0, 1)$: We have $p = 0.6$ and $P(B \leq 250) \leq$ 3.69e − 5. $M(0.01)$'s expected max-delay is then bounded above by 0.01 + 3.69e − 5.
– f is the normal distribution $N(0.5, 0.1)$ restricted to $[0, 1]$: We have $p = 0.84$ and $P(B \leq 250) \leq 7.45$e − 69. $M(0.01)$'s expected max-delay is then bounded above by 0.01 + 7.45e − 69.

On the contrary, the expected max-delay of the serial cost sharing mechanism is not approaching 0 asymptotically. For example, when $n = 500$, under $U(0, 1)$, the expected max-delay of the serial cost sharing mechanism equals 0.632.

6   Sum-Delay: Asymptotic Optimality

Theorem 2. *When the number of agents approaches infinity, the optimal single deadline mechanism is optimal among all mechanisms in terms of expected sum-delay.*

Theorem 2 can be proved by combining Proposition 4 and Proposition 5.

Proposition 2. *The optimal expected sum-delay is finite regardless of the distribution.*

Proof. We consider the following mechanism: Pick an arbitrary integer $k > 1$. We offer $\frac{1}{k}$ to the agents one by one. An agent gets the whole interval $[0,1]$ if she agrees to pay $\frac{1}{k}$ and if the project is built. Otherwise, she gets nothing. We build the project only when k agents agree. Since we approach the agents one by one, after k agents agree to pay $\frac{1}{k}$, all future agents receive the whole interval for free. This mechanism's expected sum-delay is bounded above by a constant. The constant only depends on the distribution.

The following proposition follows from Proposition 2.

Proposition 3. *Given a mechanism M and the number of agents n, let $Fail(n)$ be the probability of not building under M. We only need to consider M that satisfies $Fail(n) = O(1/n)$.*

We then propose a relaxed version of the ex post budget balance constraint, and use it to calculate the delay lower bound.

Definition 3 (Ex ante budget balance). *Mechanism M is ex ante budget balanced if and only if the expected total payment from the agents equals the probability of building (times project cost 1).*

Proposition 4. *Let $Fail(n)$ be the probability of not building the project when there are n agents. We consider what happens when we offer o for the whole interval $[0,1]$ to an individual agent. If the agent accepts o then she pays o and gets the whole interval. Otherwise, the agent pays 0 and receives nothing.*
We define the delay versus payment ratio $r(o)$ as follows:

$$r(o) = \frac{\int_0^o f(x)dx}{o \int_o^1 f(x)dx}$$

r is continuous on $(0,1)$. Due to f being Lipschitz continuous, we have $\lim_{o\to 0} r(o) = f(0)$ and $\lim_{o\to 1} r(o) = \infty$.[4] We could simply set $r(0) = f(0)$, then r is continuous on $[0,1)$. We define the optimal delay versus payment ratio $r^* = \min_{o \in [0,1)} r(o)$.
The expected sum-delay is bounded below by $r^*(1 - Fail(n))$, which approaches r^* asymptotically according to Proposition 3.

Proposition 5. *Let o^* be the optimal offer that leads to the optimal delay versus payment ratio r^*.[5]*

$$o^* = \arg \min_{o \in [0,1)} r(o)$$

---

[4] When o approaches 0, $r(o)$'s numerator is approaching $of(0)$ while the denominator is approaching o.

[5] If $o^* = 0$, then we replace it with an infinitesimally small $\gamma > 0$. The achieved sum-delay is then approaching $r(\gamma)(1 + \epsilon)$ asymptotically. When γ approaches 0, $r(\gamma)$ approaches r^*.

Let $\epsilon > 0$ be an arbitrarily small constant. The following single deadline mechanism's expected sum delay approaches $r^*(1 + \epsilon)$ asymptotically.

$$M\left(\frac{1 + \epsilon}{no^* \int_{o^*}^1 f(x)dx}\right)$$

We then use an example to show that when $n = 500$, under different distributions, the optimal single deadline mechanism's expected sum-delay is close to optimality.

Example 2. We consider $n = 500$ which is the same as Example 1. Simulations are based on $100,000$ random draws.

- f is the uniform distribution $U(0,1)$: The single deadline mechanism $M(1)$ (essentially the serial cost sharing mechanism) has an expected sum-delay of 1.006, which is calculated via numerical simulation. $Fail(500)$ is then at most 0.002. $r^* = 1$. The lower bound is 0.998, which is close to our achieved sum-delay 1.006.
- f is the normal distribution $N(0.5, 0.1)$ restricted to $[0,1]$: The single deadline mechanism $M(1)$'s expected sum-delay equals $2.3e - 4$ in simulation, which is obviously close to optimality.
- f is the beta distribution $Beta(0.5, 0.5)$: The single deadline mechanism $M(0.01)$'s expected sum-delay equals 1.935 in simulation. $Fail(500)$ is then at most 0.00387. $r^* = 1.927$. The lower bound equals $(1 - 0.00387) * r^* = 1.920$, which is very close to the achieved sum-delay of 1.935. The serial cost sharing mechanism $M(1)$ is far away from optimality in this example. The expected sum-delay of the serial cost sharing mechanism is much larger at 14.48.

7   Automated Mechanism Design for Smaller Number of Agents

For smaller number of agents, the single deadline mechanism family no longer contains a near optimal mechanism. We propose two numerical methods for identifying better mechanisms for smaller number of agents. One is by extending the single deadline mechanism family and the other is via evolutionary computation.

Definition 4 (Multiple Deadline Mechanisms). *A multiple deadline mechanism $M(d_1, \ldots, d_n)$ is characterized by n different deadlines. Agent i's non-free part is $[0, d_i]$ and her free part is $[d_i, 1]$. The mechanism's rules are otherwise identical to the single deadline mechanisms.*

We simply use exhaustive search to find the best set of deadlines. Obviously, this approach only works when the number of agents is tiny. We then present an Automated Mechanism Design approach based on evolutionary computation.

Ohseto [8] characterized all strategy-proof and individually rational mechanisms for the binary public project model (under several minor technical assumptions). We summarize the author's characterization as follows:

- *Unanimous mechanisms* (characterization for the nonexcludable model): Under an unanimous mechanism, there is a cost share vector $(c_1, c_2, \ldots, c_n)$ with $c_i \geq 0$ and $\sum_i c_i = 1$. The project is built if and only if all agents accept this cost share vector.
- *Largest unanimous mechanisms* (characterization for the excludable model): Under a largest unanimous mechanism, for every submittable condition of the agents, there is a constant cost share vector. The agents initially face the cost share vector corresponding to the grand coalition. If some agents do not accept the current cost share vector, then they are forever excluded. The remaining agents face a different cost share vector based on who are left. If at some point, all remaining agents accept, then we build the project. Otherwise, the project is not built.

We extend the largest unanimous mechanisms by adding the *release time* element.

Definition 5 (Sequential unanimous mechanisms). *A cost share vector under a sequential unanimous mechanism includes both the payments and the release time:*

$$T_1, B_1, \quad T_2, B_2, \quad \ldots, \quad T_n, B_n$$

Agent i accepts the above cost share vector if and only if her utility based on her reported valuation *is nonnegative when paying B_i for the time interval $[T_i, 1]$. That is, agent i accepts the above cost share vector if and only if* her reported valuation *is at least $\frac{B_i}{1-T_i}$. $\frac{B_i}{1-T_i}$ is called the* unit price *agent i faces. We require $B_i \geq 0$ and $\sum_i B_i = 1$.*

A sequential unanimous mechanism contains m cost share vectors in a sequence. The mechanism goes through the sequence and stops at the first vector that is accepted by all agents. The project is built and the agents' release time and payments are determined by the unanimously accepted cost share vector. If all cost share vectors in the sequence are rejected, then the decision is not to build.

The largest unanimous mechanisms (can be interpreted as special cases with binary T_i) form a subset of the sequential unanimous mechanisms. The sequential unanimous mechanisms' structure makes it suitable for genetic algorithms—we treat the cost share vectors as the *genes* and treat the sequences of cost share vectors as the *gene sequences*.

The sequential unanimous mechanisms are generally not strategy-proof. However, they can be easily proved to be strategy-proof in two scenarios:

- A sequential unanimous mechanism is strategy-proof when *the sequence contains only one cost share vector* (an agent faces a take-it-or-leave-it offer). This observation makes it easy to generate an initial population of strategy-proof mechanisms.

– If for every agent, as we go through the cost share vector sequence, the unit price an agent faces is *nondecreasing* and her release time is also *nondecreasing*, then the mechanism is strategy-proof. Essentially, when the above is satisfied, all agents prefer earlier cost share vectors. All agents are incentivized to report truthfully, as doing so enables them to secure the earliest possible cost share vector.

The sequential unanimous mechanism family *seems* to be quite expressive.[6] Our experiments show that by optimizing within the sequential unanimous mechanisms, we are able to identify mechanisms that perform better than existing mechanisms. Our approach is as follows:

– Initial population contains 200 strategy-proof mechanisms. Every initial mechanism is a sequential unanimous mechanism with only one cost share vector. The B_i and the T_i are randomly generated by sampling $U(0, 1)$.
– We perform evolution for 200 rounds. Before each round, we filter out mechanisms that are not truthful. We have two different filters:
  • Strict filter: we enforce that every agent's unit price faced and release time must be nondecreasing. With this filter, the final mechanism produced must be strategy proof. We call this variant the *Truthful Genetic Algorithm (TGA)*.
  • Loose filter: we use simulation to check for strategy-proofness violations. In every evolution round, we generate 200 random type profiles. For each type profile and each agent, we randomly draw one false report and we filter out a mechanism if any beneficial manipulation occurs. After finishing evolution, we use 10, 000 type profiles to filter out the untruthful mechanisms from the final population. It should be noted that, we can only claim that the remaining mechanisms are *probably* truthful. We call this variant the *Approximately Truthful Genetic Algorithm (ATGA)*.
– We perform crossover and mutations as follows:
  • Crossover: We call the top 50% of the population (in terms of fitness, *i.e.*, expected max-delay or sum-delay) the *elite population*. For every elite mechanism, we randomly pick another mechanism from the whole population, and perform a crossover by randomly swapping one gene segment.
  • Mutation: For every elite mechanism, with 20% chance, we randomly select one gene, modify the offer of one agent by making it worse. We insert that new cost share vector into a random position after the original position.
  • Neighbourhood Search: For every elite mechanism, with 20% chance, we randomly perturb one gene uniformly (from -10% to $+10\%$).

---

[6] Let M be a strategy-proof mechanism. There exists a sequential unanimous mechanism M' (with exponential sequence length). M' has an approximate equilibrium where the equilibrium outcome is arbitrarily close to M's outcome. To prove this, we only need to discretize an individual agent's type space $[0, 1]$ into a finite number of grid points. The number of type profiles is exponential. We place M's outcomes for all these type profiles in a sequence.

- Abandon duplication and unused genes: In every evolution round, if a cost share vector is never unanimously accepted or if two cost share vectors are within 0.0001 in L1 distance. then we remove the duplication/unused genes.

7.1 Experiments

We present the expected max-delay and sum-delay for $n = 3, 5$ and for different distributions (Table 1). ATGA is only approximately truthful. We recall that in our evolutionary process, in each round, we only use a very loose filter to filter out the untruthful mechanisms. After evolution finishes, we run a more rigorous filter on the final population (based on $10,000$ randomly generated type profiles). The percentage in the parenthesis is the percentage of mechanisms surviving the more rigorous test. The other mechanisms (TGA and Single/Multiple deadlines) are strategy-proof. SCS is the serial cost sharing mechanism from Moulin [7], which has the best known expected delays [6].

Table 1. We see that ATGA performs well in many settings. If we focus on *provable* strategy-proof mechanisms, then TGA and the optimal multiple deadline mechanism also often perform better than the serial cost sharing mechanism.

$n = 3$, sum-delay	ATGA	TGA	Single deadline	Multiple deadline	SCS
Uniform(0,1)	**1.605(95%)**	**1.605**	**1.605**	**1.605**	**1.605**
Beta(0.5,0.5)	**1.756(89%)**	**1.757**	**1.757**	**1.757**	**1.757**
Bernoulli(0.5)	**0.869(100%)**	**0.868**	1.499	1.253	1.498
50% 0, 50% 0.8	**1.699(98%)**	1.873	1.873	1.873	1.873
$n = 3$, max-delay	ATGA	TGA	Single deadline	Multiple deadline	SCS
Uniform(0,1)	**0.705(97%)**	**0.705**	**0.705**	**0.705**	**0.705**
Beta(0.5,0.5)	**0.754(87%)**	0.757	0.782	0.757	0.782
Bernoulli(0.5)	**0.5(100%)**	0.498	0.687	**0.50**	0.877
50% 0, 50% 0.8	**0.676(94%)**	0.753	0.749	0.749	0.877
$n = 5$, sum-delay	ATGA	TGA	Single deadline	Multiple deadline	SCS
Uniform(0,1)	1.462(95%)	1.503	**1.415**	**1.415**	**1.415**
Beta(0.5,0.5)	2.279(92%)	2.12	**1.955**	**1.955**	**1.955**
Bernoulli(0.5)	**1.146(100%)**	1.867	2.106	1.711	2.523
50% 0, 50% 0.8	2.432(94%)	2.845	2.323	**2.248**	2.667
$n = 5$, max-delay	ATGA	TGA	Single deadline	Multiple deadline	SCS
Uniform(0,1)	0.677(91%)	0.677	**0.662**	**0.662**	0.678
Beta(0.5,0.5)	0.754(79%)	0.75	**0.73**	**0.73**	0.827
Bernoulli(0.5)	0.506(100%)	**0.50**	0.577	**0.50**	0.971
50% 0, 50% 0.8	**0.666(80%)**	0.751	0.736	0.679	0.968

References

1. Conitzer, V., Sandholm, T.: Complexity of mechanism design. In: Darwiche, A., Friedman, N. (eds.) UAI 2002, Proceedings of the 18th Conference in Uncertainty in Artificial Intelligence, University of Alberta, Edmonton, Alberta, Canada, 1–4 August 2002, pp. 103–110. Morgan Kaufmann (2002)
2. Deb, R., Razzolini, L.: Voluntary cost sharing for an excludable public project. Math. Soc. Sci. **37**(2), 123–138 (1999)
3. Dütting, P., Feng, Z., Narasimhan, H., Parkes, D., Ravindranath, S.S.: Optimal auctions through deep learning. In: International Conference on Machine Learning, pp. 1706–1715. PMLR (2019)
4. Fisher, D.: Vupen founder launches new zero-day acquisition firm zerodium (2015), July 24, 2015 https://threatpost.com/vupen-launches-new-zero-day-acquisition-firm-zerodium/113933/
5. Greenberg, A.: Shopping for zero-days: A price list for hackers' secret software exploits (2012), 23 March 2012 online: http://www.forbes.com/sites/andygreenberg/2012/03/23/shopping-for-zero-days-an-price-list-for-hackers-secret-software-exploits/
6. Guo, M., Yang, Y., Ali Babar, M.: Cost sharing security information with minimal release delay. In: Miller, T., Oren, N., Sakurai, Y., Noda, I., Savarimuthu, B.T.R., Cao Son, T. (eds.) PRIMA 2018. LNCS (LNAI), vol. 11224, pp. 177–193. Springer, Cham (2018). https://doi.org/10.1007/978-3-030-03098-8_11
7. Moulin, H.: Serial cost-sharing of excludable public goods. Rev. Econ. Stud. **61**(2), 305–325 (1994)
8. Ohseto, S.: Characterizations of strategy-proof mechanisms for excludable versus nonexcludable public projects. Games Econ. Behav. **32**(1), 51–66 (2000)
9. Phelps, S., McBurney, P., Parsons, S.: Evolutionary mechanism design: a review. Auton. Agents Multi-agent Syst. **21**(2), 237–264 (2010)
10. Shen, W., Tang, P., Zuo, S.: Automated mechanism design via neural networks. In: Proceedings of the 18th International Conference on Autonomous Agents and MultiAgent Systems, pp. 215–223. AAMAS 2019, International Foundation for Autonomous Agents and Multiagent Systems, Richland, SC (2019)
11. Wang, G., Guo, R., Sakurai, Y., Babar, A., Guo, M.: Mechanism design for public projects via neural networks. In: 20th International Conference on Autonomous Agents and Multiagent Systems (AAMAS 2021) (2021)

Strategy Proof Mechanisms for Facility Location at Limited Locations

Toby Walsh[(✉)]

UNSW Sydney and CSIRO Data61, Sydney, Australia
tw@cse.unsw.edu.au

Abstract. Most studies of facility location problems permit a facility to be located at any position. In practice, this may not be possible. For instance, we might have to limit facilities to particular locations such as at highway exits, close to bus stops, or on empty building lots. We consider here the impact of such constraints on the location of facilities on the performance of strategy proof mechanisms for facility location. We study six different objectives: the total or maximum distance agents must travel, the utilitarian or egalitarian welfare, and the total or minimum satisfaction of agents (satisfaction is a normalized form of utility). We show that limiting the location of a facility makes all six objectives harder to approximate. For example, we prove that the median mechanism modified suitably to locate the facility only at a feasible location is strategy proof and 3-approximates both the optimal total distance and the optimal maximum distance. In fact, this is optimal as no deterministic and strategy proof mechanism can better approximate the total or maximum distances. This contrasts with the setting where the facility can be located anywhere, and the median mechanism returns the optimal total distance and 2-approximates the maximum distance.

1 Introduction

The facility location problem has been studied using tools from a wide variety of fields such as AI (e.g. [1–4]). Operations Research (e.g. [5,6]), and Game Theory (e.g. [7,8]). Our goal here is to design mechanisms that locate the facility in a way that the agents have no incentive to mis-report their true locations. Facility location models many practical problems including the location of bus or tram stops, schools, playgrounds, telephone exchanges, mobile phone masts, recycling centres, electric car charging points, shared cars, power plants, electricity substations, doctors, chemists, fire stations, and hospitals. In many of these real world settings, facilities may be limited in where they can be located. For example, a warehouse might need to be constrained to be near to the railway, or an ambulance station close to a highway. Our contribution is to demonstrate that such constraints on the location of a facility make it harder to design strategy proof mechanisms which provide high quality solutions. We measure the quality of the solution in six different ways: total or maximum distance of the agents to

© Springer Nature Switzerland AG 2021
D. N. Pham et al. (Eds.): PRICAI 2021, LNAI 13031, pp. 113–124, 2021.
https://doi.org/10.1007/978-3-030-89188-6_9

the facility, the utilitarian and egalitarian welfare, and the social or minimum satisfaction.

From a technical sense, limiting the location of a facility might appear to change little the facility location problem. We merely need to limit the space of mechanisms to the strict subset of mechanism which only locate facilities at feasible locations. We can therefore immediately inherit many impossibility results. For instance, since there is no deterministic and strategy proof mechanism for the facility problem which minimizes the maximum distance an agent travels when the facility can be located anywhere, it follows quickly that there is no such mechanism when the facility is limited in its location. However, the mechanisms excluded because they locate facilities at infeasible locations are often precisely those with good normative properties. Our contribution here is to show restricting mechanisms to locate facilities only at feasible locations often increases approximation ratios, irrespective of whether the objective is distance, welfare or satisfaction. However, the extent to which approximation ratios increases depends very much on the objective and the problem. For example, the lower bound on the best possible approximation ratio of the optimal egalitarian welfare increases from $\frac{3}{2}$ to unbounded when we limit the feasible location of a facility. On the other hand, the best possible approximation ratio of the optimal utilitarian welfare only triples in this case. Our results are summarized in Tables 1 and 2.

Table 1. Approximation ratios achievable by deterministic and strategy proof mechanisms for the single facility location problem at limited locations. **Bold** for results proved here. [Numbers] in brackets are the approximation ratios achieved for when the facility can be located anywhere.

Mechanism	Measure					
	Total distance	Max distance	Utilitarian welfare	Egalitarian welfare	Social satisfaction	Min satisfaction
Lower bound	3 [1]	**3** [2]	**3** [1]	∞ [$\frac{3}{2}$]	∞[1.07]	∞ ($\frac{4}{3}$)
MEDIAN*	3 [1]	**3** [2]	**3** [1]	∞ [∞]	∞ [$\frac{3}{2}$]	∞ [∞]

Table 2. Summary of approximation ratios achieved by ENDPOINT* mechanism for the two facility location problem at limited locations. **Bold** for results proved here. [Numbers] in brackets are the approximation ratios achieved by the corresponding ENDPOINT mechanism when the two facilities can be located anywhere.

Mechanism	Measure					
	Total distance	Max distance	Utilitarian welfare	Egalitarian welfare	Social satisfaction	Min satisfaction
ENDPOINT*	2n-3 [n-2]	3 [2]	**2** [2]	$\frac{3}{2}$ [$\frac{3}{2}$]	$\frac{3n}{4} - \frac{1}{2}$ [$\frac{n}{2} - \frac{1}{4}$]	∞ [∞]

2   Related Work

We follow the line of work initiated by Procaccia and Tennenholtz [1] that looks
to resolve the inherent tension in designing mechanisms that are strategy proof
and effective by identifying strategy proof mechanisms that are guaranteed to
return solutions within some constant factor of optimal. The most related prior
work to ours is by Feldman, Fiat, Golomb [9]. This also considers facility location problems where the facility is restricted to limited locations. There is, however, a critical difference with this work. This earlier work restricted analysis
to a single objective (sum of distances), while here we consider six objectives
(sum/maximum distance, utilitarian/egalitarian welfare, social/minimum satisfaction). Our results show that approximation ratios that can be achieved
depend critically on the objective chosen. For instance, when the facility is
restricted to limited locations, deterministic and strategy proof mechanisms can
3-approximate the optimal utilitarian welfare. However, no deterministic and
strategy proof mechanism has a bounded approximation ratio for the egalitarian welfare. By contrast, if we consider a different but related objective to the
egalitarian welfare such as the maximum distance an agent travels, then deterministic and strategy proof mechanisms exist which bound the approximation
ratio even when the facility is restricted to limited locations. In addition, when
the facility is unrestricted, there exists a deterministic and strategy proof mechanism that can $\frac{3}{2}$-approximate the optimal egalitarian welfare. The choice of
objective then reveals different aspects of the approximability of these facility
location problems.

One month after this work here first appeared as a preprint, Tang, Wang,
Zhang and Zhao published a preprint looking independently at a special case of
this problem in which facilities are limited to a finite set of locations [10]. There
are two significant technical differences between the two studies. First, the work
of Tang et al. does not capture the more general setting here where the facility
is limited to a set of subintervals. In their work, a facility is limited to a finite
set of locations. Their model cannot then describe a setting where, for example,
a school must be within 500 m of one of the neighbourhood bus stops as the
feasible set is not finite. In addition, the work of Tang et al., like the work of
Feldman et al., only considers two objectives: total and maximum cost. Here we
consider four additional objectives: utilitarian and egalitarian welfare, as well
as social and minimum satisfaction. Our results show that we can achieve very
different approximation ratios with these different objectives. Indeed, for many
of these new objectives, we cannot achieve a bounded approximation ratio with
deterministic and strategy proof mechanisms.

As in much previous work on mechanism design for facility location (e.g. [1]),
we consider the one-dimensional setting. This models a number of real world
problems such as locating shopping centres along a highway, or ferry stops along
a river. There are also various non-geographical settings that can be viewed as
one-dimensional facility location problems (e.g. choosing the temperature of a
classroom, or the tax rate for property transactions). In addition, we can use
mechanisms for the one-dimensional facility location problem in more complex

settings (e.g. we can decompose the 2-d rectilinear problem into a pair of 1-d problems). Finally, results about mechanisms for the one-dimensional problem can inform the results about mechanisms for more complex metrics. For instance, lower bounds on the performance of strategy proof mechanisms for the 1-d problem provide lower bounds for the 2-d problem.

3   Formal Background

We have n agents located on $[0, 1]$, and wish to locate one or more facilities also on $[0, 1]$ to serve all the agents. Agent i is at location x_i. Without loss of generality, we suppose agents are ordered so that $x_1 \leq \ldots \leq x_n$. A solution is a location y_j for each facility j. Agents are served by their nearest facility. We consider six different performance measures: total or maximum distance, utilitarian or egalitarian welfare, and social or minimum satisfaction.

The total distance is $\sum_{i=1}^{n} \min_j |x_i - y_j|$. The maximum distance is $\max_{i=1}^{n} \min_j |x_i - y_j|$. We suppose the utility u_i of agent i is inversely related to its distance from the facility serving it. More precisely, $u_i = 1 - \min_j |x_i - y_j|$. Utilities are, by definition, in $[0, 1]$. The utilitarian welfare is the sum of the utilities of the individual agents, $\sum_{i=1}^{n} u_i$. The egalitarian welfare is the minimum utility of any agent, $\min_{i=1}^{n} u_i$.

In [11,12], normalized utilities called "happiness factors" are introduced. The happiness h_i of agent i is $h_i = 1 - \min_j \frac{|x_i - y_j|}{d_{max}^i}$ where d_{max}^i is the maximum possible distance agent i may need to travel. Here $d_{max}^i = \max(x_i, 1 - x_i)$. Note that the happiness of an agent is, by definition, in $[0, 1]$. The social satisfaction is then the sum of the happinesses of the individual agents, $\sum_{i=1}^{n} h_i$. The minimum satisfaction is the minimum happiness of any agent, $\min_{i=1}^{n} h_i$. Our goal is to optimize one of the distance, welfare or satisfaction objectives.

We consider some particular mechanisms for facility location. Many are based on the function $median(z_1, \ldots, z_p)$ which returns z_i where $|\{j | z_j < z_i\}| < \lceil \frac{p}{2} \rceil$ and $|\{j | z_j > z_i\}| \leq \lfloor \frac{p}{2} \rfloor$. With $n - 1$ parameters z_1 to z_{n-1} representing "phantom" agents, a GENMEDIAN mechanism locates the facility at $median(x_1, \ldots, x_n, z_1, \ldots, z_{n-1})$ As we argue shortly, such mechanisms characterize an important class of strategy proof mechanisms [13]. The LEFTMOST mechanism has parameters $z_i = 0$ for $i \in [1, n)$ and locates the facility at the location of the leftmost agent. The RIGHTMOST mechanism has parameters $z_i = 1$ for $i \in [1, n)$ and locates the facility at the location of the rightmost agent. The MEDIAN mechanism has parameters $z_i = 0$ for $i \leq \lfloor \frac{n}{2} \rfloor$ and 1 otherwise, and locates the facility at the median agent if n is odd, and the leftmost of the two median agents if n is even. The MIDORNEAREST mechanism is an instance of GENMEDIAN with parameters $z_i = \frac{1}{2}$ for $i \in [1, n)$, locating the facility at $\frac{1}{2}$ if $x_1 \leq \frac{1}{2} \leq x_n$, and otherwise at the nearest x_i to $\frac{1}{2}$. The ENDPOINT mechanism locates one facility with the LEFTMOST mechanism and another with the RIGHTMOST mechanism.

We extend this model of facility location problems with constraints on the location of the facility. In particular, we suppose the interval $[0, 1]$ is decomposed into a set of feasible and disjoint (open or closed) sub-intervals, and the facility must be located within one of these sub-intervals. Our goal is to see how restricting the feasible locations of the facility in this way impacts on the performance of strategy proof mechanisms. Note that unlike [9], agents are not limited in where they can be located. We only limit where the facility (and not agents) can be located. In particular, we modify mechanisms to ensure the facility is located at a feasible location. For instance, the LEFTMOST* mechanism modifies the LEFTMOST mechanism to locate the facility at the nearest feasible location to the leftmost agent. The RIGHTMOST* mechanism modifies the RIGHTMOST mechanism in a similar fashion. Note that we cannot have agents simply report their nearest feasible location as there might be a choice of such locations. Indeed, many of our results that approximation guarantees are not bounded arise because of the difficulty of choosing between the two nearest and feasible locations to some optimal but infeasible facility location in a strategy proof way.

We consider three desirable properties of mechanisms: anonymity, Pareto optimality and strategy proofness. Anonymity is a fundamental fairness property that requires all agents to be treated alike. Pareto optimality is one of the most fundamental normative properties in economics. It demands that we cannot improve the solution so one agent is better off without other agents being worse off. Finally, strategy proofness is a fundamental game theoretic property that ensures agents have no incentive to act strategically and try to manipulate the mechanisms by mis-reporting their locations.

More formally, a mechanism is *anonymous* iff permuting the agents does not change the solution. A mechanism is *Pareto optimal* iff it returns solutions that are always Pareto optimal. A solution is *Pareto optimal* iff there is no other solution in which one agent travels a strictly shorter distance, and all other agents travel no greater distance. A mechanism is *strategy proof* iff no agent can mis-report and thereby travel a shorter distance. For instance, the MEDIAN mechanism is anonymous, Pareto optimal and strategy proof. Finally, we will consider strategy proof mechanisms that may approximate the optimal distance, welfare or satisfaction. A mechanism achieves an approximation ratio ρ iff the solution it returns is within a factor of ρ times the optimal. In this case, we say that the mechanism ρ-approximates the optimal.

Procaccia and Tennenholtz initiated the study of designing approximate and strategy proof mechanisms for locating facilities on a line [1]. With just one facility, they argue that the MEDIAN mechanism is strategy proof and optimal for the total distance, while the LEFTMOST mechanism is strategy proof and 2-approximates the optimal maximum distance, and no deterministic and strategy proof mechanism can do better.

4   Single Facility, Distance Approximations

For a single facility on the line, Moulin proved a seminal result that any mechanism that is anonymous, Pareto optimal and strategy proof is a generalized median mechanism, GENMEDIAN [13]. This locates the facility at the median location of the n agents and $n-1$ "phantom" agents. We cannot apply Moulin's result directly to our setting as a GENMEDIAN mechanism may select an infeasible location for the facility. Instead, we consider the GENMEDIAN* mechanism which locates a facility at the nearest feasible location to that returned by a GENMEDIAN mechanism. If there are two nearest and equi-distant feasible locations, then the GENMEDIAN* mechanism uses a fixed tie-breaking rule for each infeasible interval (e.g.,. always use the leftmost of the two nearest locations). Here, as indeed throughout the paper, we suppose a fixed tie-breaking rule to ensure that the modified mechanism retains anonymity and strategy proofness. However, none of our results on performance guarantees depend on the choice.

The MEDIAN* mechanism is an instance of GENMEDIAN* which locates the facility at the median agent if it is a feasible location, and otherwise at the nearest feasible location to the median agent. Massó and Moreno de Barreda prove that, when locating a single facility at limited locations, a mechanism is anonymous, Pareto efficient and strategy proof iff it is a GENMEDIAN* mechanism with at least one phantom agent at 0 and one at 1 (corollary 2 in [14]). It follows that the MEDIAN* mechanism is anonymous, Pareto efficient and strategy proof.

4.1   Total Distance

We first consider the objective of minimizing the total distance agents travel to be served. The MEDIAN* mechanism 3-approximates the optimal total distance (Lemma 21 in [9]). In fact, this is optimal. No deterministic strategy proof mechanism can better approximate the total distance in general (Lemma 19 in [9]). By comparison, when the facility can be located anywhere, the MEDIAN mechanism is strategy proof and returns the *optimal* total distance. Limiting the feasible locations of a facility therefore worsens the performance of the best possible deterministic and strategy proof mechanism. In particular, the best possible deterministic and strategy proof mechanism goes from returning an optimal solution to 3-approximating the optimal total distance.

4.2   Maximum Distance

We consider next the objective of minimizing the maximum distance any agent travels to be served. The MEDIAN* mechanism also 3-approximates the optimal maximum distance.

Theorem 1. *The* MEDIAN* *mechanism 3-approximates the optimal maximum distance for a facility location problem with limited locations.*

We contrast this with the setting where the facility can be located anywhere, and the MEDIAN mechanism 2-approximates the optimal maximum distance. In fact, when there are no constraints on where facilities can be located, the MEDIAN mechanism is optimal as no deterministic and strategy proof mechanism can do better than 2-approximate the optimal maximum distance (Theorem

3.2 of [1]). Restricting the feasible locations of a facility therefore worsens the performance of a median mechanism from a 2-approximation of the optimal maximum distance to a 3-approximation.

Can any strategy proof mechanism do better than 3-approximate the maximum distance when we limit the feasible locations of the facility? We show that no deterministic and strategy proof mechanism has a smaller approximation ratio for the optimal maximum distance.

Theorem 2. *For a facility location problem with limited locations, no deterministic and strategy proof mechanism can do better than 3-approximate the optimal maximum distance.*

Hence the MEDIAN* mechanism is optimal. No deterministic and strategy proof mechanism can do better than 3-approximate the optimal maximum distance.

5   Single Facility, Welfare Approximations

We switch now to considering how well strategy proof mechanisms approximate the utilitarian or egalitarian welfare.

5.1   Utilitarian Welfare

With no limits on the location of the facility, it is not hard to see that the MEDIAN mechanism is strategy proof and returns the optimal utilitarian welfare. However, in our setting, the MEDIAN mechanism may select an infeasible location for the facility. We consider instead the MEDIAN* mechanism which locates the facility at the nearest feasible location to the median agent.

Theorem 3. *For a facility location problem with limited locations, the MEDIAN* mechanism is strategy proof and 3-approximates the optimal utilitarian welfare.*

As with minimizing the total distance, the MEDIAN* mechanism is optimal. No deterministic and strategy proof mechanism has a better approximation guarantee.

Theorem 4. *For a facility location problem with limited locations, any deterministic and strategy proof mechanism at best 3-approximates the optimal utilitarian welfare.*

5.2   Egalitarian Welfare

We turn now to the egalitarian welfare. It is not hard to see that the MEDIAN mechanism may not bound the approximation ratio of the optimal egalitarian welfare. Similarly, when the location of facilities is limited, the corresponding MEDIAN* mechanism also may approximate the optimal egalitarian welfare poorly.

Theorem 5. *For a facility location problem with limited locations, the* MEDIAN* *mechanism does not bound the approximation ratio of the optimal egalitarian welfare.*

In fact, no deterministic and strategy proof mechanism for a facility location problem with limited locations has a bounded approximation ratio. This contrasts with the setting where the facility can be located anywhere and it is possible to show that no deterministic and strategy proof mechanism can do better than $\frac{3}{2}$-approximate the optimal egalitarian welfare, and that the MIDORNEAREST mechanism actually achieves this ratio.

Theorem 6. *For a facility location problem with limited locations, no deterministic and strategy proof mechanism has a bounded approximation ratio of the optimal egalitarian welfare.*

6 Single Facility, Satisfaction Approximations

We consider next how well strategy proof mechanisms approximate the optimal social or minimum satisfaction.

6.1 Social Satisfaction

Mei *et al.* prove that the MEDIAN mechanism $\frac{3}{2}$-approximates the optimal social satisfaction (Theorem 1 of [12]). In addition, they show that no deterministic and strategy proof mechanism has an approximation ratio of the optimal social satisfaction of less than $8 - 4\sqrt{3}$ which is approximately 1.07 (Theorem 3 of [12]). We cannot apply these results directly to our setting as the mechanisms considered in [12] may select an infeasible location for the facility. Instead, we again consider the MEDIAN* mechanism which locates the facility at the nearest feasible location to the median agent.

Theorem 7. *For a facility location problem with limited locations, the* MEDIAN* *mechanism is strategy proof and has an unbounded approximation ratio of the optimal social satisfaction.*

Unfortunately, we cannot do better. No deterministic and strategy proof mechanism has a bounded approximation ratio of the optimal social satisfaction.

Theorem 8. *For a facility location problem with limited locations, no deterministic and strategy proof mechanism has a bounded approximation ratio of the optimal social satisfaction.*

6.2 Minimum Satisfaction

We turn now to the minimum satisfaction. Mei *et al.* argue that no deterministic and strategy proof mechanism has an approximation ratio of the optimal minimum satisfaction of less than $\frac{4}{3}$ (also Sect. 3.3 of [12]). The MEDIAN mechanism has an unbounded approximation ratio for the minimum satisfaction. Consider two agents at 0 and one at 1. Not surprisingly, the MEDIAN* mechanism may also approximate the optimal minimum satisfaction poorly.

Theorem 9. *For a facility location problem with limited locations, the* MEDIAN* *mechanism does not bound the approximation ratio of the optimal minimum satisfaction.*

In fact, no deterministic and strategy proof mechanism for a facility location problem with limited locations has a bounded approximation ratio of the minimum satisfaction.

Theorem 10. *For a facility location problem with limited locations, no deterministic and strategy proof mechanism has a bounded approximation ratio of the optimal minimum satisfaction.*

7   Two Facilities, Distance Approximations

We move now from locating a single facility to locating two facilities. When facilities are not limited in their location, the only deterministic and strategy proof mechanism for locating two facilities on the line with a bounded approximation ratio for either the optimal total or maximum distance is the ENDPOINT mechanism [15]. This provides a $(n-2)$-approximation of the total distance and a 2-approximation of the maximum distance.

We suppose now that facilities are limited in their location, and consider the corresponding ENDPOINT* mechanism that locates the leftmost facility at the nearest feasible location to the leftmost agent, tie-breaking to the right, and the rightmost facility at the nearest feasible location to the rightmost agent, tie-breaking instead to the left. Tang *et al.* prove that, when the two facilities are limited in their locations, this mechanism $2n-3$-approximates the total distance [10]. Tang *et al.* also prove that the mechanism 3-approximates the maximum distance, and that no deterministic and strategy proof mechanism can do better [10].

8   Two Facilities, Welfare Approximations

When facilities are not limited in their location, the ENDPOINT mechanism offers a good approximation of both the optimal utilitarian and egalitarian welfare. In particular, it is not hard to show that it 2-approximates the optimal utilitarian welfare, and $\frac{3}{2}$-approximates the optimal egalitarian welfare,

When facilities are limited in their locations, the corresponding ENDPOINT* mechanisms provides the same approximation ratio for the utilitarian and egalitarian welfare. We contrast this with the distance objective, where limiting the location of the two facilities worsens the approximation ratio of the ENDPOINT* mechanism. We also contrast this with a single facility, where limiting the location of the facility worsens the approximation ratio for either welfare objective.

Theorem 11. *The* ENDPOINT* *mechanism 2-approximates the optimal utilitarian welfare, and $\frac{3}{2}$-approximates the optimal egalitarian welfare.*

9 Two Facilities, Satisfaction Approximations

When facilities are not limited in their location, the ENDPOINT mechanism offers a good approximation of the social satisfaction but not of the minimum satisfaction. In particular, it is not hard to show that it $\frac{n}{2} - \frac{1}{4}$-approximates the optimal social satisfaction but has no bound on the approximation ratio of the minimum satisfaction.

When facilities are limited in their locations, the corresponding ENDPOINT* mechanism provides a larger approximation ratio for the social satisfaction. We compare this with the distance objective, where limiting the location of the two facilities also worsens the approximation ratio of the ENDPOINT* mechanism. We also compare this with a single facility, where limiting the location of the facility means that the approximation ratio for the social satisfaction becomes unbounded.

Theorem 12. *The* ENDPOINT* *mechanism $\frac{3n}{4} - \frac{1}{2}$-approximates the optimal social satisfaction, but does not bound the approximation ratio of the optimal minimum satisfaction.*

10 Conclusions

We have studied the impact of constraints on the location of a facility on the performance of strategy proof mechanisms for facility location. We considered six different objectives: the total and maximum distance agents must travel, the utilitarian and egalitarian welfare, and the social and minimum satisfaction. In general, constraining facilities to a limited set of locations makes all six objectives harder to approximate in general. For example, a modified median mechanism is strategy proof and 3-approximates both the optimal total and maximum distance. No deterministic and strategy proof mechanism can do better. This contrasts with the setting in which there are no restrictions on where facilities can be located and the median mechanism returns the optimal total distance, and 2-approximates the optimal maximum distance. In future work, we intend to consider computational questions around such facility location problems (e.g. [16,17]), as well as online versions of the problem (e.g. [18]), and (Nash) equilibria in strategic settings (e.g. [19,20]).

References

1. Procaccia, A., Tennenholtz, M.: Approximate mechanism design without money. ACM Trans. Econ. Comput. **1**(4), 18:1–18:26 (2013)
2. Golowich, N., Narasimhan, H., Parkes, D.: Deep learning for multi-facility location mechanism design. In: Proceedings of the Twenty-Seventh International Joint Conference on Artificial Intelligence, IJCAI-18, International Joint Conferences on Artificial Intelligence Organization, pp. 261–267 (7 2018)
3. Aziz, H., Chan, H., Lee, B., Li, B., Walsh, T.: Facility location problem with capacity constraints: algorithmic and mechanism design perspectives. In: Conitzer, V., Sha, F. (eds.) Proceedings of the Thirty-Fourth AAAI Conference on Artificial Intelligence, AAAI Press (2020)
4. Walsh, T.: Strategy proof mechanisms for facility location with capacity limits. Technical report, CoRR archive within arXiv.org, Cornell University Library. http://arxiv.org/abs/2009.07986 (September 2020)
5. Drezner, Z., Hamacher, H. (eds.): Facility Location: Applications and Theory. Berlin, Springer (2002)
6. Jagtenberg, C., Mason, A.: Improving fairness in ambulance planning by time sharing. Eur. J. Oper. Res. **280**(3), 1095–1107 (2020)
7. Lu, P., Sun, X., Wang, Y., Zhu, Z.: Asymptotically optimal strategy-proof mechanisms for two-facility games. In: Proceedings of the 11th ACM Conference on Electronic Commerce, EC 2010, New York, pp. 315–324. ACM (2010)
8. Escoffier, B., Gourvès, L., Kim Thang, N., Pascual, F., Spanjaard, O.: Strategy-proof mechanisms for facility location games with many facilities. In: Brafman, R.I., Roberts, F.S., Tsoukiàs, A. (eds.) ADT 2011. LNCS (LNAI), vol. 6992, pp. 67–81. Springer, Heidelberg (2011). https://doi.org/10.1007/978-3-642-24873-3_6
9. Feldman, M., Fiat, A., Golomb, I.: On voting and facility location. In: Conitzer, V., Bergemann, D., Chen, Y., (eds.) Proceedings of the 2016 ACM Conference on Economics and Computation, (EC 2016), pp. 269–286. ACM (2016)
10. Tang, Z., Wang, C., Zhang, M., Zhao, Y.: Mechanism design for facility location games with candidate locations. CoRR archive within arXiv.org, Cornell University Library, Technical report (2020)
11. Mei, L., Li, M., Ye, D., Zhang, G.: Strategy-proof mechanism design for facility location games: revisited (extended abstract). In: Jonker, C.M., Marsella, S., Thangarajah, J., Tuyls, K., (eds.) Proceedings of the 2016 International Conference on Autonomous Agents & Multiagent Systems, Singapore, 9–13 May 2016, pp. 1463–1464. ACM (2016)
12. Mei, L., Li, M., Ye, D., Zhang, G.: Facility location games with distinct desires. Discrete Appl. Math. **264**, 148–160 (2019)
13. Moulin, H.: On strategy-proofness and single peakedness. Public Choice **35**(4), 437–455 (1980)
14. Massó, J., de Barreda, I.M.: On strategy-proofness and symmetric single-peakedness. Games Econ. Behav. **72**(2), 467–484 (2011)
15. Fotakis, D., Tzamos, C.: On the power of deterministic mechanisms for facility location games. In: Fomin, F.V., Freivalds, R., Kwiatkowska, M., Peleg, D. (eds.) ICALP 2013. LNCS, vol. 7965, pp. 449–460. Springer, Heidelberg (2013). https://doi.org/10.1007/978-3-642-39206-1_38
16. Walsh, T.: Challenges in resource and cost allocation. In: Proceedings of the 29th AAAI Conference on AI, Association for Advancement of Artificial Intelligence, pp. 25–30 (2015)

17. Walsh, T.: Fair division: the computer scientist's perspective. In: Bessiere, C., (ed.) Proceedings of 29th International Joint Conference on Artificial Intelligence, pp. 4966–4972 (2020)
18. Aleksandrov, M., Walsh, T.: Online fair division: a survey. In: Conitzer, V., Sha, F., (eds.) Proceedings of the Thirty-Fourth AAAI Conference on Artificial Intelligence, AAAI Press (2020)
19. Walsh, T.: Strategic behaviour when allocating indivisible goods. In: Schuurmans, D., Wellman, M., (eds.) Proceedings of the Thirtieth AAAI Conference on Artificial Intelligence, AAAI Press, pp. 4177–4183 (2016)
20. Aziz, H., Goldberg, P., Walsh, T.: Equilibria in sequential allocation. In: Rothe, J. (ed.) ADT 2017. LNCS (LNAI), vol. 10576, pp. 270–283. Springer, Cham (2017). https://doi.org/10.1007/978-3-319-67504-6_19

Applications of AI

A Consistency Enhanced Deep Lmser Network for Face Sketch Synthesis

Qingjie Sheng⬤, Shikui Tu⁽✉⁾⬤, and Lei Xu⬤

Department of Computer Science and Engineering, Shanghai Jiao Tong University,
Shanghai, China
{seansheng,tushikui,leixu}@sjtu.edu.cn

Abstract. Existing face sketch synthesis methods extend conditional generative adversarial network framework with promising performance. However, they usually pre-train on additional large-scale datasets, and the performance is still not satisfied. To tackle the issues, we develop a deep bidirectional network based on the least mean square error reconstruction (Lmser) self-organizing network, which is a further development of autoencoder by folding along the central hidden layer. Such folding makes the neurons on the paired layers between encoder and decoder merge into one. We model the photo-to-sketch mapping by an Lmser network and build a sketch-to-photo mapping by a complement Lmser sharing the same structure. The bidirectional mappings form an alternation system. We devise a supervised alternating consistency for the system, by minimizing the deviation between the alternatively mapped pattern and the ground-truth. Enhanced by the consistency constraints along the bidirectional paths, the model achieve a significant improvement in terms of Fréchet Inception Distance (FID). Experiments demonstrate the effectiveness of our method in comparison with state-of-the-art methods, and reduce the FID from 34.1 to 28.7 on the CUFS dataset and from 18.2 to 11.5 on the CUFSF dataset.

Keywords: Face sketch synthesis · Deep bidirectional network · Lmser · Supervised alternating consistency

1 Introduction

Face sketch synthesis is to represent a photo of a face into a corresponding face sketch [33]. It can be considered a subfield of image-to-image translation [7]. Enabling the judiciary to narrow down potential suspects in law enforcement and criminal cases [28], it can also be used as an auxiliary process in digital entertainment with the prevalent use of digital devices.

Supported by National Science and Technology Innovation 2030 Major Project (2018AAA0100700) of the Ministry of Science and Technology of China and Shanghai Municipal Science and Technology Major Project (2021SHZDZX0102).

D. N. Pham et al. (Eds.): PRICAI 2021, LNAI 13031, pp. 127–138, 2021.
https://doi.org/10.1007/978-3-030-89188-6_10

Advances have been made in this area, especially with the development of generative adversarial networks (GANs) [3]. As a common framework for image-to-image translation with paired images, pix2pix [7] has drawn extensive attention and benefited various subfields. Pix2pix extends GANs with an image input rather than a random noisy vector and employs convolutional neural networks (CNNs) instead of fully connected neural network to model both the generator and discriminator. Although the framework is easy to use, it tends to produce blurry outputs in face sketch synthesis. The reason is that the generators and the modules are relatively simple and insufficient to generate high-quality and perceptual realistic images.

To tackle this problem, the community further extends pix2pix with various technologies. For instance, the work by [33] employed perceptual loss [8] and face parsing [13] for face sketch synthesis. However, the two mechanisms have limitations of depending on datasets. For example, both are pre-trained on large-scale image datasets, and there may be significant differences in the pattern of data between the datasets for pre-training and training.

To develop an effective model for the generation of high-quality and perceptual realistic images, we propose a supervised-consistency (SC) enhanced deep least mean squared error reconstruction network (Lmser) [29,30], and call our model as SC-Lmser. Lmser was previously a further development of autoencoder (AE) by folding along the central hidden layer. Such folding makes the neurons on the paired layers between encoder and decoder merge into one, which induces six types of dualities to improve the performance of representation learning [31]. Two major types are duality in connection weights (DCW), which refers to using the symmetric weights in corresponding layers in encoder and decoder, and duality in paired neurons (DPN), which refers to dual roles of the neurons between the encoder and decoder. Recently, Lmser was revisited in [5] and confirmed that deep Lmser learning works well on potential functions, such as image reconstruction, association recall, and so on, as previously discuss in [30]. Moreover, it was extended to CNN based Lmser (CLmser) [6], which is more appropriate for image related tasks. DPN and DCW were extensively investigated in [6] with new findings on their relative strengths in different aspects on image reconstruction and image impainting. It has been suggested in [31] that GAN loss can be added to improve Lmser learning. The effectiveness was verified in [10] for image super-resolution and in [32] for image-to-image translation. Deep Lmser learning can be further considered in deep yIng-yAng (IA) system [31] for various tasks of image thinking, e.g., image pattern transformation. The IA system considers not only inward cognition from the actual visible world or yAng domain (A-domain) but also outward interaction from the invisible internal brain or yIng domain (I-domain) back to A-domain. Readers are referred to [31] for more details.

Specifically, we consider photo X as A-domain, sketch Y as I-domain. We model A-mapping by a Lmser network, which was trained by a conditional GAN [7] to translate X into Y. Moreover, I-mapping is also modeled to translate Y into X by a network with the same structure as A-mapping. For a paired X and Y, a fake Y (i.e., $\hat{Y}$) is generated via the A-mapping $X \rightarrow \hat{Y}$, while a fake X (i.e., $\hat{X}$)

is also a generated through the I-mapping $Y \to \hat{X}$. With the IA-alternation, it is then possible to compute the reconstruction results $\widetilde{X}$ through $\hat{Y}$ and I-mapping, and generate further reconstruction results $\widetilde{Y}$ through $\widetilde{X}$ and A-mapping. In this paper, we consider supervised consistency for two paths. One is the consistency between X and $\hat{X}$ via $Y \to \hat{X}$. The other is between the alternating outputs and their ground-truth via $X \to \hat{Y} \to \widetilde{X} \to \widetilde{Y}$. These consistencies enhance the deep Lmser representation learning, leading to improved photo-to-sketch performance.

The contributions of this study are as follows: (1) It extended a deep bidirectional network with the Lmser network [29] for face sketch synthesis, to enhance the efficiency of photo-to-sketch. (2) It demonstrated that the Lmser implemented with additive skip connections benefited the bidirectional supervised consistency system more than the concatenate one. (3) The proposed model improved the Fréchet Inception Distance (FID) from 34.1 to 28.7 on the CUFS [28] dataset and from 18.2 to 11.5 on the CUFSF [38] dataset.

2   Related Work

2.1   Face Sketch Synthesis

The method presented in [24] is the first data-driven method based on eigentransformation. They project the test photo onto the eignspace of the training photos by principal component analysis (PCA). Then the final sketch is generated from linearly combined weighted training sketches using the same projection. [12] subdivides the photo into overlapping patches and proposes to calculate the linear combination weight by searching similar neighbors in terms of Euclidean distance at the image patch level. In [28], a Markov random field (MRF) model is employed to take the neighboring consistency into account. Given that the similarity search processs is inefficient in previous data-driven methods, SSD [21] functions face sketch synthesis as a spatial sketch denoising problem, and RSLCR [25] develops a random sampling strategy to search the nearest neighboring patch. The two methods indeed improve the efficiency of synthesizing one sketch to an acceptable level. However, they are inefficient for applications, compared to the model-driven methods without similarity searching of patches.

Several studies also extend CNN models to learn a direct mapping from face photos to sketches. The method proposed in [35] employs a 7-layers fully convolutional network (FCN) and the objective of mean squared error (MSE). [34] proposes a branched fully convolutional network (BFCN) to generate structural and textual representations, and then fuse them together according to the face parsing results. Recently, many researchers focus on GANs to synthesize high-quality face sketches. For example, face sketches are generated by conditional GANs and further refined using the back projection strategy (BP-GAN) [27]. [33] extends pix2pix [7] framework by the composition information of face image to guide the generation of face sketch, and employs a compositional loss [34,37] to enhance the information of facial components and structures, leading to state-of-the-art performance in combination with a stacked strategy.

2.2   Image-to-image Translation

Face photo-to-sketch synthesis can be regarded as a subproblem of image-to-image translation. So far, image-to-image translation problem has made excellent progress using GANs [3,11], and variational auto-encoder (VAEs) [15].

Among the GAN models, there are two representative methods. A conditional GAN, called pix2pix, was presented in [7] for image-to-image translation tasks with paired training samples, such as image style transfer [1], labels to street scenes and semantic segmentation. However, obtaining paired training data is difficult or expensive. To tackle this problem, CycleGAN [39] is proposed. Cycle-GAN is designed with two cycles, $X \rightarrow \hat{Y} \rightarrow \tilde{X}$ and $Y \rightarrow \hat{X} \rightarrow \tilde{Y}$, to preserve the consistency of input and output of the cycles. CycleGAN is closely related to the network presented in this paper, but the proposed model is strengthened by conditional GAN and a further cycle following $\hat{X} \rightarrow \tilde{Y}$ mapping. As a result, the model can synthesize sketch images of higher quality from real face photos.

3   Method

3.1   Overview of Our Method

Given a set of input images $\{x_i\}_{i=1}^N$ and output images $\{y_i\}_{i=1}^N$, where x_i and y_i are paired. The aim is to learn a function of translating domain X to Y where $x_i \in X$ and $y_i \in Y$. The model consist of two networks $A : X \rightarrow Y$ (A-mapping) and $I : Y \rightarrow X$ (I-mapping), and they share the same structure. Each mapping is a Lmser with shortcuts. With the inputs X and Y, we get the generated images $\hat{Y}$ and $\hat{X}$ by A-mapping and I-mapping respectively, then a consistency constraint can be computed. According to the two paths $X \rightarrow \hat{Y}$ and $Y \rightarrow \hat{X}$, a rough model of A-mapping and a regularization model of I-mapping is first obtained. After that, with the input $\hat{Y}$, the reconstructed images $\tilde{X}$ are produced to regularize the A-mapping by the symmetrical network I-mapping in a complement direction. Moreover, $\tilde{X}$ is employed as new samples to further train A-mapping. Finally, the path $X \rightarrow \hat{Y}$ is extended as $X \rightarrow \hat{Y} \rightarrow \tilde{X} \rightarrow \tilde{Y}$. This not only provides many more samples for A-mapping, but also sets higher demands on it because the reconstructed samples do not strictly fit the real images. In addition, the adversarial discriminators D_X and D_Y are trained to distinguish between real X with fake X and real Y with fake Y respectively, in a conditional manner [7]. The overall architecture of the proposed model and the differences of paths between cycleGAN [39] and ours are illustrated in Fig. 1.

3.2   Objective

We utilize the least square adversarial loss for both mapping functions, known as LSGAN [16]. It converges easily and is useful for our model by conditional adjustment. For the A-mapping $A : X \rightarrow Y$ and the corresponding discriminator D_Y, the objective can be expressed as:

$$\mathcal{L}_{adv}(A, D_Y, X, Y) = \mathbb{E}_{x,y}[(1 - D(x,y))^2] + \mathbb{E}_x[(D(x, A(x)))^2]. \tag{1}$$

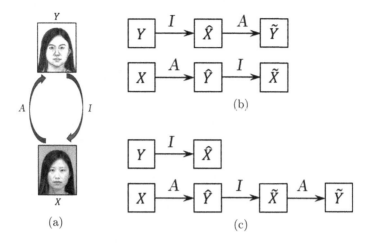

Fig. 1. (a) Overview of our model. (b) Two paths in cycleGAN. (c) Two paths in our model.

Following previous works [7,33], we adopt L_1 distance to encourage the "fake" outputs to fit the distribution of targets as:

$$\mathcal{L}_{L_1}(A, X, Y) = \mathbb{E}_{x,y}[\|A(x) - y\|_1]. \tag{2}$$

In the deep bidirectional leaning framework, $\widetilde{X}$ is regarded as the reconstruction result by the abstract representation of A-mapping's input X. We also employ L_1 distance to constrain them to be consistent. Moreover, $\widetilde{Y}$ is the abstract representation of $\widetilde{X}$ by A-mapping, and to be consistent with Y can further strengthen the learning of A-mapping. The two losses can be fused as:

$$\mathcal{L}_{SC}(A, I, X, Y) = \mathbb{E}_x[\|I(A(x)) - x\|_1] + \mathbb{E}_{x,y}[\|A(I(A(x))) - y\|_1]. \tag{3}$$

Our final objectives are:

$$(A^*, D_Y^*) = \arg\min_A \max_{D_Y} \mathcal{L}_{adv}(A, D_Y, X, Y) + \lambda \mathcal{L}_{L_1}(A, X, Y) \tag{4}$$
$$+ \beta \mathcal{L}_{SC}(A, I, X, Y),$$

$$(I^*, D_X^*) = \arg\min_I \max_{D_X} \mathcal{L}_{adv}(I, D_X, Y, X) + \lambda \mathcal{L}_{L_1}(I, Y, X), \tag{5}$$

where λ and β are weighting factors.

3.3 Network Architecture

In this paper, the Lmser are adopted with two different skip connections as the networks of A-mapping and I-mapping. Similar to U-Net [19] architecture, the residual blocks in both encoder and decoder are illustrated in Fig. 2. The ReLU activation function with a slope 0.2 is used in all ResDown blocks. The architecture of generators is illustrated in Fig. 2.

The discriminators follow 70×70 patchGAN architecture in [7].

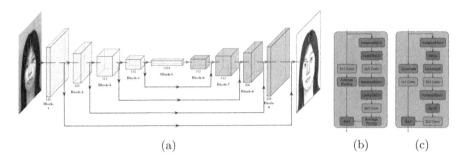

(a)   (b)   (c)

Fig. 2. (a) Network architecture for A-mapping. I-mapping has the same architecture with contrary input and output. (b) Details of ResDown block. (c) Details of ResUp block.

4 Experiments

To explore the effectiveness of the proposed method on face sketch synthesis, we conduct experiments on two extensively applied and public available datasets: CUFS dataset [28] and CUFSF dataset [38].

- CUFS: includes 606 pairs of face photos and sketches, and consists of three datasets: CUHK student dataset [23] (188 pairs), AR dataset [17] (123 pairs) and XM2VTS dataset [18] (295 pairs).
- CUFSF: includes 1194 pairs of face photos and sketches. It is more challenging relatively because of the varieties of lighting in photos and shape deformations and exaggerations in sketches.

Dataset Partition. To be consistent with representative methods, we follow the settings presented in [25] to split the datasets. We select 88 face photo-sketch pairs from the CUHK student dataset, 80 pairs from the AR dataset, and 100 pairs from the XM2VTS dataset for training, the rest are for testing. For the CUFSF dataset, 250 pairs are for training and the rest are for testing.

Data Processing. Likewise, we follow SCA-GAN [33] to crop the face images (photos and sketches) from the original using three-point geometric rectification for those that do not well aligned. The overall images are cropped to the size of 250 × 200. Photos are represented in RGB color space, and sketches are represented in gray color space.

For data augmentation, the images obtained after the data processing are padded to the size of 286 × 286 with 255 and further randomly cropped to the size of 256 × 256 for training, and cropped the center for testing. In the SCA-GAN setting, the input images is padded to the target size with zero, which significantly enhances performance, compared to resize image setting in pix2pix [7] according to their experiments. However, we observed that padding with zero could produce slight blurred effects in the generated sketch in our experimental settings.

4.1   Training Details

We optimized the generators and discriminators alternatively at every iteration. We use the Adam solver with a batch size of 1. For all the experiments, the weighting factors λ and β were set to 10 and 10, respectively. The generators and discriminators were trained with the learning rates of 0.0002 and 0.0001 respectively. We trained our model on a single Nvidia Titan X GPU. Each iteration took about 1.2 s, and it took about 18 h for training 300 epochs.

4.2   Evaluation Metrics

Evaluating the quality of synthesized images is a synthetical and thorny problem. We follow [33] and employ three criteria: *Fréchet inception distance* (FID) [4,14,33], *feature similarity index metric* (FSIM) [36] and *null-space linear discriminant analysis* (NLDA) [2].

The FID measures the earth-mover distance (EMD) between the feature of real image and generated image. Generally, the feature is produced by an Inception-v3 network [22] pre-trained on the ImageNet dataset [20]. A lower FID score means that the distribution and perception of real data and synthetic are closer. FID score has been widely applied in image translation and related tasks, and has a great impact on image quality assessment.

In FSIM, the consistency of real and synthesized image is measured by the phase congruency and the image gradient magnitude. As reported in [26], FSIM is better at evaluating the quality setbacks of photos compared with SSIM [9], however, it is not suitable for evaluating the quality of sketches. In our experiments, we still employ it since FSIM is a prevalent criterion in face sketch synthesis community.

Additionally, face recognition is a significant application of face sketch synthesis. [25] initially used NLDA [2] to conduct the face recognition experiments. We follow this setting to evaluate the face recognition accuracy by the generated and the ground-truth sketches.

4.3   Ablation Study

We conduct an ablation study to evaluate the performance of different modules in the proposed method. We extend pix2pix framework [7] with two different generators. The *concat* and *add* denote the concatenate and additive skip connections applied in generators, respectively. Figure 3 shows the qualitative effects of these modules on CUFS and CUFSF datasets. Table 1 illustrates their quantify performance. With pix2pix framework alone, the *concat* and *add* generators have almost the same performance and make significant progress compared to SCA-GAN [33]. However, they still lead to blurry effects and coarse-grained facial characteristics. Adding the deep bidirectional leaning mechanism make further improvements in the quality of results, and decrease the FID score from 14.5 and 15.2 to 12.4 and 11.5 by using *concat* and *add* respectively. It follows that the additive skip connections are fitter for the bidirectional system.

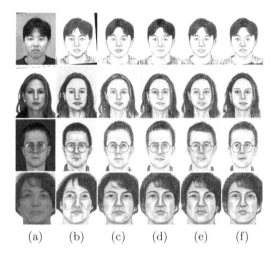

(a)   (b)   (c)   (d)   (e)   (f)

Fig. 3. Each column shows results trained under different modules. (a) Input, (b) Ground truth, (c) *concat + cGAN*, (d) *add + cGAN*, (e) *concat + cGAN + SC*, (f) *add + cGAN + SC*. From top to bottom, the examples are selected from the CUHK student dataset, AR dataset, XM2VTS dataset, and CUFSF dataset, sequentially.

Table 1. Ablation study: performance of face photo→sketch for different model modules, evaluated on the CUFS and CUFSF dataset. *add* denotes additive skip connections. *concat* denotes concatenate skip connections. The last row illuminate our final model. *cGAN* denotes pix2pix framework. *SC* denotes our bidirectional supervised-consistency mechanism.

Model	CUFS dataset			CUFSF dataset		
	FID↓	FSIM↑	NLDA↑	FID↓	FSIM↑	NLDA↑
concat + cGAN	32.2	0.7207	0.9667	14.5	0.7151	0.7885
add + cGAN	32.7	0.7203	0.9734	15.2	0.7154	0.7673
concat + cGAN + SC	29.5	0.7251	0.9712	12.4	0.7178	0.7902
add + cGAN + SC	28.7	0.7188	0.9720	11.5	0.7179	0.7968

4.4   Comparison Against Baselines

We compare the proposed method with several existing methods, including MRF [28], SSD [21], RSLCR [25], DGFL [40], BP-GAN [27], pix2pix [7] and SCA-GAN [33]. MRF, SSD and RSLCR are the representative data-driven methods, and the rest are the representative model-driven methods. Pix2pix is proposed for image-to-image translation tasks, and we implement this model for comparison on face sketch synthesis since the proposed method is also extended with it. All these methods and ours follow the same experimental settings.

Table 2 and Fig. 4 report the quantitative performance in terms of FID score, FSIM and NLDA. The proposed model obtains the lowest FID score reducing it from 34.1 and 18.2 to 28.7 and 11.5 on CUFS and CUFSF datasets, respectively, compared to the previous state-of-the-art method. In addition, it is highly competitive with previous works in terms of FSIM and NLDA. As mentioned above, FSIM is not suitable for evaluating the quality of sketches [26], and for reference only.

Figure 5 shows some face sketches that have been synthesized by different methods on the CUFS and CUFSF datasets. The incipient data-driven method (MRF) [28] fails to synthesize quality sketches and leads to deformations and blurry effects. SSD [21], RSLCR [25] and DGFL [40] produce over-smooth sketch with artifacts. BP-GAN [27] synthesizes face sketches with clear outlines and structures, but it also suffers an over-smooth problem especially in the regions of hair. Pix2pix [7] has no over-smooth problems, it, however, generates many blurry effects. SCA-GAN [33] is based on pix2pix framework and employs other mechanisms. It obviously improves the performance and the results have quality details but fails to generate several subtle structures (such as glasses) and textures. The model proposed in this paper can produce visually more realistic face sketches than previous state-of-the-art methods, especially in some subtle details. For example, as illustrated in Fig. 5, the proposed model can generate an entire glasses frame (see the examples of AR and XM2VTS datasets), facial folds (see the example of AR datasets), meticulous and plentiful textures (see

Table 2. Performance of face photo→sketch for different methods on the CUFS and CUFSF dataset. ↓ indicates lower is better, and ↑ indicates higher is better.

Criterion	Dataset	Data-driven methods			Model-driven methods				
		MRF	SSD	RSLCR	DGFL	BP-GAN	pix2pix	SCA-GAN	Ours
FID↓	CUFS	57.9	72.7	70.7	62.3	68.7	48.0	34.1	**28.7**
	CUFSF	61.5	59.9	68.5	52.5	52.0	20.8	18.2	**11.5**
FSIM↑	CUFS	0.7066	0.6946	0.6981	0.7079	0.6899	**0.7205**	0.7156	0.7188
	CUFSF	0.6967	0.6830	0.6775	0.6957	0.6814	0.7189	**0.7292**	0.7179

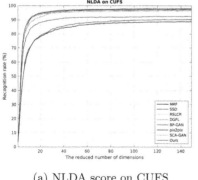

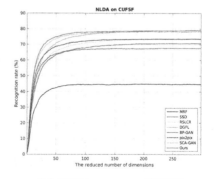

(a) NLDA score on CUFS   (b) NLDA score on CUFSF

Fig. 4. Face recognition rate against feature dimensions on CUFS dataset and CUFSF dataset.

the examples of CUHK and XM2VTS datasets), and little distortions (see the example of CUFSF datasets).

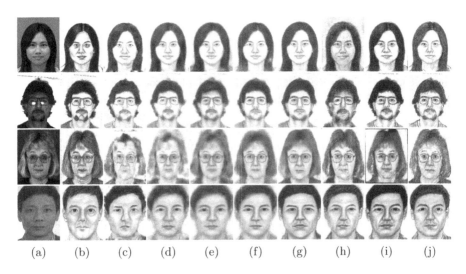

(a)   (b)   (c)   (d)   (e)   (f)   (g)   (h)   (i)   (j)

Fig. 5. Example synthesized face sketches of different methods on the CUFS and CUFSF dataset. (a) Photo, (b) corresponding sketch drawn by artist, (c) MRF, (d) SSD, (e) RSLCR, (f) DGFL, (h) pix2pix, (i) SCA-GAN, and (j) Ours. From top to bottom, the examples are selected from the CUHK student dataset, AR dataset, XM2VTS dataset, and CUFSF dataset, sequentially.

5   Conclusion

In this paper, we presented a supervised consistency enhanced Lmser network for face sketch synthesis. It contains two Lmser mappings for photo-to-sketch (A-mapping) and sketch-to-photo (I-mapping). I-mapping provides a regularization strength to A-mapping by optimizing the reconstruction of the input photo from its corresponding sketch. Moreover, we introduced the reconstructed results as complimentary samples, to further enhance the A-mapping network. This bidirectional setting benefits the presented model and achieved a state-of-the-art performance on face sketch synthesis. The experimental results on CUFS and CUFSF datasets demonstrated that the proposed method succeeds in synthesizing higher-quality sketches, in comparison with previous state-of-the-art methods. Moreover, the ablation experiments showed that the additive skip connection generator works more effectively in the deep bidirectional learning system.

References

1. Chen, D., Yuan, L., Liao, J., Yu, N., Hua, G.: Stylebank: an explicit representation for neural image style transfer. In: IEEE Conference on Computer Vision and Pattern Recognition, pp. 2770–2779 (2017)

2. Chen, L., Liao, H., Ko, M., Lin, J., Yu, G.: A new lda-based face recognition system which can solve the small sample size problem. Pattern Recogn. **33**(10), 1713–1726 (2000)
3. Goodfellow, I., et al.: Generative adversarial nets. In: Advances in Neural Information Processing Systems, vol. 27, pp. 2672–2680 (2014)
4. Heusel, M., Ramsauer, H., Unterthiner, T., Nessler, B., Hochreiter, S.: Gans trained by a two time-scale update rule converge to a local nash equilibrium. In: Advances in Neural Information Processing Systems, vol. 30, pp. 6626–6637 (2017)
5. Huang, W., Tu, S., Xu, L.: Revisit lmser from a deep learning perspective. In: Intelligence Science and Big Data Engineering. Big Data and Machine Learning, pp. 197–208 (2019)
6. Huang, W., Tu, S., Xu, L.: Deep CNN based Lmser and strengths of two built-in dualities. Neural Process. Lett. **8**, 108418–108428 (2020)
7. Isola, P., Zhu, J., Zhou, T., Efros, A.A.: Image-to-image translation with conditional adversarial networks. In: IEEE Conference on Computer Vision and Pattern Recognition, pp. 5967–5976 (2017)
8. Johson, J., Alahi, A., Li, F.F.: Perceptual losses for real-time style transfer and super-resolution. In: European Conference on Computer Vision, pp. 694–711 (2016)
9. Karacan, L., Erdem, E., Erdem, A.: Structure-preserving image smoothing via region covariances **32**(6), 176 (2013)
10. Li, P., Tu, S., Xu, L.: GAN flexible Lmser for super-resolution. In: Proceedings of the 27th ACM International Conference on Multimedia, pp. 756–764 (2019)
11. Liu, M., Tuzel, O.: Coupled generative adversarial networks. In: Advances in Neural Information Processing Systems, vol. 29, pp. 469–477 (2016)
12. Liu, Q., Tang, X., Jin, H., Lu, H., Ma, S.: A nonlinear approach for face sketch synthesis and recognition. In: IEEE Computer Society Conference on Computer Vision and Pattern Recognition, vol. 1, pp. 1005–1010 (2005)
13. Liu, S., Yang, J., Huang, C., Yang, M.: Multi-objective convolutional learning for face labeling. In: IEEE Conference on Computer Vision and Pattern Recognition, pp. 3451–3459 (2015)
14. Lucic, M., Kurach, K., Michalski, M., Gelly, S., Bousquet, O.: Are gans created equal? a large-scale study. In: Advances in Neural Information Processing Systems, vol. 31, pp. 700–709 (2018)
15. Makhzani, A., Shlens, J., Jaitly, N., Goodfellow, I., Frey, B.: Adversarial autoencoders. arXiv preprint arXiv:1511.05644 (2015)
16. Mao, X., Li, Q., Xie, H., Lau, R.Y.K., Wang, Z., Smolley, S.P.: Least squares generative adversarial networks. In: IEEE International Conference on Computer Vision, pp. 2813–2821 (2017)
17. Martinez, A., Benavente, R.: The AR face database. CVC Technical Report #24 (1998)
18. Messer, K., Matas, J., Kittler, J., Luettin, J., Maitre, G.: XM2VTSDB: The extended M2VTS database. In: Second International Conference on Audio and Video-based Biometric Person Authentication, pp. 72–77 (1999)
19. Ronneberger, O., Fischer, P., Brox, T.: U-net: convolutional networks for biomedical image segmentation. In: Navab, N., Hornegger, J., Wells, W.M., Frangi, A.F. (eds.) MICCAI 2015. LNCS, vol. 9351, pp. 234–241. Springer, Cham (2015). https://doi.org/10.1007/978-3-319-24574-4_28
20. Russakovsky, O., et al.: Imagenet large scale visual recognition challenge. Int. J. Comput. Vision **115**(3), 211–252 (2015)
21. Song, Y., Bao, L., Yang, Q., Yang, M.: Real-time exemplar-based face sketch synthesis. In: European Conference on Computer Vision, pp. 800–813 (2014)

22. Szegedy, C., Vanhoucke, V., Ioffe, S., Shlens, J., Wojna, Z.: Rethinking the inception architecture for computer vision. In: IEEE Conference on Computer Vision and Pattern Recognition, pp. 2818–2826 (2016)
23. Tang, X., Wang, X.: Face photo recognition using sketch. In: Proceedings of the International Conference on Image Processing, vol. 1, pp. I-I (2002)
24. Tang, X., Wang, X.: Face sketch synthesis and recognition. In: Proceedings Ninth IEEE International Conference on Computer Vision, vol. 1, pp. 687–694 (2003)
25. Wang, N., Gao, X., Li, J.: Random sampling for fast face sketch synthesis. Pattern Recogn. **76**, 215–227 (2018)
26. Wang, N., Gao, X., Li, J., Song, B., Li, Z.: Evaluation on synthesized face sketches. Neurocomputing **214**, 991–1000 (2016)
27. Wang, N., Zha, W., Li, J., Gao, X.: Back projection: an effective postprocessing method for GAN-based face sketch synthesis. Pattern Recogn. Lett. **107**, 59–65 (2017)
28. Wang, X., Tang, X.: Face photo-sketch synthesis and recognition. IEEE Trans. Pattern Anal. Mach. Intell. **31**(11), 1955–1967 (2009)
29. Xu, L.: Least mse reconstruction by self-organization. i. multi-layer neural-nets. In: Proceedings 1991 IEEE International Joint Conference on Neural Networks, vol. 3, pp. 2362–2367 (1991)
30. Xu, L.: Least mean square error reconstruction principle for self-organizing neural-nets. Neural Netw. **6**(5), 627–648 (1993)
31. Xu, L.: An overview and perspectives on bidirectional intelligence: Lmser duality, double IA harmony, and causal computation. IEEE/CAA J. Automatica Sinica **6**(4), 865–893 (2019)
32. Yang, H., Tu, S.: Glmser: a gan-lmser network for image-to-image translation. In: IEEE 31st International Conference on Tools with Artificial Intelligence (ICTAI), pp. 582–589 (2019)
33. Yu, J., et al.: Toward realistic face photo-sketch synthesis via composition-aided gans. IEEE Transactions on Cybernetics, pp. 1–13 (2020)
34. Zhang, D., Lin, L., Chen, T., Wu, X., Tan, W., Izquierdo, E.: Content-adaptive sketch portrait generation by decompositional representation learning. IEEE Trans. Image Process. **26**(1), 328–339 (2017)
35. Zhang, L., Lin, L., Wu, X., Ding, S., Zhang, L.: End-to-end photo-sketch generation via fully convolutional representation learning. In: Proceedings of the 5th ACM on International Conference on Multimedia Retrieval, pp. 627–634 (2015)
36. Zhang, L., Zhang, L., Mou, X., Zhang, D.: FSIM: a feature similarity index for image quality assessment. IEEE Trans. Image Process. **20**(8), 2378–2386 (2011)
37. Zhang, M., Li, J., Wang, N., Gao, X.: Compositional model-based sketch generator in facial entertainment. IEEE Trans. Syst. Man Cybern. **48**(3), 904–915 (2018)
38. Zhang, W., Wang, X., Tang, X.: Coupled information-theoretic encoding for face photo-sketch recognition. In: IEEE Conference on Computer Vision and Pattern Recognition, pp. 513–520 (2011)
39. Zhu, J., Park, T., Isola, P., Efros, A.A.: Unpaired image-to-image translation using cycle-consistent adversarial networks. In: IEEE International Conference on Computer Vision, pp. 2242–2251 (2017)
40. Zhu, M., Wang, N., Gao, X., Li, J.: Deep graphical feature learning for face sketch synthesis. In: Proceedings of the Twenty-Sixth International Joint Conference on Artificial Intelligence, pp. 3574–3580 (2017)

A Cost-Efficient Framework for Scene Text Detection in the Wild

Gangyan Zeng[1], Yuan Zhang[1], Yu Zhou[2,3(✉)], and Xiaomeng Yang[2,3]

[1] Communication University of China, Beijing, China
{zgy1997,yzhang}@cuc.edu.cn
[2] Institute of Information Engineering, Chinese Academy of Sciences, Beijing, China
zhouyu@iie.ac.cn,xiaomeng.17@intl.zju.edu.cn
[3] School of Cyber Security, University of Chinese Academy of Sciences,
Beijing, China

Abstract. Scene text detection in the wild is a hot research area in
the field of computer vision, which has achieved great progress with the
aid of deep learning. However, training deep text detection models needs
large amounts of annotations such as bounding boxes and quadrangles,
which is laborious and expensive. Although synthetic data is easier to
acquire, the model trained on this data has large performance gap with
that trained on real data because of domain shift. To address this problem, we propose a novel two-stage framework for cost-efficient scene text
detection. Specifically, in order to unleash the power of synthetic data, we
design an unsupervised domain adaptation scheme consisting of Entropy-
aware Global Transfer (EGT) and Text Region Transfer (TRT) to pre-
train the model. Furthermore, we utilize minimal actively annotated and
enhanced pseudo labeled real samples to fine-tune the model, aiming
at saving the annotation cost. In this framework, both the diversity of
the synthetic data and the reality of the unlabeled real data are fully
exploited. Extensive experiments on various benchmarks show that the
proposed framework significantly outperforms the baseline, and achieves
desirable performance with even a few labeled real datasets.

Keywords: Scene text detection · Unsupervised domain adaptation ·
Semi-supervised active learning

1 Introduction

Text spotting [39] in scene images has achieved great success with the development of deep learning, which includes two stages, namely text detection
[3,8,24,25,30,47] and text recognition [21–23,28,41], or only a single end-to-
end stage [17]. Training these models requires a large amount of annotated data,
and the annotation process is time-consuming and expensive. To alleviate the
burden, many researchers turn to create massive synthetic data whose annotations come for free. Text recognition models can be trained fully on synthetic
data and perform comparably with that trained on real data. However, for text

© Springer Nature Switzerland AG 2021
D. N. Pham et al. (Eds.): PRICAI 2021, LNAI 13031, pp. 139–153, 2021.
https://doi.org/10.1007/978-3-030-89188-6_11

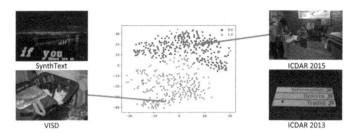

Fig. 1. Illustration of the domain shift problem. Left: synthetic text detection datasets as source domains, e.g. SynthText [9] and VISD [42]. Right: real text detection datasets as target domains, e.g. ICDAR 2015 [11] and ICDAR 2013 [12]. We visualize VISD and ICDAR 2015 image features from a text detector [10]. It exhibits a large distribution bias, which hinders the generalization between domains.

detection, there is still a large performance gap between the model trained on synthetic data and that trained on real data [9,42], which results from domain shift, as shown in Fig. 1. In the training settings of previous text detection work, it is common to pre-train the model on large-scale synthetic datasets, and then fine-tune it on the target datasets of specific scenarios. However, there are two problems overlooked.

On the one hand, in the pre-training process, the unlabeled real data of target domain is not explored. The model pre-trained only on the synthetic datasets has difficulty adapting to the distribution of the real target datasets, leading to the sub-optimal transfer learning results. Recently, Unsupervised Domain Adaptation (UDA) [4,7,46] is proposed to learn invariant representations between different domains. Inspired by this, we propose to implement domain adaptation in the pre-training step to provide better initialization. We design an Entropy-aware Global Transfer (EGT) module and a Text Region Transfer (TRT) module to deal with the domain shift at image level and region level respectively. Especially, the EGT module aligns not only image features but also discrimination entropy maps to strengthen the global transferability. Considering that foregrounds are more discriminative than backgrounds during the cross-domain text detection process, the TRT module is introduced to reduce the domain discrepancy of text regions.

On the other hand, supervised fine-tuning on the full target datasets requires enormous annotation cost. Recent studies have shown that unsupervised and self-supervised learning [14,15,18,19,38,44,45] are effective in many applications. In this work, we contend that the contributions of annotations on the target dataset may be different, and some annotations may even be redundant. We adopt a Semi-Supervised Active Learning (SSAL) approach to leveraging both the labeled and unlabeled data, targeting on maximizing performance at the lowest labeling effort. Concretely, we present an uncertainty-based active learning method to iteratively select the most informative samples for human labeling, and further utilize the left samples with reliable pseudo labels. Equipped with the proposed framework, we take full advantages of synthetic data and real data, thus creating a powerful network with less annotation cost.

In summary, the contributions of this work are as follows:

- We propose a novel text detection framework which explores the usability of the synthetic data and the unlabeled real data simultaneously with UDA and reduces the amount of annotations of real data with active learning. To the best of our knowledge, it is the first work to combine UDA and active learning for cost-efficient scene text detection.
- For UDA, we design two domain adaptation modules: EGT and TRT, to mitigate the disparities between real and synthetic domains. Furthermore, an SSAL algorithm which combines uncertainty-based sample selection and an enhanced pseudo-labeling strategy is proposed to actively annotate real data and utilize the remaining unlabeled data.
- On several benchmarks, our proposed method achieves significant improvement over traditional learning-based schemes such as fine-tuning, and obtains comparable performance to state-of-the-art text detectors with much fewer annotations.

2   Related Work

2.1   Scene Text Detection

Scene text detection has been a fundamental problem in computer vision for a long time, since it is widely applied in scene understanding, video analysis, autonomous driving, etc. Most of recent text detectors are based on CNN models, which can be roughly classified into bounding box-based and segmentation-based methods. Bounding box-based methods [16,30] are usually inherited from general object detection frameworks [27,36,37] by modifying anchors and filters to fit text instances with large aspect ratios. Segmentation-based methods [5,32,33] regard text detection as a semantic segmentation or an instance segmentation task, which classify text regions at the pixel level, thus performing well on texts of arbitrary shapes. Nevertheless, training these supervised text detectors comes at the high cost of annotated data. Thus, some weakly and semi-supervised methods are presented. WeText [29] trains a character detector with the help of word annotations which can be easily obtained in existing datasets. [26] utilizes a small amount of pixel-level annotated data and a much larger amount of rectangle-level weakly annotated data or unlabeled data to detect curved text in scene images.

2.2   Unsupervised Domain Adaptation

Unsupervised Domain Adaptation (UDA) tries to mitigate the domain disparities by transferring features and knowledge from a labeled source domain to a new unlabeled target domain. Prior work [7] explicitly estimates the domain

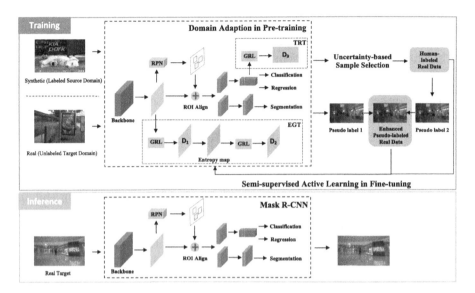

Fig. 2. Illustration of the overall framework. Top: the training process. We start with pre-training through domain adaptation from labeled synthetic data (source domain) to unlabeled real data (target domain). Then, the pre-trained model is used to perform uncertainty-based sample selection to select some informative real samples for human labeling, and the remaining real samples are pseudo-labeled with an enhanced strategy. Finally, both the human-labeled and pseudo-labeled real data are used to fine-tune the model. Bottom: the inference process. We can simply use the original Mask R-CNN architecture with adapted weights to output detection results.

gap and minimizes it. Recent work [4,46] is prone to utilize adversarial learning mechanism to achieve domain confusion.

Several efforts [1,2,35,43] are intended to address the domain shift in scene text detection. Chen et al. [1] reduce the domain gap in feature space. They apply pixel and image-level unsupervised adaptation components on a single-stage detection architecture. SyntoReal-STD [35] first aligns the feature map outputs of the backbone between synthetic and real domains, and then introduces text self-training on unlabeled real data. In contrast to previous work, our work not only improves global alignment on the image, but also takes into account fine-grained foreground region alignment and distribution alignment.

2.3 Semi-supervised Active Learning

Active Learning (AL) [31,40] is to automatically choose the most informative or representative samples for human labeling by elaborate sampling strategy. Semi-supervised Learning (SSL) [20] is to utilize both labeled and unlabeled samples for training, and in the self-training scheme, unlabeled samples are usually pseudo-labeled using model's certain prediction. These two learning paradigms are related and complementary with the potential to yield better results if combined. Leng et al. [13] introduce an SSAL method to train SVM with the labeled samples and the unlabeled class central samples. Wang et al. [34] propose to combine manifold regularization and AL, which shows that SSAL performs better than either SSL or AL using the same number of labeled samples. Our work aims to design a convincing combination of AL and SSL techniques for scene text detection.

3   Methodology

The architecture of our proposed framework is illustrated in Fig. 2, which follows Mask R-CNN [10] as the base network. It first extracts features of the input image via backbone, and then uses Region Proposal Network (RPN) to generate text proposals for the subsequent R-CNN and mask branch. The objective function of Mask R-CNN is formulated as:

$$L_{base} = L_{rpn} + L_{cls} + L_{reg} + L_{seg} \tag{1}$$

where L_{rpn}, L_{cls}, L_{reg} and L_{seg} are the loss functions of RPN, classification, regression and segmentation branches respectively.

Based on it, our proposed framework mainly consists of two components: (1) the unsupervised domain adaptation in Sect. 3.1; (2) a novel semi-supervised active learning strategy in Sect. 3.2.

3.1   Domain Adaptation in Pre-training

The goal of this section is to learn an adaptive text detector in pre-training with the labeled synthetic data and unlabeled real data. Existing work [1,35] has demonstrated the effectiveness of implementing synth-to-real domain adaptation at the image and pixel levels. However, they ignore that text is a special kind of object with larger diversity of shapes, sizes and orientations, so the adaptation only at the image or pixel level is limited.

In this work, we design Entropy-aware Global Transfer (EGT) and Text Region Transfer (TRT) to enhance the transferability at multiple levels in an adversarial way. We introduce three domain classifiers (i.e. D_1, D_2 and D_3) with their associated Gradient Reversal Layers (GRLs) [6]. During the forward process, GRL acts as an identity transform. In the backward stage, the sign of gradient is reversed when passing through the GRL layer. As a result, the domain classifiers are optimized to distinguish source and target examples, while the feature extractor learns to deceive the domain classifiers.

Entropy-Aware Global Transfer. We first eliminate the shift caused by the global image difference via aligning the feature map from the output layer of the backbone. Given an image x^s from the labeled source domain and x^t from the unlabeled target domain, $G(x_k)$ denotes the feature vector of the k-th

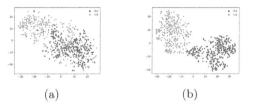

Fig. 3. Visualization of features obtained by (a) feature alignment (i.e. L_1 loss) and (b) entropy alignment (i.e. L_2 loss), where the orange points represent source samples and the blue ones represent target samples.

location in the feature map obtained from backbone G. The domain classifier D_1 is designed as a fully convolutional network. Therefore, the image feature adversarial training loss is formulated as follows,

$$L_1 = -\left[\sum_k log(D_1(G(x_k^s))) + \sum_k log(1 - D_1(G(x_k^t)))\right] \tag{2}$$

More importantly, considering that source images have labels but target images do not, the trained model tends to produce different prediction confidence levels for the two domains. Hence, we further propose to utilize the entropy map generated by D_1 to align the distribution shift between source and target domains. Specifically, the output probability of the domain classifier D_1 is represented by $d_k = D_1(G(x_k))$. We can use information entropy function $H(\cdot)$ to estimate the domain classification uncertainty (i.e. entropy) h_k of each x_k,

$$h_k = H(d_k) = -d_k \cdot log(d_k) - (1 - d_k) \cdot log(1 - d_k) \tag{3}$$

Then, D_2 is trained to predict the domain label of the entropy map via the following loss function:

$$L_2 = -\left[\sum_k log(D_2(h_k^s)) + \sum_k log(1 - D_2(h_k^t))\right] \tag{4}$$

The loss functions L_1 and L_2 are optimized to conduct global domain alignment from the perspectives of image feature and discrimination entropy, respectively. It is worth noting that both of them are indispensable, since the former is used to confuse the features across domains, and the latter can keep the different domain manifolds consistent, as shown in Fig. 3.

Text Region Transfer. There is an observation that foreground regions share more common features than backgrounds between different domains, so Regions of Interest (RoIs) are usually more important than backgrounds during domain adaptation [46]. In order to highlight the foregrounds (i.e. text proposals) and alleviate the local instance deviations across domains (e.g., text appearance, scale, deformation), the TRT component is added. Although text proposal representations can be extracted from RoI-based feature vectors after the RPN block, they always involve background noises. To reduce the negative effects, we only align features of the proposals whose text classification scores exceed 0.5.

Similar to L_1 and L_2, we utilize a domain classifier D_3 for the text region features. Let us denote the i-th text region in an image x as x_i, and its RoI feature as $F(x_i)$. The TRT loss can be written as

$$L_3 = - \left[\sum_i log(D_3(F(x_i^s))) + \sum_i log(1 - D_3(F(x_i^t))) \right] \quad (5)$$

The final training loss in pre-training is a weighted summation of each objective, denoted as:

$$L = L_{base} + \lambda_1 L_1 + \lambda_2 L_2 + \lambda_3 L_3 \quad (6)$$

For simplicity, inheriting from the domain adaptation setting for general object detection [4], λ_1, λ_2 and λ_3 are all set to 0.1 in our experiments.

3.2 Semi-supervised Active Learning in Fine-Tuning

Although the detector performance has been greatly improved by the unsupervised domain adaptation method, it is still far from satisfactory compared with the supervised counterpart. The general fine-tuning strategy is to fine-tune the pre-trained model on the full target labeled datasets, which is costly and unnecessary. In terms of self-training schema, it is common to generate pseudo labels for unlabeled data and add them into the training set without extra labor cost [20]. However, labeling all real target data with pseudo labels will mislead the model since they include many label noises. Consequently, we propose a semi-supervised active learning based approach in this section. For the real samples with the lowest certainty for the pre-trained model, we feed them to the human annotator. Meanwhile, the remaining real samples are automatically labeled with an enhanced pseudo labeling strategy.

Uncertainty-Based Sample Selection. We use the pre-trained model to select a small number of informative real samples for human labeling. It is not only to save the cost of labeling, but also to reduce information redundancy. Active Learning [31,40] is an algorithm that iteratively chooses the training data from a large unlabeled pool by elaborate strategies. Considering that the informative data points are often the samples that the model is most uncertain about, we adopt an uncertainty-based sample selection approach.

In particular, we define a classification uncertainty metric based on the entropy of text classification prediction. For each text proposal x, text detection network can predict its foreground probability p_x in the classification branch. Then we compute its entropy $H(x) = -p_x \cdot log(p_x) - (1 - p_x) \cdot log(1 - p_x)$ as the uncertainty score. Moreover, as we annotate image samples at each active

Fig. 4. Visualization examples of the enhanced pseudo-labeling strategy. The first and second columns are the predictions of the model trained with actively labeled samples and the pre-trained model respectively. These predictions often vary, but they both include a lot of false positives. The third column exhibits the final pseudo labels filtered with the IOU threshold t, which are more reliable. Best viewed in zoom. (Color figure online)

learning round, we need to take the average for all N proposals in the image I to obtain the image level uncertainty:

$$U(I) = \frac{\sum_{i=1}^{N} H(x_i)}{N} \tag{7}$$

Therefore, the model initialized by the pre-trained model conducts selection by estimating the uncertainties of images from the unlabeled pool and sampling top-K at each round. The selected samples are further labeled with human annotations (i.e. ground truth annotations) and then added into the training set for the next round. The selection process ends when the size of labeled set reaches the annotation budget.

Enhanced Pseudo Labeling. The genuine pseudo-labeling strategy uses the detection results of the pre-trained model as the pseudo labels. Unfortunately, we have found that this naive strategy causes the degradation of performance. Therefore, we propose an enhanced pseudo-labeling strategy by exploiting the complementarity of the synthetic data and real data, because the models trained by them always output different predictions for the same test image. Concretely, we use the pre-trained model and the model trained with actively labeled samples to output predictions for each unlabeled image respectively. The IOU values of these two predictions are computed, and only those predictions with the IOU value greater than threshold t (set as 0.7 in our experiments) are selected as the final pseudo labels. These enhanced pseudo labels are more reliable and notably suppress false positives. Some examples are visualized in Fig. 4. Note that we have also tried to directly use the actively trained model to generate pseudo labels, but its performance is inferior to our method.

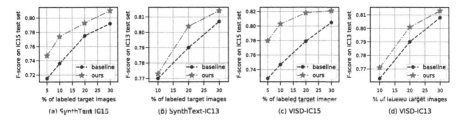

Fig. 5. Comparisons with baseline in different transfer scenarios. The x-axis indicates the percentage of human labeled target images, and the y-axis indicates the performance on the target test set.

Finally, both the actively human-labeled and enhanced pseudo-labeled real data are used to fine-tune the pre-trained model. Especially, we remove the losses of the bounding box regression and the segmentation for pseudo-labeled data, since pseudo labels are not so accurate in localization.

4   Experiments

4.1   Datasets

We evaluate our proposed method on several synthetic and real datasets.

SynthText [9] is a synthetic dataset that includes about 800K text images with 8K background images. Since the texts are rendered to blend with background images via well-designed heuristic algorithm, the images look realistic.

VISD [42] creates 10K synthetic images on different background images. It takes into account the semantic coherence of text and the embedding region, and thus is more diverse and realistic.

ICDAR 2015 (IC15) [11] is an incidental text dataset introduced from ICDAR 2015 Robust Reading Competition. It includes 1,000 training images and 500 test images, which are taken by Google Glasses without high quality.

ICDAR 2013 (IC13) [12] is a real focused text dataset whose text is often horizontal and noticeable. The dataset consists of 229 training images and 233 test images.

4.2   Implementation Details

We use ResNet-50 that pre-trained on ImageNet as the backbone model. The training is optimized by SGD and weight decay is set to 0.0001. The initial learning rate is 0.003 which decays after several epochs.

The training process contains pre-training and fine-tuning stages. In the pre-training stage, only the ground truth of source domain is accessible. At each iteration, we feed three source images and three target images to the model. In the fine-tuning stage, the batch size is set to 6. More critically, in the active learning process, we perform 5 rounds and the annotation budget in each round is equal to 1/5 of the number of the samples allowed to be labeled.

Table 1. Comparisons with existing text detectors on VISD to IC15/IC13 transfer tasks. "FOTS-Det" refers to the single detection version of FOTS [17] without recognition supervision. "Pro." indicates the proportion of human-labeled target images. "P", "R" and "F" represent Precision, Recall and F-score respectively.

Source → Target	Methods	Backbone	Pro.	P	R	F
VISD→IC15	EAST [47]	VGG16	10%	0.739	0.751	0.745
	Mask R-CNN [10]	ResNet50	10%	0.834	0.676	0.747
	PSENet [32]	ResNet50+FPN	10%	0.818	0.712	0.761
	PAN [33]	ResNet50+FPEM	10%	0.840	0.719	0.775
	Ours	ResNet50	5%	0.833	0.733	0.780
	Ours	ResNet50	10%	0.873	0.744	**0.803**
VISD→IC13	Mask R-CNN [10]	ResNet50	20%	0.820	0.763	0.790
	FOTS-Det [17]	ResNet50	20%	0.797	0.740	0.767
	Ours	ResNet50	10%	0.861	0.698	0.771
	Ours	ResNet50	20%	0.812	0.790	**0.801**

4.3 Comparison Results

Comparison with Baseline. The baseline setting in our experiments is pre-training only on all samples of the source dataset and fine-tuning on the randomly selected human-labeled samples of the target dataset. It is important to note that the performance will decrease if we perform genuine self-training, so we decide to report the baseline without pseudo-labeling strategy. Figure 5 shows the F-score curves with different annotation ratios in different domain transfer scenarios. It is obvious that our method consistently outperforms the baseline no matter how many target samples are labeled, which validates the effectiveness of our framework. Additionally, there is a common trend for all scenarios: as the number of labeled target samples increases, the performance improvement of our method over the baseline first increases and then gradually saturates. This phenomenon may result from the roles of active learning and pseudo-labeling simultaneously. When the actively labeled target samples are scarce, the pseudo labels provided by them are extremely noisy. And when the labeled samples increase to about 10% on IC15 and 20% on IC13, the improvement reaches the maximum. As shown in the Fig. 5 (c), when labeling 10% target samples, our method achieves the maximum gain of 5.6% (74.7% to 80.3%), and it is even close to the baseline with 30% labeled target samples (80.5%). Nevertheless, when the amount of labeled samples exceeds a certain value, the effect of active learning is relatively insignificant, hence the performance improvement saturates or gradually decreases.

Comparison with Existing Methods. To demonstrate the cost-effectiveness of our approach, we compare our framework with other state-of-the-art text detectors at only minimal annotation cost. The comparisons are conducted on VISD to IC15 and VISD to IC13 transfer tasks, and the results are summarized

Table 2. Comparison with other UDA methods on VISD to IC15/IC13 transfer tasks. The proportion of human-labeled target images is 10% on VISD→IC15 and 20% on VISD→IC13. "P", "R" and "F" represent Precision, Recall and F-score respectively.

Source→Target	Methods	P	R	F
VISD→IC15	Chen et al. [1]	0.894	0.700	0.785
	SyntoReal-STD [35]	0.835	0.725	0.776
	Ours	0.873	0.744	**0.803**
VISD→IC13	Chen et al. [1]	0.843	0.750	0.794
	SyntoReal-STD [35]	0.845	0.751	0.795
	Ours	0.812	0.790	**0.801**

Table 3. Ablation studies on VISD to IC15 transfer task. "USS" and "EPL" denote uncertainty-based sample selection and enhanced pseudo labeling respectively. "P", "R" and "F" represent Precision, Recall and F-score respectively.

Method	EGT	TRT	USS	EPL	P	R	F
Baseline					0.834	0.676	0.747
Ours	✓	✓	✓		0.838	0.727	0.779
	✓	✓		✓	0.872	0.674	0.760
			✓	✓	0.825	0.692	0.753
	✓		✓	✓	0.823	0.749	0.784
		✓	✓	✓	0.844	0.753	0.796
	✓	✓	✓	✓	0.873	0.744	0.803

in Table 1. Specifically, all the comparison text detectors are pre-trained on VISD dataset, and then fine-tuned on the randomly annotated IC15 or IC13 dataset. At the same annotation cost, our method which is based on Mask R-CNN without many bells and whistles is superior to other powerful text detectors. Particularly, on the VISD to IC15 task, even if PSENet [32] and PAN [33] use stronger backbones, our method with 5% human-labeled target samples performs better than them with 10% human-labeled target samples. On the VISD to IC13 task, our method surpasses FOTS-Det [17] with a 10% annotation reduction. It shows that our framework can yield appealing results with notable less annotation cost. Moreover, our framework is generic and can also be applied to other state-of-the-art text detection networks.

In addition, to evaluate the effect of our domain adaptation method (EGT & TRT) in pre-training, we compare it with other UDA methods, while uncertainty-based sample selection (USS) and enhanced pseudo labeling (EPL) are retained. Chen et al. [1] propose a pixel and image level domain adaptation scheme (PDA & IDA) to deal with cross-domain text detection problem, but these components are all feature alignments without focus. SyntoReal-STD [35] designs an adversarial text instance alignment (ATA) module to align the

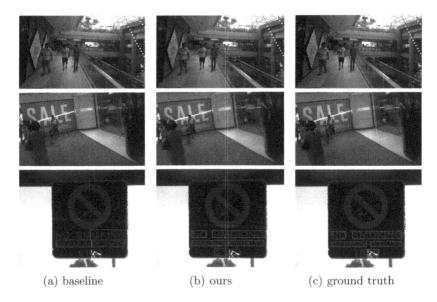

(a) baseline   (b) ours   (c) ground truth

Fig. 6. Detection examples from three transfer tasks, from top to bottom: SynthText-IC15, VISD-IC15, VISD-IC13. Best viewed in zoom. (Color figure online)

feature map outputs of the backbone, which is similar to Eq. 2. As shown in Table 2, on the VISD to IC15 task, replacing EGT & TRT modules with PDA & IDA modules and ATA module result in a 1.8% and 2.7% performance decrease respectively. And on the VISD to IC13 task, our UDA method is also superior to these competing UDA methods. It implies that entropy-aware distribution alignment and fine-grained text instance alignment are important, and these strategies are applicable to both rectangle annotations like IC13 and more complicated quadrilateral annotations like IC15. Our method enhances the model adaptability and handles the domain shift efficiently.

4.4   Ablation Study

To further evaluate the performance of each component in our framework, we conduct an overall ablation experiment on VISD to IC15 transfer task, as displayed in Table 3. Note that all comparison methods are based on 10% labeled target samples. No USS denotes random sampling, and no EPL denotes using the single pre-trained model to provide pseudo labels for the remaining samples. The results show that each component contributes to the final compelling results. In particular, the EGT module and TRT module respectively bring 3.1% and 4.3% gains compared with their ablated version (75.3%), and when integrating them, the F-score can get a 5.0% improvement. It also suggests that USS and EPL should be combined with these domain adaptation modules, since the effects of USS and EPL greatly depend on the pre-trained model.

4.5   Qualitative Analysis

Figure 6 illustrates the examples of detection results on several transfer tasks. Our framework consistently performs better than the baseline. For example, in the results of SynthText to IC15 task (Line 1), the baseline approach wrongly recognizes several background regions as texts because they have "text-like" patterns (such as fences, repetitive structured stripes, etc.), while our model suppresses this adverse impact of false positives. It not only benefits from the training of human-labeled hard samples introduced by USS, but also the minimizing of domain gap addressed by our UDA method. Additionally, our model is capable of detecting more obscured texts and producing more accurate localization results.

5   Conclusion

In this paper, we propose a two-stage cost-efficient framework for scene text detection. Unsupervised domain adaptation and semi-supervised active learning are integrated to address the problems of domain shift and data annotation respectively. Extensive experiments on public benchmarks of SynthText/VISD/ IC15/IC13 verify the effectiveness and superiority of our approach. Ablation studies demonstrate that the proposed EGT/TRT/USS/EPL all contribute to this framework. In the future, more sophisticated techniques will be explored towards training detectors purely on synthetic data.

Acknowledgments. This work is supported by the Open Research Project of the State Key Laboratory of Media Convergence and Communication, Communication University of China, China (No. SKLMCC2020KF004), the Beijing Municipal Science & Technology Commission (Z191100007119002), the Key Research Program of Frontier Sciences, CAS, Grant NO ZDBS-LY-7024, and the National Natural Science Foundation of China (No. 62006221).

References

1. Chen, D., et al.: Cross-domain scene text detection via pixel and image-level adaptation. In: ICONIP, pp. 135–143 (2019)
2. Chen, Y., Wang, W., Zhou, Y., Yang, F., Yang, D., Wang, W.: Self-training for domain adaptive scene text detection. In: ICPR, pp. 850–857 (2021)
3. Chen, Y., Zhou, Y., Yang, D., Wang, W.: Constrained relation network for character detection in scene images. In: PRICAI, pp. 137–149 (2019)
4. Chen, Y., Li, W., Sakaridis, C., Dai, D., Van Gool, L.: Domain adaptive faster r-cnn for object detection in the wild. In: CVPR, pp. 3339–3348 (2018)
5. Deng, D., Liu, H., Li, X., Cai, D.: Pixellink: detecting scene text via instance segmentation. In: AAAI, vol. 32 (2018)
6. Ganin, Y., Lempitsky, V.: Unsupervised domain adaptation by backpropagation. In: ICML, pp. 1180–1189 (2015)
7. Gong, B., Shi, Y., Sha, F., Grauman, K.: Geodesic flow kernel for unsupervised domain adaptation. In: CVPR, pp. 2066–2073 (2012)

8. Guo, Y., Zhou, Y., Qin, X., Wang, W.: Which and where to focus: a simple yet accurate framework for arbitrary-shaped nearby text detection in scene images. In: ICANN (2021)
9. Gupta, A., Vedaldi, A., Zisserman, A.: Synthetic data for text localisation in natural images. In: CVPR, pp. 2315–2324 (2016)
10. He, K., Gkioxari, G., Dollár, P., Girshick, R.: Mask r-cnn. In: ICCV, pp. 2961–2969 (2017)
11. Karatzas, D., et al.: Icdar 2015 competition on robust reading. In: ICDAR, pp. 1156–1160 (2015)
12. Karatzas, D., et al.: Icdar 2013 robust reading competition. In: ICDAR, pp. 1484–1493 (2013)
13. Leng, Y., Xu, X., Qi, G.: Combining active learning and semi-supervised learning to construct svm classifier. Knowl.-Based Syst. **44**, 121–131 (2013)
14. Li, W., Luo, D., Fang, B., Zhou, Y., Wang, W.: Video 3d sampling for self-supervised representation learning. arXiv preprint arXiv:2107.03578 (2021)
15. Li, X., et al.: Dense semantic contrast for self-supervised visual representation learning. In: ACM MM (2021)
16. Liao, M., Shi, B., Bai, X.: Textboxes++: a single-shot oriented scene text detector. TIP **27**(8), 3676–3690 (2018)
17. Liu, X., Liang, D., Yan, S., Chen, D., Qiao, Y., Yan, J.: Fots: fast oriented text spotting with a unified network. In: CVPR, pp. 5676–5685 (2018)
18. Luo, D., Fang, B., Zhou, Y., Zhou, Y., Wu, D., Wang, W.: Exploring relations in untrimmed videos for self-supervised learning. arXiv preprint arXiv:2008.02711 (2020)
19. Luo, D., et al.: Video cloze procedure for self-supervised spatio-temporal learning. In: AAAI, pp. 11701–11708 (2020)
20. Pise, N.N., Kulkarni, P.: A survey of semi-supervised learning methods. In: CIS, vol. 2, pp. 30–34 (2008)
21. Qiao, Z., Qin, X., Zhou, Y., Yang, F., Wang, W.: Gaussian constrained attention network for scene text recognition. In: ICPR, pp. 3328–3335 (2021)
22. Qiao, Z., et al.: PIMNet: a parallel, iterative and mimicking network for scene text recognition. In: ACM MM (2021)
23. Qiao, Z., Zhou, Y., Yang, D., Zhou, Y., Wang, W.: Seed: Semantics enhanced encoder-decoder framework for scene text recognition. In: CVPR, pp. 13528–13537 (2020)
24. Qin, X., et al.: Mask is all you need: Rethinking mask r-cnn for dense and arbitrary-shaped scene text detection. In: ACM MM (2021)
25. Qin, X., Zhou, Y., Guo, Y., Wu, D., Wang, W.: Fc 2 rn: a fully convolutional corner refinement network for accurate multi-oriented scene text detection. In: ICASSP. pp. 4350–4354 (2021)
26. Qin, X., Zhou, Y., Yang, D., Wang, W.: Curved text detection in natural scene images with semi-and weakly-supervised learning. In: ICDAR, pp. 559–564 (2019)
27. Ren, S., He, K., Girshick, R., Sun, J.: Faster r-cnn: towards real-time object detection with region proposal networks. TPAMI **39**(6), 1137–1149 (2016)
28. Shi, B., Bai, X., Yao, C.: An end-to-end trainable neural network for image-based sequence recognition and its application to scene text recognition. TPAMI **39**(11), 2298–2304 (2016)
29. Tian, S., Lu, S., Li, C.: Wetext: scene text detection under weak supervision. In: ICCV, pp. 1492–1500 (2017)
30. Tian, Z., Huang, W., He, T., He, P., Qiao, Y.: Detecting text in natural image with connectionist text proposal network. In: ECCV, pp. 56–72 (2016)

31. Wang, K., Zhang, D., Li, Y., Zhang, R., Lin, L.: Cost-effective active learning for deep image classification. TCSVT **27**(12), 2591–2600 (2016)
32. Wang, W., et al.: Shape robust text detection with progressive scale expansion network. In: CVPR, pp. 9336–9345 (2019)
33. Wang, W., et al.: Efficient and accurate arbitrary-shaped text detection with pixel aggregation network. In: ICCV, pp. 8440–8449 (2019)
34. Wang, X., Wen, J., Alam, S., Jiang, Z., Wu, Y.: Semi-supervised learning combining transductive support vector machine with active learning. Neurocomputing **173**, 1288–1298 (2016)
35. Wu, W., et al.: Synthetic-to-real unsupervised domain adaptation for scene text detection in the wild. In: ACCV (2020)
36. Yang, D., Zhou, Y., Wang, W.: Multi-view correlation distillation for incremental object detection. arXiv preprint arXiv:2107.01787 (2021)
37. Yang, D., Zhou, Y., Wu, D., Ma, C., Yang, F., Wang, W.: Two-level residual distillation based triple network for incremental object detection. arXiv preprint arXiv:2007.13428 (2020)
38. Yao, Y., Liu, C., Luo, D., Zhou, Y., Ye, Q.: Video playback rate perception for self-supervised spatio-temporal representation learning. In: CVPR, pp. 6548–6557 (2020)
39. Ye, Q., Doermann, D.: Text detection and recognition in imagery: a survey. TPAMI **37**(7), 1480–1500 (2014)
40. Yoo, D., Kweon, I.S.: Learning loss for active learning. In: CVPR, pp. 93–102 (2019)
41. Zeng, G., Zhang, Y., Zhou, Y., Yang, X.: Beyond OCR + VQA: involving OCR into the flow for robust and accurate TextVQA. In: ACM MM (2021)
42. Zhan, F., Lu, S., Xue, C.: Verisimilar image synthesis for accurate detection and recognition of texts in scenes. In: ECCV, pp. 249–266 (2018)
43. Zhan, F., Xue, C., Lu, S.: Ga-dan: geometry-aware domain adaptation network for scene text detection and recognition. In: ICCV, pp. 9105–9115 (2019)
44. Zhang, Y., Liu, C., Zhou, Y., Wang, W., Wang, W., Ye, Q.: Progressive cluster purification for unsupervised feature learning. In: ICPR, pp. 8476–8483 (2021)
45. Zhang, Y., Zhou, Y., Wang, W.: Exploring instance relations for unsupervised feature embedding. arXiv preprint arXiv:2105.03341 (2021)
46. Zheng, Y., Huang, D., Liu, S., Wang, Y.: Cross-domain object detection through coarse-to-fine feature adaptation. In: CVPR, pp. 13766–13775 (2020)
47. Zhou, X., et al.: East: an efficient and accurate scene text detector. In: CVPR, pp. 5551–5560 (2017)

A Dueling-DDPG Architecture for Mobile Robots Path Planning Based on Laser Range Findings

Panpan Zhao[1], Jinfang Zheng[1], Qinglin Zhou[1], Chen Lyu[1,2], and Lei Lyu[1,2(✉)]

[1] School of Information Science and Engineering, Shandong Normal University,
Jinan 250358, China
{lvchen,lvlei}@sdnu.edu.cn
[2] Shandong Provincial Key Laboratory for Distributed Computer Software Novel
Technology, Jinan 250358, China

Abstract. Planning an obstacle-free optimal path presents great challenges for mobile robot applications, the deep deterministic policy gradient (DDPG) algorithm offers an effective solution. However, when the original DDPG is applied to robot path planning, there remains many problems such as inefficient learning and slow convergence that can adversely affect the ability to acquire optimal path. In response to these concerns, we propose an innovative framework named dueling deep deterministic policy gradient (D-DDPG) in this paper. First of all, we integrate the dueling network into the critic network to improve the estimation accuracy of *Q-value*. Furthermore, we design a novel reward function by combining the cosine distance with the Euclidean distance to improve learning efficiency. Our proposed model is validated by several experiments conducted in the simulation platform Gazebo. Experiments results demonstrate that our proposed model has the better path planning capability even in the unknown environment.

Keywords: Robot path planning · Deep deterministic policy
gradient · Dueling network · Cosine distance

1 Introduction

Nowdays, a variety of mobile robots such as industrial robots [7,9,19], cleaning robots [2,10,16], family companion robots [12,15,28] are booming and playing an increasingly important role in people's lives. Path planning [3,4,29], a fundamental technique for mobile robots, it directly determines whether a robot can perform a specific task efficiently and accurately. The goal of robot path planning is to find an optimal or near-optimal obstacle-free path from the starting position to the target position. Researchers have proposed many methods for robot path planning. Traditional methods include Dijkstra algorithm [5,18,31], A-star (A*) [22,26] and artificial potential field method [14,30]. These methods rely on surrounding environment information and are difficult to work in the complex and uncertain environment. Therefore, it is essential to develop a path planning solution that has low dependence on the environment. In response to this situation, deep reinforcement learning (DRL) [27] has been proposed, which combines the perception of deep learning (DL) with the decision-making ability of reinforcement learning (RL) [6,8], agent learns through a continuous process of trial and error by interaction with the environment. Thus it can perform search and navigation tasks without relying on a priori map information, which determines that it has better flexibility even in unknown environment.

Traditional RL methods are limited by high dimensions of action space, thus they do not accommodate to continuous action space. Therefore, the deep deterministic policy gradient (DDPG), a representative of DRL algorithm, is proposed to reduce the dimensions of the action space using a deterministic policy. However, traditional DDPG has some drawbacks including inefficient learning and slow convergence, which seriously hinder its wide application in realistic robot path planning. In practice, learning by trial and error over a long period of time is very expensive, so it is important to reduce the convergence time of the model.

In response to the above concerns, we propose an innovative D-DDPG approach, which combines the dueling network with the critic network of DDPG and redesigns the reward function to improve the training efficiency of the model.

Our main contributions in this paper are summarized as follows:

- We introduce the dueling network, which represents both the state value and action advantage functions, making the estimation of Q-value more accurate and a good learning efficiency can be obtained.
- We combine the cosine distance with the Euclidean distance to generate a novel reward function. It can simultaneously control the direction and speed of robot movement and make exploration goal clearer.
- We apply our model to several realistic simulation scenarios, which give a more realistic picture of our model's path planning performance.

2 Related Work

In recent years, many RL-based approaches have been proposed for robot path planning, which can be categorized into value-based RL and policy-based RL.

Q-learning algorithm and State-Action-Reward-State-Action (SARSA) algorithm are two typical representatives of value-based RL algorithms [20,24] and have recently been implemented in various fields of robotics. The SARSA algorithm has faster convergence performance, while the Q-learning algorithm has better final performance, therefore Wang et al. [23] proposed to combine the SARSA algorithm with the Q-learning algorithm to improve the convergence effect of the algorithm. But the value-based Q-learning method has a shortcoming that it lrequires maintaining a Q-table, which takes a lot of time and space to search and store. To tackle this problem, Xin et al. [25] trained a designed deep Q network (DQN) to approximate the mobile robot state-action value function. The DQN combines Q-learning algorithm, replay buffer and convolutional neural network (CNN) [1], which is widely used in the field of path planning.

However, value-based RL algorithm is essentially an algorithm that approaches deterministic output. At best, it uses ϵ-greedy approach to exploration. This approach is not problematic in a more restrictive state environment, but may be problematic in environments with many repeated states.

Unlike the value-based RL, the policy-based algorithms directly optimize the policy and output the random policy when processing continuous states and actions. In recent years, researchers have been committed to integrating the Q function learned by the value-based algorithm and the policy function learned by the policy-based algorithm to make RL applicable to the continuous space. The Actor-Critic (AC) framework is widely used in practical RL, which integrates the value estimation algorithm and the policy search algorithm. Lillicrap et al. [17] proposed deep deterministic policy gradient (DDPG), which trains a deterministic policy to deal with the problem of continuous action by using a deep neural network on AC method. Tai et al. [21] used only ten-dimensional sparse feature values and real-time position to output the robot's linear velocity and angular velocity, which is similar to our work. As proved by Hasselt et al. [11], the traditional critic network usually overestimates the Q-$value$ and the estimated error will increase as the action increases. They proposed the Double DQN algorithm to solve this problem. However, using DQN as the underlying algorithm still has limitations when facing high dimensional space, but the DDPG will solve this problem very well. In addition, using only Euclidean distances in the reward function often suffers from the problem of unclear exploration goal in the exploration process.

Different from these works, we extend the DDPG algorithm by using a dueling network and introducing a cosine distance into the reward function. This allows the model to better implement robot path planning in a high-dimensional space.

3   The Methodology

In this section, we will give the definition of D-DDPG algorithm in detail. It adopts the Actor-Critic architecture, consisting of actor network and critic network. As shown in Fig. 1, our innovation is focused on the critic network, we introduce the dueling network to improve estimation accuracy of Q-$value$, in addition, a novel reward function is presented for optimizing the path.

3.1   DDPG Algorithm

The DDPG is based on the *Actor-Critic* framework and has good learning ability in continuous action space problems. It takes state S_t as input, and the output-action A_t is calculated by *online_action* network, after the robot performs the action, the reward value r_t is given by the reward function. Then (S_t, A_t, r_t, S_{t+1}) are stored in the replay buffer. In addition, in order to improve the exploration ability of the agent, random noise is added to the output action to increase the randomness [13]:

$$A = \mu(S; \theta) + \mathcal{N} \tag{1}$$

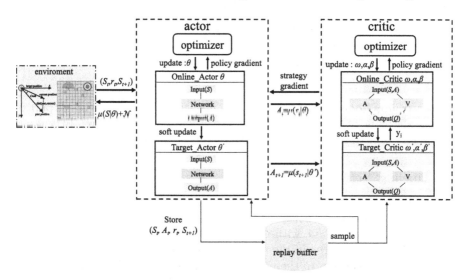

Fig. 1. The framework of the D-DDPG algorithm.

where the $\mathcal{N}$ is random noise.

A mini-batch of samples are sampled from replay buffer when updating critic and actor networks, then the loss function of critic network is calculated by target Q function and current Q function, the loss function can be defined as:

$$J(\omega) = \frac{1}{m} \sum_{t=1}^{m} (y_t - Q(S_t, A_t; \omega))^2 \tag{2}$$

where m represents the number of samples, the target Q function y_t is defined by Eq. 3:

$$y_t = \begin{cases} r_t, & is\_end \ is \ true \\ r_t + \gamma Q'(S_{t+1}, A_{t+1}; \omega'), & is\_end \ is \ false \end{cases} \tag{3}$$

where the ω is the parameter of the *online_critic* network and the ω' is the parameter of *target_critic* network, the r_t represents the reward value. γ is a discount factor, the larger the value of γ is, the larger the proportion of future income is considered in the calculation of the value generated by the current behavior, and the γ is taken as 0.99 in this paper.

The actor network is updated by the deterministic policy gradient:

$$\nabla_\theta J(\theta) \approx \frac{1}{m} \sum_{t=1}^{m} \nabla_{a_t} Q(S_t, A_t; \omega) \nabla_\theta \mu(S_t; \theta) \tag{4}$$

where ω is the parameter of the critic network and θ is the parameter of the actor network.

In order to avoid updating the parameters of network frequently and improve learning stability, the online network and the target network all use a soft update method, which the parameters of the target network are updated by a small amount in each iteration:

$$\begin{cases} \omega' \leftarrow \tau\omega + (1-\tau)\omega' \\ \theta' \leftarrow \tau\theta + (1-\tau)\theta' \end{cases} \tag{5}$$

The parameters in the target network are only scaled to update a small part of them, so the value of the update coefficient τ is small, which can greatly improve the stability of learning, we take τ as 0.001 in this paper.

3.2 Dueling Network

In D-DDPG, the actor network is served to output action using a policy-based algorithm, while the critic network is responsible for evaluating the value of the action based on its Q-value with a value-based approach. In order to generate action with higher Q-value in the same state, the actor network will adjust the policy gradient according to the evaluation of its current policy. Therefore, the estimation accuracy of Q-value has a crucial impact on the performance of the whole model. However, the original critic network tends to overestimate the Q-value, which leads to slow converge when the whole model is trained. To tackle this problem, we design a new critic network by introducing the dueling network to improve the estimation accuracy of Q-value. The framework is shown in Fig. 2.

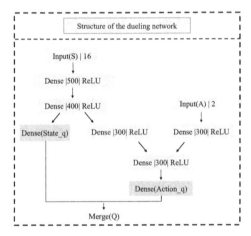

Fig. 2. The network structure of dueling network.

The dueling network is based on the fact that for many states, it is unnecessary to estimate the value of each action choice, while the estimation of state value is necessary. Therefore, in our critic network, the output is mapped to two fully connected layers, which are responsible for evaluating the state value and the action advantage, respectively. And they are merged to produce the final Q-value.

The relative advantage of action is expressed:

$$A(S, A) = Q(S, A) - V(S) \tag{6}$$

where $A(S, A)$ denotes the advantage of action A in a particular state, $V(S)$ represents the state value. As shown in Fig. 2, the *state_q* and the *action_q* are calculated by V and A, respectively

According to the Eq. 6, we construct the aggregating module to parameterize the estimation of the true Q function:

$$Q(S, A; \omega, \alpha, \beta) = A(S, A; \omega, \alpha) + V(S; \omega, \beta) \tag{7}$$

where ω is the network parameter of the common part, α and β are two parameters of the fully connected layer network.

The benefit of this is that we can realize the generalized learning of different actions without imposing any changes to the underlying RL, thereby improving the estimation accuracy of the Q-value.

3.3 Novel Reward Function

In RL, the reward function has a great effect on the convergence speed and learning effect of the algorithm. Traditional reward function is used to control the walking path of the robot indirectly only with the Euclidean distance, which ignores the moving direction of robot, thereby leading to unclear goal for the robot during exploration. To tackle this problem, we propose a novel reward function by combining the cosine distance with the Euclidean distance.

The cosine distance reflects the relative difference in direction between two vectors, while the Euclidean distance reflects the absolute difference in distance between two positions. As illustrated in Fig. 3, we use the *target position* as a reference, and control the moving direction of the robot by adjusting the angle and distance between the position of the past step (*past position*) and the position of current step (*current position*).

Specifically, the *vec1* refers to the vector that points from the *target position* to the *current position*, and the *vec2* refers to the vector that points from the *target position* to the *past position*. The angle between two vectors ranges from 0 to Π, corresponding to the cosine $[1, -1]$, which is expressed as:

$$Cos < vec1, vec2 >= \frac{vec1 \cdot vec2}{\|vec1\|_2 \|vec2\|_2} \tag{8}$$

To obtain the reward value, the cosine value is mapped to the value of $[0, 1]$ via a linear transformation. Let R_1 denote the reward value:

$$R_1 = k \times Cos < vec1, vec2 > +b \tag{9}$$

where the k and b is the linear transformation coefficient.

The reward value R_1 is always used as a negative reward to penalize the robot, in this way the greater the angle, the greater the negative reward penalty the robot receives, so that the robot will tend to move towards the target position.

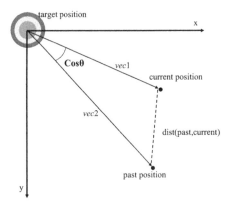

Fig. 3. Cosine distance and Euclidean distance between the past position and the current position.

Let R_2 denotes the reward value calculated from the Euclidean distance:

$$R_2 = C \times distance\_rate \tag{10}$$

where *distance_rate* represents the difference in Euclidean distance between the *current position* and the *past position* from the *target position*, the hyperparameter C is adjusted by experiment and it is set to 500 in this paper.

As a result, the reward function is obtained by combining the cosine distance with the Euclidean distance:

$$R = \begin{cases} -100, \ done \\ \ \ 120, \ arrive \\ R_2 - R_1, \ else \end{cases} \tag{11}$$

According to the Eq. 11, the robot will get a reward value of –100 when it runs into obstacles, and a reward value of 120 when the robot reaches the target position. In other cases, the reward value is determined by both the cosine distance and the Euclidean distance. We adjust the reward value during the experiment according to the experimental results.

3.4   D-DDPG Algorithm

The framework of the D-DDPG algorithm is shown in Fig. 1, in the critic network, the network structure is mapped into two fully connected layers. In this way, the loss function after introducting the dueling network is defined as:

$$J(\omega) = \frac{1}{m} \sum_{t=1}^{m} (y_t - Q(S_t, A_t; \omega, \alpha, \beta))^2 \tag{12}$$

where the Q function is defined by Eq. 13.

$$Q(S_t, A_t; \omega, \alpha, \beta) = A(S_t, A_t; \omega, \alpha) + V(S_t; \omega, \beta) \tag{13}$$

where ω and (α, β) is the parameter of the dueling network. The details of D-DDPG are described in Algorithm 1.

Algorithm 1. The D-DDPG algorithm

1: Initialize Actor net $\mu(S_t|\theta)$ and Critic net $Q(S_t, A_t; \omega, \alpha, \beta)$
2: Initialize replay buffer D
3: **for** each episode $i = 1, 2, 3, ...N$ **do**
4:     Initialize random noise $\mathcal{N}$
5:     Initialize state S_t
6:     **for** each episode $t = 1, 2, 3, ...T$ **do**
7:         Obtain action A_t in the *online_actor* network based on state S_t: $A_t = \mu(S_t; \theta) + \mathcal{N}$
8:         Perform action A_t and obtain the next state S_{t+1}
9:         Obtain the reward value r_t based on the novel reward function
10:        Store (S_t, A_t, r_t, S_{t+1}) in the replay buffer: $D \leftarrow (S_t, A_t, r_t, S_{t+1})$
11:        $S_t = S_{t+1}$
12:        Sample a mini-batch(S_t, A_t, r_t, S_{t+1}) to calculate the target Q value
13:        Update dueling network of *online_critic* by minimizing loss
14:        Update *online_actor* network by policy gradient
15:        Update *target_actor* network and *target_critic* network with soft update
16:     **end for**
17: **end for**

---

4   Experiment Results and Evaluation

In this section, we first describe the setup details for the model training. Next, to evaluate the effectiveness of our proposed method, we provide a thorough evaluation of the D-DDPG by comparing it with the DDPG.

4.1   Experiment Settings

We select Gazebo as simulation platform to creat the complex indoor environments. In the platform, we take Turtlebot3 as mobile robot, which obtains a sparse 10-dimensional range findings through laser scanning device. The linear and angular velocities are used as continuous steering commands to directly control the action of robots, which the maximum linear velocity is 0.5 m/s, and the maximum angular velocity is 1 rad/s.

In addition, we build four two-dimensional indoor environments including Env1, Env2, Env3 and Env4 to test our method, as shown in Fig. 4. The size of Env1 is 8 m × 8 m, in which there is no other obstacles except the walls around. Compared to Env1, Env2 with a size of 12 m × 12 m contains more obstacles including a long wall with a length of 4 m and a number of randomly placed cubes and spheres. In Env3, some cubes and spheres are placed indoors as obstacles and the size of Env3 is same as Env2. Env4 with a size of 8 m × 8 m is unknown to the robot and will serve as our test environment, which contains several cubes and spheres placed as obstacles.

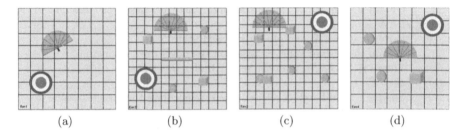

(a)   (b)   (c)   (d)

Fig. 4. Four initial simulation environments. The target position is represented by a target-shaped circle, the spheres and squares represent obstacles. (a) Env1. (b) Env2. (c) Env3. (d) Env4.

In our model, the input contains only the sparse 10-dimensional range findings, therefore our network has no convolutional layers but only fully connected layers, which including three layers in the actor network and six layers in the critic network. As shown in Fig. 2, in the critic network, the branch for calculating the $state\_q$ is composed of two hidden layers, which contain 500 and 400 hidden units, respectively. While the branch for calculating the $action\_q$ contains a hidden layer with 300 hidden units. In each hidden layer, a rectified linear unit (ReLU) activation function is set to avoid gradient explosion and gradient disappearance. In the actor network, there are two hidden layers containing 400 and 300 hidden units, respectively, and each layer is normalized. The output layer contains two units, corresponding linear velocity and angular velocity.

We use the Adam optimizer to train the network. The online network and the target network adopt soft update method, and the decay rate is set to 0.999. The learning rate of the network is set to 0.0001, the batch size of the samples is set to 128, the size of the replay buffer is set to 1×10^5. Each episode is set to a maximum of 500 steps, if the target position is not reached after more than 500 steps, the target position will be reset. When the total number of steps reaches 1×10^4 steps, the average reward value and success rate are recorded once.

4.2   Experimental Results

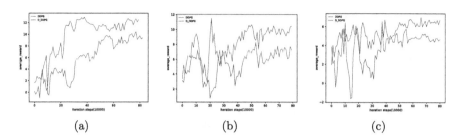

(a)   (b)   (c)

Fig. 5. The average reward value of D-DDPG and original DDPG. (a) Env1. (b) Env2. (c) Env3.

Both the original DDPG and the D-DDPG are trained for 8×10^5 steps in Env1, Env2, and Env3. From Env1 to Env3, the obstacles become increasingly complex. And there are some differences in the placement of the obstacles. As can be seen from Fig. 5(a), the average reward of D-DDPG stabilizes at around 12 in Env1, while the average reward of the original DDPG is stable around 10. Meanwhile, D-DDPG starts to converge when the iteration reaches 2×10^5 steps, while the original DDPG only starts to have a tendency to converge when the iteration reaches 6×10^5 steps. Similarly, in Env2 and Env3, our model can obtain higher average reward value and converge faster than the original DDPG model. This indicates that our algorithm can speed up the convergence of the model with good robustness.

4.3   Experimental Comparison Analysis

To investigate effectiveness of our proposed improvements and the factors influencing the performance of the model, the proposed improvements are experimentally verified separately.

Firstly, we only introduce the dueling network into the original DDPG and the extended model is named as DDPG_with_dueling. The DDPG_with_dueling and the original DDPG are all trained for 8×10^5 steps in Env1, and their average rewards are shown in Fig. 6. It can be found that applying the dueling network can speed up the convergence of the model and obtain higher reward values. This indicates that combining the advantage of action and state value can improve the accuracy of the model for Q estimation, which has a positive effect on the performance of overall model.

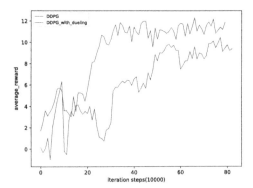

Fig. 6. Comparison of the DDPG_with_dueling and the original DDPG.

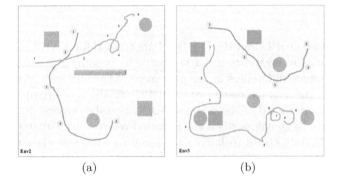

(a)   (b)

Fig. 7. The moving path of the robot in Env2 and Env3. The yellow path represents the robot movement path based on the cosine_DDPG, and the blue path represents the robot movement path based on the original DDPG. The gray objects represent obstacles. (a) Env2. (b) Env3. (Color figure online)

Secondly, we only introduce cosine distance into the original DDPG and the extended model is named as cosine_DDPG. The cosine_DDPG and the original DDPG are iterated for 8×10^5 steps in Env2 and Env3, respectively. Then, we test the trained models in the above two environments. The trajectory tracking of robot is shown in Fig. 7, we can see that the robot based the original DDPG tends to move around the target position rather than directly towards the target position when it is close to the target position, but this phenomenon does not occur when it is based on cosine_DDPG. This indicates that adding negative reward by using cosine distance as a criterion in the reward function can improve the learning efficiency of the robot and achieve an optimized path.

4.4   Generalization Experiment

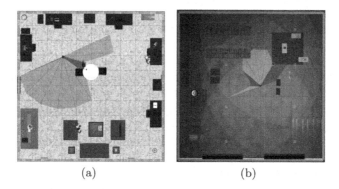

(a)   (b)

Fig. 8. The two realistic simulation scenarios. (a) A small office. (b) A warehouse.

In order to test the effectiveness of our model in an unknown environment, we train our model in Env3, then test the trained model in Env4 and several realistic simulation scenarios. These several realistic simulation scenarios are shown in Fig. 8, representing a small office and a warehouse. In the small office, our robot can deliver documents for office workers; in the warehouse, our robot can help workers move goods. The success rates of test are shown in Table 1.

Table 1. The success rate of our model tested in three scenarios.

Iteration steps(10^5)	1	2	3	4	5	6	7	8
Success rate in Env4	87%	84%	85%	84%	83%	86%	85%	87%
Success rate in office	72%	73%	75%	79%	80%	73%	74%	76%
Success rate warehouse	60%	61%	63%	55%	56%	54%	59%	60%

It can be seen from the Table 1 that our model trained in Env3 can still achieve a success rate of >80% when tested in Env4. In addition, a success rate of >50% can be obtained in the remaining two realistic simulation scenarios. The results show that the D-DDPG can achieve obstacle avoidance and path planning for robots in unknown environments with high success rate, and showed good path planning ability in several real simulation scenarios. It indicates that the D-DDPG has good generalization performance.

5   Conclusion

In this paper, we propose the D-DDPG for path planning of robots, which dueling network are used to split the *Q-value* into two parts to improve the estimation accuracy of *Q-value*. In addition, we propose a novel reward function to make the exploration goal of robot clearer by combining cosine distance with Euclidean distance. Experimental results show that our proposed method achieves higher average reward value and better convergence efficiency compared to the original DDPG, and it shows good obstacle avoidance and optimal path capabilities in unknown environment. However, there are still some aspects for improvement, such as we use ten-dimensional laser ranging findings as input and providing a low-cost solution for robot path planning with multi-range sensors in indoor scenes, but it is obvious that the advantage of it is not as great when the application scenario is a large-scale complex environment, in which we need more information about the environment.

In future work, in order to make our model more adaptable in complex environments, the picture information of the environment will be used as input. And we will evaluate the performance of the D-DDPG for path planning in real world.

Acknowledgement. This work is supported by the National Natural Science Foundation of China (61976127).

References

1. Bai, N., Wang, Z., Meng, F.: A stochastic attention CNN model for rumor stance classification. IEEE Access **8**, 80771–80778 (2020). https://doi.org/10.1109/ACCESS.2020.2990770
2. Bjørlykhaug, E., Egeland, O.: Vision system for quality assessment of robotic cleaning of fish processing plants using CNN. IEEE Access **7**, 71675–71685 (2019). https://doi.org/10.1109/ACCESS.2019.2919656
3. Capisani, L.M., Ferrara, A.: Trajectory planning and second-order sliding mode motion/interaction control for robot manipulators in unknown environments. IEEE Trans. Industr. Electron. **59**(8), 3189–3198 (2012). https://doi.org/10.1109/TIE.2011.2160510
4. Chen, Y., Bai, G., Zhan, Y., Hu, X., Liu, J.: Path planning and obstacle avoiding of the USV based on improved ACO-APF hybrid algorithm with adaptive early-warning. IEEE Access **9**, 40728–40742 (2021). https://doi.org/10.1109/ACCESS.2021.3062375
5. Chen, Y., Li, H., Liu, F.: An adaptive routing algorithm based on multiple-path-finding dijkstra's and q-learning algorithm in silicon photonic interconnects on chip. In: 2020 IEEE 20th International Conference on Communication Technology (ICCT), pp. 117–120 (2020). https://doi.org/10.1109/ICCT50939.2020.9295898
6. Cui, Z., Wang, Y.: UAV path planning based on multi-layer reinforcement learning technique. IEEE Access **9**, 59486–59497 (2021). https://doi.org/10.1109/ACCESS.2021.3073704
7. Drolshagen, S., Pfingsthorn, M., Gliesche, P., Hein, A.: Acceptance of industrial collaborative robots by people with disabilities in sheltered workshops. Front. Robot. AI **7**, 173 (2021)
8. Er, M.J., Deng, C.: Obstacle avoidance of a mobile robot using hybrid learning approach. IEEE Trans. Industr. Electron. **52**(3), 898–905 (2005). https://doi.org/10.1109/TIE.2005.847576

9. Fernandez, S.R.: Accuracy enhancement for robotic assembly of large-scale parts in the aerospace industry (2020)
10. Guo, K., Pan, Y., Yu, H.: Composite learning robot control with friction compensation: a neural network-based approach. IEEE Trans. Industr. Electron. **66**(10), 7841–7851 (2019). https://doi.org/10.1109/TIE.2018.2886763
11. Hasselt, H.V., Guez, A., Silver, D.: Deep reinforcement learning with double q-learning. Computer Science (2015)
12. Henkemans, O., Pal, S., Werner, I., Neerincx, M.A., Looije, R.: Learning with charlie: a robot buddy for children with diabetes. In: the Companion of the 2017 ACM/IEEE International Conference (2017)
13. Hessel, M., et al.: Rainbow: combining improvements in deep reinforcement learning (2017)
14. Khatib, O.: Real-time obstacle avoidance for manipulators and mobile robots. In: Proceedings. 1985 IEEE International Conference on Robotics and Automation, vol. 2, pp. 500–505 (1985). https://doi.org/10.1109/ROBOT.1985.1087247
15. Lee, S.B., Hun Yoo, S.: Design of the companion robot interaction for supporting major tasks of the elderly. In: 2017 14th International Conference on Ubiquitous Robots and Ambient Intelligence (URAI), pp. 655–659 (2017). https://doi.org/10.1109/URAI.2017.7992695
16. Li, Y., Zhang, D., Yin, F., Zhang, Y.: Cleaning robot operation decision based on causal reasoning and attribute learning*. In: 2020 IEEE/RSJ International Conference on Intelligent Robots and Systems (IROS), pp. 6878–6885 (2020). https://doi.org/10.1109/IROS45743.2020.9340930
17. Lillicrap, T.P., et al.: Continuous control with deep reinforcement learning. Computer Science (2015)
18. Luo, M., Hou, X., Yang, J.: Surface optimal path planning using an extended dijkstra algorithm. IEEE Access **8**, 147827–147838 (2020). https://doi.org/10.1109/ACCESS.2020.3015976
19. dos Santos, M.G., Petrillo, F.: Towards automated acceptance testing for industrial robots (2021)
20. Sutton, R., Barto, A.: Reinforcement Learning: An Introduction. An Introduction, Reinforcement Learning (1998)
21. Tai, L., Paolo, G., Liu, M.: Virtual-to-real deep reinforcement learning: continuous control of mobile robots for mapless navigation. In: 2017 IEEE/RSJ International Conference on Intelligent Robots and Systems (IROS), pp. 31–36 (2017). https://doi.org/10.1109/IROS.2017.8202134
22. Tang, G., Tang, C., Claramunt, C., Hu, X., Zhou, P.: Geometric a-star algorithm: an improved a-star algorithm for agv path planning in a port environment. IEEE Access **9**, 59196–59210 (2021). https://doi.org/10.1109/ACCESS.2021.3070054
23. Wang, Y.H., Li, T., Lin, C.J.: Backward q-learning: The combination of Sarsa algorithm and q-learning. Eng. Appl. Artif. Intell. **26**(9), 2184–2193 (2013)
24. Watkins, C., Dayan, P.: Technical note: Q-learning. Mach. Learn. **8**(3–4), 279–292 (1992)
25. Xin, J., Zhao, H., Liu, D., Li, M.: Application of deep reinforcement learning in mobile robot path planning. In: 2017 Chinese Automation Congress (CAC), pp. 7112–7116 (2017). https://doi.org/10.1109/CAC.2017.8244061
26. Yang, R., Cheng, L.: Path planning of restaurant service robot based on a-star algorithms with updated weights. In: 2019 12th International Symposium on Computational Intelligence and Design (ISCID), vol. 1, pp. 292–295 (2019). https://doi.org/10.1109/ISCID.2019.00074

27. Yang, Y., Li, J., Peng, L.: Multirobot path planning based on a deep reinforcement learning DQN algorithm. CAAI Trans. Intell. Technol. **5**(3), 177–183 (2020)
28. Yong, T., Wei, H., Wang, T., Chen, D.: A multi-layered interaction architecture for elderly companion robot. In: International Conference on Intelligent Robotics & Applications (2008)
29. Yuan, J., Yang, S., Cai, J.: Consistent path planning for on-axle-hitching multi-steering trailer systems. IEEE Trans. Industr. Electron. **65**(12), 9625–9634 (2018). https://doi.org/10.1109/TIE.2018.2823691
30. Zhao, T., Li, H., Dian, S.: Multi-robot path planning based on improved artificial potential field and fuzzy inference system. J. Intell. Fuzzy Syst. **39**(5), 7621–7637 (2020)
31. Zhu, D.D., Sun, J.Q.: A new algorithm based on dijkstra for vehicle path planning considering intersection attribute. IEEE Access **9**, 19761–19775 (2021). https://doi.org/10.1109/ACCESS.2021.3053169

A Fully Dynamic Context Guided Reasoning and Reconsidering Network for Video Captioning

Xia Feng[1,2], Xinyu He[1,2], Rui Huang[1], and Caihua Liu[1,2(✉)]

[1] College of Computer Science and Technology, Civil Aviation University of China, Tianjin, China
{xfeng,2019052045,rhuang,chliu}@cauc.edu.cn
[2] Information Technology Base of Civil Aviation Administration of China, CAUC, 2898 Jinbei Road, Dongli District, Tianjin 300300, China

Abstract. Visual reasoning and reconsidering capabilities are instinctively executed alternately as people watch a video and attempt to describe its contents with natural language. Inspired by this, a novel network that joints fully dynamic context guided reasoning and reconsidering is proposed in this paper. Specifically, an elaborate reconsidering module referred to as the reconsiderator is employed for rethinking and sharpening the preliminary results of stepwise reasoning from coarse to fine, thereby generating a higher quality description. And in turn, the reasoning capability of the network can be further boosted under the guidance of the context information summarized during reconsidering. Extensive experiments on two public benchmarks demonstrate that our approach is pretty competitive with the state-of-the-art methods.

Keywords: Video captioning · Fully dynamic context guidance · Stepwise reasoning · Reconsidering

1 Introduction

The video captioning task aiming to describe video contents with natural language, generally a sentence, attracts increasing interests from both computer vision and natural language processing communities. It has been widely used in varieties of areas such as human-robot interaction [15], assisting the visually-impaired [27], visual question answering [8] and so on. Formidable challenges in video captioning are mainly posed by diverse scenes, various interaction relations and intricate causal relationships.

When describing video contents, human tend to reason step by step according to perceived visual information at first. And then, each tentative reasoning

This work was supported by the Natural Science Foundation of Tianjin (No. 20JCQNJC00720) and the Fundamental Research Funds for the Central Universities, CAUC (No. 3122021052).

result will be ruminated over and over again in mind to ensure its validity. For instance, after the action *"slice"* is recognized, the *"slice"* will be refined to *"slicing"* depending on the previous words *"a woman is"* in human brains. Lastly, a fluent and grammatical sentence *"a woman is slicing an onion"* is generated via stepwise reasoning and reconsidering. Compared to humans, most existing video captioning models or deep models extremely adept at recognizing targets and lack the ability to perform visual reasoning over time, let alone further in-depth rethinking.

Recently, some research [22,33] exerts efforts to raise reasoning capacity for visual captioning models. [22] utilized a so-called neural module networks [1] to achieve stepwise reasoning and generate the description for a video clip word by word. They devised three neural modules guided by static averaging global features for executing visual reasoning. One of the preliminary reasoning results from all the neural modules was then sampled as the determined reasoning result and was used for emitting word. However, it has already been proved that the simple mean-pooling method can result in chaotic feature representations [32] and the contextual information involved in the static guidance is deficient as well as not comprehensive enough. Clearly, the model reasoning performance is inclined to degrade significantly under static and inaccurate guidance. Additionally, they directly leveraged the preliminary reasoning result to generate word and neglected the indispensable reconsidering part.

In this paper, we introduce to guide stepwise reasoning process fully dynamic context which changes from time to time. To make up for the omission of reconsidering, we design a sophisticated reconsiderator to polish the preliminary reasoning result from coarse to fine. More accurate semantic feature representations thus can be provided for emitting words and contribute to diminish the gap between visual reasoning and captions generating. Note that compared to the global averaging features derived from performing mean-pooling operation on visual feature representations, the fully dynamic context comprises more precise and richer historical information produced during reconsidering, which is capable of further augmenting the model reasoning capability.

Overall, the main contributions of our work are summarized as follows:

1) We propose a fully dynamic context guided **re**asoning and **re**considering network abbreviated as BiReNet for video captioning. It possesses both capabilities of stepwise reasoning and reconsidering simultaneously. A powerful reconsidering module called the reconsiderator is devised for refining the preliminary reasoning result to generate higher quality captions.
2) More accurate and holistic dynamic context characterized in reconsidering stage is introduced to guide stepwise reasoning process, strengthening the model reasoning ability.
3) Extensive experimental results indicate that our model outperforms the state-of-the-art methods on MSVD dataset and is quite competitive on MSR-VTT dataset.

2   Related Work

Early approaches to video captioning mainly are template-based [12,23]. They first identify objects, actions and attributes in videos with hand-crafted features respectively. And then these fragments are mapped into corresponding components in predefined syntactic templates. However, manufactured features and rigid templates are prone to generate descriptions with terrible fluency and unsatisfactory quality.

Deep sequence learning methods are proposed to replace the template-based ones with the booming development and remarkable improvement of deep learning. The encoder-decoder framework such as CNN-RNN or RNN-RNN has been the prominent architecture for video captioning. [25] performs simple averaging on visual features extracted from CNN and decodes it to captions with a RNN language model. [26] utilizes a two-layer stacked LSTM to summarize temporal structure in videos and handles input/output of variable length. To well explore the spatial-temporal dependencies in videos, a large number of approaches incorporate attention mechanisms into encoder or decoder. [32] proposes a temporal attention mechanism for assigning different weights over frame features to overcome temporal crash caused by indiscriminative mean pooling. [6] devises a motion guided attention mechanism for modeling spatial information. Recently, prior knowledge such as Part-of-Speech (POS) tags, topics and knowledge graph are applied in video captioning models to generate stylized and detailed sentences. Besides visual modality, audio or textual modalities are fused in [20,31] to complement each other.

More Recent, [7,14] introduce the deliberation network in neural machine translation (NMT) to visual captioning tasks, in which more precise semantic information is able to be acquired by refining the hidden states of the decoder. [22] holds human may have the reasoning process of locating subjects, inferring predicates and identifying objects in order when generating descriptions for videos. Thus, they adopt neural module networks on video captioning for imitating human-like stepwise reasoning and improving the model explainability. However, they take static mean-pooling global visual features as a guide for visual reasoning and directly have the preliminary reasoning result decoded without any necessary reconsidering. We argue that it is irrational to guide reasoning process using the static averaging global features since its insufficient contextual information and negative impact on temporal cues underlying videos. In contrast, we leverage more accurate and fully dynamic context to supervise the reasoning process. And motivated by [7,14], we propose a unified video captioning network that integrates stepwise reasoning and reconsidering. The preliminary reasoning result can be polished from coarse to fine with an elaborate reconsiderator.

3   Method

3.1   Overall Framework

The overall framework of our video captioning network (BiReNet) is illustrated in Fig. 1. It consists of two components, *i.e.*, **a)** an encoder with reasoning and

b) a decoder with reconsidering. Specifically, the reasoning portion **c)** of the encoder including three distinct fully dynamic context guided reasoning modules and a module selector, as the name implies, is responsible for step-by-step reasoning like humans. The reconsidering module **d)** of the decoder serves as a reconsiderator for rethinking the preliminary reasoning result on the top of a fundamental decoder. We describe the encoder with fully dynamic context guided reasoning in Sect. 3.2. The decoder with a dedicated reconsiderator is presented in Sect. 3.3. In Sect. 3.4, we detail the training process.

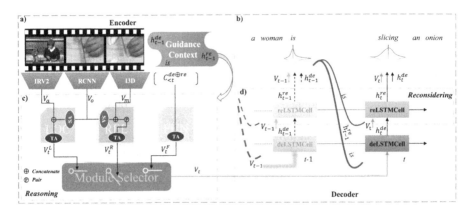

Fig. 1. The proposed BiReNet consists of **a)** an encoder with **c)** reasoning and **b)** a decoder with **d)** reconsidering. Firstly, the appearance features V_a, object features V_o and motion features V_m of an input video sequence are extracted from the pretrained 2D CNN, RCNN and 3D CNN. Secondly, three reasoning modules, **LOC**, **REL** and **FUN**, perform spatial-temporal visual reasoning on these features and the previous cell states of decoder part under fully dynamic context guidance. Thirdly, one preliminary reasoning result is sampled by a module selector and decoded by a fundamental decoder. Finally, a reconsiderator is applied to polish the preliminary reasoning result from coarse to fine for emitting a word.

3.2 Encoder with Fully Dynamic Context Guided Reasoning

Given an input video sequence, the appearance features V_a, object features V_o and motion features V_m are extracted from the pretrained 2D CNN, RCNN and 3D CNN respectively. Concretely, the InceptionResNetV2 (IRV2) [21] trained on ILSVRC-2012-CLS [19] is used to extract V_a, the Faster-RCNN [18] is adopted to extract 36 region features per frame to obtain V_o and the I3D [4] trained on Kinetics [11] is applied to extract V_m. Following [22], we employ three spatial-temporal reasoning modules which are responsible for generating words of distinct POS information, *i.e.*, **LOC** for generating visual words, **REL** for generating action words and **FUN** for generating functional words in our network. The classical additive attention [2] is performed on space and time dimensions, formulating the spatial attention $\mathbf{SA}(\mathbf{V}, \mathbf{q})$ and the temporal attention $\mathbf{TA}(\mathbf{V}, \mathbf{q})$ respectively. $\mathbf{V}$ and $\mathbf{q}$ denotes values and queries of the attention.

Different from plainly applying static averaging global features to guide the stepwise reasoning process in [22], for time t, we render a guidance context G made up of the word y_{t-1}, the hidden state of the fundamental decoder h_{t-1}^{de} and the hidden state of the reconsiderator h_{t-1}^{re} generated at last timestep as the guidance for visual reasoning (see Eq. (1), where [;] denotes concatenate operation and $E[\cdot]$ denotes embedding matrix). To this end, we take the guidance context G as the query while the extracted feature representations or the previous cell states of decoder part as the value for the spatial and temporal attention. Note that the guidance context G not only is filled with more accurate and informative context, but also dynamically evolves over time.

$$G = [h_{t-1}^{re}; h_{t-1}^{de}; E[y_{t-1}]] \tag{1}$$

Relying on the fully dynamic guidance context G, the preliminary reasoning results, *i.e.*, V_t^L, V_t^R and V_t^M, are produced by corresponding reasoning modules. Specifically, in **LOC** module, the object features V_o are first fed into the spatial attention **SA**. Then, the appearance features V_a concatenated with the prior result are fed into the temporal attention **TA**. Finally, the preliminary reasoning result V_t^L is acquired:

$$V_t^L = \mathbf{LOC}\,(V_a, V_o, G) = \mathbf{TA}\,([\mathbf{SA}\,(V_o, G)\,;V_a], G) \tag{2}$$

In **REL** module, the motion features V_m rather than the appearance features V_a are used for characterizing action information:

$$Cate = [\mathbf{SA}\,(V_o, G)\,;V_m] \tag{3}$$

$$V_t^R = \mathbf{REL}\,(V_m, V_o, G) = \mathbf{TA}\,(\mathbf{Pair}[Cate_i; Cate_j], G) \tag{4}$$

where a pairwise operation $\mathbf{Pair}[Cate_i; Cate_j]$ concatenates all of the prior concatenated results $Cate$ in pairs.

In **FUN** module, the previous cell states of the fundamental decoder and the recosniderator, *i.e.*, $C_{<t}^{de}$ and $C_{<t}^{re}$, are fed into the temporal attention **TA**:

$$C_{<t}^{de} = [c_1^{de}, c_2^{de}, \cdots, c_{t-1}^{de}], C_{<t}^{re} = [c_1^{re}, c_2^{re}, \cdots, c_{t-1}^{re}] \tag{5}$$

$$V_t^F = \mathbf{FUN}\,(C_{<t}^{de}, C_{<t}^{re}, G) = \mathbf{TA}\,([C_{<t}^{de}; C_{<t}^{re}], G) \tag{6}$$

For performing stepwise reasoning, a module selector is used to discretely sample one of the preliminary reasoning results and takes it as input to the decoder part, which is achieved by a scoring function [22] and the Gumbel Approximation strategy [10]. As it is not the core content in this work, more details please refer to [10,22]. In short, the determined preliminary reasoning result V_t is selected by a one-hot decision vector S_t:

$$V_t = S_t \otimes [V_t^L, V_t^R, V_t^F] \tag{7}$$

where $\otimes$ denotes the inner product. In practical, S_t also represents the POS tags predicted for the current word with the scoring function since the reasoning modules are corresponds to specific POS tags, *e.g.*, $S_t = [0, 1, 0]$ indicates the **REL** module is selected and V_t^R is the determined preliminary reasoning result.

3.3   Decoder with Reconsidering

The decoder part consists of a fundamental decoder and a reconsiderator, both of which are the long short term memory (LSTM) networks (denoted as **deLSTM** and **reLSTM** respectively). At time t, the fundamental decoder **deLSTM** takes the preliminary reasoning result V_t, the hidden state of the reconsiderator h_{t-1}^{re} and the word y_{t-1} generated at last timestep as input:

$$h_t^{de}, c_t^{de} = \mathbf{deLSTM}\left([V_t; h_{t-1}^{re}; E[y_{t-1}]], \left(h_{t-1}^{de}, c_{t-1}^{de}\right)\right) \tag{8}$$

Unlike immediately emitting a word using the hidden state of the fundamental decoder h_t^{de} in previous works, we devise a reconsiderator **reLSTM** on the basis of the fundamental decoder **deLSTM**. It is defined as follows:

$$h_t^{re}, c_t^{re} = \mathbf{reLSTM}\left([V_t; h_t^{de}; E[y_{t-1}]], \left(h_{t-1}^{re}, c_{t-1}^{re}\right)\right) \tag{9}$$

where the preliminary reasoning result V_t is fed into the reconsiderator again for further sharpening according to the current timestep hidden state of the fundamental decoder h_t^{de}. It is noteworthy that the preliminary reasoning result V_t actually passes through the fundamental decoder **deLSTM** and the reconsiderator **reLSTM** in a residual connection manner, which allows our network to be endowed with the reconsidering capacity based on stepwise reasoning. Besides, the hidden state of the reconsiderator h_t^{re} is more accurate and full of sufficient historical information.

For emitting the word at time t, a *softmax* function is employed to get the probability distribution of y_t:

$$P_{y_t} = softmax\left(W^T[V_t; h_t^{re}; h_t^{de}; G]\right) \tag{10}$$

where W^T denotes the learnable parameters.

3.4   Training

Cross-Entropy Loss. The cross entropy loss is the most commonly used loss function for generating sentences. Given the i-th video clip in the training dataset $\mathcal{D}$ with N samples and its ground truth caption $\hat{\mathbf{y}}_i = [y_{i1}^*, y_{i2}^*, \cdots, y_{il_i}^*]$, the cross entropy loss for the entire training dataset $\mathcal{D}$ is formulated as:

$$\mathcal{L}_{ce} = -\frac{1}{N}\sum_{i=1}^{N}\sum_{t=1}^{l_i} \log\left(P_{y_{it}}\left(y_{it}^*\right)\right) \tag{11}$$

where l_i denotes the length of the caption and y_{it} is the word emitted at timestep t for the i-th video.

Kullback-Leibler Divergence Loss. For maintaining the syntactic structure, the Part-of-Speech (POS) tags are applied to supervise module selection process. Concretely, the POS tags $\hat{\mathbf{s}}_i = [s_{i1}^*, s_{i2}^*, \cdots, s_{il_i}^*]$ of the ground truth caption $\hat{\mathbf{y}}_i = [y_1^*, y_2^*, \cdots, y_{l_i}^*]$ are labeled by Spacy Tagging Tool[1]. The **LOC** module corresponds to adjectives and nouns. The **REL** module corresponds to verbs. The **FUN** module corresponds to the rest POS tags. The Kullback Leibler (KL) divergence loss is adopted to force the module selection vector S_{it} (in Sect. 3.2) and the one-hot encoded POS tag $\Theta\left(s_{it}^*\right)$ to be as close as possible:

$$\mathcal{L}_{kl} = -\frac{1}{N} \sum_{i=1}^{N} \sum_{t=1}^{l_i} \mathbf{KL}\left(S_{it} || \Theta\left(s_{it}^*\right)\right) \tag{12}$$

Therefore, in training stage, the objective of our network is to minimize the entire loss $\mathcal{L}$:

$$\mathcal{L} = \mathcal{L}_{ce} + \lambda \mathcal{L}_{kl} \tag{13}$$

where λ is a trade-off parameter and is set to 0.1 empirically.

4 Experiments

4.1 Datasets and Settings

We evaluate our proposed method on the two most popular video captioning benchmark datasets, Microsoft Video Description (MSVD) [5] and MSR Video-to-Text (MSR-VTT) [30], using the widely used standard automatic evaluation metrics, BLEU-4 [16], METEOR [3], ROUGE-L [13] and CIDEr [24]. The MSVD dataset contains 1,970 YouTube video clips. Each video clip has roughly 41 English captions and describes a single activity in 10 s to 25 s. The MSR-VTT is a large-scale dataset which contains 10,000 video clips from 20 categories and each video clip is annotated with 20 English descriptions on average. We follow the standard training/validation/testing samples split settings in prior works [14, 17, 20, 22, 29], *i.e.*, 1,200/100/670 for MSVD and 6,513/497/2,990 for MSR-VTT.

For each video clip, 26 equally spaced frames are uniformly sampled. Each caption is truncated or zero-padded to 26 words. We convert all captions to lower case, remove punctuations and filter rare words. The numbers of unique words are 7,531 for MSVD and 9,732 for MSR-VTT. The hidden size of the LSTM is set to 512 for MSVD and 1,300 for MSR-VTT, respectively. The Adam optimizer with an initial learning rate 1e–4 is used for training. Our experiments are performed on a device with a single NVIDIA RTX5000 GPU and the batch size on both datasets is set to 8. The beam search with a beam size of 2 is employed to generate the final captions during inference.

---

[1] https://spacy.io.

4.2   Quantitative Results

We compare our method with current state-of-the-art methods in video caption-ing on MSVD and MSR-VTT dataset. The state-of-the-art methods we choose to compare and their characteristics are as follows: POS-CG [28] and Mixture [9] utilize the POS information of captions. RecNet [29] and CVI-DelNet [14] adopt a two-layer stacked LSTM. MARN [17] exploits visual context from other videos with a memory mechanism. SGN [20] takes the partially decoded caption as textual modality cues. RMN [22] is our direct baseline and is described earlier.

Table 1 shows the comparison results on MSVD dataset. We observe that our BiReNet achieves the best performance and outperforms all of the state-of-the-art methods in multiple metrics, which is mainly attributed to the proposed fully dynamic context guidance and the reconsidering for preliminary reasoning results based on stepwise reasoning. Compared to the baseline model, BiReNet not only outperforms it by 0.6%, 0.6% in terms of METEOR and ROUGE-L scores respectively, but also outperforms it by a large margin of 3.7% in terms of the CIDEr score. It is noteworthy that the CIDEr score is devised for captioning task specifically and is believed to more consistent with human judgement. BiReNet achieves the same scores with the baseline model on BLEU-4 that is designed to evaluate the matching degree between generated captions and references. It is reasonable because depending on the proposed fully dynamic context and the sophisticated reconsiderator, BiReNet tends to generate more expressive and detailed captions compared to the corresponding references. On the whole, the quantitative results in Table 1 strongly suggest the superiority of our proposed method.

Table 1. Comparisons with the state-of-the-art methods on MSVD dataset in terms of BLEU-4, METEOR, ROUGE-L and CIDEr scores (%).

Models	BLEU-4	METEOR	ROUGE-L	CIDEr
RecNet [29]	52.3	34.1	69.8	80.3
POS-CG [28]	52.5	34.1	71.3	92.0
Mixture [9]	52.8	36.1	71.8	87.8
MARN [17]	48.6	35.1	71.9	92.2
CVI-DelNet [14]	53.8	35.1	72.4	94.5
SGN [20]	52.8	35.5	72.9	94.3
Our Baseline: RMN [22]	**54.6**	36.5	73.4	94.4
Our BiReNet	**54.6**	**37.1**	**74.0**	**98.1**

Experimental results on MSR-VTT dataset is shown in Table 2. We can see that our network outperforms the reproduced baseline model by 0.9%, 0.1%, 0.8% and 0.7% in terms of BLEU-4, METEOR, ROUGE-L and CIDEr scores. It is interesting to observe that our network significantly outperforms the Mix-ture [9] model on MSVD dataset while slightly inferior to it on MSR-VTT dataset. To figure out the reason behind it, we investigate the Mixture model, delve into MSR-VTT dataset and come up with the following insights: 1)The scale of MSR-VTT is larger than MSVD and each caption in MSR-VTT is more longer. Its visual words and action words are richer and more diverse. In addition, there are a large number of other Part-of-Speech words inside the corpus of MSR-VTT. 2)In Mixture, the top 24 most frequent POS tags are adopted for training, whereas we divide all POS tags into three groups, $i.e.$, adjectives and nouns, verbs and the others, and leverage them for assisting our network to maintain the syntactic structure. Compared to Mixture in which the POS information is more granular and is of importance for generating descriptions, the POS tags merely paly an auxiliary role in our network; 3)During inference, the beam size set in Mixture is 5. Typically, the metric scores tend to fluctuate with the beam size. For making a fair comparison with the baseline model, the beam size in our experiments is set to 2.

It is noteworthy that even though the batch size adopted in all of our experiments is 8 instead of 48 in the original baseline model due to computational power limitation, our network still acquires quite competitive results and achieves nearly state-of-the-art performance. More POS tags information and versatile visual interactive relationships in videos will be focused on and explored for MSR-VTT dataset in our future work.

Table 2. Comparisons with the state-of-the-art methods on MSR-VTT dataset in terms of BLEU-4, METEOR, ROUGE-L and CIDEr scores (%). ∗ denotes our reproduced result with batch size 8.

Models	BLEU-4	METEOR	ROUGE-L	CIDEr
RecNet [29]	39.1	26.6	59.3	42.7
POS-CG [28]	42.0	28.2	61.6	48.7
Mixture [9]	**42.3**	**29.7**	**62.8**	49.1
MARN [17]	40.4	28.1	60.7	47.1
CVI-DelNet [14]	41.6	28.4	61.3	48.5
SGN [20]	40.8	28.3	60.8	**49.5**
Our Baseline: RMN∗	40.1	28.1	60.5	47.4
Our BiReNet	41.0	28.2	61.3	48.1

4.3   Ablation Study

To evaluate the effectiveness of our proposed fully dynamic context guided reasoning module and the dedicated reconsiderator, we conduct ablation studies on MSVD dataset with diverse settings networks and the comparison results of these ablated networks are illustrated in Table 3. Note that without all of the proposed components, our network degrades to the baseline model RMN [22] whose results are shown in the first row of Table 3.

Table 3. Ablation study on MSVD dataset in terms of BLEU-4, METEOR, ROUGE-L and CIDEr scores (%). RS denotes reasoning modules in encoder and RC denotes reconsidering part in decoder.

Models	BLEU-4	METEOR	ROUGE-L	CIDEr
Enc(RS)-Dec:RMN [22]	**54.6**	36.5	73.4	94.4
Enc(RS*)-Dec	54.4	36.8	73.3	95.6
Enc(RS)-Dec(RC)	54.1	36.3	73.6	97.2
Enc(RS**)-Dec(RC): Our BiReNet	**54.6**	**37.1**	**74.0**	**98.1**

To verify fully dynamic context is better than the static averaging global feature representations for guiding reasoning process, Enc(RS*)-Dec exploits fully dynamic context made up of the hidden states of decoder and the word generated at last timestep rather than static averaging global features as queries of spatial and temporal attentions to guide the stepwise reasoning. It is observed that Enc(RS*)-Dec outperforms the baseline model by 0.3% and 0.6% in terms of METEOR and CIDEr metrics respectively, which demonstrates the benefits as well as great potential of the fully dynamic context guidance.

Enc(RS)-Dec(RC) empowers the baseline model with the dedicated reconsiderator for polishing and rethinking the preliminary reasoning results. We can see that Enc(RS)-Dec(RC) performs superiorly to the baseline model on ROUGE-L and CIDEr metrics when the reconsiderator is introduced. Especially, a considerable increase, 2.8%, is obtained on CIDEr score, which implies that the reconsidering for preliminary reasoning results is necessary and useful for improving performance.

Enc(RS**)-Dec(RC) is our proposed BiReNet, where the fully dynamic context and the reconsiderator are integrated on the basis of the baseline model. Note that in addition to the hidden states of the fundamental decoder and the word generated at last timestep, the fully dynamic context within BiReNet also includes the hidden states of the reconsiderator which are more precise and filled with historical information. We can find that BiReNet makes further noticeable improvements on multiple metrics and achieves new state-of-the-art performance. This is mainly due to the following facts: 1) The preliminary reasoning results in BiReNet can be refined from coarse to fine using the elaborate reconsiderator for generating more expressive captions; 2) More accurate and fully dynamic context characterized during reconsidering is employed to guide the reasoning modules to generate more rational reasoning results; 3) BiReNet is capable of performing stepwise reasoning and reconsidering alternately and enables them to facilitate each other for boosting overall performance.

4.4   Qualitative Results

In order to intuitively perceive the superior quality of the captions generated by our proposed BiReNet, we present several representative examples in Fig. 2. In

(a)
GT: an elephant is eating
Baseline: an elephant is walking
Ours: an elephant is eating

(b)
GT: two men are dancing
Baseline: a man is dancing
Ours: two men are dancing

(c)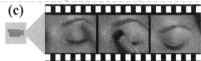
GT: a girl doing some sort of makeup
above her eyes
Baseline: a dog is making something
Ours: a woman is doing some sort
of makeup with a brush

(d)
GT: a man is doing stunts on a
motorcycle
Baseline: a man is riding a motorcycle
Ours: a man is doing stunts on a
motorcycle

(e)
GT: a man spoons sauce into a bowl
of spaghetti
Baseline: a man is cooking
Ours: a man is stirring some sauce
in a bowl

(f)
GT: a panda is laying down
Baseline: a panda is laying on the
ground
Ours: a panda is lying on the ground
and looking around

(g)
GT: the person is playing the rabbit
Baseline: a person is holding a piece
of food
Ours: a person is playing with a rat

(h)
GT: a man is putting sliced cucumbers
in a pitcher
Baseline: a man is removing
something
Ours: a man is talking about how to
make something

Fig. 2. Visualization examples for qualitative comparisons between BiReNet and the baseline model (better viewed in color). As can be seen, our proposed BiReNet is able to generate more accurate, more detailed and more descriptive captions than that generated by the baseline model, even better than the references. (Color figure online)

Fig. 2(a), the baseline model generates the wrong action word "*walking*" while BiReNet successfully infers the right verb term "*eating*". Similarly, BiReNet identifies "*two men*" instead of "*a man*" in baseline model in Fig. 2(b). It implies that more accurate descriptions can be obtained through reconisdering based on stepwise reasoning. Note that the baseline model depicts the video clip in Fig. 2(c) in a totally wrong manner, whereas our method is able to describe the video contents correctly. It demonstrates that the preliminary reasoning results need to be reconfirmed to ensure its validity, otherwise current step reasoning error may incur a collapsed sentence. In Fig. 2(d), the baseline model fails to capture the core video content and just generates *"a man is riding a motorcycle"*. In contrast, BiReNet can recognize the man actually is doing stunts rather than riding his motorcycle.

Besides, we can easily observe that the descriptions produced by BiReNet is more detailed than that generated by the baseline model. For instance, the rough caption *"a man is cooking"* is produced by the baseline model in Fig. 2(e), while BiReNet depicts the video with a detailed caption *"a man is stirring some sauce in a bowl"*. We also provide some interesting examples deserved to pay attention. In Fig. 2(f), both the reference and the baseline model miss the fine-grained action *"look around"* made by the panda. By contrast, BiReNet not only identifies the panda is lying on the ground, but also captures the subtle motion of the panda's eyes and head. The baseline model generates *"a person is holding a piece of food"* in Fig. 2(g), which apparently is a logical failure and is irrational. In fact, the hamster is holding a piece of food and the core content inside the video is that a person is playing with the hamster. BiReNet succeeds in capturing the key information expressed by the video. In Fig. 2(h), the baseline model produces a rough caption *"a man is removing something"*. Although reference makes a further step to describe it in detail, the man in the video indeed is explaining how to make a drink. The caption *"a man is talking about how to make something"* generated by BiReNet is more precise.

Overall, these visualization examples demonstrate our proposed BiReNet is capable of yielding more accurate, more detailed and more comprehensive captions. Meanwhile, the above observations validate the introduced fully dynamic context guidance and the dedicated reconsiderator significantly contribute to the quality of descriptions.

5   Conclusion

In this paper, we propose a novel fully dynamic context guided reasoning and reconsidering network (BiReNet) which is equipped with reconsidering capacity based on stepwise reasoning for video captioning. Specifically, to address reconsidering omitting, a dedicated reconsiderator is devised to rethink and polish the preliminary reasoning result rendered by stepwise reasoning modules. After reconsidering, the context filled with more accurate and dynamic historical information is leveraged to guide the reasoning process for further enhancing reasoning performance. The stepwise reasoning and reconsidering are executed alternately and facilitate each other to generate higher quality descriptions. Extensive experiments demonstrate that our proposed BiReNet achieves state-of-the-art performances on MSVD dataset and reaches quite competitive performances on MSR-VTT dataset.

References

1. Andreas, J., Rohrbach, M., Darrell, T., Klein, D.: Neural module networks. In: Proceedings of the IEEE Conference on Computer Vision and Pattern Recognition (CVPR) (2016)
2. Bahdanau, D., Cho, K., Bengio, Y.: Neural machine translation by jointly learning to align and translate. In: ICLR (2015)
3. Banerjee, S., Lavie, A.: Meteor: an automatic metric for MT evaluation with improved correlation with human judgments. In: Proceedings of the ACL Workshop on Intrinsic and Extrinsic Evaluation Measures for Machine Translation and/or Summarization, pp. 65–72 (2005)
4. Carreira, J., Zisserman, A.: Quo vadis, action recognition? a new model and the kinetics dataset. In: Proceedings of the IEEE Conference on Computer Vision and Pattern Recognition (CVPR) (2017)
5. Chen, D., Dolan, W.: Collecting highly parallel data for paraphrase evaluation. In: Proceedings of the 49th Annual Meeting of the Association for Computational Linguistics: Human Language Technologies, pp. 190–200 (2011)
6. Chen, S., Jiang, Y.G.: Motion guided spatial attention for video captioning. In: Proceedings of the AAAI Conference on Artificial Intelligence, vol. 33, pp. 8191–8198 (2019)
7. Gao, L., Fan, K., Song, J., Liu, X., Xu, X., Shen, H.T.: Deliberate attention networks for image captioning. In: Proceedings of the AAAI Conference on Artificial Intelligence, vol. 33, pp. 8320–8327 (2019)
8. Gordon, D., Kembhavi, A., Rastegari, M., Redmon, J., Fox, D., Farhadi, A.: Iqa: visual question answering in interactive environments. In: Proceedings of the IEEE Conference on Computer Vision and Pattern Recognition (CVPR) (2018)
9. Hou, J., Wu, X., Zhao, W., Luo, J., Jia, Y.: Joint syntax representation learning and visual cue translation for video captioning. In: Proceedings of the IEEE International Conference on Computer Vision (ICCV) (2019)
10. Jang, E., Gu, S., Poole, B.: Categorical reparameterization with gumbel-softmax. In: ICLR (2017)
11. Kay, W., et al.: The kinetics human action video dataset. arXiv preprint arXiv:1705.06950 (2017)
12. Kojima, A., Tamura, T., Fukunaga, K.: Natural language description of human activities from video images based on concept hierarchy of actions. Int. J. Comput. Vision $50(2)$, 171–184 (2002)
13. Lin, C.Y.: ROUGE: a package for automatic evaluation of summaries. In: Text Summarization Branches Out, pp. 74–81 (2004)
14. Lu, M., Li, X., Liu, C.: Context visual information-based deliberation network for video captioning. In: 2020 25th International Conference on Pattern Recognition (ICPR), pp. 9812–9818 (2021)
15. Nguyen, A., Kanoulas, D., Muratore, L., Caldwell, D.G., Tsagarakis, N.G.: Translating videos to commands for robotic manipulation with deep recurrent neural networks. In: ICRA (2018)
16. Papineni, K., Roukos, S., Ward, T., Zhu, W.J.: Bleu: a method for automatic evaluation of machine translation. In: Proceedings of the 40th Annual Meeting of the Association for Computational Linguistics, pp. 311–318 (2002)
17. Pei, W., Zhang, J., Wang, X., Ke, L., Shen, X., Tai, Y.W.: Memory-attended recurrent network for video captioning. In: Proceedings of the IEEE Conference on Computer Vision and Pattern Recognition (CVPR) (2019)

18. Ren, S., He, K., Girshick, R., Sun, J.: Faster r-cnn: towards real-time object detection with region proposal networks. IEEE Trans. Pattern Anal. Mach. Intell. **39**(6), 1137–1149 (2017)
19. Russakovsky, O., et al.: Imagenet large scale visual recognition challenge. Int. J. Comput. Vision **115**(3), 211–252 (2015)
20. Ryu, H., Kang, S., Kang, H., Yoo, C.D.: Semantic grouping network for video captioning. arXiv preprint arXiv:2102.00831 (2021)
21. Szegedy, C., Ioffe, S., Vanhoucke, V., Alemi, A.: Inception-v4, inception-resnet and the impact of residual connections on learning. In: Proceedings of the AAAI Conference on Artificial Intelligence, vol. 31 (2017)
22. Tan, G., Liu, D., Wang, M., Zha, Z.J.: Learning to discretely compose reasoning module networks for video captioning. In: Proceedings of the Twenty-Ninth International Joint Conference on Artificial Intelligence (IJCAI), pp. 745–752 (2020)
23. Thomason, J., Venugopalan, S., Guadarrama, S., Saenko, K., Mooney, R.: Integrating language and vision to generate natural language descriptions of videos in the wild. In: Proceedings of COLING 2014, the 25th International Conference on Computational Linguistics: Technical Papers, pp. 1218–1227 (2014)
24. Vedantam, R., Lawrence Zitnick, C., Parikh, D.: Cider: consensus-based image description evaluation. In: Proceedings of the IEEE Conference on Computer Vision and Pattern Recognition (CVPR) (2015)
25. Venugopalan, S., Xu, H., Donahue, J., Rohrbach, M., Mooney, R., Saenko, K.: Translating videos to natural language using deep recurrent neural networks. arXiv preprint arXiv:1412.4729 (2014)
26. Venugopalan, S., Rohrbach, M., Donahue, J., Mooney, R., Darrell, T., Saenko, K.: Sequence to sequence - video to text. In: Proceedings of the IEEE International Conference on Computer Vision (ICCV) (2015)
27. Voykinska, V., Azenkot, S., Wu, S., Leshed, G.: How blind people interact with visual content on social networking services. In: Proceedings of the 19th ACM Conference on Computer-Supported Cooperative Work & Social Computing, pp. 1584–1595 (2016)
28. Wang, B., Ma, L., Zhang, W., Jiang, W., Wang, J., Liu, W.: Controllable video captioning with pos sequence guidance based on gated fusion network. In: Proceedings of the IEEE International Conference on Computer Vision (ICCV) (2019)
29. Wang, B., Ma, L., Zhang, W., Liu, W.: Reconstruction network for video captioning. In: Proceedings of the IEEE Conference on Computer Vision and Pattern Recognition (CVPR) (2018)
30. Xu, J., Mei, T., Yao, T., Rui, Y.: Msr-vtt: a large video description dataset for bridging video and language. In: Proceedings of the IEEE Conference on Computer Vision and Pattern Recognition (CVPR) (2016)
31. Xu, J., Yao, T., Zhang, Y., Mei, T.: Learning multimodal attention LSTM networks for video captioning. In: Proceedings of the 25th ACM International Conference on Multimedia, MM 2017, pp. 537–545 (2017)
32. Yao, L., et al.: Describing videos by exploiting temporal structure. In: Proceedings of the IEEE International Conference on Computer Vision (ICCV) (2015)
33. Zha, Z.J., Liu, D., Zhang, H., Zhang, Y., Wu, F.: Context-aware visual policy network for fine-grained image captioning. IEEE Trans. Pattern Anal. Mach. Intell. (TPAMI), 1 (2019). https://ieeexplore.ieee.org/document/8684270

Adaptive Prediction of Hip Joint Center from X-ray Images Using Generalized Regularized Extreme Learning Machine and Globalized Bounded Nelder-Mead Strategy

Fuchang Han[1], Shenghui Liao[1(✉)], Yiyong Jiang[1], Shu Liu[1], Yuqian Zhao[2], and Xiantao Shen[3]

[1] School of Computer Science and Engineering, Central South University, Changsha, China
lsh@csu.edu.cn
[2] School of Automation, Central South University, Changsha, China
[3] Wuhan Children's Hospital, Huazhong University of Science and Technology, Wuhan, China

Abstract. The prediction of hip joint center (HJC) is an important step in hip dysplasia screening. Existing state-of-the-art identification methods focus on the development of Mose circle, functional and predictive methods. Those approaches extract few factors and ignore the adaptive HJC prediction, and their applications are not universally applicable. This paper proposes an adaptive HJC prediction model from X-ray images. The proposed network is based on generalized regularized extreme learning machine (GRELM) with three improvements: a multivariable feature extraction module, obtaining comprehensive predictive factors; an attribute optimization module based on Pearson correlation method and entropy weights, guiding the network to focus on useful information at variables; And appending a globalized bounded Nelder-Mead (GBNM) strategy to the framework to automatically and efficiently determine optimal model parameters. By integrating the above improvements in series, the models' performances are gradually enhanced. Experimental results demonstrate the effectiveness of our method. Our method can be easily connected in series with an automatic landmark detection module, and the HJC can be quickly determined based on these anatomical landmarks using the proposed model.

Keyword: Hip joint center · Generalized regularized extreme learning machine · Globalized bounded Nelder-Mead strategy

1 Introduction

Hip joint center (HJC) is an important reference point for treatment decisions in hip dysplasia, and X-ray examination has played a crucial role in its determination [1, 2]. Since the HJC landmark cannot be palpated, its location is usually manually estimated by expert orthopedists. However, this artificial identification method may bring inaccurate results due to poor personal experience or large visual blur [3, 4]. To assist early diagnosis

© Springer Nature Switzerland AG 2021
D. N. Pham et al. (Eds.): PRICAI 2021, LNAI 13031, pp. 183–196, 2021.
https://doi.org/10.1007/978-3-030-89188-6_14

in hips and improve the treatment efficiency, automatic HJC prediction is attracting much attention.

Current state-of-the-art methods for HJC prediction can be categorized into three classes. (1) The first class is Mose circle methods. Mose circle is a standardized and quantitative approach to describe the HJC by using a template of concentric circles [5], and the modified 1-mm Mose circle technique provides the most accurate approximation of the HJC [6]. However, when the ossification of the femoral skull epiphysis is insufficient, the HJC position determined by this method may be eccentric. (2) The second class is functional methods. Functional methods locate the HJC by estimating the relative motion of the thigh and pelvis [7–9]. But their accuracy is affected by two main reasons. First, the estimate of the HJC relies heavily on the quality and range of movement during calibration trials. Functional methods would result in large location errors when hip motion is substantially limited [10]. Second, due to soft tissue artifacts (STAs) and stereo photogrammetric errors, it is difficult to establish a reliable local coordinate system [11]. (3) The third class is predictive methods. Predictive methods use anthropometric-based regression equations to determine the HJC, and different pelvic dimensions and empirical regression equations have been proposed [12]. But these equations are not applicable universally since HJC-related measurements are quite variable between races or even communities. Thus, more accurate and population-comprehensive prediction approaches are desired.

However, within the context of adaptive HJC prediction from X-ray images, the challenges stem from three aspects. (1) The first aspect is limited predictive factors. Classical anatomical landmarks are the teardrop and the medial wall of the acetabulum in pelvis. However, these landmarks can be deformed or destroyed in some cases [13]. More solid reference points or predictive factors are needed. (2) The second aspect is adaptive HJC prediction. Existing HJC estimation approaches are suitable only for certain groups of people [13], and how to predict the HJC adaptively using intelligent machine learning models remains unsolved. (3) The third aspect is intraclass variations. This issue is caused by the existence of HJC instances with an unexpectedly tilted or rotated pelvis when X-ray examinations are taken. This property brings a new challenge to general classifiers.

To address the above challenging problem, we focus on adaptive machine learning approach and propose an automatic prediction model for HJC identification with the following three aspects.

(1) Comprehensive predictive factors are extracted. Our model is based on anteroposterior X-ray images and their multiscale predictive factor extraction is desired. Eight anatomical landmarks on each hip are annotated by expert orthopedists, and six pelvis-related features are calculated. Note that these anatomical landmarks can also be detected with an automatic landmark detection module, and our method can be easily appended to an automatic landmark detection module to implement the end-to-end HJC prediction.

(2) We introduce a new attribute optimization module, guiding the network to focus on meaningful information at input variables. By ranking the correlation coefficients between the input attributes and the output using the Pearson correlation method, we select the high-importance attributes and then each input attribute is weighted using

the entropy weight method. This module can be easily added to model architectures increasing prediction accuracy.

(3) The proposed method is based on generalized regularized extreme learning machine (GRELM), and our method considers the adaptive HJC prediction to tackle the problem of automated model optimization. We initialized the model with optimal parameters obtained by the globalized bounded Nelder-Mead (GBNM) strategy. Validation on a dataset from the Wuhan Women and Children's Hospital in China demonstrates the effectiveness of our method.

2   The Proposed Method

2.1   Overview

Our goal is to automatically and efficiently identify HJC from X-ray images using adaptive machine learning approaches. This goal requires that comprehensive predictive factors and adaptive optimization techniques be investigated for identifying HJC. To this end, we propose an adaptive HJC prediction model based on GRELM, as shown in Fig. 1. The proposed method involves one predictive factor extraction module that calculates anatomical landmarks and pelvis-related features, one attribute optimization module that conducts data post-processing, one adaptive GBNM module for automatic optimal model parameters, and one model establishment and analysis module to train the HJC prediction model. Next, we will describe these four modules.

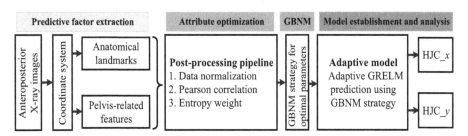

Fig. 1. The overall flowchart of our proposed method.

2.2   Predictive Factor Extraction

Comprehensive predictive factor extraction from X-ray is desired. First, eight prominent bony landmarks on each hip are annotated by orthopedists, as shown in Fig. 2 (a) and Table 1. We set up the coordinate system as shown in Fig. 3 by taking the midpoint of the line connecting landmark 1 and landmark 9 as the origin of the coordinates. Second, six pelvis-related features are calculated, as shown in Fig. 2 (b) and Table 2. Note that these anatomical landmarks annotated by orthopedists are the current gold standard, and their determination is the consensus reached by experts in many orthopedic professional fields. These anatomical landmarks can also be detected by an automatic landmark detection module [14, 15] and after automatically identifying these landmarks, our method can be appended to the automatic landmark detection module to implement the end-to-end HJC prediction. Our method can be regarded as a post-processing adaptive prediction module.

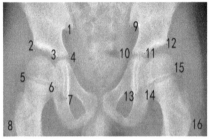

(a) Anatomical landmarks.

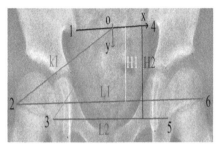

(b) Pelvis-related features.

Fig. 2. The comprehensive predictive factors.

Table 1. Annotated anatomical landmarks.

Landmarks	Definition	State
1, 9	Posterior inferior iliac spine	Static
2, 12	Outer margin of acetabulum	Static
3, 11	Inner margin of acetabulum	Static
4, 10	Apex of Y-shaped cartilage	Static
5, 15	Outer margin of epiphyseal plate	Dynamic
6, 14	Inner margin of epiphyseal plate	Dynamic
7, 13	Inferior margin of teardrop	Static
8, 16	Tip of greater trochanters	Dynamic

2.3 Attribute Optimization

To enhance the utilization of the useful information, we perform a post-processing pipeline including the data normalization, Pearson correlation analysis, and weight assignment. (1) Data normalization. All samples are normalized into [0, 1]. (2) Pearson correlation coefficient with a significance level of 0.05 is adopted to determine useful predictive features, as shown in Fig. 3. The Pearson correlation coefficient is described as Eq. (1). (3) Different weights are assigned to the input attributes based on entropy weight method. Entropy weight method uses the entropy to express the characteristics of information. When the variance of a landmark or pelvis-related feature among the

Table 2. Pelvis-related features.

Pelvic features	Definition
K1	The slope of the connection line between the coordinate origin and outer margin of epiphyseal plate
K2	The slope of the connection line between the coordinate origin and inner margin of epiphyseal plate
L1	The length of the line connecting the outer margin of epiphyseal plate on the left and right sides
L2	The length of the line connecting the inner margin of epiphyseal plate on the left and right sides
H1	The distance between the x-axis and the line of outer margin of epiphyseal plate on the left and right sides
H2	The distance between the x-axis and the line of inner margin of epiphyseal plate on the left and right sides

input samples is large, the entropy of this input attribute is small, which reveals more effective information. The weights of the input attributes are estimated as Eq. (2).

$$P_{x,y} = \frac{cov(x, y)}{\sigma_x \sigma_y} = \frac{\sum_{i=1}^{n} (x_i - \tilde{x})(y_i - \tilde{y})}{(n - 1)\sigma_x \sigma_y} \tag{1}$$

$$W_j = c_j \left/ \sum_{j=1}^{n} c_j \right. = \frac{1 + k \sum_{i=1}^{N} u_{ij} \ln u_{ij}}{\sum_{j=1}^{n} (1 + k \sum_{i=1}^{N} u_{ij} \ln u_{ij})} \tag{2}$$

where, σ represents the standard deviation of samples, $cov(x, y)$ represents the sample covariance, x represents the predictive landmarks and pelvis-related features, y represents the HJC samples, n is the sample size, C_j represents the effectiveness coefficient of jth input attribute, u_{ij} represents the normalized samples, $k = (\ln N)^{-1}$ represents the information entropy coefficient, and N is the overall sample size.

2.4 Adaptive GBNM Strategy

The manual tuning of model parameters can be a time-consuming and tedious process. Adaptive HJC prediction and fully automated model optimization are desired. The GBNM optimization strategy is appended to our GRELM architecture for better prediction, as shown in Fig. 4. The GBNM optimization strategy is a black-box local-global approach. It is based on the probabilistic restart and has been found to obtain better performance than evolutionary optimization algorithms in terms of convergence speed, accuracy of results, and ability to find optima. However, within the context of the Nelder–Mead algorithm for optimum searches, the challenges stem from two aspects: (1) Nelder–Mead algorithm may fail to converge to a local optimum, and (2) Nelder–Mead algorithm may escape a region that would be a basin of attraction for a pointwise

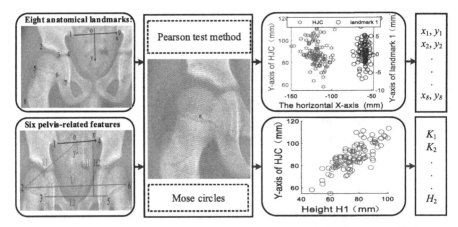

Fig. 3. The Pearson correlation analysis between the predictive factors and HJC.

descent search [16]. In this study, Nelder–Mead algorithm is enhanced with two following improvements: simplex degeneracy detection and handling through reinitialization. Note that the probabilistic restart uses an adaptive probability density to keep a memory of past local searches, whose contribution in this study is twofold: (1) repeating local searches until a fixed total cost, and (2) checking and improving the convergence of the algorithm [17]. Our optimization objective function is the average coefficient of determination (R^2) from 10-fold validation processes on the training data using the GRELM method. Finally, the GBNM strategy yields a list of candidate local optima which contain global solutions [18].

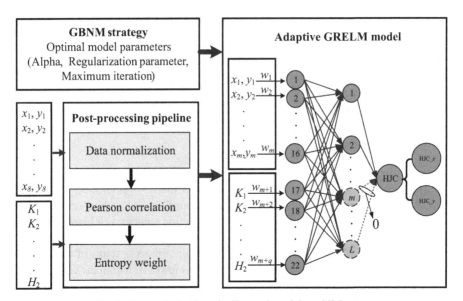

Fig. 4. The optimization pipeline and model establishment.

2.5 Model Establishment and Analysis

The selected best features with different weights are finally supplied to the adaptive GRELM model for final HJC prediction. The main idea of GRELM approach is to find a set of solutions that share a common nonzero support, which can be described as a minimization problem:

$$\underset{B}{\text{minimize}} \ \frac{C}{2} \|HB - T\|_F^2 + \lambda_1 \|B\|_{2,1} + \frac{\lambda_2}{2} \|B\|_F^2 \tag{3}$$

where λ_1, λ_2 and C represent the regularization parameters, H represents the output matrix, B represents the output weight vector, T represents the training target, $\|.\|_F$ represents the Frobenius norm, $\|B\|_{2,1} = \sum_{i=1}^{\tilde{N}} \|b_i\|$ and b_i is the ith row of B. Note that the alternating direction method of multipliers (ADMM) [19] is used to address the above minimization problem. In each iteration of ADMM, we perform the alternating minimization of augmented Lagrangian, as described in Eq. (4).

$$L(B, Z, U) = \frac{C}{2} \|HB - T\|_F^2 + \frac{\lambda_2}{2} \|B\|_F^2 + \lambda_1 \|Z\|_{2,1} + \frac{\rho}{2} \|B - Z + U\|_F^2$$
$$- \frac{\rho}{2} \|U\|_F^2 \tag{4}$$

where $U = (1/\rho)Y$ is the scaled dual variable, ρ represents the penalty parameter and Y represents the Lagrangian multiplier, Z represents the global variable that is subjected to B.

Having a smaller number of neurons in hidden layer without compromise the training and testing accuracy is realized by using GRELM model. When a row of B is zero, our method can eliminate the neuron in the hidden node associated with this row, as shown in Fig. 4. Note that once the GRELM model is established, it can be used to predict the unknown-label HJC. Moreover, the optimal model parameters (the alpha, regularization parameter, and maximum iteration) obtained by the GBNM are updated automatically during the training phase. Experimental results show that the proposed adaptive GRELM model with optimal parameters can automatically and efficiently identify HJC.

3 Experimental Results

3.1 Data Processing and Analysis

To show the effectiveness of our proposed method, we collect the X-ray dataset from the Wuhan Women and Children's Hospital in China and validate our method on this dataset. In addition, we compare it with state-of-the-art methods. The dataset includes 100 X-ray images and a total of 200 hips. This work was approved by the Ethics Committee of Wuhan Women and Children's Hospital, and complied with the tenets of the Declaration of Helsinki for clinical research. In addition, all participants in this study signed the written consent form before they are examined. Comprehensive predictive factors are extracted. We use the Pearson correlation coefficient (P) with a significance level (R) of 0.05 to determine useful predictive features. The correlation results between HJC and each predictor are shown in Table 3 and Table 4, from which we can find that the landmark points and pelvic features are highly correlated with the HJC, and we also find $P < 0.05$, indicating that the correlation results are statistically significant. Specifically, each input attribute is weighted using the entropy weight method, as shown in Table 5.

Table 3. The correlation results between HJC coordinates and anatomical landmarks.

Items	Landmark 1	Landmark 2	Landmark 3	Landmark 4
R	0.9926	0.9987	0.9988	0.9977
P	0.0000	0.0000	0.0000	0.0000
Items	Landmark 5	Landmark 6	Landmark 7	Landmark 8
R	0.9987	0.9977	0.9991	0.9934
P	0.0000	0.0000	0.0000	0.0000

Table 4. The correlation results between HJC coordinates and pelvic features.

Items	Slope K1	Slope K2	Length L1
R (HJC_x)	-0.3019	-0.3024	-0.7825
P (HJC_x)	0.0023	0.0022	0.0000
R (HJC_y)	-0.7649	-0.6939	0.4683
P (HJC_y)	0.0000	0.0000	0.0000
Items	Length L2	Height H1	Height H2
R (HJC_x)	-0.7571	-0.3718	-0.4068
P (HJC_x)	0.0000	0.0001	0.0000
R (HJC_y)	0.4946	0.7680	0.7074
P (HJC_y)	0.0000	0.0000	0.0000

Table 5. The feature weight value based on entropy weight method.

Factors	X1	Y1	X2	Y2	X3	Y3	X4	Y4
Weight	0.0374	0.0453	0.0386	0.0452	0.0509	0.0465	0.0560	0.0506
Factors	X5	Y5	X6	Y6	X7	Y7	X8	Y8
Weight	0.0255	0.0389	0.0447	0.0307	0.0524	0.0425	0.0403	0.0784
Factors	K1	K2	L1	L2	H1	H2		
Weight	0.0249	0.0189	0.0670	0.0762	0.0416	0.0477		

3.2 Experimental Setting

By considering the number of both weighted predictive features and HJC coordinates, the end-to-end parameters of our model include the input neurons size (22) and the number of output neurons (2). Note that 70% of the samples are used to train the model, and the remaining 30% are used for testing. Our optimization objective function is the average coefficient of determination (R^2) from 10-fold validation processes on the training data using the GRELM method. The model is initialized by constrained optimization strategy: the lower boundary of the parameter is set to vector (0, 0.1, 10), and the upper boundary is set to vector (1, 1500, 50). The optimal parameters obtained by the GBNM strategy include the alpha (0.9470), regularization parameter (354.7452) and maximum iteration (46).

3.3 Comparison with State-Of-The-Art Methods

The experimental results of our proposed method are shown in Fig. 5. We compare the proposed GRELM approach with state-of-the-art ELM variants such as the ELM [20, 21], RELM [22] and IRELM [23] models. Note that the parameters of these algorithms are optimal by the GBNM strategy, and their prediction error curves are shown in Fig. 6. We use the correlation coefficient (R) with a significance level (P), root mean square error (RMSE), mean absolute percentage error (MAPE) and coefficient of determination (R^2) as evaluation metrics, and the performance comparison of above state-of-the-art ELM variants are shown in Table 6 and Table 7. Obviously, (1) our GRELM obtains the largest R and R^2 values and the smallest RMSE and MAPE values, which outperforms the three state-of-the-art methods. (2) The ELM model achieves the best performance in training phase but an inferior performance in testing phase. The reason is that the ELM is a single-layer feedforward network (SLFN) and is prone to overfitting. Our proposed

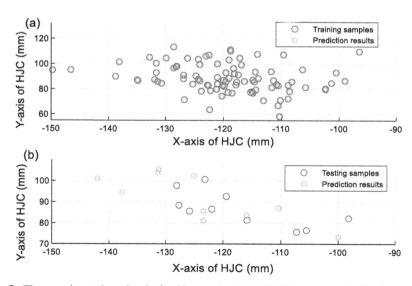

Fig. 5. The experimental results obtained by our model. (a) Training results. (b) Testing results.

strategy can greatly improve prediction performance. In addition, our GRELM features a better accuracy (RMSE = 9.4777 mm) than traditional functional methods (up to 26 mm) [10] and regression methods (25–30 mm) [8]. These findings show that our method obtains the coordinates closest to the real HJC. Like popular deep convolutional neural network (CNN) models, these CNN methods extract features from images to achieve prediction, which is completely different from our method based on anatomical landmarks, so this paper does not compare CNN models for HJC prediction.

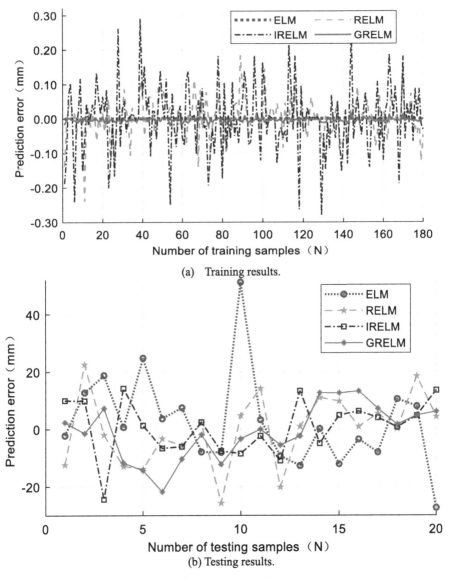

(a)   Training results.

(b) Testing results.

Fig. 6. The prediction error curves of four approaches.

Table 6. Performance comparison of state-of-the-art ELM variants in training phase.

Models	R (P)	RMSE (mm)	MAPE	R^2
ELM	1 (0)	2.4096e−09	2.4121e−09	1.0000
RELM	1 (0)	0.0580	0.0423	1.0000
IRELM	1 (0)	0.0953	0.0690	1.0000
GRELM	1 (0)	0.0069	0.0056	1.0000

Table 7. Performance comparison of state-of-the-art ELM variants in testing phase.

Models	R (P)	RMSE (mm)	MAPE	R^2
ELM	0.9890 (2.1127e-16)	16.3804	11.1469	0.9744
RELM	0.9943 (5.7097e-19)	12.2013	9.5528	0.9858
IRELM	0.9960 (2.3805e-20)	9.5539	7.8256	0.9913
GRELM	**0.9977 (1.9706e-22)**	**9.4777**	**7.6474**	**0.9914**

3.4 Ablation Analysis

To better demonstrate the effectiveness of the proposed multiscale predictive factor extraction and optimization pipeline strategy, we performed ablation experiments on our model, as shown in Fig. 7 and Table 8. The results indicate that (1) the model performance is evidently improved by combining the bone landmarks and pelvic features. It can be clearly observed that our multifeature extraction and fusion strategy can provide richer feature representations than the existing single representation methods. (2) Applying a post-processing step or a GBNM optimization strategy optimizes the HJC prediction. (3) The hybrid post-processing step and GBNM optimization strategy can further help the HJC prediction. Obviously, our proposed method greatly enhances the accuracy of HJC prediction.

Our method can be connected in series with an automatic landmark detection module. After the anatomical landmarks are detected, the HJC can be quickly predicted based on these anatomical landmarks using the proposed model. Our future work is to develop such an automatic landmark detection module, and we will test the proposed model with more labeled clinical datasets to expand the application range and improve the robustness and accuracy of the model.

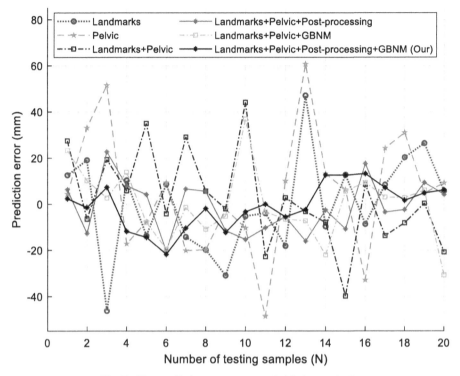

Fig. 7. The prediction error curves of ablation analysis.

Table 8. The ablation results on our proposed method.

Items	R (P)	RMSE (mm)	MAPE	R^2
Landmarks	0.9839 (6.5068e-15)	20.8599	17.4001	0.9568
Pelvic features	0.9713 (1.1445e-12)	26.6584	20.7607	0.9355
Landmarks + Pelvic features	0.9884 (3.3692e-16)	20.2609	13.5847	0.9650
Landmarks + Pelvic features + Post-processing	0.9940 (8.9410e-19)	11.3976	9.3318	0.9879
Landmarks + Pelvic features + GBNM	0.9896 (1.2988e-16)	15.0021	11.4998	0.9798
Landmarks + Pelvic features + Post-processing + GBNM (Our)	**0.9977 (1.9706e-22)**	**9.4777**	**7.6474**	**0.9914**

4 Conclusion

This paper presents an adaptive prediction model to address the problem of hip joint center (HJC) determination. A generalized regularized extreme learning machine (GRELM) with the globalized bounded Nelder-Mead (GBNM) strategy is designed to determine optimal model parameters and address the adaptive prediction. Specifically, we use one multivariable feature extraction module to obtain comprehensive predictive factors and one attribute optimization pipeline to enhance the utilization of the useful information. Validation on a dataset from the Wuhan Women and Children's Hospital in China demonstrates that the proposed method outperforms the state-of-art models.

Acknowledgments. This work was supported by the National Natural Science Foundation of China (No.61772556), National Key R&D Program of China (No.2018YFB1107100, No.2016 YFC1100600), Postgraduate Research and Innovation Project of Hunan (No.CX20200321) and Fundamental Research Funds for the Central Universities of Central South University (2020 zzts140).

References

1. Schofer, M.D., Pressel, T., Heyse, T.J., Schmitt, J., Boudriot, U.: Radiological determination of the anatomic hip centre from pelvic landmarks. Acta Orthop. Belg. **76**(4), 479–485 (2010)
2. Myers, C.A., Huff, D.N., Mason, J.B., Rullkoetter, P.J.: Effect of intraoperative treatment options on hip joint stability following total hip arthroplasty. J. Orthop. Res. (2021). https://doi.org/10.1002/jor.25055
3. Kawahara, S., et al.: Digitalized analyses of intraoperative acetabular component position using image-matching technique in total hip arthroplasty. Bone Joint Res. **9**(7), 360–367 (2020)
4. Dorr, L.D., Callaghan, J.J.: Death of the Lewinnek "Safe Zone." J. Arthroplasty **34**(1), 1–2 (2019)
5. Mose, K.: Methods of measuring in Legg-Calvé-Perthes disease with special regard to the prognosis. Clin. Orthop. Relat. Res. **150**, 103–109 (1980)
6. Cuomo, A.V., Fedorak, G.T., Moseley, C.F.: A practical approach to determining the center of the femoral head in subluxated and dislocated hips. J. Pediatr. Orthop. **35**(6), 556–560 (2015)
7. Adewuyi, A., Levy, E.T., Wells, J., Chhabra, A., Fey, N.P.: Kinematic simulations of static radiographs provides discriminating features of multiple hip pathologies. In: 2020 42nd Annual International Conference of the IEEE Engineering in Medicine and Biology Society (EMBC), pp. 4992–4995. IEEE (2020)
8. Camomilla, V., Cereatti, A., Vannozzi, G., Cappozzo, A.: An optimized protocol for hip joint centre determination using the functional method. J. Biomech. **39**(6), 1096–1106 (2006)
9. Bennett, H.J., Valenzuela, K.A., Fleenor, K., Weinhandl, J.T.: A normative database of hip and knee joint biomechanics during dynamic tasks using four functional methods with three functional calibration tasks. J. Biomech. Eng. **142**(4), 041011 (2020)
10. Piazza, S.J., Erdemir, A., Okita, N., Cavanagh, P.R.: Assessment of the functional method of hip joint center location subject to reduced range of hip motion. J. Biomech. **37**(3), 349–356 (2004)
11. Heller, M.O., Kratzenstein, S., Ehrig, R.M., Wassilew, G., Duda, G.N., Taylor, W.R.: The weighted optimal common shape technique improves identification of the hip joint center of rotation in vivo. J. Orthop. Res. **29**(10), 1470–1475 (2011)

12. Krishnan, S.P., Carrington, R.W., Mohiyaddin, S., Garlick, N.: Common misconceptions of normal hip joint relations on pelvic radiographs. J. Arthroplasty **21**(3), 409–412 (2006)
13. Bombaci, H., Simsek, B., Soyarslan, M., Murat Yildirim, M.: Determination of the hip rotation centre from landmarks in pelvic radiograph. Acta Orthop. Traumatol. Turc. **51**(6), 470–473 (2017)
14. Wang, L., Ma, L., Li, Y., Niu, K., He, Z.: A DCNN system based on an iterative method for automatic landmark detection in cephalometric X-ray images. Biomed. Signal Process. Control **68**, 102757 (2021)
15. Juneja, M., et al.: A review on cephalometric landmark detection techniques. Biomed. Signal Process. Control **66**, 102486 (2021)
16. Abdel-Basset, M., Mohamed, R., Mirjalili, S.: A novel whale optimization algorithm integrated with Nelder–Mead simplex for multi-objective optimization problems. Knowl.-Based Syst. **212**, 106619 (2021)
17. Inaba, F.K., Salles, E.O.T., Perron, S., Caporossi, G.: DGR-ELM: distributed generalized regularize ELM for classification. Neurocomputing **275**, 1522–1530 (2018)
18. Luersen, M.A., Le Riche, R.: Globalized Nelder-Mead method for engineering optimization. Comput. Struct. **82**(23–26), 2251–2260 (2004)
19. Boyd, S., Parikh, N., Chu, E., Peleato, B., Eckstein, J.: Distributed optimization and statistical learning via the alternating direction method of multipliers. Found. Trends Mach. Learn. **3**(1), 1–122 (2010)
20. Huang, G.B., Zhou, H.M., Ding, X.J., Zhang, R.: Extreme learning machine for regression and multiclass classification. IEEE Trans. Syst. Man Cybern. Part B-Cybern. **42**(2), 513–529 (2012)
21. Huang, G.-B., Zhu, Q.-Y., Siew, C.-K.: Extreme learning machine: theory and applications. Neurocomputing **70**(1–3), 489–501 (2006)
22. Martínez-Martínez, J.M., Escandell-Montero, P., Soria-Olivas, E., Martín-Guerrero, J.D., Magdalena-Benedito, R., Gómez-Sanchis, J.: Regularized extreme learning machine for regression problems. Neurocomputing **74**(17), 3716–3721 (2011)
23. Xu, Z.X., Yao, M., Wu, Z.H., Dai, W.H.: Incremental regularized extreme learning machine and it's enhancement. Neurocomputing **174**, 134–142 (2016)

Adversarial Training for Image Captioning Incorporating Relation Attention

Tianyu Chen[1], Zhixin Li[1(✉)], Canlong Zhang[1], and Huifang Ma[2]

[1] Guangxi Key Lab of Multi-source Information Mining and Security,
Guangxi Normal University, Guilin 541004, China
lizx@gxnu.edu.cn
[2] College of Computer Science and Engineering, Northwest Normal University,
Lanzhou 730070, China

Abstract. Image captioning methods with attention mechanism are leading this field, especially models with global and local attention. But there are few conventional models to integrate the relationship information between various regions of the image. In this paper, this kind of relationship features are embedded into the fused attention mechanism to explore the internal visual and semantic relations between different object regions. Besides, to alleviate the exposure bias problem and make the training process more efficient, we combine Generative Adversarial Network with Reinforcement Learning and employ the greedy decoding method to generate a dynamic baseline reward for self-critical training. Finally, experiments on MSCOCO datasets show that the model can generate more accurate and vivid image captioning sentences and perform better in multiple prevailing metrics than the previous advanced models.

Keywords: Image captioning · Fused attention mechanism · Generative Adversarial Network · Reinforcement Learning · Self-critical training

1 Introduction

Automatic image captioning intends to generate a descriptive sentence that verbalizes the visual content of an image. With the rapid development of deep learning, the current encoder-decoder model based on Convolutional Neural Network (CNN) with attention mechanism and Recurrent Neural Network (RNN) has been leading this field. However the RNN model faces a common problem in dealing with the sequence generation problem: Exposure Bias. Which will influence the result inevitably.

As far as we know, most traditional global attention mechanisms allocate attention weights only to CNN's low-level coarse features. It may cause the object mistakenly identified. What's more important, the crucial potential clues of the relationship between different objects are also neglected. Concerning the caption

© Springer Nature Switzerland AG 2021
D. N. Pham et al. (Eds.): PRICAI 2021, LNAI 13031, pp. 197–211, 2021.
https://doi.org/10.1007/978-3-030-89188-6_15

generation part, there are certain drawbacks associated with the application of Generative Adversarial Network (GAN) [4] in discrete token generation. A major reason is that the generative model's discrete outputs make it difficult to pass the gradient update from the discriminative model to the generative model. The solution was then assayed for SeqGAN [25] model, which combines GAN with policy gradient algorithm [15]. Nevertheless, when the policy is already powerful, the model may still sample a bad sentence. The probability of this sentence will even increase because it still has a reward value.

This paper proposes a Fused Attention Network (FAN) and extra allocate attention weights to objects' regional relation features to more effectively excavate the image's information. Besides, the GAN and Reinforcement Learning (RL) [14] algorithm is combined in the proposed self-critical GAN (SC-GAN) to solve the exposure bias problem. The main contributions of this paper are as follow:

- The relation features containing visual similarity and semantic information between different regions are integrated with the fused attention mechanism. Subsequently, the relation features are weighted together with the object's local features. These three kinds of features complement each other to more fully excavate and represent the feature information of the image.
- In the language part, the RL algorithm is combined with GAN. It replaces the output of the discriminator with the reward value of the generated word to solve the problem that discrete data can not propagate the gradient back. Simultaneously, the greedy decoding method is applied to optimize the model structure through self-critical training by providing a dynamic baseline reward value.
- The experimental results on the MSCOCO dataset show that either of the two methods can enhance the experiment performance. Furthermore, when they are integrated together, the improvement is more salient. The ablation and qualitative experiments show that our model is comparable even more superior to many of the existing approaches in mostly metric.

2   Related Work

We mainly introduce the application of neural networks with attention mechanism. Besides, some sequence-level learning methods and transformer-based methods are described.

2.1   Attention Mechanism

Inspired by soft-attention mechanism which can focus on diverse parts of input when generating different words proposed by Bahdanau [2], Xu et al. [22] apply soft-attention to image captioning; when generating different words, the model will focus on different parts of the image to select the most useful information. You et al. [24] initiated semantic attention. They abstracted important global semantic information from the image to enhance image information. Later, Wang et al. [19] proposed a hierarchical attention network, which combines patch, target, and text semantic features to enhance image information. Anderson et al. [1] believed the salient targets in the image should receive more attention, so he improved the traditional method of evenly distributing attention to each region of the image and added bottom up attention through Faster R-CNN [12]. Yao et al. [23] initiated the GCN-LSTM architecture, which novelly integrates both semantic and spatial object relationships into image encoder. Huang et al. [7] innovatively made use of the internal annotation knowledge to assist the calculation of visual attention, then introduced a new strategy to inject external knowledge extracted from knowledge graph into the encoder-decoder framework to facilitate meaningful captioning. The original self-attention proposed by [16] is regard as a great innovation in both Computer Vision and Natural Language Processing. It has the advantage to catch the global long-distance relation information and compute parallelly. Wei et al. [21] combined sentence-level attention with word-level attention for obtaining more detail and accurate captions. Huang et al. [8] firstly considered whether or how well the attended vector and the given attention query are related, and proposed an "Attention on Attention" (AoA) module which extends the conventional attention mechanisms to determine the relevance between attention results and queries. Liu et al. [10] proposed an Interactive Dual Generative Adversarial Network (IDGAN), which mutually combined the retrieval-based and generation-based methods to learn a better image captioning ensemble. The experiment results showed the great effectiveness of this model. Zhou et al. [26] conducted Part-of-Speech enhanced image-text matching model named POS-SCAN, as the effective knowledge distillation for more grounded image captioning. Wang et al. [18] introduced the recall mechanism to integrate the prior knowledge of the similar image captions, they first used the text retrieval model to calculate the similarity between the image and other captions in the training set, and the words in the first five captions are selected as recall words to guide the sentence generation.

2.2 Sequence-Level Training

With the aim to solve the exposure bias problem caused by the traditional RNN based decoder, Ranzato et al. [11] introduced policy gradient algorithm into RNN based sequence generation model for the first time and used Reinforcement Learning combined with the Monte Carlo sampling method for training. Although evaluating the generated result on the sentence-level can alleviate the exposure bias problem to a certain extent, their performance on metric with recall is still unsatisfactory, Chen et al. [3] proposed the SLL-SLE and added a sequence-level exploration term to the conventional loss function to boost recall. It guides the model to explore more plausible captions in the training phase. By this means, the proposed sequence-level learning objective takes both the precision and recall sides of generated captions into account. Rennie et al. [13] proposed a self-critical sequence training method, which employs the sentences generated by the current model as the baseline to reduce the variance of gradient estimation. By this way the model can generate better description sentences than the auxiliary sentences. Yu et al. [25] innovatively changed the output passed by the discriminator to the generator into a continuous probability value, which presents the probability that generated sentence is ground truth. Referring to the idea of self-critical sequence training (SCST) [13], we propose SC-GAN and provide a dynamic baseline reward generated by the greedy decoding method, which can not only reduce the high variance of the reward obtained by roll-out sampling, but also make the model converges faster, and optimize the reward and punishment of each generated sample more clear. Through the comparative experiments on the MSCOCO dataset, it is found that the above two methods can effectively improve the quality of generated sentences in the most popular metric.

3   Method

Given an image I, image captioning aims to generate a text description $Y = \{Y_1, Y_2, ...Y_T\}$, where T is the length of sentence. As depicted in Fig. 1, our model consists of the FAN and the SC-GAN. We detail these parts in subsection.

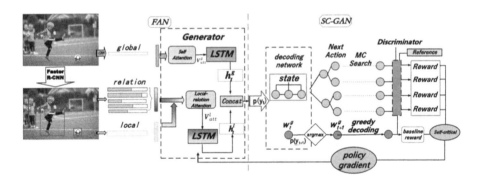

Fig. 1. The overview of our proposed system Fused Attention Network (FAN) and Self-critical GAN (SC-GAN). The FAN is composed of self-attention mechanism and local-relation mechanism. After deriving the next word probability $p(y_t)$ from the FAN to the SC-GAN, the Discriminator of SC-GAN completes the generated sentence and updates the parameter of Generator by policy gradient strategy.

3.1   Fused Attention Network (FAN)

Directly processing by CNN is the main non-invasive method used for extracting the global features in traditional attention mechanism. But in FAN, a variant of self-attention is adopted to obtain further in-depth information of global static features. We replace the original formula in [16] for computing the similarity coefficients of the vector Q and the vector K with a single neural network. As shown in Fig. 2. Firstly, the input image is encoded into a spatial feature vector $I = (i_1, i_2, ..., i_L)$ by CNN, where L is the number of image space regions. $i_{1:L} \in \mathbb{R}^C$ represents the feature of regions and $L = n \times n$. Afterward three 1×1 convolutional layers W_q, W_k, and W_v are used to transform I into three spatial features Q, K, and V. Then the attention weights a on V is calculated by fusing Q and K. The final global feature V_{att}^g is obtained by multiplying the attention weights a by V. The global attention mechanism can expressed by the following formula:

$$Q = W_q I, K = W_k I, V = W_v I$$
$$a = f(Q, K) = W_s(relu(Q \odot K)) + b_s$$
$$a = softmax(a^T)$$
$$V_{att}^g = V*a$$

(1)

Where $W_q \in \mathbb{R}^{C' \times C}$, $W_k \in \mathbb{R}^{C' \times C}$ and $W_v \in \mathbb{R}^{C'' \times C}$. We combine the Q and K by a single neural network. The $W_s \in \mathbb{R}^{C'}$ in this network is the transformation matrix and $\odot$ is the dot-product operation. The a, V have the same space size, that is, $n \times n$. The obtained V_{att}^g which represent the global features with regions' relation information is passed to the first Long short-term memory (LSTM) [6] network in FAN. Then the corresponding LSTM hidden state h_t^g is generated.

Faster R-CNN [12] did the synthesis of local features and relation features between different objects, the detected object regions are expressed as $R_{1:K}$. If these regional features are all assigned with attention weight, it will inevitably lead to overfitting. At the meantime, it is hard to burden the computation when calculating the relation features. Hence the Top-k ROIs are selected. The obtained local features are represented as F_i^l. The relation feature continues to be a great impetus to optimize the attention mechanism. In our FAN, the relation feature of region R_i is represented as F_i^r. For the target region R_i, the visual similarity between itself and other regions is calculated by dot-product, as shown in Fig. 3, hereafter the relation coefficient of other regions is obtained by softmax normalization:

$$f(F_i^l, F_j^l) = \frac{exp(F_i^l \cdot F_j^l)}{\sum_{j \neq i}^k exp(F_i^l \cdot F_j^l)}$$

(2)

In this way, the visual relationship between different regions are expressed. It is generally acknowledged that in addition to the visual information visible to the human eye, the semantic information between different regions in the image is also very crucial to guide the generation of caption sentences. According to human commonsense, the regions with long-distance or great visual difference also contain important semantic relations, such as "football" and "doorframe", "people" and "football" in Fig. 3, each pair of them should play a key role when generating the other one. So the region relation matrix $f(F_i^l, F_j^l)$ is set as trainable parameter matrix like W_s, W_a, and represent it as W_{ij}^r. The initial value of it before training is set according to the visual relationship coefficient

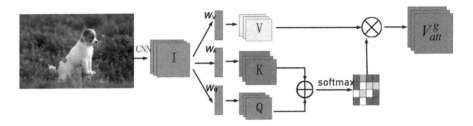

Fig. 2. The illustration of the global attention mechanism in FAN, after processed by three 1 * 1 convolution layer, we get the global feature with assigned weights.

obtained by (2). During the train process, the $\boldsymbol{W}_{ij}^{r}$ can be updated by back propagation. By this means the FAN can integrate the regional semantic relation with visual relation, the region relation feature $\boldsymbol{F}_{i}^{r}$ of the region R_i is obtained by this formula:

$$\boldsymbol{F}_{i}^{r} = \sum_{j \neq i}^{k} f(\boldsymbol{F}_{i}^{l}, \boldsymbol{F}_{j}^{l})\boldsymbol{F}_{j}^{l} = \boldsymbol{W}_{ij}^{r}\boldsymbol{F}_{j}^{l} \qquad (3)$$

So far, the model has extracted the local feature and relation feature of each region R_i. The image features integrated into the second LSTM at time step t in this local-relation attention mechanism are represented as $\boldsymbol{V}_{att}^{l}$, the calculation formula is as follows:

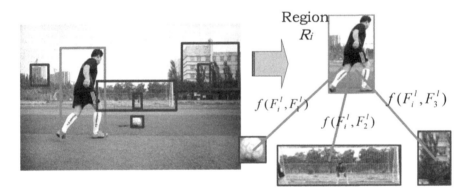

Fig. 3. The illustration of calculating the relation feature of the region R_i, the weight $f(R_i^l, R_j^l)$ of each other area is obtained by dot-product and softmax operation.

$$\boldsymbol{V}_{att}^{l} = \sum_{i=1}^{k} \gamma_{i}^{t}(\boldsymbol{F}_{i}^{l} + \boldsymbol{F}_{i}^{r}) \qquad (4)$$

γ_{i}^{t} is the attention weight of region R_i at time step t, $\sum_{i}^{k} \gamma_{i}^{t} = 1$, which represents the focusing degree of each ROI of the image with its closely related ROIs. It is determined by the connection with the LSTM hidden layer information h_{t-1} at the previous time. The calculation method is as follows:

$$\gamma_i^t = softmax(\boldsymbol{W}_q^T tanh(\boldsymbol{W}_h h^{t-1} + \boldsymbol{W}_f(\boldsymbol{F}_i^l + \boldsymbol{F}_i^r) + \boldsymbol{b}_l)) \tag{5}$$

$\boldsymbol{W}_q$, $\boldsymbol{W}_h$, $\boldsymbol{W}_f$ and b_l are the parameters to be learned by training, which are shared by all functions in all time steps. The decoding process is as follow:

$$h_t^g = LSTM([x_t; \boldsymbol{V}_{att}^g], h_{t-1}^g)$$
$$h_t^l = LSTM([x_t; \boldsymbol{V}_{att}^l], h_{t-1}^l) \tag{6}$$
$$h_t^{out} = Concat(h_t^g, h_t^l)$$

After concatenating the output hidden layer state h_t at timestep t, the probability vector $\boldsymbol{p}(y_t)$ of the next word is calculated following the traditional LSTM operation in (7). So far, the output of the image caption generator to the discriminator is completed. We denote the all the parameters of FAN including our $\boldsymbol{W}_{ij}^r$ as θ. In traditional MLE training, parameters θ are learned by minimizing the cross entropy loss (XE) in (8). While in our model, the parameters θ are learned by self-critical adversarial training in SC-GAN and the MLE method is used to pre-train our generator.

$$p_\theta(y_t|I, y_{1:t-1}) = softmax(\boldsymbol{W}_p h_t^{out}) \tag{7}$$

$$L(\theta) = -\sum_{t=1}^{T} log(p_\theta(y_t|y_{1:t-1})) \tag{8}$$

3.2   Self-critical Generative Adversarial Network (SC-GAN)

Following traditional GAN structure combined with RL, the sequence $(y_1,...,y_{t-1})$ is denoted as state s, action a is the next selected word y_t, and policy is generator $G_\theta(y_t|y_1, ..., y_{t-1})$. After the next action is chosen, the state transition is determined. The flow of the training is shown in the Algorithm 1. What is worth mentioning is that the parameter θ and φ are random values at begin. First of all, G_θ should be pre-trained on the sequence dataset s by MLE method. Secondly, the same amount of generated samples and ground truth samples are transferred to D_φ for pre-training, then G_θ and D_φ will be trained alternately. Because there is no intermediate reward, the goal of the generator (policy) G_θ is to generate a sequence from the initial state s_0 to maximize its expected end reward:

$$J(\theta) = \boldsymbol{E}[R_T|s_0, \theta] = \sum_{y_1 \in Y} G_\theta(y_1|s_0) * Q_{D_\varphi}^{G_\theta}(s_0, y_1) \tag{9}$$

where R_T is the reward for a complete sentence given by the discriminator D_φ, $Q_{D_\varphi}^{G_\theta}(s_0, y_1)$ is the action-value function of a sequence. The expected accumulative reward starting from state s, taking an action a, and then following policy

G_θ. The objective of the generator is to generate a sequence which would make the discriminator consider it is real.

We follow the REINFORCE algorithm and consider the estimated probability of being real given by the discriminator $D_\varphi(Y_{1:T})$ as the reward. Formally, it is:

$$Q_{D_\varphi}^{G_\theta}(s_0, y_1)(a = y_t, s = Y_{1:T-1}) = D_\varphi(Y_{1:T}) \tag{10}$$

Since the discriminator can only judge the complete sentence, as shown in right part of Fig. 1, we adopt Monte Carlo search with a roll-out policy G_β to sample the future last T-t tokens. We represent an N-time search for each sampled token to evaluate the action-value for an intermediate state. The roll-out policy G_β is set the same as the generator. In this way the $Q_{D_\varphi}^{G_\theta}(s_0, y_1)$ is formulated as:

$$Q_{D_\varphi}^{G_\theta}(s_{t-1}, y_t) \begin{cases} \frac{1}{N}\sum_{n=1}^{N} D_\varphi(Y_{1:T}^n), \ Y_{1:T}^n \in MC^{G_\beta}(Y_{1:t};N) & for \ t<T \\ D_\varphi(Y_{1:t}) & for \ t=T \end{cases} \tag{11}$$

We connect the FAN and the SC-GAN with the policy gradient algorithm. The policy gradient algorithm is applied to update the parameters in FAN including W_q, W_{ij}^r. Different from traditional cross entropy based method, RL method takes the expectation of the reward from the discriminator as the objective function. Refer to (9), the goal of generator training is to maximize the objective function. The reward given by D_φ is a non-negative probability value. Even if a worse result is generated, the discriminator will not punish the bad result, which will only reduce the probability of samples with less reward. However, due to uncontrollable factors such as incomplete sampling, the unclear reward and punishment system may make the training of the generator unfair. Therefore, the traditional greedy decoding algorithm is introduced to select the word with the highest probability. Then D_φ will output this auxiliary sentence probability of being ground truth $D_\varphi(w_{1:T}^g)$ and present it as the baseline reward:

$$w_t^g = \arg\max p(w_t|h_t^{out})$$
$$r_{baseline} = D_\varphi(w_{1:T}^g) \tag{12}$$

The $Q_{D_\varphi}^{G_\theta}$ in (11) is supposed to be updated: each D_φ score of sentence sampled by N-time Monte Carlo search $D_\varphi(Y_{1:T}^n)$ should subtract $D_\varphi(w_{1:T}^g)$. Finally, the generator's parameters θ can be derived as (13), referring to likelihood ratios, we further build an unbiased estimation:

$$\nabla J(\theta) \approx \sum_{t=1}^{T} \nabla_\theta G_\theta(y_t|Y_{1:t-1}) * \frac{1}{N}\sum_{n=1}^{N}(D_\varphi(Y_{1:T}^n) - D_\varphi(w_{1:T}^g))$$
$$= \sum_{t=1}^{T} G_\theta * \nabla_\theta log G_\theta * \frac{1}{N}\sum_{n=1}^{N}(D_\varphi(Y_{1:T}^n) - D_\varphi(w_{1:T}^g)) \tag{13}$$
$$= \sum_{t=1}^{T} E_{y_t \sim G_\theta}[\nabla_\theta log G_\theta * \frac{1}{N}\sum_{n=1}^{N}(D_\varphi(Y_{1:T}^n) - D_\varphi(w_{1:T}^g))]$$

As the expectation $\mathbf{E}$ can be approximated by sampling, then we can update the generator's parameters as:

$$\theta \leftarrow \theta + a_t \nabla \theta J(\theta) \tag{14}$$

Here a_t denotes the corresponding learning rate at time step t. Once G_θ generates a more realistic sample, the model will retrain the discriminator D_φ according to the following formula:

$$\nabla_\theta J(\theta) = \mathbf{E}_{Y \sim p(data)}[log D_\varphi Y] - \mathbf{E}_{Y \sim G_\theta}[log(1 - D_\varphi(Y))] \tag{15}$$

D_φ and G_θ are trained alternatively after pre-train stage. When G_θ has been trained for g-steps, the D_φ needs to be re-trained for d-steps to keep in good pace with G_θ, which means G_θ should provide d different negative samples. The number of the positive samples from dataset S is set to the same as the negative samples from generator in each d-step D_φ re-training. With each pair of fused samples, we train D_φ for n epochs.

Algorithm 1. Image Captioning Based on Self-critical Adversarial Training.

Require: generator policy G_θ; roll-out policy G_β; discriminator D_φ; a sequence dataset S.

1: Initialize the G_θ and D_φ with random weights θ, φ
2: Pre-train G_θ on S on MLE
3: **repeat**
4:     **for** 1-steps **do**:
5:         Generate a sequence $Y_{1:T}$
6:         **for** t in 1:T **do**
7:             Compute $Q(a = y_t, s = Y_{1:t-1})$ by (11)
8:         **end for**
9:         Compute baseline reward $r_{baseline}$ based on greedy decoding
10:        Update generator parameters including W_{ij}^r by (13)
11:    **end for**
12:    **for** 5-steps **do**:
13:        Use current G_θ to generate negative samples and combine with ground truth one
14:        Train D_φ for 3 epochs by (15) on each group of sentences.
15:    **end for**
16:    $\beta \leftarrow \theta$
17: **until** SC-GAN converges

---

4 Experimental Results and Analysis

4.1 Implementation Details

We use the popular MSCOCO dataset to validate the performance of the proposed method. In the phase of extracting global features, we adapt ResNet-101 without the last two layers, and fine-tune their parameters on the MSCOCO. The extracted image feature I has a fixed size of $2048 * 14 * 14$. In more details, the number of neurons in LSTM sets to 512, the number of neurons in the three $1 * 1$ convolutional layers W_q, W_k, W_v are set to 64, 64, 512 separately. The attention weights α has the same space size with V, which is $14 * 14$. We also retrieve local object features using a Faster R-CNN pre-trained on the MSCOCO dataset. The top-15 detected object features are selected. We conduct our experiment on the Pytorch platform.

Following the optimal parameters setting in SeqGAN, the g, d and n in SC-GAN are set as 1, 5 and 3 separately and the maximum length of input sentence is set to 20. We firstly pre-train the G_θ for 10 epochs by MLE and subsequently pre-train the D_φ for 2500 iterations. Then the G_θ and D_φ can follow the adversarial training scheme. The batch size is set to 32 and learning rating is 0.001. All experiments are conducted on a server embedded with NVIDIA RTX2080Ti GPU and Ubuntu16.04 system.

4.2 Result and Analysis

Ablation Experiments. In order to independently verify the effectiveness of FAN, we first integrate the traditional MLE training method to conduct experiments. Compared with other advanced models that also used the cross-entropy method for training, the experimental results show in Table 1. What stands out in the table is that the FAN with the cross-entropy loss training method brings improvement in the major metric, which proves that it can make more reasonable use of the image feature information and excavate the potential internal relationship of the image regions.

To verify the effectiveness of SC-GAN, we further combine it with the FAN and compare the performance with the model that only contains FAN. The improvement is evident by comparing the results of Table 1 and Table 2. In addition, we also conduct comparative experiments with some advanced RL-based methods to verify the capacity of the whole model. As can be seen from the Table 2, when the SC-GAN is combined with FAN, there is a more significant increment in most metrics, our model can also bring comparable even better results compared with start-of-the-art methods in recent years, including several prevailing transformer-based models. The effectiveness of our proposed modules is more clearly reflected in Table 3.

Qualitative Analysis. In order to show our model's effect more intuitively, we visualize the attention weights in Fig. 4 to demonstrate that our model can accurately simulate human perception. We first expand our attention weight

Table 1. Performance of our model and other advanced models based on cross-entropy, where B@N, M, R, C and S are short for BLEU@N, METEOR, ROUGE-L, CIDEr-D and SPICE scores.

Methods	B@1	B@4	M	R	C	S
SCST [13]	–	30.0	25.9	53.4	00.4	–
HAN [19]	77.2	36.2	27.5	56.6	114.8	20.6
DAIC [21]	73.7	34.2	26.4	54.8	106.2	–
Up-Down [1]	77.2	36.2	27.0	56.4	113.5	20.3
RFNet [9]	76.4	35.8	27.4	56.8	112.5	20.5
GCN-LSTM [23]	77.3	36.8	27.9	57.0	116.3	20.9
AoANet [8]	77.4	37.2	**28.4**	57.5	**119.8**	21.3
ARL [17]	75.9	35.8	27.8	56.4	111.3	–
CL-topdown [20]	–	37.08	27.85	57.22	117.10	–
Ours (FAN)	**78.3**	**37.9**	27.8	**58.5**	119.6	**21.5**

Table 2. Performance comparison with other advanced models based on Reinforcement Learning. [†] means the original model is ensembled with self-critical training.

Methods	B@1	B@4	M	R	C	S
SCST:Att2all [13]	–	34.2	26.7	55.7	114.0	–
G-GAN [5]	–	29.7	22.4	47.5	79.5	–
DAIC[†] [21]	77.6	35.4	26.7	56.5	116.8	–
HAN[†] [19]	80.9	37.6	27.8	58.1	121.7	21.5
UP-DOWN[†] [1]	79.8	36.3	27.7	56.9	120.1	21.4
GCN-LSTM[†] [23]	80.5	38.2	28.5	58.3	127.6	22.0
IIEK[†] [7]	79.3	37.3	27.7	56.9	120.4	–
IDGAN [10]	81.3	38.5	28.5	58.8	123.5	–
AoANet[†] [8]	81.6	40.2	29.3	**59.4**	**132.0**	22.8
SLL-SLE [3]	–	–	27.0	–	119.6	19.9
POS-SCAN [26]	80.2	38.0	28.5	–	126.1	22.2
Ours (FAN+SC-GAN)	**82.1**	**40.9**	**29.6**	59.1	129.6	**22.9**

Table 3. Performance of our key modules combined with other baseline module.

Methods	B@1	B@4	M	R	C	S
FAN+cross-entropy training	78.3	37.9	27.8	58.5	119.6	21.5
HAN[19]+SC-GAN	80.2	38.6	28.5	58.7	125.9	22.1
FAN+SC-GAN	**82.1**	**40.9**	**29.6**	**59.1**	**129.6**	**22.9**

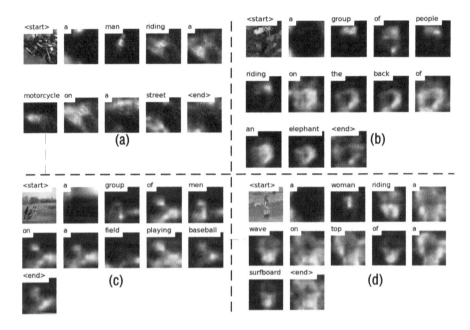

Fig. 4. Examples illustrate word prediction when attending on different image regions.

24 times and adjust it to the same size as the input image by the Gaussian filter. Closer inspection of Fig. 4 shows that the model can not only focus on the corresponding target image area when generating the main object, but also grasp the key areas in the graph when generating the words describing the relationship between different objects. For example, in Fig. 4(a), when generating the word "riding", the model obviously focuses on the image part connected to the person and the motorcycle. In Fig. 4(c), when generating the word "baseball", the image not only pays attention to the word "baseball" itself, but also pays adequate attention to the baseball cap on the head. These demonstrates the model can utilize the semantic information effectively.

The effect of our model at the sentence level is presented in Fig. 5, we compare the ground-truth sentences, descriptions generated by the MLE training-based model, and the generated sentences. The red texts are the sentences generated by the proposed model, which are more accurate and natural than the MLE-based model, which are shown in blue. Significantly, the proposed model shows superior performance in detecting the fine-grained properties of the image. For example, in Fig. 5(c), we successfully detect the "barrel", and in (d) the keyword "ball" is obtained. What's more, we successfully excavate the critical relationship between image areas. In Fig. 5(a), the successful detection of the verb "riding" shows the importance of relation features. Besides, it is believed that the word "barrel" plays a crucial role in generating the word "wine", which indicated our local-relation attention mechanism could effectively take advantage of the potential information between regions again. Our model has impressive performance in generating the words that describe the regional relationship to obtain a more vivid and appropriate image caption.

(a)

Ground Truth: a couple of men riding horses on top of a green field
MLE: a group of people in a field with a Horse
Ours: two man are riding their horses in a green field

(b)

Ground Truth: woman cutting pizza with fork and knife sitting next to young girl
MLE: a woman sitting at a table with a pizza
Ours: a woman and a boy are sitting at a tabel with a pizza in front of them

(c)

Ground Truth: the people are samplin g wine at a wine tasting
MLE: a group of people sitting at a table with a food
Ours: a group of people tasting wine next to some barrels

(d)

Ground Truth: two people playing tennis in a neighborhood park
MLE: a man holding a tennis ball on a tennis court
Ours: two people on the tennis court one serves the ball

Fig. 5. Visualization of the generated descriptions. All samples are randomly selected.

5   Conclusion

In this paper, we propose a new fused attention mechanism, integrating global attention achieved by self-attention and local-relation attention. For each region, the relation features are assigned with attention weights together with the local features to better excavate the potentially important information of the image. Besides, we also improve the traditional GAN with a self-critical training method. In this way, the reward and punishment system becomes more explicit. The model training process can be more stable and effective. Experiments on the MSCOCO dataset demonstrate both of the two innovations can boost the quality of the generated sentences.

Acknowledgement. This work is supported by National Natural Science Foundation of China (Nos. 61966004, 61866004, 61762078), Guangxi Natural Science Foundation (Nos. 2019GXNSFDA245018, 2018GXNSFDA281009), Innovation Project of Guangxi Graduate Education (No. XYCBZ2021002), Guangxi "Bagui Scholar" Teams for Innovation and Research Project, Guangxi Talent Highland Project of Big Data Intelligence and Application, and Guangxi Collaborative Innovation Center of Multi-source Information Integration and Intelligent Processing.

References

1. Anderson, P., et al.: Bottom-up and top-down attention for image captioning and visual question answering. In: Proceedings of the IEEE Conference on Computer Vision and Pattern Recognition, pp. 6077–6086 (2018)

2. Bahdanau, D., Cho, K., Bengio, Y.: Neural machine translation by jointly learning to align and translate. arXiv preprint arXiv:1409.0473 (2014)
3. Chen, J., Jin, Q.: Better captioning with sequence-level exploration. In: Proceedings of the IEEE/CVF Conference on Computer Vision and Pattern Recognition, pp. 10890–10899 (2020)
4. Creswell, A., White, T., Dumoulin, V., Arulkumaran, K., Sengupta, B., Bharath, A.A.: Generative adversarial networks: an overview. IEEE Signal Process. Mag. **35**(1), 53–65 (2018)
5. Dai, B., Fidler, S., Urtasun, R., Lin, D.: Towards diverse and natural image descriptions via a conditional GAN. In: Proceedings of the IEEE International Conference on Computer Vision, pp. 2970–2979 (2017)
6. Hochreiter, S., Schmidhuber, J.: Long short-term memory. Neural Comput. **9**(8), 1735–1780 (1997)
7. Huang, F., Li, Z., Wei, H., Zhang, C., Ma, H.: Boost image captioning with knowledge reasoning. Mach. Learn. **109**(12), 2313–2332 (2020)
8. Huang, L., Wang, W., Chen, J., Wei, X.Y.: Attention on attention for image captioning. In: Proceedings of the IEEE/CVF International Conference on Computer Vision, pp. 4634–4643 (2019)
9. Jiang, W., Ma, L., Jiang, Y.-G., Liu, W., Zhang, T.: Recurrent fusion network for image captioning. In: Ferrari, V., Hebert, M., Sminchisescu, C., Weiss, Y. (eds.) ECCV 2018. LNCS, vol. 11206, pp. 510–526. Springer, Cham (2018). https://doi.org/10.1007/978-3-030-01216-8_31
10. Liu, J., et al.: Interactive dual generative adversarial networks for image captioning. In: Proceedings of the AAAI Conference on Artificial Intelligence, vol. 34, pp. 11588–11595 (2020)
11. Ranzato, M., Chopra, S., Auli, M., Zaremba, W.: Sequence level training with recurrent neural networks. arXiv preprint arXiv:1511.06732 (2015)
12. Ren, S., He, K., Girshick, R., Sun, J.: Faster R-CNN: towards real-time object detection with region proposal networks. In: Advances in Neural Information Processing Systems, pp. 91–99 (2015)
13. Rennie, S.J., Marcheret, E., Mroueh, Y., Ross, J., Goel, V.: Self-critical sequence training for image captioning. In: Proceedings of the IEEE Conference on Computer Vision and Pattern Recognition, pp. 7008–7024 (2017)
14. Sutton, R.S., Barto, A.G.: Reinforcement Learning: An Introduction. MIT Press, Cambridge (2018)
15. Sutton, R.S., McAllester, D.A., Singh, S.P., Mansour, Y., et al.: Policy gradient methods for reinforcement learning with function approximation. In: Advances in Neural Information Processing Systems, pp. 1057–1063 (1999)
16. Vaswani, A., et al.: Attention is all you need. In: Advances in Neural Information Processing Systems, pp. 5998–6008 (2017)
17. Wang, J., Wang, W., Wang, L., Wang, Z., Feng, D.D., Tan, T.: Learning visual relationship and context-aware attention for image captioning. Pattern Recogn. **98**, 107075 (2020)
18. Wang, L., Bai, Z., Zhang, Y., Lu, H.: Show, recall, and tell: image captioning with recall mechanism. In: Proceedings of the AAAI Conference on Artificial Intelligence, vol. 34, pp. 12176–12183 (2020)
19. Wang, W., Chen, Z., Hu, H.: Hierarchical attention network for image captioning. In: Proceedings of the AAAI Conference on Artificial Intelligence, vol. 33, pp. 8957–8964 (2019)
20. Wang, Z., Huang, Z., Luo, Y.: Human consensus-oriented image captioning. In: IJCAI, pp. 659–665 (2020)

21. Wei, H., Li, Z., Zhang, C., Ma, H.: The synergy of double attention: combine sentence-level and word-level attention for image captioning. Comput. Vis. Image Underst. **201**, 103068 (2020)
22. Xu, K., et al.: Show, attend and tell: neural image caption generation with visual attention. In: International Conference on Machine Learning, pp. 2048–2057. PMLR (2015)
23. Yao, T., Pan, Y., Li, Y., Mei, T.: Exploring visual relationship for image captioning. In: Ferrari, V., Hebert, M., Sminchisescu, C., Weiss, Y. (eds.) Computer Vision – ECCV 2018. LNCS, vol. 11218, pp. 711–727. Springer, Cham (2018). https://doi.org/10.1007/978-3-030-01264-9_42
24. You, Q., Jin, H., Wang, Z., Fang, C., Luo, J.: Image captioning with semantic attention. In: Proceedings of the IEEE Conference on Computer Vision and Pattern Recognition, pp. 4651–4659 (2016)
25. Yu, L., Zhang, W., Wang, J., Yu, Y.: SeqGAN: sequence generative adversarial nets with policy gradient. In: Proceedings of the AAAI Conference on Artificial Intelligence, vol. 31, pp. 2852–2858 (2017)
26. Zhou, Y., Wang, M., Liu, D., Hu, Z., Zhang, H.: More grounded image captioning by distilling image-text matching model. In: Proceedings of the IEEE/CVF Conference on Computer Vision and Pattern Recognition, pp. 4777–4786 (2020)

Element Re-identification in Crowdtesting

Li Zhang[1]([✉])[ID] and Wei-Tek Tsai[1,2,3,4,5]

[1] Digital Society and Blockchain Laboratory, Beihang University, Beijing, China
[2] Arizona State University, Tempe, AZ 85287, USA
[3] Beijing Tiande Technologies, Beijing, China
[4] Andrew International Sandbox Institute, Qingdao, China
[5] IOB Laboratory, National Big Data Comprehensive Experimental Area, Guizhou, China

Abstract. Software usually provides different GUI layouts for different devices for a better user experience. This increases the workload of testing, so crowdsourced testing is needed to reduce costs. The crowdsourced testing will perform similar test steps for each GUI layout and record them. After the software is updated, each GUI layout can be automatically tested according to these test records. A test record contains several steps, and each step contains an operation and an element. The automated test is to find the element according to the recorded element attributes and then perform the recorded operation. The idea of manually testing one GUI layout and then automatically testing other GUI layouts does not work. Because an element may have different attributes in different GUI layouts, the attributes recorded in one GUI layout cannot guarantee that the elements will be found correctly in another GUI layout. However, humans can easily find the same element in different GUI layouts. This is because the appearance of the same element in different GUI layouts is similar. Humans can easily perceive this with their eyes, and so can AI. To achieve this, we propose an approach of visually re-identifying elements. Specifically, our method consists of two convolutional neural networks, Element Re-Identification Network (ERINet) and UNet. ERINet can identify whether two elements are the same or different. UNet provides ERINet with attention masks of elements and backgrounds which can help improve the accuracy. Furthermore, we introduce a new dataset for element re-identification, which contains 31,098 element images and 170 background images. Our method achieves excellent performance on this dataset. Our code and dataset are made publicly available at https://github.com/laridzhang/ERINet.

Keywords: Crowdtesting · Element re-identification · Convolutional neural network · Attention mechanism

1 Introduction

A lot of software requires long-term updates to fix bugs and add new features. In order to attract more users, the software also needs to run on different devices

© Springer Nature Switzerland AG 2021
D. N. Pham et al. (Eds.): PRICAI 2021, LNAI 13031, pp. 212–225, 2021.
https://doi.org/10.1007/978-3-030-89188-6_16

(different hardware or operation systems). Every version of the software needs to be fully tested on all kinds of devices. This will lead to a substantial increase in testing workload, especially the testing of software with GUI. In order to reduce costs, more and more test platforms use crowdsourcing to complete the test, and we call them the crowdsourced test (CST) platforms. In this paper, we only discuss the testing of software that has a GUI.

We investigated several CST platforms such as TestProject [16], Testim [15], Applitools [2], Testsigma [17], TestBirds [14], and AppQuality [3]. At first, the CST platforms would allow multiple testers to complete all the tests. Subsequently, the CST platforms found that only the first round of testing was required to complete by testers. If they record the first round of testing, most of the later versions of the software can be tested automatically, although some test steps will fail. These failed test steps require testers to test again. Recently, the CST platforms have discovered that artificial intelligence (AI) can fix most of these failed test steps in automated testing.

Automated testing is performed based on test records. The first test record was manually created by the crowdsourced testers. The test record contains the information of the elements (such as user avatars, buttons, logos, images, and links) and operations (such as click and drag) of each test step. Most failed test steps are caused by missing elements. For example, elements in web pages are located by identifiers such as XPath, CSS selector, name, and id. Once the GUI layout changes, the identifier of the element also changes. Then the element cannot be found according to the previously recorded identifier.

Some crowdsourced test platforms [15,16] increase the probability of finding the element by recording several or hundreds of identifiers and then rely on a recommendation algorithm to sort these identifiers according to the likelihood of finding the element to improve efficiency. This did have some effect. But think about this question: why humans can find the same elements in different GUI layouts completely correctly. This is because the same elements in different GUI layouts look the same or similar, which humans know at a glance. And this is exactly the task that AI is good at, specifically, the computer vision methods based on deep learning.

With the element images recorded in the previous test, the process for humans to find the element is to match the corresponding element in the GUI of this test according to the image, which is a task of image matching. Using a screenshot of the area where the element is located is the best way to record the element, because screenshots can be used for all types of elements in the GUI. But using screenshots to match elements also makes this different from other image matching tasks.

When an element changes its position due to updates or different devices, the background on which the element is located may change. In other words, the background area of the element screenshot may change in different tests while the element area stays the same. Common image matching algorithms can be misled by changing backgrounds. The algorithm for finding elements needs to be able to identify the same elements in different backgrounds, that is, element re-identification. Element re-identification is a different task from image matching. It needs to distinguish the subjects and backgrounds in the two images. Then it matches the subjects in the two images, and ignore the similarities or differences in the backgrounds.

We propose a novel method for element re-identification based on deep learning in this paper. To achieve this, we collect a new dataset for element re-identification in GUI. Experiments prove that our method has achieved high accuracy. We apply an attention mechanism to our method for distinguishing elements and background, and it achieves better accuracy. We also analyzed the results of the experiment in detail.

The contributions of this paper are summarized as follows.

(1) We propose a novel convolutional neural network (CNN) model for the re-identification of elements in GUI.
(2) We propose a method to realize the attention mechanism for element re-identification. It can focus the model's attention on the element itself instead of the background when it needs to be identified.
(3) We collected a new dataset for the re-identification of elements in the GUI.

This paper is organized as follows: Sect. 2 introduces related work; Sect. 3 presents our elements re-identification method, which mainly includes a dataset and a CNN model with an attention mechanism for re-identifying elements in previous tests; Sect. 4 introduces the experiments and results of our method; Sect. 5 concludes this paper.

2   Related Work

Each test step in the record is an operation (such as clicking, dragging, typing characters) for an element (such as button, link, icon, avatar, textbox). Elements are identified by recorded attributes (such as ID, name, XPath, CSS selector). All these CST platforms [15,16] use attributes to find elements and none of them uses visual methods.

2.1   Element Attribute Recommendation

To increase the possibility of finding elements, these CST platforms [15,16] record multiple attributes of each element. The number of recorded attributes varies from a few to hundreds. In the next test, they look for available ones from these records. This can improve the success rate of automated tests. The greater the number of attributes recorded, the higher the success rate. But the time consuming to find available records will increase. To solve this problem, some CST platforms have introduced AI-based recommendation algorithms or ranking algorithms. They use AI to recommend the attributes that are most likely to be available.

None of these crowdsourced test platforms disclose the specific AI algorithm to achieve this function. But they mentioned that they would rank each attribute of the element or assign weights to these attributes. Similar algorithms can refer to RankNet [5], LambdaRank [6], LambdaMART [7].

These CST platforms provide a simple solution to avoid the invalidation of a single attribute by recording multiple attributes. But this does not prevent the invalidation of all recorded attributes. A better solution of element re-identification is through vision. If the layout of a web page changes, humans can still easily find the previous element. Humans use vision to judge, and computers can do it too. Since we can use screenshots to record visual information of all types of elements, using screenshots to find the elements is the most conducive to all situations.

One good idea is to use an image comparison algorithm to determine whether the current screenshot of the element is consistent with the recorded screenshot. It should be noted that the current image comparison algorithms cannot distinguish between the subject (element) and the background in the image. If the background of the element is changed due to various reasons, these algorithms will give wrong results.

2.2   Real World Image Comparison

There are many approaches to judge the similarity of two images. Most of these methods focus on judging real-world images, rather than software GUI screenshots. In addition, these methods compare the entire image, not the subject in the image.

Traditional methods have used SIFT [11] or similar hand-craft methods [18,19] to extract features. To compare the distances of features more conveniently, these methods usually use dimensionality reduction methods [4] before calculating the distances.

Convolutional neural networks (CNNs) have achieved many exciting results in computer vision tasks. MC-CNN [21,22] inspired by this can determine whether the two image patches match, so as to achieve the stereo matching. However, MC-CNN can only match very similar image patches. Elements that change positions in the GUI may have completely different backgrounds, so MC-CNN will not be competent. Similar to this, there are methods [1,20] for calculating the similarity of image pairs.

The current image comparison methods, whether they are traditional methods or CNN methods, cannot be used to solve the problem of element re-identification. Different GUI layouts or dynamic GUI and other reasons will cause the background in the element screenshot to change. Therefore, it is inappropriate to use these methods to determine whether the elements in the two screenshots match. The difficulty of element re-identification is how to judge whether the elements in the images match, while avoiding the influence of the backgrounds in the images. A good element re-identification method requires the ability to distinguish between the elements and the backgrounds in the images. This is precisely what is difficult to achieve with current image comparison or matching methods.

3   Element Re-identification

We propose a multi-task method based on deep learning to solve this problem. Our idea is to find the element based on the visual information of the element in the screenshot. This method is the same as the way humans find the elements, so it is very reliable.

In this section, we first introduce a dataset that can be used for element re-identification. Then we introduce an Element Re-Identification Network (ERINet) for identifying the same elements in different backgrounds. We also introduce an attention mechanism for reducing the adverse effect of background on element re-identification.

3.1   Dataset

We collected 31,098 images of various types of GUI elements and 170 high-resolution background images from the Internet. The resolution of element images ranges from 32×32 to 512×512, which covers common element sizes. These element images have various shapes and colors. Some samples of the element images are shown in Fig. 1(a).

(a) Elements   (b) Backgrounds

Fig. 1. Some samples of element images and some samples cropped from the background images in the dataset.

The resolution of background images ranges from 225×225 to 5369×7994. The background images contain various colors and textures. These images will be randomly cropped into small patches as the background of the element images. Some samples cropped from the background images are shown in Fig. 1(b).

The same element image with different background patches stands for GUI changes. Different element images with any background patches stand for different elements in GUI.

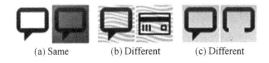

(a) Same   (b) Different   (c) Different

Fig. 2. Some samples of the same or different elements with backgrounds.

Some samples of the same or different elements with the background are shown in Fig. 2. Figure 2(a) shows a pair of the same elements with different backgrounds and its label is the "Same" . Similarly, the same elements with the same background will also be labeled as the "Same". Figure 2(b) shows a pair of different elements with the same background and its label is the "Different" . Similarly, different elements with different backgrounds will be labeled as the "Different". Figure 2(c) shows another pair of different elements. It should be noted that this pair of different elements comes from the same element image, but part of the element on the right is removed. All of these samples and labels can be generated from the element images and background images of the dataset.

3.2   The Element Re-identification Network

We propose the Element Re-Identification Network (ERINet) for identifying the same elements in different backgrounds. The structure of this network is inspired by the success of the VGG [13] and the feature extraction method of the ASNet [8]. The input of our ERINet will be two images of elements with backgrounds. To reduce the amount of network calculation, we use two shared weights backbone networks for feature extraction. Specifically, we removed the deepest pooling layer, all fully-connected layers, and the softmax layer of the VGG-16 [13] and then put rest convolutional layers and max pool layers as the backbone network. This makes our network a fully convolutional network and is good for adding attention. To obtain the desired label output, we used a combination of convolutional layers, a transposed convolutional layer, an average pooling layer, and a softmax layer to map the features to the label. The ERINet architecture is presented in Fig. 3.

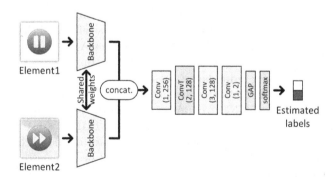

Fig. 3. The configurations of the Element Re-Identification Network (ERINet).

There are four new convolutional layers on top of the backbone. The first one has convolutional kernels with a size of 1×1 and has 256 output channels. The second one is a deconvolutional layer that has 2×2 kernels with a stride of 2 pixels. The third one has 3×3 kernels and 128 output channels. The fourth one has 1×1 kernels and 2 output maps. Then these two feature maps are mapped to the labels through the global average pooling layer and the softmax layer.

3.3 The Attention Mechanism

As we can see, the background area in the element images may adversely affect the estimation result of ERINet. We will elaborate on this adverse effect in the section of the experiment. We expect ERINet to focus on extracting the features of the element areas in the image, rather than the background. Therefore, we propose an attention mechanism that can be used in ERINet.

Benefiting from the alpha channel in the original element images, we can accurately distinguish the element area and background area in the images. Some element images and corresponding ground truth masks are shown in Fig. 4. Figure 4(a) shows the element images. Figure 4(b) shows the ground truth masks. The black areas in the masks represent the background areas, and their values are 0. The white areas in the masks represent the element areas, and their values are 1.

Fig. 4. Some samples of element images and corresponding ground truth masks.

Using these element images and masks, we propose an attention mechanism based on distinguishing background and element areas. Inspired by the success of UNet [12] in medical image segmentation, we use its network structure to provide ERINet with an attention mechanism. We apply the attention masks to the feature maps of the ERINet to remove the adverse effects of the background. The structure of the ERINet with attention (ERINet-A) is shown in Fig. 5.

The attention masks are generated using UNet. In order to make the estimated masks have some redundancy, we dilate the masks by 10 pixels. Then they are used to set the feature values in the background areas of the feature maps generated by the ERINet to 0. After this, all the feature values that affect the estimated labels come from the element area. ERINet's attention will be focused on the element area and ignore the influence of the background area. The feature maps applied with attention masks will be processed by the global average pooling layer and the softmax layer to obtain the estimated labels.

4   Experiments

In this section, we will first introduce the data settings for training and testing. Then we will introduce the details of the experiment of the ERINet and the UNet for attention mechanism. Finally, we will introduce the training details and test results of the ERINet-A.

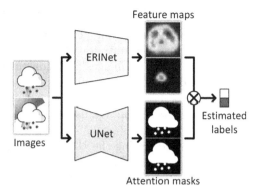

Fig. 5. The configurations of the ERINet with attention (ERINet-A).

4.1 Basic Data Settings

There is a total of 31,098 element images in the dataset. We use about 10% of the randomly selected element images as the test set and the rest as the training set. There are 27988 element images in the training set and 3110 element images in the test set. All element images are resized to 128 pixels on the long side with a ratio fixed. All background images are resized to no more than 1024 pixels on the long side and no less than 256 pixels on the short side with a ratio fixed. If the long side and short side of the original background image meet this range, it will not be resized. When scaling the background image, give priority to ensuring that the short side meets the requirements.

Before using an element image for training or testing, we need to attach a background image to it. We will randomly select a background image and randomly crop a small area as the background. The length and width of this small area are 20 pixels larger than that of the element image. The element image is placed in the center of the cropped background image. Since the background is random every time the element image is used, we used the same original background image in training and testing.

4.2 Training and Testing Settings

Every element image for training or testing is generated using an element image and a patch cropped from a background image. There are four types of generated data. The first category is same element images and different backgrounds. The corresponding ground truth label is "same". This category accounts for about 40% of the total data. The second category is same element image and same background. But one of the element images will be partially removed at a random location. As a result, one of the elements is original, while the other is partially missing. Therefore, from the perspective of human vision, these two element images are different. In the actual software GUI, two elements like this will have different meanings. So the corresponding ground truth label is "different".

This category accounts for about 20% of the total data. The third category is different element images and same background. The corresponding ground truth label is "different". This category accounts for about 20% of the total data. The fourth category is different element images and different backgrounds. The corresponding ground truth label is "different". This category accounts for about 20% of the total data. The ground truth labels used to calculate the loss will be converted into a two-digit representation. We use (1, 0) to mean "same", and (0, 1) to mean "different".

The data used for training and testing the UNet is the element images and the corresponding ground truth masks. The ground truth masks are generated based on the alpha channel in the element images. In the mask, the value of pixels belonging to the background is 0, and the value of pixels belonging to the element is 1.

4.3   Evaluation and Analysis

Below we will introduce the test results of the ERINet, the UNet for attention mechanism, and the ERINet-A.

ERINet. We loop the test 20 times on the entire test set, and the average correct rate of the ERINet was **99.38%**. Some samples of test results are shown in Fig. 6. The "GT" and "ET" in the upper left corner of each test result image represent the ground truth label and estimated label, respectively. Each test result image is composed of four small images. The upper row is two element images input to the network. The bottom row is two feature maps output by the last convolutional layer of the ERINet. The original feature maps are grayscale images (single-channel images containing response values). For better visualization, we map them to heat maps. The red in the heat maps represents the high response value, and the blue represents the low response value. It can be seen that the areas with high response values in the two feature maps represent similar and dissimilar areas respectively. In detail, the similar parts in the two input images have high response values at corresponding positions in the left feature map. The dissimilar parts have high response values in the corresponding positions in the right feature map. Because there is no attention mechanism, there are some high response values in the area corresponding to the background in the feature maps of the ERINet. The response values in the feature maps will affect the final estimated labels. In other words, these abnormal response values in the background area may lead to incorrectly estimated labels. Obviously, if the attention mechanism is added, the influence of the background is less, and the estimation result of ERINet can be more stable and accurate. Therefore, below we introduce the experiment of adding attention mechanism through the UNet.

UNet for Attention Mechanism. We loop the test 20 times on the entire test set, and the average Intersection-over-Union (IoU) of the UNet was **97.30%**. Some samples of test results are shown in Fig. 7. Each test result is composed of

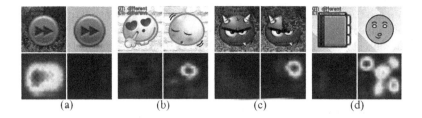

Fig. 6. Some samples of ERINet test results. (Color figure online)

three images. The images in the first row are element images that input to the network. The second row is the ground truth masks. The third row is the binary estimated masks that output by the network. The accuracy of the estimated masks is very high. Whether it is a regular-shaped element image, or a complex-shaped element image, or even an element image drawn by lines, the estimated mask can well segment elements from the background. On this basis, we can eliminate the influence of the background areas in the feature maps of ERINet according to the estimated masks. Below we will introduce the experiment results of the ERINet-A.

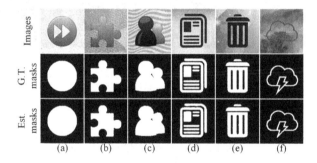

Fig. 7. Some samples of attention mask test results.

ERINet-A. We loop the test 20 times on the entire test set, and the average correct rate of the ERINet-A was **99.84%**. Compared with the ERINet, there is a significant improvement. On average, in a test of 3110 samples, the estimated results of more than 3101 samples are correct. Some samples of test results are shown in Fig. 8. The layout of each sub-image is the same as the above ERINet test results. This time, due to the support of the attention mechanism, no matter what background the input image is, the background part of the feature maps no longer have an obvious response value. In Fig. 8(a), there are samples of the same element image with different backgrounds. The left feature maps of these samples only have high response values in the element area, because the two elements are the same. The feature map on the right shows the different parts of the input image, but there is almost no response value, even if their backgrounds are different. This is because the network's attention is completely focused on the element areas while ignoring the differences in the backgrounds. In Fig. 8(b) and (c), there are samples of different elements with different backgrounds. The background areas of both feature maps do not have any response value. The response values are concentrated in the element areas. Therefore, the attention mechanism in these samples is also successful. In Fig. 8(d), there are samples of different elements with the same background. The feature map on the left shows the similarity of the two input images. The reason why there is no obvious response value is that the attention mechanism makes the network ignore the same background. Since the elements are not similar, there is no obvious response value in the left feature map. In addition, the response values in the right feature map are concentrated in the element area. There is no response value in the background area. This shows that the attention mechanism also performs well in this type of sample.

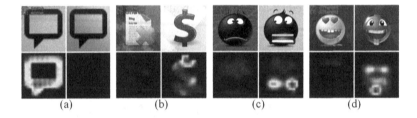

Fig. 8. Some samples of ERINet-A test results.

Based on the analysis of the results of the above three models, the following summary can be drawn. Firstly, the ERINet can achieve good element re-identification accuracy. However, it can be observed from its feature maps that the backgrounds have adverse effects on the estimation result. Secondly, the UNet used for the attention mechanism can accurately distinguish between the elements and the backgrounds in the images, even if the appearances of the elements and the backgrounds are complex and changeable. Finally, the ERINet-A can achieve higher accuracy of element re-identification. The main reason for this is that the attention mechanism helps the network reduce the adverse effects of the backgrounds.

4.4   Ablation Study

To quantify the effect of the attention mask, we counted the distribution of feature values in the ground truth background area of the feature maps before and after applying the mask. When there are nonzero values in the ground truth background area, they may have negative effects on the accuracy. The ideal situation is that the feature values of the background are all zeros, and the values of the foreground are relatively high. This means that the network concentrates its attention entirely on the elements, rather than the background. Therefore, we can understand the effectiveness of the network's attention mechanism by observing the distribution of feature values in the ground truth background area. To avoid the effect of random backgrounds, we also tested 20 cycles on the entire test set and calculate the averages. We first normalize the maximum value of the feature map to 1. Then the distribution of the normalized feature values in the ground truth background area of the feature map is counted and shown in Table 1. The ratio values in the table have been rounded. After applying the attention masks, the number of zero feature values has significantly increased from 64.42% to 90.40%, which means that the total number of non-zero feature values has been significantly reduced. In the ten equally spaced intervals from 0 to 1, the proportion of the number of non-zero feature values decreased from 27.79% to a maximum of 82.73%. The fewer the non-zero feature value of the background area, the more the network ignores the background area because of its attention.

Table 1. The distribution of feature values in the ground truth background area.

Value intervals	Ratio in background		Reduction ratio
	w/o attention	w/attention	
0	64.42%	90.40%	–
(0, 0.1]	20.57%	3.55%	82.73%
(0.1, 0.2]	6.20%	1.78%	71.22%
(0.2, 0.3]	3.15%	1.26%	60.07%
(0.3, 0.4]	1.90%	0.87%	54.15%
(0.4, 0.5]	1.27%	0.64%	49.64%
(0.5, 0.6]	0.90%	0.50%	45.03%
(0.6, 0.7]	0.65%	0.39%	40.39%
(0.7, 0.8]	0.46%	0.29%	36.53%
(0.8, 0.9]	0.29%	0.19%	34.00%
(0.9, 1.0]	0.19%	0.13%	27.79%

As mentioned in the Sect. 4.2, we divided the element images into four categories. The proportions of these four categories in training data and test data are similar. In order to clarify the correct rate of ERINet-A on each category of data, we conducted tests on each category of test data separately. Since the data is randomly generated, we also conducted multiple rounds of testing and averaged the results. The results are shown in Table 2. The correct rate shown in the table has been rounded. These results show that ERINet-A has the highest correct rate when the original element images are different. When the original element images are the same, the correct rate is slightly lower. The partially missing element image is very similar to the original element image, only the missing part is different from the original. This is very challenging and will slightly reduce the correct rate of ERINet-A.

Table 2. The distribution of feature values in the ground truth background area.

Category	Correct rate	Data proportion
1	99.78%	40%
2	99.67%	20%
3	99.99%	20%
4	99.97%	20%
Ave.	99.84%	–

5 Conclusion

In this article, we propose to use visual methods to solve the problem of re-identification of elements in software testing. To this end, we propose an Element Re-Identification Network (ERINet) and its attention mechanism. In order to train and validate our proposed method, we also introduce a new dataset for element re-identification. Extensive experiments on this dataset have proved that the method has excellent performance.

Acknowledgement. This work is supported by Chinese Ministry of Science and Technology (Grant No. 2018YFB1402700). This work is also supported by National Key Laboratory of Software Environment at Beihang University, National 973 Program (Grant No. 2013CB329601) and National Natural Science Foundation of China (Grant No. 61690202).

References

1. Appalaraju, S., Chaoji, V.: Image similarity using deep CNN and curriculum learning. arXiv preprint arXiv:1709.08761 (2017)
2. Applitools: Automated visual testing with visual AI. [EB/OL]. https://applitools.com/. Accessed 22 May 2021
3. AppQuality: Appquality: real crowd, digital quality. [EB/OL]. https://www.app-quality.com/. Accessed 22 May 2021
4. Brown, M., Hua, G., Winder, S.: Discriminative learning of local image descriptors. IEEE Trans. Pattern Anal. Mach. Intell. **33**(1), 43–57 (2010)
5. Burges, C., et al.: Learning to rank using gradient descent. In: Proceedings of the 22nd International Conference on Machine Learning, pp. 89–96 (2005)
6. Burges, C., Ragno, R., Le, Q.: Learning to rank with nonsmooth cost functions. Adv. Neural Inf. Process. Syst. **19**, 193–200 (2006)

7. Burges, C.J.: From ranknet to lambdarank to lambdamart: an overview. Learning **11**(23–581), 81 (2010)
8. Jiang, X., et al.: Attention scaling for crowd counting. In: Proceedings of the IEEE/CVF Conference on Computer Vision and Pattern Recognition, pp. 4706–4715 (2020)
9. Kaggle: Carvana image masking challenge. [EB/OL]. https://www.kaggle.com/c/carvana-image-masking-challenge/. Accessed 22 May 2021
10. Kingma, D.P., Ba, J.: Adam: a method for stochastic optimization. arXiv preprint arXiv:1412.6980 (2014)
11. Lowe, D.G.: Distinctive image features from scale-invariant keypoints. Int. J. Comput. Vis. **60**(2), 91–110 (2004)
12. Ronneberger, O., Fischer, P., Brox, T.: U-Net: convolutional networks for biomedical image segmentation. In: Navab, N., Hornegger, J., Wells, W.M., Frangi, A.F. (eds.) MICCAI 2015. LNCS, vol. 9351, pp. 234–241. Springer, Cham (2015). https://doi.org/10.1007/978-3-319-24574-4_28
13. Simonyan, K., Zisserman, A.: Very deep convolutional networks for large-scale image recognition. arXiv preprint arXiv:1409.1556 (2014)
14. Testbirds: Home of crowdtesting: Ux and usability testing. [EB/OL]. https://www.testbirds.com/. Accessed 22 May 2021
15. Testim: Automated functional testing - software testing tool. [EB/OL]. https://www.testim.io/. Accessed 22 May 2021
16. TestProject: Free test automation for all. [EB/OL]. https://testproject.io/. Accessed 22 May 2021
17. Testsigma: Cloud-based automation testing tool for web and mobile. [EB/OL]. https://testsigma.com/. Accessed 22 May 2021
18. Tola, E., Lepetit, V., Fua, P.: A fast local descriptor for dense matching. In: IEEE Conference on Computer Vision and Pattern Recognition, pp. 1–8. IEEE (2008)
19. Trzcinski, T., Christoudias, C.M., Lepetit, V., Fua, P.: Learning image descriptors with the boosting-trick. In: Conference and Workshop on Neural Information Processing Systems (2012)
20. Zagoruyko, S., Komodakis, N.: Learning to compare image patches via convolutional neural networks. In: Proceedings of the IEEE Conference on Computer Vision and Pattern Recognition, pp. 4353–4361 (2015)
21. Zbontar, J., LeCun, Y.: Computing the stereo matching cost with a convolutional neural network. In: Proceedings of the IEEE Conference on Computer Vision and Pattern Recognition, pp. 1592–1599 (2015)
22. Zbontar, J., LeCun, Y., et al.: Stereo matching by training a convolutional neural network to compare image patches. J. Mach. Learn. Res. **17**(1), 2287–2318 (2016)

Flame and Smoke Detection Algorithm for UAV Based on Improved YOLOv4-Tiny

Ruinan Wu[1] , Changchun Hua[2(✉)], Weili Ding[2], Yifan Wang[2] ,
and Yubao Wang[1]

[1] School of Information Science and Engineering, Yanshan University,
Qinhuangdao, China
wyb@ysu.edu.cn
[2] School of Electrical Engineering, Yanshan University, Qinhuangdao, China
{cch,weiye51}@ysu.edu.cn

Abstract. Aiming at the current YOLOv4-tiny network's insufficient feature fusion capability and low utilization of feature extraction in flame and smoke detection tasks, a flame and smoke detection algorithm based on improved YOLOv4-tiny is proposed. Firstly, a new effective feature layer is added to obtain more detailed feature information and improve the accuracy of small target detection of flame and smoke. Then, the DWCSP feature fusion structure is proposed to improve the network's ability to integrate and utilize multi-scale feature information on the basis of minimizing the increment of parameters. Finally, the CBAM attention mechanism is embedded to improve the network's channel and spatial feature expression ability, and enhance the ability to perceive the target. The algorithm is embedded in the UAV equipment. In the detection task of self built flame and smoke data set, the mAP@0.5 reaches 71.11%, which is 6.48% higher than the original algorithm, and meets the needs of FPS and lightweight.

Keywords: Flame and smoke detection · YOLOv4-tiny · Feature fusion · CBAM · UAV

1 Introduction

Among various disasters, fire is one of the most frequent and common major disasters threatening public safety and social development, causing immeasurable losses to people's lives and property [1]. If the flame and smoke are identified and dealt with in time before the fire spreads, losses can be greatly reduced and disasters can be avoided.

Supported by National Key R & D Program of China (2019YFB1312104), Key R & D Program of Hebei Province (20311803D), Key R & D Program of Hebei Province (F2021203054), and the Fund of the Natural Science Foundation of Hebei Province (F2020203099).

D. N. Pham et al. (Eds.): PRICAI 2021, LNAI 13031, pp. 226–238, 2021.
https://doi.org/10.1007/978-3-030-89188-6_17

At present, fire monitoring system can be divided into two categories, that is, traditional fire monitoring system and automatic fire monitoring system. Most of the traditional fire monitoring systems use sensors such as flame and smoke sensors to monitor, which has relatively low detection accuracy, sensitivity, and response speed, and it is only suitable for indoor scenes [2]. For outdoor large-scale scenes, monitoring personnel mainly use lookout, patrol and other ways, which consume a lot of manpower and material resources [3]. It has become urgent to explore new automatic fire monitoring methods. In this regard, several fire monitoring technologies and systems have been proposed, such as Wire-less Sensor Networks (WSNs) [4], remote camera monitoring systems [5] and the Unmanned Aerial Vehicles (UAVs) monitoring systems [6]. With the rapid development of image processing technology, the method of using UAV equipped with intelligent algorithm for fire monitoring has been widely concerned by researchers. It has the advantages of wide detection range, fast speed, high degree of intelligence, small interference to the environment and so on. At the same time, it can provide rich on-site information for firefighters and improve the efficiency of fire fighting and rescue.

Considering the real-time requirements of embedded devices, and the fact that YOLOv4-tiny [7] is one of the latest and most excellent lightweight target detection algorithms, this paper is based on YOLOv4-tiny algorithm and carries out the following work for flame and smoke detection: 1) In order to solve the problem of poor flame detection of small targets in the early stage of fire, a new effective feature layer is introduced; 2) In order to improve the feature fusion capability of the network, the DWCSP module is proposed; 3) In order to improve the channel and spatial feature expression ability of the network and enhance the target perception ability, the convolutional block attention module (CBAM) are embedded in the backbone network; 4) The improved algorithm is transplanted to the UAV embedded device, and the real machine experiment is carried out. The results show that in the flame and smoke detection tasks of UAV, the improved algorithm's mAP@0.5 reaches 71.11%, which is an increase of 6.48% compared to the original algorithm, and it meets the real-time and lightweight requirements of detection.

2   Related Work

In recent years, there are two kinds of fire detection methods based on image processing: traditional method and deep learning method.

The traditional method is based on the hand-crafted of flame, according to the color, shape, texture and other visual features of the flame, combined with the classification algorithm in pattern recognition, to determine whether there is flame in the image. Wang et al. [8] proposed a flame detection method based on KNN background subtraction combining the flame color feature and the local feature. Ashraf et al. [9] proposed a smoke and fire detection method based on LBP and SVM. These hand-crafted methods have fast detection speed, but poor stability and generalization ability. It is easy to cause false detection and missing detection when detecting the objects with similar color to the flame and the flame with color beyond the set threshold.

Deep learning method uses neural network to achieve the task of image feature extraction and pattern classification, which can easily process high-dimensional data and automatically extract features without adding other manual features. Compared with the traditional flame detection methods, the technology based on deep convolution neural network has higher accuracy, recall and stronger generalization ability. Zhikai Yang et al. [10] proposed a Indoor video detection method, which used CNN combined with SRU model to extract scene content, extracted dynamic characteristics of fire from continuous frames, and improved the accuracy of fire detection. However, in practice, there are many missed detection, low robustness, and large amount of computation lead to the difficulty of application of embedded equipment. Hongyi pan et al. [11] proposed an additive neural network for forest fire detection, which can save the detection time of flame and smoke by using the highly efficient additive deep neural network. But the actual detection accuracy is not high enough. ChaoXia et al. [12] proposed an improved Faster R-CNN flame detection method. This method uses the color features of the flame to define the limit of the anchor, and uses a parallel network to generate image global information to guide the detection. However, the reasoning speed of two-stage algorithm is slower than that of one-stage algorithm, and its real-time performance cannot be guaranteed.

3   Method

3.1   YOLOv4-Tiny Network Structure

The YOLOv4-tiny backbone network is CSPDarknet53-Tiny, which mainly includes CBL, CSP and maxpooling. The first two layers of CBL mainly compress the height and width of the image, and the last layer of CBL integrates the features of the image. The CSP divides the feature map of the base layer into two parts, and merges them through cross-layer connections, which enhances the learning ability of the convolutional neural network, reduces the amount of calculation, and ensures a higher accuracy rate. Among them, the benefits of cross-layer connection are as follows: 1) feature mapping is formed, feature reuse is achieved to obtain more semantic information, and detection accuracy is improved; 2) calculation bottleneck is reduced, and memory overhead is reduced. The structure of CBL and CSP is shown in Fig. 1. Each CSP structure is followed by maxpooling to compress the height and width of the image.

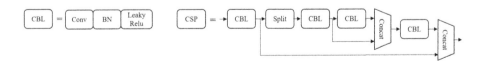

Fig. 1. CBL and CSP structure.

In the neck part, the backbone network leads to two effective feature layers of 13×13 and 26×26, adopts the FPN [13], builds a feature pyramid, and enhances the feature fusion between images of different scales. In the head part, YOLO-Head uses the acquired features to make predictions. YOLOv4-tiny extracts a total of 13×13 and 26×26 feature layers for target detection. The specific network structure of YOLOv4-tiny is shown in Fig. 2.

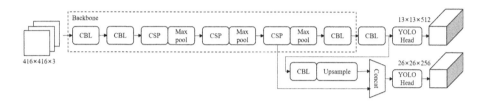

Fig. 2. YOLOv4-tiny network structure.

3.2 Feature Layer Improvement

When the CSPDarknet53-Tiny network extracts feature information, the shallow feature map has a smaller grid division and mainly provides position information; the deep feature map has a larger grid division and mainly provides semantic information. YOLOv4-tiny uses two scale feature maps of 13×13 and 26×26 when extracting multiple feature layers for target detection. Compared with the input image of 416×416 pixels, the fineness of the grid division is lower. After the product is calculated, part of the feature information will be lost, and the shallow feature information is not well used, resulting in the low accuracy of the algorithm for detecting small targets. In the early stage of a fire, the area of flames and smoke observed by UAVs at high altitudes is small, and higher detection accuracy of small targets is required at the application level.

In response to the above problems, this paper improves the multi-scale detection network of YOLOv4-tiny, and increases the 52×52 feature scale with a smaller resolution to fully learn the shallow features and improve the multi-scale feature fusion ability of the network.

3.3 DWCSP Feature Fusion Structure

The neck part of the YOLOv4-tiny network uses the feature pyramid of the FPN, and there are multiple feature maps of different sizes for fusion. But since the network itself has a small number of convolutional layers and only uses conventional convolution, the prediction ability of multi-scale feature fusion is insufficient.

Inspired by the structure of CSPNet [14], this paper designs a DWCSP structure that enhances the feature fusion capability, as shown in Fig. 3. The DWCSP structure is mainly formed by the fusion of DWCBL and 1×1 convolution. In order to reduce the amount of network parameters, the bottleneck structure is used, and the residual unit inside the original CSPNet structure is cancelled. After cross-layer connection and concat, further feature integration is performed through the BN layer, the leakyrelu activation function and the DWCBL unit.

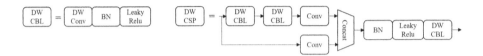

Fig. 3. DWCSP structure.

The DWCBL unit is composed of 3×3 depthwise separable convolution [15], BN layer and Leaky Relu activation function. Depthwise separable convolution is mainly composed of depthwise convolution and pointwise convolution. Depthwise convolution is responsible for filtering, composed of M $3 \times 3 \times 1$ convolution kernels, which act on each input channel, where M is the number of input feature map channels; Pointwise convolution is responsible for converting channels, composed of N $1 \times 1 \times M$ convolution kernels, which act on the output feature map of depthwise convolution, where N is the number of output feature map channels. Then the ratio of the parameter amount between the depthwise separated convolution (DWConv) and the standard convolution (Conv) is Eq. (1):

$$\frac{DWConv}{Conv} = \frac{3 \times 3 \times 1 \times M + 1 \times 1 \times M \times N}{3 \times 3 \times M \times N} = \frac{1}{N} + \frac{1}{9} \tag{1}$$

It can be seen from Eq. (1) that compared with standard convolution, depthwise separable convolution can greatly reduce network parameters and calculations, and the speed of prediction and detection is improved to a certain extent.

3.4   CBAM Attention Mechanism

CBAM [16] is an attention mechanism proposed in ECCV2018. The attention map of network feature map is calculated from the dimension of channel and space, and then the attention map is multiplied by the feature graph to carry out adaptive feature learning. Then the features are re-weighted, and the features with high weights are the focus of attention. CBAM can improve the channel and spatial feature expression ability of the network, and enhance the perception ability of the target.

Both flames and smoke are targets without a fixed form, but they are distinguishable from the background environment information. The attention mechanism is needed to extract the target more accurately from the environment. Therefore, the performance and detection ability of the network can be improved by the addition of CBAM. The network structure of CBAM is shown as in Fig. 4.

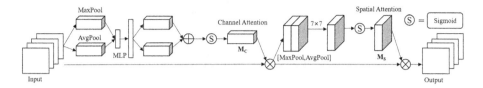

Fig. 4. CBAM network structure.

Channel attention is an attention mechanism that considers the relationship between the feature map channels. The input feature map is respectively passed through global max pooling and global average pooling based on width and height, and then passed through MLP. The features output by MLP are added and sigmoid to generate channel attention features. The channel attention features are shown in Eq. (2).

$$
\begin{aligned}
M_c\left(F\right) &= \sigma\left(MLP\left(Avgpool\left(F\right)\right) + MLP\left(Maxpool\left(F\right)\right)\right) \\
&= \sigma\left(W_1\left(W_0\left(F_{avg}^c\right)\right) + W_1\left(W_0\left(F_{max}^c\right)\right)\right), \\
W_0 &\in \mathbb{R}^{C/r \times C} \qquad W_1 \in \mathbb{R}^{C \times C/r}
\end{aligned}
\tag{2}
$$

Among them, σ is the sigmoid operation, r represents the reduction rate, and the Relu activation is required after W_0. The feature is multiplied with the input feature to generate the input feature map required by the spatial attention module.

Different from channel attention, spatial attention can make the neural network pay more attention to the pixel areas in the image that are decisive for classification and ignore the insignificant areas. The feature map output by the channel attention module is used as the input feature map of this module. Global max pooling and global average pooling based on channel are implemented first, and then these two results are subjected to channel concat operation. After 7×7 convolution, the dimension is reduced into 1 channel, and then the spatial attention features are generated through sigmoid. The spatial attention features are shown in Eq. (3).

$$
\begin{aligned}
M_s\left(F\right) &= \sigma\left(f^{7\times7}\left(\left[Avgpool\left(F\right); MaxPool\left(F\right)\right]\right)\right) \\
&= \sigma\left(f^{7\times7}\left(\left[F_{avg}^s; F_{max}^s\right]\right)\right)
\end{aligned}
\tag{3}
$$

Among them, 7×7 represents the size of the convolution kernel. The feature is multiplied with the input feature of the module to obtain the final output feature map.

4 Experiment

4.1 Data Set Establishment

At present, there are not many public data sets related to flames and smoke, so this experiment uses self-built flame and smoke data sets. The main component of the data set is the public flame and smoke pictures crawled on the Internet through crawler technology. At the same time, the relevant pictures taken in the laboratory and outdoors are added to enrich the data set. The self-built data set of this experiment has a total of 19,819 images, including 13,873 in the training set, 1982 in the validation set, and 3964 in the test set.

4.2 Evaluation Index

In this experiment, when using the test set to test the trained model, a relatively authoritative indicator in the target detection field is used to evaluate the performance of the model using the mean Average Precision (mAP), and the IOU threshold of mAP is set to 0.5 (mAP@0.5). The mAP is shown in Eq. (4):

$$Precision = \frac{TP}{TP + FP}$$
$$Recall = \frac{TP}{FP + FN} \tag{4}$$
$$mAP = \frac{1}{N} \sum AP$$

Among them, TP (True Positive) is the number of correctly detected targets, FP (False Positive) is the number of falsely detected targets, FN (False Negative) is the number of missed targets; AP (Average Precision) is the average accuracy of each type of object, and its value is equal to the area under the Precision-Recall curve; N is the total number of categories.

Considering the practical application of embedded devices, this experiment adds the indicators of parameters, model size and FPS to evaluate the lightness of the model and the real-time detection. Among them, due to the limitation of camera and the complexity of video detection environment, the real-time FPS is not good as an evaluation index, so the FPS test method in the literature [17] is adopted. The FPS test method selects network reasoning, score threshold screening and NMS part, and tests the FPS of a single flame and smoke picture. In practice, the reading frequency of the camera is limited, and the process includes pre-processing and drawing parts, so the FPS detected by the camera will be relatively low. In addition, the evaluation index of computational time is replaced by the FPS in this experiment, which is convenient for comparative experiment and practical application.

4.3 Experimental Conditions

This experiment is based on the pytorch deep learning framework. The training of the network model is completed on a computer with Intel Core i9-10980HK CPU, NVIDIA 2070Super 8G GPU, and a memory capacity of 16 GB. Then transplant the model to a self-organizing UAV development platform equipped with NVIDIA TX2 onboard computer to complete the comparative experiment. The UAV platform is shown in Fig. 5.

Fig. 5. Self-organizing UAV development platform.

4.4   Comparative Experiment

Feature Layer Comparison Experiment. The third effective feature layer, with a scale of 52×52, is derived from backbone, and added into the FPN network to rebuild the feature pyramid to enhance the feature fusion between feature layers of different sizes.

The effective feature layer of each size matches 3 anchors. After the introduction of the third effective feature layer, the number of anchors is increased from 6 to 9. Therefore, this paper uses the K-means clustering algorithm to recalculate the anchors. The 13×13 size feature layer has the largest receptive field, matching large-size anchors, suitable for detecting large-size target; The 26×26 size feature layer has medium receptive fields, matching medium-sized anchors, suitable for detecting medium-sized target; The 52×52 size feature layer has the smallest receptive field, but is more detailed in terms of details. It matches small-size anchors, suitable for detecting small-size target.

The comparison experiment in this part takes the original YOLOv4-tiny as baseline, compared with the algorithm of adding the 52×52 effective feature layer. The results are shown in Table 1. It can be seen that with a small increase in parameters and a small decrease in FPS, mAP@0.5 has been improved to a certain extent.

Table 1. Comparative experiment results of effective feature layer.

Model	mAP@0.5 (%)	Params (M)	Size (MB)	FPS
Baseline	64.63	5.92	22.4	18.4
With a new feature	**65.31**	6.17	23.4	18.0

DWCSP Feature Fusion Structure Comparison Experiment. Since DWCSP is a module designed to enhance feature fusion, it is set after the 13×13 effective feature layer and the concat of different feature layers of the feature pyramid to enhance the feature fusion of different features and improve the comprehensive prediction ability.

The comparison experiment in this part takes the algorithm introducing 52×52 effective feature layer as baseline. The DWCSP module, and the CSP structure of CSPNet are added at the same position to compare the results. The results are shown in Table 2. It can be seen that after adding the DWCSP structure, the increase in parameters and the decrease in the FPS are within the acceptable range, while mAP has increased by 3.14%, which has been greatly improved.

Table 2. Comparative experiment results of DWCSP.

Model	mAP@0.5 (%)	Params (M)	Size (MB)	FPS
Baseline	65.31	6.17	23.4	18.0
With CSP	67.87	8.30	31.6	15.4
With DWCSP	**68.45**	7.33	27.8	15.8

CBAM Attention Mechanism Comparison Experiment. There is no appropriate theory as to where the mechanisms of attention embedded in a network might be more effective in specific situations. This part will compare the performance of the CBAM attention mechanism embedded in different positions in the network model. The structure of introducing 52×52 effective feature layer and DWCSP feature fusion module into the network is taken as the baseline, the following four structures of embedded CBAM are given: 1) Three modules are embedded in the part where three effective feature layers are derived from the backbone network; 2) Three modules are embedded in front of the three DWCSP modules; 3) Three modules are embedded in front of the three YOLO Heads; 4) Two modules are embedded before and after the three CSP-Maxpooling structures in the backbone. The results of the comparative experiment are shown in Table 3. In contrast, model 4 has the highest mAP@0.5 and FPS, which can increase the mAP@0.5 by 2.66% compared to the baseline. Therefore, the CBAM embedded before and after the three CSP-Maxpooling structures of the backbone has the best effect.

Comparison Between Improved Algorithm and Mainstream Algorithm. Based on the above comparative experiments, this paper proposes an improved algorithm based on YOLOv4-tiny (hereafter called YOLOv4-tiny Super) for flame and smoke detection. The network structure is shown in Fig. 6.

In order to further analyze the algorithm performance of the improved algorithm, YOLOv4-tiny Super was compared with SSD [18], YOLOv4 [19], YOLOv4-tiny, Efficientdet-d2 [20] and Faster R-CNN [21] algorithm for self-built flame and smoke data sets. The algorithm test results are shown in Table 4.

Table 3. Comparative experiment results of CBAM.

Model	mAP@0.5 (%)	Params (M)	Size (MB)	FPS
Baseline	68.45	7.33	27.8	15.8
1	69.12	7.41	28.0	13.6
2	69.09	7.40	28.0	13.5
3	69.07	7.40	28.0	13.3
4	**71.11**	7.39	27.9	14.2

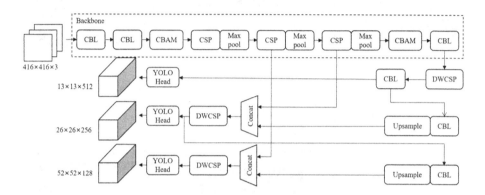

Fig. 6. Network structure of YOLOv4-tiny Super.

Table 4. Comparison experiment results with mainstream algorithms.

Model	Backbone	mAP@0.5 (%)	Params (M)	Size (MB)	FPS
SSD	VGG	69.46	23.9	91.1	9.72
YOLOv4	CSPDarknet53	71.02	63.9	244	4.50
YOLOv4-tiny	CSPDarknet53-Tiny	64.63	5.92	22.4	18.4
Efficientdet-d2	Efficientnet	66.43	8.09	31.2	2.36
Faster R-CNN	Resnet50	67.04	28.3	108	1.67
YOLOv4-tiny Super	–	**71.11**	7.39	27.9	14.2

As can be seen from the Table 4, for flame and smoke detection, the mAP@0.5 of YOLOv4-tiny Super has reached the detection level of the YOLOv4. The parameter amount is only 1/9 of the latter, and the FPS exceeds the latter by 67. Compared with the mainstream algorithms in other tables, the performance of YOLOv4-tiny Super is better from mAP@0.5, parameters, model size and FPS. In addition, It is not as good as the YOLOv4-tiny in FPS performance, but its mAP@0.5 exceeds 6.48%. When FPS meets actual needs, the actual detection effect is greatly improved. In summary, compared with the mainstream algorithms in the table, YOLOv4-tiny Super meets the requirements of FPS and lightweight, and can have better results for flame and smoke detection.

UAV Detection Effect Experiment. The self-assembled UAV platform is equipped with a three-axis pod gimbal for stability, which is suitable for flame and smoke detection. YOLOv4-tiny and YOLOv4-tiny Super are compared for UAV detection effect, and the results are shown in Fig. 7 and Fig. 8 respectively.

(a) Near target.   (b) Distant target.   (c) Multi-target.

Fig. 7. Flame and smoke detection effect of YOLOv4-tiny.

(a) Near target.   (b) Distant target.   (c) Multi-target.

Fig. 8. Flame and smoke detection effect of YOLOv4-tiny Super.

It can be seen from Fig. 7 that YOLOv4-tiny has a serious failure to detect when the smoke is not thick and the color is lighter (such as (a)); In the case of smoke interference, its flame detection effect is poor (such as (b)); In the case of a small target flame, its detection effect is not good enough, and there are many cases of missed detection (such as (c)). In Fig. 8, YOLOv4-tiny Super can achieve better detection results in the above-mentioned situations. The comparison shows that its actual detection results are much better than the original algorithm, and the FPS can also meet the detection requirements of UAV.

5   Conclusion

In this paper, a lightweight flame and smoke detection network YOLOv4-tiny for UAV is proposed. Firstly, the new effective feature layer is introduced and a new FPN feature pyramid is constructed. Then, the DWCSP feature fusion structure is proposed, which makes the network better integrate and utilize multi-scale feature information. Finally, CBAM attention mechanism is embedded in the backbone network to make the network pay more attention to the target information from the environment. The results of UAV experiments show that the mAP@0.5 of YOLOv4-tiny Super reaches 71.11%, which is 6.48% higher than YOLOv4-tiny. When FPS meets actual needs, the actual detection effect is greatly improved. Compared with other mainstream target detection algorithms, YOLOv4-tiny Super performs better in mAP@0.5, parameters, model size, and FPS. Aiming at the problem that the real-time FPS of camera is not as good as the test FPS caused by the limitation of camera equipment, the next work will improve and optimize these limiting factors to reduce the loss of real-time FPS of camera.

References

1. Sahar, O.: Wildfires in Algeria: problems and challenges. IFOREST **8**(6), 818–826 (2015)
2. Cowlard, A., Jahn, W., Abecassis-Empis, C., et al.: Sensor assisted fire fighting. Fire Technol. **46**, 719–741 (2010)
3. Abid, F.: A survey of machine learning algorithms based forest fires prediction and detection systems. Fire Technol. **57**, 559–590 (2021)
4. Karray, F., Jmal, M.W., Abid, M., BenSaleh, M.S., Obeid, A.M.: A review on wireless sensor node architectures. In: Proceedings of 9th International Symposium on Reconfigurable and Communication-Centric Systems-on-Chip (ReCoSoC), pp. 1–8. IEEE (2014)
5. Zhong, Z., Wang, M., Shi, Y., et al.: A convolutional neural network-based flame detection method in video sequence. SIViP **12**, 1619–1627 (2018)
6. Jiang, B., Qu, R., Li, Y., Li, C.: Survey of object detection in UAV imagery based on deep learning. Acta Aeronautica et Astronautica Sinica **42**(4), 137–151 (2021)
7. YOLOv4-tiny. https://github.com/AlexeyAB/darknet. Accessed 28 June 2020
8. Wang, X., Li, Y., Li, Z.: Research on flame detection algorithm based on multi - feature fusion. In: 2020 IEEE 4th Information Technology, Networking, Electronic and Automation Control Conference (ITNEC), pp. 184–189. IEEE (2020)
9. Russo, A.U., Deb, K., Tista, S.C., Islam, A.: Smoke detection method based on LBP and SVM from surveillance camera. In: 2018 International Conference on Computer, Communication, Chemical, Material and Electronic Engineering (IC4ME2), pp. 1–4. IEEE (2018)
10. Yang, Z., Bu, L., Wang, T., et al.: Indoor video flame detection based on lightweight convolutional neural network. Pattern Recogn. Image Anal. **30**, 551–564 (2020)
11. Pan, H., Badawi, D., Zhang, X., et al.: Additive neural network for forest fire detection. SIViP **14**, 675–682 (2020)
12. Chaoxia, C., Shang, W., Zhang, F.: Information-guided flame detection based on faster R-CNN. IEEE Access **8**, 58923–58932 (2020)
13. Lin, T., Dollár, P., Girshick, R., He, K., Hariharan, B., Belongie, S.: Feature pyramid networks for object detection. In: 2017 IEEE Conference on Computer Vision and Pattern Recognition (CVPR), pp. 936–944. IEEE (2017)
14. Wang, C., Mark Liao, H., Wu, Y., Chen, P., Hsieh, J., Yeh, I.: CSPNet: a new backbone that can enhance learning capability of CNN. In: 2020 IEEE/CVF Conference on Computer Vision and Pattern Recognition Workshops (CVPRW), pp. 1571–1580. IEEE (2020)

15. Howard, A.G., Zhu, M., Chen, B., et al.: MobileNets: efficient convolutional neural networks for mobile vision applications. arXiv preprint arXiv:1704.04861 (2017)
16. Woo, S., Park, J., Lee, J.-Y., Kweon, I.S.: CBAM: convolutional block attention module. In: Ferrari, V., Hebert, M., Sminchisescu, C., Weiss, Y. (eds.) ECCV 2018. LNCS, vol. 11211, pp. 3–19. Springer, Cham (2018). https://doi.org/10.1007/978-3-030-01234-2_1
17. FPS   test.   https://github.com/zylo117/Yet-Another-EfficientDet-Pytorch. Accessed 12 Dec 2020
18. Liu, W., et al.: SSD: single shot MultiBox detector. In: Leibe, B., Matas, J., Sebe, N., Welling, M. (eds.) ECCV 2016. LNCS, vol. 9905, pp. 21–37. Springer, Cham (2016). https://doi.org/10.1007/978-3-319-46448-0_2
19. Bochkovskiy, A., Wang, C.Y., Liao, H.Y.M.: YOLOv4: optimal speed and accuracy of object detection. arXiv preprint arXiv:2004.10934 (2020)
20. Tan, M., Pang, R., Le, Q.V.: EfficientDet: scalable and efficient object detection. arXiv preprint arXiv:1911.09070 (2020)
21. Ren, S., He, K., Girshick, R., Sun, J.: Faster R-CNN: towards real-time object detection with region proposal networks. arXiv preprint arXiv:1506.01497 (2016)

Improving Protein Backbone Angle Prediction Using Hidden Markov Models in Deep Learning

Fereshteh Mataeimoghadam[1](✉), M. A. Hakim Newton[1,2](✉), Rianon Zaman[1], and Abdul Sattar[1,2]

[1] School of Information and Communication Technology, Griffith University, Nathan, Australia
fereshteh.mataeimoghadam@griffithuni.edu.au,
mahakim.newton@griffith.edu.au
[2] Institute of Integrated and Intelligent Systems, Griffith University, Nathan, Australia

Abstract. Protein Structure Prediction (PSP) is one of the most challenging problems in bioinformatics and biomedicine. PSP has obtained significant improvement lately. This is from the growth of the protein data bank (PDB) and the use of Deep Neural Network (DNN) models since DNNs could learn more accurate patterns from more known protein structures in the PDB. Hidden Markov Models (HMM) are a widely used method to extract underlying patterns from given data. HMM profiles of proteins have been used in existing DNN models for protein backbone angle prediction (BAP), but their full potential is yet to be exploited amid the complexities involed with those DNN models. In this paper, for BAP, we propose a simple DNN model that more effectively exploits HMM profiles as features beside other features. Our proposed method significantly outperforms existing state-of-the-art methods SAP, OPUS-TASS, and SPOT-1D, and obtains mean absolute error (MAE) values of 15.45, 18.33, 6.00, and 20.68 respectively for four types of backbone angles ϕ, ψ, θ, and τ. The differences in MAE values for all four types of angles are between 1.15% to 1.66% compared to the best known results.

Keywords: Protein structure prediction · Deep neural network · Protein backbone angle prediction

1 Introduction

Protein Structure Prediction (PSP) is one of the most challenging issues in the bioinformatics area, especially in drug design. PSP is determining the three-dimensional structure of a protein just from its amino acid sequence. The fast growth of protein sequence information in comparison with the slow growth of

---

F. Mataeimoghadam and M. A. H. Newton—Contributed equally to this work.

© Springer Nature Switzerland AG 2021
D. N. Pham et al. (Eds.): PRICAI 2021, LNAI 13031, pp. 239–251, 2021.
https://doi.org/10.1007/978-3-030-89188-6_18

protein structure knowledge indicates a huge demand of effective methods in determining protein structures. In vitro methods such as X-ray Crystallography, Nuclear Magnetic Resonance (NMR), and Electron microscopy (EM) are time consuming, costly, and in some cases impossible. To address these issues, computational methods have been proposed [5–7,9,11,18]. However, the computational approaches are also difficult because of the inevitability of searching an astronomically large conformation space and the absence of a highly accurate energy function to evaluate potential protein conformations [11,20].

Proteins are chains of amino acids linked by peptide bonds. Every amino acid consists of three parts: an amine functional group ($-NH_2$), a carboxyl functional group (-COOH), and an R group or side-chain specific to each amino acid. These groups are linked to a C atom, which is referred to as C_α. The backbone of the protein is made up of C and N atoms of every two consecutive amino acids. Hence, dihedral angles ϕ, ψ, and ω can represent protein backbone structures, which are respectively defined by taking every four consecutive atoms from the sequence C_{i-1}, N_i, C_{α_i}, C_i, N_{i+1}, $C_{\alpha_{i+1}}$ [11]. Protein structures can also be represented by θ and τ angles, where θ is a planar angle defined by three consecutive C_α atoms, τ is a dihedral angle defined by four consecutive C_α atoms [11]. Since, ω is fixed at 180° for the majority of proteins [2]. The ϕ and ψ, or θ and τ values are essential for constructing protein structures. In this work, we predict all of these four backbone angles using HMM profiles besides other informative features within a fully connected neural network (FCNN).

Protein backbone angle prediction (BAP) methods in recent years are mostly based on DNNs. SPIDER [9] applies a stacked sparse auto-encoder DNN with three hidden layers and 150 nodes in each layer for predicting θ and τ angles. The input features in SPIDER are position-specific scoring matrices (PSSM) produced by PSI-BLAST [1], seven physico-chemical properties (7PCP), predicted three probability values for secondary structures (SS3) helix, sheet, and coils, and predicted solvent accessible surface area (ASA) from SPINE-X [3]. SPIDER also applied a window size of 21 in order to capture local interactions. SPIDER2 [6] takes advantage of an iterative training process to improve protein backbone angles and SS predictions. SPIDER2's features are PSSM and 7PCP. Besides, SPIDER2 reuses predicted backbone torsion angles, predicted SS, and predicted ASA of one DNN as input features of another DNN, and SPIDER2 thus has three successive DNNs in total in a series.

SPIDER3 [7] is another BAP method, which employs bidirectional recurrent neural networks (BRNN) to predict ϕ, ψ, θ, and τ. Like SPIDER2, SPIDER3 also uses an iterative training method to train BRNNs, and it's input features are PSSM, 7PCP, and Hidden Markov Model (HMM) profiles produced by HHBlits [15]. In addition, SPIDER3 reuses predicted backbone torsion angles, predicted SS, and predicted ASA for the iterative training process. SPOT-1D [5] uses the same features used in SPIDER3 [7] and utilises an ensemble of 9 Long Short Term Memory (LSTM) BRNN and Residual Network (ResNet) models to predict ϕ, ψ, θ, and τ. OPUS-TASS [18] employs a DNN model consists of Convolutional Neural Networks (CNN), LSTM, and Transformer [17] layers to predict ϕ and ψ. OPUS-TASS also applies multitask learning to improve the generalization of neural networks by introducing related tasks into the training process [18]. OPUS-TASS's input features contain all SPOT-1D's input features plus PSP19 [19]. SAP [11], as a state-of-the-art BAP, insists on using a simpler model with fewer features. SAP employs an FCNN, with three hidden layers and it's input features are PSSM, 7PCP, 8-state SS (SS8) predicted by SSPro8 [10]. SAP predicts ϕ, ψ, θ, and τ. In this paper, we use a simple DNN model as SAP does but we include HMM profiles as additional features and investigate the effectiveness.

HMM profiles are one powerful statistical modelling technique to extract underlying patterns from the high dimensional data. Bioinformatic researchers over the years have used HMM profiles to analyse chromatin folding patterns in order to distinguish cancer variant mutations [13] and to extract patterns from protein sequences [1,15] for various purposes that include BAP methods [4–7,9,11,18]. However, the full potential of HMM profiles in BAP is yet to be exploited. In this work, for BAP, we propose a simple DNN model that more effectively exploits HMM profiles as features beside other features such as PSSM, HMM, 7PCP, and SS8 predicted by SSpro8 [10]). Our proposed method significantly outperforms existing state-of-the-art methods SAP, OPUS-TASS, and SPOT-1D, and obtains mean absolute error (MAE) values of 15.45, 18.33, 6.00, and 20.68 respectively for four types of backbone angles ϕ, ψ, θ, and τ. The differences in MAE values for all four types of angles are between 1.15% to 1.66% compared to the best known results.

2   Methods

We explain the DNN model and the dataset used in our method.

2.1   Input Features

We describe each residue as an window of a number of residues around it: half before and half after. Each residue in such a window is represented by 65 features. 30 features are from HMM profiles generated by HHblists [12] with the Uniprot sequence profile database from October 2017. Next, 20 features are from PSSM profiles generated by three iterations of PSI-BLAST [1] against the UniRef90 sequence database updated in April 2018. Then, 8 features are from encoded one-hot vector of SS8 prediction by SSpro8 [10]. Lastly, 7 features are from physicochemical properties of each amino acid.

Secondary Structure. Local structures named secondary structures (SS) are formed in protein segments by hydrogen bonds. There are three overall kinds of protein secondary structures: helies, sheets, and coils. Helices and sheets have regular patterns while coils have irregular structures. There is also an eight-class classification for secondary structures (SS8). The eight labels are 3–10 helix (G), α-helix (H), π-helix (I), β-sheet (E), β-bridge(B), turn (T), bend (S), and coil (C). In this work, we use SS8 prediction of SSpro8 [10] as input features, then we encode each SS type prediction by a one-hot vector.

Position-Specific Scoring Matrix. In PSSM, using multiple sequence alignment (MSA), for each position in a protein's sequence, a substitution score is computed for each amino acid. For a protein with length L, PSSM is a matrix with size $L \times 20$. The (i, j)th entry of the matrix shows the mutation score of the ith residue to the jth amino acid. Scores are represented by positive and negative values. Positive values mean the chance of occurrence is higher than random selection while negative values show less probability of occurrence.

Hidden Markov Model. HMMs are widely used in modelling the correlations between adjacent symbols, domains, or events [14]. HHM describes the observable events that depend on internal factors and include two stochastic processes: an invisible process of hidden states and a visible process of observable symbols. The hidden states form a Markov chain, and the probability distribution of the observed symbol depends on the underlying state. For this reason, HMM is also called a doubly-embedded stochastic process [14]. HMM essentially accumulates the substitution scores with penalties for insertions and deletions. These can be estimated from the frequencies of insertions and deletions in the MSA [1,16]. For a protein with length L, HMM is a matrix with size $L \times 30$, where first 20 columns show the residue substitution values while the last 10 columns illustrate the transition frequency and the number of effective homologous sequences.

Seven Physicochemical Properties. 7PCP are another informative features used in PSP. Each amino acid has its own physicochemical properties. Just like the other BAP methods [5–7,9,11,18], for each amino acid, we only consider seven properties as physicochemical features. These are steric parameter (graph shape index), hydrophobicity, volume, polarizability, isoelectric point, helix probability, and sheet probability.

2.2   Predicted Outputs

Although most recent BAP methods use sine and cosine ratios for each angle to tackle the periodicity issue (angles must be in range $[-180°, 180°]$), our method predict direct angle values for one residue at a time. For each residue, we have four regression outputs that predict the direct values of ϕ, ψ, θ, and τ. Similar to SAP, we address the periodicity issue within the loss function of the DNN.

2.3   Neural Networks

We use SAP's DNN, which is an FCNN with three hidden layers, and 150 neurons in each layer, as shown in Fig. 1. An FCNN consists of neurons with learnable weights and biases. Each neuron's output is produced by computing the product of the weights at the inputs and applying a nonlinear activation function to provide results. Generally, inputs pass through the hidden layers. Each hidden layer consists of several neurons that are connected to all neurons in the previous layer. Each layer's neurons work independently without any contact with each other. The output layer is the last layer, which usually estimates the output or displays each class's score. In our method, we use `Python` language with `Keras` library to implement our DNN. We apply an `SGD optimiser` with `momentum 0.9` as an optimiser. We use `linear` as the activation function for the last layer and `sigmoid` as the activation function for the input and hiden layers. MAE and MSE (Mean Square Error) are the common loss functions in regression problems. We use MAE as the loss function since it is better with outlier predictions than MSE; the square function in MSE causes more emphasis to be put on outliers. Besides, recent BAPs [5–7,9,11,18] utilise the MAE as their loss function. To tackle the periodicity issue, we calculate absolute error (AE) as the following procedure. For each predicted angle (P) and native angle (N), we compute $D = |P - N|$. The absolute error is defined by $AE = \min(D, |360 - D|)$. In addition, we ignore the angles at the beginning or at the end of the protein since they are not defined.

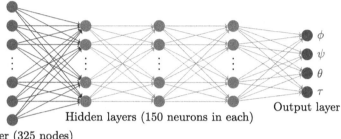

Fig. 1. The fully connected deep neural network used in our method. It has three hidden layers, each has 150 neurons.

2.4   Benchmark Datasets

We use the same dataset used by SPOT-1D [5]. This dataset is collected with the constraints such as high resolution ($<2.5\,\text{A}°$), R-free < 0.25, and sequence identity cutoff of 25% according to BlastClust [1]. Moreover, we have used filters similar to SAP [11] to handle proteins with mismatches in their amino acid sequences from various data source files (e.g. .t, .pssm, .dssp, and .fasta files). We have used 8-state SS predictions from SSpro8 [10], then perform another filtering and remove 3259 proteins from SPOT-1D's proteins using Blast [1] against SSpro8's training set with e-value 0.01. Table 1 demonstrates the numbers of proteins and residues in training, validation, and testing datasets, after applying the above mentioned filtering.

Table 1. Numbers of proteins and residues in training, validation, and testing datasets.

Datasets	Training	Validation	Testing	Total
Proteins	6721	667	1205	8593
Residues	1670605	165530	282317	2118452

3   Results

In order to understand the effect of HMM and window size, we perform various settings of our method to find the best settings. Besides, we show various other analyses of the results obtained for the best settings.

3.1   Determining Best Settings

We select the SAP setting as our baseline and try to add HMM features to check the effectiveness. Besides, we assess the performance by examining two window sizes 5 and 9 (the best window sizes in SAP). In addition, based on the SAP's experimental results, we apply range based normalisation as feature input encoding, direct angle value as output representation. Table 2 shows the MAE value for each setting for each angle.

Table 2. Performance of our experimental settings on 1205 testing proteins. The column HMM denotes whether HMM is used (Yes/No), column WS shows the window size. The boldened values are the best values over the four settings.

Features	Window size	ϕ MAE		ψ MAE		θ MAE		τ MAE	
HMM	WS	Test	Valid	Test	Valid	Test	Valid	Test	Valid
N	5	15.65	16.04	18.59	18.80	6.07	6.16	21.03	21.18
N	9	15.82	16.16	18.83	19.06	6.14	6.24	21.25	21.40
Y	5	**15.45**	**15.78**	**18.33**	**18.52**	**6.00**	**6.09**	**20.68**	**20.80**
Y	9	15.47	15.79	18.41	18.57	6.03	6.12	20.72	20.81

As we see from Table 2, there is only one setting which is the best for all four types of angles. In summary, the best setting has the following parameters.

- Input Features: SS prediction from SSPro8, PSSM, 7PCP, HMM
- Window Size: 5
- Input Encoding: Range-based normalisation
- Output Representation: Direct angle prediction

To evaluate the robustness of our method, we perform 10-fold cross validation and independent testing with the best setting. The results from the 10 runs are not statistically significantly different from each other as per 95% confidence level of the Analysis of Variance (ANOVA) testing.

3.2   Comparison with State-of-the-Art Predictors

As shown in Table 3, we compare our method with existing state-of-the-art BAP methods. MAE values for all BAP methods are shown in Table 3 for ϕ, ψ, θ, and τ. By computing improvement $= \dfrac{\text{2nd Best MAE} - \text{Our Method MAE}}{\text{2nd Best MAE}}$, we compare relative improvements in MAE values and it shows our method is better than the existing methods in all cases in terms of MAE. We do not strictly compare the running time of the competing methods since obtaining better accuracy is a key focus in PSP. Moreover, execution time would depend on the implementation, the language, and the hardware used. Further, the training programs are not available to us for OPUS-TASS and SPOT-1D. Both for SAP and the method proposed in this paper, given the input features are already computed, each DNN model needs up to four hours for training and a few seconds for each protein in testing.

Table 3. Performances of SPOT-1D, OPUS-TASS, SAP, and our method on our testing dataset. The emboldened values are the winning numbers for the corresponding types of angles and datasets. OPUS-TASS does not predict θ and τ angles.

Dataset	Proteins	Residues	Method	ϕ MAE	ψ MAE	θ MAE	τ MAE
Testing	1205	282317	SPOT-1D	16.23	23.22	6.77	24.57
			OPUS-TASS	15.74	22.41	–	–
			SAP	15.65	18.59	6.07	21.03
			Our Method	**15.45**	**18.33**	**6.00**	**20.68**
			Improvement	1.27%	1.40%	1.15%	1.66%

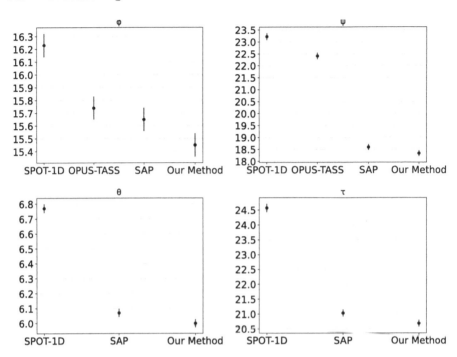

Fig. 2. 95% confidence intervals of AE values (y-axis) for various methods (x-axis).

By analysing each method's Absolute Error (AE) using ANOVA at 95% confidence level, we see that at least one method is significantly different from other methods. Then, in order to check pairwise differences at 95% confidence level, we perform Tukey's Honest Significant Difference (HSD) test. Figure 2 shows our method significantly outperforms the other BAPs for all four angles. (except for ϕ the prediction of OPUS-TASS and SAP has overlapping)

3.3 Comparison on Protein Length Groups

Figure 3 shows the performance of our method, SAP, OPUS-TASS, and SPOT-1D by categorising test proteins based on their lengths. Overall, for all methods, performance decrease when the protein length increases (slight exception for proteins with length between 200 to 300 residues). In all protein lengths, our method achieves better MAE values than the other methods.

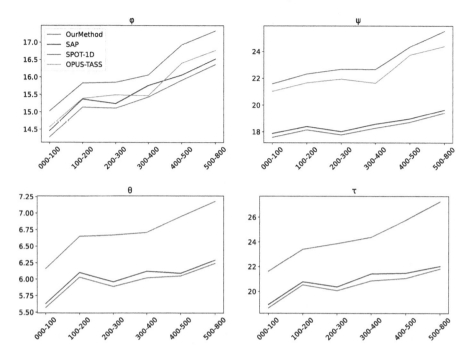

Fig. 3. Performance of our method, SAP, OPUS-TASS, and SPOT-1D when test proteins are grouped based on their length

3.4   Comparison on Secondary Structure Groups

Figure 4 illustrates the distribution of the residues over the native SS types. H, E, and C with respectively 34.3%, 21.6%, and 19.9% cover the big portions of residues while, the amount of G, B, and I are negligible. One way to assess each method's performance is by examining them based on the specific SS types. Overall, the SS classification is associated with angle ranges. On one hand, Helices and sheets have narrow ranges for ϕ and ψ [8,11] and so prediction for them is easier than prediction for coil residues. On the other hand, coils contain a big portion of residues. Therefore, assessing a method's performance

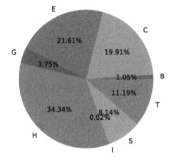

Fig. 4. Distribution of residues over 8-state secondary structure types on our test set

based on the SS value brings more opportunities to have a better understanding of each method's weakness. Figure 5 shows the performance of our method, SAP, OPUS-TASS, and SPOT-1D when test proteins are grouped based on the native 8-state secondary structures and the horizontal line in each chart shows the overall MAE value for our method. Notice that all methods have worse MAE for coils while the best MAEs are achieved for helices.

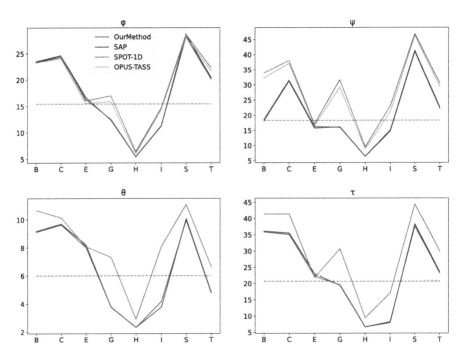

Fig. 5. Performance of our method, SAP, OPUS-TASS, and SPOT-1D on the testing proteins when residues are grouped based on their SS types. In the charts, y-axis shows MAE values and x-axis shows SS types. The dashed horizontal line in each chart shows the overall MAE value for our method.

3.5   Protein Structure Generation and Refinement

The ultimate aim of BAP methods is achieving accurate protein structures. However existing BAP methods still need to be improved and they are far from this goal. In this work, we have tried to generate entire protein structures from the predicted values of ϕ and ψ from our method, SAP, OPUS-TASS, and SPOT-1D by considering $\omega = 180°$. Figure 6 shows the Root Mean Square Deviation (RMSD) values obtained by our method, SAP, OPUS-TASS, and SPOT-1D for 27 proteins that are from Critical Assessment of Structure Prediction (CASP) competition 2018 and are also in our test set. Moreover, Fig. 7, shows the 3D structures of two sample proteins 5cesA (first row) and 5dleA (second row), reconstructed by the predicted ϕ and ψ from our method, SAP, OPUS-TASS, and SPOT-1D. Both proteins have helixes and sheets in their structures. The native structures are shown in green colour. No method has the desired predictions for sheet, but our method has better RMSD values than the others.

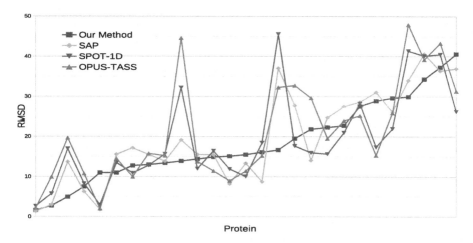

Fig. 6. RMSD values obtained by our method, SAP, OPUS-TASS, and SPOT-1D on our 27 test proteins (sorted on RMSD of our method) from CASP2018.

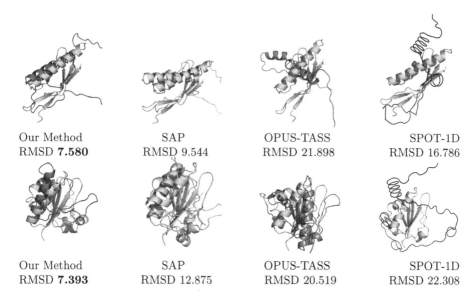

Fig. 7. Sample 3D structures of 5cesA (first row) and 5dleA (second row), reconstructed using the predicted ϕ and ψ from our method, SAP, OPUS-TASS, and SPOT-1D. Each method's $RMSD$ value is reported below each figure. The lower the $RMSD$, the better the performance. The emboldened values are the better reconstruction. The green colour indicates the native structure. (Color figure online)

4   Conclusion

In this paper, we improve the accuracy of backbone angle prediction for proteins by employing HMM profiles as input features of a simple deep neural network.

HMM is a statistical method to extract hidden models that are available in the alignment of proteins. Although HMM profiles have been used in the litertaure, but their full potential is yet to be exploited. In this work, we have used HMM profiles besides other features like PSSM, 7PCP, and predicted secondary structures. On a set of standard benchmark proteins, our method achieves better MAE than the state-of-the-art methods.

Acknowledgements. This research is partially supported by Australian Research Council Discovery Grant DP180102727. We gratefully acknowledge the support of the Griffith University eResearch Service & Specialised Platforms team and the use of the High Performance Computing Cluster "Gowonda" to complete this research.

Author Contributions Statement. F.M. and M.A.H.N. contributed equally and in all parts of the work. R.Z. helped run experiments. A.S. took part in discussions and reviewed the manuscript.

References

1. Altschul, S.F., et al.: Gapped BLAST AND PSI-BLAST: a new generation of protein database search programs. Nucleic Acids Res. **25**(17), 3389–3402 (1997)
2. Cutello, V., Narzisi, G., Nicosia, G.: A multi-objective evolutionary approach to the protein structure prediction problem. J. Roy. Soc. Interface **3**(6), 139–151 (2005)
3. Faraggi, E., Zhang, T., Yang, Y., Kurgan, L., Zhou, Y.: SPINE X: improving protein secondary structure prediction by multistep learning coupled with prediction of solvent accessible surface area and backbone torsion angles. J. Comput. Chem. **33**(3), 259–267 (2012)
4. Hanson, J., Paliwal, K., Litfin, T., Yang, Y., Zhou, Y.: Accurate prediction of protein contact maps by coupling residual two-dimensional bidirectional long short-term memory with convolutional neural networks. Bioinformatics **34**(23), 4039–4045 (2018)
5. Hanson, J., Paliwal, K., Litfin, T., Yang, Y., Zhou, Y.: Improving prediction of protein secondary structure, backbone angles, solvent accessibility and contact numbers by using predicted contact maps and an ensemble of recurrent and residual convolutional neural networks. Bioinformatics **35**(14), 2403–2410 (2018)
6. Heffernan, R., et al.: Improving prediction of secondary structure, local backbone angles, and solvent accessible surface area of proteins by iterative deep learning. Sci. Rep. **5**, 11476 (2015)
7. Heffernan, R., Yang, Y., Paliwal, K., Zhou, Y.: Capturing non-local interactions by long short-term memory bidirectional recurrent neural networks for improving prediction of protein secondary structure, backbone angles, contact numbers and solvent accessibility. Bioinformatics **33**(18), 2842–2849 (2017)
8. Kabsch, W., Sander, C.: Dictionary of protein secondary structure: pattern recognition of hydrogen-bonded and geometrical features. Biopolym. Orig. Res. Biomol. **22**(12), 2577–2637 (1983)
9. Lyons, J., et al.: Predicting backbone $c\alpha$ angles and dihedrals from protein sequences by stacked sparse auto-encoder deep neural network. J. Comput. Chem. **35**(28), 2040–2046 (2014)

10. Magnan, C.N., Baldi, P.: SSpro/ACCpro 5: almost perfect prediction of protein secondary structure and relative solvent accessibility using profiles, machine learning and structural similarity. Bioinformatics **30**(18), 2592–2597 (2014)
11. Mataeimoghadam, F., et al.: Enhancing protein backbone angle prediction by using simpler models of deep neural networks. Sci. Rep. **10**(1), 1–12 (2020)
12. Mirdita, M., von den Driesch, L., Galiez, C., Martin, M.J. Söding, J., Steinegger, M.: Uniclust databases of clustered and deeply annotated protein sequences and alignments. Nucleic Acids Res. **45**(D1), D170–D176 (2017)
13. Perez-Rathke, A., Mali, S., Du, L., Liang, J.: Alterations in chromatin folding patterns in cancer variant-enriched loci. In: 2019 IEEE EMBS International Conference on Biomedical & Health Informatics (BHI), pp. 1–4. IEEE (2019)
14. Rabiner, L.R.: A tutorial on hidden Markov models and selected applications in speech recognition. Proc. IEEE **77**(2), 257–286 (1989)
15. Remmert, M., Biegert, A., Hauser, A., Söding, J.: HHblits: lightning-fast iterative protein sequence searching by HMM-HMM alignment. Nat. Methods **9**(2), 173 (2012)
16. Steinegger, M., Meier, M., Mirdita, M., Vöhringer, H., Haunsberger, S.J., Söding, J.: HH-suite3 for fast remote homology detection and deep protein annotation. BMC Bioinform. **20**(1), 1–15 (2019)
17. Vaswani, A., et al.: Attention is all you need. In: Advances in Neural Information Processing Systems, pp. 5998–6008 (2017)
18. Xu, G., Wang, Q., Ma, J.: OPUS-TASS: a protein backbone torsion angles and secondary structure predictor based on ensemble neural networks. Bioinformatics (Oxf. Engl.) **36**, 5021–5026 (2020)
19. Xu, G., Ma, T., Zang, T., Sun, W., Wang, Q., Ma, J.: OPUS-DOSP: a distance-and orientation-dependent all-atom potential derived from side-chain packing. J. Mol. Biol. **429**(20), 3113–3120 (2017)
20. Zhou, Y., Duan, Y., Yang, Y., Faraggi, E., Lei, H.: Trends in template/fragment-free protein structure prediction. Theor. Chem. Acc. **128**(1), 3–16 (2011)

Magic Mirror Stealth: Interactive Automatic Picture Editing System

MengDi Zhou[1,2(✉)], BoHeng Hu[3], and Si Liu[4]

[1] Institute of Information Engineering, Chinese Academy of Sciences, Beijing, China
zhoumengdi@iie.ac.cn
[2] University of Chinese Academy of Sciences, Beijing, China
[3] Beijing No. 8 High School, Beijing, China
[4] BeiHang University, Beijing, China
liusi@buaa.edu.cn

Abstract. This paper builds an interactive automatic picture editing system based on the most advanced algorithms in the field of multi-modality. It removes a specific area or entity in the image according to the natural language expression, which is like a magic mirror that can make the target invisible. The system is composed of two core processing modules: a referring image segmentation module based on natural language expressions and an automatic image inpainting module. The two modules cooperate to precisely control the editing area and generate the editing results based on the image semantics, which can ensure that the edited images are natural, realistic, and meet the editing needs of users. The two modules of the system are trained on open-source datasets separately. Experimental results demonstrate that the system can help users quickly edit images by a natural language expression.

Keywords: Interactive automatic picture editing system · Referring image segmentation · Image inpainting

1 Introduction

With the development of the mobile Internet and the popularization of smartphones, photo sharing has become an important part of everyday life. Many photo editing tools have been developed to assist the user to process the picture. However, some tools often require users to have certain background knowledge and professional skill; the function of others is too single and is difficult to satisfy the user. For example, we came to the snow mountain to ski and took pictures during the vacation. We came and went in a hurry, so we couldn't check the photo in time. When we are preparing to post these photos on social media, we find one of our favorite photos broke into one stranger which affects the beauty of the photo, as shown on the left side of Fig. 1. It's a pity that the photo is abandoned and we don't have a retake opportunity. At this time, if we do not

---

B. Hu and S. Liu—Contributed equally to this research.

D. N. Pham et al. (Eds.): PRICAI 2021, LNAI 13031, pp. 252–265, 2021.
https://doi.org/10.1007/978-3-030-89188-6_19

have a professional image editing technique, we have to face the problem of post an unsatisfactory photo or abandon the photo. If there is an automatic picture editing system, like a magic mirror, helps the user automatically "invisible" strangers by interacting with the user, so that the difficulty of photo editing will be greatly reduced, and the user experience will be improved.

The rapid development of artificial intelligence provides a technological basis for the magic mirror stealth system. Deep learning technology has achieved great success in many research fields such as computer vision and natural language processing [1,2]. Cross-modal or multimodal research has also received extensive attention and in-depth exploration [3]. Researchers are concerned about how to interact and align the information between different modalities and put forward a lot of many new research directions, such as referring image segmentation and image repair. The new directions are derived from the actual needs of applications.

This paper proposes a magic mirror stealth system to achieve stealth like a magic mirror. It is an interactive automatic picture editing system based on multi-model technology and algorithm. This system receives natural language expressions as instructions, aligns the text with the regions or entities in the image, and automatically realizes accurate editing of the picture. Using a picture and a text instruction describing the target operation as inputs, the system can remove a specific area or entity in the image and repair the image. At the same time, the system should maintain the image visually realistic and semantically correct. We present an example in Fig. 1. The inputs are a picture and a text instruction "remove the man in blue". The output is an automatically edited photo, and the edited part of the photo can be well integrated with the surrounding scenery.

Fig. 1. An example of magic mirror stealth system. (Color figure online)

2   Related Work

Deep learning has made significant progress in the fields of computer vision and natural language processing [4–6]. How to combine different research to build a useful and efficient system has important significance for application. In this paper, we investigate and use the advanced solutions to build a multimodal end-to-end interactive image editing system, Magic Mirror Stealth System. The system mainly involves two tasks: referring image segmentation tasks and automatic image inpainting tasks.

The purpose of referring image segmentation tasks is to segment the part from the image which includes entities described by input expression. Compared with traditional semantic segmentation, the referring image segmentation is a more challenging task, because the natural language has complex forms of expression, such as various coreference relations. Early work [7] used a simple pipeline method to integrate visual and language features to solve this problem. Some later work [8,9] further uses attention between different modalities or self-attention mechanism to learn visual embedding or visual text embedding and model context information.

Image inpainting is another important task in computer vision. The challenge of image inpainting is how to generate pixels that are consistent with surrounding pixels for a specified area to achieve visually realistic and semantically reasonable. Early work [4,10] tried to solve the problem with texture generation [11,12], which was achieved by matching and copying background color blocks. These methods are particularly effective in background repair tasks and have been deployed in practical applications [4]. However, the method assumes that the removed and missing pixels can be found somewhere in the background area, so it cannot generate novel image content that is significantly different from other background areas, nor can they solve the complex and non-repetitive painting areas, such as faces. Moreover, these methods cannot capture high-level semantics. Recently, inspired by the rapidly developing Deep Convolutional Neural Network (CNN) and Generative Adversarial Network (GAN) [13], The work [6,14,15] take image inpainting as the conditional image generation and use a convolutional encoder-decoder network to generate pixels, which is jointly trained with the adversarial network to improve the consistency between the generated pixels and the existing pixels. The generated results prove these methods can generate reasonable new content in highly structured images, such as faces, objects, and complex scenes.

3   The Interactive Automatic Image Editing System

Given a picture and a natural language expression, the goal of the system is to remove the corresponding part of the image, repair the image according to the description of the expression, and maintain the picture visually realistic and semantically correct. The system mainly includes two parts: referring image segmentation module and image inpainting module. The architecture of the system is shown in Fig. 2. The image segmentation aims to understand natural language expression, recognize entities in the image that match the expression, and use masks for identification. This part obtains the image mask matching the language expression, which is described in detail in Sect. 3.1. The image inpainting inputs the original image and the mask, removes the part of the image covered by the mask, and uses the background information to repair the image to obtain the edited image, which is described in detail in Sect. 3.2.

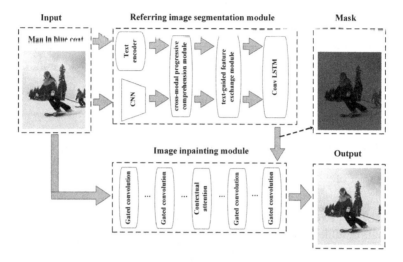

Fig. 2. Structure of magic mirror stealth system.

3.1   Referring Image Segmentation Module

The overall structure of the image segmentation module is shown in Fig. 3. First, the pre-trained convolutional network is used to extract the visual features of the image and the text encoder is used to extract the language features. Then, the cross-modal progressive comprehension (CMPC) sub-module is used to identify the entities in the text and images, and highlight the entities referred to by the text expression and suppress other entities by the relational words. After that, a text-guided feature exchange (TGFE) sub-module is used to implement the communication between multi-level features. Finally, the ConvLSTM neural network is used to integrate multimodal features to obtain the prediction result of the image mask that matches the text expression.

Image and Text Feature Extraction. Following prior research [7,9], The multi-level visual features are extracted with a pre-trained CNN and respectively fused with an 8-D spatial coordinate feature $O \in R^{H \times W \times 8}$ using a 1×1 convolution. The dimension of visual features is $R^{H \times W \times C_v}$, where H, W and C_v are the height, width and channel dimension respectively. The transformed image features are denoted as $\{X_3, X_4, X_5\}$, which respectively correspond to the 3rd, 4th, and 5th stage output of pre-trained CNN. To simplify the representation, we will use X to represent the visual features of a single layer later. Text

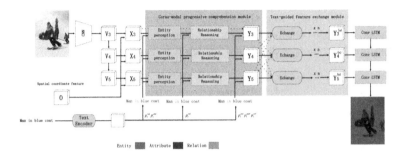

Fig. 3. The referring image segmentation module.

features $L = \{l_1, l_2, ..., l_T\}$ is extracted with a LSTM, where T is the length of the input text, $l_i \in R^{C_l}$ ($i \in \{1, 2, ..., T\}$) denotes i-th words features, C_l denotes the dimension of word features.

Cross-Modal Progressive Comprehension (CMPC) Module. The CMPC sub-module is mainly divided into two stages: entity perception and relationship reasoning. The structure is shown in Fig. 4. In the entity perception stage, the text features of the entity words and attribute words are fused with the visual features through the bilinear fusion strategy to obtain multimodal features $M \in R^{H \times W \times C_m}$, where C_m is the channel dimension in the multimodal feature size. In the relationship reasoning stage, a fully connected graph is constructed based on multimodal features M and relational words. Relation words serve as routers connecting vertices in the graph. Each vertex corresponds to a spatial region in M. By reasoning in the graph, the entities referred to in the text are highlighted and other irrelevant entities are suppressed. Finally, an enhanced multimodal feature $\overline{M}_g$ which further integrates visual features and text features are obtained.

Text-Guided Feature Exchange (TGFE) Module. As shown in Fig. 3, the input of the TGFE submodule is Y_3, Y_4, Y_5 and text feature $L = [l_1, l_2, ...l_T]$, where multimodal features $Y_3, Y_4, Y_5 \in R^{H \times W \times C_m}$. After n rounds of feature exchange, the output is $Y_3^{(n)}, Y_4^{(n)}, Y_5^{(n)}$.

Through n rounds of iterative feature exchange, the features of each level are refined. The model finally uses ConvLSTM to integrate the features Y_3, Y_4, Y_5 to predict the final image mask.

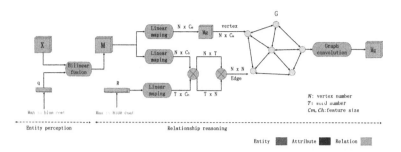

Fig. 4. The cross-modal progressive comprehension (CMPC) submodule.

3.2 Image Inpainting Module

The image inpainting uses the image and mask information to remove the mask coverage part of the image, and generates new pixels to repair the image. The image inpainting module structure is shown in Fig. 5, which is mainly based on the work [16] Coarse-to-fine model structure. The coarse inpainting part is an encoder-decoder network composed of gate convolution, which can deal with valid and blank pixels in the image more effectively than the traditional convolution. Because the shape of the mask is irregular and the position is uncertain, a variant of generative adversarial networks (SN-PatchGAN) is proposed in the refinement part. This network is simple in formulation, fast and stable in training.

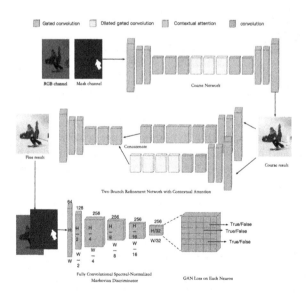

Fig. 5. The automatic image inpainting module.

Gated Convolution. The traditional convolution structure applies the same convolution kernel to any spatial position in the image. About the image inpainting task, image pixels include valid pixels and invalid pixels (a mask covers some pixels). Some problems will be caused by traditional convolution, such as color discrepancy, blurriness. In the deep layer of traditional CNN, the mask part will disappear.

To deal with the problem, a gated convolution is used, as shown in Fig. 6. Gated convolution uses a soft parameter update method, as shown in the following formula:

$$Gatting_{y,x} = \sum_{i=-k'_h}^{k'_h} \sum_{j=-k'_w}^{k'_w} W^g_{k'_h+i,k'_w+j} I_{y+i,x+j}$$

$$Feature_{y,x} = \sum_{i=-k'_h}^{k'_h} \sum_{j=-k'_w}^{k'_w} W^f_{k'_h+i,k'_w+j} I_{y+i,x+j}$$

$$O_{y,x} = \phi\left(Feature_{y,x}\right) \odot \sigma\left(Gatting_{y,x}\right)$$

where x and y represent the coordinates x and y of output, k_h and k_w are the height and width of the convolution kernel, $k'_h = \frac{k_h-1}{2}$, $k'_w = \frac{k_w-1}{2}$, W^g $W^f \in R^{k_h \times k_w \times C' \times C}$ represent different convolution kernels, $I_{y+i,x+j} \in R^C$ and $O_{y,x} \in R^{C'}$ represent input and output respectively, C represents channel dimension, C' represents the number of convolution kernals, Σ is a sigmoid function. The *Gatting* part range is $[0, 1]$, ϕ is a activation function.

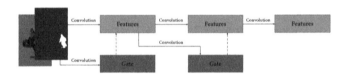

Fig. 6. Structure of gated convolution.

Gated convolution can learn a dynamic feature selection method for different image positions and channels. In the deep layer, the value of the gate structure not only includes the features of the mask part but also includes semantic features in some channels.

Spectral Normalized Markovian Discriminator (SN-PatchGAN). The model needs to deal with masks with various shapes that appear in any position and to stabilize the training process, the model uses a spectral normalized markovian discriminator [17].

A convolutional network is used as the discriminator where the input consists of image and mask, and the output is a three-dimensional features feature of shape $R^{H \times W \times C_{v'}}$ representing the height, width, and the number of channels respectively. Six convolutions with kernel size 5 and stride 2 are stacked to captures the feature. Then GANs directly applied for each feature element in this feature map, formulating $H \times W \times C_{v'}$ number of GANs focusing on different locations and different semantics (represented in different channels) of the input image. The receptive field of each neuron in the output map can cover the entire input image in our training setting, thus there is no need for a global discriminator.

The loss function of generator L_G and the loss function of discriminator $L_{D^{sn}}$:

$$L_G = -E_{z \sim P(z)}[D^{sn}(G(z))],$$
$$L_{D^{sn}} = E_{x \sim P_{data(x)}}[ReLU(1 - D^{sn}(x))]$$
$$+ E_{z \sim P_z(z)}[ReLU(1 + D^{sn}(G(z)))]$$

where D^{sn} represents the discriminator, G is the image inpainting network, $ReLU$ represents the ReLU activation function, and $P_{data(x)}$ represents the probability distribution of real image data, $P_z(z)$ represents the probability distribution of the input data of the image inpainting network.

The final image inpainting network loss function is composed of pixel-wise reconstruction loss and SN-PatchGAN loss function.

4   Experiments

4.1   Datasets

We choose a high-quality open-source dataset to train the model and supplement a part of self-built data. The open-source UNC dataset [3] is used to train the referring image segmentation module. The automatic image inpainting module is trained on the challenging Places2 dataset [18]. We randomly divide the UNC dataset and Places2 dataset into training set, validation set and test set, the statistics data of dataset in Table 1, the data example in Table 2 and Table 3. We built a Magic Mirror Stealth System (MMSS) test dataset, which includes a subset of the test set in the UNC dataset and self-built data, which are specifically used to test the overall system performance. The dataset includes 1132 pieces of data and the example is shown in Table 4.

Table 1. Details of UNC and Places2 dataset

Dataset	Training	Validation	Test
UNC	120624	10834	5657
Places2	1434967	36500	328500

4.2   Experimental Setup

First, we separately train and evaluate the two modules of the system. The referring image segmentation module is trained on the dataset UNC and uses

Table 2. An example of UNC dataset

original image	text expression	reference output
	woman in white on the left	

Table 3. An example of Places2 dataset

input mask	referrence output

Overall IoU and Prec@X as evaluation metrics. The automatic inpainting module is trained on the dataset Places2, and the average absolute error (MAE) and mean square error (MSE) are used as evaluation metrics. Then, we integrate the two modules to construct a magic mirror stealth system and evaluate the system on the self-build test set.

The backbone of the CMPC module is DeepLab-101 [19] pre-trained on the PASCAL-VOC [1] dataset. The output of Res3, Res4, and Res5 is used as multi-level features. The size of input image is $320 * 320$. The channel dimension is set to $C_v = C_l = C_m = 1000$. ConvLSTM hidden layer size is set to 500. The hyperparameter of bilinear fusion is $a = 5$. The number of feature exchange iterations is set to $n = 3$. The GloVe is used as word embedding. The layer of GCN is set to 1. We use Adam optimizer wiht the initial learning rate of $2.5e^{-4}$ and the weight decay of $5e^{-4}$. During the training process, the CNN backbone is frozen. The loss function is cross-entropy loss averaged over all pixels. Finally, DenseCRF [20] is used to refine the segmentation mask.

Table 4. An example of magic mirror stealth system dataset

original image	mask	referrence output

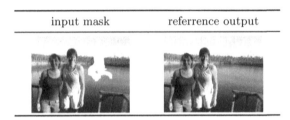

The input image size of the automatic image inpainting module is 256 * 256, and the largest mask size is 128 * 128. Because the module is based on convolutional neural networks, the model can adapt to different resolutions.

4.3   Results of Referring Image Segmentation Module

According to previous research [8], overall Intersection-over-Union (Overall IoU) and Prec@X are adopted as metrics to evaluate the performance of the image segmentation module. Overall IoU calculates total intersection regions over total union regions of all the test samples. Prec@X measures the percentage of predictions whose IoU are higher than the threshold $X \in \{0.5, 0.6, 0.7, 0.8, 0.9\}$. The experimental results are shown in Table 5.

Table 5. The experimental results of referring image segmentation module

Metric (%)	pre@0.5	pre@0.6	pre@0.7	pre@0.8	pre@0.9	Overall IoU
UNC validation	63.82	56.13	45.88	31.28	9.72	57.74
UNC test	66.44	58.79	48.91	33.00	10.44	59.89

The results shown in Table 5 demonstrate the trained module has achieved good results on both the validation set and the test set of UNC data, indicating the effectiveness of the CMPC and TGFE submodule.

4.4   Results of Image Inpainting Module

The results shown in Table 6 demonstrate the trained module has achieved good results on both the Places2 validation set and the test set, indicating the effectiveness of the automatic image inpainting module.

Table 6. The experimental results of image inpainting module

Metric	Places2 validation	Places2 test
MAE (%)	7.89	7.95
MSE (%)	2.25	2.28

4.5   Results of Magic Mirror Stealth System

We evaluate the entire system on the MMSS test dataset. The experimental results are shown in Table 7. The results demonstrate both the first phase test and the second phase test have achieved good results, which can be considered consistent with the single module test results. And it further shows that although two modules are trained independently, the entire system still maintains effectiveness and robustness in the integration test.

Table 7. The experimental results of magic mirror stealth system

Metric (%)	pre@0.5	pre@0.6	pre@0.7	pre@0.8	pre@0.9	overall IoU	MAE	MSE
MMSS test	64.36	56.90	46.18	32.90	10.81	59.44	7.45	2.92

4.6   Results of Manual Evaluation

To further evaluate the actual users' demand and satisfaction with the system, we designed a questionnaire, which contains the following three question:

(1) Question 1: Have you encountered any dissatisfaction with taking photos (often, occasionally, never)?
(2) Question 2: Do you think you need an interactive automatic image editing system to help you solve the problem of dissatisfaction with taking pictures (necessary, a little, no need)?
(3) There are 10 sets of data randomly selected in the system test results, (including original image, expression, and corresponding output image). Please give an image quality score for each set of data (1–5).

We have released an online system that requires users to fill out a questionnaire after using the system. We got a total of 120 valid questionnaires. The results of questionnaires are shown in Table 8. The results show that 74% of users often or occasionally encounter unsatisfied photos, and 94% of users think an interactive automatic editing system is useful. The result of these two questions illustrates the rationality and necessity of our magic mirror stealth system. 74% of the generated images have a score of no less than 3, which shows that our Magic Mirror Stealth System can handle images in most scenes. The system can meet the needs of users and generate a satisfactory image for users.

Table 8. The results of manual evaluation

Question	Result				
1	Often		Occasionally		Never
	27%		47%		26%
2	Necessary		Reasonable		No need
	45%		49%		6%
3	1	2	3	4	5
	17%	9%	13%	25%	36%

We randomly select some example images generated by the system, as shown in Table 9. The example image shows that our system can well use entities and attribute words to perceive the candidate entities referred to by the expression, and with the information of relation words for graph-based reasoning. Then the correct target can be distinguished among similar entities (for example, in the "bird at the bottom" picture, the system keeps the bird at the top). The feature exchange module in our system can also make good use of text information and selectively integrate multiple levels of features to improve mask prediction (for example, in the "ball on the bottom" picture, the system can also identify the shadow of the ball). Our system can also make good use of surrounding texture and structure to generate more realistic results by the context's attention mechanism (for example, in the "The man at the edge of the picturey" picture, the system uses the texture of the surrounding).

Table 9. Examples of image edited by magic mirror stealth system

text expresion	input image	mask	inpainting image
ball on the bottom			
boy on the left			
bird at the bottom			
The man at the edge of the picture			

5 Conclusion

To solve the practical problem, reduce the difficulty for users of editing images, and improve the quality of the editing results, multimodal technology and algorithms are applied to realize an end-to-end interactive automatic editing system, the Magic Mirror Stealth system. The system includes two sub-modules: referring image segmentation module and image inpainting module. The system was evaluated qualitatively and quantitatively, which proved that the system has good interactive automatic editing performance.

In this paper, we only realize the end-to-end reasoning. Considering the difficulty of system implementation, training was divided into two phases. We hope to achieve end-to-end training to achieve better results in the future work.

References

1. Everingham, M., Van Gool, L., Williams, C.K.I., Winn, J.M., Zisserman, A.: The pascal visual object classes (VOC) challenge. Int. J. Comput. Vis. **88**(2), 303–338 (2010)
2. Shi, X., Chen, Z., Wang, H., Yeung, D.-Y., Wong, W.-K., Woo, W.: Convolutional LSTM network: a machine learning approach for precipitation nowcasting. In: Advances in Neural Information Processing Systems, pp. 802–810 (2015)
3. Yu, L., Poirson, P., Yang, S., Berg, A.C., Berg, T.L.: Modeling context in referring expressions. In: Leibe, B., Matas, J., Sebe, N., Welling, M. (eds.) ECCV 2016. LNCS, vol. 9906, pp. 69–85. Springer, Cham (2016). https://doi.org/10.1007/978-3-319-46475-6_5
4. Barnes, C., Shechtman, E., Finkelstein, A., Goldman, D.B.: PatchMatch: a randomized correspondence algorithm for structural image editing. ACM Trans. Graph. **28**(3), 24 (2009)
5. Simakov, D., Caspi, Y., Shechtman, E., Irani, M.: Summarizing visual data using bidirectional similarity. In: 2008 IEEE Conference on Computer Vision and Pattern Recognition, pp. 1–8. IEEE (2008)
6. Yeh, R.A., Chen, C., Lim, T.-Y., Hasegawa-Johnson, M., Do, M.N.: Semantic image inpainting with perceptual and contextual losses. CoRR, abs/1607.07539 (2016)
7. Liu, C., Lin, Z., Shen, X., Yang, J., Lu, X., Yuille, A.: Recurrent multimodal interaction for referring image segmentation. In: Proceedings of the IEEE International Conference on Computer Vision, pp. 1271–1280 (2017)
8. Chen, D.-J., Jia, S., Lo, Y.-C., Chen, H.-T., Liu, T.-L.: See-through-text grouping for referring image segmentation. In: Proceedings of the IEEE International Conference on Computer Vision, pp. 7454–7463 (2019)
9. Ye, L., Rochan, M., Liu, Z., Wang, Y.: Cross-modal self-attention network for referring image segmentation. In Proceedings of the IEEE Conference on Computer Vision and Pattern Recognition, pp. 10502–10511 (2019)
10. Hays, J., Efros, A.A.: Scene completion using millions of photographs. Commun. ACM **51**(10), 87–94 (2008)
11. Efros, A.A., Freeman, W.T.: Image quilting for texture synthesis and transfer. In: Proceedings of the 28th Annual Conference on Computer Graphics and Interactive Techniques, pp. 341–346 (2001)
12. Efros, A.A., Leung, T.K.: Texture synthesis by non-parametric sampling. In: Proceedings of the 7th IEEE International Conference on Computer Vision, vol. 2, pp. 1033–1038. IEEE (1999)
13. Goodfellow, I.J., Pouget-Abadie, J., Mirza, M., Xu, B., Warde-Farley, D.: Generative adversarial nets. In: Advances in Neural Information Processing Systems (NIPS) (2014)
14. Iizuka, S., Simo-Serra, E., Ishikawa, H.: Globally and locally consistent image completion. ACM Trans. Graph. **36**(4), 107:1–107:14 (2017)

15. Li, Y., Liu, S., Yang, J., Yang, M.-H.: Generative face completion. In: Proceedings of the IEEE Conference on Computer Vision and Pattern Recognition, pp. 3911–3919 (2017)
16. Yu, J., Lin, Z., Yang, J., Shen, X., Lu, X., Huang, T.S.: Generative image inpainting with contextual attention. In: Proceedings of the IEEE Conference on Computer Vision and Pattern Recognition, pp. 5505–5514 (2018)
17. Yu, J., Lin, Z., Yang, J., Shen, X., Lu, X., Huang, T.S.: Free-form image inpainting with gated convolution. In: Proceedings of the IEEE International Conference on Computer Vision, pp. 4471–4480 (2019)
18. Zhou, B., Lapedriza, A., Khosla, A., Oliva, A., Torralba, A.: Places: a 10 million image database for scene recognition. IEEE Trans. Pattern Anal. Mach. Intell. **40**(6), 1452–1464 (2017)
19. Chen, L.-C., Papandreou, G., Kokkinos, I., Murphy, K., Yuille, A.L.: DeepLab: semantic image segmentation with deep convolutional nets, atrous convolution, and fully connected CRFs. IEEE Trans. Pattern Anal. Mach. Intell. **40**(4), 834–848 (2017)
20. Krähenbühl, P., Koltun, V.: Efficient inference in fully connected CRFs with gaussian edge potentials. In: Advances in Neural Information Processing Systems, pp. 109–117 (2011)

Off-TANet: A Lightweight Neural Micro-expression Recognizer with Optical Flow Features and Integrated Attention Mechanism

Jiahao Zhang[1,2], Feng Liu[1,2,3(✉)], and Aimin Zhou[1,2,3(✉)]

[1] School of Computer Science and Technology, East China Normal University,
Shanghai, China
lsttoy@163.com, amzhou@cs.ecnu.edu.cn
[2] Shanghai Institute for AI Education, East China Normal University,
Shanghai, China
[3] Shanghai Key Laboratory of Mental Health and Psychological Crisis Intervention,
Shanghai, China

Abstract. Micro-expression recognition is a video sentiment classification task with extremely small sample size. The transience and spatial locality of micro-expressions bring difficulties to constructing large micro-expression databases and designing micro-expression recognition algorithms. To reach the balance between classification accuracy and model complexity in this domain, we propose a lightweight neural micro-expression recognizer, Off-TANet, which is based on apex-onset optical flow features. The neural network contains a simple yet powerful triplet attention mechanism, and the powerfulness of this design could be interpreted in 2 aspects, FACS AU and matrix sparseness. The model evaluation is conducted with a LOSO cross-validation strategy on a combined database including 3 mainstream micro-expression databases. With obviously fewer total parameters (59,403), the results of the experiment indicate that the model achieves an average recall of 0.7315 and an average F1-score of 0.7242, exceeding other major architectures in this domain. A series of ablation experiments are also conducted to ensure the validity of our model design.

Keywords: Micro-expression recognition · Attention module · Self-attention mechanism · Optical flow features · Convolutional neural networks · Computational affection

This study supported by The Research Project of Shanghai Science and Technology Commission (20dz2260300) and The Fundamental Research Funds for the Central Universities. also supported by the Science and Technology Commission of Shanghai Municipality (No. 19511120601).

D. N. Pham et al. (Eds.): PRICAI 2021, LNAI 13031, pp. 266–279, 2021.
https://doi.org/10.1007/978-3-030-89188-6_20

1   Introduction

Micro-expression is a very brief and rapid facial motion that is provoked involuntarily, which could reveal an individual's true emotions even when true feelings are deliberately concealed. Due to the affinity between micro-expression and true emotions, micro-expression has a wide range of applications in mental disorder treatment, such as emotion recognition ability recovery for Schizophrenia patients [20,21] and Alexithymia diagnosis [24]. Compared with regular facial expressions (macro-expression), micro-expression is more subtle both temporally and spatially. To be more specific, the duration of a micro-expression is rather low (between $1/25$ s and $1/5$ s) [33], and a micro-expression only occurs in limited facial regions [13]. The nature of micro-expression not only brings challenges to automated micro-expression recognition but also causes data creation difficulties including human data labeling, sample video capturing, and micro-expression induction. As a consequence, the process of constructing large micro-expression datasets is severely delayed, and micro-expression recognition is still a small sample size problem even to this day.

In recent years, the MEGCs (Micro-Expression Grand Challenge) [22,32] accelerates the development of this domain. In MEGC 2019 [22], lightweight neural micro-expression classification approaches started to completely supersede handcrafted feature (LBP-TOP [8], etc.) based approaches with the help of the widely-used 'Less is more' onset-apex optical flow method [13]. In 2020, deep learning-based algorithms with more advanced techniques, such as graph neural networks and dilated convolution, are led into this domain [10,16]. These models, though drastically inflating the parameter scale, show better recognition accuracy than proposed methods in 2019. Nevertheless, neural micro-expression recognition models in these years still reflect some disadvantages, and the main demerit is that the balance between parameter scale and classification performance is fairly unsatisfying for those models.

To solve the parameter-accuracy balance problem mentioned above, we propose a novel optical flow-based neural network architecture called Off-TANet (Optical flow feature-Triplet Attention Net) for micro-expression sentiment classification. We design a triplet attention module including spatial attention, channel attention, and self-attention, and applied this attention module on a minimalist residual network. We summarize our main contributions as follows:

- We design a powerful triplet attention mechanism and find an interpretation for the powerfulness of the novel attention module based on FACS AU [3] and matrix sparsity.
- This paper proposes a simplified neural network architecture, Off-TANet, with the triplet attention mechanism. The architecture could prevent overfitting and greatly reduce the number of parameters.
- In a combined micro-expression database including $CASME$ [31], $CASME\ II$ [30] and $CAS(ME)^2$ [19], two evaluation metrics, UAR and UF1, are verified in experiments. In comparison to the listed mainstream models and ablation study results, our network, with an extremely low number of parameters, could reach the state-of-the-art.

2   Related Work

Owning to the difficulty to construct a micro-expression dataset, research of micro-expressions are based on some public databases with a limited number of samples. The mainstream databases are SAMM [1], SMIC [11], $CASME$ [31], $CASME\ II$ [30] and $CAS(ME)^2$ [19]. The total number of micro-expression image sequences in all the datasets mentioned above is extremely low (less than 1000). In those datasets, despite being unitary in ethnics, the three $CASME$ datasets with higher image resolution and better preprocessing, including face region segmentation and apex frame detection, are more capable of training neural micro-expression recognizers.

Micro-expression recognition is a new domain in computer vision. Automated micro-expression recognition firstly appears in 2009 [18], which is much later than the burgeon of macro-expression recognition algorithms since the 1990s. After the early explorations of handcrafted feature-based micro-expression recognition, the innovative 'Less is more' apex-onset optical flow method is proposed [13], and neural micro-expression classifiers began to emerge in 2019. ResNet-18 with adversarial training and expression magnification and reduction [14] shows a relatively satisfying performance in MEGC 2019. Several novel CNN structures are also mentioned in MEGC 2019, such as Off-ApexNet [4], Dual-Inception [34], and STSTNet [12]. In 2020, Lo et al. proposed a graph convolution network-based model called MER-GCN [16], which applies a GCN on top of a 3D convolution network to explore the dependencies among different FACS AUs. A real-time micro-expression recognizer, MACNN [10], with residual blocks and atrous convolutions is proposed by Lai et al.to categorize a micro-expression in a low response time. Wang et al. try to improve the performance of ResNet [5] in micro-expression recognition by adding micro-attention modules.

Attention mechanism plays a significant role in human perception. Computer vision researchers have made several previous attempts of leading attention mechanisms into convolutional networks to improve the performance of feature extraction. The spatial transformer is a typical form of spatial attention mechanism, which means the mechanism applies the same warping to each channel [9]. This structure could rotate and scale the feature map and focus on the regions with important features. By contrast, channel attention mechanism allocates the weight of every channel instead of calculating the importance of every pixel in each feature map. An instance of channel attention mechanism is the "Squeeze-and-Excitation" (SE) block, which adaptively recalibrates channel-wise feature responses by explicitly modelling interdependencies between channels [7]. The fusion of spatial and channel attention also shows satisfying performance [27,29]. Self-attention, as the essential operator of Transformers [25], was first widely used in the NLP (Natural Language Processing) tasks [25]. The early application of self-attention blocks in computer vision is the non-local neural network [28]. These days, the success of visual Transformers, including ViT [2], BoTNet [23], and Swin Transformer [15], also proves the effectiveness of this simple but powerful design.

3   Proposed Method

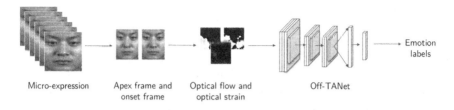

Micro-expression   Apex frame and   Optical flow and   Off-TANet   Emotion
                      onset frame   optical strain   labels

Fig. 1. The whole picture of our two-stage proposed method.

3.1   Optical Flow Feature Extraction

Considering that the facial movements in a micro-expression are extremely sub-tle, the difference between every two consecutive frames is inconspicuous. Instead of taking all frames as an input of the neural network, our micro-expression recog-nition pipeline (Fig. 1) includes two main steps: onset-apex optical flow feature extraction and neural representation learning. This optical flow method firstly mentioned in [13] could memorably reduce the dimension of input features.

Let u and v denote the horizontal and vertical components of the optical flow vector field. In our feature extraction pipeline, the image partial derivatives are calculated by the Sobel operator, and u and v are solved by the TV-L1 optical flow algorithm [17].

Another optical flow-based feature called optical strain is also used in our work. It is capable of approximating the intensity of facial deformation [12], and can be defined as:

$$u = [u, v]^T \tag{1}$$

$$\epsilon(x,y) = \frac{1}{2}[\nabla u + (\nabla u)^T] \tag{2}$$

$$= \begin{bmatrix} \frac{\partial u}{\partial x} & \frac{1}{2}(\frac{\partial u}{\partial y} + \frac{\partial v}{\partial x}) \\ \frac{1}{2}(\frac{\partial v}{\partial x} + \frac{\partial u}{\partial y}) & \frac{\partial v}{\partial y} \end{bmatrix} \tag{3}$$

The magnitude of optical strain is:

$$|\epsilon(x,y)| = \sqrt{(\frac{\partial u}{\partial x})^2 + (\frac{\partial v}{\partial y})^2 + \frac{1}{2}(\frac{\partial u}{\partial y} + \frac{\partial v}{\partial x})^2} \tag{4}$$

The optical flow features $\{u, v, |\epsilon|\}$ could be seen as a 3 channel image, and our neural network will take that 'image' as an input.

3.2 The Attention Mechanism

Spatial and Channel Attention Module. Experiments show that the convolutional block attention module (CBAM) is expected to boost the accuracy of lightweight networks [29]. We applied this argument-saving yet powerful structure to enhance the process of high-level feature extraction.

The CBAM includes two separated mechanisms: spatial attention and channel attention. In the spatial attention operator, the features are aggregated between different channels by both average and max pooling operations. Then the two spatial context descriptors are concatenated and convolved. In the channel attention operator, the features in each channel are aggregated by the two pooling operations, and then transformed by a shared MLP and merged by an element-wise summation. The spatial and channel attention map $SpA(\cdot)$ and $CA(\cdot)$ in our proposed method can be summarized as:

$$SpA(x) = Sigmoid(Conv([AvgPool(x); MaxPool(x)])) \tag{5}$$
$$CA(x) = Sigmoid(MLP(AvgPool(x)) + MLP(MaxPool(x))) \tag{6}$$

where $Conv$ denotes a convolution operator with a 3×3 kernel and MLP denotes a shared one-hidden layer perceptron. After the attention maps are calculated, the attention map could be applied by an element-wise multiplication on the input tensor.

Multi-head Self-attention Module. The burgeoning of visual Transformers showed the potential of the self-attention mechanism in computer vision tasks. Compared with spatial attention, which applies an identical map on each channel, the self-attention map on each channel differs. We applied this module after the CBAM module to construct a more powerful triplet attention mechanism.

The self-attention module in our network is similar to the self-attention block in NLP tasks. Specifically, the input tensor is transformed to three different representations query q, key k, and value v by three linear transformation matrices W_q, W_k, and W_v. Then we can calculate the output of the self-attention module as follows:

$$Attention(q, k, v, r) = Softmax(qk^T + qr^T) * v \tag{7}$$
$$r_{x,y} = PE(x, featureMapSize) + PE(y, featureMapSize) \tag{8}$$
$$PE(2i, d) = sin(1/10000^{2i/d}) \tag{9}$$
$$PE(2i+1, d) = cos(1/10000^{2i/d}) \tag{10}$$

where r denotes the positional code, x and y represent pixel positions. The 2-D image positional code is constructed by adding the results of two 1-D sinusoidal positional code PE [25]. The attention map is then calculated by the element-wise summation of query-key matrix product and query-positional code matrix product. To obtain better performance, a multi-head self-attention mechanism is also applied by concatenating the output from self-attention blocks with unequal weights.

3.3   Network Architecture

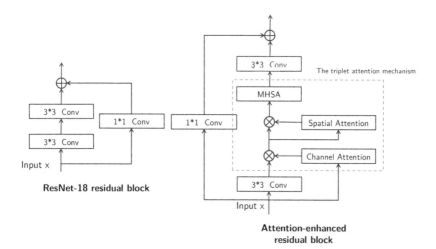

Fig. 2. The attention-enhanced residual block of our network, based on a ResNet-18 residual block. The triplet attention mechanism is added between the two convolution layers in a ResNet-18 residual block.

According to the experiments in BoTNet [23], apply an attention mechanism in the last residual block could improve the performance of ResNets. We replaced the last residual block in a minimalist residual convolutional network with a novel attention-enhanced residual block (Fig. 2). Compared with the CBAM [29] attention module, our triplet attention module is expected to focus more on the important facial regions, as the CBAM channel and spatial attention extract features in a larger granularity, while the self-attention map differs both between different spatial positions and different channels.

The input apex images and onset images are firstly normalized to 112×112 with a cubic interpolation algorithm, then the $3 \times 112 \times 112$ optical flow features are extracted and sent to the network. The network architecture is shown in Fig. 3. The number of channels in this architecture is under strict control to reduce the scale of parameters. The low-level features are extracted by a 7×7 convolution layer, and then the tensor is sent to two ResNet-18 style residual blocks. The attention-enhanced residual block with a triplet attention mechanism extracts the high-level representations. The output channels in the last residual block are reduced to shrink the FC layer, which could cause over-fitting problems. More details about the network can be found in the published source code.

4   Experiments and Analysis

To validate the validity of our approach on micro-expression sentiment classification, we conduct experiments on a combined database including $CASME$ [31],

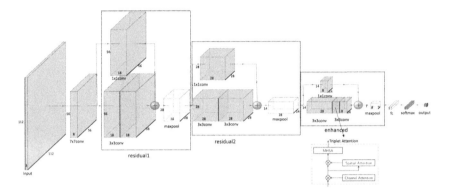

Fig. 3. The overall architecture of our network. The operator type and the output tensor shape in each layer are shown in this picture.

$CASME\ II$ [30] and, $CAS(ME)^2$ [19]. Considering that mainstream models are tested on dissimilar benchmarks and datasets, all the models mentioned in Table 2 are re-implemented and tested on this novel combined dataset with a 'MEGC 2019-like' benchmark.

Source code in Python, .csv format combined dataset (without images) and our running environments are available on https://github.com/ECNU-Cross-Innovation-Lab/PRICAI2021-Off-TANet.

4.1 Data Preparation

The datasets used in our work are $CASME$ [31], $CASME\ II$ [30], and $CAS(ME)^2$ [19] respectively. The sentiment label, apex frame, onset frame of each micro-expression image sequence is provided by those datasets. Images are also properly cropped to get rid of the interference from pixels containing non-facial information. The input image will be normalized to different sizes with inter-cubic interpolation to adapt the input layer of each model, and RGB images are turned black and white before optical flow feature extraction.

To avoid confusing the learning process, We apply two 'MEGC 2019-like' data preparation methods. Among all the datasets, only main sentiment categories, which contain abundant micro-expression samples, are selected to form the combined dataset. Apart from that, macro-expression samples in $CAS(ME)^2$ [19] and 'Others' samples in $CASME\ II$ [30] are not used. To weaken the classification bias between datasets, we map those original labels to only three classes. Categorization information about the database can be seen in Table 1.

4.2 Algorithm Comparison

In this paper, all the methods mentioned in Table 2 are tested with a LOSO (Leave One Subject Out) protocol, and our metrics, UAR (Unweighted Average

Table 1. Categorization information about the databases.

Label	Total samples	Number of samples			Original label
		$CASME$ [31]	$CASME\ II$ [30]	$CAS(ME)^2$ [19]	
Positive	48	10	32	6	Happiness
Negative	194	85	88	21	Disgust Repression Sadness
Surprise	52	19	25	8	Surprise

Recall) and UF1 (Unweighted F1-Score) are the same as metrics used in MEGC 2019 [22].

The LOSO protocol is a cross-validation strategy that repeats evaluation for 49 times by splitting out samples in each subject group in the 49-subject combined database. This widely used protocol effectively mimics realistic scenarios and ensures subject-independent evaluation.

The combined dataset is obviously imbalanced in category distribution, so class-balanced metrics are used in our experiments. The computation methods of UAR and UF1, which are also called balanced accuracy and macro-averaged F1-score, are as follows:

$$UAR = \frac{\sum_{c \in C} \frac{TP_c}{n_c}}{|C|} \qquad (11)$$

$$UF1 = \frac{1}{|C|} \sum_{c \in C} \frac{2TP_c}{2TP_c + FP_c + FN_c} \qquad (12)$$

In these two formulas, C is the set of sentiment classes, n_c represents number of samples in class c, and TP_c, FP_c, FN_c means True Positive, False Positive, and False Negative. We assume that each left-out subject is of the same importance, so the final UAR and UF1 is the unweighted mean of all UARs and UF1s calculated in the 49-fold cross-validation.

Table 2. Results of mainstream approaches (sorted by UAR).

Model	UAR	UF1	Params	Flops	MemR+W
Off-ApexNet (2019) [4]	0.5832	0.5650	2.66M	3.87M	10.35 MB
STSTNet (2019) [12]	0.5584	0.5399	162,051	526.98K	0.76 MB
Dual-Inception (2019) [34]	0.6167	0.5814	6.45M	12.64M	25.67 MB
MACNN (2020) [10]	0.6835	0.6660	70.57M	793.67M	1140.00 MB
Micro-Attention (2020) [26]	0.7086	0.7003	53.38M	1.0G	237.97 MB
Off-TANet (ours)	**0.7315**	**0.7242**	**59,403**	**30.08M**	**5.64 MB**

The results of mainstream approaches are illustrated in Table 2. **UAR**, **UF1**, the number of total parameters (**Params**), the total floating-point operation

(**FLOPs**), and the total memory read/write (**MemR+W**) are listed in the table. Parameter numbers and memory usage are measured by the **torchstat** Python package.

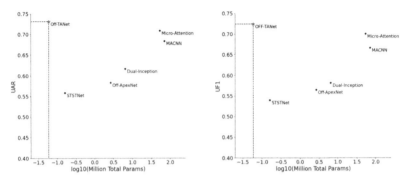

(a) TotalParams-UAR scatter diagram (b) TotalParams-UF1 scatter diagram

Fig. 4. The scatter plot of the test results. Our model reaches the highest UAR and UF1 with the lowest parameter number.

The hyperparameters of optimizers and the training process can be found in the code of this paper. The train epochs of re-implemented models are selected by a grid search to accommodate our new dataset, and other hyperparameters are determined according to the original papers. The architectures of MACNN [10] and Micro-Attention [26] are slightly adjusted to speed up the training process, avoid over-fitting and save GPU memory.

Table 2 and its corresponding scatter diagram Fig. 4 directly shows the advantages of our architecture. With the lowest **Total Params (59,403)** and an obviously low **Total MemR+W (5.64 MB)**, Off-TANet reached the highest **UAR (0.7315)** and **UF1 (0.7242)**.

4.3   Ablation Study

To ensure the validity of our model design, we have carried out a series of ablation experiment.

First of all, the effectiveness of the optical strain feature is examined. In the no optical strain experiment, we change the number of input channels of the first convolution layer and remove the optical strain feature from the input. The result also indicates the superiority of optical flow features compared with the end-to-end approach, which takes the raw onset and apex image as the input.

Despite the experiments in BotNet [23] show that the attention-enhancement should only be applied on the last residual block, we still compare the performance between Off-TANet and a network with identical output tensor shape in each block which change all the residual blocks with the triplet attention residual

Table 3. Results of ablation experiments on the input feature and the number of enhanced blocks.

Model	UAR	UF1
Off-TANet + no optical flow features	0.6631	0.6440
Off-TANet + no optical strain	0.7180	0.7078
Off-TANct + all residual block attention-enhanced	0.6895	0.6814
Off-TANet (ours)	**0.7315**	**0.7242**

Table 4. Results of ablation experiments on the design of the last attention-enhanced residual block.

Model	UAR	UF1
No enhancement	0.6804	0.6745
+ CBAM [29]	0.6903	0.6744
+ multi-head self-attention	0.6943	0.6857
+ bottleneck Transformer [23]	0.7045	0.6937
Off-TANet (ours)	**0.7315**	**0.7242**

block. The accuracy of Off-TANet exceeds the accuracy of its counterpart which could cause overfitting problems (Tables 3 and 4).

The design of the attention-enhanced block is also discussed in this paper. On the original ResNet-18 residual block, we applied three different attention-enhancement approaches including only self-attention, only CBAM and bottleneck transformer. As visual Transformers are more data-hungry, the bottleneck transformer shows a less satisfying performance on micro-expression recognition – a small sample size problem. The self-attention enhancement and the CBAM approach also show their weakness compared with our design.

4.4   Off-TANet Attention Mechanism Analysis

Compared with raw CNN features, the attention features are more interpretable when visualized. To explore the intrinsic mechanism of our integrated attention block, we visualized the attention maps of our model (Fig. 5) when inferencing sample EP01-5 from *CASME* Subject 1. The attention maps are firstly resized to 112×112. The model is pre-trained on the training set of the first cross-validation fold (leaving *CASME* Subject 1 out).

Sample EP01-5 contains a positive micro-expression with human-annotated FACS Action Unit [3] 'AU12', which means the lip corner puller and its related facial regions are colored red on the AU picture. The validity of the integration of CBAM [29] and self-attention can be seen from the figure, as the spatial attention map is general and vague, while the self-attention map only focuses on the most important facial areas. In addition, the self-attention map and the FACS AU facial regions correspond on the nasolabial fold, the right mouth corner, and

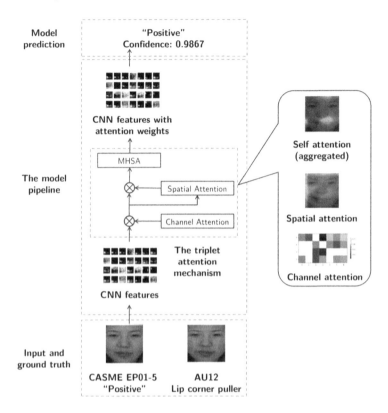

Fig. 5. The attention maps of Off-TANet when inferencing sample EP01-5. The CNN features are extracted by layers before the triplet attention mechanism. The spatial and self-attention maps are visualized by two heat maps. All the self-attention maps are aggregated by a channel-wise maximization to get exactly one attention map, and then the attention map is multiplicated on the spatial-attention map and visualized. Other details about the visualization process can be found in the source code.

the left cheekbone, and this shows the affinity between the Off-TANet triplet attention mechanism and human perception.

Despite the effectiveness of the fusion of channel attention and spatial attention is ensured by the experiments in [29], the lead-in of the self-attention module still needs more support phenomenons besides merely accuracy numbers. A possible explanation is that the self-attention enhanced CBAM [29] could further discriminate the spatial regions with significant features in comparison with the original CBAM [29]. This could mean that compared with the CBAM [29] spatial attention map, the attention map after the self-attention enhancement has greater matrix sparseness, as the attention weights for unimportant spatial positions are suppressed to zero. We applied two sparseness evaluation metrics in our experiment, soft 0-norm (the number of elements smaller than the threshold) and Hoyer sparseness [6]. Their definitions are as follows:

$$Soft_t(x) = |\{i|x_i < t\}| \tag{13}$$

$$Hoyer(x) = \frac{\sqrt{n} - (\Sigma|x_i|)/\sqrt{\Sigma x_i^2}}{\sqrt{n} - 1} \tag{14}$$

where x denotes the matrix, x_i denotes its element and t denotes a threshold. We validate the mean value of these two indicators in multiple cross-validation folds (Table 5), and the sparseness assumption is confirmed.

Table 5. The sparseness of the self-attention map. Only folds with large test set sizes are contained.

Cross-val fold	Test set size	Spatial attention		Self-attention	
		$Soft_{0.01}$	$Hoyer$	$Soft_{0.01}$	$Hoyer$
1	22	0	0.0088	1470	0.1195
4	13	0	0.0154	1161	0.1768
6	23	0	0.0172	845	0.1196
41	31	0	0.0161	1036	0.1313

5 Conclusion

The integration of innovative neural network architectures and micro-expression recognition is an attractive topic. In our paper, we proposed a novel neural optical flow processor called Off-TANet for micro-expression sentiment classification. In this architecture based on a minimalist ResNet, a triplet attention mechanism is used to improve its classification performance. We test our model on a combined dataset with a LOSO protocol and showed that the UAR and UF1 of our design exceed the counterparts of other mainstream approaches. We also conduct a series of ablation experiments to ensure the validity of our design. We also give an possible interpretation for the intrinsic mechanism of the triplet attention module. Though this paper only explored the application of the triplet attention mechanism in micro-expression recognition, this design could be a general design for lightweight neural networks and we hope to release the potential of this simple yet powerful architecture on other tasks in our future work.

References

1. Davison, A.K., Lansley, C., Costen, N., Tan, K., Yap, M.H.: SAMM: a spontaneous micro-facial movement dataset. IEEE Trans. Affect. Comput. **9**(1), 116–129 (2016)
2. Dosovitskiy, A., et al.: An image is worth 16 × 16 words: transformers for image recognition at scale. arXiv preprint arXiv:2010.11929 (2020)

3. Ekman, P., Friesen, W.V.: Nonverbal leakage and clues to deception. Psychiatry **32**(1), 88–106 (1969)
4. Gan, Y., Liong, S.T., Yau, W.C., Huang, Y.C., Tan, L.K.: OFF-ApexNet on micro-expression recognition system. Sig. Process. Image Commun. **74**, 129–139 (2019)
5. He, K., Zhang, X., Ren, S., Sun, J.: Deep residual learning for image recognition. In: Proceedings of the IEEE Conference on Computer Vision and Pattern Recognition, pp. 770–778 (2016)
6. Hoyer, P.O.: Non-negative matrix factorization with sparseness constraints. J. Mach. Learn. Res. **5**(9), 1457–1469 (2004)
7. Hu, J., Shen, L., Sun, G.: Squeeze-and-excitation networks. In: Proceedings of the IEEE Conference on Computer Vision and Pattern Recognition, pp. 7132–7141 (2018)
8. Huang, X., Zhao, G., Hong, X., Zheng, W., Pietikäinen, M.: Spontaneous facial micro-expression analysis using spatiotemporal completed local quantized patterns. Neurocomputing **175**, 564–578 (2016)
9. Jaderberg, M., Simonyan, K., Zisserman, A., Kavukcuoglu, K.: Spatial transformer networks. arXiv preprint arXiv:1506.02025 (2015)
10. Lai, Z., Chen, R., Jia, J., Qian, Y.: Real-time micro-expression recognition based on ResNet and atrous convolutions. J. Ambient. Intell. Humaniz. Comput., 1–12 (2020). https://doi.org/10.1007/s12652-020-01779-5
11. Li, X., Pfister, T., Huang, X., Zhao, G., Pietikäinen, M.: A spontaneous micro-expression database: inducement, collection and baseline. In: 2013 10th IEEE International Conference and Workshops on Automatic Face and Gesture Recognition (FG), pp. 1–6. IEEE (2013)
12. Liong, S.T., Gan, Y., See, J., Khor, H.Q., Huang, Y.C.: Shallow triple stream three-dimensional CNN (STSTNet) for micro-expression recognition. In: 2019 14th IEEE International Conference on Automatic Face & Gesture Recognition, FG 2019, pp. 1–5. IEEE (2019)
13. Liong, S.T., See, J., Wong, K., Phan, R.C.W.: Less is more: micro-expression recognition from video using apex frame. Sig. Process. Image Commun. **62**, 82–92 (2018)
14. Liu, Y., Du, H., Zheng, L., Gedeon, T.: A neural micro-expression recognizer. In: 2019 14th IEEE International Conference on Automatic Face & Gesture Recognition, FG 2019, pp. 1–4. IEEE (2019)
15. Liu, Z., et al.: Swin transformer: hierarchical vision transformer using shifted windows. arXiv preprint arXiv:2103.14030 (2021)
16. Lo, L., Xie, H.X., Shuai, H.H., Cheng, W.H.: MER GCN: micro-expression recognition based on relation modeling with graph convolutional networks. In: 2020 IEEE Conference on Multimedia Information Processing and Retrieval (MIPR), pp. 79–84. IEEE (2020)
17. Pérez, J.S., Meinhardt-Llopis, E., Facciolo, G.: TV-L1 optical flow estimation. IPOL **2013**, 137–150 (2013)
18. Polikovsky, S., Kameda, Y., Ohta, Y.: Facial micro-expressions recognition using high speed camera and 3D-gradient descriptor (2009)
19. Qu, F., Wang, S.J., Yan, W.J., Li, H., Wu, S., Fu, X.: CAS(ME)^2: a database for spontaneous macro-expression and micro-expression spotting and recognition. IEEE Trans. Affect. Comput. **9**(4), 424–436 (2017)
20. Russell, T.A., Chu, E., Phillips, M.L.: A pilot study to investigate the effectiveness of emotion recognition remediation in schizophrenia using the micro-expression training tool. Br. J. Clin. Psychol. **45**(4), 579–583 (2006)

21. Russell, T.A., Green, M.J., Simpson, I., Coltheart, M.: Remediation of facial emotion perception in schizophrenia: concomitant changes in visual attention. Schizophr. Res. **103**(1–3), 248–256 (2008)
22. See, J., Yap, M.H., Li, J., Hong, X., Wang, S.J.: MEGC 2019-the second facial micro-expressions grand challenge. In: 2019 14th IEEE International Conference on Automatic Face & Gesture Recognition, FG 2019, pp. 1–5. IEEE (2019)
23. Srinivas, A., Liu, T.Y., Parmar, N., Shlens, J., Abbeel, P., Vaswani, A.: Bottleneck transformers for visual recognition. arXiv preprint arXiv:2101.11605 (2021)
24. Swart, M., Kortekaas, R., Aleman, A.: Dealing with feelings: characterization of trait alexithymia on emotion regulation strategies and cognitive-emotional processing. PLOS ONE **4**(6), e5751 (2009)
25. Vaswani, A., et al.: Attention is all you need. arXiv preprint arXiv:1706.03762 (2017)
26. Wang, C., Peng, M., Bi, T., Chen, T.: Micro-attention for micro-expression recognition. Neurocomputing **410**, 354–362 (2020)
27. Wang, F., et al.: Residual attention network for image classification. In: Proceedings of the IEEE Conference on Computer Vision and Pattern Recognition, pp. 3156–3164 (2017)
28. Wang, X., Girshick, R., Gupta, A., He, K.: Non-local neural networks. In: Proceedings of the IEEE Conference on Computer Vision and Pattern Recognition, pp. 7794–7803 (2018)
29. Woo, S., Park, J., Lee, J.-Y., Kweon, I.S.: CBAM: convolutional block attention module. In: Ferrari, V., Hebert, M., Sminchisescu, C., Weiss, Y. (eds.) ECCV 2018. LNCS, vol. 11211, pp. 3–19. Springer, Cham (2018). https://doi.org/10.1007/978-3-030-01234-2_1
30. Yan, W.J., et al.: CASME II: an improved spontaneous micro-expression database and the baseline evaluation. PLOS ONE **9**(1), e86041 (2014)
31. Yan, W.J., Wu, Q., Liu, Y.J., Wang, S.J., Fu, X.: CASME database: a dataset of spontaneous micro-expressions collected from neutralized faces. In: 2013 10th IEEE International Conference and Workshops on Automatic Face and Gesture Recognition (FG), pp. 1–7. IEEE (2013)
32. Yap, M.H., See, J., Hong, X., Wang, S.J.: Facial micro-expressions grand challenge 2018 summary. In: 2018 13th IEEE International Conference on Automatic Face & Gesture Recognition, FG 2018, pp. 675–678. IEEE (2018)
33. Zhang, M., Fu, Q., Chen, Y.H., Fu, X.: Emotional context influences micro-expression recognition. PLOS ONE **9**(4), e95018 (2014)
34. Zhou, L., Mao, Q., Xue, L.: Dual-inception network for cross-database micro-expression recognition. In: 2019 14th IEEE International Conference on Automatic Face & Gesture Recognition, FG 2019, pp. 1–5. IEEE (2019)

Pulmonary Nodule Classification of CT Images with Attribute Self-guided Graph Convolutional V-Shape Networks

Xiangbo Zhang[1,2], Kun Wang[1,2], Xiaohong Zhang[1,2(✉)], and Sheng Huang[1,2]

[1] Key Laboratory of Dependabel Service Computing in Cyber Physical Society, Ministry of Education, Chongqing University, Chongqing 400044, China
{zhangxiangbo,kun.wang,xhongz,huangsheng}@cqu.edu.cn
[2] The School of Big Data and Software Engineering, Chongqing University, Chongqing 401331, China

Abstract. Accurate identification and early diagnosis of malignant pulmonary nodules are critical to improving the survival rate of lung cancer patients. Recently, deep learning methods have been proved to be successful in computer-aided diagnosis tasks. However, most advanced research work does not fully utilized valuable attribute prior knowledge for semantic reasoning to guide the network. Therefore, it lacks interpretability and hence is difficult for clinical radiologists to understand and apply. To comprehensively tackle these challenges, we propose a novel Attribute Self-guided Graph Convolutional V-shape Networks (AS-GCVN) for pulmonary nodules classification with steps as follows. We first develop a sub-network for representation learning, which can effectively extract image-level features. Second, we construct a graph convolution V-shape network to model the semantic information of attributes to guide the classification of benign and malignant pulmonary nodules accurately. Moreover, an Attribute Self-guided Feature Enhancement (ASFE) module is proposed to improve the ability of graph semantic reasoning, which can map the image features extracted by the convolutional neural network to attribute features through adaptive learning. Finally, the two sub-networks effectively integrate attribute inference knowledge and representation learning to enable end-to-end training. This way can further improve the interpretability and robustness of pulmonary nodule classification. Extensive experimental results on the LIDC-IDRI dataset demonstrate that our approach obviously outperforms other existing state-of-the-art methods.

Keywords: Pulmonary nodule classification · Graph convolution network · Attribute learning · Computed tomography (CT)

1 Introduction

Medical image analysis is an important link in computer-aided diagnosis. Lung computed tomography (CT) is a kind of medical image that can directly observe

© Springer Nature Switzerland AG 2021
D. N. Pham et al. (Eds.): PRICAI 2021, LNAI 13031, pp. 280–292, 2021.
https://doi.org/10.1007/978-3-030-89188-6_21

pulmonary nodules. Lung CT can clearly observe the structural information of lung nodules, such as shape, size, texture, etc. The Lung CT provides an effective measure for doctors to evaluate whether the pulmonary nodules have canceration. Bray [3] and Torre [19] have shown that lung cancer is the leading cause of cancer death globally, and its morbidity and mortality are both high. Early diagnosis of lung cancer is the key to reducing mortality. Therefore, it is significant to propose a reliable computer-aided diagnosis method to analyze lung CT images to help doctors effectively and accurately classify lung nodules.

Despite the development of approaches for lung nodule classification in recent years, it remains a challenging task for the following reasons. First, the visual features of some nodules and their surrounding tissues have low contrast (see Fig. 1(a) (P2 and P5)). Second, different types of nodules have different visual characteristics (see Fig. 1(a) (P3 and P4, P1 and P5)). For these reasons, the lung nodule classification model is still not reliable in terms of accuracy and robustness. With the development of deep learning technology, convolution neural network (CNN) is widely proposed for image classification models. Some researchers have tried to apply CNN to extract image features from lung CT. These image features with rich discriminative information adapted to different vision tasks. Most previous works focused on image features to pulmonary nodules classification tasks. Shen [18] used a convolutional neural network to identify benign and malignant pulmonary nodules, and a multi-crop convolutional neural network was proposed. To diagnose pulmonary benign and malignant nodules more efficiently, Causey [4] proposed NoduleXNet, which can extract features from all CT at one time. Al-Shabi [1] proposed to use convolution kernel with different scales as local and global feature extractors for pulmonary nodules to extract local and global features of nodules, respectively. However, these methods can only output the malignant grade of lung nodules. Thus, they cannot be explained. In order to make the network interpretable, some researches output attribute scores and malignant scores. Shen [16] divided the process of deep neural learning of pulmonary nodule diagnosis into the low task and high task. Low and high tasks predict attribute scores and malignant scores, respectively. LaLonde [11] utilized a capsule network to predict the attributes scores and malignancy scores of pulmonary nodules. Unfortunately, these methods rely on image features to judge the malignant degree of pulmonary nodules and ignore the important prior knowledge based on the attributes of pulmonary nodules. Thus, for the robust and interpretable lung nodule classification model, a method that can jointly analyze image information and attribute information to judge the malignant degree and output the attribute scores is indispensable.

To address the above challenge, we propose a novel method based on Graph Convolutional Network (GCN), which joint analysis the attribute features and image features of lung nodules. This work motivates by experts' clinical experience that many features explained by radiologists from CT scans are considered when assessing the pulmonary nodule's malignancy [6,9] as illustrated in Fig. 1(b). These features are called attribute features in this study. Examples of such attributes include margin, sphericity, texture, *et al.* Therefore, the joint

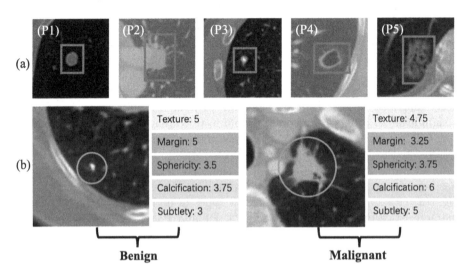

Fig. 1. (a) Example CT images of lung nodules in different positions and shapes: (1) common isolated nodule. (2) juxtapleural nodule. (3) cavitary nodule. (4) calcific nodule. (5) ground-glass opacity (GGO) nodule. (b) The attributes of benign and malignant pulmonary nodules are different. Thus these attributes can be used as an important basis for judging benign and malignant pulmonary nodules. The six nodule characteristics are diagnostic features and attribute features, including calcification, subtlety, sphericity, margin, texture. For each characteristic, we take the average value of four radiologists.

analysis of attribute characteristics and image characteristics will help improve the ability to distinguish pulmonary nodules. Specifically, we first design a sub-network to perform representation learning on lung CT images, which can extract image-level features. Second, we utilize the GCN to model the attribute semantic information of lung nodules, and then design a second sub-network to extract attribute-level features. Moreover, we propose the Attribute Self-guided Feature Enhancement (ASFE) module that can map image-level features extracted by CNN to attribute features, which enhances the semantic inference ability of graph convolutional neural networks. Finally, the information extracted by the two subnets is jointly optimized. This way also echoes our motivation that use the images and attributes of lung nodules to analyze together, which makes the final classification results more robust and accurate.

Our main contributions can be summarized as follows:

- To the best of our knowledge, we are the first to propose a novel end-to-end interpretable classification framework for pulmonary nodules based on GCN attribute features and CNN image features. The proposed framework employs GCN to yield attribute scores for pulmonary nodule's benign and malignant assist-proofs diagnosis.
- We propose an attribute self-guided feature enhancement (ASFE) module that can adaptively learn the low-level features of interdependent attributes

to enhance the reasoning ability of the graph semantic so as to guide the classification of pulmonary nodules better. Moreover, this module can be seamlessly embedded in the network for end-to-end learning.
– Experimental results on the LIDC-IDRI dataset using 5-fold cross-validation demonstrate that our AS-GCVN yields superior performance over the previous competing approaches.

2   Method

2.1   Overview

Our proposed diagnosis of benign and malignant pulmonary nodules via attribute adaptive guided graph convolutional v-shape networks (AS-GCVN) consists of two components. The overall pipeline of our model show in Fig. 2.

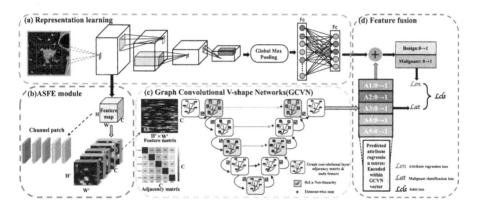

Fig. 2. Overview of the proposed method. The framework that we proposed can be divided into four parts: (a) Representation learning module. This module extracts the image feature through convolutional neural networks. (b) Attribute self-guided feature enhancement (ASFE) module. The input of the ASFE module is the image-level feature map. (c) GCVN fuses attribute features with prior knowledge and then conducts attribute classification. (d) Feature fusion module. This module fuses image-level features with attribute-level features.

The first component applies ResNet-50 to extract the overall images' visual features, and obtains the image-level feature vector $\hat{y}_{im} \in \mathbb{R}^{B \times C}$ (B is the number of batch size and C is the number of the attribute) through global average pooling and fully connection (FC) layer; see the (a) frame in Fig. 2. Thus, if an input image is with the $B \times 50 \times 50 \times 1$ resolution, we can obtain $B \times 5$ feature vector from the FC layer.

The second component's input is the feature map of the image in the first stage after layer1 (the first block of the ResNet-50). The feature map transforms the image-level features into attribute features through the ASFE module. Then attribute feature and attribute adjacency matrix are used as inputs to obtain attribute level vector $\hat{y}_{at} \in \mathbb{R}^{B \times C}$ through graph convolutional v-shape networks (GCVN), as illustrated in the bottom part of Fig. 2. Thus, if an input feature is with the $B \times 5 \times 11 \times 11$ resolution, we can obtain the $B \times 5$ feature vector from the GCVN.

Next, $\hat{y}_{im}$ and $\hat{y}_{at}$ are added to obtain the feature vector enhanced by the attribute level feature. Finally, the enhanced vector is passed through the FC layer to obtain the benign and malignant results $\hat{y} \in \mathbb{R}^{B \times 2}$.

2.2 Attribute Self-guided Feature Enhancement Module

To better guide the classification of benign and malignant pulmonary nodules, we design an attribute self-guided feature enhancement (ASFE) module that numerically maps image low-level features into attribute-level features utilizing attribute learning. ASFE module numerically characterizes the low-level image features extracted from the deep convolution neural network through adaptive weight.

The ASFE module's input is the image feature $I \in \mathbb{R}^{B \times S \times H \times W}$ (S is the number of image feature channel and H and W represent the height and width of the feature map respectively). After one layer of convolution, the dimension of the image level features becomes $I_{im} \in \mathbb{R}^{B \times C \times H' \times W'}$. Then we transform the image features of each category by weight adaptive, which can be expressed as:

$$I^i_{ASFE} = \Phi\left(f\left(I^i_{im}, E^i_{ASFE}\right)\right) \tag{1}$$

where I^i_{im} represents the ith image feature channel patch of I_{im}, E^i_{ASFE} that have the same dimension as I^i_{im} is the adaptive transformation matrix and $f(\cdot)$ represents the Hadamard product of the matrix, $\Phi(\cdot)$ represents the ReLu activation function.

Finally, we stretch the I_{ASFE} to get the attribute features $A \in \mathbb{R}^{B \times C \times D}(D = H' \times W')$.

2.3 Graph Convolutional V-Shape Networks

Graph Convolutional Network (GCN) was introduced in [10] to perform semi-supervised classification. Unlike standard image convolution operations, the purpose of graph convolution is to convolve the feature and adjacency matrix constructed by attributes. In the graph convolutional operations, the aim of the network is to learn a series of weight matrices W which are acting on the graph G, and then the nonlinear transformation $\mathcal{F}$ is used to extract the features. In GCN, the feature matrix $A \in \mathbb{R}^{B \times C \times D}$ and the adjacency matrix $X \in \mathbb{R}^{C \times C}$ are used as inputs. In the network calculation, the network calculates the weight matrix and the characteristic matrix to get the feature matrix H of this layer and then transfers the feature matrix to the next layer. The calculation of the feature matrix of each layer is the same operation. And then the GCN operation of [10] can be represented as

$$H^1 = \mathcal{F}\left(XAW^1\right), H^{l+1} = \mathcal{F}\left(XH^lW^{l+1}\right) \tag{2}$$

where H^l is the feature graph of the output of each layer in GCN and $W^l \in \mathbb{R}^{dim \times d'}$ is the weight matrices.

For the adjacency matrix X of the attribute, we build the adjacency matrix between the nodes by mining the relationship between the attributes in the dataset, for example, $P\left(C_j|C_i\right)$ represents the probability of $P\left(C_j\right)$ in the case of $P\left(C_i\right)$. As shown in Fig. 2, $P\left(C_j|C_i\right)$ is not equal to $P\left(C_i|C_j\right)$. Therefore, the adjacency matrix between nodes is asymmetric.

To establish the adjacency matrix between nodes, firstly, we counted the number of lesions per type. According to the doctor's label, the grade of the lesion is greater than or equal to 3, which is considered as this kind of lesion. The adjacency matrix can be represented as:

$$P\left(C_i|C_j\right) = \frac{\Sigma(C_{ij})}{\Sigma(C_j)} \tag{3}$$

In the experience of deep neural networks, multi-parameter learning can achieve satisfactory performance. However, the excessive overlay of the GCN model will lead to the problem of over-smoothing. Over-smoothing may cause the nodes in GCN to be consistent. Unfortunately, the output results may become indistinguishable. To solve the problem of over-smoothing, we propose a novel V-shaped graph convolutional network framework, which distributes the semantic information of high and low levels more evenly in the GCVN to overcome the problem of over-smoothing.

GCVN expands the node information and then encodes and decodes the node information. The purpose of encoding and decoding the node information is to make the semantic information more evenly distributed in the deep graph convolution network. To integrate and distribute the node information evenly in the deeper graph convolution network, we fuse the low-level and high-level semantic information of GCVN with each other. Thus, we utilize the element-wise summation operation to fuse the semantic information as follows:

$$H^l = sum\left(H^l, H^{L-l}\right) \tag{4}$$

where L is the number of GCVN layers. In this paper, we set L to 4 empirically.

2.4   Joint Loss Function of AS-GCVN

Our proposed AS-GCVN combines attribute features and image features for joint analysis. This fusion of semantic information of attribute regression with benign and malignant image features renders a mutual influence between the classification and regression. Therefore, our final loss function is the joint loss function $\mathcal{L}_{cls}$, which can be expressed as:

$$\mathcal{L}_{\text{cls}} = \psi_1 \mathcal{L}_{en} + \psi_2 \mathcal{L}_{at} \tag{5}$$

where $\mathcal{L}_{en}$ and $\mathcal{L}_{at}$ can be expressed as:

$$\mathcal{L}_{en}(\hat{\boldsymbol{y}}, \boldsymbol{y}) = -\sum \boldsymbol{y}_i \log \left(\exp(\hat{\boldsymbol{y}}_i) / \sum \exp(\hat{\boldsymbol{y}}_j) \right), \tag{6}$$

$$\mathcal{L}_{at}(\hat{\boldsymbol{y}}_{at}, \boldsymbol{y}_{at}) = \frac{1}{C} \sum \|\hat{\boldsymbol{y}}_{at} - \boldsymbol{y}_{at}\|_2^2 \tag{7}$$

In the above formula, $\mathcal{L}_{at}$ is attribute regression loss function and $\mathcal{L}_{en}$ is the benign and malignant classification loss function. Where ψ_1, ψ_2 represent the weight factors of $\mathcal{L}_{en}$ and $\mathcal{L}_{at}$, respectively.

3   Experiments

3.1   Dataset

The lung image database combined with image collection (LIDC-IDRI) [2] includes marker annotation lesions for diagnosis and lung cancer screening by chest CT. For each lesion attribute, a total of four radiologists were labeled independently. Therefore, we took the average value of four radiologists for each attribute as the final label [7,8]. We excluded the benign and malignant mean label values equal to exactly 3 similar to other works [4,5,20]. Therefore, a total of 1593 lung nodules were left for evaluation (1092 benign(mean label < 3) and 501 malignant (mean label > 3)).

Besides malignancy, five semantic attributes (subtlety, calcification, sphericity, margin, texture) were scored in the LIDC-IDRI dataset. Most of the Most features were rated in the range of 1–5, while the calcification were given scores in the range of 1–6. We also take the average score to obtain the ground truth attribute score similar to other works [13].

3.2   Implementation Detail

The overall network structure consists of baseline and AAFE module, GCVN, among which baseline is the ResNet50. The output of ResNet50 and GCVN is 5×1 vector, and the final output of the whole network is obtained by adding the output of ResNet50 and GCVN. During training and testing, we perform a five-fold cross-validation on the dataset. The input of ResNet50 network is a 50×50 image, and the input of GCVN is the adjacency matrix $\boldsymbol{X} \in \mathbb{R}^{5 \times 5}$. We crop The original data's image into 50×50 according to the coordinates of the node center point provided in the dataset. Moreover, we rescaled the average truth attribute scores from 1–5, 1–6 to 1-0 for normalization. The weight factors of loss function are set empirically to 1. During the training, the mini-batch size is set as 32. And a total of 80 epochs are trained. For network optimization, we use SGD as the optimizer. The momentum parameter is set to 0.9. The initial learning rate is 0.01. We implement the network based on PyTorch [15] and train on an Nvidia Tesla V100 GPU with 32G memory.

3.3   Evaluation Metrics and Results

To compare with other state-of-the-art methods, we report the accuracy(ACC), sensitivity(SEN), specificity(SPE), and AUC of benign and malignant classification. which are expressed as:

$$ACC = (TP + TN)/(TP + TN + FP + FN) \tag{8}$$

$$SEN = TP/(TP + FN) \tag{9}$$

$$SPE = TN/(FP + TN) \tag{10}$$

$$AUC = \frac{\sum_{i \in p} \text{rank}_i + N_p * (N_p + 1)}{N_p * N_n} \tag{11}$$

where TP is true positive, FN is false negative, FP is false positive, and TN is true negative. N_p, N_p are the numbers of positive samples and negative samples, respectively. rank_i is the rank of the ith positive example. $i \in p$ denotes the ith example from the positive sample [14].

Table 1. The performance of the classification results on LIDC-IDRI dataset. ACC, SEN, SPE, AUC indicate accuracy, sensitivity, specificity and ROC respectively. The ↑ indicates that the higher value, the better.

Method	ACC (%)↑	SEN (%)↑	SPE (%)↑	AUC↑
Li et al. [12]	82.15	–	–	–
Shen et al. [16]	84.20	70.50	88.90	85.60
LaLonde et al. [11]	86.39	–	–	–
Shen et al. [17]	86.84	–	–	–
Ours	**88.01**	**75.45**	**93.78**	**90.26**

The results of pulmonary nodule classification are shown in Table 1. Concretely, the proposed AS-GCVN obtains 88.01% mean ACC, 75.45% mean SEN, 93.78% mean SPE, 90.26% mean AUC, which the mean ACC outperforms state-of-the-art by 1.17%. Experiments show that this method is effective. Besides, our method's superiority is demonstrated by the visualization of the feature, as shown in Fig. 3.

Figure 4 shows the interpretability of the model for the analysis of benign and malignant pulmonary nodules by attribute. Attributes were associated with nodule's prediction as benign or malignant, such as the absence of calcification, sharp edges, roundness, a marked contrast with the surrounding environment, and solid consistency. The regression scores and benign and malignant predictions of the five attributes of pulmonary nodules are consistent with the true labels. The regression predictions of the attributes are consistent with our knowledge of benign and malignant pulmonary nodules. Unlike the benign case, our model predicts the malignant nodule having indistinct margins or even partially sharp margins, a partial ground glass, and an irregular shape.

Fig. 3. t-SNE visualizations. Red dots and blue dots represent the benign and malignant pulmonary nodules. **(Left):** feature of the nodules from the original image pixel; **(Right):** deep features from our proposed method. (Color figure online)

3.4   Ablation Studies

We applied five-fold cross-validation to conduct the ablation studies to objectively evaluate the ASFE module's effectiveness and GCVN on benign and malignancy pulmonary nodule classification.

Table 2. Results of the ablation studies for analyzing the GCVN and ASFE module. We compare our method to the GCVN and ASFE module. The best results are highlighted in bold.

Baseline	GCN	GCVN	ASFE	Metrics (%)			
				ACC	SEN	SPE	AUC
✔				83.96	62.77	92.86	84.35
✔	✔			85.75	71.67	92.09	89.96
✔		✔		86.62	73.75	92.45	90.02
✔		✔	✔	**88.01**	**75.45**	**93.78**	**90.26**

To verify the ASFE module and GCVN perform the notable effect, we first compare our method with the baseline. After this, the GCVN framework in our method is the novel network framework to alleviate the over-smoothing problems, which can perform well on regression prediction. We compare GCVN with results from the normal GCN framework on the baseline. Besides, the ASFE module is the adaptive learning attribute feature module, which can enhance GCVN reasoning power. Thus, we compare our method with the framework, which contains the baseline and GCVN. Ablation studies are shown in Table 2.

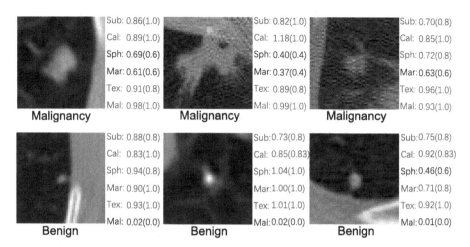

Fig. 4. pulmonary nodule diagnosis results of our proposed model. The score on each pulmonary nodule's right side was the five attribute scores and the benign and malignant (Mal) grade predicted by our proposed model. The bracket after the predicted score contains the true score for each attribute. The five attributes are calcification (Cal), subtlety (Sub), sphericity (Sph), margin(Mar), texture (Tex).

Our method improves the mean ACC score from 83.96% (compared with baseline) to 88.01%; raises the mean SEN score from 62.77% (compared with baseline) to 75.45%. The mean ACC score of the GCVN framework proposed in this paper has been improved from 85.75% to 86.62% compared with the sequential GCN framework. The mean accuracy of the baseline model, which contains GCVN and ASFE, has reached 88.01%, while the accuracy of the baseline model with GCVN is 86.62%. GCVN has also outperformed the baseline by around 5.91% area under the curve. The experimental results demonstrate the effectiveness of the ASFE module and GCVN. Figure 5 shows the receiver operating characteristic (ROC) curve plots comparing AS-GCVN versus ablation studies. The closer the ROC curve is to the upper left corner, the higher the accuracy of the model. The curve near the upper left corner shows the superior performance of our model.

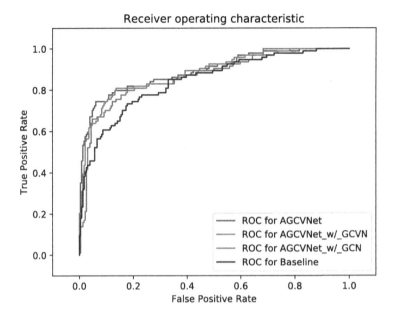

Fig. 5. The receiver operating characteristic curve (ROC curve) of our AS-GCVN and the ablation studies. It can be seen that the ROC of our AS-GCVN is very competitive compared to the other ablation studies.

4   Conclusion

In this study, we propose a novel end-to-end AS-GCVN under the structure of GCN, with a joint analysis strategy for the classification of lung nodules. In order to improve the semantic reasoning ability of graph convolutional neural networks, we introduced the ASFE module, which converts image-level features from self-guided into attribute-level features. In addition, we designed the GCVN model, which evenly distributes the information between nodes to solve the over-smoothing problem. Experimental results and ablation results show that our proposed model is superior to other methods in the classification of benign and malignant lung nodules, reaching the latest level. Both quantitative and qualitative results show that our AS-GCVN has excellent robustness and accuracy in the classification of lung nodules. In the future, we will explore our method in interpretable medical image computing.

References

1. Al-Shabi, M., Lan, B.L., Chan, W.Y., Ng, K.H., Tan, M.: Lung nodule classification using deep local-global networks. Int. J. Comput. Assis. Radiol. Surg. **14**(10), 1815–1819 (2019)
2. Armato, S.G., III., et al.: The lung image database consortium (LIDC) and image database resource initiative (IDRI): a completed reference database of lung nodules on CT scans. Med. Phys. **38**(2), 915–931 (2011)

3. Bray, F., Ferlay, J., Soerjomataram, I., Siegel, R.L., Torre, L.A., Jemal, A.: Global cancer statistics 2018: Globocan estimates of incidence and mortality worldwide for 36 cancers in 185 countries. CA Cancer J. Clin. **68**(6), 394–424 (2018)
4. Causey, J.L., et al.: Highly accurate model for prediction of lung nodule malignancy with CT scans. Sci. Rep. **8**(1), 1–12 (2018)
5. Chen, S., Ni, D., Qin, J., Lei, B., Wang, T., Cheng, J.-Z.: Bridging computational features toward multiple semantic features with multi-task regression: a study of CT pulmonary nodules. In: Ourselin, S., Joskowicz, L., Sabuncu, M.R., Unal, G., Wells, W. (eds.) MICCAI 2016. LNCS, vol. 9901, pp. 53–60. Springer, Cham (2016). https://doi.org/10.1007/978-3-319-46723-8_7
6. Erasmus, J.J., Connolly, J.E., McAdams, H.P., Roggli, V.L.: Solitary pulmonary nodules: Part i. morphologic evaluation for differentiation of benign and malignant lesions. Radiographics **20**(1), 43–58 (2000)
7. Hussein, S., Cao, K., Song, Q., Bagci, U.: Risk stratification of lung nodules using 3D CNN-based multi-task learning. In: Niethammer, M., Styner, M., Aylward, S., Zhu, H., Oguz, I., Yap, P.-T., Shen, D. (eds.) IPMI 2017. LNCS, vol. 10265, pp. 249–260. Springer, Cham (2017). https://doi.org/10.1007/978-3-319-59050-9_20
8. Hussein, S., Gillies, R., Cao, K., Song, Q., Bagci, U.: TumorNet: lung nodule characterization using multi-view convolutional neural network with Gaussian process. In: 2017 IEEE 14th International Symposium on Biomedical Imaging (ISBI 2017), pp. 1007–1010. IEEE (2017)
9. Kim, H., Park, C.M., Goo, J.M., Wildberger, J.E., Kauczor, H.U.: Quantitative computed tomography imaging biomarkers in the diagnosis and management of lung cancer. Invest. Radiol. **50**(9), 571–583 (2015)
10. Kipf, T.N., Welling, M.: Semi-supervised classification with graph convolutional networks. arXiv preprint arXiv:1609.02907 (2016)
11. LaLonde, R., Torigian, D., Bagci, U.: Encoding visual attributes in capsules for explainable medical diagnoses. arXiv, arXiv:1909.05926 (2019)
12. Li, Y., Gu, D., Wen, Z., Jiang, F., Liu, S.: Classify and explain: an interpretable convolutional neural network for lung cancer diagnosis. In: ICASSP 2020–2020 IEEE International Conference on Acoustics, Speech and Signal Processing (ICASSP), pp. 1065–1069. IEEE (2020)
13. Liu, L., Dou, Q., Chen, H., Qin, J., Heng, P.A.: Multi-task deep model with margin ranking loss for lung nodule analysis. IEEE Trans. Med. Imaging **39**(3), 718–728 (2019)
14. Lobo, J.M., Jiménez-Valverde, A., Real, R.: AUC: a misleading measure of the performance of predictive distribution models. Global Ecol. Biogeogr. **17**(2), 145–151 (2008)
15. Paszke, A., et al.: Automatic differentiation in PyTorch (2017)
16. Shen, S., Han, S.X., Aberle, D.R., Bui, A.A., Hsu, W.: An interpretable deep hierarchical semantic convolutional neural network for lung nodule malignancy classification. Expert Syst. Appl. **128**, 84–95 (2019)
17. Shen, W., Zhou, M., Yang, F., Yang, C., Tian, J.: Multi-scale convolutional neural networks for lung nodule classification. In: Ourselin, S., Alexander, D.C., Westin, C.-F., Cardoso, M.J. (eds.) IPMI 2015. LNCS, vol. 9123, pp. 588–599. Springer, Cham (2015). https://doi.org/10.1007/978-3-319-19992-4_46
18. Shen, W., Zhou, M., Yang, F., Yu, D., Dong, D., Yang, C., Zang, Y., Tian, J.: Multi-crop convolutional neural networks for lung nodule malignancy suspiciousness classification. Pattern Recogn. **61**, 663–673 (2017)

19. Torre, L.A., Siegel, R.L., Jemal, A.: Lung cancer statistics. In: Ahmad, A., Gadgeel, S. (eds.) Lung Cancer and Personalized Medicine. AEMB, vol. 893, pp. 1–19. Springer, Cham (2016). https://doi.org/10.1007/978-3-319-24223-1_1
20. Xie, Y., Xia, Y., Zhang, J., Feng, D.D., Fulham, M., Cai, W.: Transferable multi-model ensemble for benign-malignant lung nodule classification on chest CT. In: Descoteaux, M., Maier-Hein, L., Franz, A., Jannin, P., Collins, D.L., Duchesne, S. (eds.) MICCAI 2017. LNCS, vol. 10435, pp. 656–664. Springer, Cham (2017). https://doi.org/10.1007/978-3-319-66179-7_75

Semantic Structural and Occlusive Feature Fusion for Pedestrian Detection

Hui Wang[1] , Yu Zhang[1] , Hongchang Ke[2,3](✉) , Ning Wei[1],
and Zhongyu Xu[1]

[1] The College of Computer Science and Engineering, Changchun University
of Technology, Changchun 130012, China
email_wanghui@126.com

[2] The School of Computer Technology and Engineering, Changchun Institute
of Technology, Changchun 130012, China

[3] National and Local Joint Engineering Research Center for Intelligent Distribution
Network Measurement Organization Control and Safe Operation Technology of
National Development and Reform Commission, Changchun Institute of Technology,
Changchun 130012, China

Abstract. Pedestrian detection under occlusion scenes remains a formidable challenge in computer vision. Recently, anchor-free approach has been raised on the object detection and pedestrian detection field, anchor-free detector Center and Scale Prediction (CSP) has been proposed in pedestrian detection without special measures for occlusion. In this paper, we propose an anchor-free detector named OCSP with powerful occlusion handling ability to existing anchor-free detection network. OCSP integrates prior information into the network to handle occlusion. This high-fusion prior information gives the detector a hint about identifying the structural features of pedestrians. OCSP becomes more robust with the prior information which fusion the semantic head, the visible part, and the size and center body for each pedestrian. The detector enhances the perception of occlusion by predicting the semantic head and visible part. Besides, we design a head branch and add predicting the visible box to achieve a similar result. Experiments show that this fusion of prior information represents a suitable combination. We compare our OCSP with state-of-arts models on the Citypersons dataset, the proposed OCSP detector achieves the state-of-arts result on the CityPersons benchmark.

Keywords: Pedestrian detection · Anchor-free · Convolutional neural networks · Semantic head

1 Introduction

Pedestrian detection is of fundamental importance in computer vision, which serves as the basis of autonomous driving, pedestrian re-identification, video surveillance, robotics, and so on. Pedestrian detection is related to people's personal safety, so the performance of pedestrian detection needs to be improved.

© Springer Nature Switzerland AG 2021
D. N. Pham et al. (Eds.): PRICAI 2021, LNAI 13031, pp. 293–307, 2021.
https://doi.org/10.1007/978-3-030-89188-6_22

However, pedestrians usually are occluded in real scenes, and the detector should accurately detect pedestrians in any situation, no matter how high the occlusion rate is. Pedestrian detection evolved from anchor-based to anchor-free inspired by the development of object detection. CSP [14] is an anchor-free detector, which was first proposed in pedestrian detection, but the accuracy needs to improve when in an occlusion scene.

Generally speaking, part-based pedestrian detection usually exploits the parts of each pedestrian and integrates them to achieve a new balance. The detector learns the pedestrian structure through five or four pedestrian parts, in this way, the detector has the ability to identify the occluded pedestrians. However, the five or four parts of pedestrian wouldn't often precisely represent the pedestrian structure for the pedestrian annotation is a rectangle box, not pixel level mask and the common dataset often lacks the parts of the pedestrian annotations. However, the head remains a distinguishing feature of the pedestrian structure and occupies a significant part of the human body. Even at various angles, the head is also a distinguishing feature, the occlusion rate of the head is lower than that of the human body. Therefore, we predict the head center of each pedestrian. In this way, the detector can recognize a person's head to identify a pedestrian when the pedestrian visible part includes the head region, the detector becomes more sensitive to the pedestrian head and more stable. However, the annotation of the head in the datasets frequently lacking, similar to PSC-Net [25], OR-CNN [29] and PehHunter [2], calculating the weak annotations of the semantic head with the proportion of head area to the human body.

In addition, prior information is useful for the detector to better classify the characteristics of pedestrians. In CityPersons [28], there have bounding box annotations and visible box annotations, to make full use of these two annotations, we predict the body center and the visible part simultaneously. Further, the relationship between the body center and the visible part center tells the detector information when pedestrians in the occlusion scene. There are many detectors adopt visible part to improve the performance, like BCNet [19] and 0.5-stage [23]. As follows, we predict the visible and body center simultaneously to improve the ability to deal with occlusion.

We propose OCSP aim to handle the occlusion with some strategies. OCSP integrates prior information which includes the semantic head, the visible part and the center and size of the body to aware occlusion and improves the performance and robustness. After adding these strategies, we observe that predicting the width and height of the pedestrian can improve the result. On the basis of these strategies, we find that predicting the visible box can also improve the result, besides, we design a head branch that outside the box prediction also improves the result.

The summary of our work are as follows:

We provide the performance-enhancing combination, combining the visible part, the body box and the semantic head center to improve the capability of handling occlusion. OCSP learns discrimination feature of the semantic head in each pedestrian. The detector learns to identify occlusion features by the difference between the visible part center and the body center.

We straight predict the logarithm of height and width of each pedestrian to learn the slight difference when the aspect ratio is not 0.41, this way the detector divides more attention to the size map, predicting the width and height combine center heat-map reserve space information of the pedestrian. We use ResNeSt [26] as the backbone to extract feature.

We conduct some alternative experiments with similar results, such as, adding predicting the visible box which achieves 7.77% on the partial subset; designing a head branch outside the body center prediction which achieves 8.35% on the Reasonable subset and 4.63% on the Bare subset.

Our result clearly shows that OCSP provides an improvement on Citypersons [28] dataset. OCSP achieves 39.98% on the Heavy subset, 9.38% on the Reasonable subset, 8.49% on the Partial subset, 5.57% on the Bare subset.

2   Related Work

2.1   Anchor-Based

With the development of anchor-based object detection, anchor-based pedestrian detection also improved greatly. The two-stage detectors RCNN [6], Fast-RCNN [5] and Faster-RCNN [17] are the classical algorithm. Recently, Zoom-Net [20] added an extra branch to the ResNet [8] backbone, the extra branch composed of two convolution layers, which mainly handled the small scale of the pedestrian. HBAN [15] adopted semantic head to make the detector more robust.

There are many detectors based on part pedestrian detection to handle the occlusion, i.e. PehHunter [2], PSC-Net [25] and OR-CNN [29]. PehHunter [2] proposed occlusion-simulated data augmentation which randomly occluded the part of the pedestrian beside the head with the mean-value of ImageNet [18] to increase the occlusion ratio of a dataset, it also proposed a head mask guide which utilized the head location to learn more discriminative occlusion features. PSC-Net [25] proposed a dedicated module which exploited the topological structure of pedestrian, this module explicitly obtained the inter and intra-part co-occurrence information of pedestrian parts to handle occlusion. OR-CNN [29] proposed an occlusion-aware region of interest pooling unit which integrated the prior structure information (parts of the body) of the human body with visible prediction to handle occlusion, it divided the human body into five areas to improve the robustness of the detector.

2.2   Anchor-Free

Recently, anchor-free object detector has introduced in the object detection field, i.e. CornerNet [11] and CenterNet [30]. In pedestrian detection, CSP [14] was first proposed in an anchor-free method, it predicted the center and size of

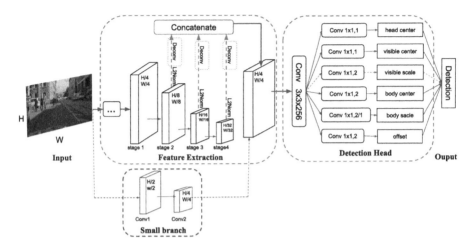

Fig. 1. The overall architecture of OCSP, which mainly includes three components, i.e. the feature extraction, small branch and detection head. In the feature extraction, the detector concatenates the different level feature come from the backbone (ResNeSt101 [26]). The detection head has five prediction layers, each of them is a 1×1 convolutional layer, the Conv 1×1, 2 indicates the kernel size is 1×1, the output channel is 2. The 2/1 indicates 2 or 1. The small branch includes two layers. (Color figure online)

each person. There are many improvements based on CSP [14], i.e. ACSP [24], BCNet [19], PP-Net [1] and APD [27]. ACSP [24] changed the backbone from ResNet-50 to ResNet-101. BCNet [19] predicted the fusion center which was the weighted sum of the body center and the visible part center. PP-Net [1] proposed a pyramid-like structure to aggregate multi-level information. APD [27] proposed an attribute-aware Non-Maximum Suppression to refine box and encode both density and diversity pedestrian in dense scenes.

3   Proposed Method

3.1   Overall Architecture

The proposed OCSP model is illustrated in Fig. 1 which is based on CSP [14] architecture. The architecture includes two parts: feature extraction and detection head. The image put into the backbone to extract different levels of features, fuse these features, attach two convolutional layers, then we obtain the output, the architecture is simple and straight.

We use the ResNeSt-101 [26] to extract different levels features, the output feature of the backbone has four stages, the four stages are downsampled by 4, 8, 16, 32 times to the input size. Our input size of image is (512,1024), 1024 indicate width, 512 indicate height, the original size of the input is (1024,2048), we resize the original size to (512,1024), the size of the input is (512,1024) with 3 channels input, after feeding into the backbone, the size of stage 1 is (128,256) with 256 output channels, the size of stage 2 is (64,128) with 512 output channels, the size of stage 3 is (32,64) with 1024 output channels, the size of stage 4 is (16,32) with 2048 output channels. Following [14], OCSP concatenate the stage 3, stage 4 and stage 5. Next, three stages adopt L2-normalization. To fusion the lower feature and high feature, these three stages upsampling 2, 4, 8 times to $(\frac{H}{4}, \frac{W}{4})$, these three upsampling with 256 output channels, then concatenate three stages together in channel dimensions get the fusion feature concatenation. The size of this fusion feature map is (128,256) with 768 input channels and 256 output channels.

This fusion concatenation feature map follows a 3×3 convolutional layer, then attach five 1×1 convolutional layers set as the output of the architecture. The five output represent the semantic head center map, the visible center map, the visible size map, the body center map, the scale map, and the offset map. The size of these output maps is $(\frac{H}{r}, \frac{W}{r})$ with 1 or 2 output channel, where r is set as 4. The detector predicts the body center with one output channel, the visible center with one output channel, the semantic head center with one output channel, the offset map with two channels, and the size map with one or two channels. When the detector predicts the width and height, the output channel of the scale map is two, one is for the width map, another is for the height map. When the detector only predicts height, the output channel is one for height. The offset map has two output channels, the offset map refines the coordinates of the body center, one for refining the x coordinate of the body center, another for refining the y coordinate of the body center. When the detector predicts the center and size of the visible box, the output of the visible size map was applied, visible size map with two output channels, one for the height map, another for the width map.

Semantic Head. There have many occlusion situations, pedestrians become incomplete under occlusion. Because of this situation, the detector needs to understand that part of the body equally represents a pedestrian, so the pedestrian detector learns the parts feature of the pedestrian, compare with the other part of the body, the head is a more discriminative part, so the head location assists the detector to learn more discriminative features for occluded pedestrians. There have many detectors utilize the semantic head to assist detector identify the pedestrian, i.e. OR-CNN [29], HBAN [15], PSC-Net [25] and PehHunter [2]. Consequently, we predict the semantic head center, with feeding the detector prior information, the detector learns the discrimination feature of the head. However, the dataset lack annotations for the precise head region, as follows, taking the upper center part of the human body as the semantic head.

Similar to PSC-Net [25], OR-CNN [29] and PehHunter [2], the definition of semantic head box contains the head and shoulder area. Assume $B = (x_1, y_1)$, $C = (x_2, y_2)$, B is the left upper of the pedestrian, C is the right bottom of the pedestrian, we assume the area of the head region is $(0.7w, 0.2h)$ of the body region, where w and h represent the width and height of body box, the head is at the top center of the body. The left upper relative coordinates of semantic head is $(0.85x_1 + 0.15x_2, y_1)$, the right bottom relative coordinates of semantic head is $(0.85x_2 + 0.15x_1, 0.8y_1 + 0.2y_2)$. In this way, the detector can get the feature of the semantic head. What'more, predicting the semantic head only in training stages, it not spends extra cost when in the inference stage.

There have two styles of adding semantic head prediction seen in Fig. 1 and Fig. 2 Detection Head part. At first, the prediction of the semantic head center and the prediction of the body center share a 3×3 convolutional layer. Since the head area adopts the proportion of the human body, we design a semantic head branch outside the predicting the center and size of the body, the architecture shown in Fig. 2.

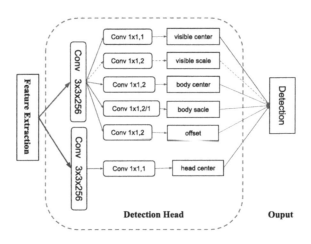

Fig. 2. The semantic head map is outside of the body prediction map, and the deep magenta arrow point path is the head branch. The result is shown in Table 4 after adopting the head branch. (Color figure online)

Visible Part. The visible part box is different from the body bounding box when pedestrians in occlusion scenes, there are many types of visible parts, which caused by both inter-class occlusion and intra-class occlusion. The visible part center is different from the body center when in the occlusion situation. The visible part of the pedestrian indicates the difference between the foreground target and background target when in intra-class occlusion. Both anchor-free detectors and anchor-based detectors predicted the visible part center of the pedestrian, i.e. BCNet [19] and 0.5-stage [23]. The annotation provides the visible pedestrian include the upper left corner and the right bottom corner. The way obtains the visible boxes from the annotation is the same as gain the body boxes. After predicting the visible center and the body center simultaneously, the detector becomes more capable to deal with occlusion. What's more, to let the detector learn the feature of the visible part area and to make full use of the visible part, we do further experiment to predict the center and size of the visible part. Predicting the center and size of the visible part can make the detector more capable of handling occlusion. The visible part size map is seen in Fig. 1. In the detection head, the output of the visible size map indicates by the dotted line.

Extra Branch. The lower feature map contains detailed edge information, to make full use of the lower level feature, we add an extra branch to the backbone as shown in Fig. 1 the green dotted line, the input of the extra branch is the images, the extra branch maintains two layers, and then fusion to the fusion feature map. ZoomNet [20] proposed to add an extra branch to the network. Our extra branch is two convolutional layers, the first layer is the same as ZoomNet [20], the first layer is the ResNet-101's [8] or ResNeSt's [26] first layer without the max pooling. We define the second convolutional layer with 3×3 kernel and 2 strides, the output channel of feature map is 128. Then attach BachNormlization [9] and PReLU [7]. When the small extra branch is appended, the input channel of the fusion feature map adds 128 which is the Conv2's output channel, so its input channel is 896. The extra branch adds to the backbone only in the ablation experiment.

3.2   Training

Loss Function. The loss function includes three parts: center loss, scale loss and offset loss.

Center Loss. As in [14], we predict the heatmap of center, the center indicates the body center, the visible part center, and the semantic head center. Each heatmap has 3 channels, one is the heatmap generated using the Eq. 2, the other is the ground-truth of the center, which is set as 1 in the center and outside the center are set as 0, and the last map within the box of each pedestrian are set as 1 and outside are assigned as 0. The size of center map is $(\frac{H}{r}, \frac{W}{r})$. The center heatmap using a $2D$ Gaussian. It is defined as:

$$M_{ij} = \max_{k=1,2,...K} G(i, j; x_k, y_k, \sigma_{w_k}, \sigma_{h_k}) \tag{1}$$

$$G(i, j, x, y, \sigma_w, \sigma_h) = e^{-(\frac{(i-x)^2}{2\sigma_w^2} + \frac{(j-y)^2}{2\sigma_h^2})} \tag{2}$$

where K is the total number of pedestrian in each image, (x_k, y_k, w_k, h_k) is the ground-truth center coordinates divided by r of the kth pedestrian. If two Gaussians overlap, we apply the element-wise maximum [14] values in the overlapped location.

$$L_c = -\frac{1}{K} \sum_{i=1}^{\frac{W}{r}} \sum_{j=1}^{\frac{H}{r}} \alpha_{ij}(1 - \hat{p}_{ij})^\gamma log(\hat{p}_{ij}) \tag{3}$$

where

$$\hat{p}_{ij} = \begin{cases} p_{ij} & if \ y_{ij} = 1 \\ 1 - p_{ij} & otherwise \end{cases} \tag{4}$$

$$\alpha_{ij} = \begin{cases} 1 & if \ y_{ij} = 1 \\ (1 - M_{ij})^\beta & otherwise \end{cases} \tag{5}$$

In the above, y_{ij} is the ground-truth of the pedestrian center. The M_{ij} is in Eq. 1, p_{ij} represents the score at location (i, j) in the predicte map. The size of predicting map is $(\frac{H}{r}, \frac{W}{r})$, so the i is from 1 to $\frac{W}{r}$, the j is from 1 to $\frac{H}{r}$. The center loss combines the focal loss [12] and 2D Gaussian map. The σ is set as 2 and β is set as 4, similar as suggested in [11].

For the loss function of the semantic head, visible center, and body center, we formulate it as center loss, which is denoted as L_{head}, L_{vis} and $L_{bodycenter}$. The center loss is defined as:

$$L_{center} = \lambda_c L_{bodycenter} + \lambda_v L_{vis} + \lambda_h L_{head} \tag{6}$$

where λ_c, λ_v, λ_h are set as 1, 0.5, 1.

Scale Loss. For scale prediction, the scale loss function consists of two parts, the L_{width} and the L_{height}. We formulate the L_{width} and L_{height} as a regression task via L1 loss [5]. In the ground-truth of scale map, there include three channels, the two use surrounding 2 pixels of the body center are set as the logarithm of width and height, the last map are set as 1 in the same location of the two maps but other location are set as 0. When testing, the height and width take the exponent of the predicting width and height. The scale loss is defined as:

$$L_{width} = \frac{1}{K} \sum_{k=1}^{K} L1(s_k, t_k) \tag{7}$$

where s_k and t_k represent the detector's prediction of width map and the ground-truth of width map. The loss function of L_{height} is also formulated in the Eq. 7. The total loss of scale loss is the sum of L_{height} and L_{width}.

$$L_{scale} = L_{height} + L_{width} \tag{8}$$

When predicting the size of the visible part box, the loss function about the scale of the visible part is marked as $L_{visibleScale}$. The $L_{visibleScale}$ also includes two parts, one for the height, anchor for the width. The loss $L_{visibleScale}$ formulates above function.

Offset Loss. The offset loss not only refines the center of the body but also refines deviation during the process of rounding down. The offset loss is defined as:

$$L_{offset} = \frac{1}{K} \sum_{k=1}^{K} SmoothL1(o_k, \hat{o}_k) \tag{9}$$

where o_k and $\hat{o}_k$ are the ground truth offset and predicted offset respectively. The o_k include o_{kx} and o_{ky}. $o_{kx} = \frac{x_k}{r} - \lfloor \frac{x_k}{r} \rfloor$, $o_{ky} = \frac{y_k}{r} - \lfloor \frac{y_k}{r} \rfloor$, where r is set as 4.

The total loss function is denoted as:

$$L = \lambda_l L_{center} + \lambda_s L_{scale} + \lambda_o L_{offset} \tag{10}$$

where λ_l, λ_s, λ_o are set as 0.01, 0.05, 0.1.

If the detector predicts the size of visible box, the total loss function can be denoted as:

$$L = \lambda_l L_{center} + \lambda_s L_{scale} + \lambda_{sv} L_{visibleScale} + \lambda_o L_{offset} \qquad (11)$$

where λ_l, λ_s, λ_{sv}, λ_o are set as 0.01, 0, 005, 0.0025, 0.1.

Inference. During testing, even adding prior information, the prediction of pedestrian straight comes from the center map, size map and offset map. In the body center prediction map, following [14], the score above 0.1 are kept. If the detector predicts the width and height, the scale map has two output channels, then keep the responding exponent of height and width in the prediction scale map. NMS is also adopted 0.5 to filter the box. If the detector only predicts the width, the scale map has only one channel, the width adopts 0.41 times the height unless extra emphasis.

4   Experiments

4.1   Experiment Settings

Dataset. CityPersons [28] Dataset was proposed in the 2017 year, which annotated on the CityScapes benchmark [3]. The background includes 27 cities. It has 5,000 images altogether. We use the 2975 images for training and 500 validation subset images for testing. The input size of images is 1× when testing. The evaluation metric is MR^{-2} [4], which is log-average Miss Rate over False Per Image (FPPI) ranging in $[10^{-2}, 100]$.

Training Details. The OCSP is realized in Pytorch [16]. The ResNeSt101 [26] is the backbone of the network, which pre-trained on ImageNet [7]. The detector adopts Adam [10] optimizer to optimize the network. The moving average weights [22] is adopted to achieve stable training and perfect result. A mini-batch contains 4 images with one GPU. The type of GPU is Tesla V100-SXM2. The input size of the image is 512×1024 which is 0.5 times the original size in the datasets. The learning rate is set as 4e−4 and is unchanging during the training unless otherwise stated. The epoch of the training is 150.

4.2   Ablation Study

Our experiment conducts on the CityPersons [28] datasets. We try different strategy portfolios to reduce the MR^{-2}. In these experiments, we select the best result within 150 epoch. In the Table 3, we first do the experiment on the backbone ResNet-101 [8], to improve the evaluation result, the detector add predicting the semantic head center, the visible center and a small branch to the network, however, the result needs to be improved, then we change the backbone from ResNet101 [8] to ResNeSt101 [26]. We conduct the ablation study to find a better balance after changed the backbone, we first add each strategy individually to the backbone, then add pairwise strategy, then add total strategy to the networks. Furthermore, we predict the width and height to get a better result rather than only predict the height. Finally, the experiment result shows that predicting the semantic head center, the visible center, predicting the width and height with the ResNeSt101 [26] backbone is a fine combination.

Table 1. Comparison between different backbones. The experiment sets both add semantic head, visible center. The semantic head and small extra branch add in ResNeSt50, the experiment of ResNeSt269 include visible center, semantic and one GPU with 2 images. The learning rate is set as 2e−4 with the backbone ResNeSt101 [26].

Backbone	Reasonable
ResNeSt50	11.30%
ResNeSt101	9.26%
ResNeSt200	10.41%
ResNeSt269	11.16%

What is the Influence of the Backbone? First, the result of own running ACSP [24] is show in Table 3 first row, which is different to the [24], because of the different experiment setting, ACSP [24] adopt two GPU with two images, we adopt one GPU with 4 images. To find the appropriate backbone for the OCSP, we also use the ResNeSt50 [26], ResNeSt101 [26], ResNeSt200 [26] and ResNeSt269 [26] backbone to extract feature, in the Table 1, experiments shows that the ResNeSt101 [26] is fit for the OCSP. Comparisons are conducted in Table 3, the result is improved when only change the backbone from ResNet101 [8] to ResNeSt101 [26] with the result from 52.9% to 47.92% on the Heavy subset, on the basis of the backbone, adding the semantic head, the result comes from 10.82% to the 10.09% on the reasonable subset.

Table 2. Comparison between the different regions of the head. The backbone is ResNeSt101, using the visible center and the semantic head.

Semantic head	Heavy
(0.7w,0.2h)	44.44%
(2/3w,1/3h)	46.13%

What is the Influence of the Semantic Head Center when Training? The semantic head is strong prior information for the detector. In the HBAN [15], the definition of the semantic head is $(2/3w, 1/3h)$, in the PSC-Net [25], OR-CNN [29] and PedHunter [2], the definition of the semantic head is $(0.7w, 0.23h)$, the two areas of the head are different, so it is significant to do the experiment to find a better result. Both experiments add the semantic head and visible center, the Table 2 shows that the $(0.7w, 0.2h)$ receives a relatively good result. So the region of the head area is $(0.7w, 0.2h)$. In fourth row of the Table 3, MR^{-2} is 10.09% on the reasonable subset when predicting semantic head on the basis of backbone ResNeSt101. In the penultimate row of the Table 3, the result is 44.22% when predicting semantic head heatmap and visible part center heatmap. These two results show that the semantic head is important to the detector.

In the Table 3, we make these strategies in a different combination, the result shows that the ResNeSt-101, visible center, the semantic head and add predicting width is the best combination with the result 42.55% on the heavy subset. In Table 3, we observe that the evaluation result is 43.98% and 43.66% on the Heavy subset after adding a small branch, so adding a small branch improves the result.

Table 3. Comparisons with different prior information had or not. The performance is measured by MR^{-2}. The +semantic head indicates that the detector predicts the semantic head center, the +visible center indicates that the detector predicts visible center, the +extra branch indicates that adds an extra branch to the fusion feature map, the $-$log indicates that the detector predicts the width and the ground truth of the width and height without the logarithm, the +width indicates that the detector predicts the width with the logarithm. In the first and second row, the detector adopt backbone ResNet101 [8]. In the remaining lines, the detector adopt ResNeSt101 [26].

+Semantic head	+Visible center	+Extra branch	$-$log	+width	Reasonable	Heavy
×	×	×	×	×	13.14%	52.22%
✓	✓	✓	×	×	11.10%	52.90%
×	×	×	×	×	10.82%	47.92%
✓	×	×	×	×	10.09%	46.67%
×	✓	×	×	×	10.45%	45.81%
×	×	✓	×	×	11.0%	43.98%
✓	✓	✓	×	×	9.63%	44.21%
✓	✓	✓	✓	×	9.58%	43.66%
×	✓	✓	×	×	8.93%	45.27%
✓	×	✓	×	×	9.70%	44.03%
✓	✓	×	×	×	9.26%	44.22%
✓	✓	×	×	✓	9.11%	42.55%

What is the Influence of Predict Width and Height? In the first row of the Table 4, we find the detector achieve the best result in the 125 epoch, the MR^{-2} on the heavy subset is 42.55% in 125 epoch, the learning rate reduced

Table 4. The OCSP(w) indicates that the detector predicts the width and height of each pedestrian, with adding predicting the semantic head center and the visible center. The initial learning rate is set as 4e−4, decrease learning rate ten times after 125 epochs. Don't use moving average weights after 125 epochs. The OCSP$^+$ predict visible box which predicts the visible center and visible width and visible height, the learning rate is unchanging during training. In OCSP*, the batch size is 4, but the loss update is 16, because the backbone is a split attention network and it suits the larger batch size, OCSP* adopts the head branch output in the head detection seen in Fig. 2. The other experiment setting is the same as the OCSP(w).

Method	Epoch	LR	Reasonable	Heavy	Partical	Bare
OCSP (w)	125	4e−4	9.11%	42.55%	8.72%	5.17%
OCSP (w)	144	4e−5	9.38%	39.94%	8.49%	5.57%
OCSP (w)	120	4e−5	9.54%	42.98%	8.52%	6.41%
OCSP$^+$	144	4e−4	8.99%	43.00%	7.77%	5.51%
OCSP*	115	4e−4	8.35%	45.07%	8.05%	4.63%

by ten times after 125 epoch, what's more, the moving average weights don't adopt after 125 epoch, after changing these and continuing training, the MR^{-2} on the heavy subset is 39.94% in 144 epoch. In the third row of the Table 4, we use the learning rate 4e−5 to training the detector, these two experiments only the learning rate are different, these two experiments both predict the width and height, semantic head center and visible part center. The result shows that the MR^{-2} increase 0.43% in the reasonable subset, so the smaller learning rate is not fit the detector because of the poor performance. In the fourth row of the Table 4, the detector predicts the semantic head center, the center and size of the visible and full pedestrian box, each box predict the width and height, this two result show that the OCSP$^+$ represents a good balance with 43.00% on the heavy subset, 7.77% on the partial subset, 5.51% on the bare subset, the partial result and bare result is the state of art result. We also use the head branch outside the body prediction which is shown in Fig. 2, the result of this experiment show in the last line of the Table 4, the result outperforms the OCSP* with the 8.35% on the Reasonable subset.

4.3 Comparison with the State of the Arts

We compare our OCSP with all existing state-of-the-art detectors on the validation set of CityPersons. All methods are trained on Citypersons training set without any extra data (except ImageNet) and test on Citypersons validation set. The result is observed in Table 5. The evaluation metric is MR^{-2}. From the table, we can figure out that our OCSP achieves a state-of-art result. When predicting the center and center and size of visible part, the semantic head center, the center and size of body box and each box predict width and height, the MR^{-2} is 43.00% on the heavy subset, the MR^{-2} is 8.99% on the reasonable subset, the MR^{-2} is 7.77% on the partial subset, the MR^{-2} is 5.51% on the bare subset. When add predicting the width and height, the semantic head center and the visible part center to the predicting body center box, the MR^{-2} is 39.94% on the heavy subset. We achieve 8.35% on the Reasonable subset, when adopting the head branch outside the prediction of the body.

Table 5. Comparisons with state-of-the-arts on Citypersons datasets.

Method	Backbone	Reasonable	Heavy	Partial	Bare
FRCNN [28]	VGG-16	15.4%	–	–	–
FRCNN+Seg [28]	VGG-16	14.8%	–	–	–
TLL [21]	ResNet-50	15.5%	53.6%	17.2%	10.0%
ALF [13]	ResNet-50	12.0%	51.9%	11.4%	8.4%
OR-CNN [29]	VGG-16	12.8%	55.7%	15.3%	6.7%
CSP [14]	ResNet-50	11.0%	49.3%	10.8%	8.1%
BCNet [19]	ResNet-50	9.8%	53.3%	9.2%	5.8%
ACSP [24]	ResNet-101	9.3%	46.3%	8.7%	5.6%
OCSP(w) (ours)	ResNeSt-101	9.38%	39.94%	8.49%	5.57%
OCSP$^+$ (ours)	ResNeSt-101	8.99%	43.00%	7.77%	5.51%
OCSP* (ours)	ResNeSt-101	8.35%	45.07%	8.05%	4.63%

5   Conclusion

In this paper, we propose OCSP which is an anchor-free approach to handle occlusion. A lot of prior information is provided to the detector, in this way, the detector directly obtains the structural feature of the pedestrian. We model the pedestrian as the semantic head center, visible center or visible box, body center and scale, the scale includes the width and height. The detector not only predicts the center and size of the pedestrian, but also predicts the semantic head center and the visible part, these two extra predictions can make the detector more robust and effective to deal with the occlusion. OCSP maintains the perception of occlusion by predicting the semantic head and visible part. We also try other possibilities such as adding predicting the visible box and adopting a head branch, which achieves similar results. We manage to explain why we carry out these changes. Experiments are conducted on the Citypersons, OCSP achieves state-of-the-art evaluation results.

Acknowledgments. This work was supported by the National Nature Science Foundation of China (61841602, 61806024), the Jilin Province Education Department Scientific Research Planning Foundation of China (JJKH20210753KJ, JJKH20200618KJ).

References

1. Cai, J., et al.: Pedestrian as points: an improved anchor-free method for center-based pedestrian detection. IEEE Access **8**, 179666–179677 (2020)
2. Chi, C., Zhang, S., Xing, J., Lei, Z., Li, S.Z., Zou, X.: PedHunter: occlusion robust pedestrian detector in crowded scenes. In: Proceedings of the AAAI Conference on Artificial Intelligence, vol. 34, pp. 10639–10646 (2020)
3. Cordts, M., et al.: The cityscapes dataset for semantic urban scene understanding. In: Proceedings of the IEEE Conference on Computer Vision and Pattern Recognition, pp. 3213–3223 (2016)
4. Dollar, P., Wojek, C., Schiele, B., Perona, P.: Pedestrian detection: an evaluation of the state of the art. IEEE Trans. Pattern Anal. Mach. Intell. **34**(4), 743–761 (2011)
5. Girshick, R.: Fast R-CNN. In: Proceedings of the IEEE International Conference on Computer Vision, pp. 1440–1448 (2015)
6. Girshick, R., Donahue, J., Darrell, T., Malik, J.: Rich feature hierarchies for accurate object detection and semantic segmentation. In: Proceedings of the IEEE Conference on Computer Vision and Pattern Recognition, pp. 580–587 (2014)
7. He, K., Zhang, X., Ren, S., Sun, J.: Delving deep into rectifiers: surpassing human-level performance on ImageNet classification. In: Proceedings of the IEEE International Conference on Computer Vision, pp. 1026–1034 (2015)
8. He, K., Zhang, X., Ren, S., Sun, J.: Deep residual learning for image recognition. In: Proceedings of the IEEE Conference on Computer Vision and Pattern Recognition, pp. 770–778 (2016)
9. Ioffe, S., Szegedy, C.: Batch normalization: accelerating deep network training by reducing internal covariate shift. In: International Conference on Machine Learning, pp. 448–456. PMLR (2015)
10. Kingma, D.P., Ba, J.: Adam: a method for stochastic optimization. arXiv preprint arXiv:1412.6980 (2014)
11. Law, H., Deng, J.: CornerNet: detecting objects as paired keypoints. In: Ferrari, V., Hebert, M., Sminchisescu, C., Weiss, Y. (eds.) Computer Vision – ECCV 2018. LNCS, vol. 11218, pp. 765–781. Springer, Cham (2018). https://doi.org/10.1007/978-3-030-01264-9_45
12. Lin, T.Y., Goyal, P., Girshick, R., He, K., Dollár, P.: Focal loss for dense object detection. In: Proceedings of the IEEE International Conference on Computer Vision, pp. 2980–2988 (2017)
13. Liu, W., Liao, S., Hu, W., Liang, X., Chen, X.: Learning efficient single-stage pedestrian detectors by asymptotic localization fitting. In: Ferrari, V., Hebert, M., Sminchisescu, C., Weiss, Y. (eds.) Computer Vision – ECCV 2018. LNCS, vol. 11218, pp. 643–659. Springer, Cham (2018). https://doi.org/10.1007/978-3-030-01264-9_38
14. Liu, W., Liao, S., Ren, W., Hu, W., Yu, Y.: High-level semantic feature detection: A new perspective for pedestrian detection. In: Proceedings of the IEEE/CVF Conference on Computer Vision and Pattern Recognition, pp. 5187–5196 (2019)
15. Lu, R., Ma, H., Wang, Y.: Semantic head enhanced pedestrian detection in a crowd. Neurocomputing **400**, 343–351 (2020)
16. Paszke, A., et al.: Automatic differentiation in PyTorch (2017)
17. Ren, S., He, K., Girshick, R., Sun, J.: Faster R-CNN: Towards real-time object detection with region proposal networks. arXiv preprint arXiv:1506.01497 (2015)

18. Russakovsky, O., et al.: ImageNet large scale visual recognition challenge. Int. J. Comput. Vis. **115**(3), 211–252 (2015)
19. Sha, M., Boukerche, A.: Semantic fusion-based pedestrian detection for supporting autonomous vehicles. In: 2020 IEEE Symposium on Computers and Communications (ISCC), pp. 1–6. IEEE (2020)
20. Shang, C., Ai, H., Zhuang, Z., Chen, L., Xing, J.: ZoomNet: deep aggregation learning for high-performance small pedestrian detection. In: Asian Conference on Machine Learning, pp. 486–501. PMLR (2018)
21. Song, T., Sun, L., Xie, D., Sun, H., Pu, S.: Small-scale pedestrian detection based on topological line localization and temporal feature aggregation. In: Ferrari, V., Hebert, M., Sminchisescu, C., Weiss, Y. (eds.) ECCV 2018. LNCS, vol. 11211, pp. 554–569. Springer, Cham (2018). https://doi.org/10.1007/978-3-030-01234-2_33
22. Tarvainen, A., Valpola, H.: Weight-averaged, consistency targets improve semi-supervised deep learning results. CoRR vol. abs/1703 2017 (1780)
23. Ujjwal, U., Dziri, A., Leroy, B., Bremond, F.: A one-and-half stage pedestrian detector. In: Proceedings of the IEEE/CVF Winter Conference on Applications of Computer Vision, pp. 776–785 (2020)
24. Wang, W.: Adapted center and scale prediction: more stable and more accurate. arXiv preprint arXiv:2002.09053 (2020)
25. Xie, J., Pang, Y., Cholakkal, H., Anwer, R., Khan, F., Shao, L.: PSC-Net: learning part spatial co-occurrence for occluded pedestrian detection. Sci. China Inf. Sci. **64**(2), 1–13 (2021)
26. Zhang, H., et al.: ResNeSt: split-attention networks. arXiv preprint arXiv:2004. 08955 (2020)
27. Zhang, J., et al.: Attribute-aware pedestrian detection in a crowd. IEEE Trans. Multimedia **23**, 3085–3097 (2020)
28. Zhang, S., Benenson, R., Schiele, B.: CityPersons: a diverse dataset for pedestrian detection. In: Proceedings of the IEEE Conference on Computer Vision and Pattern Recognition, pp. 3213–3221 (2017)
29. Zhang, S., Wen, L., Bian, X., Lei, Z., Li, S.Z.: Occlusion-aware R-CNN: detecting pedestrians in a crowd. In: Ferrari, V., Hebert, M., Sminchisescu, C., Weiss, Y. (eds.) ECCV 2018. LNCS, vol. 11207, pp. 657–674. Springer, Cham (2018). https://doi.org/10.1007/978-3-030-01219-9_39
30. Zhou, X., Wang, D., Krähenbühl, P.: Objects as points. arXiv preprint arXiv:1904.07850 (2019)

VTLayout: Fusion of Visual and Text Features for Document Layout Analysis

Shoubin Li[1,2]([✉]), Xuyan Ma[1,2], Shuaiqun Pan[2], Jun Hu[2], Lin Shi[2],
and Qing Wang[2]

[1] University of Chinese Academy of Sciences, Beijing, China
maxuyan@bjtu.edu.cn
[2] The Institute of Software, Chinese Academy of Sciences, Beijing, China
{shoubin,hujun,shilin,wq}@iscas.ac.cn, shuaiqun@ualberta.ca

Abstract. Documents often contain complex physical structures, which make the Document Layout Analysis (DLA) task challenging. As a pre-processing step for content extraction, DLA has the potential to capture rich information in historical or scientific documents on a large scale. Although many deep-learning-based methods from computer vision have already achieved excellent performance in detecting *Figure* from documents, they are still unsatisfactory in recognizing the *List, Table, Text* and *Title* category blocks in DLA. This paper proposes a VTLayout model fusing the documents' deep visual, shallow visual, and text features to localize and identify different category blocks. The model mainly includes two stages, and the three feature extractors are built in the second stage. In the first stage, the Cascade Mask R-CNN model is applied directly to localize all category blocks of the documents. In the second stage, the deep visual, shallow visual, and text features are extracted for fusion to identify the category blocks of documents. As a result, we strengthen the classification power of different category blocks based on the existing localization technique. The experimental results show that the identification capability of the VTLayout is superior to the most advanced method of DLA based on the PubLayNet dataset, and the F1 score is as high as 0.9599.

Keywords: Document layout analysis · Fusion of visual and text · VTLayout · PubLayNet

1 Introduction

With the development of science and technology, more and more scientific achievements are published, and the abundant academic literature makes it difficult for scientists to extract cutting-edge innovations. Therefore, it is highly critical to extract the information needed by researchers effectively and accurately from a large amount of scientific literature. As a pre-processing step of the document understanding system, the high-performance DLA model can accurately locate and identify different category blocks in the documents. In practice, a good

DLA result can improve the performance for document retrieval, text recognition, and other tasks in the field of natural language processing (NLP).

Based on the observation of the images from the PubLayNet dataset [29], the layout usually contains five categories: *Figure, List, Table, Text*, and *Title*. According to the recent literature review, the recognition of the *List* can be a challenge which the previous methods always can not perform well on *List* compared with other categories [29]. Besides, identifying the *Title* is also one of the most difficult tasks because *Title* always appears with fewer words. Therefore, to fully understand the content of scientific literature, automatically identifying the layout of document structure well has become a top priority.

The current widespread object detection and classification approaches often rely on Deep Convolutional Neural Networks (DCNNs) to obtain features. Although the *Figure, List*, and *Table* in DLA are different from the objects in traditional object detection tasks, some deep-learning-based models can still perform well, such as Faster R-CNN [22], Mask R-CNN [29], SSD [15], and YOLO [21]. Based on the observations of the images from the PubLayNet dataset, each category has its unique feature. Therefore, we believe a DCNNs-based approach can extract these unique features for fusion to effectively enhance the performance of DLA. Besides, some intuitive perceptual features can help classify the category blocks for the document pages with a single background color. For example, people often notice that the *Title* usually presents in a bolder form than other text paragraphs. Based on these observations, we believe that the statistical pixel values of each category block can be used as a feature to classify different category blocks. Therefore, this intuitive perceptual feature is considered in our proposed model, also called the shallow visual feature in this paper. The ablation experiments prove that the extraction and recognition of shallow visual features can effectively enhance the recognition of different category blocks.

Inspired by Asim M N [2], the model we finally propose that considers not only the visual features but also the text features of the documents. In order to improve the classification power based on the previous methods, the Faster R-CNN and Mask R-CNN models are reproduced to find out which categories are easily incorrectly classified. It can be found that the *Title* can not be recognized well by both Faster R-CNN and Mask R-CNN models based on the PublayNet dataset. Therefore, after considering the text features of the *Title*, we decide to apply a traditional feature extraction technique in text mining as one of the feature extraction techniques in our final proposed model.

Based on the motivations mentioned above, a novel two-stage model for DLA is proposed. The first stage is designed to locate each category block accurately. In the second stage, different category blocks are classified, including three different units related to the deep visual feature, shallow visual feature, and text features. In order to extract deep visual features from different category blocks, MobileNetV2 [23], a lightweight DCNNs, is applied in our proposed model. Furthermore, the shallow visual feature is extracted based on the statistical pixel values of each category block. In addition, Term Frequency - Inverse Document

Frequency (TF-IDF) [20] is also applied as a weighting method to reinforce the distinction between text format category blocks.

The contributions of our work can be summarized as follows:

- A document layout analysis model, VTLayout, based on the fusion of deep visual, shallow visual, and text features, is proposed to solve the low recognition rate of different document category blocks.
- A Shallow Visual Feature Extractor is proposed to obtain intuitive perceptual features from document images.
- Experimental results show that the VTLayout model achieves the state-of-the-art performance on the PubLayNet dataset.

The paper is structured as follows: In this section, the motivations of DLA and contributions of this paper are introduced. The second section summarizes the latest literature review in DLA. Then, the third section briefly describes the structure of the VTLayout model with different feature extractors in detail, and the PubLayNet dataset is introduced in Sect. 4. In the next section, the experiment settings are listed in detail and we present the experimental results of the VTLayout model on the PubLayNet dataset with some further analysis in Sect. 6. The last section concludes the VTLayout model and future research in DLA.

2   Related Work

Scientists have already proposed some methods for DLA. For example, a method for page layout analysis has been proposed based on the bottom-up, nearest-neighbor clustering of page components [17]. Meanwhile, this method generated precise measures of skew, within-line, and between-line spacings. Besides, text lines and blocks were also located. Another traditional page segmentation technique has been proposed based on the recursive X-Y [7]. Moreover, the black pixels were used for connected components instead of using image pixels. In 2007, Namboodiri and Jain [16] proposed a workflow of the document layout and structure analysis system that includes the pre-processing, layout, and structure analysis, segmented document, and evaluation steps.

In recent years, Zhong et al. [29] published a huge dataset named the PubLayNet. It was created for DLA by automatically matching the XML representation, and the content includes more than one million PDF articles publicly available on PubMed Central. Based on the PubLayNet dataset, three more experiments were also made to investigate. Firstly, it has been demonstrated that Faster R-CNN and Mask R-CNN models can perform well on this dataset, although there was much room for improvement. Next, the Faster R-CNN and Mask R-CNN models were pre-trained on PubLayNet by researchers and fine-tuned successfully to tackle the ICDAR 2013 Table Recognition Competition. Thirdly, experimental results have demonstrated that the PublayNet dataset can be used for transfer learning in distant domains.

Furthermore, the researchers proposed a series of new methods based on the DCNNs [3,4,26]. For document image classification, Kang et al. [11] applied a DCNNs architecture on the Tobacco 3482 benchmark dataset to learn from the raw image pixels. The experimental result has demonstrated that the proposed method can surpass the performance of the simple structure-based approach. In 2018, Kavasidis et al. [12] proposed a method that combined the DCNNs, graphical models, and saliency concepts to solve the table and chart detection task. Siddiqui et al. [25] solved the table structure recognition task from the domain of semantic segmentation. In addition, a method of prediction tiling based on the consistency assumption was proposed for the tabular structure, which achieved excellent performance on the ICDAR-13 image-based table structure recognition dataset. Sun et al. [27] proposed a table detection method based on the Faster R-CNN architecture combined with the corner location method.

In addition, some researchers believe that combining the semantic text information of the documents is a benefit for DLA. In 2017, Yang et al. [28] proposed an end-to-end, multimodal, and fully convolutional network for document semantic structure. Meanwhile, the unified model classified pixels not only by their appearance as in the traditional page segmentation task but also by the content of the underlying text. In 2019, a novel two-stream approach was proposed based on the feature-ranking algorithm for document image classification [2]. Meanwhile, an average ensembling method was applied to concatenate the textual and visual stream in the proposed approach. Jain and Wigington [10] proposed another method for DLA based on the multimodal feature fusion combining a feature representation of the visual and text modalities.

3   Methodology

This section introduces the workflow of VTLayout in detail. VTLayout consists of two stages for DLA. A proven efficient object detection model has been applied directly to localize different category blocks in the first stage. Then, a novel classification approach has been proposed in the second stage based on the fusion of the deep visual, shallow visual, and text features. Figure 1 exhibits the two stages of the VTLayout model.

3.1   Category Block Localization

In the first stage, the document images are sent to the Cascade Mask R-CNN model [5], where all the different category blocks are localized. The Cascade Mask R-CNN model extends the Cascade R-CNN by adding a mask head to the cascade. In object detection, the intersection over union (IoU) [5] threshold is required to define positives and negatives, and it is expected that some existing methods can not perform well when the IoU threshold increases. Therefore, the Cascade R-CNN is proposed for solving this problem with a multi-stage object detection architecture trained with increasing IoU thresholds.

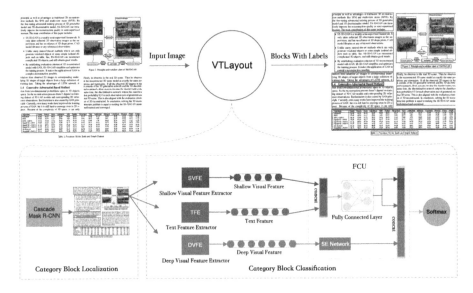

Fig. 1. The structure of the VTLayout consists of two stages, Category Block Localization and Category Block Classification. The Category Block Localization stage localizes the different categories from scientific documents using the Cascade Mask R-CNN model. The DVFE, SVFE, and TFE have been built to extract different features in the Category Block Classification stage. The DVFE is built with the MobileNetV2 model to extract the deep visual feature from all the category blocks. The SVFE extracts the shallow visual feature based on the statistical pixels of different category blocks. The TFE is implemented with the TF-IDF feature extraction technique to extract the text features from the category blocks.

3.2   Category Block Classification

Although it is demonstrated that Cascade Mask R-CNN is shown to surpass all the single-model object detectors on the challenging COCO dataset [14], due to the similarity of *List*, *Text*, *Title*, it can locate each category block rather well but can not classify them correctly in the PubLayNet dataset. Therefore, in the second stage, a novel approach is proposed to improve the classification power of the category blocks based on the fusion of the deep visual, shallow visual, and text features. The Deep Visual Feature Extractor (DVFE) is built with the MobileNetV2 model to extract the deep visual feature from all the category blocks. The shallow visual feature is also extracted by the Shallow Visual Feature Extractor (SVFE) based on the statistical pixels of different category blocks. To extract the text features from the category blocks, the TF-IDF feature extraction technique is applied as the primary technology in the Text Feature Extractor (TFE). Then, a Squeeze-and-Excitation (SE) network [9] is applied with the MobileNetV2 model to weigh each feature map extracted by the MobileNetV2 model. Meanwhile, the extracted shallow visual feature and text feature vectors are concatenated and sent to a fully connected layer for further classification.

The following subsections, the DVFE, SVFE, TFE, and Feature Concatenation Unit (FCU), are introduced with more details.

Deep Visual Feature Extractor

MobileNetV2 model is selected as the backbone architecture, which has been proved to achieve excellent results in multiple tasks and benchmarks. Compared with other proposed architectures, MobileNetV2 is a lightweight DCNNs architecture, which delivers high accuracy results with small numbers of parameters and mathematical operations. The basic structure of the MobileNetV2 is a bottleneck depth-separable convolution with residuals and contains the initial fully convolution layer [23]. Based on the MobileNetV1 model [8], researchers found that removing non-linearities in the narrow layers is essential to maintain the representational power and the experimental results proved its feasibility.

Shallow Visual Feature Extractor

Based on the experimental results from the Category Block Localization stage, *List*, *Text* and *Title* can be misclassified by the Cascade Mask R-CNN. For most images, pixel values range from 0 (black) to 255 (white). As Fig. 2 shows, the statistical pixels of *Figure*, *List*, *Table*, *Text* and *Title* are plotted as line graphs for comparison based on all the category blocks from the PubLayNet training dataset. The horizontal axis represents the pixel values range from 0 to 255, and the vertical axis represents the number of pixels for each pixel value. Based on the line graph of pixels, it is easy to find that the pixel values between 0 to 255 have distinct characteristics to classify different category blocks. Therefore, the SVFE is proposed as one of the units, and all the feature vectors are in length 256.

Text Feature Extractor

Text Feature Extractor (TFE) is built for extracting the text features of all the different category blocks. Since every word needs to be extracted for text features, all the category blocks are applied with the PaddleOCR [24]. In particular, as *Title* blocks are always in small formats and even difficult to be identified by human naked eyes, we particularly enlarge each category block eightfold. Then, the TF-IDF feature extraction technique is applied with the output of PaddleOCR to determine the importance of each word in the textual content. Finally, a vector is built for each category block which represents the text feature.

Feature Concatenation Unit

The DVFE can extract important feature maps that cannot be directly observed, while SVFE can extract features that may be missed by the network in the process of convolution. Furthermore, the features extracted by TFE can enhance the discriminant capability of text format category blocks. Considering the three kinds of extracted features, increasing the weights of the more valuable features by the whole classifier automatically becomes the next research key point.

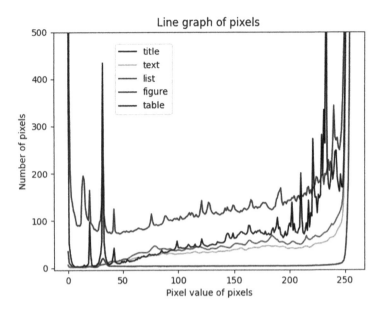

Fig. 2. Statistical pixels of different category blocks.

Researchers have found that enhancing the quality of spatial encodings throughout its feature hierarchy is a proper way to strengthen the representational power of CNN. In this work, the SE block has been proposed to recalibrate the channelwise feature adaptively [9]. Since the SE block has been proved that it can improve the performance of CNNs at a small additional computational cost, we apply the SE block with the MobileNetV2 model.

Besides the deep visual feature, the shallow visual feature and the text features are merged into a single larger vector. Then, the concatenated vector is put into a four-layer, fully connected deep neural networks (DNNs) with the number of neurons [512, 256, 128, 64], and the output is concatenated with the output of the SE block.

4   Dataset

This section introduces the dataset used in our experiments in detail. The PubLayNet dataset is the largest dataset ever for DLA task. It contains more than 360,000 document images with five annotated document layout categories. Table 1 shows the statistics of the whole PubLayNet dataset, which includes the training and validation dataset. As Table 1 shows, the *Text* category contains an enormous amount of data compared to other categories, which is expected because the amount of *Text* is often much more extensive than other categories in scientific literature.

Meanwhile, it is easy to find that the amount of data in *Title* is ranked as the second, and the number of *List* is the smallest in the entire dataset.

For experiments of reproducing the baselines and the VTLayout models, all the images from the PubLaynet dataset are used. As the test dataset is not published so far, we use all the images from the training dataset for training, and the whole validation dataset is used for inference. Therefore, there are 335,703 images for training and 11,245 images for inference.

Table 1. Statistic of the PubLayNet dataset.

Categories of the dataset	Training dataset	Validation dataset
Text	2,376,702	88,625
Title	633,359	18,801
List	81,850	4,239
Table	103,057	4,769
Figure	116,692	4,327
Total	3,311,660	120,761

5 Experimental Settings

This section describes all the experimental settings of this paper. In the beginning, we compare the performance of our proposed VTLayout model with the Faster R-CNN, Mask R-CNN baselines published in the paper of PubLayNet dataset [29]. Besides, we also compare the Cascade Mask R-CNN experimental results with the VTLayout model to observe the effectiveness of fusing the visual and text features for DLA. As we want to compare the classification power of the VTLayout model with the baselines, we reproduce the baselines based on their experimental settings and analyze their classification results without localization results. Therefore, precision, recall, and F1 score [6] are applied as the primary evaluation metrics to evaluate the models in this experiment instead of the MAP @ IOU [0.50:0.95] evaluation metric applied in the paper of PubLayNet dataset.

In our VTLayour model, the Cascade Mask R-CNN model is implemented by Pytorch framework [18]. Then, the resNeXt-101-64x4d model is selected as the backbone network, initialized with the model pre-trained on the ImageNet dataset. The model is trained for 30 epochs with a batch size of 8, one sample per GPU. Moreover, SGD optimizer [13] is used with the initial learning rate of 0.02, the momentum of 0.9, and the weight-decay of 0.0001. In DVFE, the mobileNetV2 model is applied with the TensorFlow framework [1] and all the category blocks are resized to 128×128 by padding. The mobileNetV2 is pre-trained by the ImageNet dataset without the fully connected layer at the top of the network. Besides, the three input channels are set as (128, 128, 3), and the global average pooling is applied to the output of the last convolutional block. In the SVFE, all the color images are firstly converted to grayscale images. In the first step of TFE, the chinese_ocr_db_crnn_mobile [30] from PaddleOCR is applied to identify the words from the documents. Then, the TF-IDF feature extraction technique is applied with the Sklearn library [19]. Finally, the Adam optimizer [13] is used with the initial learning rate of 0.001, and the cross-entropy is used as the loss function.

Besides comparing the VTLayout model with the baselines, a series of stability checking experiments are built based on a small-sized dataset. In order to test our proposed VTLayout model on a small dataset, we only train the Category Block Classification stage with 25,000 randomly selected images for *Text* and *Title*, 10,000 randomly selected images for *Figure*, *List* and *Table* from the output of the Cascade Mask R-CNN instead of all of the training dataset. Based on the statistics of the PubLayNet training dataset, there are around seven *Text* blocks, and two *Title* blocks can be extracted from one page. As around four pages can contain one *List*, three pages can contain one *Table* and one *Figure*, 30,000 images from the PubLayNet training dataset are randomly selected to train the Faster R-CNN and Mask R-CNN to see the classification capability of each model. The results of the comparative experiment are presented in the Result section.

Meanwhile, a five-fold cross-validation experiment is also applied to test the stability of our VTLayout model on the same small-sized dataset. In the experiments, the dataset is randomly divided into five parts on average and takes out four of them as the new training dataset and the remaining one as the test dataset each time. Besides, each fold of data is required to be the test dataset once. Finally, in the ablation experiments, a series of experiments are implemented to see whether all the three feature extractors can affect the master model and what kind of feature can contribute most to the VTLayout model. In particular, if the DVFE is not implemented as one of the units in the VTLayout model, the SE network will also not be applied. If the SVFE or TFE are not applied in the VTLayout model, their feature vectors will not be concatenated and put into the fully connected layer. F1 score is selected as the only evaluation metric for the stability experiments and ablation experiments.

6   Results and Analysis

Table 2 shows that our proposed VTLayout model achieves a state-of-the-art performance than the baseline models on the PubLayNet dataset with the F1 score of 0.9599. The excellent F1 score means that our model has both low false positives and low false negatives, and the low precision and recall values also prove the effectiveness of the VTLayout model.

Moreover, we compare the F1 scores of the Faster R-CNN, Mask R-CNN, Cascade Mask R-CNN, and our proposed VTLayout model based on each category block. As Table 3 shows, it can be found that our proposed VTLayout model achieve the state-of-the-art performance on identifying the *Table*, *Text* and *List*. Compared with the Cascade Mask R-CNN model, our VTLayout model can perform better in most categories, although there is a small drop in recognition

Table 2. VTLayout performance compared with the baselines.

Model	Precision	Recall	F1 score
Faster R-CNN	0.9319	0.9130	0.9224
Mask R-CNN	0.9379	0.9410	0.9385
Cascade Mask R-CNN	0.9515	0.9506	0.9510
VTLayout (ours)	**0.9584**	**0.9618**	**0.9599**

of *Figure* with the F1 score of 0.9824 only. In particular, the VTLayout model successfully made up for the inaccuracy of Cascade Mask R-CNN in *Title*'s recognition which increases the F1 score from 0.9166 to 0.9411, although Faster R-CNN model can work better on recognition of the *Title* with the F1 score of 0.9425. Meanwhile, we can find that the identification capability of the *List* is the worst among the five categories in baselines, but our proposed model greatly improves the recognition power of the *List* with the F1 score of 0.9177.

Table 3. F1 score comparison on different categories.

	Faster R-CNN	Mask R-CNN	Cascade mask R-CNN	VTLayout (ours)
Text	0.9475	0.9475	0.9688	**0.9751**
Title	**0.9425**	0.9406	0.9166	0.9411
List	0.8150	0.8874	0.9055	**0.9177**
Figure	0.9663	0.9617	**0.9846**	0.9824
Table	0.9376	0.9553	0.9794	**0.9833**

Based on the paper of PubLayNet dataset, the MAP @ IOU [0.50:0.95] values of the *Title* were the worst compared with other categories by Faster R-CNN and Mask R-CNN models. However, according to our reproduction of the two models, the experimental results from Table 3 show that *Title* can be recognized better than *List*. Thus, it proves that *Title* can be well recognized but localizing the *Title* can be challenging because it can be recognized easily as part of the *Text*.

Correction of the Wrong Cases

As shown in Fig. 3, two images have been shown as examples of the corrections based on our proposed VTLayout model. These two images are wrong predictions by the Cascade Mask R-CNN. On the left-hand side, the *Title* is recognized wrongly by the Cascade Mask R-CNN, and the VTLayout model predicts the *Title* correctly. On the right-hand side, Cascade Mask R-CNN predicts the *List* as *Text*, but our VTLayout model corrects this error successfully.

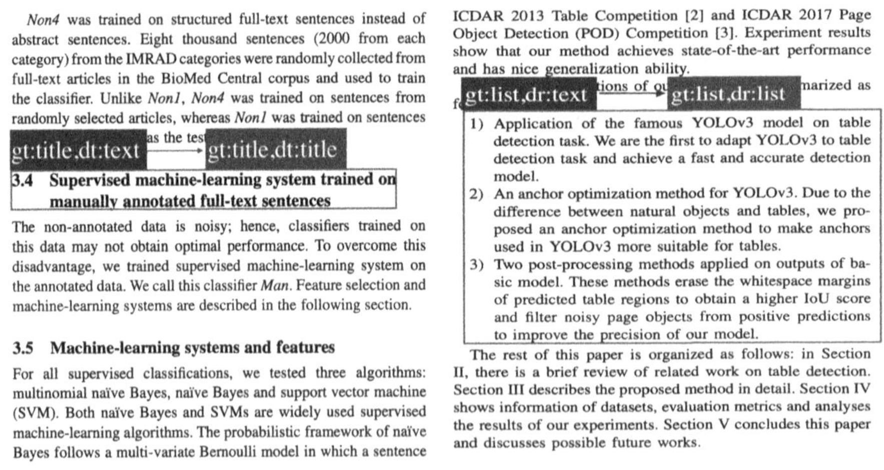

Non4 was trained on structured full-text sentences instead of abstract sentences. Eight thousand sentences (2000 from each category) from the IMRAD categories were randomly collected from full-text articles in the BioMed Central corpus and used to train the classifier. Unlike Non1, Non4 was trained on sentences from randomly selected articles, whereas Non1 was trained on sentences as the test

gt:title,dt:text ⟶ gt:title,dt:title

3.4 Supervised machine-learning system trained on manually annotated full-text sentences

The non-annotated data is noisy; hence, classifiers trained on this data may not obtain optimal performance. To overcome this disadvantage, we trained supervised machine-learning system on the annotated data. We call this classifier *Man*. Feature selection and machine-learning systems are described in the following section.

3.5 Machine-learning systems and features

For all supervised classifications, we tested three algorithms: multinomial naïve Bayes, naïve Bayes and support vector machine (SVM). Both naïve Bayes and SVMs are widely used supervised machine-learning algorithms. The probabilistic framework of naïve Bayes follows a multi-variate Bernoulli model in which a sentence

ICDAR 2013 Table Competition [2] and ICDAR 2017 Page Object Detection (POD) Competition [3]. Experiment results show that our method achieves state-of-the-art performance and has nice generalization ability.

tions of qu   marized as f

gt:list,dr:text   gt:list,dr:list

1) Application of the famous YOLOv3 model on table detection task. We are the first to adapt YOLOv3 to table detection task and achieve a fast and accurate detection model.
2) An anchor optimization method for YOLOv3. Due to the difference between natural objects and tables, we proposed an anchor optimization method to make anchors used in YOLOv3 more suitable for tables.
3) Two post-processing methods applied on outputs of basic model. These methods erase the whitespace margins of predicted table regions to obtain a higher IoU score and filter noisy page objects from positive predictions to improve the precision of our model.

The rest of this paper is organized as follows: in Section II, there is a brief review of related work on table detection. Section III describes the proposed method in detail. Section IV shows information of datasets, evaluation metrics and analyses the results of our experiments. Section V concludes this paper and discusses possible future works.

Fig. 3. Corrections of the wrong cases.

Stability Checking on Small-Sized Dataset

The experiment of checking the VTLayout model on the small-sized dataset shows that the overall F1 score decreases slightly from 0.9599 to 0.9546 on the whole validation dataset. For the stability checking experiment on Faster R-CNN, the F1 score decreases from 0.9224 to 0.9168 with a drop around 0.0056. Meanwhile, the F1 score of Mask R-CNN also decreases from 0.9385 to 0.9361, with a drop of around 0.0024. These experimental results demonstrate that our proposed VTLayout model has excellent stability on the small-sized dataset as well as the Faster R-CNN and Mask R-CNN model.

Table 4 shows the experimental results of the five-fold cross-validation experiment, which demonstrates that the F1 score of all kinds is relatively stable. Overall, all the experimental results prove that the stability of the VTLayout model is high, and the contingency is low.

Table 4. Results of the five-fold cross-validation experiment of F1 scores on different categories of the VTLayout model.

	Text	List	Title	Figure	Table	Average
Fold1	0.9450	0.9648	0.9295	0.9560	0.9472	0.9495
Fold2	0.9428	0.9746	0.9056	0.9878	0.9735	0.9569
Fold3	0.9402	0.9760	0.9347	0.9627	0.9512	0.9532
Fold4	0.9562	0.9810	0.9537	0.9848	0.9626	0.9678
Fold5	0.9376	0.9687	0.9195	0.9591	0.9425	0.9458
Average	0.9444	0.9286	0.9730	0.9701	0.9554	0.9546

Ablation Experiments

Table 5 shows the F1 scores of the VTLayout model and all the ablation experiments, in which DVFE denotes the Deep Visual Feature Extractor, SVFE represents the Shallow Visual Feature Extractor, and TFE represents the Text Feature Extractor. Meanwhile, $VTLayout_{DVFE+SVFE+TFE}$ represents our proposed VTLayout model, and $VTLayout_{DVFE+SVFE}$ denotes the VTLayout model without the Text Feature Extractor. The experimental results demonstrate that all the components impact the master model because the loss of any component results in performance degradation. In particular, the $VTLayout_{DVFE}$ experiment shows that although DVFE can work well on the recognition of the *Text* with an F1 score of 0.9789, the loss of SVFE and TFE can result in a decrease of F1 score on identifying the *List* to 0.7881. Besides, we also can conclude that the DVFE makes the most significant contribution to our model. While TFE has the worst recognition rate for category blocks, it is still necessary because it can make the overall performance of the model better.

Table 5. The ablation experimental results of F1 scores of the VTLayout model.

No.	Model	Text	Title	List	Figure	Table	Average
1	$VTLayout_{DVFE+SVFE+TFE}$	0.9751	0.9411	0.9177	0.9824	0.9833	0.9599
2	$VTLayout_{DVFE+SVFE}$	0.9638	0.9296	0.8725	0.9834	0.9678	0.9440
3	$VTLayout_{DVFE+TFE}$	0.9230	0.8633	0.7635	0.9625	0.9656	0.8956
4	$VTLayout_{SVFE+TFE}$	0.8412	0.7699	0.6944	0.9308	0.9261	0.8455
5	$VTLayout_{DVFE}$	0.9789	0.9273	0.7881	0.9801	0.9576	0.9272
6	$VTLayout_{TFE}$	0.3657	0.3635	0.1030	0.1990	0.1505	0.3198
7	$VTLayout_{SVFE}$	0.8913	0.8391	0.3753	0.9275	0.9273	0.8209

Overall, based on the experimental results and analysis above, we demonstrate that our proposed VTLayout model is superior to the current most advanced methods of DLA. The reasons can be summarized as follows. Firstly, our VTLayout model fuses three different kinds of features, deep visual, shallow visual, and text features from the PublayNet dataset, which can boost the performance of identifying different category blocks. In particular, the experimental results of the ablation experiments have demonstrated that all three features are beneficial and necessary for DLA. Secondly, with the great success of deep learning in object detection, researchers have neglected the importance of traditional shallow visual features. Our proposed extractor for the shallow visual feature is one of the most important contributions in this paper. Thirdly, the experimental results prove that the VTLayout model has excellent stability on randomly selected small datasets.

In addition, our proposed method still has some deficiencies, which the recognition of *Title* and *List* need to be further improved. Based on these findings and recent literature review, the recognition of *List* still remains challenging compared with other different category blocks, and it can be predicted wrongly as *Text* category easily. Therefore, improving the identification rate of the *List* has become our next focus, and we believe that the bullet points in the *List* can be the key to solving this problem. One of the main reasons for inaccurate recognition of *Title* is that many of the *Titles* in the text have only one or two words, so the *Titles* are often appear in small sizes and even the human cannot accurately identify them with naked eyes. In the experiments, although we enlarge the size of *Title* blocks before applying with the PaddleOCR, the blurring caused by the amplification still makes the recognition rate of *Title* less than ideal.

7   Conclusion

A VTLayout model is proposed for DLA task based on the fusion of deep visual, shallow visual, and text features. The experimental results show that the proposed VTLayout model is superior to the most advanced classification methods in the PublayNet dataset, and the F1 score is 0.9599. Meanwhile, we find that the intuitive perceptual feature is beneficial to the DLA. As we mentioned in the introduction, the accuracy of the DLA can determine the performance of many NLP-related tasks. An accurate and efficient DLA model can accurately locate a category block and extract it from many complex datasets for future work. As far as I know, in the field of applied chemistry, some researchers prefer to pay more attention to the *Tables* only from the literature. Our work could significantly shorten the time it takes researchers to find *Tables* in thousands of academic papers. In addition, DLA can be beneficial to the evaluations of grant applications. In recent years, government and top research institution funding agencies gradually started to apply AI techniques to assist manual evaluating of grant applications. Our proposed VTLayout model has been applied to extract the *Text* and *Tables* from thousands of grant applications for further evaluation.

Although the VTLayout model achieves the state-of-the-art performance in identifying different categories in DLA, there is still much room for improvement in both localization and classification of different category blocks. Firstly, compared with the traditional DCNN-based object detection models, Transformer-based backbones start to show up and achieve remarkable results in a series of traditional public datasets for object detection. Therefore, applying the Transformer-based method to DLA will be our next research direction. Secondly, assign features that have more influence on classifier performance with more weights can be another key consideration in the future. We believe that the model's performance can be improved by self-adjusting the weights of deep visual, shallow visual, and text features. Next, the accuracy of OCR is self-evident for the VTLayout model. In recent years, the research of scene text recognition has made significant progress. Complex background conditions, text color, font size, and irregular text representation are no longer obstacles in recognizing the scene text. Therefore, we believe that the achievements of scene text recognition can meet our requirements for OCR's accuracy. Fourthly, we will continue to explore further the research of multimodal fusion in DLA to optimize the extraction of deep visual, shallow visual and text features of documents. In addition, we also seek to come up with an end-to-end, lighter DLA model.

References

1. Abadi, M., et al.: Tensorflow: large-scale machine learning on heterogeneous distributed systems. arXiv preprint arXiv:1603.04467 (2016)
2. Asim, M.N., Khan, M.U.G., Malik, M.I., Razzaque, K., Dengel, A., Ahmed, S.: Two stream deep network for document image classification. In: 2019 International Conference on Document Analysis and Recognition (ICDAR), pp. 1410–1416. IEEE (2019)
3. Augusto Borges Oliveira, D., Palhares Viana, M.: Fast CNN-based document layout analysis. In: Proceedings of the IEEE International Conference on Computer Vision Workshops, pp. 1173–1180 (2017)
4. Binmakhashen, G.M., Mahmoud, S.A.: Document layout analysis: a comprehensive survey. ACM Comput. Surv. (CSUR) **52**(6), 1–36 (2019)
5. Cai, Z., Vasconcelos, N.: Cascade R-CNN: delving into high quality object detection. In: Proceedings of the IEEE Conference on Computer Vision and Pattern Recognition, pp. 6154–6162 (2018)
6. Goutte, C., Gaussier, E.: A probabilistic interpretation of precision, recall and F-score, with implication for evaluation. In: Losada, D.E., Fernández-Luna, J.M. (eds.) ECIR 2005. LNCS, vol. 3408, pp. 345–359. Springer, Heidelberg (2005). https://doi.org/10.1007/978-3-540-31865-1_25
7. Ha, J., Haralick, R.M., Phillips, I.T.: Recursive xy cut using bounding boxes of connected components. In: Proceedings of 3rd International Conference on Document Analysis and Recognition, vol. 2, pp. 952–955. IEEE (1995)
8. Howard, A.G., et al.: Mobilenets: Efficient convolutional neural networks for mobile vision applications. arXiv preprint arXiv:1704.04861 (2017)
9. Hu, J., Shen, L., Sun, G.: Squeeze-and-excitation networks. In: Proceedings of the IEEE Conference on Computer Vision and Pattern Recognition, pp. 7132–7141 (2018)
10. Jain, R., Wigington, C.: Multimodal document image classification. In: 2019 International Conference on Document Analysis and Recognition (ICDAR), pp. 71–77. IEEE (2019)
11. Kang, L., Kumar, J., Ye, P., Li, Y., Doermann, D.: Convolutional neural networks for document image classification. In: 2014 22nd International Conference on Pattern Recognition, pp. 3168–3172. IEEE (2014)
12. Kavasidis, I., et al.: A saliency-based convolutional neural network for table and chart detection in digitized documents. arXiv preprint arXiv:1804.06236 (2018)
13. Keskar, N.S., Socher, R.: Improving generalization performance by switching from Adam to SGD. arXiv preprint arXiv:1712.07628 (2017)
14. Lin, T.Y., et al.: Microsoft COCO: common objects in context. In: Fleet, D., Pajdla, T., Schiele, B., Tuytelaars, T. (eds.) ECCV 2014. LNCS, vol. 8693, pp. 740–755. Springer, Cham (2014). https://doi.org/10.1007/978-3-319-10602-1_48
15. Liu, W., et al.: SSD: single shot multibox detector. In: Leibe, B., Matas, J., Sebe, N., Welling, M. (eds.) ECCV 2016. LNCS, vol. 9905, pp. 21–37. Springer, Cham (2016). https://doi.org/10.1007/978-3-319-46448-0_2
16. Namboodiri, A.M., Jain, A.K.: Document structure and layout analysis. In: Chaudhuri, B.B. (eds.) Digital Document Processing. Advances in Pattern Recognition. Springer, London (2007). https://doi.org/10.1007/978-1-84628-726-8_2
17. O'Gorman, L.: The document spectrum for page layout analysis. IEEE Trans. Pattern Anal. Mach. Intell. **15**(11), 1162–1173 (1993)

18. Paszke, A., et al.: PyTorch: an imperative style, high-performance deep learning library. arXiv preprint arXiv:1912.01703 (2019)
19. Pedregosa, F., et al.: Scikit-learn: machine learning in Python. J. Mach. Learn. Res. **12**, 2825–2830 (2011)
20. Ray, S., Chandra, N.: Domain based ontology and automated text categorization based on improved term frequency-inverse document frequency. Int. J. Mod. Educ. Comput. Sci. **4**(4), 28 (2012)
21. Redmon, J., Divvala, S., Girshick, R., Farhadi, A.: You only look once: unified, real-time object detection. In: Proceedings of the IEEE Conference on Computer Vision and Pattern Recognition, pp. 779–788 (2016)
22. Ren, S., He, K., Girshick, R., Sun, J.: Faster R-CNN: towards real-time object detection with region proposal networks. arXiv preprint arXiv:1506.01497 (2015)
23. Sandler, M., Howard, A., Zhu, M., Zhmoginov, A., Chen, L.C.: MobileNetV2: inverted residuals and linear bottlenecks. In: Proceedings of the IEEE Conference on Computer Vision and Pattern Recognition, pp. 4510–4520 (2018)
24. Shi, B., Bai, X., Yao, C.: An end-to-end trainable neural network for image-based sequence recognition and its application to scene text recognition. IEEE Trans. Pattern Anal. Mach. Intell. **39**(11), 2298–2304 (2016)
25. Siddiqui, S.A., Khan, P.I., Dengel, A., Ahmed, S.: Rethinking semantic segmentation for table structure recognition in documents. In: 2019 International Conference on Document Analysis and Recognition (ICDAR), pp. 1397–1402. IEEE (2019)
26. Soto, C.X., Soto, C.X.: Visual detection with context for document layout analysis. Technical report, Brookhaven National Lab. (BNL), Upton, NY (United States) (2019)
27. Sun, N., Zhu, Y., Hu, X.: Faster R-CNN based table detection combining corner locating. In: 2019 International Conference on Document Analysis and Recognition (ICDAR), pp. 1314–1319. IEEE (2019)
28. Yang, X., Yumer, E., Asente, P., Kraley, M., Kifer, D., Lee Giles, C.: Learning to extract semantic structure from documents using multimodal fully convolutional neural networks. In: Proceedings of the IEEE Conference on Computer Vision and Pattern Recognition, pp. 5315–5324 (2017)
29. Zhong, X., Tang, J., Yepes, A.J.: PubLayNet: largest dataset ever for document layout analysis. In: 2019 International Conference on Document Analysis and Recognition (ICDAR), pp. 1015–1022. IEEE (2019)
30. Zhou, X., et al.: East: an efficient and accurate scene text detector. In: Proceedings of the IEEE Conference on Computer Vision and Pattern Recognition, pp. 5551–5560 (2017)

An Initial Study of Machine Learning Underspecification Using Feature Attribution Explainable AI Algorithms: A COVID-19 Virus Transmission Case Study

James Hinns[1], Xiuyi Fan[1(✉)], Siyuan Liu[1], Veera Raghava Reddy Kovvuri[1], Mehmet Orcun Yalcin[2], and Markus Roggenbach[1]

[1] Computer Science Department, Swansea University, Swansea, UK
xiuyi.fan@swansea.ac.uk
[2] Department of Data Science and Knowledge Engineering, Maastricht University, Maastricht, The Netherlands

Abstract. From a dataset, one can construct different machine learning (ML) models with different parameters and/or inductive biases. Although these models give similar prediction performances when tested on data that are currently available, they may not generalise equally well on unseen data. The existence of multiple equally performing models exhibits *underspecification* of the ML pipeline used for producing such models. In this work, we propose identifying underspecification using feature attribution algorithms developed in Explainable AI. Our hypothesis is: **by studying the range of explanations produced by ML models, one can identify underspecification**. We validate this by computing explanations using the Shapley additive explainer and then measuring statistical correlations between them. We experiment our approach on multiple datasets drawn from the literature, and in a COVID-19 virus transmission case study.

Keywords: Underspecification · Explainable AI · COVID-19

1 Introduction

Underspecification has been identified as a major challenge in machine learning (ML) research. Roughly speaking, an ML pipeline is underspecified *"when it can return many predictors with equivalently strong held-out performance in the training domain."* [4] Having multiple different predictors is problematic in real-world applications as the current practice often treats such predictors as equivalent (based on their training performances), while they usually give different behaviours in deployment. Thus, we see that ML models sometimes exhibit unexpectedly poor behaviours when they are used in real-world applications when such multi-predictor phenomenon occurs.

© Springer Nature Switzerland AG 2021
D. N. Pham et al. (Eds.): PRICAI 2021, LNAI 13031, pp. 323–335, 2021.
https://doi.org/10.1007/978-3-030-89188-6_24

Table 1. Two simple string datasets, D_1, and D_2 for underspecification illustration.

	Data	POS Explanation Pattern (s)
D_1	POS: 01101, 11101, 11111, 01111	$\cdot 1 \cdots$, $\cdot\cdot 1 \cdot\cdot$, $\cdots\cdot 1$
	NEG: 00000, 00010, 10010, 10000	
D_2	POS: 01101, 11101, 11111, 01111, 01001, 11100	$\cdot 1 \cdots$
	NEG: 00000, 00010, 10010, 10000, 00001, 10111	

The first step of addressing underspecification is to identify it. To this end, stress tests measuring prediction performances - evaluations that probe a predictor by observing its outputs on specifically designed inputs - have been reported in the literature [4]. However, with a few exceptions, as we discuss in Sect. 4, existing approaches identify underspecification solely with traditional prediction metrics such as accuracy and root mean square error, which will make underspecification not fully identified in many situations.

In this work, we present an alternative approach: identifying underspecification with explanations. In a nutshell, given a dataset, we construct a set of predictors and study explanations generated using a feature attribution algorithm [14] from these predictors. We identify underspecification when observing "too many" different explanations form such predictors on the dataset. We observe that: **if a dataset can be explained in multiple ways, then a ML pipeline built from it is likely underspecified.**

Our core idea can be illustrated with the following example. Consider two binary classification datasets, D_1 and D_2, shown in Table 1. D_1 and D_2 contain eight and twelve 5-bit strings as data instances, respectively, on the alphabet $\{0, 1\}$. Each string is labelled either POS (positive) or NEG (negative). D_2 contains all strings of D_1 and four additional strings. Both datasets are balanced with each containing the same number of POS and NEG strings. If we consider each bit in a string representing a feature, which can be a potential explanation for a string's positivity, then there are three "1-bit explanations" for the positivity of strings in D_1 as follows:

- $\cdot 1 \cdots$: *a string is* POS *because its second bit is 1*,
- $\cdot\cdot 1 \cdot\cdot$: *a string is* POS *because its third bit is 1*, and
- $\cdots\cdot 1$: *a string is* POS *because its fifth bit is 1*.

There are no reasons to prefer any one of these explanations to the others given the dataset D_1. However, with the four additional strings introduced in D_2, we see that both explanations $\cdot\cdot 1 \cdot\cdot$ and $\cdots\cdot 1$ are ruled out, as 10111 and 00001 are both NEG. So there is a single explanation left for all strings in D_2:

- $\cdot 1 \cdots$: *a string is* POS *because its second bit is 1*.

Thus, we observe that D_2 with more data yields fewer 1-bit explanations than D_1 and can better specify prediction models than D_1.

Various explanation construction techniques have been developed in Explainable AI (XAI) [18]. These techniques produce explanations of different types, see e.g., [19] for an overview. In this work, we use a feature attribution explanation method, SHapley Additive exPlanations (SHAP) [14], which computes explanations to data instances in the form of "feature weights", to facilitate underspecification identification. SHAP is chosen in this work for its sound mathematical foundation and its ease of implementation.

SHAP is based on the coalitional game theory concept *Shapley value*, which is assigned to each feature of a data instance. Shapley values are defined to answer the question: "What is the fairest way for a coalition to divide its payout among the players"? It assumes that payouts should be assigned to players in a game depending on their contribution towards total payout. In a machine learning context, feature values are "players"; and the prediction is the "total payout". In this setting, the Shapley value of a feature represents its contribution to the prediction and thus explains the prediction. SHAP is model-agnostic and thus independent of underlying prediction models. For a data instance x, SHAP computes the marginal contribution of each feature to the prediction of x.

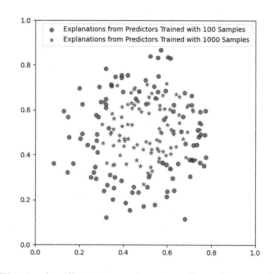

Fig. 1. An illustration of explanations from predictors trained with different sample sizes. Predictors trained with more data - hence less underspecified ML pipelines - produce more agreeable explanations. Red stars are placed closer to each other than blue dots are. (Blue dots and red stars represent explanations obtained from predictors trained with 100 and 1000 randomly selected samples in the COVID-19 dataset respectively. Within each set, the coordinates $\mathbf{x}_i$ are computed with a stochastic hill climbing algorithm that solves $\arg\min_{\mathbf{x}_i, \mathbf{x}_j} \sum |L_2(\mathbf{x}_i, \mathbf{x}_j) - D_\tau(\hat{\mathbf{x}}_i, \hat{\mathbf{x}}_j)|$, where L_2 is the L2 norm, D_τ is the Kendall distance of each pair of explanations $(\hat{\mathbf{x}}_i, \hat{\mathbf{x}}_j)$.) (Color figure online)

Given a prediction model $P \in \mathcal{P}$, where $\mathcal{P}$ is the set of models, let $\mathbf{y} = P(\mathbf{x})$ be the prediction made by P on the input $\mathbf{x} = \langle x_1, \ldots, x_M \rangle \in \mathbb{R}^M$, SHAP gives an explanation $\langle \phi_1, \ldots, \phi_M \rangle \in \mathbb{R}^M$ (for $\mathbf{y} = P(\mathbf{x})$); ϕ_i can be viewed as the contribution of x_i for this prediction. We can think SHAP as a function $\Pi : \mathcal{P} \times \mathbb{R}^M \mapsto \mathbb{R}^M$. From a dataset, we train a set of models $\mathcal{P} = \{P_1, \ldots, P_n\}$. For the same input $\mathbf{x}$, we compute a set of explanations $\Phi = \{\Pi(P_i, \mathbf{x}) | P_i \in \mathcal{P}\}$.

By looking at how "compact" Φ is, we identify underspecification of the ML pipeline - if explanations in Φ are close to each other, that means models in $\mathcal{P}$ are agreeable with each other, thus less underspecified. Otherwise, explanations in Φ are apart from each other, then models in $\mathcal{P}$, although might be making the same prediction $\mathbf{y}$, make predictions for different reasons, hence more underspecified.

To put things into a concrete setting, we study how underspecification occurs in the context of predicting COVID-19 virus transmission. To this end, we construct a dataset containing daily confirmed cases between March 2020 and January 2021 and non-pharmaceutical control measures used in the UK and predict whether the infectious rate is growing on a given day. As illustrated in Fig. 1, underspecification is observed when explanations generated from models are far apart from each other; whereas when explanations are close to each other and form compact clusters, there is less underspecification.

Overall, the proposed approach to identifying underspecification with explanations has the following advantages:

1. It is model-agnostic and applicable to any data types and ML models as long as such a model can be analysed with a model-agnostic explainer.
2. It is self-contained and does not require any additional information such as domain knowledge or human expert inputs.
3. It is simple and does not require any special treatment to the dataset, e.g., stratification or alteration, to estimate underspecification.

Our contributions in this work are as follows:

– We formulate underspecification identification as a problem of measuring correlations between explanations.
– We perform the explanation distance measurement using a well studied statistical metric, Kendall Rank Correlation Coefficient.
– We demonstrate our approach on both existing datasets in the literature and a real-world COVID-19 dataset.

The rest of this paper is organised as follows. Section 2 introduces our main approach with results produced from a synthesised dataset. Section 3 introduces the virus transmission case study in detail. Section 4 discusses some related work. We conclude in Sect. 5.

2   Our Approach

As introduced in [4], we consider underspecification in a supervised learning setting. Specifically, we consider an ML pipeline with a dataset D that produces a model (predictor) P, drawn from a set of predictors $\mathcal{P}$. Regardless of the method used to construct P, it is evaluated with some performance measures such as accuracy or root mean square error on D. An ML pipeline is *underspecified* if it can return multiple different predictors such that they give similar performances, while encoding substantially different inductive biases that can result in different generalisation behaviours on datasets beyond D (Out-of-Distribution).

Since predictors can contain a vast amount of parameters and/or have different internal structures, it is not straightforward to directly compare two predictors and determine how similar they are. Thus, in order to determine whether an ML pipeline is underspecified, we study explanations obtained from predictors produced by the ML pipeline, and use those as a proxy to estimate the differences between predictors.

Our Core Assumption is That:

If two predictors give the same explanation to a prediction, then they encode the same inductive bias; hence they should be considered the same.

In this setting, given predictors $\mathcal{P} = \{P_1, \ldots, P_K\}$ produced by an ML pipeline with dataset D, we first use the SHAP explainer Π to compute *global* explanations $\boldsymbol{\Phi}_P$ for each predictor $P \in \mathcal{P}$ on the entire dataset D:

$$\boldsymbol{\Phi}_P = \sum_{\mathbf{x} \in D} \Pi(P, \mathbf{x}). \tag{1}$$

The rank of explanations from P is the ranked list calculated over $\boldsymbol{\Phi}_P$. For example, if SHAP values $\boldsymbol{\Phi}_P$ were [0.1, 0.2, 0.4, 0.3] the ranked list would be [4, 3, 1, 2]. This process of generating models and then computing their rank of explanations is shown in Algorithm 1. Note that the parameter θ used in line 3 is to ensure that all predictors trained in $\mathcal{P}$ have similar and high performances. K is the parameter that controls the number of predictors in experiments.

Algorithm 1. GenModels(D, K, θ) **return R**

Input: The number of models K, Dataset D, Prediction Performance Threshold θ
Output: Global Explanation ranks **R**

1: $\mathbf{R} = []$
2: **while** $|\mathbf{R}| < K$ **do**
3:     Train a predictor P with D such that the performance of P is greater than θ
4:     $\boldsymbol{\Phi}_P = \langle 0, \ldots, 0 \rangle$ with $|\boldsymbol{\Phi}_P|$ the number of features in D
5:     **for** each $\mathbf{x} \in D$ **do**
6:       $\boldsymbol{\Phi}_P = \boldsymbol{\Phi}_P + \Pi(P, \mathbf{x})$
7:     Append the ranked list of $\boldsymbol{\Phi}_P$ to **R**
8: **return R**

With explanation rank lists **R** computed for all predictors, to identify underspecification, we compute

$$\mathcal{T} = \frac{2}{K(K-1)} \sum_{i=0}^{K} \sum_{j>i}^{K} \tau_{i,j}, \tag{2}$$

where $\tau_{i,j}$ is the pair-wise Kendall rank correlation coefficient over ranks of explanations generated from predictors P_i and P_j. $\mathcal{T}$ is the average Kendall rank correlation coefficient between all explanation pairs in $\mathcal{P}$. We can see that:

- $-1 \leq \mathcal{T} \leq 1$ for any ML pipelines and datasets; and
- the larger $\mathcal{T}$ is, the closer explanations are, hence less underspecification.

Table 2. Datasets for experiments.

Dataset	# of samples	# of POS samples	# of feature	Type of features
String [31]	9,623	4,410	20	Categorical
House Price [3]	1,461	728	79	Mixed
Abalone [5]	4,178	2,081	8	Mixed
Mushroom [5]	8,124	3,916	22	Categorical

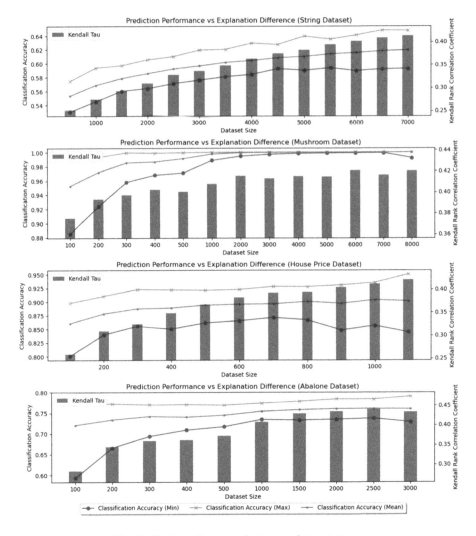

Fig. 2. Explanation correlation vs dataset sizes.

Table 3. Non-pharmaceutical COVID control measures.

Meeting Friends/Family (Indoor)	Meeting Friends/Family (Outdoor)
Domestic Travel Control	International Travel Control
Cafes and Restaurants Control	Pubs and Bars Control
Sports and Leisure Closure	Hospitals/Care and Nursing Home Visits
Non-Essential Shops Closure	School Closure

We test our approach on four datasets found in the literature, string classification [31], house price [3], abalone age [5] and mushroom [5]. Characteristics of these four datasets are summarised in Table 2.

To investigate how underspecification changes with different dataset sizes, we stratify each dataset into multiple smaller datasets in different sizes. For each of these smaller dataset lengths we trained $K = 100$ random forest predictors and test their performances on the whole dataset, comparing their explanation correlations with classification accuracy. This experiment was then repeated 10 times with averages shown in Fig. 2. In this figure, we can see that for all four datasets, as we increase the dataset size, the explanation correlation increases. This means that with a larger dataset, explanations become more similar. Both the explanation correlations and classification accuracy plateau for larger dataset sizes indicating that once the dataset size reaches a certain threshold, introducing more samples does not reduce underspecification.

3 COVID-19 Virus Transmission Case Study

In this section, we apply our approach to a coronavirus virus transmission case study. This case study can be viewed as a realistic experiment modelled after the epidemiological model that demonstrates underspecification in [4]. In a nutshell, the model in [4] illustrates that at early stages of an epidemic, there is insufficient amount of data to fully specify an accurate prediction model; so multiple prediction trajectories can be formed based on the insufficient training data, consequentially the predictions becomes largely arbitrary.

From the Public Health England website[1], we collected daily infection numbers reported across 12 regions in UK: East Midlands, East of England, London, North East, North West, Northern Ireland, Scotland, South East, South West, Wales, West Midlands as well as Yorkshire and The Humber. Non-pharmaceutical control measure data was composed based on UK's COVID policies as summarised in Table 3. Data was corrected from various sources including Wikipedia and major news agencies. Control Measures were coded based on level of severity (e.g., "High", "Moderate", "Low") for all control measures excluding Non-essential shops and School closures, which are coded as binary choices ("Open" and "Closed"). Data points for temperature and humidity were

---

[1] https://www.gov.uk/government/organisations/public-health-england.

extracted from the weather website Raspisaniye Pogodi Ltd[2]. In total 4,257 data points were collected between February 2020 and February 2021.

From daily infection numbers, we estimate R_t using the method reported in [7,30]. R_t is one of the most important quantities used to measure the epidemic spread. If $R_t > 1$, then the epidemic is expanding at time t, whereas if $R_t < 1$, then it is shrinking at time t. A *serial interval distribution*, which is a Gamma distribution $g(\tau)$ with mean 7 and standard deviation 4.5, is used to model the time between a person getting infected and them subsequently infecting another person on day τ. The number of new infections c_t on a day t is computed as:

$$c_t = R_t \sum_{\tau=0}^{t-1} c_\tau g_{t-\tau}, \tag{3}$$

where c_τ is the number of new infections on day τ,

$$g_1 = \int_{\tau=0}^{1.5} g(\tau)d\tau,$$

and for $s = 2, 3, \ldots$,

$$g_s = \int_{\tau=s-0.5}^{s+0.5} g(\tau)d\tau.$$

From Eq. 3, we have:

$$R_t = \frac{c_t}{\sum_{\tau=0}^{t-1} c_\tau g_{t-\tau}} \tag{4}$$

For $x = t$ and τ, c_x is the difference between the confirmed case on day x and the confirmed case on day $x - 1$, which is available from the dataset directly.

With this data, we pose a simple classification question:

Given the infection number and control measures implemented on a day t, is $R_t \geq 1$?

To account the fact that control measures take time to affect the infection rate, we expand the dataset to include the duration of control measure implementation for all control measures. For example, *"Meeting Indoors (High) = 5"* means that *"it is the 5th day that meeting indoors has been banned completely"*. Similarly, *International Travel (Low) = 0* means that *"there is no restriction implemented on international travel"*. We also drop instances before March 15, 2020 across all 12 regions in our dataset due to the low number of infections.[3] In this way, we form a data file with 25 features and 3,937 instances with 2,288 positive ones.

---

[2] https://rp5.ru/Weather_in_the_world.
[3] As can be seen from Eq. 4, when c_x is small, R_t can flatulate in a unrealistically large range and generate noises in the dataset.

To demonstrate the effect of underspecification, we stratify the dataset D into 11 random groups with sizes 100 to 3500, respectively. We train 100 random forest predictors with each group in D and compute explanation correlations using the process described in Sect. 2. In addition, we also calculate the classification accuracy over the remaining dataset. Figure 3 shows the results from these experiments. We observe that as the dataset size increases, both the classification performance and explanation correlation increase, as expected.

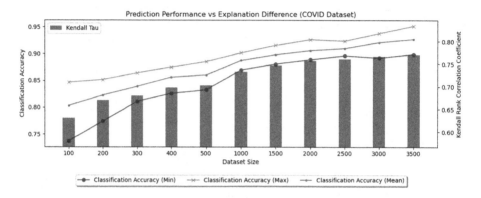

Fig. 3. COVID-19 R_t classification case study.

4   Related Work

As briefly discussed in the Introduction, stress tests have been used to identify underspecification [4]. In particular, stratified performance evaluations, testing whether different strata of a dataset give similar performance on a predictor (see e.g., [1,21]), shifted performance evaluation, testing whether the average performance of a predictor generalises when the test distribution differs in a specific way from the training distribution (see e.g., [11,28]), and contrastive evaluation, testing whether a particular modification of the input causes the output of the model to change in unexpected ways (see e.g., [10,24]) are notable approaches. Comparing with these, our work studies underspecification from a different angle.

Underspecification has been studied in the ML literature in different notions. In deep learning, the discussion focuses on the local geometric properties of objective functions [2], and the geometry of loss surfaces in model averaging and network pruning [8,9,13,29]. Recently there have been analyses of overparameterisation in theoretical and real deep learning models, where underspecificaiton is considered to be caused by potential more degrees of freedom than datapoints induce [17,20]. In [6,15,25,26], underspecificaiton is treated as different near-optimal solutions for a single learning problem specifications having different properties such as interpretability or fairness.

Our idea of looking at underspecification from the explanation dimension is highly relevant but also orthogonal to the line of recent works on "right for the right reason", for example [25] and [16]. In [25], domain knowledge capturing "right explanations" and human experts are introduced in an ML pipeline to directly assist the prediction and select the most suitable predictor from a group of predictors based on their explanations, respectively. In [16], predictors for natural language inference tasks are tested against a set of common but sometimes wrong reasons, encoded as learning heuristics benchmarks. Comparing with these, we do not attempt to increase prediction performance or develop datasets for benchmarking; instead, we focus on studying the relation between explanations and underspecification and show that the number of "distinct" explanations, or the "average distance" between explanations, generated from different predictors is a good indicator for the degree of underspecification.

5   Conclusion

In this work, we present an alternative approach that identifies underspecification by investigating explanation correlation. Simply put, given a set of equally high performing predictors trained from an ML pipeline, if they produce highly correlated explanations to their predictions, then the ML pipeline is not underspecified; otherwise, the pipeline is underspecified. We illustrate our approach in multiple classification tasks and in a real-world case study. Our results show that having more data usually helps to address underspecification.

As an early work in studying underspecification, there are several limitations of this work we plan to address in the future. Firstly, we believe that the concept of *underspecification* must be further refined. The current state-of-the-art as represented by [4] suggests underspecification is a qualitative concept without precise quantification. However, to advance this field, measurable quantification is needed so researchers can compare two different ML pipelines and compare their degrees of underspecification quantitatively so "improvement" can be discussed meaningfully. We believe explanation correlation suggested in this work could be such a metric, yet a deeper study is needed.

Secondly, additional explanation generation algorithms should be considered. As feature attribution algorithms are in rapid development, there are techniques other than SHAP, e.g., LIME [23], that also compute feature weights. Although SHAP shows certain superiority over LIME as found in some studies [12,14, 22,27], it would be interesting to see whether our SHAP-based results can be reproduced with LIME, or some other interesting behaviours can be discovered.

Thirdly, other forms of machine learning should be studied. This work has focused on classification tasks in supervised learning. We need to consider regression and unsupervised learning tasks. We believe some of the techniques introduced in this work could be carried over to a regression setting. However, carefully planned experiments are necessary to validate such approaches. For analysing underspecification in unsupervised learning, some theoretical work is needed to clearly define and scope the problem.

Lastly, this work focuses solely on identifying underspecification. Ultimately, we would like to have a technique that addresses underspecification with data that is currently available. To this end, the technique needs to select predictors with the "correct" inductive bias. We would like to explore whether explanation properties can be used for such identification.

Acknowledgments. This work is supported by the Welsh Government Office for Science, Ser Cymru III programme – Tackling Covid-19.

References

1. Buolamwini, J., Gebru, T.: Gender shades: intersectional accuracy disparities in commercial gender classification. In: Friedler, S.A., Wilson, C. (eds.) FAT. Proceedings of Machine Learning Research, vol. 81, pp. 77–91. PMLR (2018)
2. bibitemch24chaudhari2019entropy Chaudhari, P., et al.: Entropy-SGD: biasing gradient descent into wide valleys. J. Stat. Mech: Theory Exp. **2019**(12), 124018 (2019)
3. Cock, D.D.: Ames, iowa: Alternative to the Boston housing data as an end of semester regression project. J. Stat. Educ. **19**(3) (2011)
4. D'Amour, A., et al.: Underspecification presents challenges for credibility in modern machine learning. CoRR abs/2011.03395 (2020)
5. Dua, D., Graff, C.: UCI machine learning repository (2017). http://archive.ics.uci.edu/ml
6. Fisher, A., Rudin, C., Dominici, F.: All models are wrong, but many are useful: Learning a variable's importance by studying an entire class of prediction models simultaneously. J. Mach. Learn. Res. **20**(177), 1–81 (2019)
7. Flaxman, S., et al.: Report 13: estimating the number of infections and the impact of non-pharmaceutical interventions on covid-19 in 11 European countries. Technical report, Imperial College London (2020)
8. Fort, S., Hu, H., Lakshminarayanan, B.: Deep ensembles: a loss landscape perspective. arXiv preprint arXiv:1912.02757 (2019)
9. Frankle, J., Dziugaite, G.K., Roy, D., Carbin, M.: Linear mode connectivity and the lottery ticket hypothesis. In: International Conference on Machine Learning, pp. 3259–3269. PMLR (2020)
10. Garg, S., Perot, V., Limtiaco, N., Taly, A., Chi, E.H., Beutel, A.: Counterfactual fairness in text classification through robustness. In: Conitzer, V., Hadfield, G.K., Vallor, S. (eds.) Proceedings of the 2019 AAAI/ACM Conference on AI, Ethics, and Society, AIES 2019, Honolulu, HI, USA, 27–28 January 2019, pp. 219–226. ACM (2019)
11. Hendrycks, D., Dietterich, T.G.: Benchmarking neural network robustness to common corruptions and perturbations. CoRR abs/1903.12261 (2019)
12. Honegger, M.: Shedding light on black box machine learning algorithms: Development of an axiomatic framework to assess the quality of methods that explain individual predictions. CoRR abs/1808.05054 (2018)
13. Izmailov, P., Podoprikhin, D., Garipov, T., Vetrov, D., Wilson, A.G.: Averaging weights leads to wider optima and better generalization. arXiv preprint arXiv:1803.05407 (2018)

14. Lundberg, S.M., Lee, S.: A unified approach to interpreting model predictions. In: Guyon, I., von Luxburg, U., Bengio, S., Wallach, H.M., Fergus, R., Vishwanathan, S.V.N., Garnett, R. (eds.) Advances in Neural Information Processing Systems 30: Annual Conference on Neural Information Processing Systems 2017, 4–9 December 2017, pp. 4765–4774. Long Beach, CA, USA (2017)

15. Marx, C., Calmon, F., Ustun, B.: Predictive multiplicity in classification. In: International Conference on Machine Learning, pp. 6765–6774. PMLR (2020)

16. McCoy, T., Pavlick, E., Linzen, T.: Right for the wrong reasons: diagnosing syntactic heuristics in natural language inference. In: Korhonen, A., Traum, D.R., Màrquez, L. (eds.) Proceedings of the 57th Conference of the Association for Computational Linguistics, ACL 2019, Florence, Italy, July 28- August 2, 2019, Volume 1: Long Papers, pp. 3428–3448. Association for Computational Linguistics (2019)

17. Mei, S., Montanari, A.: The generalization error of random features regression: Precise asymptotics and double descent curve. arXiv preprint arXiv:1908.05355 (2019)

18. Miller, T.: Explanation in artificial intelligence: insights from the social sciences. Artif. Intell. **267**, 1–38 (2019)

19. Molnar, C.: Interpretable Machine Learning (2019). https://christophm.github.io/interpretable-ml-book/

20. Nakkiran, P., Kaplun, G., Bansal, Y., Yang, T., Barak, B., Sutskever, I.: Deep double descent: Where bigger models and more data hurt. arXiv preprint arXiv:1912.02292 (2019)

21. Obermeyer, Z., Powers, B., Vogeli, C., Mullainathan, S.: Dissecting racial bias in an algorithm used to manage the health of populations. Science **366**(6464), 447–453 (2019)

22. Rathi, S.: Generating counterfactual and contrastive explanations using SHAP. CoRR abs/1906.09293 (2019)

23. Ribeiro, M.T., Singh, S., Guestrin, C.: "why should I trust you?": explaining the predictions of any classifier. In: Proceedings of the 22nd ACM SIGKDD International Conference on Knowledge Discovery and Data Mining, San Francisco, CA, USA, 13–17 August 2016, pp. 1135–1144. ACM (2016)

24. Ribeiro, M.T., Wu, T., Guestrin, C., Singh, S.: Beyond accuracy: Behavioral testing of NLP models with checklist. In: Jurafsky, D., Chai, J., Schluter, N., Tetreault, J.R. (eds.) Proceedings of the 58th Annual Meeting of the Association for Computational Linguistics, ACL 2020, Online, 5–10 July 2020, pp. 4902–4912. Association for Computational Linguistics (2020)

25. Ross, A.S., Hughes, M.C., Doshi-Velez, F.: Right for the right reasons: training differentiable models by constraining their explanations. In: Sierra, C. (ed.) Proceedings of the Twenty-Sixth International Joint Conference on Artificial Intelligence, IJCAI 2017, Melbourne, Australia, 19–25 August 2017, pp. 2662–2670. ijcai.org (2017)

26. Semenova, L., Rudin, C., Parr, R.: A study in rashomon curves and volumes: a new perspective on generalization and model simplicity in machine learning. arXiv preprint arXiv:1908.01755 (2019)

27. Slack, D., Hilgard, S., Jia, E., Singh, S., Lakkaraju, H.: Fooling LIME and SHAP: adversarial attacks on post hoc explanation methods. In: Markham, A.N., Powles, J., Walsh, T., Washington, A.L. (eds.) Proceedings of AIES, pp. 180–186. ACM (2020)

28. Wang, H., Ge, S., Lipton, Z.C., Xing, E.P.: Learning robust global representations by penalizing local predictive power. In: Wallach, H.M., Larochelle, H., Beygelzimer, A., d'Alché-Buc, F., Fox, E.B., Garnett, R. (eds.) Advances in Neural Information Processing Systems 32: Annual Conference on Neural Information Processing Systems 2019, NeurIPS 2019, 8–14 December 2019, Vancouver, BC, Canada, pp. 10506–10518 (2019)
29. Wilson, A.G., Izmailov, P.: Bayesian deep learning and a probabilistic perspective of generalization. arXiv preprint arXiv:2002.08791 (2020)
30. Wu, J.T., et al.: Estimating clinical severity of covid-19 from the transmission dynamics in Wuhan, China. Nature Medicine, pp. 1–5 (2020)
31. Yalcin, O., Fan, X., Liu, S.: Evaluating the correctness of explainable AI algorithms for classification. CoRR abs/2105.09740 (2021)

Generation of Environment-Irrelevant Adversarial Digital Camouflage Patterns

Xu Teng[1], Hui Zhang[2(✉)], Bo Li[1], Chunming Yang[1], and Xujian Zhao[1]

[1] School of Computer Science and Technology, Southwest University of Science and Technology, Mianyang 621010, Sichuan, China
[2] School of Science, Southwest University of Science and Technology, Mianyang 621010, Sichuan, China
zhanghui@swust.edu.cn

Abstract. Digital camouflage is the most common and effective means to combat military reconnaissance. Traditional digital camouflage generation methods must regenerate camouflage images according to the current environment. When the environment changes, generated camouflage images may be detected by neural network classification models. We present a digital camouflage generation model based on disentangled representation, which can decompose images into a content space and a style space, thereby recombining the current content of the environment image with different digital camouflage styles. When the environment changes, our model can generate digital camouflage images based on the original environment content and the corresponding digital camouflage style, without obtaining the current environment image. To counter the detection of the classification models, we design a category reordering function to mislead the classification result of the classification model. Experiments show that the proposed method can generate digital camouflage images in different seasons and successfully implement an adversarial attack on the classification model.

Keyword: Camouflage generation · Disentangled representation · Style transfer · Adversarial attack

1 Introduction

Digital camouflage technology is an important military protection method which coats the designed camouflage patterns on the surface of the moving target, in order to decrease the saliency of the target and conceal the target in the background environment [1]. Traditional digital camouflage generation methods mainly include three aspects: selection of the main color, design of camouflage spots and combination of the generated spots. However, traditional digital camouflage generation methods may have appealing camouflage performance in the specified environment, but with the environment changes, the

---

Supported by Key Project of Sichuan Provincial Department of Science and Technology (2021YFG0031).

D. N. Pham et al. (Eds.): PRICAI 2021, LNAI 13031, pp. 336–346, 2021.
https://doi.org/10.1007/978-3-030-89188-6_25

camouflage performance will be considerably weakened. At the same time, generated camouflage may be detected by neural network models [2].

Several efforts have been made to combine digital camouflage generation with deep neural networks. In [3], a deep convolution adversarial auto-encoder network is used to extract and describe the configuration features of the spots in the background. In [4], a new digital camouflage spots extraction and reproduction method based on generative adversarial network is proposed to directly fit the distribution of deformation camouflage pattern spots. However, the above methods only use deep neural networks to extract better patterns of digital camouflage, cannot generate digital camouflage images based on the same environment adapting to the changes of different environmental characteristics. Moreover, the threat of neural network classification models has also not been considered in digital camouflage generating methods.

In this work, we propose an environment-irrelevant digital camouflage generation model which can generate without environmental change and resist the detection of neural network image classification models. We assume that the digital camouflage images in domain X and the environment images in domain Y share the same content space and also have specific style space. This model learns the features of digital camouflage patterns from different environments and maps them to the same background content to generate digital camouflage. At the same time, we propose an adversarial sample category loss to mislead the classification model with incorrect classification.

2 Related Work

Digital Camouflage Generation and Detection. Alfimtsev et al. [5] design a camouflage pattern generation system based on the characteristics of the deep neural network recognition system and human observers. Zheng et al. [6] propose a model through the Dense Deconvolution Network to accurately detect hidden camouflage people. Experimental results show that the proposed method outperforms the classical camouflaged object detection method and general CNN-based detection methods. In this work, we propose an environment-irrelevant digital camouflage generation method for the digital camouflage generation. Different from the aforementioned digital generation methods, our method generates digital camouflage without the need for the current environment image.

Disentangled Representations. Disentangled representation aims at modeling the factors of data variation. In [7], Mathieu et al. use labeled data to factorize representations into class-related and class-independent components. In [8, 9], Gatys et al. demonstrate that texture synthesis and image style can be extracted by convolutional neural networks. Similar to MUNIT [10] and DRIT [11], we first encode the environmental images and digital camouflage images into a shared content space and then encode the digital camouflage images with varying environmental characteristics into a specific style space. To better align the environmental content and the digital camouflage content, we apply an alignment feature loss to generate digital camouflage images which combine different environmental features with the same environmental content features.

Adversarial Attacks. Szegedy et al. [12] find that new samples obtained by adding slight disturbances to the original data enable the machine learning model to output incorrect classifications with high confidence. Traditional adversarial attack methods usually add special perturbations to the original image to accomplish an attack. However, the purpose of generating digital camouflage is to damage the surface structure of the camouflaged target, and the camouflaged target can be integrated with the surrounding environment through the fine patches of the digital camouflage. Therefore, we cannot simply add perturbations to the original images to achieve an adversarial attack. In this paper, we treat digital camouflage as a special perturbation and define a reordered function to constrain the classification results of the adversarial samples.

3 Proposed Method

For generate digital camouflage with different environmental characteristics and attack image classification models, we first propose a design scheme for an adversarial digital camouflage generation model based on disentangled representation in Sect. 3.1. The proposed adversarial sample category loss that enables the image classification model misclassification is described in Sect. 3.2. Finally, we will detail the other loss functions in Sect. 3.3.

3.1 Model Overview

Let $x \in X$, $y \in Y$ as images from the environment image domain and the digital camouflage domain. As we regard the generation of digital camouflage as a mapping from the background environment domain to the digital camouflage domain, where our framework consists of content encoders $\{E_X^c, E_Y^c\}$, style encoders $\{E_X^s, E_Y^s\}$, generators $\{G_X, G_Y\}$, and domain discriminators $\{G_X, G_Y\}$ for two domains. The environmental image x is first encoded into the shared content space $(c_x = E_X^c(x))$ and the digital camouflage image y is encoded into the specific style space $(s_y = E_Y^s(y))$. In MUNIT and DRIT, they translate one domain to another domain through the generator to recombine the content features and the style feature. However, due to the large structural difference between the environment image and the digital camouflage, the environment content feature c_x cannot be properly integrated with the digital camouflage style feature s_y. In order to better align the features between environment images and digital camouflage images, we aligned content features from the background environment domain X and the digital camouflage domain Y by the content alignment function Map_c. After aligning the content feature by:

$$c_{xtoy} = Map_{c_{share}2c_y}(c_x, c_y), \tag{1}$$

we can generate better digital camouflage images by $y_{xtoy} = G_y(c_{xtoy}, s_y)$. However, it is difficult to define he content alignment function Map_c precisely. In this paper, we use the feature alignment loss L_{remain}^y to learn the alignment function. For finding the alignment function Map_c, we require that the feature alignment loss L_{remain}^y to force the content feature c_{down_y} obtained by down sampling which is similar to the aligned content feature

c_{xtoy}. Therefore, the content feature c_{xtoy} could align with the digital camouflage style better (Fig. 1). The feature alignment loss L^y_{remain} is defined as:

$$L^y_{remain} = E_{y \sim p(y)}[|||c_{down\_y} - Map_{c_{share}2c_y}(c_x, c_y)||]_1 \qquad (2)$$

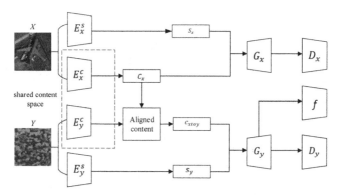

Fig. 1. The framework of the digital camouflage generation method.

3.2 Adversarial Sample Category Loss

We expect the generated camouflage images could mislead the image classification model to output incorrect results, so we introduce the adversarial sample recognition module to attack the image classification model. We use the VGG-16 [13] to classify the generated digital camouflage samples. The classification results are reordered to constrain the classification categories of adversarial samples that were previously used for classification purposes. The structure of the adversarial sample recognition module is illustrated in Fig. 2.

The generated digital camouflage will damage the original image representation to a certain extent, and the purpose of the generated adversarial samples is to mislead the classification model. However, if the classify labels of the adversarial samples deviate too much from the original labels, the generation model may fail to fit the distribution of the original images. To address this problem, we set some constraints on the category loss to ensure the classification result of the adversarial sample deviate not far from the original category. The purpose of the adversarial attack is to make the classification model misclassify the image x. Assuming that there are N categories, the output vector. is defined as $T_N(x) = [l_1, l_2, \ldots, l_i, \ldots, l_N](l_1 + l_2 + \cdots + l_N = 1)$, where the l_i represents the probability of x belong to i th category. We randomly select a category t 1 which different with the true category of the image x as the target category. We set $l_t =$ in the output vector and introduce a reordering function:

$$Reorder(x) = softmax([l_1, l_2, \ldots, l_t, \ldots, l_{true}, \ldots, l_N]) \qquad (3)$$

The reordering function ensures the output of the target category is maximized while maintaining the original classification result as much as possible. In this way, we can maintain the original classification result to a certain extent and ensure the target category has the highest classification score. The adversarial sample category loss combined with the reordering function is defined as:

$$L_{adv}^{label} = E_{x \sim X}[\sum_{i=1}^{N} -f(x) \log(Reorder(G_y(c_x, s_x))) - (1 - f(x)) \log(1 - Reorder(G_y(c_x, s_x)))] \quad (4)$$

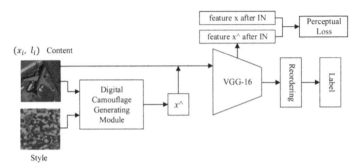

Fig. 2. The overall structure of the adversarial sample recognition module.

3.3 Other Losses

In addition to the proposed adversarial sample category loss, we also use several other loss functions to facilitate network training. The used loss functions include functions for style transfer and functions for image-to-image translation.

Image Reconstruction Loss. Since the generation model adopts the structure of the encoder and the decoder, the image reconstruction loss is used to ensure the generator can perform the image reconstruction. Therefore, we define the loss of image reconstruction for the generators as follows:

$$L_{recon}^{x} = E_{x \sim p(x)}[||G_x(c_x, s_x) - x||_1] \quad (5)$$

$$L_{recon}^{y} = E_{y \sim p(y)}[||G_y(c_{xtoy}, s_y) - y||_1] \quad (6)$$

Style Reconstruction Loss. In order to enable the model to learn specific style features of images, we defined the style reconstruction loss L_{recon}^{s}. When different kinds of digital camouflage (such as forest camouflage, desert camouflage, snow camouflage, etc.) are used as the style features, the loss function enables the model to generate diverse digital camouflage output under the same background environment.

$$L_{recon}^{s_x} = E_{x \sim p(x)}[||E_x^s(G_x(c_x, s_x)) - s_x||_1] \quad (7)$$

$$L_{recon}^{s_y} = E_{y \sim p(y)}[||E_y^p(G_y(c_{xtoy}, s_y)) - s_y||_1] \quad (8)$$

Adversarial Loss. Since the structure of generating countermeasure network is adopted to ensure that the data distribution of the generated image is consistent with that of the original image. The adversarial loss is used to ensure that the discriminator D_x and D_y can distinguish the difference between the real image and the generated image, so that the generated model can generate more real images.

$$L_{adv}^{domain} = E_{x \sim X}\left[\log D_x(x)\right] + E_{c_x, s_x}\left[\log(1 - D_x(G_x(c_x, s_x)))\right] + E_{y \sim Y}\left[\log D_y(y)\right]$$
$$+ E_{c_{xtoy}, s_y}\left[\log(1 - D_y(G_y(c_{xtoy}, s_y)))\right]$$
(9)

Cross-cycle Consistency Loss. We hope that after generating the digital camouflage based on the background image, the generated image can still be converted to the original background image. As the cyclic consistency loss proposed by Unpaired Image-to-Image Translation using Cycle-Consistent Adversarial Networks (CycleGAN) [14] makes the generation model maintain the original spatial image features in the cross-domain image generation problem, we adopt the cyclic consistency loss function in our model.

$$L_{cycle}^x = E_{x \sim X}[||x_{x \sim y \sim x} - x||_1]$$
(10)

$$L_{cycle}^y = E_{y \sim Y}[||y_{y \sim x \sim y} - y||_1]$$
(11)

Perceptual Loss. In order to perform cross domain image conversion better, we use the perceptual loss to retain the content features of the original image.

$$L_{per}^x = E_{x, xtoy}\left[||E_y^c(xtoy) - E_x^c(x)||_1\right]$$
(12)

$$L_{per}^y = E_{y, ytox}[||E_x^c(ytox) - E_y^c(y)||_1]$$
(13)

Total Loss. We jointly train the encoders, decoders, and discriminators to optimize thefinal objective, which is a weighted sum of the adversarial loss and the bidirectional reconstruction loss terms.

$$\min_{E_x, E_y, G_x, G_y D_x, D_y} \max L(E_x, E_y, G_x, G_y, D_x, D_y) = \lambda_{map}\left(L_{remain}^y\right) + \lambda_{image}\left(L_{recon}^x + L_{recon}^y\right)$$
$$+ \lambda_s\left(L_{recon}^{s_x} + L_{recon}^{s_y}\right) + \lambda_{cc}\left(L_{cycle}^x + L_{cycle}^y\right) + \lambda_{adv}\left(L_{adv}^x + L_{adv}^y\right) + \lambda_{label}L_{adv}^{label} + \lambda_{pre}(L_{per}^x + L_{per}^y)$$
(14)

where $\lambda_{map}, \lambda_{image}, \lambda_s, \lambda_{cc}, \lambda_{adv}, \lambda_{label}$ are weights that control the importance of reconstruction terms.

4 Experimental Results

4.1 Datasets

We select a variety of natural background images and digital camouflage images from the Internet as experimental datasets, including 1000 natural background images and 1000 digital camouflage images, as well as 300 tank images and 300 aircraft images. In order to unify the input of the datasets, all images are cropped to 256 * 256 pixels after image preprocessing. Because there are no uniform labels for the natural background images, only the labeled tank and aircraft data sets are used in the adversarial attack training.

4.2 Compared Methods

We compare our method with MUNIT and DRIT for comparative experiments. Both of them learn multi-modal mappings between two domains. For multi-domain comparisons, we train these models multiple times for every pair of image domains. All the methods are trained using the implementations provided by the authors.

4.3 Qualitative Comparisons

We use Canny edge detector to measure the visual camouflage effect of the generated digital camouflage. Canny edge detector uses a multi-stage algorithm to detect a wide range of edges in images and also detect and extract the spots in the background region.

When using the same environment image as the input of the model, the outputs of digital camouflage maintain certain structural characteristics and have different seasonal characteristics (such as the snow season, desertification and other climate conditions under the same background). Figure 3 shows the digital camouflage generated from different seasons within the same background environment, where the first row is the semi-desertification area, the second row is the desert environment and the third row is the grassland. Figure 3(a) is the natural image, Fig. 3(b) is the digital camouflage generated by the proposed model, Fig. 3(c) and Fig. 3(d) are images generated from MUNIT and DRIT.

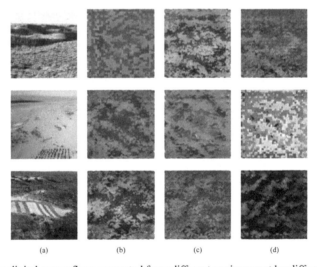

(a)   (b)   (c)   (d)

Fig. 3. The digital camouflage generated from different environment by different models.

Figure 4 shows the results of digital camouflage and edge detection. The first row shows the input environment image and the generated digital camouflage, the second row shows the Canny edge detection results corresponding to the images shown in first row. The third row and the fourth row are same with the first and the second row. Figure 4(a) is the input background image, Fig. 4(b) is the digital camouflage generated by the

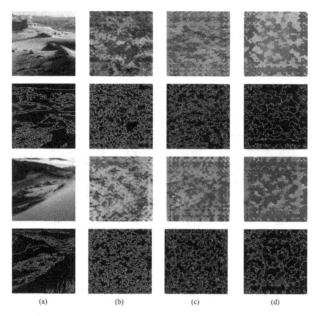

(a)   (b)   (c)   (d)

Fig. 4. The generation of digital camouflage and edge detection results by different models.

proposed model, Fig. 4(c) is the digital camouflage generated by MUNIT, and Fig. 4(d) is the digital camouflage generated by DRIT. From the generated digital camouflage and edge detection images, it can be seen that the digital camouflage generated by DRIT and MUNIT have more regular edges, which make the camouflage easier to be detected by the edge detection model. However, the above two models use the content features of background image without alignment which resulted in more overlapping textures around the generated digital camouflage. The digital camouflage generated by the proposed model has more irregular image edges, leading the generated digital camouflage by the proposed model has better camouflage effects than that generated by MUNIT and DRIT.

4.4 Quantitative Comparison

Due to the particularities of camouflage, compared with ordinary images, camouflage should blend with the surrounding background as much as possible while retaining the original texture structure of the background. We choose the SSIM [15] structural similarity algorithm to quantitatively evaluate the digital camouflage generated by different models, and the results are shown in Table 1. Lower SSIM scores indicate better camouflage effects. From Table 1 we can see that the proposed model has the lowest SSIM score thus achieves the best camouflage effect. Both of the qualitative comparison results and the quantitative comparison results show that the proposed model obtains the best camouflage effects.

(a)   (b)   (c)

Fig. 5. The camouflage image obtained by the aircraft and tank images

Table 1. SSIM evaluation score of edge detection results from different models

	The proposed model	MUNIT	DRIT
SSIM score	0.318	0.394	0.469

For the adversarial attack problem of neural network classification model, the tanks and aircraft images are used which are commonly used in military. The adversarial sample category loss function is used in training to reduce the output accuracy of the correct category of the classifier and improve the output accuracy of the target category. If the accuracy of the target category is the highest, it demonstrates that the attack is success. The image classification model uses the VGG-16 model which has been pretrained by ImageNet, and the target categories are also selected from the categories owned by ImageNet. Figure 5 shows the camouflage images obtained by the fusion of digital camouflage generated based on camouflage targets (aircraft and tank). Figure 5(a) shows the origin aircraft and tank images, Fig. 5(b) shows the digital camouflage styles, Fig. 5(c) shows the generated digital camouflage with adversarial attack on Fig. 5(a).

Table 2. Classification accuracy of the tank dataset with different conditions

Target category	Real category	Target category after attacking	Real category after attacking
Amphibian	95.58	87.81	8.27
Automobile	95.58	79.42	13.20

Table 2 and Table 3 show the accuracy of classifying the target categories to the origin categories after adversarial attack in tank dataset and aircraft dataset. We choose amphibian and automobile as the target categories in Table 2, we choose folding chair and pinwheel as the target categories in Table 3. In Table 2 and Table 3, the first column

Table 3. Classification accuracy of the aircraft dataset with different conditions

Target category	Real category	Target category after attacking	Real category after attacking
Folding chair	79.91	65.39	17.21
Pinwheel	79.91	72.19	14.78

shows the specified target categories, the second column shows the accuracy of the real category without attack, the third column shows the accuracy of the target category after attacking and the fourth column shows the accuracy of the real category after attacking.

The classification model without adversarial attack has high classification accuracy. The purpose of proposed reordering function is to use specified target category to replace the role of the real category. Leading the classification model to produce wrong output and realize the purpose of adversarial attack. Therefore, the classification accuracy after adversarial attack should be greatly reduced for the real category, while the classification accuracy for the specified target category should be greatly increased.

As shown in the second column to the fourth column in Table 2 and Table 3, after the adversarial attacking, the target categories we appointed have higher accuracy. The accuracy of real category decreases greatly after adversarial attacking. The results show that the proposed adversarial attack method achieves the expected objective.

5   Conclusion

In this paper, we propose an environment-irrelevant adversarial digital camouflage generation model. It deconstructs the content features and style features from different domains, and aligns the content features of the environment images to the digital camouflage content features, improving the generalization effects of digital camouflage. In order to implement an adversarial attack on the classification model, we propose an adversarial sample category loss to mislead the classification model. Qualitative and quantitative results show that the proposed model produces better digital camouflage than other works. The experimental results show that the proposed adversarial attack method reduces the accuracy of the real category successfully.

References

1. Cuthill, I.C.: Camouflage. J. Zool. **308**(2), 75–92 (2019)
2. Zhuo, L., Chen, X.Q., Xie, Z.P., Jiang, X.J., Bi, D.K.: Simulation learning method for discovery of camouflage targets based on deep neural networks. Laser Optoelectron. Progress **56**(7), 071102 (2019)
3. Yang, X., Xu, W.D., Jia, Q., Li, L.: Research on digital camouflage pattern generation algorithm based on adversarial autoencoder network. Int. J. Pattern Recogn. Artif. Intell. **34**(06), 2050017 (2020)
4. Yang, X., et al.: Research on extraction and reproduction of deformation camouflage spots based on generative adversarial network model. Defence Technol. **16**(3), 555–563 (2020)

5. Alfimtsev, A.N., Sakulin, S.A., Loktev, D.A., Kovalenko, A.O., Devyatkov, V.V.: Hostis humani ET mashinae: adversarial camouflage generation. J. Adv. Res. Dyn. Control Syst. **11**(2), 506–516 (2019)

6. Zheng, Y., Zhang, X., Wang, F., Cao, T., Sun, M., Wang, X.: Detection of people with camouflage pattern via dense deconvolution network. IEEE Signal Process. Lett. **26**(1), 29–33 (2018)

7. Mathieu, M., Zhao, J., Sprechmann, P., Ramesh, A., LeCun, Y.: Disentangling factors of variation in deep representations using adversarial training. In: NeurIPS (2016)

8. Gatys, L., Ecker, A.S., Bethge, M.: Texture synthesis using convolutional neural networks. In: NeurIPS (2015)

9. Gatys, L.A., Ecker, A.S., Bethge, M.: Image style transfer using convolutional neural networks. In: CVPR (2016)

10. Huang, X., Liu, M.-Y., Belongie, S., Kautz, J.: Multimodal unsupervised image-to-image translation. In: Ferrari, V., Hebert, M., Sminchisescu, C., Weiss, Y. (eds.) ECCV 2018. LNCS, vol. 11207, pp. 179–196. Springer, Cham (2018). https://doi.org/10.1007/978-3-030-01219-9_11

11. Lee, H.-Y., Tseng, H.-Y., Huang, J.-B., Singh, M., Yang, M.-H.: Diverse image-to-image translation via disentangled representations. In: Ferrari, V., Hebert, M., Sminchisescu, C., Weiss, Y. (eds.) ECCV 2018. LNCS, vol. 11205, pp. 36–52. Springer, Cham (2018). https://doi.org/10.1007/978-3-030-01246-5_3

12. Szegedy, C., et al.: Intriguing properties of neural networks. In: ICLR (2014)

13. Simonyan, K., Zisserman, A.: Very deep convolutional networks for large-scale image recognition. In: ICLR (2015)

14. Zhu, J.Y., Park, T., Isola, P., Efros, A.A.: Unpaired image-to-image translation using cycle-consistent adversarial networks. In: ICCV (2017)

15. Wang, Z., Bovik, A.C., Sheikh, H.R., Simoncelli, E.P.: Image quality assessment: from error visibility to structural similarity. IEEE Trans. Image Process. **13**(4), 600–612 (2004)

Magnitude-Weighted Mean-Shift Clustering with Leave-One-Out Bandwidth Estimation

Yuki Yamagishi[1,2(✉)], Kazumi Saito[2], Kazuro Hirahara[2], and Naonori Ueda[2]

[1] Faculty of Informatics, Shizuoka Institute of Science and Technology,
Fukuroi, Japan
yamagishi.yuki@sist.ac.jp
[2] Center for Advanced Intelligence Project, RIKEN, Kyoto, Japan
{yuki.yamagishi.ks,kazumi.saito,kazuro.hirahara,naonori.ueda}@riken.jp

Abstract. In this paper, we address the problem of clustering earthquakes in a catalog, which is also known as declustering in seismology, i.e., a task of classifying each earthquake into foreshock, mainshock, or aftershock. For this purpose, we newly propose a magnitude-weighted mean-shift clustering algorithm equipped with a leave-one-out procedure for estimating its bandwidth parameter. Although there exist a wide variety of clustering techniques in machine learning, we employ the mean-shift approach because each spatio-temporal event with magnitude can be naturally regarded as a weighted Gaussian kernel function, and the number of clusters can be automatically determined by a bandwidth parameter, where some standard statistical resampling techniques can estimate this parameter. In our experiments, we generated our dataset of earthquakes with magnitudes ≥ 3.0 in 1997–2016 from the earthquake catalog of the Japan Meteorological Agency that covered the whole of Japan and selected 24 major earthquakes which caused significant damage or casualties in Japan. In our experimental comparison with three representative clustering methods in seismology, i.e., the window method, single-link method, and correlation-metric method, we mainly show that concerning the clusters containing the 24 major earthquakes, the sizes of these clusters obtained by our proposed method are consistently smaller than those of the window or correlation-metric method, but larger than those of the single-link method. These results suggest that our proposed method is vital and has a promising characteristic.

Keywords: Declustering · Mean-shift clustering · Bandwidth estimation

1 Introduction

In seismology, there is a pressing need for understanding the relationships of earthquakes in an extensive catalog. Especially, earthquake declustering [20], which is tasked with classifying each earthquake into foreshock, mainshock, or

D. N. Pham et al. (Eds.): PRICAI 2021, LNAI 13031, pp. 347–358, 2021.
https://doi.org/10.1007/978-3-030-89188-6_26

aftershock, plays an essential role in many critical applications such as forecasting future earthquakes, modeling seismic activities, and so forth. Note that this declustering task can also be formalized as a standard clustering problem, which identifies each cluster containing a mainshock together with its foreshocks and aftershocks. Meanwhile, in machine learning, many sophisticated clustering techniques have been developed. One ultimate goal in this research is to explore advanced declustering algorithms under such sophisticated clustering techniques.

In this paper, by focusing on mean-shift clustering [4], we newly propose a magnitude-weighted mean-shift clustering algorithm equipped with a leave-one-out procedure for estimating its bandwidth parameter. Although there are many clustering techniques in machine learning, we employ the mean-shift approach for two reasons. First, since each earthquake in a catalog is expressed as a spatio-temporal event with magnitude, we can naturally formulate it as a weighted Gaussian kernel function. Second, although determining an adequate number of clusters might be challenging for some clustering techniques such as hierarchical clustering or k-means algorithm, this number can be automatically determined by a bandwidth parameter, and some standard statistical resampling techniques can estimate this parameter. In our experiments, we generated our dataset from an earthquake catalog that covered Japan and selected 24 major earthquakes which caused significant damage or casualties in Japan. In our experimental comparison with three representative clustering methods in seismology, i.e., the window method, single-link method, and correlation-metric method, we compare the clustering results containing the above 24 major earthquakes in terms of the cluster sizes, similarity matrices, and earthquake visualization results.

An outline of this paper is given below. Section 2 describes related conventional algorithms for earthquake declustering and mean-shift clustering. As preliminaries, Sect. 3 details the conventional declustering algorithms used in our experimental evaluation for comparison purposes. After that, Sect. 4 presents our magnitude-weighted mean-shift clustering algorithm, equipped with a leave-one-out procedure for estimating its bandwidth parameter. In Sect. 5, we report our experimental results using an existing Japanese earthquake catalog and discuss notable characteristics of our proposed method. Finally, Sect. 6 gives concluding remarks and future problems.

2   Related Work

One of the representative clustering methods is hierarchical cluster analysis such as linkage methods [17–19], and the other is partitioning methods such as the k-means algorithm [13]. In seismology, declustering algorithms (e.g., [22]) focusing partitioning seismicity into groups closer in space and time than expected in a purely random distribution have been studied. Yamagishi et al. [21] proposed a clustering method using linkage based on the declustering algorithms in the Japanese earthquake catalog, but it suffers from the same problem that cannot determine an adequate number of clusters as the representative methods described above. Therefore, we adopt the mean-shift algorithm described below, automatically determining the number of clusters by a bandwidth parameter.

In seismology, declustering is the task of classifying each earthquake in a catalog into foreshock, mainshock, or aftershock, and tremendous efforts have been devoted to developing effective algorithms for this task [20]. Knopoff & Gardner [9,12] proposed a pioneering algorithm known as the window method, which identifies aftershocks by assigning a window with some length and duration parameters to each earthquake regarded as a mainshock. Reasenberg [16] proposed another algorithm known as the cluster method, which assumes an interaction zone centered on each earthquake. Zhuang et al. [24–26] proposed a stochastic declustering algorithm also known as stochastic reconstruction using the ETAS (epidemic-type aftershock sequence) model [14,15]. Frohlich and Davis [5,8] proposed another declustering algorithm, also known as the single-link cluster analysis, which utilizes a spatio-temporal distance with respect to given two earthquakes. Baiesi & Paczuski [1] proposed a spatio-temporal distance known as correlation-metric, and based on this metric, Zaliapin et al. [23] proposed another declustering algorithm, which identifies background earthquakes (mainshocks) by rescaling its distance and time.

The mean-shift algorithm is a recursive computing procedure using a nonparametric probability density estimator based on the Parzen window kernel function [4]. The detailed mathematical derivation of the mean-shift procedure is given in the study of a robust approach for characterizing multi-layered forests using airborne laser scanning (ALS) data [7]. Mean-shift works by placing a kernel on each point in the data set. The kernel, a function that determines the weight of nearby points for re-estimating the mean, is iteratively shifted with a bandwidth (namely the diameter of the hyper-sphere) to a denser region until it converges to a stationary point. Namely, the choice of the kernel bandwidth h is very critical. Many adaptive or variable bandwidth selection techniques have been proposed for the mean-shift concerning 2D imagery analysis. Comaniciu [3] proposed a variable bandwidth technique that imposes a local structure on the data to extract reliable scale information by maximizing the magnitude of the normalized mean-shift-vector. Huang and Zhang [11] proposed that separability in feature space or local homogeneity can be exploited to adaptively select bandwidth parameters for remote-sensing image classification and object recognition. Bo et al. [2] proposed that the neighborhood's local scale and structure information around individual samples can also be utilized to calibrate the kernel bandwidth in an adaptive mean-shift procedure to find arbitrary density, size, and shape clusters in remote sensing imagery.

3 Declustering Algorithms for Earthquake Data

For the i-th observed event (earthquake), we denote its occurrence position, occurrence time, and magnitude by r_i, t_i, and m_i, in this order, where r_i is a 3-dimensional vector obtained as $r_i = (longitude_i, latitude_i, depth_i)$. Then, we express the set of observed events as $\mathcal{D} = \{(r_i, t_i, m_i) \mid 1 \leq i \leq N\}$, where $t_i < t_j$ if $i < j$. Namely, we assign the index i to each event in chronological order from oldest to most recent ones. In this paper, among representative clustering (declustering) methods developed in seismology, we focus on the window method [9,12], the single-link method [5,8], and the correlation-metric method [1,23], which are referred to as WI, SL, and CM, respectively. Now, we explain these methods as a unified graph decomposition algorithm. Namely, we first construct a directed graph $G = (\mathcal{V}, \mathcal{E})$ by connecting the pairs of related events according to the definition of each method, where $\mathcal{V} = \{1, \cdots, N\}$ and $\mathcal{E} \subset \mathcal{V} \times \mathcal{V}$ denote the sets of nodes and links, respectively. Then, by decomposing the constructed graph G into weakly connected components, we can obtain the clusters of events as the sets of nodes belonging to the same components.

For each event i, the WI method defines the spatio and temporal metrics, $d(i)$ [km] and $t(i)$ [days], as

$$d(i) = 10^{0.1238*m_i + 0.983}, \quad t(i) = \begin{cases} 10^{0.032*m_i + 2.7389}, & \text{if } m_i \geq 6.5 \\ 10^{0.5409*m_i - 0.547}, & \text{else} \end{cases}, \quad (1)$$

and then compute the set $\mathcal{V}^{WI}(i)$ of events belonging to the window of event i, as $\mathcal{V}^{WI}(i) = \{j \mid i < j \leq N, \ \|r_i - r_j\| \leq d(i), \ t_j - t_i \leq t(i)\}$. The WI method constructs a graph G by selecting the following link set, $\mathcal{E}^{WI} = \{(i,j) \mid 1 \leq i \leq N, \ j \in \mathcal{V}^{WI}(i)\}$. Note that the event $j \in \mathcal{V}_i^{WI}$ is regarded as the child node (aftershock) of i.

For each pair of two events i and j, the SL method defines the spatio-temporal metric $d(i,j)$ as $d(i,j) = \sqrt{\|r_i - r_j\|^2 + C^2(t_j - t_i)^2}$, where the spatio-temporal scaling constant C is set to $C = 1$ [km/day] [5,8]. The SL method constructs a graph G by selecting the following link set, $\mathcal{E}^{SL} = \{(i^{SL}(j),j) \mid 2 \leq j \leq N, \ d(i^{SL}(j),j) < D\}$, where $i^{SL}(j) = \arg\min\{d(i,j) \mid 1 \leq i < j\}$, $D = 9.4\sqrt{S} - 25.2$, and S is the median of all $d(i^{SL}(j),j)$ distances. Note that the event $i^{SL}(j)$ is regarded as the parent node (foreshock) of j.

For each pair of two events i and j such that $i < j$, by using the rescaled distance $R(i,j)$ and time $T(i,j)$,

$$R(i,j) = \|r_i - r_j\|^{d_f} 10^{-b\,m_i/2}, \quad T(i,j) = (t_j - t_i)10^{-b\,m_i/2}. \quad (2)$$

the CM method defines the spatio-temporal metric as $n(i,j) = T(i,j) \times R(i,j)$, where the fractal dimension d_f is set to $d_f = 1.6$ and the parameter b of the Gutenberg-Richter law is set to $b = 0.95$ [1]. The CM method first classifies $\mathcal{X} = \{(T(i^{CM}(j),j), R(i^{CM}(j),j)) \mid 2 \leq j \leq N\}$ into the background and cluster components, $\mathcal{BX}$ and $\mathcal{CX}$, i.e., $\mathcal{X} = \mathcal{BX} \cup \mathcal{CX}$, by applying a Gaussian mixture clustering procedure, and then constructs a graph G by selecting the following link set, $\mathcal{E}^{CM} = \{(i^{CM}(j),j) \mid 2 \leq j \leq N, \ (T(i^{CM}(j),j), R(i^{CM}(j),j)) \in \mathcal{CX}\}$, where $i^{CM}(j) = \arg\min\{n(i,j) \mid 1 \leq i < j\}$. Note that the event $i^{CM}(j)$ is regarded as the parent node (foreshock) of j. Finally, it should be mentioned that according to the standard machine learning approach, we classify the observed events into $\mathcal{BX}$ and $\mathcal{CX}$ by selecting the class with the largest posterior probability, rather than determining some threshold value to the metric $n(i,j)$.

4   Proposed Method

We propose a magnitude-weighted mean-shift clustering algorithm equipped with a leave-one-out procedure for estimating its bandwidth parameter h. For each observed event i, we introduce an $(M = 4)$-dimensional vector $\boldsymbol{x}_i$ constructed by arranging $\boldsymbol{r}_i$ and t_i for the i-th observed event, i.e., $\boldsymbol{x}_i = (\boldsymbol{r}_i, t_i)$, where we adopt a scaling to be 1 [km/day] as performed in the SL method. Then, we assign the following Gaussian kernel function to each event i,

$$g_i(\boldsymbol{u}; h) = \frac{1}{(2\pi h)^{M/2}} \exp\left(-\frac{1}{2h}||\boldsymbol{u} - \boldsymbol{x}_i||^2\right), \tag{3}$$

where $\boldsymbol{u}$ means an arbitrary M-dimensional vector. Now, by using a weight value $w_i = 10^{m_i}$ for the i-th kernel function, we define the following magnitude-weighted Gaussian mixture probability density function, i.e.,

$$G(\boldsymbol{u}; h) = \frac{\sum_{i=1}^{N} w_i g_i(\boldsymbol{u}; h)}{\sum_{i=1}^{N} w_i}. \tag{4}$$

Note that the spatio-temporal event i with magnitude m_i can be naturally regarded as the above weighted kernel function. According to Gutenberg-Richter (GR) law [10], the frequency of earthquakes with the magnitude m_i is proportional to $10^{-b\,m_i}$, where b is called b-value and close to 1.0. Therefore, this weighting factor of $w_i = 10^{m_i}$ compensates for the earthquake frequency dependent on the magnitude. Now, we briefly explain the clustering procedure by the mean-shift algorithm. Namely, after setting $\boldsymbol{u}^{(0)} \leftarrow \boldsymbol{x}_j$ for each event j and $s \leftarrow 0$, by repeatedly performing the following mean-shift operation,

$$\boldsymbol{u}^{(s+1)} \leftarrow \frac{\sum_{i=1}^{N} w_i g_i(\boldsymbol{u}^{(s)}; h)\boldsymbol{x}_i}{\sum_{i=1}^{N} w_i g_i(\boldsymbol{u}^{(s)}; h)}, \tag{5}$$

and $s \leftarrow s+1$, we can obtain the converged vector $\boldsymbol{u}(\boldsymbol{x}_j)$. Finally, we can produce a resultant cluster as the following set of events.

$$\mathcal{R}_j = \{k \mid 1 \leq k \leq N, \boldsymbol{u}(\boldsymbol{x}_k) = \boldsymbol{u}(\boldsymbol{x}_j)\}. \tag{6}$$

Thus, we can see that the number of clusters is automatically determined from a given bandwidth h. Hereafter, we referred to our magnitude-weighted mean-shift clustering method as MS.

We describe our leave-one-out procedure for estimating the bandwidth parameter h. Namely, by excluding the i-th kernel function, we introduce our leave-one-out magnitude-weighted Gaussian mixture probability density function.

$$G_i(\boldsymbol{u}; h) = \frac{\sum_{j=1, j\neq i}^{N} w_j g_j(\boldsymbol{u}; h)}{\sum_{j=1, j\neq i}^{N} w_j}, \tag{7}$$

Then, we define the following leave-one-out logarithmic likelihood function.

$$L(h) = \sum_{i=1}^{N} \log G_i(\boldsymbol{x}_i; h). \tag{8}$$

Based on likelihood maximization by the EM algorithm [6], we can obtain the following update formula to maximize $L(h)$ concerning h.

$$h \leftarrow \frac{1}{NM} \sum_{i=1}^{N} \sum_{j=1, j\neq i}^{N} q_{i,j}(h)||\boldsymbol{x}_i - \boldsymbol{x}_j||^2, \tag{9}$$

where the posterior probability $q_{i,j}(h)$ is defined as

$$q_{i,j}(h) = \frac{w_j g_j(\boldsymbol{x}; h)}{\sum_{k=1, k\neq i}^{N} w_k g_k(\boldsymbol{x}_i; h)} = \frac{w_j \exp(-||\boldsymbol{x}_i - \boldsymbol{x}_j||^2/(2h))}{\sum_{k=1, k\neq i}^{N} w_k \exp(-||\boldsymbol{x}_i - \boldsymbol{x}_k||^2/(2h))}. \tag{10}$$

Below we summarize our proposed algorithm.

Step1. Set h_0 to some initial value and $s \leftarrow 0$.
Step2. Update h_s as $h_{s+1} \leftarrow \frac{1}{NM} \sum_{i=1}^{N} \sum_{j=1, j\neq i}^{N} q_{i,j}(h_s)||\boldsymbol{x}_i - \boldsymbol{x}_j||^2$.
Step3. Output h_{s+1} as $\hat{h}$ and terminate if $|h_{s+1} - h_s|/h_s < \epsilon$; otherwise set $s \leftarrow s+1$ and return to Step2.

In our experiments described later, by setting $h_0 \leftarrow 1,000$ and $\epsilon = 0.0001$, we obtained the estimated value as $\hat{h} = 16.37$. Note that instead of $L(h)$ defined in Eq. (8), by maximizing $\tilde{L}(h) = \sum_{i=1}^{N} \log G(\boldsymbol{x}_i; h)$ with respect to h, we can obtain a standard maximum likelihood estimation result without using the leave-one-out procedure. However, since Eq. (10) changes as follows:

$$\tilde{q}_{i,j}(h) = \frac{w_j \exp(-||\boldsymbol{x}_i - \boldsymbol{x}_j||^2/(2h))}{w_i + \sum_{k=1, k\neq i}^{N} w_k \exp(-||\boldsymbol{x}_i - \boldsymbol{x}_k||^2/(2h))}, \tag{11}$$

we can see that in the case of the standard maximum likelihood estimation, the bandwidth h typically converges to 0 as an overfitted result.

5   Experimental Evaluation

We generated an original dataset from an earthquake catalog of the Japan Islands containing source parameters determined by the Japan Meteorological Agency[1] for experimental evaluation. Namely, we selected $N = 104,343$ events by restricting the minimum magnitude, maximum depth, and period to $M_{\min} = 3.0$, $D_{\max} = 100$ km, and Oct. 01, 1997, to Dec. 31, 2016, respectively. From this dataset, we selected 24 major earthquakes which caused significant damage or casualties in Japan. Table 1 shows the list of these earthquakes and their information about origin times, locations (longitude, latitude and depth), magnitudes, and names, where their *ids* are assigned according to the occurrence times.

First of all, with respect to the clusters obtained by the four methods, WI, CM, SL, and MS, we examine the basic statistics of their sizes. Figure 1 compares their distributions depicted by the size of clusters (SC) and the number

---

[1] https://www.data.jma.go.jp/svd/eqev/data/bulletin/hypo.html.

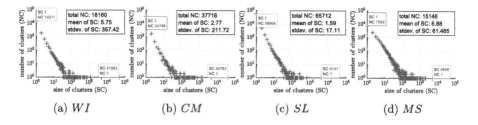

Fig. 1. Distribution and basic statistics of cluster sizes

of clusters (NC) corresponding to the horizontal and vertical axes, respectively, where Figs. 1a, 1b, 1c, and 1d show those obtained by WI, CM, SL, and MS, in this order, together with the total number, mean, and standard deviation of the cluster sizes. From these results, we can observe that the largest size of clusters obtained by WI is 47, 592 and 40, 789 by CM, which amount to almost half of the total number of observed events, c.f., $N = 104, 343$, and the number of single-member clusters obtained by SL is 56, 906, which also amounts to almost half of the total number N. On the other hand, we can see that the depicted result of MS is most likely to be approximated by a balanced power low distribution among these four methods.

Next, we focus on the clusters which contain the selected 24 major earthquakes shown in Table 1. For each method denoted by $mtd \in \{WI, CM, SL, MS\}$, let $\mathcal{R}_{id}^{mtd}$ be an obtained cluster which includes the major earthquake with $id \in \{1, \cdots, 24\}$ shown in Table 1. Also, for each cluster $\mathcal{R}_{id}^{mtd}$, we consider the following two subclusters, $\mathcal{RB}_{id}^{mtd} = \{h \in \mathcal{R}_{id}^{mtd} \mid t_h < t_{id}\}$ and $\mathcal{RA}_{id}^{mtd} = \{j \in \mathcal{R}_{id}^{mtd} \mid t_j > t_{id}\}$, i.e., the sets of events that occurred before and after the major earthquakes, respectively. Note that $|\mathcal{R}_{id}^{mtd}| = |\mathcal{RB}_{id}^{mtd}| + |\mathcal{RA}_{id}^{mtd}| + 1$.

Table 2 compares the size of these clusters obtained by the four methods. From our experimental results, we can obtain the following three observations. First, we can observe that in the cases of the three id pairs of 4 & 5, 14 & 15, and 22 & 23, the same clustering results were obtained by any $mtd \in \{WI, CM, MS\}$, i.e., $\mathcal{R}_4^{mtd} = \mathcal{R}_5^{mtd}$, $\mathcal{R}_{14}^{mtd} = \mathcal{R}_{15}^{mtd}$, and $\mathcal{R}_{22}^{mtd} = \mathcal{R}_{23}^{mtd}$. In fact, as described in Table 1, these are the well-known pairs of foreshocks and mainshocks about the 2004 Kii-Peninsula, 2011 Tohoku, and 2016 Kumamoto earthquakes. We consider that these results might show the part of the validity of these clustering methods.

Second, we can observe that for each $mtd \in \{WI, CM\}$, after the earthquake with $id \geq 14$, the same clustering results were obtained, i.e., $\mathcal{R}_{14}^{mtd} = \mathcal{R}_{id}^{mtd}$ except for the results with $id = 22$ and 23, as well as $id = 19$ of WI. Here we should note that the sizes of the clusters obtained by WI and CM might be too large. In fact, the chronological order of the earthquake with $id = 14$ is $i = 47, 744$ for the total number of events $N = 104, 343$, and thus the number of events after this earthquake is 56, 599 and those covered by these clusters amount to

Table 1. List of selected 24 major earthquakes

id	Time	Lon.	Lat.	Depth	Mag.	Name
1	10/6/2000 13:30	133.349	35.2742	8.96	7.3	2000 Tottori earthquake
2	12/18/2001 13:02	122.8152	23.8935	8.00	7.3	2001 Yonaguni Island inshore earthquake
3	9/26/2003 4:50	144.0785	41.7785	45.07	8	2003 Tokachi-oki earthquake
4	9/5/2004 19:07	136.7977	33.0332	37.58	7.1	2004 Kii Peninsula earthquake 1
5	9/5/2004 23:57	137.1413	33.1375	43.54	7.4	2004 Kii Peninsula earthquake 2
6	10/23/2004 17:56	138.8672	37.2925	13.08	6.8	2004 Chuetsu earthquake
7	3/20/2005 10:53	130.1763	33.7392	9.24	7	2005 Fukuoka earthquake
8	8/16/2005 11:46	142.2778	38.1495	42.04	7.2	2005 Miyagi earthquake
9	3/25/2007 9:41	136.686	37.2207	10.70	6.9	2007 Noto earthquake
10	7/16/2007 10:13	138.6095	37.5568	16.75	6.8	2007 Chuetsu offshore earthquake
11	6/14/2008 8:43	140.8807	39.0298	7.77	7.2	2008 Iwate-Miyagi Nairiku earthquake
12	8/11/2009 5:07	138.4993	34.7862	23.32	6.5	2009 Shizuoka earthquake
13	2/27/2010 5:31	128.68	25.9187	37.00	7.2	2010 Ryukyu Islands earthquake
14	3/9/2011 11:45	143.2798	38.3285	8.28	7.3	2011 Tohoku earthquake 1
15	3/11/2011 14:46	142.861	38.1035	23.74	9	2011 Tohoku earthquake 2
16	3/11/2011 15:08	142.7668	39.8207	32.02	7.4	2011 Iwate offshore earthquake
17	3/11/2011 15:15	141.2525	36.1208	42.70	7.6	2011 Ibaraki offshore earthquake
18	3/11/2011 15:25	144.751	37.9143	11.00	7.5	2011 Sanriku offshore earthquake
19	3/12/2011 3:59	138.5978	36.986	8.38	6.7	2011 Nagano earthquake
20	4/7/2011 23:32	141.9202	38.2042	65.89	7.2	2011 Miyagi earthquake
21	4/11/2011 17:16	140.6727	36.9457	6.42	7	2011 Fukushima earthquake
22	4/14/2016 21:26	130.8087	32.7417	11.39	6.5	2016 Kumamoto earthquake 1
23	4/16/2016 1:25	130.763	32.7545	12.45	7.3	2016 Kumamoto earthquake 2
24	11/22/2016 5:59	141.6042	37.3547	24.50	7.4	2016 Fukushima earthquake

$42,196$ and $40,782$, where the cover rates are around 0.75 and 0.72. Moreover, in case of the 2011 Tohoku earthquakes with $id = 15$, the number of events in its window is $|\mathcal{V}^{WI}(id15)| = 13,599$ for WI, and the number of its direct child events is $|\{j \mid i^{CM}(j) = id15\}| = 31,101$ for CM. Namely, we consider that some large clusters are constructed by mutually connecting these sets of events for the major earthquakes. Thus, compared to these existing methods, WI and CM, we can expect that our proposed MS method is likely to have a relatively high separability. Hereafter, for our evaluation purpose, as indicated at the rightmost column in Table 2, we refer to the set of the earthquakes before $id = 14$ as group 1 $(G = 1)$, and the rest of those as group 2 $(G = 2)$, respectively. Here recall that the earthquake with $id = 14$ is the foreshock of the 2011 Tohoku earthquake.

Third, we can observe that in the case of $id \in \{1, \cdots, 24\}$ except for $id = 19$, the following inequalities for the cluster sizes hold with reasonable precision,

$$|\mathcal{R}_{id}^{WI}| \geq |\mathcal{R}_{id}^{CM}| > |\mathcal{R}_{id}^{MS}| > |\mathcal{R}_{id}^{SL}|, \tag{12}$$

although $|\mathcal{R}_{id}^{WI}|$ and $|\mathcal{R}_{id}^{CM}|$ are almost comparable in the case of $id \in \{4,5,7\}$, and we can see the following inequalities for the cluster sizes about $|\mathcal{RB}^{mtd}|$,

$$|\mathcal{RB}^{WI}| \geq |\mathcal{RB}^{MS}| \geq |\mathcal{RB}^{CM}| \geq |\mathcal{RB}^{SL}|. \tag{13}$$

Here we should note that the sizes of the clusters obtained by SL might be too small compared to those obtained by the other methods. Actually, in case

Table 2. Size of clusters obtained by four methods

id	WI			CM			SL			MS			G
	$|\mathcal{R}|$	$|\mathcal{RB}|$	$|\mathcal{RA}|$	$|\mathcal{R}|$	$|\mathcal{RB}|$	$|\mathcal{RA}|$	$|\mathcal{R}|$	$|\mathcal{RB}|$	$|\mathcal{RA}|$	$|\mathcal{R}|$	$|\mathcal{RB}|$	$|\mathcal{RA}|$	
1	340	0	339	337	0	336	172	0	171	278	0	277	1
2	781	37	743	465	1	463	66	1	64	305	7	297	1
3	4718	1925	2792	1460	0	1459	7	0	6	440	5	101	1
4	700	1	120	740	0	739	27	0	26	666	0	665	1
5	726	58	667	740	58	681	68	2	65	666	58	607	1
6	591	4	586	550	0	549	298	0	297	520	6	513	1
7	294	0	293	295	0	294	127	0	126	280	1	278	1
8	47592	2643	44948	282	0	281	4	0	3	75	10	64	1
9	445	0	444	410	0	409	206	0	205	352	1	350	1
10	144	0	143	123	0	122	16	0	15	119	2	116	1
11	581	2	578	567	0	566	272	0	271	473	4	468	1
12	141	0	140	30	0	29	4	0	3	29	0	28	1
13	515	11	503	464	0	463	56	0	55	310	4	305	1
14	47592	5396	42195	40782	0	40781	1	0	0	1964	32	1931	2
15	47592	5587	42004	40782	190	40591	1	0	0	1964	216	1747	2
16	47592	5601	41990	40782	217	40564	1	0	0	418	7	410	2
17	47592	5607	41984	40782	226	40555	65	0	64	2134	24	2109	2
18	47592	5620	41971	40782	239	40542	1	0	0	325	1	323	2
19	207	0	206	40782	1002	39779	36	0	35	159	0	158	2
20	47592	16593	30998	40782	11373	29408	195	32	162	905	288	616	2
21	47592	17302	30289	40782	12085	28696	256	31	224	1386	400	985	2
22	1253	0	1252	1243	0	1242	74	0	73	1184	0	1183	2
23	1253	175	1077	1243	175	1067	74	18	55	1184	175	1008	2
24	47592	46663	928	40782	39872	909	181	1	179	923	57	865	2

of the 2011 Tohoku earthquakes with $id = 15$, the spatio-temporal metric $d(i^{SL}(id15), id15) = 40.76$ was larger than the threshold value $D = 7.10$.

To further examine our experimental results, we compare the visual event distribution results of the events in the clusters obtained by the four methods. Figure 2 shows the visualization results for $id = 2$, as a typical example in group 1, where Figs. 2a, 2b, 2c, and 2d are those obtained by WI, CM, SL, and MS, in this order. Here note that a red cross denotes the location of the major earthquake, and while the location of events in $\mathcal{RA}$ and $\mathcal{RB}$ are depicted by orange and blue triangles, respectively. From these results, we can easily confirm the inequalities of the cluster sizes shown in Eqs. 12 and 13.

Figure 3 shows the visual event distribution results for $id = 15$, as a typical example in group 2, where Figs. 3a, 3b, 3c, and 3d are those obtained by WI, CM, SL, and MS, in this order, and we use the same marker notations as explained in Fig. 2. From these results, we can visually confirm that the cluster members of WI and CM are somehow different where recall that the size of cluster obtained by the SL is 1, i.e., $|\mathcal{R}_{id}^{SL}| = 1$ as shown in Table 2. From these results, we can also confirm the differences among these four methods. We believe that our proposed MS method is vital and has a promising characteristic.

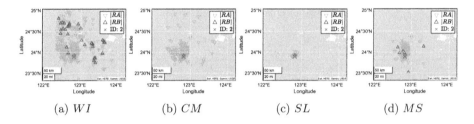

(a) WI (b) CM (c) SL (d) MS

Fig. 2. Event distribution evaluation of the clusters ($id = 2$) (Color figure online)

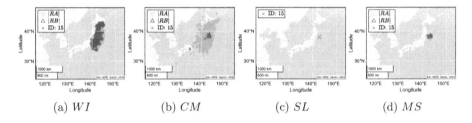

(a) WI (b) CM (c) SL (d) MS

Fig. 3. Event distribution evaluation of the clusters ($id = 15$)

6   Conclusion

In this paper, we addressed the problem of clustering earthquakes in a catalog, which is also known as declustering in seismology, i.e., a task of classifying each earthquake into foreshock, mainshock, or aftershock. This declustering task can also be formalized as a standard clustering problem, which identifies each cluster containing a mainshock together with its foreshocks and aftershocks. To this end, we proposed a magnitude-weighted mean-shift clustering algorithm, equipped with a leave-one-out procedure for estimating its bandwidth parameter. In our experimental evaluation, we generated our dataset from an earthquake catalog that covered the whole of Japan and selected 24 major earthquakes that caused significant damage or casualties in Japan. In our experimental comparison with three representative clustering methods in seismology, i.e., the window method, single-link method, and correlation-metric method, we compared the clustering results containing the above 24 major earthquakes in terms of the size of cluster, similarity matrices, and earthquake visualization results. As a result, we observed that concerning the clusters containing the 24 major earthquakes, the sizes of these clusters obtained by our proposed method were consistently smaller than those of the window or correlation-metric method but larger than those of the single-link method.

As a future task, we plan to conduct experiments by tuning the C of SL and the b-value of CM, which are also used in the proposed method MS by estimating the optimal values from the earthquake catalog, and extend our clustering method by employing more general distance settings in the Gaussian kernel function, such as a Mahalanobis distance. A further empirical study to confirm the validity of the clustering results obtained by our method is another future work.

Acknowledgement. This work was supported by JSPS Grant-in-Aid for Scientific Research (C) (No. 18K11441).

References

1. Baiesi, M., Paczuski, M.: Scale-free networks of earthquakes and aftershocks. Physical Review E, Statistical, nonlinear, and soft matter physics 69 (2004)
2. Bo, S., Ding, L., Li, H., Di, F., Zhu, C.: Mean shift-based clustering analysis of multispectral remote sensing imagery. Int. J. Remote Sensing **30**(4), 817–827 (2009)
3. Comaniciu, D.: An algorithm for data-driven bandwidth selection. IEEE Trans. Pattern Anal. Mach. Intell. **25**(2), 281–288 (2003)
4. Comaniciu, D., Meer, P.: Mean shift: a robust approach toward feature space analysis. IEEE Trans. Pattern Anal. Mach. Intell. **24**(5), 603–619 (2002)
5. Davis, S.D., Frohlich, C.: Single-link cluster analysis, synthetic earthquake catalogues, and aftershock identification. Geophys. J. Int. **104**(2), 289–306 (1991)
6. Dempster, A.P., Laird, N.M., Rubin, D.B.: Maximum likelihood from incomplete data via the EM algorithm. J. Roy. Stat. Soc. Ser. B (Methodological) **39**(1), 1–38 (1977)
7. Ferraz, A., Bretar, F., Jacquemoud, S., Gonçalves, G., Pereira, L., Tomé, M., Soares, P.: 3-D mapping of a multi-layered mediterranean forest using ALS data. Remote Sensing Environ. **121**, 210–223 (2012)
8. Frohlich, C., Davis, S.D.: Single-link cluster analysis as a method to evaluate spatial and temporal properties of earthquake catalogues. Geophys. J. Int. **100**(1), 19–32 (1990)
9. Gardner, J.K., Knopoff, L.: Is the sequence of earthquakes in southern California, with aftershocks removed, poissonian? Bull. Seismological Soc. Am. **64**(5), 1363–1367 (1974)
10. Gutenberg, B., Richter, C.F.: Frequency of earthquakes in California*. Bull. Seismological Soc. Am. **34**(4), 185–188 (10 1944)
11. Huang, X., Zhang, L.: An adaptive mean-shift analysis approach for object extraction and classification from urban hyperspectral imagery. IEEE Trans. Geosci. Remote Sensing **46**(12), 4173–4185 (2008)
12. Knopoff, L., Gardner, J.K.: Higher seismic activity during local night on the raw worldwide earthquake catalogue. Geophys. J. Int. **28**, 311–313 (1972)
13. MacQueen, J.B.: Some methods for classification and analysis of multivariate observations. In: In 5-th Berkeley Symposium on Mathematical Statistics and Probability, pp. 281–297 (1967)
14. Ogata, Y.: Statistical models for earthquake occurrences and residual analysis for point processes. Journal of the American Statistical Association **83**(401), 9–27 (1988)
15. Ogata, Y.: Space-time point-process models for earthquake occurrences. Annals of the Institute of Statistical Mathematics **50**, 379–402 (1998)
16. Reasenberg, P.: Second-order moment of central california seismicity, 1969–1982. Journal of Geophysical Research **90**, 5479–5495 (1985)
17. Sneath, P.H.A.: The application of computers to taxonomy. Journal of general microbiology **17**(1), 201–226 (1957)
18. Sokal, R.R., Michener, C.D.: A statistical method for evaluating systematic relationships. University of Kansas Science Bulletin **38**, 1409–1438 (1958)
19. Sokal, R.R., Sneath, P.H.A.: Principles of Numerical Taxonomy. Freeman, San Francisco (1963)

20. van Stiphout, T., Zhuang, J., Marsan, D.: Seismicity declustering. Community Online Resource for Statistical Seismicity Analysis (2012)
21. Yamagishi, Y., Saito, K., Hirahara, K., Ueda, N.: Spatio-temporal clustering of earthquakes based on average magnitudes. In: The 9th International Conference on Complex Networks and Their Applications (ComplexNetwork 2020), pp. 627–637. Lecture Notes in Computer Science, Springer (2020)
22. Zaliapin, I., Ben-Zion, Y.: A global classification and characterization of earthquake clusters. Geophys. J. Int. **207**(1), 608–634 (2016)
23. Zaliapin, I., Gabrielov, A., Keilis-Borok, V., Wong, H.: Clustering analysis of seismicity and aftershock identification. Phys. Rev. Lett. **101**(1), 1–4 (2008)
24. Zhuang, J.: Multi-dimensional second-order residual analysis of space-time point processes and its applications in modelling earthquake data. J. Royal Stat. Soc. **68**(4), 635–653 (2006)
25. Zhuang, J., Ogata, Y., Vere-Jones, D.: Stochastic declustering of space-time earthquake occurrences. J. Am. Stat. Assoc. **97**(458), 369–380 (2002)
26. Zhuang, J., Ogata, Y., Vere-Jones, D.: Analyzing earthquake clustering features by using stochastic reconstruction. J. Geophys. Res. **109**, B05 (2004)

Pervasive Monitoring of Gastrointestinal Health of Newborn Babies

Insu Song[1], Yi Huang[1(✉)], Tieh Hee Hai Guan Koh[2], and Victor Samuel Rajadurai[3]

[1] James Cook University, Singapore, Singapore
insu.song@jcu.edu.au, yi.huang3@my.jcu.edu.au
[2] Townsville Hospital, Townsville, QLD, Australia
guan.koh@health.qld.gov.au
[3] KK Women's and Children's Hospital, Singapore, Singapore
victor.samuel@kkh.com.sg

Abstract. Babies needing intensive care are at risk of developing gastrointestinal problems, such as feed intolerance and necrotizing enterocolitis (NEC). Monitoring, early detection, and prevention of bowel diseases in newborn may improve outcomes. However, continuous monitoring of the gastrointestinal health of babies is not currently available. We develop an innovative miniature Bowel Sounds Sensor (BoSS) for term babies and a bowel sound analyzer, called Recurrent Local Relation Encoder Classifier (ReLATEC), for real-time, visual monitoring of bowel functions in NICUs. ReLATEC detects types and locations of bowel sounds from a continuous audio stream of bowel activities recorded in noisy hospital environments. ReLATEC combines the advantages of CNN and RNN by using local attention with recurrent layers. We collected 171 bowel sound recordings from 113 newborn babies at two NICUs to evaluate our approach. The bowel sound detector was then trained using weak labels. The detector performed 7% better than conventional approaches. It was shown a sensitivity of 91% and specificity of 71% in detecting short burst bowel sounds. It showed a sensitivity of 97% and specificity of 72% in detecting long burst bowel sounds. Despite the model being trained with weak labels, it detected the boundaries of the two bowel sounds reliably for real-time visual monitoring.

Keywords: Deep learning · Semantic segmentation · Biomedical engineering · Computerized diagnosis

1 Introduction

Babies needing intensive care are at risk of developing gastrointestinal problems, such as feed intolerance and necrotizing enterocolitis (NEC). Necrotizing enterocolitis (NEC) occurs in nearly 10% of premature infants, accounts for 1% to 5% of neonatal intensive care unit (NICU) admissions [1]. Due to the rapid progression of NEC, early diagnosis of NEC remains challenging [2]. Monitoring, early detection, and prevention of bowel diseases in newborn may improve outcomes. Bowel sound monitoring provides a non-invasive clinical diagnosis [3]. The absence of bowel sound often indicates NEC [1].

© Springer Nature Switzerland AG 2021
D. N. Pham et al. (Eds.): PRICAI 2021, LNAI 13031, pp. 359–369, 2021.
https://doi.org/10.1007/978-3-030-89188-6_27

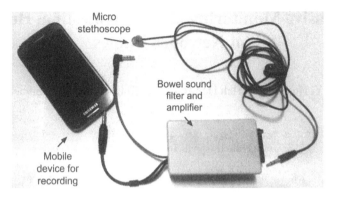

Fig. 1. Bowel Sound Sensor (BoSS) based on Docentron Acorn sensor

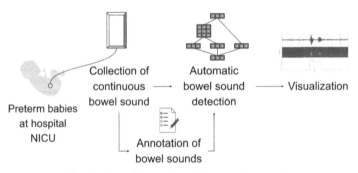

Fig. 2. Overall procedure of proposed approach

However, currently, there are no known approaches that can provide real-time, visual monitoring of bowel functions of newborn babies. Diagnosis of NEC is currently made manually using a stethoscope that is often uncomfortable and invasive for young children [4–6]. Furthermore, due to the irregular pattern and occurrence of bowel sounds, locating and detecting bowel sounds from digital recordings of bowel sounds remains a challenge [7, 8]. Manually annotating and analyzing bowel sounds is time-consuming, especially when noise exists. Even doctors can only identify a few random events [7].

Therefore, we develop an innovative miniature Bowel Sounds Sensor (BoSS) for term babies shown in Fig. 1. The 3D-printed micro stethoscope of BoSS allows continuous monitoring of bowel sounds of newborn babies with minimal discomfort. The recorded bowel sounds are then analyzed using deep learning algorithms.

Deep learning approaches achieve outstanding performance in recent years. However, existing approaches have two significant shortcomings for analyzing streams of bowel sounds. RNN updates its hidden state along the input sequence. As the gradient of the hidden state accumulates, a long sequence may lead to vanishing or exploding gradients. On the other hand, CNN learns the features like templates, which match input features with a fixed spatial or temporal distribution.

Therefore, we propose Recurrent Local Relation Encoder Classifier (ReLATEC) for detecting the locations and types of bowel sounds. ReLATEC combines the advantage of CNN and RNN by using local attention with recurrent layers.

Figure 2 illustrates how BoSS and ReLATEC are used to solve the problems. BoSS continuously records bowel sounds of newborn babies using the micro stethoscope sensor. The bowel sounds locations are then labeled for training the bowel sound detector. The labels are converted into weak labels with a lower temporal resolution because it is difficult for human listeners to identify all bowel sounds accurately due to hospital environmental noises. A ReLATEC model is then trained to detect the locations and two types of bowel sounds: short bursts and long bursts. The trained detector then provides real-time annotation of bowel sounds with locations, types, and statistics of bowel sound activities.

In our study, ReLATEC achieved a sensitivity of 91% and specificity of 71% in detecting short burst bowel sounds, and a sensitivity of 97% and specificity of 72% in detecting long burst bowel sounds. Despite the model was trained with weak labels, it recalled most of bowel sound locations labeled by human listeners reliably and also discovered new bowel sound locations.

The main contributions of our work are as follows. For the first time, we developed a miniature bowel sound sensor for preterm babies at NICUs for continuous real-time monitoring of bowel functions. A total of 171 bowel sounds of newborn babies were successfully recorded from 113 newborns at two different NICUs, and 1,267 bowel activities were successfully identified and labeled from the recordings. A new novel deep-learning approach was developed to detect the locations and types of bowel sound activities automatically.

The paper is organized as follows. In Sect. 2, we introduce our dataset and details of ReLATEC. In Sect. 3, the result is displayed and discussed. Section 4 concludes with highlights of our discoveries.

2 Proposed Method

2.1 Dataset

A total of 171 bowel sounds were collected using BoSS (Fig. 1) from 86 newborns at KK Women's and Children's Hospital in Singapore and Townsville hospital in Australian over a period of 5 months. The doctors and nurses of the hospitals were responsible for data collection. The total recordings were 852 min including 439 min of records of pre-feed and 413 min of recordings of post-feed.

BoSS was designed to amplify and filter continuous bowel sounds from preterm babies non-invasively, as shown in Fig. 1 and Fig. 2. The micro stethoscope is specifically designed to be small, soft, and comfortable for newborn babies. The bowel sound processing module filters and amplifies audio signals within the frequency range of 100 Hz and 1 kHz. The sensor module is designed to be compatible with the microphone input of mobile phones and tablets. KOPO[1] mobile audio recorder is used for recording, visualization, and annotation of bowel sounds.

---

[1] https://www.kopo.com/da/.

2.2 Data Processing

Regions of Interests (ROIs) that contain bowel sounds were then manually selected as an initial step of weak labeling. A total of 5 IT-students from James Cook University participated in data labelling. They were first trained with different types of bowel sounds both with real and simulated bowel sounds. The first group of four performed the initial labeling followed by cross verification and reclassification. The remaining one student then revalidated the labels. A total of 592 ROIs were selected from the 171 recordings by the first group. Each ROI contained at least three to four bowel activities. We then classified the bowel activities into two types: short burst and long burst (also called grumble). Figure 3 shows examples of the two types of sounds. Short bursts have a higher pitch, shorter duration, and sharp shape, while grumble sounds have a lower pitch and longer duration. We resampled the data to 8000 Hz and generated a spectrogram representation.

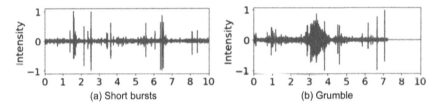

(a) Short bursts   (b) Grumble

Fig. 3. Examples of (a) short burst bowel sound and (b) long burst (grumble) bowel sound

Then, the start and the end time locations of bowel activities were manually marked and each was classified into the two types: short burst and long burst. A total of 1,267 bowel activities were marked: 971 for short bursts and 296 for long bursts, as shown in Table 1.

Due to noises and the length of the recordings, not all bowel activities could be identified by human listeners. Often bowel activities last less than a second. Therefore, we used weak labeling approach: the labelling is not complete, but all identified bowel actives are correct.

To generate weak labels, we first generated positional one-hot labels using the marks. The one-hot labels were further segmented using a 0.75 s maximum pulling sliding window. Each segment was then labeled as one or zero, whereas one means there is a bowel sound at that location. This generated 7575 weak labels for each types of bowel sound. The total number of positive weak labels indicating the presence of any short bursts at the location is 1,796 and the total number of positive weak labels indicating the presence of any long bursts at the location is 704 as shown in Table 2 and Table 3.

For training and testing, we have divided the ROIs into 10 s of input segments. Each input segment was then converted into a spectrogram feature data. Corresponding label data were also generated for each feature data. A total of 303 feature and label data pairs were generated: 242 for training and 61 for testing.

A single model was trained for both types of bowel sounds. For evaluation, we divided the dataset into the training dataset (80%) and the testing dataset (20%). Table 4 shows the mean durations of bowel activities that are manually labelled. It shows that durations of long bursts are longer than short bursts. The durations of post-feed long bursts are longer than pre-feed long bursts.

Table 1. The number of bowel activities labeled manually for training and testing

Dataset split	Short brust	Long burst (grumble)	Total
Training set	707	252	959
Testing set	264	44	308
Total	971	296	1267

Table 2. The weak labels of short bursts generated for training and testing

Dataset split	Positive	Negative	Total
Training set	1319	4731	6050
Testing set	477	1048	1525
Total	1796	5779	7575

Table 3. The weak labels of long bursts generated for training and testing

Dataset split	Positive	Negative	Total
Training set	599	5451	6050
Testing set	105	1420	1525
Total	704	6871	7575

Table 4. Mean durations of bowel activities marked manually

Measurement	Mean duration (seconds)
Pre-feed (short burst)	0.1810
Post-feed (short burst)	0.1803
Pre-feed (long burst)	0.2383
Post-feed (long burst)	0.3759

2.3 Recurrent Local Relation Transformer (ReLATEC)

Figure 4 describes the comparison between Vanilla Transformers and Recurrent Local Relation Transformer (ReLATEC) for detecting the location and types of the bowel sounds (bowel activities) from an audio stream. The length of input and output data is 10 s. The input feature data is then embedded at the embedding layer comprising of a linear layer, a pooling layer, and another linear layer. Then positional encoding is performed to encode time locations of the features values. The position values and the embedded feature data are then used to calculate attention. The resulting attention data is then used to generate the output. The upsampling layer is used to generate 10 s length of data corresponding to the input data. The output values are the probability of existence of bowel activities at the locations in the output data.

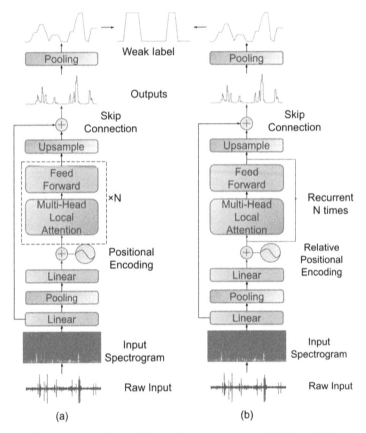

Fig. 4. Comparison of (a) vanilla transformers and (b) ReLATEC

A Transformer Network consists of self-attention layers and Feed Forward Neural Networks [9, 10]. Transformers learn features from the relationships of inputs that are robust to a different distribution. The multi-head attention mechanism is shown below:

$$Attention(Q, K, V) = softmax\left(\frac{QK^T}{\sqrt{d_k}}\right)V \tag{1}$$

$$MHA(Q, K, V) = concat(head_0, \dots head_h)W_o \tag{2}$$

$$head_i = Attention(QW_i^q, KW_i^k, VW_i^v) \tag{3}$$

where Q, K, V denote the query, key and value of input, dk denotes the dimensions of embedding, W denotes parameters, and i denotes the index of inputs. ReLATEC only uses the encoder structure of Transformer. The encoder of Transformer uses self-attention, where all Q, K, V are the input sequence, to relate different time steps among input sequence [9]. For our data, Q, K and V are the feature vector sequence. For each query vector, the energy A is calculated with all the key vector. Each value vector is multiplied by the softmax of energy A and then added up.

ReLATEC uses local relation to constrain the aggregation window of self-attention. Local Relation Network (LR-Net) [10] was also shown to be successful in modeling pixel-to-pixel relations from images with aggregation window. Instead of using entire sequence to calculate attention, only the adjacent feature vector is used to calculate attention. In LR-Net, the aggregation window is curial for learning features by introducing an information bottleneck. In this approach, we treated the time domain of audio spectrogram as one-dimensional images to apply this aggregation window. Local Attention function is shown as Eq. (4) and (5):

$$Local\ Attention(Q, K, V) = mask\left(softmax\left(\frac{QK^T}{\sqrt{d_k}}\right)\right)V \tag{4}$$

$$mask\left(E_{i,j}\right) = \begin{cases} E_{i,j}, |i - j| < \frac{windowsize}{2} + 1 \\ 0, otherwise \end{cases} \tag{5}$$

Position encodings are added to the embeddings to represent the relative positions of each time step feature vector. Position encoding provides positional information to Transformer as Eq. (6) and (7):

$$pos(2i) = sin\left(\frac{pos}{base^{\frac{2i}{d}}}\right) \tag{6}$$

$$pos(2i + 1) = cos\left(\frac{pos}{base^{\frac{2i}{d}}}\right) \tag{7}$$

where pos denotes position, base is a hyperparameter, and i denotes the index of dimension.

In vanilla Transformer configuration, the base is 10000. Figure 5(a) shows the position encoding when base is 10000. The higher dimensions do not have repeating patterns and indicate absolute positional information. The absolute positional information is meaningless in our task since breath sound is a periodical signal. Thus, we set the base to 2 for ReLATEC. Figure 5(b) shows that all dimensions of ReLATEC relative positional encoding have repeating patterns. Figure 5(c) shows that ReLATEC relative positional encoding still indicates the local positional information.

Instead of using multiple independent layers, ReLATEC recurrent one layer with a given number as Eq. (8) and (9):

$$X_i = ReLATEC\ layer(X_{i-1}) \tag{8}$$

$$ReLATEC \ layer(X_i) = FFN(X_i + MHA(X_i, X_i, X_i)) \tag{9}$$

In another interpretation, ReLATEC is Transformer with cross-weight layer sharing. Previous approaches, such as UT and ALBERT, have shown that recurrent structure the superior to multiple layer structure [11, 12]. The recurrent structure not only reduces the number of parameters but also introduces recurrent bias like RNN.

After that, the output is upsampled to the original length to provide semantic segmentation of pixels. The skip connection allows gradients flow directly through the network to prevent exploding or vanishing gradients. The length of classification layer is 1333 and dimension is two for two classes.

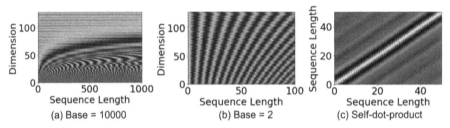

(a) Base = 10000   (b) Base = 2   (c) Self-dot-product

Fig. 5. Positional encoding when *base* is 10000 (a), *base* is 2 (b)and self-dot-product of ReLATEC Positional Encoding (c)

3   Result

3.1   Bowel Activity Location Prediction

Table 5. Performance results of predicting bowel activities using different approaches

Approach	Long burst			Short burst		
	Sensitivity	Specificity	Accuracy	Sensitivity	Specificity	Accuracy
RNN	88.47%	**71.56%**	76.85%	90.48%	71.69%	72.98%
Transformer	85.53%	70.04%	74.89%	95.24%	72.82%	74.36%
Recurrent Transformer	88.26%	70.04%	75.74%	96.19%	**72.96%**	**74.56%**
ReLATEC	**90.99%**	70.90%	**77.18%**	**97.14%**	72.25%	73.97%

Table 5 shows that ReLATEC archived 90.99% sensitivity and 70.90% specificity for short burst while it achieved 97.14% sensitivity and 72.25% specificity for long burst.

To see if ReLATEC performs better than existing approaches, we fixed the specificity to 70% by adjusting the decision boundary threshold and compared sensitivity values. ReLATEC achieved significantly higher sensitivity compared to existing approaches.

Especially for short burst activities, it showed 6.66% improvement. Figure 6 shows the ROC curves of short burst and long burst detections. ReLATEC achieved the highest AUC. The AUC for detecting long bursts was 93.1%, and the AUC for detecting short bursts was 88.5%. ReLATEC was superior to the conventional RNN baseline, Vanilla Transformer, and recurrent Transformer.

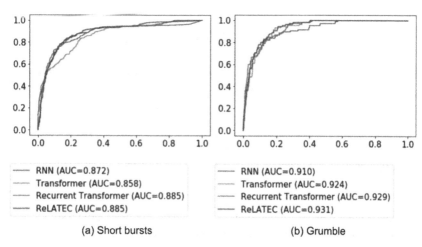

(a) Short bursts

(b) Grumble

Fig. 6. ROC of different models to classifying (a) short burst and (b) grumble locations

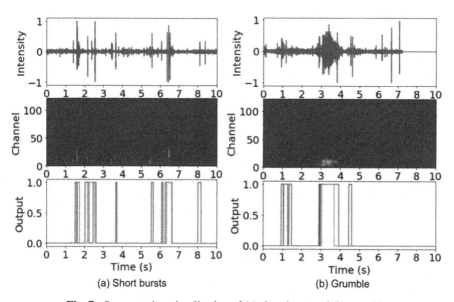

(a) Short bursts

(b) Grumble

Fig. 7. Segmentation visualization of (a) short burst and (b) grumble

Figure 7 shows the raw signal, spectrogram, ground truth, and prediction of short bursts and grumbles. The orange lines indicate labels by human listeners, and the blue lines indicate predictions. ReLATEC detected almost all bowel sounds (bowel activities) marked by human listeners. Furthermore, ReLATEC also discovered and detected bowel sound activities that human listeners did not initially detect.

3.2 Clinical Statistics

Table 6. Physiological measurements calculated from ReLATEC prediction

Measurement	Mean rate (per minute)	Std. rate	Mean duration (seconds)	Mean gap (seconds)
Pre-feed (burst)	2.0413	1.6095	0.2130	1.7597
Post-feed (burst)	3.1754	3.8070	0.2248	1.6668
Pre-feed (grumble)	1.5280	0.8269	0.2517	2.1221
Post-feed (grumble)	1.9666	0.9137	0.2955	2.1579

Displayed equations are centered and set on a separate line. Table 6 shows physiological measurements of the bowel activities based on ReLATEC predictions. Similar to the measurements done using the manual labels in Table 4, the mean durations of long burst bowel activities are larger than the short burst bowel activities. The mean rates of short bust bowel activities are higher than the post-feed rates. However, due to high variance the differences are not significant.

4 Conclusion

The main contributions of our work are as follows. Our proposed method provides non-invasive bowel activity detection and classification. The new innovative miniature bowel sound sensor successfully recorded a large number of bowel sounds and bowel activities at two different NICUs by nurses. The 3D-printed micro stethoscope was comfortable for newborn babies for continuous monitoring of bowel functions. A new novel deep-learning approach, ReLATEC, showed significant improvement in distinguishing and detecting bowel activities even with hospital environmental noises. It provided reliable and accurate boundaries of the two types of bowel activities with high sensitivity.

Furthermore, ReLATEC discovered and detected the bowel sound activities that human listeners were failed to detect initially. It can be trained with noisy labels and provide predictions with higher accuracy. The combinations of recurrent natures like RNN and self-attention from Transformer in ReLATEC achieved better performance than RNN and Transformer. Despite of the limitations of the imbalanced data, it was able to produce good specificity values and good ROC curves with AUCs of 0.87 and 0.91 for short burst and long burst, respectively, indicating robust and reliable performance for medical applications.

Acknowledgements. We would like to thank Chua MC, Sim KHZ, and Dela Puerta R for data collection at KK Women's Children's hospital Singapore, Mcinnes H and Vengabati V for data collection at JCU Townsville hospital, and the JCU Master of Information Technologies students participated in bowel sound labeling and annotation. We also like to thank the parents and the hospital staff for their support and assistant.

References

1. Thompson, A.M., Bizzarro, M.J.: Necrotizing enterocolitis in newborns. Drugs **68**, 1227–1238 (2008)
2. Gregory, K.E., DeForge, C.E., Natale, K.M., Phillips, M., Van Marter, L.J.: Necrotizing enterocolitis in the premature infant: neonatal nursing assessment, disease pathogenesis, and clinical presentation. Adv. Neonatal Care **11**, 155 (2011)
3. Sheu, M.J., Lin, P.Y., Chen, J.Y., Lee, C.C., Lin, B.S.: Higher-order-statistics-based fractal dimension for noisy bowel sound detection. IEEE Signal Process. Lett. **22**, 789–793 (2015)
4. Song, I.: Diagnosis of pneumonia from sounds collected using low cost cell phones. In: 2015 International Joint Conference on Neural Networks (IJCNN), pp. 1–8 (2015)
5. Huang, Y., Song, I., Rana, P., Koh, G.: Fast diagnosis of bowel activities. In: 2017 International Joint Conference on Neural Networks (IJCNN), pp. 3042–3049 (2017)
6. Huang, Y., Song, I.: Indexing Biosignal for integrated health social networks. In: ICBBE 2019. ACM, International Conference Proceedings by ACM (2019)
7. Ranta, R., Louis-Dorr, V., Heinrich, C., Wolf, D., Guillemin, F.: Principal component analysis and interpretation of bowel sounds. In: Proceeding of the 26th Annual International Conference of the IEEE EMBS, pp. 227–230 (2004)
8. Sazonov, E.S., Makeyev, O., Schuckers, S., Lopez-Meyer, P., Melanson, E.L., Neuman, M.R.: Automatic detection of swallowing events by acoustical means for applications of monitoring of ingestive behavior. Biomed. Eng. IEEE Trans. **57**, 626–633 (2010)
9. Vaswani, A., et al.: Attention is all you need. In: Advances in Neural Information Processing Systems, pp. 5998–6008 (2017)
10. Hu, H., Zhang, Z., Xie, Z., Lin, S.: Local relation networks for image recognition. In: Proceedings of the IEEE International Conference on Computer Vision, pp. 3464–3473 (2019)
11. Lan, Z., Chen, M., Goodman, S., Gimpel, K., Sharma, P., Soricut, R.: Albert: a lite bert for self-supervised learning of language representations. arXiv preprint arXiv:1909.11942 (2019)
12. Dehghani, M., Gouws, S., Vinyals, O., Uszkoreit, J., Kaiser, Ł.: Universal transformers. arXiv preprint arXiv:1807.03819 (2018)

Price and Time Optimization
for Utility-Aware Taxi Dispatching

Yuya Hikima[(✉)], Masahiro Kohjima, Yasunori Akagi, Takeshi Kurashima,
and Hiroyuki Toda

NTT Human Informatics Laboratories, NTT Corporation, 1-1 Hikari-no-oka,
Yokosuka-Shi, 239-0847 Kanagawa, Japan
{yuuya.hikima.ys,masahiro.kohjima.ev,yasunori.akagi.cu,
takeshi.kurashima.uf,hiroyuki.toda.xb}@hco.ntt.co.jp

Abstract. The recent enhancement of taxi dispatch services with information technology has enabled data-driven pricing and dispatch. However, existing studies failed to address differences in individual priorities as regards money savings and time savings, leading to non-optimal taxi pricing and dispatch. In this paper, we formulate a new optimization problem that yields optimized price and time proposals for each requester according to their priorities. To consider the requester's priorities, we introduce an individual requester's acceptance probability model for price and required time, which is widely used in transportation economics. The proposals of price and time combinations yielded by our method enhance both the requester's satisfaction and the service provider's profit. Since the optimization problem is difficult to solve because its objective values are hard to evaluate and discontinuous, we construct a fast approximation algorithm by utilizing the characteristics of the problem. Simulations using real-world datasets show that the proposed framework increases both the requester's satisfaction and service provider's profit.

Keywords: Ride-hailing · Price optimization · Taxi dispatching · Utility

1 Introduction

In recent years, many ride-hailing companies have introduced mobile applications for taxi ordering, and extensive data on the movement of people by taxi is being collected. The data is being actively analyzed to develop more effective taxi dispatch operations. For example, studies have yielded useful taxi dispatch and pricing technologies to maximize profit [16,22] and to minimize waiting time [14,21].

However, work to date does not consider the differences in requester priorities with regard to money savings and time savings. Many studies have shown that money savings and time savings are important factors in the utility of

© Springer Nature Switzerland AG 2021
D. N. Pham et al. (Eds.): PRICAI 2021, LNAI 13031, pp. 370–381, 2021.
https://doi.org/10.1007/978-3-030-89188-6_28

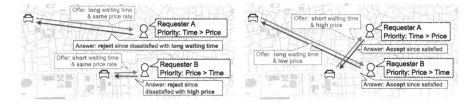

Fig. 1. Conventional taxi dispatch   **Fig. 2.** Proposed taxi dispatch

transportation services [9,20], and different individuals have different priorities [1,23]. For example, requesters who prioritize time savings (e.g. business travelers and high-income earners) want to move around the city in the shortest possible time, even if the price is high. On the other hand, requesters who prioritize money savings (e.g. non-business travelers and average income earners) want to move as cheaply as possible and their time constraints are not severe. Existing studies do not consider these differences and provide average services to all requesters. Thus, they fail to satisfy a significant number of requesters. Also, requester dissatisfaction triggers a decrease in requests, leading to a drop in profits.

Figure 1 shows the problem caused by failing to consider individual priorities as regards money savings and time savings. Here, we assume the policy that determines a price rate (the price per unit distance) charged for taxi requests for each area at each time [4,22] and executes shortest distance dispatch [14,21]. In Fig. 1, the same price rate is offered to Requester A and B since they are in the same area at the same time. By the shortest distance dispatch, a distant taxi is assigned to Requester A, while a closer taxi is assigned to Requester B. Requester A is dissatisfied with the long waiting time because (s)he prioritizes time savings over money savings. Also, Requester B is dissatisfied with the price because (s)he has the reverse priorities.

To resolve this issue, we propose a new optimization problem of optimizing price and time proposals for each requester according to their priorities. To consider the requester's priorities, we introduce a discrete choice model [18] based on generalized cost [9,20], which is widely used in transportation economics, as the requester's acceptance probability model. Our formulation can achieve both high requester satisfaction and high service provider profits for the following reasons: (i) Since desirable proposals in terms of price and time are created for each requester, the acceptance probability is high; (ii) As the proposals are less likely to be rejected, service provider profit can be expected to increase.

Figure 2 shows the improvement possible by solving our new optimization problem. The solution offers a shorter waiting time and a higher price to Requester A, who prioritizes time savings. Conversely, the solution offers a lower price and a longer waiting time to Requester B, who prioritizes money savings. As a result, both requester satisfaction and the service provider's profit are improved.

Although our new optimization problem is effective in improving the profit of the service provider and requester satisfaction, it faces two main difficulties. First, it is difficult to evaluate the objective value (expected profit of the service provider) since it requires solving 2^n bipartite matching problems, where n is the number of requesters. This is because the objective value is the expectation of the profit from the taxi-requester matching, which varies according to each of the 2^n patterns of the requester's acceptance or rejection. Second, the objective function is discontinuous with respect to times offered to requesters. This is because the taxis that can be dispatched to a requester discontinuously change depending on the time offered to the requester.

To overcome these difficulties, we propose a fast approximation algorithm based on the characteristics of the optimization problem, that is, the monotonic decreasing property of the acceptance probability model and the convexity of the optimal value of the bipartite matching problem. The proposed algorithm can output an L-approximate solution in polynomial time, $O(n \cdot (n^3 + m^3))$. Here, the approximation ratio, L, is a hyper-parameter that determines the relative weighting of requester satisfaction and the service provider's profit. In real operation, since L is set high enough to keep the requesters satisfied, the approximation ratio will be high as well.

We conducted experiments using real taxi data from New York City. The experiments show that the proposed framework has the potential to increase daily profit and improve requester satisfaction. Moreover, the computation time is within 1 s, which is short enough to be practical in real service.

2   Related Work

Existing studies on optimization for ride-hailing/taxi platforms mainly cover two topics: (a) optimization of the proposals (e.g., price, waiting time) offered to the requesters before orders are confirmed [3,4,6,7,11,13,22,25]. and (b) optimization of the taxi allocation to the requesters who accept proposals after orders are confirmed [2,8,12,14,16,17,19,21,24,26–28]. Our main focus is (a); by making appropriate proposals to requesters whose orders have not yet been confirmed, we can increase the acceptance rate and earn higher profits.

Among the studies on optimization of the proposals, [6,22] are similar to our work. In [22], price is determined with consideration of the taxi acceptance probability of the requester in each area. [6] determines the price by the LinUCB algorithm [15] which takes into account the dispatch strategy. They assume the same dispatch process as our study. However, these studies differ from our study in terms of contents of proposals. They do not propose the waiting time for each requester, and only impose the constraint that each requester can be assigned a taxi only if it is within a fixed radius of x km from the requester location. In this paper, we propose not only price but also time by considering the differences in individual price and time priorities.

3   Problem Formulation

3.1   Process of Proposal Offer and Taxi Dispatch

We explain the system of proposal offer and taxi dispatch assumed in this paper. We divide the time horizon into multiple time steps, and assume that there are multiple requesters $I := \{1, 2, ..., n\}$ and multiple taxis $J := \{1, 2, ..., m\}$ at each time step. We consider that proposal offering and taxi dispatching are performed at each time step. The process in each time step is as follows, see Fig. 3:

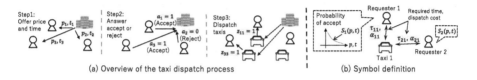

(a) Overview of the taxi dispatch process   (b) Symbol definition

Fig. 3. Taxi dispatch process and symbol definition

Step 1: The taxi operator offers price p_i and total time taken t_i to each requester $i \in I$. Here, 'price' refers to the total payment (including both pick-up and transfer costs), and the 'total time taken' refers the sum of the requester's wait for the taxi and travel time from origin to destination in the taxi. Let $p \in \mathbb{R}^n$ and $t \in \mathbb{R}^n$ be vectors with p_i and t_i with requester index i, respectively.

Step 2: Each requester, $i \in I$, accepts or rejects the offer with a probability of $S_i(p_i, t_i)$. Function S_i is the requester's acceptance probability model. We discuss this function in detail in Sect. 4. Let $a \in \{0,1\}^n$ be a discrete random vector where $a_i = 1$ indicates acceptance and $a_i = 0$ indicates rejection by requester i.

Step 3: The taxi operator then dispatches a taxi to the accepting requester. We assume the operator solves the following profit maximization problem (P_a) and dispatches taxis according to the solution:

$$(P_a) \quad \max_z \sum_{i,j} (p_i - \alpha_{ij}) \cdot a_i \cdot z_{ij}$$

$$\text{s.t.} \sum_j z_{ij} \leq 1 \quad \forall i \in I, \quad \sum_i z_{ij} \leq 1 \quad \forall j \in J$$

$$z_{ij} \in \{0,1\} \quad \forall i \in I \; \forall j \in J$$

$$z_{ij} = 0 \quad \forall (i,j) \in \{(i,j) \mid t_i < \tau_{ij}\},$$

where $z_{ij} \in \{0,1\}$ indicates whether taxi j is allocated to requester i ($z_{ij} = 1$) or not ($z_{ij} = 0$), α_{ij} is the total cost paid by taxi operator (or taxi driver) to dispatch taxi j to requester i, and τ_{ij} is the total time taken by taxi j to satisfy the request of i, that is, the total time required to move to the requester's location and to travel to the requester's destination. Let $U(a, p, z)$ and $Z(t)$ be the objective function and the feasible region in (P_a), respectively.

We provide a detailed explanation of the optimization problem (P_a) in Step 3. (P_a) is a weighted bipartite matching problem. In the objective function, $(p_i - \alpha_{ij})$ is the profit gained if the matching is successful. If $a_i = 1$ and $z_{ij} = 1$, the matching succeeds and profit is obtained. First and second constraints are the matching problem constraints, and the third constraint is for the dispatch of taxis to requesters within the total offered time taken.

3.2 Price and Time Optimization

To maximize the expected profit and heighten requester's utility, we decide price and time proposals by solving the following optimization problem:

$$(P) \quad \max_{p,t} \mathbb{E}_{a \sim D(p,t)}[\max_{z \in Z(t)} U(a, p, z)]$$

$$\text{s.t.} \quad S_i(p_i, t_i) \geq L \quad \forall i \in I,$$

where $U(a, p, z) = \sum_{i,j}(p_i - \alpha_{ij}) \cdot a_i \cdot z_{ij}$, which is the objective function of (P_a); $Z(t)$ is the feasible region of (P_a); $L \in [0, 1)$; $D(p, t)$ is the probability distribution of $a \in \{0, 1\}^n$, and its probability mass function is $\Pr(a \mid p, t) = \prod_{i=1}^{n} \left\{ S_i(p_i, t_i)^{a_i}(1 - S_i(p_i, t_i))^{(1-a_i)} \right\}$.

The objective function of (P) represents the expected profit of the service provider. The constant, L, is a hyper-parameter that can be freely determined by the taxi operator, and constraint, $S_i(p_i, t_i) \geq L$ $(i \in I)$, keeps each requester's acceptance probability high. Section 4 formally defines S_i and requester's utility function, and shows that achieving a high probability of taxi acceptance heightens requester's utility. When L is close to 0, the constraints are loose and the objective value (the service provider's profit) takes precedence; when L is close to 1, the constraints are tight and keeping the requester's utility high is the priority. Section 4 provides further explanation of L setting.

4   Utility and Taxi Acceptance Probability

We discuss in detail $S_i(p_i, t_i)$, the requester's acceptance probability model that appeared in Sect. 3. It plays a critical role in our study since we use it to optimize price and time for each requester.

We introduce generalized cost [9, 20] as the utility function. Generalized cost is a measure that encapsulates several disutilities related to travel. We set $C_i(p, t)$ as the generalized cost to individual i for the use of a taxi with price p and total time taken t. The simplest generalized cost [9] is defined as $C_i(p, t) := p + \phi_i \cdot t + \xi_i$. Here, $\phi_i \geq 0$ reflects the priority requester i places on her time; it is used to convert t into a monetary value, C_i. Parameter ξ_i represents costs with regard to other factors such as weather and date, which is fixed in the optimization process because only the price and time can be controlled in the short term.

In this paper, we assume that $C_i(p,t)$ is a monotonically increasing function with respect to p, t. This assumption is quite natural because no one prefers expensive or time-consuming taxis.

Then, we base our taxi acceptance probability model on a discrete choice model [18]. We define $S_i(p,t) := \frac{\exp(-C_i(p,t))}{\exp(-C_i(p,t))+\sum_{k \in K} \exp(-C_i(p_{ik},t_{ik}))}$ as the probability of requester i committing to a taxi offer, where K is the set of alternative transportation modes (i.e., other than taxi), such as trains and buses, and p_{ik} and t_{ik} are the price and total time taken by the k-th transportation mode for requester i. Under the setting, increasing the acceptance probability $S_i(p,t)$ by adjusting p, t leads to a decrease in generalized cost $C_i(p,t)$. Hence, the constraint of (P) keeps the generalized cost low, that is, requester's utility high, and hyper-parameter L in (P) determines the strength of the constraint. We expect to set $L \geq 0.5$ in real-world operations, where the taxi service has a lower generalized cost than any alternative transportation options included in K.

Lemma 1. *When $C_i(p,t)$ monotonically increases w.r.t. p, t, function $S_i(p,t)$ monotonically decreases w.r.t. p, t.*

Note that we can use another acceptance probability function instead of $S_i(p,t)$, as long as the function monotonically decreases w.r.t. p, t for all $i \in I$; this does not invalidate the following discussions.

5   Optimization

We have to solve the problem (P) quickly to realize real-time proposals, but there are two difficulties: (i) Random variable a takes 2^n values in $\{0,1\}^n$, and so it is necessary to solve 2^n instances of $\max_{z \in Z(t)} U(a,p,z)$ to calculate the objective value $(\mathbb{E}_{a \sim D(p,t)}[\max_{z \in Z(t)} U(a,p,z)])$; (ii) For given p, the objective function has at most m^n discontinuities with respect to t, since the closed region $Z(t)$ varies in the case of at most m^n according to t.

5.1   Approximation of the Objective Function of (P)

We introduce the following problem:

$$(\text{AP}) \quad \max_{p,t,z} U(\mathbb{E}_{a \sim D(p,t)}[a], p, z) = \sum_{i,j} (p_i - \alpha_{ij}) \cdot S_i(p_i, t_i) \cdot z_{ij}$$
$$\text{s.t. } S_i(p_i, t_i) \geq L \;\; \forall i \in I, \;\; z \in Z(t).$$

Here, (AP) is obtained by replacing objective function $\mathbb{E}_{a \sim D(p,t)}[\max_{z \in Z(t)} U(a,p,z)]$ with $\max_{z \in Z(t)} U(\mathbb{E}_{a \sim D(p,t)}[a], p, z)$ for (P).

We show the following lemma and theorem from the features of our problem:

Lemma 2. $\max_{z \in Z(t)} U(x, p, z)$ *is convex in* $x \in \mathbb{R}^n$ *for given* p, t.

proof. We fix p, t. Since $U(x, p, z)$ is convex in $x \in \mathbb{R}^n$ for any $z \in Z(t)$, $\max_{z \in Z(t)} U(x, p, z)$ is convex in $x \in \mathbb{R}^n$ from [5, Section 3.2.3]. $\qquad\square$

Theorem 1. *Let* (p^*, t^*) *be an optimal solution of problem (P) and* $(\hat{p}, \hat{t}, \hat{z})$ *be an optimal solution of problem (AP). Then,* $L \cdot \mathbb{E}_{a \sim D(p^*, t^*)}[\max_{z \in Z(t^*)} U(a, p^*, z)] \leq \mathbb{E}_{a \sim D(\hat{p}, \hat{t})}[\max_{z \in Z(\hat{t})} U(a, \hat{p}, z)]$.

proof. Let $f(a, p, t)$ be $\max_{z \in Z(t)} U(a, p, z)$. For any feasible solution p, t of (P) and (AP), we find that $f(\mathbb{E}_{a \sim D(p, t)}[a], p, t) = \max_{z \in Z(t)} \{\sum_{i,j} (p_i - \alpha_{ij}) \cdot S_i(p_i, t_i) \cdot z_{ij}\} \geq L \cdot \max_{z \in Z(t)} \{\sum_{i,j} (p_i - \alpha_{ij}) \cdot z_{ij}\} \geq L \cdot \mathbb{E}_{a \sim D(p, t)}[f(a, p, t)]$, where the first inequality follows from $S_i(p_i, t_i) \geq L$, and the second inequality holds from $a_i \in \{0, 1\}$. Lemma 2 and Jensen's inequality give $\mathbb{E}_{a \sim D(p, t)}[f(a, p, t)] \geq f(\mathbb{E}_{a \sim D(p, t)}[a], p, t)$. Then, $L \cdot \mathbb{E}_{a \sim D(p^*, t^*)}[f(a, p^*, t^*)] \leq f(\mathbb{E}_{a \sim D(p^*, t^*)}[a], p^*, t^*) \leq f(\mathbb{E}_{a \sim D(\hat{p}, \hat{t})}[a], \hat{p}, \hat{t}) \leq \mathbb{E}_{a \sim D(\hat{p}, \hat{t})}[f(a, \hat{p}, \hat{t})]$, where the second inequality holds because $\hat{p}$, $\hat{t}$ is the optimal solution for (AP) and p^*, t^* is a feasible solution for (AP). $\qquad\square$

Therefore, we can find the L-approximation solution of (P) by solving (AP).

5.2 Efficient Algorithm for (AP)

We propose an efficient algorithm for solving (AP) by utilizing Lemma 1. We consider a new optimization problem as follows:

$$(\mathrm{AP}_z) \quad \max_z \sum_{i,j} (p_{ij} - \alpha_{ij}) \cdot S_i(p_{ij}, \tau_{ij}) \cdot z_{ij}$$

$$\text{s.t.} \sum_j z_{ij} \leq 1 \ \ \forall i \in I, \ \sum_i z_{ij} \leq 1 \ \ \forall j \in J$$

$$z_{ij} \in \{0, 1\} \ \ \forall i \in I \ \forall j \in J,$$

where $p_{ij} \in \arg\max_{p \in \{p \mid S_i(p, \tau_{ij}) \geq L\}} \{(p - \alpha_{ij}) \cdot S_i(p, \tau_{ij})\}$.

(AP_z) is the maximum weight matching problem and can be solved by the existing method of [10]. In addition, we can easily determine p_{ij} by solving the univariate optimization problem of $(\max_{p \in \{p \mid S_i(p, \tau_{ij}) \geq L\}} \{(p - \alpha_{ij}) \cdot S_i(p, \tau_{ij})\})$.

We show that the optimal solution of (AP) can be found by solving (AP_z). Based on optimal solution $\hat{z}$ of problem (AP_z), we determine $\hat{p}$ and $\hat{t}$ as follows:

1. For i that satisfies $\exists j \ \hat{z}_{ij} = 1$, let $\hat{p}_i = p_{ij}, \hat{t}_i = \tau_{ij}$.
2. For other i, set arbitrary values $(\hat{p}_i, \hat{t}_i)$ that satisfy $S_i(\hat{p}_i, \hat{t}_i) \geq L$.

Then, the following theorem holds:

Theorem 2. $(\hat{p}, \hat{t}, \hat{z})$ *is an optimal solution of (AP).*
proof. If the feasible region of optimization problem (AP_z) *is taken to be* $\boldsymbol{Z}^c$, *the following lemma holds.*

Lemma 3. *For all* $z' \in \boldsymbol{Z}^c$, *we consider optimization problem* $(\mathrm{AP}(z'))$ *by fixing* z *to* z' *in (AP). We set* p', t' *by (i)* $p'_i = p_{ij}$, $t'_i - \tau_{ij}$ *for* i *which satisfies* $\exists j \; z'_{ij} = 1$, *and (ii) arbitrary value* p'_i, t'_i *that satisfies* $S_i(p'_i, t'_i) \geq L$ *for other* i. *Then,* (p', t') *is an optimal solution of* $(\mathrm{AP}(z'))$ *and the optimal value is* $\sum_{ij}(p_{ij} - \alpha_{ij}) \cdot S_i(p_{ij}, \tau_{ij}) \cdot z'_{ij}$.

proof. First, (p'_i, t'_i) is a feasible solution of $(\mathrm{AP}(z'))$ by definition. Let $M := \{(i,j) \mid z'_{ij} = 1\}$ and $h_{ij}(p,t) := (p - \alpha_{ij}) \cdot S_i(p,t)$. For arbitrary feasible solution (p_i, t_i) of $(\mathrm{AP}(z'))$, $\sum_{(i,j)} h_{ij}(p'_i, t'_i) \cdot z'_{ij} = \sum_{(i,j) \in M} h_{ij}(p_{ij}, \tau_{ij}) = \sum_{(i,j) \in M} \max_p\{h_{ij}(p, \tau_{ij}) \mid S_i(p, \tau_{ij}) \geq L\} \geq \sum_{(i,j) \in M} \max_p\{h_{ij}(p, t_i) \mid S_i(p, t_i) \geq L\} \geq \sum_{(i,j) \in M} h_{ij}(p_i, t_i) = \sum_{i,j} h_{ij}(p_i, t_i) \cdot z'_{ij}$. This indicates (p'_i, t'_i) is an optimal solution of $(\mathrm{AP}(z'))$. Note that the first inequality holds since $t_i \geq \tau_{ij}$, and $S_i(p,t)$ monotonically decreases in t from Lemma 1.   □

Lemma 3 shows that we can solve (AP) by solving optimization problem $\max_{z' \in \boldsymbol{Z}^c} \sum_{ij}(p_{ij} - \alpha_{ij}) \cdot S_i(p_{ij}, \tau_{ij}) \cdot z'_{ij}$ and deciding p, t by the process described in Lemma 3. This optimization problem is equivalent to (AP_z). □

5.3 Further Improvement of Objective Value

The algorithm explained in Sect. 5.2 cannot determine price and time for requesters for whom optimum matching fails, that is, $\{i \mid \forall j \; \hat{z}_{ij} = 0\}$ (the algorithm outputs arbitrary feasible values). We need a policy to decide the proposals offered to those requesters. We further consider the following problem:

$$(\mathrm{RP}_z) \quad \max_z \sum_{i \in I', j} w_j \cdot (p_{ij} - \alpha_{ij}) \cdot S_i(p_{ij}, \tau_{ij}) \cdot z_{ij}$$

$$\text{s.t.} \sum_j z_{ij} \leq 1 \; \forall i \in I', \; \sum_{i \in I'} z_{ij} \leq 1 \; \forall j \in J$$

$$z_{ij} \in \{0,1\} \; \forall i \in I' \; \forall j \in J,$$

where I' is the set of remaining requesters and w_j is a weight representing the probability that taxi j will be available.

We propose a policy to recursively solve (RP_z) while updating I' and w_j to determine the price and time of all requesters. First, we set $w_j := 1$ and $I' := I$, that is, (RP_z) corresponds to (AP_z). After solving (RP_z), form a new (RP_z) as follows: Remove index $i \in I'$ and set $w_j := w_j \cdot (1 - S_i(p_i, t_i))$ for (i,j) included in the previous matching. Here, the reason for multiplying the edge weights by $1 - S_i(p_i, t_i)$ is that the edges connected to j cannot be used if requester i accepts (with probability $S_i(p_i, t_i)$) and taxi j is matched. The weight can be regarded as an approximation of the expected weight that considers the probability of

---

Algorithm 1. Price and time optimization

Input: τ_{ij}, α_{ij}, S_i, and L
Output: p and t
1: Initialize: $w_j := 1$, $E := \{(i,j) \mid i \in I, \ j \in J\}$.
2: Let $p_{ij} \in \arg\max_p \{(p - \alpha_{ij}) \cdot S_i(p, \tau_{ij}) | S_i(p, \tau_{ij}) \geq L\}$.
3: **while** $\exists (i,j) \in E, (p_{ij} - \alpha \cdot \tau_{ij}) \cdot S_i(p_{ij}, \tau_{ij}) > 0$ **do**
4:    Find the optimal solution $\hat{z}$ of the (RP_z).
5:    Let $p_i := \{p_{ij} \mid \hat{z}_{ij} = 1\}$, $t_i := \{\tau_{ij} \mid \hat{z}_{ij} = 1\}$ and remove $\{i \mid \exists j, \hat{z}_{ij} = 1\}$ from I.
6:    Let $w_j := w_j \cdot (1 - S_i(p_{ij}, \tau_{ij}))$ for each $\{(i,j) \mid \hat{z}_{ij} = 1\}$
7: **end while**
8: **return** p, t

---

the corresponding taxi being surplus. Here, every time (RP_z) is solved, we can determine price and time for some of the remaining requesters from optimal solution $\hat{z}$ for (RP_z) as done in Sect. 5.2.

Algorithm 1 describes our overall algorithm. The algorithm is guaranteed to output an L-approximate solution from Theorem 1 and 2. The time complexity of the proposed algorithm is bounded by $O(n(n^3 + m^3))$ because (i) the maximum number of iterations of lines 3–7 is n since at least one index i is removed from I with each iteration, and (ii) each iteration of lines 3–7 takes $O(n^3 + m^3)$ time to solve a weighted bipartite matching [10].

6   Experiments

We conduct experiments to show that the followings hold: (i) Proposed method improves both requester's utilities and service provider's profit; (ii) Proposed method solves the problem quickly. All experiments were run on a computer with Xeon Platinum 8168 with $4 \times 2.7\,\mathrm{GHz}$, $1\,\mathrm{TB}$ memory, and CentOS 7.6.

Experiment Setup. First, we explain the data used in our experiments. We use ride data gathered in New York[1]. Each record of the data consists of pick-up area, pick-up time, drop-off area, drop-off time. We reproduce the situations of taxi ordering and dispatching by the data. We use the data from September 8 and 12, 2019, which are holidays and weekdays in a randomly chosen week. The target regions are Manhattan and Queens. We simulate 600 dispatch processes every minute from 10:00 to 20:00 by the data. We assume the other transportation set is $\{train, bus, walking\}$. Locations of stations and bus stops are taken from subway stations data[2] and bus stops data[3].

Then, we set the inputs as follows.
(i) τ_{ij}: It is calculated from the locations of requesters/taxis.
(ii) α_{ij}: Assume that there are no differences in taxi capability and no regional differences; $\alpha_{ij} := 18.0 \cdot \tau_{ij}$, which is based on taxi driver income.

---

[1] https://www1.nyc.gov/site/tlc/about/tlc-trip-record-data.page.
[2] https://data.cityofnewyork.us/Transportation/Subway-Stations/arq3-7z49.
[3] https://data.cityofnewyork.us/Transportation/Bus-Stop-Shelters/qafz-7myz.

(iii) S_i: Let $C_i(p,t) := p + \phi_i \cdot t$ and $S_i(p,t) := \frac{\exp(-C_i(p,t))}{\exp(-C_i(p,t)) + \sum_{k \in K} \exp(-C_i(p_{ik}, t_{ik}))}$, as already explained in Sect. 4. We use $C_i(p,t)$ without the effect ξ_i of other factors for simplicity. We take the value of time ϕ_i for each request i from a uniform distribution of $10 \leq \phi_i \leq 17$, which is a plausible range of values of time in U.S.A[4]. For other transportation k, we set p_{ik}, t_{ik} from the published facts[5].
(iv) L: we set $L := 0.85$ as the hyper-parameter of the proposed method.

Metrics. We use two metrics to measure how well each approach (i) improves the service provider's profits and (ii) meets the requester's priorities. The first metric is the approximated expected revenue of the service provider calculated by the Monte Carlo method: $\text{ER} := \frac{1}{N} \sum_{d=1}^{N} \max_{z \in Z(t)} U(a^d, p, z)$, where $(a^d)_{d=1}^{N}$ is a set of independent, identically distributed realizations of a, which are acceptance results. The second is the approximation of the expected generalized cost reduction calculated by the Monte Carlo method: $\text{EGCR} := \frac{1}{N} \sum_{d=1}^{N} \{\sum_{i \in X^d} G_i^{all} - G_i^{other}\}$, where $G_i^{other} := \min_{k \in K}\{C_i(p_{ik}, t_{ik})\}$, $G_i^{all} := \min\{G_i^{other}, C_i(p_i, t_i)\}$, and X^d is the set of requesters assigned taxis according to a^d. G_i^{other} is the generalized cost of optimal transportation modes when each requester can use transportation modes other than taxis, and G_i^{all} is that when each requester can use all transportation modes including taxis. It evaluates how much the taxi service reduces the generalized cost. Our goal is to increase the value of these two metrics. We set $N := 10^2$.

Compared Methods. We compared the proposed method with five baselines.
(i) MAPS [22]: It is an approximation algorithm for area basis pricing. We use it to determine prices that are offered to requesters together with a fixed waiting time θ. This method requires an acceptance probability function for each area, so we added up the individual probability functions for each area. We use the most profitable $\theta \in \{0.05, 0.075, 0.10\}$ for each region and each date.
(ii) LinUCB [15]: It is the generic contextual bandit algorithm adopted by [6]. We use it to determine prices and offer the prices and the fixed waiting time $\theta = 0.075$ to requesters. As features for learning, we use (pick-up areas, drop-off areas, hours, trip distance).
(iii) FPFT (Fixed Price and Fixed Time): It offers a fixed price rate σ and a fixed waiting time θ to all requesters. We use the most profitable combination (σ, θ) in $\sigma \in \{1.0, 1.5, 2.0, 2.5\}$ and $\theta \in \{0.05, 0, 1\}$ for each region and each date.
(iv) FPS (Fixed Price and Shortest distance dispatch): It offers a fixed price rate σ and times based on shortest distance dispatch to requesters. We use the most profitable $\sigma \in \{1.0, 1.5, 2.0, 2.5\}$ for each region and each date.
(v) FPP (Fixed Price and Profitable distance dispatch): It offers a fixed price rate σ and times based on profit-maximizing dispatch to requesters. We use the most profitable $\sigma \in \{1.0, 1.5, 2.0, 2.5\}$ for each region and each date.

Results. Table 1 shows the simulation results. The proposed method outperforms the baselines w.r.t. both ER and EGCR for all dates and regions. The

---

[4] https://www.transportation.gov/sites/dot.gov/files/docs/2016%20Revised
%20Value%20of%20Travel%20Time%20Guidance.pdf.
[5] https://new.mta.info/fares-and-tolls/subway-bus-and-staten-island-railway.

Table 1. Simulation results. Each result represents the average of 600 dispatches.

Place &	Day	n (requesters)		m (taxis)		Proposed			MAPS			LinUCB		
		MEAN	SD	MEAN	SD	ER	EGCR	time (s)	ER	EGCR	time (s)	ER	EGCR	time (s)
Manhattan	9/8 (Sun)	95.5	11.9	94.1	14.1	**123**	**111**	0.498	112	45.2	0.0886	77.0	67.1	13.1
	9/12 (Thu)	116	30.7	112	27.9	**141**	**134**	0.936	126	50.0	0.105	88.3	76.7	16.1
Queens	9/8 (Sun)	60.6	10.1	59.7	9.93	**107**	**58.4**	0.109	78.8	37.4	0.0473	58.9	41.6	7.48
	9/12 (Thu)	56.0	11.4	58.1	11.9	**93.0**	**53.1**	0.0854	68.6	32.5	0.0442	51.7	34.5	6.96

Place &	Day	n (requesters)		m (taxis)		FPFT			FPS			FPP		
		MEAN	SD	MEAN	SD	ER	EGCR	time (s)	ER	EGCR	time (s)	ER	EGCR	time (s)
Manhattan	9/8 (Sun)	95.5	11.9	94.1	14.1	89.7	39.1	-	106	46.7	4.78	110	47.1	2.82
	9/12 (Thu)	116	30.7	112	27.9	104	47.0	-	125	57.9	9.47	132	59.6	5.24
Queens	9/8 (Sun)	60.6	10.1	59.7	9.93	63.7	46.5	-	68.5	52.6	1.32	70.7	48.1	0.488
	9/12 (Thu)	56.0	11.4	58.1	11.9	55.8	40.0	-	62.1	47.1	1.15	65.0	44.3	0.351

differences between the proposed method and all other methods are significant for ER and EGCR (two-sided t-test: $p < 0.0001$) in each region and date. In addition, the computation times of the proposed method range from 0.08 to 1.0 s, which is short enough for practical use.

7   Conclusion

In this paper, we address the optimization of proposals offered to requesters in taxi services considering the individual price and time priorities. We formulated a price and time optimization problem that considers requester's service acceptance probability; we also constructed a fast approximation algorithm that offers performance guarantees. Simulations on real datasets showed that the proposed method increases both the expected profit and the satisfaction of requesters, and outputs the solutions fast enough to be practical.

References

1. Abrantes, P.A.L., Wardman, M.R.: Meta-analysis of UK values of travel time: an update. Transp. Res. Part A: Policy Practice **45**(1), 1–17 (2011)
2. Alonso-Mora, J., Samaranayake, S., Wallar, A., Frazzoli, E., Rus, D.: On-demand high-capacity ride-sharing via dynamic trip-vehicle assignment. Natl. Acad. Sci. **114**(3), 462–467 (2017)
3. Asghari, M., Deng, D., Shahabi, C., Demiryurek, U., Li, Y.: Price-aware real-time ride-sharing at scale: an auction-based approach. In: SIGSPATIAL, pp. 1–10 (2016)
4. Asghari, M., Shahabi, C.: Adapt-pricing: a dynamic and predictive technique for pricing to maximize revenue in ridesharing platforms. In: SIGSPATIAL, pp. 189–198 (2018)
5. Boyd, S., Vandenberghe, L.: Convex Optimization. Cambridge University Press, Cambridge (2004)
6. Chen, H., et al.: Inbede: integrating contextual bandit with td learning for joint pricing and dispatch of ride-hailing platforms. In: ICDM, pp. 61–70 (2019)
7. Chen, L., Zhong, Q., Xiao, X., Gao, Y., Jin, P., Jensen, C.S.: Price-and-time-aware dynamic ridesharing. In: ICDE, pp. 1061–1072 (2018)

8. Dickerson, J.P., Sankararaman, K.A., Srinivasan, A., Xu, P.: Allocation problems in ride-sharing platforms: online matching with offline reusable resources. In: AAAI, pp. 1007–1014 (2018)
9. de Dios Ortúzar, J., Willumsen, L.G.: Modelling Transport. Wiley (2011)
10. Galil, Z.: Efficient algorithms for finding maximum matching in graphs. ACM Comput. Surv. **18**(1), 23–38 (1986)
11. Gan, J., An, B., Wang, H., Sun, X., Shi, Z.: Optimal pricing for improving efficiency of taxi systems. In: IJCAI, pp. 2811–2818 (2013)
12. Jin, J., et al.: Coride: joint order dispatching and fleet management for multi-scale ride-hailing platforms. In: CIKM, pp. 1983–1992 (2019)
13. Kleiner, A., Nebel, B., Ziparo, V.A.: A mechanism for dynamic ride sharing based on parallel auctions. In: IJCAI, pp. 266–272 (2011)
14. Lee, D.H., Wang, H., Cheu, R.L., Teo, S.H.: Taxi dispatch system based on current demands and real-time traffic conditions. Transp. Res. Rec. **1882**(1), 193–200 (2004)
15. Li, L., Chu, W., Langford, J., Schapire, R.E.: A contextual-bandit approach to personalized news article recommendation. In: WWW, pp. 661–670 (2010)
16. Li, M., et al.: Efficient ridesharing order dispatching with mean field multi-agent reinforcement learning. In: WWW, pp. 983–994 (2019)
17. Lowalekar, M., Varakantham, P., Jaillet, P.: Online spatio-temporal matching in stochastic and dynamic domains. Artif. Intell. **261**, 71–112 (2018)
18. McFadden, D.: Economic choices. Am. Econ. Rev. **91**(3), 351–378 (2001)
19. Seow, K.T., Dang, N.H., Lee, D.H.: A collaborative multiagent taxi-dispatch system. IEEE Trans. Autom. Sci. Eng. **7**(3), 607–616 (2009)
20. Small, K.A., Verhoef, E.T., Lindsey, R.: The economics of urban transportation. Routledge (2007)
21. Tong, Y., She, J., Ding, B., Chen, L., Wo, T., Xu, K.: Online minimum matching in real-time spatial data: experiments and analysis. VLDB Endowment **9**(12), 1053–1064 (2016)
22. Tong, Y., Wang, L., Zhou, Z., Chen, L., Du, B., Ye, J.: Dynamic pricing in spatial crowdsourcing: a matching-based approach. In: SIGMOD, pp. 773–788 (2018)
23. Wardman, M.: The value of travel time: a review of British evidence. JTEP **32**(3), 285–316 (1998)
24. Xu, Z., et al.: Large-scale order dispatch in on-demand ride-hailing platforms: a learning and planning approach. In: KDD, pp. 905–913 (2018)
25. Zha, L., Yin, Y., Xu, Z.: Geometric matching and spatial pricing in ride-sourcing markets. Transp. Res. Part C Emerg. Technol. **92**, 58–75 (2018)
26. Zhang, L., Ye, Z., Xiao, K., Jin, B.: A parallel simulated annealing enhancement of the optimal-matching heuristic for ridesharing. In: ICDM, pp. 906–915 (2019)
27. Zhang, L., et al.: A taxi order dispatch model based on combinatorial optimization. In: KDD, pp. 2151–2159 (2017)
28. Zhao, B., Xu, P., Shi, Y., Tong, Y., Zhou, Z., Zeng, Y.: Preference-aware task assignment in on-demand taxi dispatching: an online stable matching approach. In: AAAI, pp. 2245–2252 (2019)

VAN: Voting and Attention Based Network for Unsupervised Medical Image Registration

Zhiang Zu[1], Guixu Zhang[1], Yaxin Peng[2], Zhen Ye[3], and Chaomin Shen[1,4(✉)]

[1] School of Computer Science, East China Normal University, Shanghai, China
`cmshen@cs.ecnu.edu.cn`
[2] Department of Mathematics, Shanghai University, Shanghai, China
[3] Shanghai Electric Central Research Institute, Shanghai, China
[4] Shanghai Key Laboratory of Multidimensional Information Processing,
East China Normal University, Shanghai, China

Abstract. In this paper, a novel unsupervised network for medical image registration called VAN (Voting and Attention based Network) is proposed, in which the final deformation field is determined by the voting process between multiple registration branches. To reduce model parameters, multiple registration branches share one encoder. Besides, the attention mechanism is introduced, which further improves the network accuracy. We also adopt the method of single training and multiple-registrations to deal with the problem of the large deformation field. The experimental results show that the registration effect of our proposed network outperforms the baselines VoxelMorph and Symmetric Normalization (SyN) on three brain MRI image datasets.

Keywords: Medical image registration · Voting process · Attention mechanism · Multiple-registrations

1   Introduction

Medical image registration is a fundamental task in medical image studies, which can be regarded as a basic procedure in medical image analysis. Doctors can better observe the changes of lesions through the images after registration. In short, the task of image registration is to align one image with another, so that the similarity between the aligned images is the highest. It is a prerequisite for medical imaging applications concerning comparison.

More specifically, given a moving (source) image I_M and a fixed (target) image I_F, medical image registration aims to predict a displacement field u, and the corresponding deformation field ϕ from the moving image to the fixed image, so that the warped moving image $I_W = I_M \circ \phi$ and the fixed image are as similar as possible. The transformation of pixel (voxel) position p can be expressed as

© Springer Nature Switzerland AG 2021
D. N. Pham et al. (Eds.): PRICAI 2021, LNAI 13031, pp. 382–393, 2021.
https://doi.org/10.1007/978-3-030-89188-6_29

$\phi(\boldsymbol{p}) = \boldsymbol{p} + \boldsymbol{u}(\boldsymbol{p})$ [2]. The proper deformation field ϕ^* is obtained by minimizing the image dissimilarity, i.e.,

$$\phi^* = \arg\min_{\phi} \text{ dissim} (I_M \circ \phi, I_F) + \lambda \text{ reg}(\phi),$$

where dissim$(\cdot, \cdot)$ represents the dissimilarity between images, reg$(\cdot)$ is the regularization term, and λ is the weight to balance the above two items.

The deformation field predicted by a single registration branch may be inaccurate enough due to various reasons. Therefore, this paper uses multiple registration branches to generate multiple deformation fields at the same time, and the final deformation field is generated by voting between these deformation fields. Besides, multiple registration branches share the same encoder to reduce the model parameters.

In general, the deformation can be classified as large-scale and small-scale deformations. Most registration methods can only deal with small-scale deformation. For example, VoxelMorph [2] is a typical deep learning method for small-scale deformation, so it is necessary to perform pre-registration (affine alignment) for the images. To handle the large-scale deformation, one intuitive solution is to decompose the large-scale deformation into a series of small-scale deformations. Some papers adopted the method of stacking multiple registration networks to achieve large deformation prediction. In these networks, each registration network predicts a small deformation and each of them is combined to form a large deformation. However, the accuracy of this layer-by-layer training method is no longer improved after the stacked layers reach a certain number [21].

In this paper, we provide our solution to the large-scale deformation by single training and multiple-registrations, i.e., in the training stage the model is trained once, and in the testing stage registrations are conducted multiple times.

The contributions of this paper can be summarized as follows:

- We predict the final deformation field by the voting process between multiple registration branches, which are constructed by multiple decoders sharing the same encoder to reduce model parameters;
- We use multiple-registrations to solve the problem of large deformation registration in the testing stage;
- We introduce the attention mechanism into registration, which improves the registration effect while adding a few parameters.

2   Related Work

In this section, we summarize the similarities and differences between traditional and learning-based registration methods.

2.1   Traditional Registration Methods

Medical registration can be divided into traditional registration methods and learning-based registration methods. The traditional registration methods refer to the model-driven methods. These methods are explainable, however, they are time-consuming as iterative methods are needed for implementation. Besides, these methods neglect the inherent registration patterns shared across images from the same dataset, so do not make full use of the information from other images in registration.

The popular examples of these algorithmic are Large Deformation Diffeomorphic Metric Matching (LDDMM) [3], Diffeomorphic Demons [16] and Symmetric image Normalization method (SyN) [1].

2.2   Learning-Based Registration Methods

The learning-based registration methods refer to the data-driven models constructed by neural networks. Firstly, a model is trained with a large amount of data, and then a new pair of images are registered with the trained model. These methods are in general more accurate than the traditional methods, although they are less explainable. Besides, their registration process in the testing stage is much faster than the traditional methods. The learning-based registration methods can be further divided into supervised and unsupervised methods.

Supervised Registration Methods

Supervised registration needs ground truth. In general, the ground truth can be obtained in two ways. One is to use the deformation field derived from the traditional registration methods [14]. In this case, the effect of the model will not exceed that of the traditional methods in theory. The other is to randomly deform an image to form the ground truth [15]. The original image is taken as the moving image, the deformed image as the fixed image, and the artificial deformation field as the ground truth. The disadvantage of supervised registrations is that the available high-quality supervision data are deficient, and the annotation process is costly.

VoxelMorph realized both unsupervised and supervised registrations, in which the segmentation masks are used as the supervised information. We use this registration methods as one of our baselines. Based on VoxelMorph, BIRNet [6] has made a lot of modifications to the registration network.

Unsupervised Registration Methods

Unsupervised registration is a hot topic in recent years. Image registration is essentially an unsupervised task, as it only needs to optimize the similarity between two images. However, these methods have certain requirements for the selection of image similarity metrics. Recently, many unsupervised registration models using the Generative Adversarial Networks (GANs) [7] were proposed. The advantage of these models is that they do not need a specific image similarity metric, which avoids the generality problem of fixed image similarity metrics due to the different distributions of datasets.

DIRNet [17], the first unsupervised end-to-end deep learning registration model, introduced Spatial Transformer Network (STN) [8] into registration. ICNet [19] and SYMNet [12] avoided the overlapping of the deformation field by ensuring that the deformation field is a diffeomorphism. Which is a reversible, differentiable and smooth transformation. CycleMorph [10] combined the bidirectional registration and the cycle-consistent registration to make the deformation field diffeomorphism. These models usually have many parameters and long training time. ASNet [5] and Deform-GAN [20] used GAN to solve the problem of mono-modal and multi-modal registration respectively. However, the GAN-based model is hard to converge in training.

3 Methodology

This section describes our methodology for the medical registration network called Voting and Attention based Network (VAN), as it uses the voting and attention mechanism, which will be discussed in detail later. We also introduce the loss function.

3.1 Network Framework

VAN has a training network and a testing network, which are similar but not identical. The training network is illustrated in Fig. 1, and the testing network in Fig. 3. Both networks consist of three modules: the registration module, the STN module and the Convolutional Block Attention Module (CBAM) [18]. The input of the whole network is the stacked image composed of the moving and fixed images, and the output is the warped image.

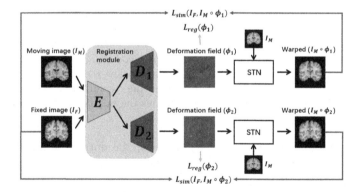

Fig. 1. Structure of the training phase. To be concise, only two registration branches are shown, and CBAM is not shown.

The moving image and fixed image are firstly concatenated in the channel dimension to obtain a 2-channel 3D image, and then it is inputted into the encoder to extract the features of the concatenated image. Then, two mappings from the moving image to the fixed image are predicted by two decoders respectively. The features obtained by the encoders are propagated to the corresponding layer of the encoder through the skip connection. After the registration field is obtained, the moving image is processed by STN and two warped images are obtained by trilinear interpolation.

Registration Module
The process of the registration module can be described as $u = R_\theta(I_F, I_M)$, where $R_\theta(\cdot)$ is the registration module and θ indicates the network parameters. The registration module consists of an encoder and multiple decoders, and each decoder outputs a deformation field. Different from the task of using multiple registration branches with the same structure and different parameters, multiple decoders share the same encoder as the input, and they have the same structure and different parameters after learning caused by different initial values. This greatly reduces the model parameters while achieving high registration results.

The encoder can extract the features of the fixed image and the moving image at the same time, while in the decoder part, the features extracted by the decoder part are used to predict registration fields from the moving image to the fixed image. The encoder and its decoder constitute a complete U-Net [13] like structure as shown in Fig. 2. Each convolution block consists of the convolution operation with the kernel size of 3 by 3 and the ReLU activation function.

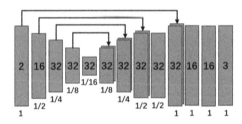

Fig. 2. The U-Net structure is constituted by an encoder and its decoder. Each rectangle represents a 3D volume; the numbers in and below the rectangle represent the number of channels and the relationship between the resolution of the original image respectively. The solid line with an arrow indicates the skip connection.

In the testing stage as illustrated in Fig. 3, the output of the registration module is a final deformation field generated by the voting process between these deformation fields. More specifically, the voting process means that after obtaining the multiple predicted deformation fields, each voxel value of the final deformation field is obtained by the average of voxels in the same position of the multiple deformation fields.

The output of the registration modules served as one of the two inputs of the STN module.

STN Module
For the 3D image with the size of $[D, W, H]$, the displacement field is a tensor with the size of $[D, W, H, 3]$. STN is used to warp the moving image according to the deformation field generated by the registration network. First, a normalized sampling grid (registration field) is obtained, and then the registration field is

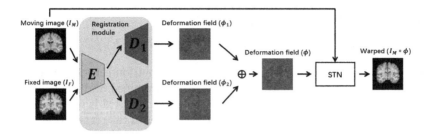

Fig. 3. Overview of the testing phase. Different from the training stage, the final deformation field is generated by the voting of multiple predicted deformation fields.

used to sample the moving image. Here the trilinear interpolation is used. This process can be expressed as $I_W = \mathrm{STN}(I_M, \phi)$, where $\mathrm{STN}(\cdot)$ is a model without parameters, and its interpolation process is differentiable, which ensures that the parameters of the whole network can be updated through back-propagation.

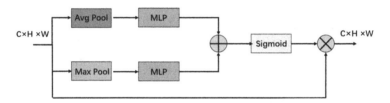

Fig. 4. Overview of the channel attention and spatial attention part in CBAM. The pooling operations are channel-based and spatial-based respectively. $\oplus$ denotes the sum and concatenation operation respectively.

Convolutional Block Attention Module

The attention mechanism in deep learning is generated by imitating human attention. When we look at an image, our attention will focus on some parts of the image (such as the face of the person), while others may be ignored. The attention mechanism is equivalent to giving a weight to every pixel. CBAM includes two parts as shown in Fig. 4: channel attention and spatial attention, which adds attention to the image in the spatial and channel dimensions of the feature map. Because CBAM does not change the size of the feature map, CBAM can be inserted into any position in the network.

The channel attention part can be expressed as

$$\mathbf{M_c}(\boldsymbol{F}) = \sigma(\mathrm{MLP}(\mathrm{Avg\ Pool}(\boldsymbol{F})) + \mathrm{MLP}(\mathrm{Max\ Pool}(\boldsymbol{F}))),$$

where $\boldsymbol{F}$ is the input feature map, $\mathrm{AvgPool}(\cdot)$ and $\mathrm{MaxPool}(\cdot)$ are the average and maximum pooling operations respectively, $\mathrm{MLP}(\cdot)$ is a multi-layer perceptron, and $\sigma(\cdot)$ represents the sigmoid activation function.

The spatial attention part can be expressed as

$$\mathbf{M_s}(\mathbf{F}) = \sigma \left(f^{7 \times 7}([\text{AvgPool}(\mathbf{F}); \text{Max Pool}(\mathbf{F})]) \right),$$

where $f^{7 \times 7}$ is the convolution operation with convolution kernel size of 7×7.

To our best knowledge, CBAM has not been combined into the registration yet. In our paper, we attempt to combine them. The CBAM is inserted into the outputs of the 2nd, 3rd and 4th layers of the encoder in the registration module.

Multiple-Registrations

In the testing stage, given a moving image and a fixed image, we can obtain a warped image. However, this warped image may not be sufficiently accurate. Thus, the testing network should be conducted again, with the modification that in the input the moving image is replaced by the warped image. This process is called multiple-registrations.

3.2 Loss Function

The loss function consists of the image similarity loss $\mathcal{L}_{sim}(I_F, I_M \circ \phi)$ and the smoothness regularization loss $\mathcal{L}_{reg}(\phi)$.

There are many kinds of image similarity losses, such as correlation coefficient (CC), normalized correlation coefficient (NCC), mutual information (MI), mean square error (MSE) and so on. The normalized correlation coefficient (NCC) loss is adopted in this paper, which is

$$\mathcal{L}_{sim}(I_F, I_M \circ \phi) = -\text{NCC}(I_F, I_M \circ \phi)$$

$$= -\sum_{p \in \Omega} \frac{\sum_{p_i} \left(I_F(p_i) - \bar{I}_F(p) \right) \left(I_M(\phi(p_i)) - \bar{I}_M(\phi(p)) \right)}{\sqrt{\sum_{p_i} \left(I_F(p_i) - \bar{I}_F(p) \right)^2 \sum_{p_i} \left(I_M(\phi(p_i)) - \bar{I}_M(\phi(p)) \right)^2}},$$

where p_i denotes the position within a $9 \times 9 \times 9$ local window centered at position p, $\bar{I}_F$ and $\bar{I}_M$ are the local means of I_F and I_M at p respectively, and Ω is a 3D domain.

The smoothness regularization loss is used to measure the smoothness of the deformation field to prevent the overlap and to ensure the smoothness of deformation fields. The formula for smoothness regularization loss is

$$\mathcal{L}_{reg}(\phi) = \sum_{p \in \Omega} \|\nabla \phi(p)\|^2.$$

Therefore, the total loss of the network is

$$\mathcal{L}(I_F, I_M, \phi) = -\frac{1}{2}[\text{NCC}(I_F, I_M \circ \phi_1) + \text{NCC}(I_F, I_M \circ \phi_2)]$$

$$+ \frac{1}{2}\lambda[\sum_{p \in \Omega} \|\nabla \phi_1(p)\|^2 + \sum_{p \in \Omega} \|\nabla \phi_2(p)\|^2],$$

where λ is the regularization trade-off parameter.

4   Experiments and Analysis

In this part, we first introduce the datasets, baselines and data preprocessing. Then the model validity is analyzed by baseline comparison and ablation experiments.

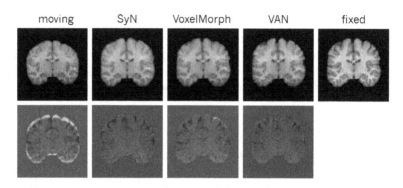

Fig. 5. Example results (top row) and difference images (bottom row) on the LPBA40 dataset.

4.1   Dataset and Preprocessing

Three brain MRI datasets LPBA40, IBSR18 and MGH10 are selected for the experiments, which include 40, 18 and 10 subjects respectively, and the Dice Similarity Coefficient (DSC) is calculated on 54, 96 and 106 brain ROIs.

We focus on the atlas-based registration, which selects an image as the fixed image, and randomly selects an image as a moving image for registration in each iteration. The fixed images used in different models and methods are the same.

For the LPBA40 and IBSR18 datasets, one image is selected as the fixed image, 30 and 13 images as the training sets, and the remaining as the testing sets. For the MGH10 dataset, one image is selected as the fixed image, the remaining are used as the testing set to verify the generality of our model.

We carry out the standard pre-processing of 3D medical image registration, including brain extraction using FreeSurfer and affine image alignment using FMRIB Software Library (FSL) [9]. Then we unify the voxel spacing to 1mm×1mm×1mm. The intensity is locally normalized for each image. Each pixel value minus the minimum value of the image pixel value, and divided by the maximum value of the image pixel value. In addition, to make full use of memory, we also use the method proposed in nnU-Net [4] to remove the redundant background part and keep only the brain area, to reduce the memory cost and training time. For LPBA40 dataset, because the images do not contain skulls and have been aligned to the MNI305 space, we do not carry out brain extraction and affine alignment.

4.2   Implementation Details

In the training parse, we use the Adam optimizer [11] and set the batch size to 1. The initial learning rate and λ for LPBA40 are 4e−4 and 4, for IBSR18 are 2e−4 and 11, respectively. The training stage runs for 15,000 iterations.

4.3   Baselines

We choose a traditional registration method and a learning-based registration method as the baseline models. The traditional registration method is symmetric normalization [1] (SyN) registration algorithm in ANTs toolkit, while the learning-based registration method is VoxelMorph registration network.

4.4   Experimental Results

The experimental results are shown in Table 1. We used three different registration methods to do experiments on three brain MRI datasets. VAN achieves the best results on LPBA40 and IBSR18 datasets compared with the SyN and VoxelMorph. Figure 5 shows an example on the LPBA40 dataset. The warped images generated by VAN registration are closer to the fixed image, which demonstrates that VAN yields better structural alignment. Besides, to verify the transferability of VAN, we apply VAN trained on the IBSR18 dataset to directly register images in the MGH10 dataset, and find that its registration effect is 0.84 (from 33.83 to 34.67) higher than VoxelMorph. This shows that our model has good robustness across different datasets.

Table 1. Average DSC of different registration methods on three datasets. (parentheses: standard deviations across subjects.)

	Affine only	SyN	VoxelMorph	VAN
LPBA40	53.86(0.04)	69.42(0.01)	68.77(0.02)	**69.98(0.02)**
IBSR18	38.38(0.05)	41.19(0.03)	41.43(0.03)	**41.51(0.03)**
MGH10	33.27(0.04)	34.65(0.06)	33.83(0.05)	**34.67(0.04)**

Table 2. Average inference time and the number of parameters for different registration methods. (parentheses: standard deviations across subjects.)

	SyN	VoxelMorph	VAN
Time(s)	17.66(1.18)	**1.32(0.04)**	1.62(0.22)
Parameter	–	**396,457**	626,908

Table 2 shows the computational time and the number of parameters for different algorithms. As mentioned earlier, learning-based registration methods take less time than traditional registration methods. The time required for VoxelMorph and VAN is much lower than the SyN. Because VAN has 230,451 (from 396,457 to 626,908) more parameters than VoxelMorph, it takes 300 ms extra time.

Due to the limitation of memory, only two registration branches are used to vote the final deformation field. Theoretically, the more registration branches participated in the voting, the better the registration results.

4.5 Ablation Experiments

Table 3. Results of ablation experiments. VAN-1 means that registration is conducted once, while VAN-2 means twice.

	VAN-1	VAN-2	VAN-2 w/o CBAM
Avg. DSC	69.18 (0.02)	**69.88 (0.02)**	62.34 (0.04)

To verify the effect of multiple-registrations and CBAM, we also conduct the ablation experiments. As shown in Table 3, for the LPBA40 dataset, a better result is obtained when 2-registrations are performed, which is 0.70 (from 69.18 to 69.88) higher than 1-registrations in terms of average DSC. This verifies the effectiveness of the multiple-registrations method. The registration effect before and after removing CBAM is also shown in Table 3. It can be found that the addition of CBAM improves registration accuracy. This shows that the addition of attention mechanism is helpful to improve the registration results.

5 Conclusion

We have presented a voting and attention based registration network, in which the final deformation field is generated by the voting process of multiple registration branches. To reduce the number of model parameters, the registration module is constructed by multiple decoders sharing an encoder. Besides, we introduce the attention mechanism to medical image registration. This voting method achieves higher registration accuracy compared with SyN and VoxelMorph. The attention mechanism improves the accuracy of the model while adding a few parameters. In addition, we use multiple-registrations method to deal with the problem of large deformation field prediction.

Acknowledgment. This work was supported by Shanghai Science and Technology Innovation Action Plan (18441909000, 20511100200), Science and Technology Commission of Shanghai Municipality (14DZ2260800), and OSTF foundation. The authors would like to thank Prof. Meng Yao of East China Normal University for fruitful discussion.

References

1. Avants, B.B., Epstein, C.L., Grossman, M., Gee, J.C.: Symmetric diffeomorphic image registration with cross-correlation: evaluating automated labeling of elderly and neurodegenerative brain. Med. Image Anal. **12**(1), 26–41 (2008)
2. Balakrishnan, G., Zhao, A., Sabuncu, M.R., Guttag, J., Dalca, A.V.: VoxelMorph: a learning framework for deformable medical image registration. IEEE Trans. Med. Imaging **38**(8), 1788–1800 (2019)
3. Beg, M.F., Miller, M.I., Trouv'e, A., Younes, L.: Computing large deformation metric mappings via geodesic flows of diffeomorphisms. Int. J. Comput. Vision **61**(2), 139–157 (2005)
4. Fabian, I., et al.: nnU-Net: self-adapting framework for u-net-based medical image segmentation. arXiv preprint arXiv:1809.10486 (2018)
5. Fan, J.F., Cao, X.H., Wang, Q.W., Yap, P.T., Shen, D.G.: Adversarial learning for mono- or multi-modal registration. Med. Image Anal. **58**, 101545 (2019)
6. Fan, J.F., Cao, X.H., Yap, P.T., Shen, D.G.: BIRNet: brain image registration using dual-supervised fully convolutional networks. Med. Image Anal. **54**, 193–206 (2019)
7. Goodfellow, I., et al.: Generative adversarial nets. In: Advances in Neural Information Processing Systems, vol. 27, pp. 2672–2680 (2014)
8. Jaderberg, M., Simonyan, K., Zisserman, A., Kavukcuoglu, K.: Spatial transformer networks. In: Advances in Neural Information Processing Systems, vol. 28, pp. 2017–2025 (2015)
9. Jenkinson, M., Smith, S.: A global optimisation method for robust affine registration of brain images. Med. Image Anal. **5**(2), 143–156 (2001)
10. Kim, B., Kim, D.H., Park, S.H., Kim, J., Lee, J.G., Ye, J.C.: CycleMorph: cycle consistent unsupervised deformable image registration. arXiv preprint arXiv:2008.05772 (2020)
11. Kingma, D.P., Ba, J.: Adam: a method for stochastic optimization. In: International Conference on Learning Representations (2015)
12. Mok, T.C.W., Chung, A.C.S.: Fast symmetric diffeomorphic image registration with convolutional neural networks. In: Proceedings of the IEEE Conference on Computer Vision and Pattern Recognition, pp. 4644–4653 (2020)
13. Ronneberger, O., Fischer, P., Brox, T.: U-Net: Convolutional networks for biomedical image segmentation. In: Medical Image Computing and Computer-Assisted Intervention, pp. 234–241 (2015)
14. Shan, S.Y., Guo, X.Q., Yan, W., Chang, E.I., Fan, Y.B., Xu, Y.: Unsupervised end-to-end learning for deformable medical image registration. arXiv preprint arXiv:1711.08608 (2017)
15. Sokooti, H., de Vos, B., Berendsen, F., Lelieveldt, B.P.F., Išgum, I., Staring, M.: Nonrigid image registration using multi-scale 3D convolutional neural networks. In: Medical Image Computing and Computer Assisted Intervention, pp. 232–239 (2017)
16. Vercauteren, T., Pennec, X., Perchant, A., Ayache, N.: Diffeomorphic demons: efficient nonparametric image registration. Neuroimage **45**(1), S61–S72 (2009)
17. de Vos, B.D., Berendsen, F.F., Viergever, M.A., Staring, M., Išgum, I.: End-to-end unsupervised deformable image registration with a convolutional neural network. In: Deep Learning in Medical Image Analysis and Multimodal Learning for Clinical Decision Support, pp. 204–212 (2017)

18. Woo, S., Park, J., Lee, J.Y., Kweon, I.S.: Cbam: convolutional block attention module. In: Proceedings of the European Conference on Computer Vision (2018)
19. Zhang, J.: Inverse-consistent deep networks for unsupervised deformable image registration. arXiv preprint arXiv:1809.03443 (2018)
20. Zhang, X.Y., Jian, W.J., Chen, Y., Yang, S.: Deform-GAN: An unsupervised learning model for deformable registration. arXiv preprint arXiv:2002.11430 (2020)
21. Zhao, S.Y., Dong, Y., Chang, E.I.C., Xu, Y.: Recursive cascaded networks for unsupervised medical image registration. In: Proceedings of the IEEE International Conference on Computer Vision, pp. 10600–10610 (2019)

Data Mining and Knowledge Discovery

MGEoT: A Multi-grained Ensemble Method for Time Series Classification

Ziyi Wang[1,2], Yujie Zhou[1,2], Chun Li[1,2], Lin Shang[1,2(✉)], and Bing Xue[3]

[1] State Key Laboratory for Novel Software Technology,
Nanjing University, Nanjing 210023, China
[2] Department of Computer Science and Technology, Nanjing University,
Nanjing 210023, China
{zywang,yujiezhou,lichun}@smail.nju.edu.cn, shanglin@nju.edu.cn
[3] Victoria University of Wellington, Wellington, New Zealand
bing.xue@ecs.vuw.ac.nz

Abstract. Classification of time series has attracted substantial interest over past decades. Methods based on Dynamic Time Warping (DTW), Symbolic Aggregate approXimation (SAX) and Shapelets are widely used and have achieved success in various real-world scenarios. However most existing time series classification methods either focus on global variation (e.g. DTW, SAX) or local variation (e.g. Shapelets). In this paper, we propose a Multi-Grained Ensemble Method for time series classification (MEGoT), which can make use of the variation of multi-grained data at the same time. In MEGoT, unstable base learners (Neural Networks) are assigned different weights to combine the ensemble. Different learners represent the learning features of different subsequences in time series, which can discover the discriminative regions, providing interpretability for classification. The training process of MGEoT is simpler and apt to parallel implementation. In the experiments, we conduct empirical evaluations and comparisons with various existing methods on 25 benchmark datasets. The final results show that dividing samples into smaller granularity is able to improve the diversity of ensemble, and MGEoT is competitive in accuracy under the Nemenyi test. Furthermore, MGEoT can discover the discriminative regions in time series, which may be neglected in the global methods.

Keywords: Time series classification · Multi-grained · Ensemble learning

1 Introduction

A time series is a set of ordered observations on a quantitative characteristic of a phenomenon at equally spaced time points [17], which is recorded from sensors and other input sources over time. There are a lot of possible application

© Springer Nature Switzerland AG 2021
D. N. Pham et al. (Eds.): PRICAI 2021, LNAI 13031, pp. 397–410, 2021.
https://doi.org/10.1007/978-3-030-89188-6_30

domains including Electro Encephalogram (EEG) in medicine, business, human walking motions [17], finance, politics, and a lot of others.

Classification is essential in time series, which assigns time series pattern to a specific category. Time series classification methods include 1-NN with Euclidean distance (ED) [6], 1-NN with Dynamic Time Warping (DTW) [2] and Symbolic Aggregate approXimation (SAX) [9], all of which only focus on the differences in the global shape. These methods can use all the information of the data as much as possible to classify different samples, but they do not concern which regions of data are important to classification. [17] mentioned that the differences of time series data in the global shape are very subtle. The Euclidean distance or DTW distance methods do not significantly outperform random guessing on some time series datasets, which is due to the fact that data is somewhat noisy, and such noisy is enough to swamp the subtle difference in the shapes. Most shapelet-based methods focus on the difference in the subsequences. Moreover, beyond mere classification accuracy, shapelet-based methods can yield some insight into the data. However if we only use the discriminative regions to classify different samples, we may lose some useful information. Therefore, it is useful to combine the information of different granularities of data at the same time.

In this paper, we propose MGEoT (Multi-Grained Ensemble), a new ensemble method for time series classification. The information of different granularities of data can be used at the same time to classify different samples. In MGEoT, we get N new training datasets by dividing the raw training datasets with different granularities. Then N unstable base learners are trained on each new dataset to improve the diversity of the ensemble. The training process of MGEoT is apt to parallel implementation, and all base learners can be trained at the same time. In MGEoT, different base learners represent the learning results of training data in different regions, which can help to discover the discriminative regions. During the testing process, base learners are assigned different weights according to their performance on the validation set. Testing data are divided same as the training data and we can get N results through the N trained base learners, which are weighted as the output.

Our contributions can be summarized as follows: (1) We propose a new multi-grained ensemble method for time series classification, which trains base learners by dividing the training sets with different granularities. (2) We conduct empirical evaluation with various existing methods on a large number of benchmark datasets, and achieve better performance than state-of-the-art methods. (3) The proposed multi-grained ensemble method can discover the discriminative regions and can be interpretable.

2   Multi-grained Ensemble Method

In this section, we propose the multi-grained ensemble method. Firstly, we define the concept of multi-grained division on raw samples and present the method to discover the discriminative regions, and then introduce how to select suitable classifier as the base learner, followed by weight calculation of different base learners. Finally, we introduce four metrics, which can measure the diversity between base learners trained by different granularities. Figure 1 shows the framework of MGEoT.

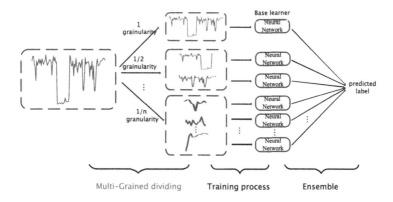

Fig. 1. The framework of MGEoT

In the training process, N different datasets are generated by dividing all data samples on different granularities, which are used to train N different base learners. In the testing process, testing data are divided based on different granularities in the same way as the training data. The divided testing data are input to the trained base learners, and the final results are obtained by weighting the output of each base learner.

2.1   Multi-gained Dividing

Data sample manipulation is the most popular mechanism in ensemble to improve the ensemble diversity [18]. Generally, the data sample manipulation is based on sampling approaches, e.g., Bagging adopts bootstrap sampling [16], AdaBoost adopts sequential sampling, etc. In MGEoT, data sample manipulation is achieved by dividing data samples with different granularities. We define $\frac{1}{n}$ granularity, that is, equally divide a time series into n subsequences.

A time series sample with a length of L will be divided into n samples of length $\lfloor \frac{L}{n} \rfloor$ after the $\frac{1}{n}$ granularity division (as shown in Fig. 2).

N different datasets are generated by dividing all samples to different granularities. In contrast to bootstrap sampling and sequential sampling, the datasets in MGEoT do not contain the same samples. Furthermore, dividing data by multi-grained in MGEoT preserves the context information of data. Different base learners represent the learning features of different subsequences in time series, which indicate the importance of different regions in raw data. Generally, the classification accuracy of the base classifier is higher, the region is more important in raw data.

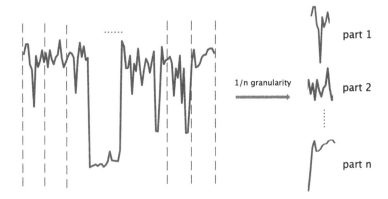

Fig. 2. $\frac{1}{n}$ granularity division of a time series sample

Most of time series data contain redundancy, so it is necessary to pay more attention on the subsequence that can discriminate the different class of the samples. The traditional brute force algorithms for finding shapelet are computationally expensive, and the classification accuracy is limited by the number of shapelets. In MGEoT, all samples are divided to different granularities to train different base learners. The base learner is assigned a larger weight if the base learner has a higher classification accuracy on the validation set, and all the base learners construct an ensemble.

2.2   Base Learner Selection

Ensemble diversity, that is, the difference among the individual learners, is a fundamental issue in ensemble methods [18]. In general, there are four popular mechanisms to improve the ensemble diversity, which include manipulating the data samples, input features, learning parameters, and output representations [18].

To construct an ensemble, different categories of base learners need to be chosen for different ensemble mechanisms. Most of base learners fall into stable base learners and unstable base learners. The stable base learners, such as SVM, Naive Bayes and KNN, which are insensitive to data sample manipulation. For many unstable base learners, such as decision tree, neural networks and so on, training sample slightly change may result in significant changes in the learner. In MGEoT, samples divided into different granularities can be considered as the sample manipulation mechanism to improve the ensemble diversity, therefore unstable base learners are needed to combine the ensemble. Time series is a kind of unstructured data, then we use neural networks as the base learner.

Multi-layer perceptron (MLP) is a simpler neural network model than Convolutional Neural Network (CNN). According to Occam's razor, when there is no significant difference between the accuracy of MLP and CNN on raw dataset, we select MLP as the base learner. To construct a good ensemble, it is known that individual learners should be accurate and diverse. Therefore, when the accuracy of CNN on the raw dataset is significantly higher than MLP, we select CNN as the base learner. In the experiments, we compare the accuracy of CNN and MLP on each datasets and select the appropriate base learners.

2.3 Weight Calculation

In MGEoT, raw samples are divided into different granularities and these datasets are used to train different base learners. Since the importance of different regions for time series classification is different, the weights of each base learner should be set differently. Output of all base learners are weighted to get the final classification result. Two issues are considered: (1) How many base learners we need to train? (2) How to calculate the weight of each base learner?

It is widely recognized that there is a negative correlation between the number of base learners and test error when using bagging scheme to carry out ensemble learning. Note that the test error is not monotonically decreasing with the increase of the number of base learners. [19] revealed that it may be better to ensemble *many* instead of *all* of the neural networks.

In MGEoT, two strategies can be used to determine the number of base learners.

Strategy 1: Given a parameter n, we can obtain N ($N = \sum_{i=1}^{n} i$) different datasets, which are used to train N base learners.

Strategy 2: Given a parameter N_{max} as the maximum number of base learners, as long as $N \leqslant N_{max}$ and the accuracy of the ensemble is higher than previous, we divide raw dataset into smaller granularity.

Strategy 1 is a static strategy, and strategy 2 is a dynamic strategy. Strategy 2 is more flexible than strategy 1, but it also tends to fall into a local minimum.

In the experiments, we relax the requirement for strategy 2. Provided that the accuracy of the ensemble after dividing the samples into smaller granularity is not reduced too much ($acc^n - acc^{n-1} \geqslant \varepsilon$, ε is a negative hyper-parameter), we continue to divide the samples into smaller granularity.

Weight w_i is the accuracy of each base learner on the validation set. Weight $C_i = w_i - \frac{1}{c}$, c represents the number of classes, and $\frac{1}{c}$ represents the accuracy of random guessing under the class-balance. We use the C_i as the final weight of the i-base classifier. When the base learner is not better than random guess ($C_i < 0$), the learner is removed. Compared with w_i, using C_i as the final weight of each base learner implies that this combination strategy prefers the strong learners.

2.4 Diversity Measure

To measure ensemble diversity, a classical approach is to measure the pairwise similarity/dissimilarity between two learners, and then average all the pairwise measurements for the over all diversity [18]. We introduce four metrics that can measure the diversity of base learners and take the binary classification task as an example. For binary classification, we have the contingency table (as shown in Table 1) for two classifiers l_i and l_j, where the $a+b+c+d = m$ is the number of samples.

Table 1. Contingency table for two classifers l_i and l_j

	$l_i = +1$	$l_i = -1$
$l_j = +1$	a	c
$l_j = -1$	b	d

Four metrics $(dis_{i,j}, \rho_{i,j}, Q_{i,j}, \kappa)$ of ensemble diversity are shown in Table 2. The value of $dis_{i,j}$ is in $[0,1]$, the larger value, the larger diversity. In statistics, the correlation coefficient is used for referring to the correlations between the entries of two random vectors X and Y. The value of $\rho_{i,j}$ is in $[-1,1]$, where $\rho_{i,j} = 0$ represents that l_i is independent of l_j, $\rho_{i,j} > 0$ represents positive correlation, and $\rho_{i,j} < 0$ represents negative correlation. The $Q_{i,j}$ is similar to $\rho_{i,j}$ and $|Q_{i,j}| \geq |\rho_{i,j}|$. p_1 and p_2 are the probabilities that the two classifiers agree and agree by chance, which can be calculated as equation (1). When l_i and l_j are totally same, $\kappa = 1$.

Table 2. Four metrics of ensemble diversity

	$dis_{i,j}$	$\rho_{i,j}$	$Q_{i,j}$	κ
Formula	$\frac{b+c}{m}$	$\frac{ad-bc}{\sqrt{(a+b)(a+c)(c+d)(b+d)}}$	$\frac{ad-bc}{ad+bc}$	$\frac{p_1-p_2}{1-p_2}$

$$p_1 = \frac{a+d}{m}, \quad p_2 = \frac{(a+b)(a+c)+(c+d)(b+d)}{m^2} \tag{1}$$

3   Experiments

3.1   Datasets

Table 3 shows the information of 25 time series datasets from UCR archive [3]. We randomly select 20% training samples as the validation set to select the number of hidden neurons. Strategy 2 ($\varepsilon = -0.05, n = 8$) is used to determine the number of base learners that we need to combine.

Figure 3 shows the validation accuracy of MLP and CNN on 25 time series datasets. We can see that, the validation accuracy of CNN is significantly higher MLP on dataset 2, 4, 7 and 12, and there is no significant difference between MLP and CNN on other time series datasets.

Therefore we use CNN as the base learner on dataset 2, 4, 7 and 12, whereas use the MLP as the base learner on other datasets.

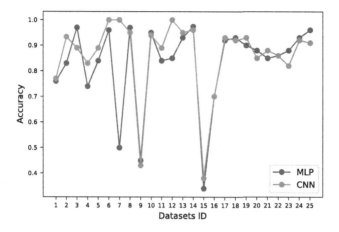

Fig. 3. The validation accuracy of MLP and CNN on 25 time series datasets

Table 3. 25 real-word time series datasets

ID	Datasets	#Train	#Test	#Classes	Length	Base learners
1	Adaic	390	391	37	176	MLP
2	Beef	30	30	5	470	CNN
3	CBF	30	900	3	128	MLP
4	ChlorineCon	467	3840	3	166	CNN
5	CinCECGTor	40	1380	4	1639	MLP
6	Coffee	28	28	2	286	MLP
7	CricketX	390	390	12	300	CNN
8	DiatomSizeR	16	306	4	345	MLP
9	Haptics	155	308	5	1092	MLP
10	ECGFiveDays	23	861	2	136	MLP
11	FaceAll	560	1690	14	131	MLP
12	FaceFour	24	88	4	350	CNN
13	Gun_Point	50	150	2	150	MLP
14	ItalyPower	67	1029	2	24	MLP
15	InlineSkate	100	550	7	1882	MLP
16	MedicalImages	381	760	10	99	MLP
17	NonInvTho1	1800	1965	42	750	MLP
18	NonInvTho2	1800	1965	42	750	MLP
19	OliveOil	30	30	4	570	MLP
20	MoteStrain	20	1252	2	84	MLP
21	SwedishLeaf	500	625	15	128	MLP
22	SonyAIBORI	20	601	2	70	MLP
23	SonyAIBORII	27	953	2	65	MLP
24	StarLightCur	1000	8236	3	1024	MLP
25	TwoLeadECG	23	1139	2	82	MLP

3.2   Baselines

As the baselines introduced in [4], two classical baseline methods: 1-NN with Euclidean distance (ED) [6] and 1-NN DTW [2]. 10 existing methods with state-of-the-art results published in the recent years, including: DTW with a warping window constraint set through cross validation (DTW CV) [11], SAX with vector space model (SV) [15], Bag-of-SFA-Symbols (BOSS) [13], Shotgun Classifier (SC) [12], Elastic Ensemble (PROP) [10], 1-NN Bag-Of-SFA-Symbols in Vector Space (BOSSVS) [14], Learn Shapelets Model (LTS) [8], and the Shapelet Ensemble (SE) model [1]. COTE, an ensemble model proposed by Bagnall et al. [1], which uses the weighted votes over 35 different classifiers. Multi-Scale Convolutional Neural Networks (MCNN) [4] is a deep learning model for time series classification.

These classifiers can be grouped into two categories: ensemble classifiers and non-ensemble classifiers. The ensemble based classifiers include BOSS, SE, COTE, BOSSVS, PROP and the others can be regarded as non-ensemble classifiers.

3.3   Results

Table 4. Test error for 25 ucr time series datasets

Dataset	DTW	ED	DTWCV	SV	BOSS	SC	BOSSVS	PROP	LTS	SE	COTE	MCNN	MGEoT
Adiac	0.396	0.389	0.389	0.417	0.22	0.373	0.302	0.353	0.437	0.435	0.233	0.231	**0.202**
Beef	0.367	0.467	0.333	0.467	0.2	0.133	0.267	0.367	0.24	0.167	0.133	0.367	**0.0677**
CBF	0.003	0.148	0.006	0.007	**0**	0.01	0.001	0.002	0.006	0.003	0.001	0.002	0.033
ChlorineCon	0.352	0.35	0.35	0.334	0.34	0.312	0.345	0.36	0.349	0.3	0.314	0.203	**0.17**
CinCECGTorso	0.349	0.103	0.07	0.344	0.125	**0.021**	0.13	0.062	0.167	0.154	0.064	0.058	0.094
Coffee	**0**	**0**	**0**	**0**	**0**	**0**	0.036	**0**	**0**	**0**	**0**	0.036	**0**
CricketX	0.246	0.423	0.228	0.308	0.259	0.297	0.346	0.203	0.209	0.218	0.154	0.182	**0**
DiatomSizeR	0.033	0.065	0.065	0.121	0.046	0.069	0.036	0.059	0.033	0.124	0.082	**0.023**	**0.023**
Haptics	0.623	0.63	0.588	0.575	0.536	0.607	0.584	0.584	0.532	0.523	0.488	0.53	**0.474**
ECGFiveDays	0.232	0.203	0.203	0.003	**0**	0.055	**0**	0.178	**0**	0.001	**0**	**0**	0.023
FaceAll	0.192	0.286	0.192	0.244	0.21	0.247	0.241	0.152	0.217	0.263	0.105	0.235	**0.099**
FaceFour	0.17	0.216	0.114	0.114	**0**	0.034	0.034	0.091	0.048	0.057	0.091	**0**	**0**
GunPoint	0.093	0.087	0.087	0.013	**0**	0.06	**0**	0.007	**0**	0.02	0.007	**0**	0.007
ItalyPower	0.05	0.045	0.045	0.089	0.053	0.053	0.086	0.039	0.03	0.048	0.036	0.03	**0.026**
InlineSkate	0.616	0.658	0.613	0.593	**0.511**	0.653	0.573	0.567	0.573	0.615	0.551	0.618	0.55
MedicalImage	0.263	0.316	0.253	0.516	0.288	0.305	0.474	0.245	0.27	0.396	0.258	0.26	**0.221**
NonInvThorax1	0.21	0.171	0.189		0.161	0.174	0.138	0.178	0.131	0.1	0.093	**0.064**	**0.064**
NonInvThorax2	0.135	0.12	0.12		0.101	0.118	0.13	0.112	0.089	0.097	0.073	0.06	**0.059**
OliveOil	0.167	0.133	0.133	0.133	0.1	0.133	0.133	0.133	0.56	0.1	0.1	0.133	**0.033**
MoteStrain	0.165	0.121	0.134	0.117	**0.073**	0.113	0.115	0.114	0.087	0.109	0.085	0.079	0.102
SwedishLeaf	0.208	0.213	0.154	0.275	0.072	0.12	0.141	0.085	0.087	0.093	0.046	0.066	**0.045**
SonyAIBORobot	0.275	0.305	0.304	0.306	0.321	0.238	0.265	0.293	**0.103**	0.067	0.146	0.23	0.115
SonyAIBORobotII	0.169	0.141	0.141	0.126	0.098	**0.066**	0.188	0.124	0.082	0.115	0.076	0.07	0.104
StarLightCurves	0.093	0.151	0.095	0.108	**0.021**	0.093	0.096	0.079	0.033	0.024	0.031	0.023	0.025
TwoLeadECG	**0**	0.09	0.002	0.004	0.004	0.029	0.015	**0**	0.003	0.004	0.015	0.001	0.031
#best	2	1	1	1	8	3	2	2	4	1	2	5	**15**
rank mean	9.54	10.66	8.5	10.12	5.2	7.8	8.06	6.56	5.98	6.74	4.2	4.2	**3.44**

We show the test error in the Table 4. The experimental results of the first 15 baseline are reported in [4]. All datasets of UCR are divided into training sets and testing sets. As can be seen, convolutional neural network (CNN) has better performance than MLP on FaceFour and CricketX, therefore we used CNN as the base classifier on these two datasets. Table 4 shows the ensemble based classifiers are significantly better than that non-ensemble classifiers. Among all of the ensemble based classifiers, MGEoT is the most competitive, achieving the highest accuracy on 15 datasets. In contrast to other ensemble learning methods designed specifically for TSC, MGEoT is much easier to train. In MGEoT, we divide the samples according to strategy 2, and different base learners are trained according to different training sets. The training process is simple and stable.

To perform comparisons of predictive performances in more well-founded ways, Friedman test is used which is a favorable statistical test for comparing more than two methods over multiple datasets [7].

$$F_F = \frac{(N-1)\chi_F^2}{N(s-1) - \chi_F^2}, \quad \chi_F^2 = \frac{12N}{s(s+1)}\left(\sum_{j=1}^{s} R_j^2 - \frac{s(s-1)^2}{4}\right) \tag{2}$$

The Friedman statistic F_F can be calculated by Eq. (2), based on that there are s comparing methods and N datasets. R_j is the average rank of the j-th method on all datasets. When the value Friedman statistic F_F is significantly greater than critical value, Friedman test at 0.05 significance level rejects the hypothesis of "equal" performance among all the comparing methods, and then we can adopt Nemenyi test to further analysis which methods are different. Figure 6 shows the critical difference diagram, which was proposed in [5]. The broken lines shown in Fig. 6 are the average rank of each classifiers. Bold lines (CD = 3.65) indicate group of classifiers which are not significantly different under Nemenyi test. The results indicate that MGEoT achieves statistically significantly superior classification performance against ED, SV, DTW, DTWCV, BOSSVS and SC. Although there is no statistically significant differences between MGEoT, COTE, MCNN, BOSS, LTS, PROP and SE, MGEoT achieves the smallest average rank among all time series classification methods. We can conclude that, MGEoT achieves competitive performance on time series classification.

3.4 Discriminative Regions

As shown with extensive empirical evaluations in diverse domains, algorithms based on the time series shapelet can be interpretable [17]. Shapelet can be regarded as the discriminative regions between different classes of time series data. The accuracy of three base learners on five validation sets are shown in Table 5.

Table 5. The accuracy of three base learners on five validation sets

Dataset	$learner1$	$learner2$	$learner3$
Beef	0.833	**0.867**	0.8
CinCECGTorso	0.843	**0.905**	0.766
ChlorineCon	0.743	0.648	**0.781**
GunPoint	0.933	0.887	**0.96**
OliveOil	0.9	**0.967**	0.867

$learner1$ is trained on the raw dataset. As mentioned in Sect. 2.1, we can get two datasets after the $\frac{1}{2}$-granularity division of raw dataset, which can be used to train $learner2$ and $learner3$. We can see that, the accuracy of learners trained on the whole sequences lower than the learners trained on subsequences. $learner2$ achieved highest classification accuracy on Beef, CinCECGTorso and OliveOil. $learner3$ achieved highest classification accuracy on ChlorineCon and GunPoint. In MGEoT, different learners represent the learning features of training data in different subsequences in time series. For example, $learner3$ has higher classification accuracy than $learner2$ on GunPoint, so we conclude that shapelet can be found in the latter part of the data. In order to validate the conjecture, we refer to the results of finding shapelet on the GunPoint in [17]. The result shows that shapelet is found in the latter part of the GunPoint dataset.

In our method MGEoT, the subsequence corresponding to the base learner with highest accuracy on the validation set can be regarded as the discriminative regions in the raw time series data. The discriminative regions provide interpretability for time series classification.

3.5   Diversity Measure

Ensemble diversity is a fundamental issue in ensemble methods [18]. In this section, we compare the diversity among different base learners. Experiments are conducted on three datasets, which are SonyAIBORobot, ECGFiveDays and MoteStrain.

In these three datasets, ten base learners are combined to construct the MGEoT. As mentioned in Sect. 2.4, there are four metrics that can measure the diversity of base learners. $dis_{i,j}$ ($0 \leq dis_{i,j} \leq 1$) is a disagreement measure, the larger the value, the larger the diversity. $\rho_{i,j}$ ($-1 \leq \rho_{i,j} \leq 1$) is a correlation measure, the smaller the value of $|\rho_{i,j}|$, the larger the diversity. $Q_{i,j}$ is similar to $\rho_{i,j}$. κ ($-1 \leq \kappa \leq 1$) is a classical statistical measure, the smaller the value of $|\kappa|$, the larger the diversity. The results of four diversity measures on three datasets are shown in Fig. 4. We can see that, the values of ρ and κ are very close. The trend of ρ, κ and Q are similar, which is contrary to the trend of dis. Moreover, the diversity of learners can be improved by dividing samples into smaller granularity, such as, $dis_{1,3} < dis_{1,5} < dis_{1,8}$ on MoteStrain, $dis_{1,2} < dis_{1,6} < dis_{1,8}$ on SonyAIBORobot and $dis_{1,2} < dis_{1,4}$ on ECGFiveDays. The

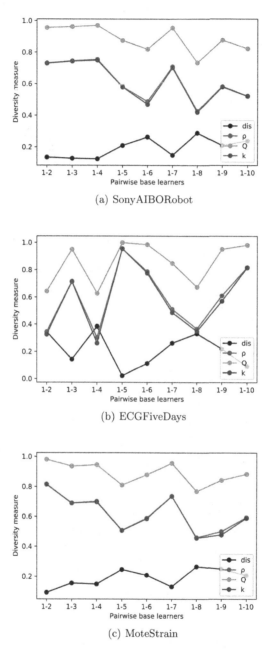

(a) SonyAIBORobot

(b) ECGFiveDays

(c) MoteStrain

Fig. 4. Four diversity measures of nine pairwise base learners on three datasets: learner 1 trained on the raw dataset, second to third learners trained on the datasets divided by $\frac{1}{2}$-granularity, fourth to sixth learners trained on the datasets divided by $\frac{1}{3}$-granularity, seventh to tenth learners trained on the datasets divided by $\frac{1}{4}$-granularity.

accuracy of different learners on testing data is shown in Fig. 5. We can see that, MGEoT achieves the highest accuracy on these datasets, which indicates that ensemble can improve the classification accuracy.

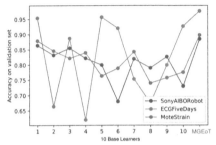
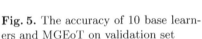
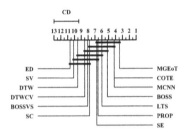

Fig. 5. The accuracy of 10 base learners and MGEoT on validation set

Fig. 6. Critical Difference Diagram over the mean rank of MGEoT and other baselines. The critical difference is 3.65.

4   Conclusion

In this paper, we propose a multi-grained ensemble method (MGEoT) for time series classification. In MGEoT, we manipulate the data samples to improve the ensemble diversity, which is implemented by dividing the raw samples into different granularities. Unstable base learners (Neural Networks) are assigned different weights to combine the ensemble. Note that, the training process of MGEoT is simpler and apt to parallel implementation. In experiments, we conduct empirical evaluation and comparisons with various existing methods on 25 benchmark datasets. The final results show that dividing samples into smaller granularity is able to improve the diversity of ensemble, and the MGEoT is competitive in accuracy under the Nemenyi test. The training result of different base learners can help to find discriminative regions, which provide interpretability for time series classification.

Acknowledgement. This work is supported by the National Natural Science Foundation of China (No. 51975294).

References

1. Bagnall, A., Lines, J., Hills, J., Bostrom, A.: Time-series classification with COTE: the collective of transformation-based ensembles. In: 32nd IEEE International Conference on Data Engineering, ICDE 2016, Helsinki, Finland, 16–20 May 2016, pp. 1548–1549 (2016). https://doi.org/10.1109/ICDE.2016.7498418

2. Berndt, D.J., Clifford, J.: Using dynamic time warping to find patterns in time series. In: Knowledge Discovery in Databases: Papers from the 1994 AAAI Workshop, Seattle, Washington, July 1994. Technical Report WS-94-03, pp. 359–370 (1994)

3. Chen, Y., Keogh, E., Hu, B., Begum, N., Bagnall, A., Mueen, A., Batista, G.: The UCR time series classification archive, July 2015

4. Cui, Z., Chen, W., Chen, Y.: Multi-scale convolutional neural networks for time series classification. CoRR abs/1603.06995 (2016)

5. Demsar, J.: Statistical comparisons of classifiers over multiple data sets. J. Mach. Learn. Res. **7**(1), 1–30 (2006)

6. Faloutsos, C., Ranganathan, M., Manolopoulos, Y.: Fast subsequence matching in time-series databases. In: Proceedings of the 1994 ACM SIGMOD International Conference on Management of Data, Minneapolis, Minnesota, May 24–27, 1994, pp. 419–429 (1994). https://doi.org/10.1145/191839.191925

7. Friedman, M.: A correction: the use of ranks to avoid the assumption of normality implicit in the analysis of variance. Publ. Am. Stat. Assoc. **32**(200), 675–701 (1939)

8. Grabocka, J., Schilling, N., Wistuba, M., Schmidt-Thieme, L.: Learning time-series shapelets. In: The 20th ACM SIGKDD International Conference on Knowledge Discovery and Data Mining, KDD 2014, New York, NY, USA, 24–27 August 2014, pp. 392–401 (2014). https://doi.org/10.1145/2623330.2623613

9. Lin, J., Keogh, E.J., Lonardi, S., Chiu, B.Y.: A symbolic representation of time series, with implications for streaming algorithms. In: Proceedings of the 8th ACM SIGMOD Workshop on Research Issues in Data Mining and Knowledge Discovery, DMKD 2003, San Diego, California, USA, 13 June 2003, pp. 2–11 (2003). https://doi.org/10.1145/882082.882086

10. Lines, J., Bagnall, A.: Ensembles of elastic distance measures for time series classification. In: Proceedings of the 2014 SIAM International Conference on Data Mining, Philadelphia, Pennsylvania, USA, 24–26 April 2014, pp. 524–532 (2014). https://doi.org/10.1137/1.9781611973440.60

11. Rakthanmanon, T., et al.: Searching and mining trillions of time series subsequences under dynamic time warping. In: The 18th ACM SIGKDD International Conference on Knowledge Discovery and Data Mining, KDD 2012, Beijing, China, 12–16 August 2012, pp. 262–270 (2012). https://doi.org/10.1145/2339530.2339576

12. Schäfer, P.: Towards time series classification without human preprocessing. In: Machine Learning and Data Mining in Pattern Recognition - 10th International Conference, MLDM 2014, St. Petersburg, Russia, 21–24 July 2014. Proceedings, pp. 228–242 (2014). https://doi.org/10.1007/978-3-319-08979-9_18

13. Schäfer, P.: The BOSS is concerned with time series classification in the presence of noise. Data Min. Knowl. Disc. **29**(6), 1505–1530 (2014). https://doi.org/10.1007/s10618-014-0377-7

14. Schäfer, P.: Scalable time series classification. Data Min. Knowl. Disc. **30**(5), 1273–1298 (2015). https://doi.org/10.1007/s10618-015-0441-y

15. Senin, P., Malinchik, S.: SAX-VSM: interpretable time series classification using SAX and vector space model. In: 2013 IEEE 13th International Conference on Data Mining, Dallas, TX, USA, 7–10 December 2013, pp. 1175–1180 (2013). https://doi.org/10.1109/ICDM.2013.52

16. Sivaganesan, S.: An introduction to the bootstrap (bradley efron and robert j. tibshirani). SIAM Rev. **36**(4), 677–678 (1994). https://doi.org/10.1137/1036171

17. Ye, L., Keogh, E.J.: Time series shapelets: a new primitive for data mining. In: Proceedings of the 15th ACM SIGKDD International Conference on Knowledge Discovery and Data Mining, Paris, France, 28 June–1 July 2009, pp. 947–956 (2009). https://doi.org/10.1145/1557019.1557122
18. Zhou, Z.H.: Ensemble Methods: Foundations and Algorithms. CRC Press (2012)
19. Zhou, Z., Wu, J., Tang, W.: Ensembling neural networks: many could be better than all. Artif. Intell. **137**(1–2), 239–263 (2002). https://doi.org/10.1016/S0004-3702(02)00190-X

Mining Skyline Frequent-Utility Itemsets with Utility Filtering

Wei Song[1]([✉]) [ID], Chuanlong Zheng[1], and Philippe Fournier-Viger[2] [ID]

[1] School of Information Science and Technology, North China University of Technology,
Beijing 100144, China
songwei@ncut.edu.cn
[2] School of Humanities and Social Sciences, Harbin Institute of Technology (Shenzhen),
Shenzhen 518055, China

Abstract. Skyline frequent-utility itemsets (SFUIs) can provide more actionable information for decision-making with both frequency and utility considered. In this paper, the problem of mining SFUIs by filtering utilities from different perspectives is studied. First, filtering by frequency is considered. The max utility array (MUA) structure is designed, which is proved to have a size no larger than the size of arrays in state-of-the-art algorithms. Using the MUA, the utility-list is verified to prune unpromising itemsets and their extensions. Second, filtering using transaction-weighted utilization is applied. The minimum utility of SFUIs is proposed and the proof that this concept can be used as a pruning strategy in the early stage of search space traversal is provided. Finally, filtering using utility itself is also considered. The minimum utility of extension is presented, and its use as a pruning strategy during the extension stage of search space traversal is validated. Based on these filtering methods, a novel algorithm called SFUIs mining based on utility filtering (SFUI-UF) is proposed. Extensive experimental results show that the SFUI-UF algorithm can discover all correct SFUIs with high efficiency and low memory usage.

Keywords: Skyline frequent-utility itemsets · Max utility array · Minimum utility of SFUIs · Minimum utility of extension

1 Introduction

Itemset mining is a core task in data mining. Several types of itemsets [10] have been proposed, among which, frequent itemsets (FIs) and high utility itemsets (HUIs) are the two most influential. FIs are itemsets that have high frequency [6], whereas HUIs are itemsets that have high profit [11].

To meet users' multiple needs and provide them with more informative knowledge, researchers have been paying increasing attention to combining FIs and HUIs. In [12], the utility-frequent itemset (UFI) and its mining algorithm were proposed considering both utility and support. Setting a single threshold of FIs or HUIs is a difficult problem, let alone two thresholds that are needed simultaneously. Furthermore, the algorithm's

© Springer Nature Switzerland AG 2021
D. N. Pham et al. (Eds.): PRICAI 2021, LNAI 13031, pp. 411–424, 2021.
https://doi.org/10.1007/978-3-030-89188-6_31

efficiency is another challenging issue for mining UFIs because the downward closure property does not hold when support and utility are considered together.

To solve this problem, skyline frequent-utility itemsets (SFUIs) were proposed [2]. An itemset is an SFUI if it is not dominated by any other itemset in the database considering both frequency and utility. Using both frequency and utility is meaningful. For example, parents of students may choose to rent houses for the students according to the price and distance of the houses from the school to save the time that it takes for students to travel to and from school. In this case, the distance from the house to the school and the price of the house are contrasted; that is, a house that is close to the school normally has a higher price than a house that is far from the school.

In the first SKYMINE algorithm [2], a tree structure was used to transform the original information. To improve efficiency, the utility-list (UL) structure was used in SFU-Miner [8], SKYFUP-D [3], and SKYFUP-B [3] algorithms. Because mining SFUIs does not require either a support threshold or utility threshold, the algorithm's efficiency is still the most challenging issue for the SFUI mining (SFUIM) problem.

We propose an SFUIM algorithm called SFUI-UF. First, we design the max utility array (MUA) structure, which is smaller than arrays in mainstream algorithms. Using this array, we propose a UL-based pruning strategy to omit unpromising itemsets and their extensions. Second, we propose the minimum utility of SFUIs (MUS), which is the highest utility of single items that have the highest frequency. Considering transaction-weighted utilization, the MUS is an effective strategy that can prune unpromising single items and all their extensions. Third, we present the minimum utility of extension (MUE), which is the utility of the itemset that generates the enumeration itemsets. The MUE is an effective pruning strategy for search space traversal. Finally, we conducted extensive experiments. Our results showed that the proposed algorithm is efficient and memory-saving compared with mainstream algorithms.

2   SFUIM Problem

Let $I = \{i_1, i_2,..., i_m\}$ be a finite set of items. Set $X \subseteq I$ is called an *itemset*, or a k-itemset if it contains k items. Let $D = \{T_1, T_2, ..., T_n\}$ be a transaction database. Each transaction $T_d \in D$ ($1 \le d \le n$), where d is a unique identifier, is a subset of I. The *frequency* of itemset X, denoted by $f(X)$, is defined as the number of transactions in which X occurs as a subset.

The *internal utility* $q(i_p, T_d)$ represents the quantity of item i_p in transaction T_d. The *external utility* $p(i_p)$ is the unit profit value of item i_p. The *utility* of item i_p in transaction T_d is defined as $u(i_p, T_d) = p(i_p) \times q(i_p, T_d)$. The utility of itemset X in transaction T_d is defined as $u(X, T_d) = \sum_{i_p \in X} u(i_p, T_d)$. The utility of itemset X in D is defined as $u(X) = \sum_{X \subseteq T_d \wedge T_d \in D} u(X, T_d)$. The *transaction utility* (TU) of transaction T_d is defined as $TU(T_d) = u(T_d, T_d)$. Because utility is not a measure that maintains the downward closure property, Liu et al. [5] proposed the *transaction-weighted utilization* (TWU) model. TWU can be used as the upper bound of utility, and it is proved that an itemset is not an HUI if its TWU is lower than the minimum utility threshold. Formally, the TWU of itemset X is the sum of the TUs of all the transactions containing X, which is defined as $TWU(X) = \sum_{X \subseteq T_d \wedge T_d \in D} TU(T_d)$.

Considering both frequency and utility factors, an itemset X *dominates* another itemset Y in D, if $f(X) \geq f(Y)$ and $u(X) > u(Y)$, or $f(X) > f(Y)$ and $u(X) \geq u(Y)$, which is denoted by $X \succ Y$. An itemset X in a database D is an SFUI if it is not dominated by any other itemsets in the database considering both frequency and utility factors. An itemset X is considered as a *potential SFUI* (PSFUI) if there is no itemset Y such that $f(Y) = f(X)$, and $u(Y) > u(X)$, and it was proved that all SFUIs are PSFUIs [8]; hence, we can enumerate the PSFUIs first, and then filter the actual SFUIs from the PSFUIs.

Based on the above definitions, the SFUIM problem is to discover all the non-dominated itemsets in the database by considering both frequency and utility factors.

Table 1. Example database

TID	Transactions	TU
1	(B, 1), (D, 1)	7
2	(A, 1), (B, 1), (C, 1), (D, 1), (E, 1)	18
3	(B, 2), (D, 1), (E, 1)	13
4	(D, 1), (E, 1)	9
5	(A, 4), (B, 1), (D, 1), (E, 2)	39
6	(B, 4), (E,1)	12
7	(C, 2)	2

Table 2. Profit table

Item	A	B	C	D	E
Profit	6	2	1	5	4

As a running example, consider the transaction database in Table 1 and the profit table in Table 2. For convenience, an itemset {D, E} is denoted by DE. In the example database, the utility of item E in transaction T_2 is $u(E, T_2) = 4 \times 1 = 4$, the utility of itemset DE in transaction T_2 is $u(DE, T_2) = 5 + 4 = 9$, and the utility of itemset DE in the transaction database is $u(DE) = u(DE, T_2) + u(DE, T_3) + u(DE, T_4) + u(DE, T_5) = 40$. The TU of T_2 is $TU(T_2) = u(ABCDE, T_2) = 18$, and the utilities of the other transactions are shown in the third column of Table 1. Because DE is contained by transactions T_2, T_3, T_4, and $T_5, f(DE) = 4$, and $TWU(DE) = TU(T_2) + TU(T_3) + TU(T_4) + TU(T_5) = 79$. Because an itemset that has a frequency of 4 and utility greater than 40 does not exist, DE is considered as a PSFUI. We can further verify that DE is not dominated by any other itemsets, so it is an SFUI.

3 Related Work

Yeh et al. [12] first proposed the concept of UFIs and designed a two-phase algorithm for mining UFIs. Then, the FUFM algorithm was proposed to mine UFIs more efficiently [9]. Both frequency and utility thresholds are required to discover UFIs. However, it is difficult for non-expert users to set these two appropriate thresholds.

To consider both frequency and utility without setting thresholds, Goyal et al. introduced SFUIs and proposed the SKYMINE algorithm for mining them [2]. Considering both frequency and utility, SFUIs are itemsets that are not dominated by any other itemsets. Thus, neither the frequency threshold nor utility threshold is needed. The UP-tree structure is used in the SKYMINE algorithm to transform the original data for mining SFUIs using a pattern-growth approach.

Using the UL structure [4], Pan et al. proposed the SFU-Miner algorithm to discover SFUIs [8]. Compared with the UP-tree, the UL can identify SFUIs directly without candidates. Furthermore, the umax array has been proposed to store information about the maximal utility for each occurrence frequency, which can be used to identify the non-dominated itemsets efficiently based on the utility and frequency measures. With the above structures, the SFU-Miner is more efficient than SKYMINE algorithm.

Lin et al. proposed two algorithms, that is, SKYFUP-D and SKYFUP-B, for mining SFUIs by depth-first and breadth-first traversing the search space, respectively [3]. In these two algorithms, the UL is also used, and the utility-max structure is designed to keep the maximal utility among the itemsets if their frequency is no lower than the index parameter.

Different from the UL, Nguyen et al. designed an extent utility list (EUL) structure in their FSKYMINE algorithm for mining SFUIs [7]. For EUL, the utility of the expanded itemset in UL is decomposed into two fields: the utility of the itemset before extension and the utility of the item before appending to the enumeration itemset. Using EUL, new pruning strategy is proposed to speed up the mining process of SFUIs.

Compared with existing methods, we design new array structure with frequency, and propose three utility filter strategies to prune the search space. Thus, the overall performance is improved.

4 Proposed Algorithm

4.1 UL Structure

The same as the methods in [3, 8], we also use the UL to transform the original data. Let $\rhd$ be the total order (e.g., lexicographic order) of items in the database D. The UL of an itemset X, denoted by $X.UL$, is a set of triads, in which each triad consists of three fields denoted by $(tid, iutil, rutil)$, where tid is the ID of a transaction containing X; $iutil$ is the utility of X in T_{tid}, that is, $iutil(X, T_{tid}) = u(X, T_{tid})$; and $rutil$ is the remaining utility of all the items after X in T_{tid}. Let T_{tid} / X be the set of items after all items of X in T_{tid} according to $\rhd$, $rutil(X, T_{tid}) = \sum_{i \in (T_{tid}/X)} u(i, T_{tid})$.

4.2 Max Utility Array

We propose an array to store utility with respect to frequency.

Definition 1 (Max utility array). Let f_{max} be the maximal frequency of all 1-itemsets in D. The MUA is an array that contains f_{max} elements. The element that has frequency f ($1 \leq f \leq f_{max}$) is defined as

$$\text{MUA}(f) = max\{u(X) \mid f(X) \geq f\},\qquad(1)$$

where X is an itemset. The MUA is similar to utilmax [3]; the difference between them is the size of the array. According to [3], the size of utilmax is $|D|$, that is, the number of transactions in D, whereas the size of MUA is f_{max}.

Theorem 1. *For the same transaction database D, the MUA covers all frequencies and $|MUA| \leq |utilmax|$, where $|MUA|$ and $|utilmax|$ are the number of elements in the MUA and utilmax, respectively.*

Proof. The frequency measure satisfies the downward closure property; that is, for any two itemsets X and Y, if $X \subseteq Y, f(X) \geq f(Y)$.

We first prove that the maximal frequency of 1-itemsets, f_{max}, is also the maximal frequency of all the itemsets. We prove this by contradiction. Let $i_x i_y$ be a 2-itemset that has the highest frequency of all the itemsets. Because $i_x \subset i_x i_y, f(i_x) \geq f(i_x i_y)$. Because f_{max} is the maximal frequency of 1-itemsets, $f_{max} \geq f(i_x) \geq f(i_x i_y)$. This contradicts the assumption. Similarly, for any k-itemset Z, we also have $f_{max} \geq f(Z)$. Thus, f_{max} is also the maximal frequency of all the itemsets.

According to Definition 1, all frequencies between 1 and f_{max} correspond to an element of the MUA. Because f_{max} is also the maximal frequency of all the itemsets, the MUA covers all frequencies in D. Furthermore, $|MUA| = f_{max} \leq |D| = |utilmax|$. $\square$

In real-world transaction databases, very few itemsets appear in every transaction. Thus, the size of the MUA is no larger than that of utilmax, in most cases, and memory consumption can be saved.

Theorem 2. *Let X be an itemset. If the sum of all iutil and rutil values in $X.UL$ is less than $MUA(f(X))$, then X and all the extensions of X are not SFUIs.*

Proof. According to the assumption, there exists an itemset Y such that $u(Y) = MUA(f(X))$; that is, $u(Y) > \sum_{d \in X.tids} (iutil(X, T_d) + rutil(X, T_d))$, where $X.tids$ denotes the set of tids in $X.UL$. Thus,

$$u(Y) > \sum_{d \in X.tids} iutil(X, T_d) = u(X).\qquad(2)$$

Based on Definition 1, $f(Y) \geq f(X)$. Thus, Y dominates X and X is not an SFUI.

Let Z be arbitrary extension of X. Then $X \subset Z$; hence, $f(Z) \leq f(X)$. Because $f(X) \leq f(Y), f(Z) \leq f(Y)$ holds. Similarly,

$$u(Y) > \sum_{d \in X.tids} (iutil(X, T_d) + rutil(X, T_d)) \geq u(Z).\qquad(3)$$

Thus, Y also dominates Z and Z is not an SFUI. $\square$

Based on Theorem 2, we can prune the search space effectively using MUA.

4.3 Pruning Strategies

We also propose two pruning strategies. They are used in the initial stage and extension stage of the SFUI-UF algorithm.

Definition 2 (Minimum utility of SFUIs). Let D be a transaction database. The minimum utility of SFUIs (MUS) in D is the maximal utility of single items that have the highest frequency, which is defined as

$$MUS = max\{u(i) \mid f(i) = f_{max}\}, \tag{4}$$

where i is an item in D and f_{max} is the maximal frequency of all 1-itemsets in D.

In the running example, three items have the highest frequency: $f(B) = 5, f(D) = 5$, and $f(E) = 5$. Since $u(B) = 18, u(D) = 25$, and $u(E) = 24$, MUS $= 25$.

Theorem 3. *Let i_x be a 1-itemset. If $TWU(i_x) < MUS$, i_x and all itemsets containing i_x are not SFUIs.*

Proof. Let i_c be the 1-itemset with $f(i_c) = f_{max}$ and $u(i_c) = MUS$. Because $u(i_x) \leq TWU(i_x) < MUS = u(i_c)$ and $f(i_x) \leq f_{max} = f(i_c)$, i_x is dominated by i_c. Thus, i_x is not an SFUI.

Consider an arbitrary itemset X containing i_x: $u(X) \leq TWU(i_x) < MUS = u(i_c)$, and $f(X) \leq f(i_x) \leq f_{max} = f(i_c)$. Thus, X is dominated by i_c and X is not an SFUI.   □

Using Theorem 3, once a 1-itemset is found to have TWU lower than the MUS, this itemset and all its supersets can be pruned safely. In our algorithm, the MUS is set to the initial values of each element in the MUA, whereas for umax [8] and utilmax [3], all initial values are set to zero.

Definition 3 (Minimum utility of extension). Let X be an itemset, i_x be an item, and $X \cup i_x$ be an extension of itemset X. Then $u(X)$ is defined as the minimum utility of extension (MUE) of $X \cup i_x$, which is denoted by $MUE(X \cup i_x)$.

Consider itemset A and its extension AD in the running example: $MUE(AD) = u(A) = 30$.

Theorem 4. *Let X be an itemset and Y be an extension of X. If $u(Y) < MUE(Y)$, Y is not an SFUI.*

Proof. Because Y is an extension of X, $X \subset Y$. Hence, $f(Y) \leq f(X)$. Because $u(Y) < MUE(Y) = u(X)$, Y is dominated by X. Thus, Y is not an SFUI.   □

Using Theorem 4, we can prune those unpromising extensions during search space traversal.

4.4 Algorithm Description

Algorithm 1 describes the proposed SFUI-UF algorithm.

The transaction database is first scanned once to determine the maximal frequency of all 1-itemsets and the MUS (Step 1). According to Theorem 3, Step 2 prunes unpromising items using the MUS, and then the TWU values of the remaining items are updated in

Step 3. The loop from Step 4 to Step 9 sorts the items in ascending order of TWU in each transaction and builds the UL of each item. The next loop (Steps 10–12) initializes each element of the MUA as the MUS. S-PSFUI and S-SFUI denote the sets of PSFUIs and SFUIs, and they are initialized as empty sets in Steps 13 and 14, respectively. The procedure P-Miner (described in Algorithm 2), which determines all PSFUIs, is called in Step 15. The function $tail(X)$ is the set of items after all items in X according to the total order of items, denoted by $\triangleright$. Specifically, $tail(X) = \{j \in I \mid \text{for } \forall i \in X, i \triangleright j\}$. In the SFUI-UF algorithm, ascending order of TWU is used. Then Step 16 calls the function S-Miner (described in Algorithm 3) to return all SFUIs. Finally, Step 17 outputs all the discovered SFUIs.

Algorithm 1	SFUI-UF
Input	Transaction database D
Output	All SFUIs
1	Scan D once to calculate f_{max} and MUS;
2	Delete items with TWU values lower than MUS;
3	Calculate the TWU values of the remaining items;
4	**for** each transaction $T_d \in D$ **do**
5	Sort items in T_d using TWU-ascending order;
6	**for** each item $i \in T_d$ in D **do**
7	Update i.UL;
8	**end for**
9	**end for**
10	**for** j=1 to f_{max} **do**
11	MUA(j) = MUS;
12	**end for**
13	S-PSFUI = $\varnothing$;
14	S-SFUI = $\varnothing$;
15	S-PSFUI $\leftarrow$ P-Miner($\varnothing$, $tail(\varnothing)$, MUA);
16	S-SFUI $\leftarrow$ S-Miner(S-PSFUI);
17	Output all SFUIs.

Algorithm 2 generates the PSFUIs by extending the enumerating itemset via depth-first search space traversal. For each item i in $tail(X)$, Step 2 first formulates a candidate itemset by appending i after X. According to Theorem 4, the new candidate is not processed until its utility is no lower than the MUE (Steps 3–12). If the utility of the candidate is no lower than the corresponding element in the MUA, the MUA is updated using the utility and frequency of the candidate in Step 5, and the candidate is determined as a PSFUI in Step 6. When a new itemset is inserted, some itemsets already in S-PSFUIs may be dominated by the newly inserted itemset. The dominated itemsets are removed from S-PSFUIs in Step 7. If the sum of all the *iutil* and *rutil* values in the UL of the new candidate is no lower than the corresponding value in the MUA, the P-Miner procedure is called recursively to determine the new PSFUIs in Step 10. Finally, the updated S-PSFUI is returned in Step 14.

Algorithm 2	P-Miner (X, tail(X), MUA)
Input	an itemset X, set of items can be extended tail(X), MUA
Output	PSFUIs generated by appending an item to X

1	for each item $i \in tail(X)$ do
2	$X' = X \cup i$;
3	if $u(X') \geq MUE(X')$ then
4	if $u(X') \geq MUA(f(X'))$ then
5	Update MUA according to $f(X')$ and $u(X')$;
6	S-PSFUI $\leftarrow X'$;
7	remove Y from S-PSFUI if $(f(Y) == f(X'))$;
8	end if
9	if $\sum_{d \in X.tids}(iutil(X', T_d) + rutil(X', T_d)) \geq MUA(f(X'))$ then
10	S-PSFUI $\leftarrow$ P-Miner $(X', tail(X'), MUA)$;
11	end if
12	end if
13	end for
14	return S-PSFUI.

In Algorithm 3, all itemsets in the S-PSFUI are checked individually. Only those itemsets that are not dominated by other PSFUIs are verified to be the actual SFUIs.

Algorithm 3	S-Miner (S-PSFUI)
Input	S-PSFUI
Output	All SFUIs

1	for each itemset X in S-PSFUI do
2	for each itemset Y in S-PSFUI do
3	if $(f(X) \geq f(Y)$ and $u(X) > u(Y))$ or $(f(X) > f(Y)$ and $u(X) \geq u(Y))$ then
4	remove Y from S-PSFUI;
5	end if
6	end for
7	end for
8	S-SFUI $\leftarrow$ S-PSFUI;
9	return S-SFUI.

4.5 Illustrated Example

We use the transaction database in Table 1 and profit table in Table 2 to explain the basic idea of the SFUI-UF algorithm. When D is scanned once, $f_{max} = 5$ and MUS = 25. Because $TWU(C) = 20 <$ MUS, C is deleted from the database. Then, the TWU values of remaining items are recalculated, and the results are $TWU(A) = 56$, $TWU(B) = 88$, $TWU(D) = 85$, and $TWU(E) = 90$.

Thus, according to TWU-ascending order, the remaining four items are sorted as A▷D▷B▷E. With this order, each transaction in the database is reorganized, and the result is shown in Table 3.

Table 3. Reorganized database

TID	Transactions	TU
1	(D, 1), (B, 1)	7
2	(A, 1), (D, 1), (B, 1), (F, 1)	17
3	(D, 1), (B, 2), (E, 1)	13
4	(D, 1), (E, 1)	9
5	(A, 4), (D, 1), (B, 1), (E, 2)	39
6	(B, 4), (E,1)	12

Then, the constructed UL structures for all remaining 1-itemsets are shown in Fig. 1. The MUA contains five elements, and each element is initialized as 25.

We take A as an example. We can calculate $u(A) = 30$ by summing up its *iutils* in Fig. 1. Furthermore, $f(A) = 2$ and $u(A) > $ MUA(2). Then MUA(2) is updated to 30. Accordingly, MUA(1) is also updated to 30. At this moment, MUA = {30, 30, 25, 25, 25}. Then, A is added into the S-PSFUI as a PSFUI. Because $iutil(A, T_2) + rutil(A, T_2) + iutil(A, T_5) + rutil(A, T_5) = 56 > $ MUA(2), the procedure P-Miner is called recursively taking A, $tail(A) = $ DBE, and the MUA as parameters.

A			D			B			E		
tid	iutil	rutil	tid	iutil	rutil	tid	iutil	rutil	tid	iutil	rutil
2	6	11	1	5	2	1	2	0	2	4	0
5	24	15	2	5	6	2	2	4	3	4	0
			3	5	8	3	4	4	4	4	0
			4	5	4	5	2	8	5	8	0
			5	5	10	6	8	4	6	4	0

Fig. 1. ULs of the remaining 1-itemsets

Then, we can obtain a new candidate AD by extending A using D. Similarly, $f(AD) = 2$ and $u(AD) = 40$. Because $u(AD) > $ MUA(2), the MUA is updated to {40, 40, 25, 25, 25}. Then, AD is added into the S-PSFUI as a PSFUI. Because itemset A is already in the S-PSFUI, and $f(A) = f(AD)$, A is then deleted from the S-PSFUI.

We perform these operations recursively until all items are processed. Finally, MUA = {56, 56, 40, 40, 25}, and the discovered SFUIs are shown in Table 4. The search space of the running example is shown in Fig. 2.

In Fig. 2, the blue nodes containing a red cross are pruned. C and all its child nodes are pruned according to Theorem 3, whereas ABE is pruned according to Theorem 2.

Table 4. Discovered SFUIs

SFUI	Frequency	Utility
ADBE	2	56
DE	4	40
D	5	25

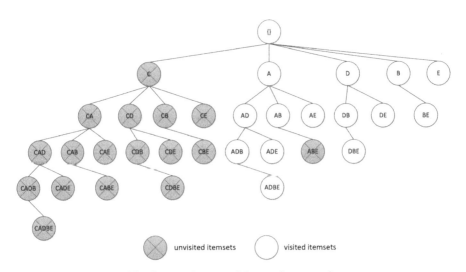

Fig. 2. Search space of the running example

5   Performance Evaluation

In this section, we evaluate the performance of our SFUI-UF algorithm and compare it with SFU-Miner [8], SKYFUP-D [3], and SKYFUP-B [3]. The source code of SFU-Miner was downloaded from the SPMF data mining library [1], and the source codes of SKYFUP-D and SKYFUP-B were provided by the author.

Our experiments were performed on a computer with a 4-Core 3.40 GHz CPU and 8 GB memory running 64-bit Microsoft Windows 10. Our programs were written in Java. We used six datasets for performance evaluation, five real datasets downloaded from the SPMF data mining library [1], and one synthetic dataset generated using the transaction utility database generator provided on the SPMF[1]. We present the characteristics of the datasets in Table 5.

The five real datasets, Chess, Foodmart, Mushroom, Ecommerce, and Connect, contain utility information. The synthetic dataset T25I100D50k do not contain the utility value or quantity of each item in each transaction. Using a random transaction database generator provided in SPMF [1], we generated the unit profit for items following a Gaussian distribution.

Table 5. Characteristics of the datasets

Dataset	#Trans	#Items	Avg. Trans. Len	Max. Trans. Len
Chess	3,196	76	37	37
Foodmart	4,141	1,559	4.42	14
Mushroom	8,124	120	23	23
Ecommerce	14,975	3,803	15.4	29
Connect	67,557	129	43	43
T25I100D50k	50,000	100	25	25

5.1 Search Space Size

We first compare the sizes of the search spaces of the four algorithms, where the size of an algorithm's search space refers to the number of nodes this algorithm visited. We show the results in Table 6.

Table 6. Comparison of the sizes of the search spaces

Dataset	#SFUIs	Sizes of search spaces			
		SFU-Miner	SKYFUP-D	SKYFUP-B	SFUI-UF
Chess	35	15,433,601	3,750,820	122,363	915,101
Foodmart	1	1,307,831	1,232,033	773,580	773,400
Mushroom	17	810,440	79,710	9,910	22,710
Ecommerce	2	22,309,811	18,590,045	3,471	2,731
Connect	46	-	13,335,429	-	4,349,427
T25I100D50k	6	193,981,690	2,123,115	-	1,595,532

For the six datasets, the proposed SFUI-UF algorithm and SKYFUP-D algorithm returned correct results in all cases, whereas the other two algorithms could not on the Connect dataset. Furthermore, SKYFUP-B algorithm could also not find any results on T25I100D50k dataset. Specifically, SFU-Miner did not return any results after 12 h, and the problem of memory leakage occurred for the SKYFUP-B algorithm. We use "-" for these three entries.

Table 6 clearly shows that the number of SFUIs is very scarce, which is in sharp contrast to the huge search space. Thus, mining SFUIs is a truly challenging problem. Among these four algorithms, SFU-Miner performed worst. This is mainly because the elements of the umax array only recorded the maximal utility of a specific frequency, whose pruning effect was worse than those of the other two array structures. The search spaces of SFUI-UF were always smaller than those of SFU-Miner and SKYFUP-D. The search spaces of SFUI-UF were comparable to those of SKYFUP-B. This shows that the MUS was effective for search space pruning. This is because once a top-ranked item was pruned using the MUS, a large number of its child nodes were pruned. Thus, the search space was reduced greatly.

5.2 Runtime

We demonstrate the efficiency of our algorithm and the comparison algorithms. We show the comparison results in Table 7.

For the same reason mentioned in Sect. 5.1, we do not report the runtime of SFU-Miner for the Connect dataset, and the runtimes of SKYFUP-B for the Connect and T25I100D50k datasets. Table 7 shows that SFUI-UF was always more efficient than SFU-Miner and SKYFUP-D. Furthermore, SFUI-UF is demonstrated to be more efficient than SKYFUP-B except for the Ecommerce dataset. More importantly, SFUI-UF successfully discovered SFUIs on all six datasets, whereas SKYFUP-B encountered the problem of memory leakage on two datasets. This shows that, in addition to the MUS, the MUE was effective for avoiding generating unpromising candidates. Thus, efficiency improved.

Table 7. Runtime of the compared algorithms

Unit (Sec)	SFU-Miner	SKYFUP-D	SKYFUP-B	SFUI-UF
Chess	169.50	40.14	37.35	29.28
Foodmart	0.57	0.44	0.46	0.34
Mushroom	9.30	2.10	2.22	1.73
Ecommerce	7.37	5.54	0.39	1.20
Connect	-	6,643.63	-	4,176.86
T25I100D50k	2781.29	139.02	-	108.85

5.3 Memory Consumption

We compare the memory usage of the four algorithms. We measured memory usage using the Java API, and show the results in Table 8. SFUI-UF performed best on most datasets, except Foodmart and Connect. Additionally, besides the reasons mentioned in Sect. 5.1 and Sect. 5.2, the MUA structure was also an important factor for saving memory. As stated in Sect. 4.2, the size of the MUA equals the maximal frequency of the 1-itemset, whereas for umax in SFU-Miner [8], and utilmax in SKYFUP-D and SKYFUP-B [3], their sizes are both equivalent to the number of transactions in the database. To show the effect of the MUA, we compared the sizes of the three arrays, and show the results in Table 9.

Table 8. Memory usage of the compared algorithms

Unit (MB)	SFU-Miner	SKYFUP-D	SKYFUP-B	SFUI-UF
Chess	128.24	154.31	1,754.45	41.30
Foodmart	12.48	12.48	85.45	50.70
Mushroom	52.49	123.02	110.50	22.72
Ecommerce	75.08	80.43	69.52	23.50
Connect	-	409.12	-	574.91
T25I100D50k	155.34	128.69	-	90.91

Table 9. Sizes of arrays of the compared algorithms

Dataset	umax	utilmax	MUA
Chess	3,196	3,196	3,195
Foodmart	4,141	4,141	25
Mushroom	8,124	8,124	8,124
Ecommerce	14,975	14,975	1,104
Connect	67,557	67,557	67,473
T25I100D50k	50,000	50,000	12706

The results in Table 9 show that the sizes umax and utilmax were always equivalent to each other on all the six datasets, whereas the size of the MUA was only equivalent to those of umax and utilmax for the Mushroom dataset. The superiority of the MUA was obvious on the three datasets: Foodmart, Ecommerce and T25I100D50k. Particularly, for Foodmart, the size of the MUA was two orders of magnitude smaller than that of the other two arrays. This is because, for most part, the items in the dataset do not appear in every transaction, the length of the MUA will always be less than or equal to the length of umax and utilmax, and the more sparse the dataset, the more significant the difference will be.

6   Conclusion

In this paper, we solve the SFUIM problem by proposing a novel algorithm called SFUI-UF. Because the frequency measure satisfies the downward closure property, we focused our algorithm on utility, similar to other SFUIM algorithms. The main idea of SFUI-UF is to filter utilities from three perspectives, that is, frequency, TWU, and utility itself, which have been formally proved. The SFUI-UF algorithm uses the UL structure to transform the original database, and traverses the search space in a depth-first manner. The experimental results on both real and synthetic datasets showed that SFUI-UF can discover accurate SFUIs with high efficiency and low memory usage.

Acknowledgments. We would like to thank Prof. Jerry Chun-Wei Lin for providing the source codes of the SKYFUP-D and SKYFUP-B algorithms. This work was partially supported by the National Natural Science Foundation of China (61977001), and Great Wall Scholar Program (CIT&TCD20190305).

References

1. Fournier-Viger, P., et al.: The SPMF open-source data mining library version 2. In: Berendt, B., et al. (eds.) ECML PKDD 2016. LNCS (LNAI), vol. 9853, pp. 36–40. Springer, Cham (2016). https://doi.org/10.1007/978-3-319-46131-1_8

2. Goyal, V., Sureka, A., Patel, D.: Efficient skyline itemsets mining. In: Proceedings of the Eighth International C* Conference on Computer Science & Software Engineering, pp.119–124 (2015)

3. Lin, J.C.-W., Yang, L., Fournier-Viger, P., Hong, T.-P.: Mining of skyline patterns by considering both frequent and utility constraints. Eng. Appl. Artif. Intell. **77**, 229–238 (2019)

4. Liu, M., Qu, J.: Mining high utility itemsets without candidate generation. In: Proceedings of the 21st ACM International Conference on Information and Knowledge Management, pp.55–64 (2012)

5. Liu, Y., Liao, W.-K., Choudhary, A.: A two-phase algorithm for fast discovery of high utility itemsets. In: Ho, T.B., Cheung, D., Liu, H. (eds.) PAKDD 2005. LNCS (LNAI), vol. 3518, pp. 689–695. Springer, Heidelberg (2005). https://doi.org/10.1007/11430919_79

6. Luna, J.M., Fournier-Viger, P., Ventura, S.: Frequent itemset mining: a 25 years review. Wiley Interdiscip. Rev. Data Min. Knowl. Discov. **9**(6) (2019)

7. Nguyen, H.M., Phan, A.V., Pham, L.V.: FSKYMINE: a faster algorithm for mining skyline frequent utility itemsets. In: Proceedings of the 6th NAFOSTED Conference on Information and Computer Science, pp.251–255 (2019)

8. Pan, J.-S., Lin, J.C.-W., Yang, L., Fournier-Viger, P., Hong, T.-P.: Efficiently mining of skyline frequent-utility patterns. Intell. Data Anal. **21**(6), 1407–1423 (2017)

9. Podpecan, V., Lavrac, N., Kononenko, I.: A fast algorithm for mining utility-frequent itemsets. In: Proceedings of International Workshop on Constraint-Based Mining and Learning, pp. 9–20 (2007)

10. Song, W., Jiang, B., Qiao, Y.: Mining multi-relational high utility itemsets from star schemas. Intell. Data Anal. **22**(1), 143–165 (2018)

11. Song, W., Zhang, Z., Li, J.: A high utility itemset mining algorithm based on subsume index. Knowl. Inf. Syst. **49**(1), 315–340 (2015). https://doi.org/10.1007/s10115-015-0900-1

12. Yeh, J.-S., Li, Y.-C., Chang, C.-C.: Two-phase algorithms for a novel utility-frequent mining model. In: Proceedings of the International Workshops on Emerging Technologies in Knowledge Discovery and Data Mining, pp.433–444 (2007)

Network Embedding with Topology-Aware Textual Representations

Jiaxing Chen[1], Zenan Xu[1], and Qinliang Su[1,2,3(✉)]

[1] School of Computer Science and Engineering, Sun Yat-sen University,
Guangzhou, China
{chenjx227,xuzn}@mail2.sysu.edu.cn, suqliang@mail.sysu.edu.cn
[2] Guangdong Key Laboratory of Big Data Analysis and Processing,
Guangzhou, China
[3] Key Laboratory of Machine Intelligence and Advanced Computing,
Ministry of Education, Guangzhou, China

Abstract. Textual network embedding aims to learn meaningful low-dimensional representations for vertices with the consideration of the associated texts. When learning the representations for texts in network embedding, existing methods mostly only exploit information from neighboring texts (*i.e.*, contexts), while rarely taking advantages of the valuable network topological (structural) information. To bridge the gap, in this paper, a model based on adaptive-filter convolutional neural networks (CNN) is developed, in which the filters are adapted to local network topologies, rather than clamped to fixed values as in traditional CNNs. The dependency enables the learned text representations to be aware of local network topologies. It is shown that the proposed *topology-aware* representations can be viewed as a complement to existing *context-aware* ones. When the two are used together, experimental results on three real-world benchmarks demonstrate that significant performance improvements on the tasks of link prediction and vertex classification.

Keywords: Textual network embedding · Network topology · Topology-aware · Context-aware

1 Introduction

Networks provide a nature way to organize the relational information like that in the social and citation networks [23,24]. The huge amount of information contained in the networks can benefit downstream applications significantly if it is exploited appropriately, such as friends recommendation in social network, precise products advertisement in e-commerce and so on. However, as networks become increasingly large, extracting information from them directly becomes too expensive to be feasible. Thus, investigating how to efficiently extract useful information from huge networks turn out to be a problem of practical importance.

© Springer Nature Switzerland AG 2021
D. N. Pham et al. (Eds.): PRICAI 2021, LNAI 13031, pp. 425–439, 2021.
https://doi.org/10.1007/978-3-030-89188-6_32

Network embedding aims to learn a low-dimensional representation for every network vertex so that the neighboring information of vertices can be preserved in the low-dimensional representations as much as possible. If we want to extract some information (*e.g.* similarity information) from the networks, we only need to work on the low-dimensional representations, instead of the original huge networks, increasing the computational efficiency significantly. So far, many efforts have been devoted to this area. In DeepWalk [22], by viewing sequences of vertices obtained by randomly walking on the network as sentences, word embedding technique Skip-Gram [18] is used to learn the embeddings for network vertices. To consider second-order proximities of networks, LINE [27] is proposed to encourage the representations of vertices that share many common neighbors to be also similar. Node2vec [8] generalizes the concept of neighborhood, and propose an efficient sampling algorithm biasing towards important vertices.

To take the influence of texts into account, TADW [35] proposes a way to absorb texts into the vertex embeddings under the framework of matrix factorization (MF), after discovering the close connection between MF and DeepWalk. On the other side, CENE[26] achieves the goal by treating the texts as another type of vertices, and then use the aforementioned structure-only methods to learn the embeddings. To generate robust embeddings for attributed networks, some researchers propose an outlier-aware network embedding algorithm (ONE) [2] which minimizes the effect of the outlier nodes. Noticing that the exact meaning of a piece of texts highly depends on the contexts it resides in, a context-aware network embedding (CANE) method is later developed in [29], which employs the attention mechanism to model the impacts from the contexts to the interested texts. To capture the fine-grained relations between the interested texts and contexts, word alignment mechanism is further proposed to use in WANE [25]. The influence of contexts is further investigated under the optimal transport metric in [7]. However, we argue that in addition to the contexts, network topologies also play an important role in uncovering the true meanings of texts. As illustrated in Fig. 1, the meaning of a sentence 'The main business of our company is to sell apples.' can only be recognized unless we resort to their social connections, *i.e.*, the network topologies. If the connections include many high-profile businessmen, it more likely means selling Apple electronic products. Otherwise, if lots of farmers are connected, it may refer to the fruit apple.

To have the textual representations being aware of network topologies, in this paper, adaptive-filer convolutional neural networks (CNN) are proposed to capture the complex relations between the network topologies and texts. Specifically, filters of the CNN are generated from a deconvolutional neural network (DCNN) by taking the local network topologies representation as input. As a result, the filters are *adapted* to the local topologies, rather than clamped to fixed values as in traditional CNNs. The adaptive filters enable the learned textual representations being aware of the network's local topologies. In this proposed model, the same text that is associated with different network topologies will lead to different representations. The topology-aware textual representations can be understood as a *complement* to the previous context-aware textual

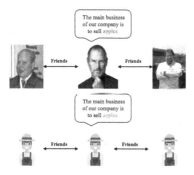

Fig. 1. Illustration of how social connections help to understand the semantic meaning of a sentence.

representations in [25,29], which provides a different view to the texts. When the proposed topology-aware representations are used together with the existing context-aware ones, substantial performance gains are observed on the tasks of link prediction [15] and vertex classification [4], demonstrating the importance of network topologies in learning textual representations for network embedding.

2 Related Work

2.1 Network Embedding.

Network embedding is designed to efficiently analyze and extract information from large networks. Traditional network embedding is regarded as a process of dimension reduction [6], and many methods focus on exploiting the properties of the Laplacian and adjacency matrices [3,28,34]. However, due to the high computational complexity, these methods are difficult to scale to large networks. Later, a large number of more sophisticated and efficient methods emerged. LINE [27] was proposed to explicitly preserve the first-order and second-order proximities [28,30] of the network. Similar to the idea of Skip-Gram [18], DeepWalk [22] employs a random walk strategy over networks to learn vertex embeddings. Further, in order to explore the network structure more efficiently, node2vec [8] introduces a biased random walk strategy in place of the random walk strategy in DeepWalk. By leveraging community structure and microscopic structure of the network, M-NMF [31] learns network embeddings from the view of Nonnegative Matrix Factorization [12].

2.2 Textual Network Embedding

TADW [35] leverages the equivalence between DeepWalk and matrix decomposition and proposes to integrate textual features into DeppWalk, which can be solved by matrix decomposition to learn the latent representation from structural information and textual information jointly. Proposed in [26], CENE optimizes the loss of vertex-vertex links and vertex-content links jointly by regarding text content as a special type of vertices. TriDNR [21] and ASNE [14] consider information from three parties: node structure, node content, and node labels (if available) to learn optimal node representation with different models [11,22] comprehensively. Considering the impact of contextual information from neighbor texts, CANE is further proposed in [29], which employs a mutual attention mechanism to adaptively encode texts conditioned on neighboring texts. Recently, NEIFA in [33] takes into account the mutual influence between structural and textual information by effectively fusing them into one information. In [32], how to embed dynamic networks is further considered by tracking the evolution of network changes over time. However, all of the aforementioned methods ignore the impact from local topology information of network for the understanding of semantic information.

3   Preliminaries

3.1   Framework of Textual Network Embedding

A textual network is defined as $\mathbb{G} = (\mathcal{V}, \mathcal{E}, \mathcal{T})$, where $\mathcal{V}$ is the set of N vertices; $\mathcal{T}$ is the set of texts associated with vertices; and $\mathcal{E} \in \mathcal{V} \times \mathcal{V}$ is the set of edges. Textual network embedding aims to learn a low-dimensional representation for each vertex and its associated texts, with the neighboring information preserved as much as possible. To this end, a structural and textual representation is learned for each vertex by optimizing the objective [25,29]:

$$
\mathcal{L} = - \sum_{\{u,v\}\in\mathcal{E}} \log p\left(\boldsymbol{h}_u^s | \boldsymbol{h}_v^s\right) - \lambda_1 \sum_{\{u,v\}\in\mathcal{E}} \log p\left(\boldsymbol{h}_u^t | \boldsymbol{h}_v^t\right)
$$
$$
- \lambda_2 \sum_{\{u,v\}\in\mathcal{E}} \left(\log p\left(\boldsymbol{h}_u^s | \boldsymbol{h}_v^t\right) + \log p\left(\boldsymbol{h}_u^t | \boldsymbol{h}_v^s\right) \right),
\tag{1}
$$

where $\boldsymbol{h}_u^s, \boldsymbol{h}_u^t \in \mathbb{R}^d$ denote the structural and textual representation of vertex u, respectively; $p(\boldsymbol{h}_u | \boldsymbol{h}_v) \triangleq \frac{\exp\left(\boldsymbol{h}_u^T \boldsymbol{h}_v\right)}{\sum_{i=1}^{|\mathcal{V}|} \exp\left(\boldsymbol{h}_i^T \boldsymbol{h}_v\right)}$; the four terms in right hand side (r.h.s.) of (1) are used to account for the structure-to-structure, text-to-text, text-to-structure and structure-to-text influences, respectively; λ_1 and λ_2 are used to control the relative importance of different terms. Here, the structural representation $\boldsymbol{h}_u^s$ is mainly used to capture local network topological information around vertex u, while the textual representation $\boldsymbol{h}_u^t$ mainly captures the information in the texts of vertex u. Given $\boldsymbol{h}_u^s$ and $\boldsymbol{h}_u^t$, the network embedding of vertex u is obtained by directly concatenating the two vectors like

$$
\boldsymbol{h}_u = [\boldsymbol{h}_u^s; \boldsymbol{h}_u^t].
\tag{2}
$$

In the objective (1), the structural representation $\boldsymbol{h}_u^s$ is randomly initialized, while the textual representation $\boldsymbol{h}_u^t$ is set to be the output of a function, that is,

$$
\boldsymbol{h}_u^t = \mathcal{F}_\theta\left(\boldsymbol{t}_u\right),
\tag{3}
$$

where $\boldsymbol{t}_u$ denotes the sequence of words associated with vertex u and the function $\mathcal{F}_\theta(\cdot)$ maps raw texts to their representations. This paper mainly focuses on how to learn a good mapping.

3.2   Context-Aware Textual Representation Learning

One simple way to obtain a textual representation is to pass the text through a neural network. When learning text representations, since the semantic meaning of texts often depends on the context it resides in, it is suggested to consider the influences from the texts of neighboring vertices as well. Therefore, a mapping function with the following form is proposed

$$h_u^t = \mathcal{F}_\theta(t_u, t_v), \qquad (4)$$

where the first argument t_u is the text of interest, while the second argument t_v serves as its context for any $(u, v) \in \mathcal{E}$. Textual representations obtained from a mapping like (4) are often dubbed as *context-aware representations*.

The first context-aware network embedding model (CANE) is proposed in [29]. It computes a correlation matrix $G_u \in \mathbb{R}^{m \times n}$ between the target text t_u and one of its neighboring texts t_v as follows

$$G_u = \tanh\left(X_u^T A X_v\right), \qquad (5)$$

where $X_u \in \mathbb{R}^{d \times m}$ and $X_v \in \mathbb{R}^{d \times n}$ denote the word embedding matrices of texts in vertices u and v, respectively; m and n are the number of words in the texts of vertices u and v, while d is the dimension of textual representation; and $A \in \mathbb{R}^{m \times n}$ is a trainable affinity matrix used to align the two feature matrices [5]. Then, the context-aware representation of texts in vertex u is computed as

$$h_u^t = X_u \alpha_u, \qquad (6)$$

where $\alpha_u = \text{softmax}(\text{Mean}(G_u))$ is the attention weight; and $\text{Mean}(\cdot)$ means taking the average over matrix rows. Obviously, the i-th element of α_u represents the relative importance of the i-th word of text t_u when it is placed under the context of t_v.

Later, fine-grained word alignment mechanism is further employed to capture the subtle relation between interested text and its contexts, leading to a model named word-alignment network embedding (WANE) [25]. WANE works similarly to CANE, except the method of computing the attention weight α_u and the way on how to obtain the final textual representation h_u^t in (6). Please refer to [25] for more details. In both of the CANE and WANE models, attention mechanism is the key to absorb the influence of contexts into the final textual representations.

4   Topology-Aware Textual Representation Learning

In addition to the contexts, as stated in the Sect. 1, network topologies also play an important role in uncovering the exact meanings of texts. The simplest way to take the influences of topologies into account is to extend the existing context-aware methods to handle the topologies. Specifically, we can represent

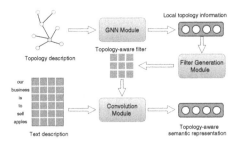

Fig. 2. Illustration of the procedure to learn topology-aware textual representations.

the local topological information of vertex u using the structural representations of vertex u and its neighbors as

$$H_u = \left[h_u^s, h_{u_1}^s, \cdots, h_{u_k}^s \right], \tag{7}$$

where u_k denotes the k-th neighbor of vertex u; and h_u^s is the structural representation of vertex u. H_u can be understood as the embedding matrix of vertices, and plays a similar role as the word embedding matrix X_v in (5). We can simply replace the X_v in (5) with H_u to obtain a topology-aware textual representation. However, we notice that the two information sources of X_v and H_u come from different domains (text and network topology). This may prevent the simple model from producing high-quality representations since attention mechanism generally works most effectively only when the information sources come from similar domains.

4.1   Topology-Aware CNN-Based Method

To have the textual representations being aware of the local network topologies, adaptive CNNs are proposed to capture the complex relations between texts and their local topologies. The key is that the CNN filters here are not clamped to fixed values, but are *adapted* to local network topologies. Supposing that the local topological information of vertex u can be summarized by a vector s_u (we will discuss how to obtain it in the next subsection), a set of CNN filters can be specifically generated for vertex u as

$$F_u = \text{Generator}\left(s_u\right), \tag{8}$$

where the tensor $F_u \in \mathbb{R}^{c \times w \times d}$ is the collection of CNN's filters, with c and $w \times d$ representing the filter number and kernel size, respectively. The Generator($\cdot$) is realized mainly by a deconvolutional operator, which transforms small patches/matrices to large ones through zero-padding and convolutional operations [20]. More specifically, the filter tensor F_u is generated by passing the local topological information vector s_u through a deconvolutional operator and performing some reshaping.

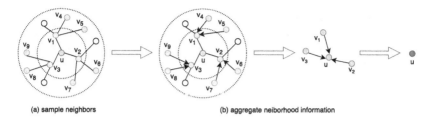

Fig. 3. Illustration of the process of local topology information extraction. (a) Sample multi-hops neighbors of node u, where blue and green nodes are 1-hop and 2-hop neighbors of u. (b) Aggregate neighborhood information: we first aggregate 2-hop neighbors' information (green) to 1-hop neighbors (blue), so we can obtain new representations for 1-hop neighbors (purple); finally we obtain new representations of node u by aggregating information from 1-hop neighbors. (Color figure online)

Given the topology-dependent filters $\boldsymbol{F}_u$, we then pass the word embedding matrix $\boldsymbol{X}_u$ of vertex u through a one-layer CNN equiped with $\boldsymbol{F}_u$ as

$$\boldsymbol{M}_u = \mathrm{Conv}(\boldsymbol{F}_u, \boldsymbol{X}_u) + \boldsymbol{b}, \tag{9}$$

where $\boldsymbol{M}_u$ denotes the CNN's feature map of vertex u; and $\boldsymbol{b}$ is the bias term. Taking an average-pooling and nonlinear transformation $\tanh(\cdot)$ over $\boldsymbol{M}_u$ gives the final textual representation

$$\boldsymbol{h}_u^{s \to t} = \tanh(\mathrm{Mean}(\boldsymbol{M}_u)), \tag{10}$$

where $\boldsymbol{h}_u^{s \to t}$ denotes the topology-aware textual representation, with the superscript representing from structure (*i.e.* topology information) to text. This is contrast to the context-aware textual representation, which is denoted as $\boldsymbol{h}_u^{t \to t}$ in the subsequent, where the superscript represents from text to text. The most intriguing part here is that the CNN filters are not fixed, but are dependent on the local network topology, which allows the model to learn topology-aware representations for texts. The advantage of such parametrization will be demonstrated in the experiments. Figure 2 illustrates the whole process of how to extract topology-aware textual representations.

4.2 Extracting Local Topological Information by Graph Neural Networks

One simple way to extract local topological information $\boldsymbol{s}_u$ used in (8) is to collect the structural representations of vertex u as well as its neighbors' $\{\boldsymbol{h}_k^s\}_{k \in \{u, \mathcal{N}(u)\}}$, and then take an average as $\boldsymbol{s}_u = \mathrm{Mean}(\boldsymbol{H}_u)$, where $\boldsymbol{H}_u$ is defined in (7). Inspired by the extraordinary performance of graph neural networks (GNN) in learning graph representations [9], a GNN-based method is adopted here. Specifically, for each vertex, we first select a fixed number (*e.g.* 10) of neighbors (they could be multi-hop away from the considered vertex), inducing a small subgraph. The structural representations of vertices in outer layers are then propagated towards inner ones layer-by-layer until the innermost vertex u, as illustrated in Fig. 3. More precisely, we divide vertices in the subgraph into different layers according to their number of hops to vertex u, and mark the outermost layer as the 0-th layer, and the one next to the outermost as 1-th layer and so on. For any vertex i from the ℓ-th layer with $\ell = 1, 2, \cdots, L$, we execute the following updates

$$Z_i^\ell = \text{Aggregate} \left(z_v^{\ell-1}, \forall v \in \mathcal{N}_{\ell-1}(i) \right), \tag{11}$$

$$z_i^\ell = \sigma \left(W_\ell \cdot \text{Mean}(Z_i^\ell) + W_\ell' h_i^s \right), \tag{12}$$

where z_v^0 is initialized by h_v^s; W_ℓ and W_ℓ' are the GNN's parameters; Aggregate($\cdot$) assembles all vectors to constitute a matrix; $\mathcal{N}_{\ell-1}(i)$ denotes the neighbors of i that are in the $(\ell-1)$-th layer; L is the maximum number of hops to the vertex u; and σ is the sigmoid function. After L steps, the obtained z_u^L is used to represent the local topological information, that is,

$$s_u = z_u^L. \tag{13}$$

This information s_u is then fed into the filter generator module as shown in (8).

5   The Whole Model

The topology-aware model views the texts from a perspective different from the context-aware models, thus is possible to extract some extra information not contained in the context-aware representations. To obtain a more comprehensive textual representation, we can merge the two. For simplicity, only a linear combination is considered here

$$h_u^t = \gamma h_u^{t \to t} + (1 - \gamma) h_u^{s \to t}, \tag{14}$$

where $h_u^{t \to t}$ could be obtained by using the existing CANE [29] or WANE [25] methods; and $\gamma \in [0,1]$ is a learnable parameter that controls the relative importance of the two representations. In the experiments, this parameter is learned together with other model parameters automatically. Given the structural and textual representations h_u^s and h_u^t, the network embedding of vertex u is obtained by directly concatenating them

$$h_u = [h_u^s; h_u^t].$$

In the subsequent, the whole model proposed above is abbreviated as TANE, standing for Topology-Aware Network Embedding Model.

Training Details. To train the model, we need to optimize the objective function (1), which requires to repeatedly evaluate the probabilities $p(z_u|z_v) \triangleq \frac{\exp (z_u^T z_v)}{\sum_{i=1}^{|\mathcal{V}|} \exp (z_i^T z_v)}$, where $|\mathcal{V}|$ is number of vertices. For large-scale networks, this would be computationally prohibitive. To address this problem, the negative sampling strategy [19] that samples only a subset of negative edges for each evaluation is introduced. As a result, the probability is approximated as $\log p(z_u|z_v) \approx \log \sigma(z_u^T z_v) + \sum_{k=1}^{K} \mathbb{E}_{k \sim p(w)}[\log \sigma(-z_k^T z_v)]$, where $\sigma(\cdot)$ is the sigmoid function; K is the number of negative samples. Following [19], the distribution is set to be $p(w) \propto d_w^{3/4}$, where d_w denotes the out-degree of vertex $w \in \mathcal{V}$. During the whole training process, the Adam algorithm [10] is used.

6 Experiments

6.1 Datasets, Baselines and Setups

Datasets. To evaluate the performance of the proposed methods, we conduct experiments on the following three benchmark datasets.

- *Zhihu* [26]: A social network crawled from the largest Q&A website in China, including 10000 active users, 43896 connection relationships, as well as the users' descriptions on their interested topics.
- *Cora* [17]: A paper citation network consisting of 2277 machine learning papers collected from 7 research areas, and 5214 citation relationships.
- *HepTh* [13]: A citation network made up of 1038 papers associated with abstract information, and 1990 citation relationships between them.

Baselines. To demonstrate the effectiveness of our proposed method, two types of competitive baselines are adopted for comparison. The first type employs the structure information only, including MMB [1], DeepWalk [22], LINE [27] and node2vec [8], while the second type leverages both the structure and text information, including the naive combination method, TADW [35], CENE [26], CANE[29] as well as the WANE [25].

Experiment Setups. For a fair comparison, following the settings in [29], we also set the dimension of network embedding h_u to 200, with the dimensions of structural and textual representations h_u^s and h_u^t both set to 100. Adam [10] is employed for optimizing the model parameters, with the mini-batch size set to 64. Dropout is used on the word embedding layer to alleviate overfitting. For the local topology information extraction, we sample up to 25 one-hop neighbors and 10 two-hop neighbors for each node. Moreover, to speed up the convergence and obtain better results, we learn the structural representation h_u^s alone for several epochs first, and then learn both the structural and textual representations simultaneously using the Adam algorithm.

6.2 Comparison with Other Methods

Link Prediction. We randomly delete certain proportions, ranging from 15% to 95%, of edges from the networks, and then use the learned embeddings of vertices to predict the existence of unobserved (deleted) edges between two vertices. The

Table 1. AUC values on Zhihu.

% Training edges	15%	25%	35%	45%	55%	65%	75%	85%	95%
MMB [1]	51.0	51.5	53.7	58.6	61.6	66.1	68.8	68.9	72.4
DeepWalk [22]	56.6	58.1	60.1	60.0	61.8	61.9	63.3	63.7	67.8
LINE [27]	52.3	55.9	59.9	60.9	64.3	66.0	67.7	69.3	71.1
node2vec [8]	54.2	57.1	57.3	58.3	58.7	62.5	66.2	67.6	68.5
Naive Combination	55.1	56.7	58.9	62.6	64.4	68.7	68.9	69.0	71.5
TADW [35]	52.3	54.2	55.6	57.3	60.8	62.4	65.2	63.8	69.0
CENE [26]	56.2	57.4	60.3	63.0	66.3	66.0	70.2	69.8	73.8
CANE [29]	56.8	59.3	62.9	64.5	68.9	70.4	71.4	73.6	75.4
TANE-ATT	50.4	51.2	51.8	52.0	53.1	55.0	55.4	58.3	60.5
TANE[1]	**61.0**	**68.0**	**72.4**	**76.4**	**76.9**	**77.6**	**78.4**	**78.5**	**78.8**
WANE [25]	58.7	63.5	68.3	71.9	74.9	77.0	79.7	80.0	82.6
TANE[2]	**66.2**	**69.3**	**73.5**	**75.4**	**78.1**	**80.0**	**81.2**	**82.5**	**82.8**

task is established on the assumption that the embeddings of two originally connected vertices should be closer. We follow the procedures in CANE [29] and WANE [25] to compute the accuracy of link prediction, in which the AUC metric is used. The performance of the proposed models, along with the baselines, on the three benchmark datasets Zhihu, HepTh and Cora are reported in Table 1, Table 2 and Table 3, respectively. In the tables, TANE[1] and TANE[2] represent the TANE models that use the context-aware textual representations from CANE and WANE, respectively, while TANE-ATT denotes the TANE model based on the attention mechanism.

It can be seen from Tables 1, 2 and 3 that when the proposed adaptive TANE is used together with existing context-aware methods, no matter it is the CANE or WANE, performance improvements can be observed consistently on all three datasets. This may be because the topology-aware representations successfully extract from texts some extra information that is not contained in the context-aware representations. Thus, when they are used together, improvements can be observed. This also demonstrate the importance of topologies and contexts in understanding the subtle meanings of texts. But as seen from the tables, the attention-based TANE performs poorly on all the three datasets. This confirms our previous conjecture that the attention mechanism is not suitable to capture the complex relation between texts and network topologies that come from two totally different domains. We also notice that the proposed TANE models sometimes perform a little worse than the CANE or WANE models at small proportions of observed edges. This is because under this scenario, the obtained topological information is too little to represent the true local network structure. Interestingly, we observe that in Zhihu dataset, the learnable parameter γ converges to a small value (*e.g.* 0.2), while in the other two datasets, it converges to a relatively large value (*e.g.* 0.9). This indicates that the topology-aware rep-

Table 2. AUC values on HepTh.

% Training edges	15%	25%	35%	45%	55%	65%	75%	85%	95%
MMB [1]	54.6	57.9	57.3	61.6	66.2	68.4	73.6	76.0	80.3
DeepWalk [22]	55.2	66.0	70.0	75.7	81.3	83.3	87.6	88.9	88.0
LINE [27]	53.7	60.4	66.5	73.9	78.5	83.8	87.5	87.7	87.6
node2vec [8]	57.1	63.6	69.9	76.2	84.3	87.3	88.4	89.2	89.2
Naive Combination	78.7	82.1	84.7	88.7	88.7	91.8	92.1	92.0	92.7
TADW [35]	87.0	89.5	91.8	90.8	91.1	92.6	93.5	91.9	91.7
CENE [26]	86.2	84.6	89.8	91.2	92.3	91.8	93.2	92.9	93.2
CANE [29]	**90.0**	91.2	92.0	93.0	94.2	94.6	95.4	95.7	96.3
TANE-ATT	60.3	78.2	82.0	83.4	83.5	85.6	89.7	90.8	91.9
TANE[1]	84.9	**92.6**	**93.7**	**94.9**	**96.6**	**96.7**	**98.3**	**98.2**	**99.3**
WANE [25]	**92.3**	94.1	95.7	96.7	97.5	97.5	97.7	98.2	98.7
TANE[2]	86.5	**94.7**	**96.0**	**97.2**	**98.2**	**97.7**	**98.5**	**98.4**	**99.1**

Table 3. AUC values on Cora.

% Training edges	15%	25%	35%	45%	55%	65%	75%	85%	95%
MMB [1]	54.7	57.1	59.5	61.9	64.9	67.8	71.1	72.6	75.9
DeepWalk [22]	56.0	63.0	70.2	75.5	80.1	85.2	85.3	87.8	90.3
LINE [27]	55.0	58.6	66.4	73.0	77.6	82.8	85.6	88.4	89.3
node2vec [8]	55.9	62.4	66.1	75.0	78.7	81.6	85.9	87.3	88.2
Naive Combination	72.7	82.0	84.9	87.0	88.7	91.9	92.4	93.9	94.0
TADW [35]	86.6	88.2	90.2	90.8	90.0	93.0	91.0	93.4	92.7
CENE [26]	72.1	86.5	84.6	88.1	89.4	89.2	93.9	95.0	95.9
CANE [29]	**86.8**	**91.5**	92.2	93.9	94.6	94.9	95.6	96.6	97.7
TANE-ATT	75.4	77.3	80.2	83.1	84.7	85.6	88.0	90.1	91.3
TANE[1]	85.2	89.6	**93.1**	**94.4**	**94.8**	**95.2**	**95.8**	**97.5**	**98.2**
WANE [25]	**91.7**	**93.3**	94.1	95.7	96.2	96.9	97.5	98.2	99.1
TANE[2]	89.4	92.1	**94.3**	**95.9**	**96.6**	**97.3**	**97.8**	**98.4**	**99.2**

resentation is more important in Zhihu dataset, while less in the other two, suggesting that Zhihu may contain more topological information.

Multi-label Vertex Classification. For this task, we train a linear SVM classifier on the learned network embeddings of the Cora dataset. The proportions of embeddings used for training vary from 10% to 50%. The classification accuracy on the remaining embeddings is reported as the final performance. Figure 4(a) shows the test accuracies of the proposed and baseline models under different percentages of training data. Note that due to the similarities between CANE

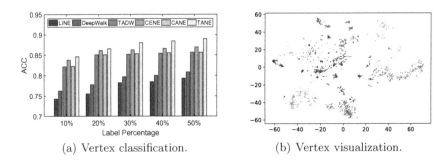

(a) Vertex classification.   (b) Vertex visualization.

Fig. 4. Vertex classification and visualization on Cora

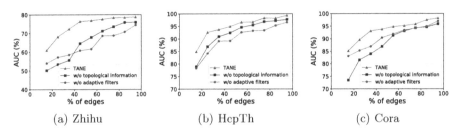

(a) Zhihu   (b) HepTh   (c) Cora

Fig. 5. Ablation study of TANE on different datasets in terms of link prediction.

and WANE, only the TANE model using CANE context-aware representations is considered in subsequent experiments. It can be seen that the proposed model TANE performs the best under all percentages, demonstrating the effectiveness of the proposed network embedding method. This further supports the argument that the topology-aware and context-aware representations emphasize different aspects of the texts, and integrating them could lead to more comprehensive representations.

6.3 Further Analysis

Ablation Study. To investigate the importance of topological information and the adaptive filter CNN in the proposed TANE model, we carry out an ablation study on different datasets in the link prediction task. Specifically, in addition to the original TANE model, we also experiment with its two variants: i) TANE (w/o topological information), in which the topological information is replaced by random vectors; ii) TANE (w/o adaptive filters), in which the adaptive filters are replaced by a set of fixed filters as in the traditional CNNs. The experimental results are shown in Fig. 5. It can be observed that if we replace the topological information with random vectors, the performance decreases a lot, which implies that the topological information does contribute a lot to produce high-quality network embeddings. On the other hand, by replacing the adaptive filters with a set of fixed filters, a significant performance drop is also observed. This confirms the effectiveness of adaptive filter CNN in learning semantic representations that are aware of local structures.

Visualization Analysis. To show an intuitive understanding on the quality of network embeddings learned by the proposed TANE method, we apply t-SNE [16] to project the embeddings into a two-dimensional space, and then visualize them in the coordinate system. We conduct this experiment on Cora dataset whose vertices are labelled. As shown in Fig. 4(b), each point denotes a vertex (paper) in the network and its color indicates the category it belongs to. It can be seen that most of the embeddings with the same label are clustered relatively closer than those with different labels. This may explain the superior performance of our proposed topology-aware network embedding method.

7   Conclusions

In this paper, we present the topology-aware textual network embedding (TANE) model for the first time. It seeks to eliminate the semantic ambiguities and boost the quality of text representation in network embedding by leveraging the network topological information. To this end, an adaptive CNN based model is developed, in which the filters are adapted to the local topology information, rather than fixed in traditional CNNs. An graph neural network is also proposed to extract the local topology information. It is found that the proposed model is able to extract from texts some additional information which is not preserved in the existing context aware representations. When the proposed model is used with existing context-aware models like CANE and WANE, significant performance improvements are observed.

Acknowledgement. This work is supported by the National Natural Science Foundation of China (No. 61806223, U1811264), Key R&D Program of Guangdong Province (No. 2018B010107005), National Natural Science Foundation of Guangdong Province (No. 2021A1515012299), Science and Technology Program of Guangzhou (No. 202102021205).

References

1. Airoldi, E.M., Blei, D.M., Fienberg, S.E., Xing, E.P.: Mixed membership stochastic blockmodels. J. Mach. Learn. Res. **9**, 1981–2014 (2008)
2. Bandyopadhyay, S., Lokesh, N., Murty, M.N.: Outlier aware network embedding for attributed networks. In: Proceedings of the 33rd AAAI Conference on Artificial Intelligence, pp. 12–19 (2019)
3. Belkin, M., Niyogi, P.: Laplacian eigenmaps and spectral techniques for embedding and clustering. In: Proceedings of the 15th Annual Conference on Neural Information Processing Systems, pp. 585–591 (2001)
4. Bhagat, S., Cormode, G., Muthukrishnan, S.: Node classification in social networks. In: Social Network Data Analytics, pp. 115–148 (2011)

5. Chen, D., Bolton, J., Manning, C.D.: A thorough examination of the cnn/daily mail reading comprehension task. arXiv:1606.02858 (2016)
6. Chen, H., Perozzi, B., Al-Rfou, R., Skiena, S.: A tutorial on network embeddings. arXiv:1808.02590 (2018)
7. Chen, L., et al.: Improving textual network embedding with global attention via optimal transport. In: Proceedings of the 57th Annual Meeting of the Association for Computational Linguistics, pp. 5193–5202 (2019)
8. Grover, A., Leskovec, J.: node2vec: scalable feature learning for networks. In: Proceedings of the 22nd ACM SIGKDD International Conference on Knowledge Discovery and Data Mining, pp. 855–864. ACM (2016)
9. Hamilton, W.L., Ying, R., Leskovec, J.: Inductive representation learning on large graphs. In: Advances in Neural Information Processing Systems, pp. 1025–1035 (2017)
10. Kingma, D.P., Ba, J.: Adam: a method for stochastic optimization. arXiv:1412.6980 (2014)
11. Le, Q., Mikolov, T.: Distributed representations of sentences and documents. In: Proceedings of the 31st International Conference on Machine Learning, pp. 1188–1196 (2014)
12. Lee, D.D., Seung, H.S.: Algorithms for non-negative matrix factorization. In: Advances in Neural Information Processing Systems, pp. 556–562 (2001)
13. Leskovec, J., Kleinberg, J., Faloutsos, C.: Graphs over time: densification laws, shrinking diameters and possible explanations. In: Proceedings of the 11th ACM SIGKDD International Conference on Knowledge Discovery in Data Mining, pp. 177–187 (2005)
14. Liao, L., He, X., Zhang, H., Chua, T.S.: Attributed social network embedding. IEEE Trans. Knowl. Data Eng. **30**(12), 2257–2270 (2018)
15. Liben-Nowell, D., Kleinberg, J.: The link-prediction problem for social networks. J. Am. Soc. Inform. Sci. Technol. **58**(7), 1019–1031 (2007)
16. Maaten, L.v.d., Hinton, G.: Visualizing data using t-sne. J. Mach. Learn. Res. **9**, 2579–2605 (2008)
17. McCallum, A.K., Nigam, K., Rennie, J., Seymore, K.: Automating the construction of internet portals with machine learning. Inf. Retrieval **3**(2), 127–163 (2000)
18. Mikolov, T., Chen, K., Corrado, G., Dean, J.: Efficient estimation of word representations in vector space. arXiv:1301.3781 (2013)
19. Mikolov, T., Sutskever, I., Chen, K., Corrado, G.S., Dean, J.: Distributed representations of words and phrases and their compositionality. In: Proceedings of the 27th Annual Conference on Neural Information Processing Systems, pp. 3111–3119 (2013)
20. Noh, H., Hong, S., Han, B.: Learning deconvolution network for semantic segmentation. In: Proceedings of the IEEE International Conference on Computer Vision, pp. 1520–1528 (2015)
21. Pan, S., Wu, J., Zhu, X., Zhang, C., Wang, Y.: Tri-party deep network representation. Network **11**(9), 12 (2016)
22. Perozzi, B., Al-Rfou, R., Skiena, S.: Deepwalk: online learning of social representations. In: Proceedings of the 20th ACM SIGKDD International Conference on Knowledge Discovery and Data Mining, pp. 701–710 (2014)
23. Qazvinian, V., Radev, D.R.: Scientific paper summarization using citation summary networks. In: Proceedings of the 22nd International Conference on Computational Linguistics, pp. 689–696 (2008)
24. Scott, J.: Social network analysis. Sociology **22**(1), 109–127 (1988)

25. Shen, D., Zhang, X., Henao, R., Carin, L.: Improved semantic-aware network embedding with fine-grained word alignment. arXiv:1808.09633 (2018)
26. Sun, X., Guo, J., Ding, X., Liu, T.: A general framework for content-enhanced network representation learning. arXiv:1610.02906 (2016)
27. Tang, J., Qu, M., Wang, M., Zhang, M., Yan, J., Mei, Q.: Line: large-scale information network embedding. In: Proceedings of the 24th International Conference on World Wide Web, pp. 1067–1077 (2015)
28. Tenenbaum, J.B., Silva, V.D., Langford, J.C.: A global geometric framework for nonlinear dimensionality reduction. Science **290**(5500), 2319–2323 (2000)
29. Tu, C., Liu, H., Liu, Z., Sun, M.: Cane: context-aware network embedding for relation modeling. In: Proceedings of the 55th Annual Meeting of the Association for Computational Linguistics, pp. 1722–1731 (2017)
30. Wang, D.X., Cui, P., Zhu, W.W.: Structural deep network embedding. In: Proceedings of the 22nd ACM SIGKDD International Conference on Knowledge Discovery and Data Mining, pp. 1225–1234 (2016)
31. Wang, X., Cui, P., Wang, J., Pei, J., Zhu, W., Yang, S.: Community preserving network embedding. In: Proceedings of the 31st AAAI Conference on Artificial Intelligence (2017)
32. Xu, Z., Ou, Z., Su, Q., Yu, J., Quan, X., Lin, Z.: Embedding dynamic attributed networks by modeling the evolution processes. In: COLING (2020)
33. Xu, Z., Su, Q., Quan, X., Zhang, W.: A deep neural information fusion architecture for textual network embeddings. In: Proceedings of the 2019 Conference on Empirical Methods in Natural Language Processing and the 9th International Joint Conference on Natural Language Processing (EMNLP-IJCNLP), pp. 4698–4706 (2019)
34. Yan, S., Xu, D., Zhang, B., Zhang, H., Yang, Q., Lin, S.: Graph embedding and extensions: A general framework for dimensionality reduction. IEEE Trans. Pattern Analysis Mach. Intell. **29**(1), 40–51 (2007)
35. Yang, C., Liu, Z., Zhao, D., Sun, M., Chang, E.: Network representation learning with rich text information. In: Proceedings of the 24th International Joint Conference on Artificial Intelligence (2015)

Online Discriminative Semantic-Preserving Hashing for Large-Scale Cross-Modal Retrieval

Jinhan Yi[1,2,4], Yi He[1,3,4], and Xin Liu[1,2,3(✉)] (iD)

[1] Department of Computer Science and Technology, Huaqiao University,
Xiamen 361021, China
xliu@hqu.edu.cn
[2] Key Laboratory of Intelligent Perception and Systems for High-Dimensional
Information of Ministry of Education, Nanjing University of Science and Technology,
Nanjing 210094, People's Republic of China
[3] Xiamen Key Laboratory of Computer Vision and Pattern Recognition,
Xiamen, China
[4] Fujian Key Laboratory of Big Data Intelligence and Security, Xiamen, China

Abstract. Cross-modal hashing has drawn increasing attentions for efficient retrieval across different modalities, and existing methods primarily learn the hash functions in a batch based mode, i.e., offline methods. Nevertheless, the multimedia data often comes in a streaming fashion, which makes the batch based learning methods uncompetitive for large-scale streaming data due to the large memory consumption and calculation. To address this problem, we present an Online Discriminative Semantic-Preserving Hashing (ODSPH) method for large-scale cross-modal retrieval, featuring on fast training speed, low memory consumption and high retrieval accuracy. Within the proposed ODSPH framework, we utilize the newly coming data points to learn the hash codes and update hash functions in a stream manner. When new data comes, the corresponding hash codes are obtained by regressing the class label of the training examples. For hash function, we update it with the accumulated information from each round. Besides, we design a novel momentum updating method to adaptively update the hash function and reduce quantization loss, which can produce discriminative hash codes for high retrieval precision. Extensive experiments on three benchmark datasets show that the proposed ODSPH method improves the retrieval performance over the state-of-the-arts.

Keywords: Cross-modal hashing · Online semantic-preserving hashing · Stream manner · Momentum updating

Supported by the National Science Foundation of Fujian Province (Nos. 2020J01083 and 2020J01084), and Program (JYB202102) of Key Laboratory of Intelligent Perception and Systems for High-Dimensional Information of Ministry of Education, Nanjing University of Science and Technology.

D. N. Pham et al. (Eds.): PRICAI 2021, LNAI 13031, pp. 440–453, 2021.
https://doi.org/10.1007/978-3-030-89188-6_33

1   Introduction

In recent years, with the explosive growth of various kinds of multimedia data on the Internet, cross-modal retrieval algorithm is popular to return semantically relevant results of one modality in response to a query of different modality [1]. Hashing method has been widely applied in cross-modal retrieval due to its advantages of low storage and fast query [2,3]. In general, cross-modal hashing methods can be categorized into unsupervised fashion [4–6] and supervised fashion [7–9]. The unsupervised cross-modal hashing methods directly learn the hash codes from original feature space to Hamming space, so they ignore the label discrimination and the their retrieval performances are a bit poor. Remarkably, the label information is able to well correlate the semantic information between different modalities, and supervised cross-modal hashing approaches often produce more compact hash codes to boost the retrieval performance, typical methods including Semantic Correlation Maximization (SCM) [10], Semantic-Preserving Hashing (SePH) [11], Generalize Semantic Preserving Hashing (GSePH) [12], Fusion Similarity Hashing (FSH) [13], Discrete Cross-modal Hashing (DCH) [14].

It is noted that most cross-modal hashing methods mainly attempt to learn hash functions in a batch based mode, and all training data points should be available before hash functions learning process. If the training data is increasingly accumulated, the batch based learning method must recalculate the hash functions on the whole database, which involve expensive computation and large memory cost [15]. Works [16,17] solve this problem with an online learning scheme. Nevertheless, these online methods often accumulates large quantization error when learning hash codes and their retrieval performances need further improvements. Therefore, it is particularly important to develop an efficient online cross-modal retrieval method to deal with the streaming multimedia database.

In this paper, we propose an Online Discriminative Semantic-Preserving Hashing (ODSPH) for fast retrieval of streaming data, which improves the state-of-the-art methods by providing following contributions:

- We propose to regress the class labels of training examples to their corresponding hash codes in a streaming fashion, and only utilize the newly coming data to adaptively learn the hash functions.
- An efficient momentum updating method is presented to optimize the descending direction of hash function, which can significantly reduce the quantization loss for compact hash codes learning.
- The proposed ODSPH algorithm seamlessly correlates the heterogeneous modalities in the online learning process and preserves the semantic correlations both in the old data points and new data points.
- Experimental results show its comparable performance in comparison with existing online cross-modal hashing and other offline counterparts.

2   Related Work

In this section, we briefly review the related works of cross-modal hashing (CMH), including offline CMH and online CMH works.

2.1   Offline CMH Works

Many efforts have been devoted to offline cross-modal hashing, which can be broadly divided into supervised and unsupervised cases. Unsupervised CMH learns the unified hash codes directly from the paired training data so as to preserve the inter-modality and intra-modality information. For instance, Ding et al. [18] present a collective matrix factorization hashing (CMFH) to learn cross-view hash functions and achieve cross-modal retrieval. In addition, Inter-Media Hashing (IMH) [19] defines two selection matrices to deal with unpaired data, and obtains the hash function by linear projection and threshold method. Fusion Similarity Hashing (FSH) [13] constructs a graph to simulate the fusion similarity between different patterns, and learns the binary codes embedded with this fusion similarity. Supervised CMH leverages the label information to promote the hash codes learning, which generally produces better performance. Along this line, [10] presents a Semantic Correlation Maximization (SCM) [10] maximizes the semantic correlation by utilizing the label information. Supervised Matrix Factorization Hashing (SMFH) [20] improves accuracy by embedding tags to supervise the collective matrix decomposition. Generalized Semantic Preserving Hashing (GSePH) [12] constructs an affinity matrix using the tag information to obtain more discriminative hash codes. Discrete Cross-modal Hashing (DCH) [14] retains discrete constraints when learning hash codes. In recent years, deep-networks-based cross-modal hashing methods [21,22] can represent high-level semantics more efficiently and accurately compared to the method of extracting hand-crafted features. Although these cross-modal methods are effective in the search process, they are all offline learning methods. In real application, multimedia data points often continuously arrive in a stream fashion, which makes these methods hard to retrain hash functions on all available data points.

2.2   Online CMH Works

Online retrieval algorithm can be applied to deal with the streaming data points, and most online hashing methods mainly focus on single modality [23–26], which cannot be directly extended to cross-modal retrieval scenarios. To address this issue, Online Cross-Modal Hashing (OCMH) [16] updates hash codes online, and decomposes the hash codes matrix to a shared latent codes matrix and a dynamic matrix. Online Collective Matrix Factorization Hashing (OCMFH) [27] performs collaborative matrix decomposition in an online manner. However, these unsupervised methods often deliver a bit poor retrieval performance. To embedding the label supervision, Online Latent Semantic Hashing (OLSH) [17] maps discrete tags to a continuous latent semantic space, while updating hash functions based on only newly arriving multimedia data points. This approach has produced promising retrieval performances to sequentially process the streaming data points, but its performance is not very stable. Therefore, it is still desirable to develop an efficient online cross-modal hash algorithm.

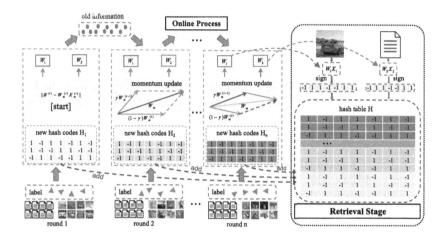

Fig. 1. The graphical illustration of the proposed ODSPH framework.

3   Proposed ODSPH Algorithm

In this section, we present the proposed online discriminative semantic-preserving hashing (ODSPH) algorithm in detail, and the graphical illustration of ODSPH is shown in Fig. 1. The proposed ODSPH approach aims to overcome the limitation of batch based model by developing an online cross-modal hashing learning scheme. Without loss of generality, we focus on online hash learning for image and text, and the proposed framework can be easily extended to more modalities.

3.1   Problem Formulation

Suppose the training database consists of multiple streaming image-text data pairs. During the training, a new data chunk $\mathbf{X}^{(t)} = [\mathbf{X}_1^{(t)}, \mathbf{X}_2^{(t)}]$ of size N_t is added to the database at each round t, where $\mathbf{X}_1^{(t)} \in R^{d_1 \times N_t}$, $\mathbf{X}_2^{(2)} \in R^{d_2 \times N_t}$ denote the feature matrices of image and text data, respectively. Let $\mathbf{L}^{(t)} \in R^{c \times N_t}$ represents the class label matrix of new data chunk, where c is the number of all categories. At round t, N is utilized to denote the size of the all data that has been obtained. So we can define the old data as $\widehat{\mathbf{X}}^{(t-1)} = [\widehat{\mathbf{X}}_1^{(t-1)}, \widehat{\mathbf{X}}_2^{(t-1)}]$, the old label as $\widehat{\mathbf{L}}^{(t-1)} \in R^{c \times (N-N_t)}$, where $\widehat{\mathbf{X}}_1^{(t-1)}$, $\widehat{\mathbf{X}}_2^{(t-1)}$ denote all cumulative image features and text features that have been obtained at round $t - 1$. For simplicity, we can utilize $\widehat{\mathbf{X}} = [\widehat{\mathbf{X}}_1, \widehat{\mathbf{X}}_2]$ denotes all cumulative data that have been obtained at round t, $\widehat{\mathbf{L}}$ denotes all the label that have been obtained at round t, where $\widehat{\mathbf{X}}_m = [\widehat{\mathbf{X}}_m^{(t-1)}, \mathbf{X}_m^{(t)}]$, $\widehat{\mathbf{L}} = [\widehat{\mathbf{L}}^{(t-1)}, \mathbf{L}^{(t)}]$.

3.2 Objective Function

Our ultimate goal is to learn the mapping matrix corresponding to the heterogeneous data, and map the heterogeneous data into a shared hamming space, where the similarity between the different modalities can be calculated. For image-text data pair, we study two mapping matrices $\mathbf{W}_1$, $\mathbf{W}_2$, which can map the feature data of two modalities into binary hash codes. When the new data arrives, the hash function is formulated as:

$$h_m(\mathbf{X}_m) = \mathrm{sgn}(\mathbf{W}_m \mathbf{X}_m) \tag{1}$$

where $h_m(\mathbf{X}_m)$ denotes the hash codes of the data $\mathbf{X}_m$, $\mathrm{sgn}(\cdot)$ is a sign function. For the paired data, the hash codes of different modalities should share same hash codes to maintain the similar semantic information. Therefore, the following expression can be obtained:

$$\min ||\mathbf{B}^{(t)} - \mathbf{W}_1^{(t)} \mathbf{X}_1^{(t)}||_F^2 + ||\mathbf{B}^{(t)} - \mathbf{W}_2^{(t)} \mathbf{X}_2^{(t)}||_F^2 \quad s.t. \mathbf{B} \in \{-1, 1\}^{r \times N_t} \tag{2}$$

where $|| \cdot ||_F$ denotes the Frobenius norm. To solve Eq. (2), most methods usually abandon the discrete constraint of learning binary codes and adopt relaxed quantization method to approximate binary solutions, which often degrades the retrieval performance. In order to learn more discriminative binary codes, we refer to work [28] and directly regress the tag information to the corresponding hash codes, while retaining the discrete constraint to reduce the quantization loss. The corresponding expression is formulated as:

$$\min ||\mathbf{B}^{(t)} - \mathbf{U}^T \mathbf{L}^{(t)}||_F^2 \quad s.t. \mathbf{B}^{(t)} \in \{-1, 1\}^{r \times N_t} \tag{3}$$

Where $\mathbf{U} \in \mathbb{R}^{r \times c}$ is a auxiliary matrix. Note that the solution of Eq. (3) has a closed solution for hash codes learning, which only needs one step to learn the hash codes. Therefore, such hash codes learning scheme is computationally efficient in comparison with iterative learning model. By combining Eq. (2) and Eq. (3), considering the online scenario, when new data is added in each round of training, our cumulative objective function is:

$$\widehat{\mathbf{G}} = \widehat{\mathbf{G}}^{(t-1)} + ||\mathbf{B}^{(t)} - \mathbf{U}^T \mathbf{L}^{(t)}||_F^2 + \sum_{m=1}^{2} \mu_m ||\mathbf{B}^{(t)} - \mathbf{W}_m \mathbf{X}_m^{(t)}||_F^2$$
$$+ \sum_{m=1}^{2} \lambda_m ||\mathbf{W}_m||_F^2 + \lambda_3 ||\mathbf{U}||_F^2 \quad s.t. \mathbf{B}^{(t)} \in \{-1, 1\}^{r \times n} \tag{4}$$

where

$$\widehat{\mathbf{G}}^{(t-1)} = ||\widehat{\mathbf{B}}^{(t-1)} - \mathbf{U}^T \widehat{\mathbf{L}}^{(t-1)}||_F^2 + \sum_{m=1}^{2} \mu_m ||\widehat{\mathbf{B}}^{(t-1)} - \mathbf{W}_m \widehat{\mathbf{X}}_m^{(t-1)}||_F^2$$
$$+ \sum_{m=1}^{2} \lambda_m ||\mathbf{W}_m||_F^2 + \lambda_3 ||\mathbf{U}||_F^2 \quad s.t. \widehat{\mathbf{B}}^{(t)} \in \{-1, 1\}^{r \times n} \tag{5}$$

3.3   Online Optimization

In this section we discuss the online optimization of Eq. (4). At each learning round t, a new data chunk $[\mathbf{X}_1^{(t)}, \mathbf{X}_2^{(t)}]$ is added into the training set for online updating, and the optimization process is as follows:

Compute $\mathbf{B}^{(t)}$: Learn $\mathbf{B}^{(t)}$ by fixing other variables. $\mathbf{B}^{(t)}$ is only relevant to the new data. So the objective function related to $\mathbf{B}^{(t)}$ can be written as follow:

$$\min_{\mathbf{B}} ||\mathbf{B}^{(t)} - \mathbf{U}^T\mathbf{L}^{(t)}||_F^2 + \sum_{m=1}^{2} \mu_m ||\mathbf{B}^{(t)} - \mathbf{W}_m\mathbf{X}_m^{(t)}||_F^2 \quad s.t. \mathbf{B} \in \{-1,1\}^{r \times n} \quad (6)$$

where $\mathbf{B}^{(t)}$ denotes the hash codes of the new data obtained at round t. For the solution of $\mathbf{B}^{(t)}$, we refer to work [28] and directly regress the tag information of training examples to the corresponding hash codes, so as to speed up the algorithm and retain the discrete constraint. The trace of the matrix is denoted by $tr(\cdot)$, and Eq. (6) can be expressed as:

$$\begin{aligned} \min_{\mathbf{B}} & tr\left((\mathbf{B}^{(t)} - \mathbf{U}^T\mathbf{L}^{(t)})^T (\mathbf{B}^{(t)} - \mathbf{U}^T\mathbf{L}^{(t)})\right) \\ +\mu_1 & tr\left((\mathbf{B}^{(t)} - \mathbf{W}_1^T\mathbf{X}_1^{(t)})^T (\mathbf{B}^{(t)} - \mathbf{W}_1^T\mathbf{X}_1^{(t)})\right) \\ +\mu_2 & tr\left((\mathbf{B}^{(t)} - \mathbf{W}_2^T\mathbf{X}_2^{(t)})^T (\mathbf{B}^{(t)} - \mathbf{W}_2^T\mathbf{X}_2^{(t)})\right) \\ & s.t. \mathbf{B} \in \{-1,1\}^{r \times n} \end{aligned} \quad (7)$$

Since $tr(\mathbf{B}^{(t)T}\mathbf{B}^{(t)})$ is a constant, Eq. (7) is equivalent to:

$$\min_{\mathbf{B}} -tr(\mathbf{B}^{(t)T}(\mathbf{U}^T\mathbf{L}^{(t)} + \mu_1\mathbf{W}_1^T\mathbf{X}_1^{(t)} + \mu_2\mathbf{W}_2^T\mathbf{X}_2^{(t)})) \quad s.t. \mathbf{B} \in \{-1,1\}^{r \times n} \quad (8)$$

Therefore, $\mathbf{B}^{(t)}$ can obtain the following analytic solution:

$$\mathbf{B}^{(t)} = sign(\mathbf{U}^T\mathbf{L}^{(t)} + \mu_1\mathbf{W}_1^T\mathbf{X}_1^{(t)} + \mu_2\mathbf{W}_2^T\mathbf{X}_2^{(t)}) \quad (9)$$

The solution is only related to the new data, so the time complexity is $O(N_t)$.

Update $\mathbf{U}$: Learn $\mathbf{U}$ by fixing other variables. $\mathbf{U}$ is related to all accumulated data. So Eq. (4) can be written as follow:

$$\min_{\mathbf{U}} ||\widehat{\mathbf{B}} - \mathbf{U}^T\widehat{\mathbf{L}}||_F^2 + \lambda_3 ||\mathbf{U}||_F^2 \quad (10)$$

where $\widehat{\mathbf{B}} = [\widehat{\mathbf{B}}^{(t-1)}, \mathbf{B}^{(t)}]$ denotes all hash codes that have been obtained at round t, $\widehat{\mathbf{B}}^{(t-1)}$ denotes all hash codes that have been obtained at round $t-1$. By setting the derivative of Eq. (10) w.r.t $\mathbf{U}$ to 0, the analytic solution can be obtained by:

$$\mathbf{U} = (\widehat{\mathbf{L}}\widehat{\mathbf{L}}^T + \lambda_3 I)^{-1}\widehat{\mathbf{L}}\widehat{\mathbf{B}}^T \quad (11)$$

where

$$\widehat{\mathbf{L}}\widehat{\mathbf{L}}^T = \left[\widehat{\mathbf{L}}^{(t-1)}, \mathbf{L}^{(t)}\right]\left[(\widehat{\mathbf{L}}^{(t-1)})^T (\mathbf{L}^{(t)})^T\right] = \widehat{\mathbf{L}}^{(t-1)}(\widehat{\mathbf{L}}^{(t-1)})^T + \mathbf{L}^{(t)}(\mathbf{L}^{(t)})^T \quad (12)$$

$$\widehat{\mathbf{L}\mathbf{B}}^T = \left[\widehat{\mathbf{L}}^{(t-1)}, \mathbf{L}^{(t)}\right]\left[(\widehat{\mathbf{B}}^{(t-1)})^T(\mathbf{B}^{(t)})^T\right] = \widehat{\mathbf{L}}^{(t-1)}(\widehat{\mathbf{B}}^{(t-1)})^T + \mathbf{L}^{(t)}(\mathbf{B}^{(t)})^T \quad (13)$$

By substituting Eq. (12) and Eq. (13) into Eq. (11), the online solution expression of $\mathbf{U}$ can be obtained:

$$\mathbf{U} = (pLL + \mathbf{L}^{(t)}(\mathbf{L}^{(t)})^T + \lambda_3 I)^{-1}(pLB + \mathbf{L}^{(t)}(\mathbf{B}^{(t)})^T) \quad (14)$$

where $pLL = \widehat{\mathbf{L}}^{(t-1)}(\widehat{\mathbf{L}}^{(t-1)})^T$ and $pLB = \widehat{\mathbf{L}}^{(t-1)}(\widehat{\mathbf{B}}^{(t-1)})^T$ are constants, and they can be obtained in the previous round. So this step only needs to calculate $\mathbf{L}^{(t)}(\mathbf{L}^{(t)})^T$ and $\mathbf{L}^{(t)}(\mathbf{B}^{(t)})^T$. Therefore, the time complexity is $O(N_t)$.

Update $\mathbf{W}_1, \mathbf{W}_2$: Learn $\mathbf{W}_1$ by fixing other variables, Eq. (5) can be written as follow:

$$\min_{\mathbf{W}_1} \mu_1 ||\widehat{\mathbf{B}} - \mathbf{W}_1 \widehat{\mathbf{X}}_1||_F^2 + \lambda_1 ||\mathbf{W}_1||_F^2 \quad (15)$$

By setting the derivative of Eq. (15) w.r.t $\mathbf{W}_1$ to 0 respectively, the analytic solution can be obtained as follows:

$$\mathbf{W}_1 = \widehat{\mathbf{B}}\widehat{\mathbf{X}}_1^T (\widehat{\mathbf{X}}_1\widehat{\mathbf{X}}_1^T + \lambda_1 I)^{-1} \quad (16)$$

Similarly, $\widehat{\mathbf{X}}_1\widehat{\mathbf{X}}_1^T$ and $\widehat{\mathbf{X}}_1\widehat{\mathbf{B}}^T$ in Eq. (16) can be calculated as follows:

$$\widehat{\mathbf{B}}\widehat{\mathbf{X}}_1^T = \left[\widehat{\mathbf{B}}^{(t-1)}, \mathbf{B}^{(t)}\right]\left[\begin{matrix}(\widehat{\mathbf{X}}_1^{(t-1)})^T \\ (\mathbf{X}_1^{(t)})^T\end{matrix}\right] = \widehat{\mathbf{B}}^{(t-1)}(\widehat{\mathbf{X}}_1^{(t-1)})^T + \mathbf{B}^{(t)}(\mathbf{X}_1^{(t)})^T \quad (17)$$

$$\widehat{\mathbf{X}}_1\widehat{\mathbf{X}}_1^T = \left[\widehat{\mathbf{X}}_1^{(t-1)}, \mathbf{X}_1^{(t)}\right]\left[\begin{matrix}(\widehat{\mathbf{X}}_1^{(t-1)})^T \\ (\mathbf{X}_1^{(t)})^T\end{matrix}\right] = \widehat{\mathbf{X}}_1^{(t-1)}(\widehat{\mathbf{X}}_1^{(t-1)})^T + \mathbf{X}_1^{(t)}(\mathbf{X}_1^{(t)})^T \quad (18)$$

By substituting Eq. (17) and Eq. (18) into Eq. (16), the online solution expression of $\mathbf{W}_1^{(t)}$ can be obtained:

$$\mathbf{W}_1^{(t)} = (pB1 + \mathbf{B}^{(t)}(\mathbf{X}_1^{(t)})^T)(pX1 + \mathbf{X}_1^{(t)}(\mathbf{X}_1^{(t)})^T + \lambda_1 I)^{-1} \quad (19)$$

where $pB1 = \widehat{\mathbf{B}}^{(t-1)}(\widehat{\mathbf{X}}_1^{(t-1)})^T$ and $pX1 = \widehat{\mathbf{X}}_1^{(t-1)}(\widehat{\mathbf{X}}_1^{(t-1)})^T$ are constants, and their values can be obtained in the previous round. Therefore, the time complexity of this step is $O(N_t)$.

Similar to $\mathbf{W}_1^{(t)}$, the solution expression for $\mathbf{W}_2^{(t)}$ is

$$\mathbf{W}_2^{(t)} = (pB2 + \mathbf{B}^{(t)}(X_2^{(t)})^T)(pX2 + \mathbf{X}_2^{(t)}(\mathbf{X}_2^{(t)})^T + \lambda_2 I)^{-1} \quad (20)$$

where $pB2 = \widehat{\mathbf{B}}^{(t-1)}(\widehat{\mathbf{X}}_2^{(t-1)})^T$, $pX2 = \widehat{\mathbf{X}}_2^{(t-1)}(\widehat{\mathbf{X}}_2^{(t-1)})^T$. Therefore, the time complexity is $O(N_t)$.

Momentum Updating: Due to $\mathbf{W}_1, \mathbf{W}_2$ is constantly updated at each round t, which is similar to gradient descent process. One problem with this process is that it is difficult for the model to reach the optimal value if the descending speed is too slow, while it may skip the global optimal value if the

---

Algorithm 1. Optimizing of ODSPH at round t

Input: $\mathbf{X}_1^{(t)}, \mathbf{X}_2^{(t)}, \mathbf{L}^{(t)}, \mathbf{W}_1, \mathbf{W}_2, pLL, pLB, pX1, pB1, pX2, pB2$
Output: $\mathbf{W}_1, \mathbf{W}_2, \mathbf{B}, pLL, pLB, pX1, pB1, pX2, pB2$

1: Initialize $\mathbf{B}^{(t)}$ randomly
2: **for** iter $<= T_{iter}$ **do**
3:    Compute $\mathbf{B}^{(t)}$ according to Eq.(9);
4:    Update $\mathbf{U}$ according to Eq.(14);
5:    Update $\mathbf{W}_1$ according to Eq.(19)(21);
6:    Update $\mathbf{W}_2$ according to Eq.(20)(21);
7: **end for**
8: Update $\mathbf{B}$ by $\mathbf{B} = [\mathbf{B}; \mathbf{B}^{(t)}]$;
9: Update $pLL, pLB, pX1, pB1, pX2, pB2$;

---

descending speed is too fast. To tackle this problem, we propose a momentum updating method to adapt the proposed online learning framework. More specifically, we perform exponential weighted moving average processing on the variable, and the result $\mathbf{W}_m$ at round t is the linear combination of the variable $\mathbf{W}_m^{t-1}$ calculated at round $t-1$ and the variable $\mathbf{W}_m^t$ calculated at round t:

$$\mathbf{W}_m = (1 - \gamma)\mathbf{W}_m^{(t)} + \gamma \mathbf{W}_m^{(t-1)} \tag{21}$$

where γ is the balance parameter. To adapt online learning, we learn its values adaptively instead of assigning a fixed value. That is, γ is given by the change in the mapping matrix $\mathbf{W}_m$ at each round of t. However, it is difficult to quantify its variation by itself. Considering that the ultimate purpose of calculating the mapping matrix is to get the appropriate hash codes, we utilize the hash codes calculated by both the mapping matrix and the training data, as the calculation standard. The solution equation of γ is obtained by:

$$\gamma = \nu_m \frac{\sum_{i,j} |B_P[i,j] - B_Q[i,j]|}{r \cdot N_t} \tag{22}$$

where ν_m denotes an auxiliary parameter. $B_P = \mathbf{W}_m^t \mathbf{X}_m^{(t)}$ denotes the hash codes computed from the current $\mathbf{W}_m^t$. Similarly, $B_Q = \mathbf{W}_m^{(t-1)} \mathbf{X}_m^{(t)}$ represents the hash codes computed from the previous $\mathbf{W}_m^{t-1}$. The difference between the two methods is quantified to obtain the proportion of different places within the hash codes matrices, which is taken as the value of γ.

Complexity Analysis: The whole optimization process of ODSPH at each round t is shown in Algorithm 1. The time complexity of computing $\mathbf{U}, \mathbf{W}_1, \mathbf{W}_2$ is $O(N_t)$, which is linear to the size of new data. Comparing with batch based methods, the proposed ODSPH algorithm is more computational efficient.

4 Experiments

4.1 Datasets and Features

In order to confirm the superiority of our method, we conduct a series of quantitative experiments on three datasets: MIRFlickr dataset and NUS-WIDE dataset.

MIRFlickr dataset [29] consists of 25,000 image-text pairs collected from the popular Flickr website, where the images are annotated with one or more of 24 semantic labels. We use the 4,096-dimensional feature vector of fc7 layer extracted by VGG-16 as the image feature, while the text is represented by a 1,386-dimensional feature vector derived from its binary tagging vector. As suggested in [11], we remove the instances whose textual tags appear less than 20 times, then 20,015 image-text pairs are kept. We take out 2,000 instances as the query set and the remaining parts as the training set.

NUS-WIDE dataset [30] contains 269,648 image-text pairs with 81 concepts that can be used for evaluation. Specifically, we use a 500-dimensional SIFT feature vector as the feature of the image, and the text is described by a 1000-dimensional bag-of-words (BoW) vector. We select pictures of the 10 categories with the highest frequency as the experimental data set, and obtain 186,577 pictures. As NUS-WIDE-all is a larger dataset, it needs to occupy a large amount of computing resources. Then we randomly select 100,000 images and associated texts in this experiment. We take out 5% of the dataset as the query set and the remaining parts as the training set.

4.2 Baseline and Experimental Settings

Within the proposed method, we empirically set $\lambda_1 = \lambda_2 = 10^{-2}$, $u_1 = u_2 = 10^{-5}$ and $\lambda_3 = 1$. In Algorithm 1, we set $T_{iter} = 1$ since each variable has been optimized by old data at each round.

For online cross-modal methods, i.e., OCMH [16], OCMFH [27], OLSH [17] and our ODSPH, they learn hash functions with streaming data, and the training hash codes are directly used in retrieval task. To simulate streaming data, referring to [17], the training set of MIRFlickr is split to 19 data chunks, each of the first 18 chunks contains 1,000 pairs, and the last chunk contains 15 pairs. The training set of NUS-WIDE is split to 10 data chunks, each of the first 9 chunks contains 10,000 pairs, and the last chunk contains 5,000 pairs.

Besides, our proposed ODSPH algorithm is also compared with some popular batch based methods, such as CCA [31], SCM [10], CMFH [18], SMFH [20], FSH [13], SePH [11], IMH [19], DCH [14], GSePH [12]. For these batch based methods, we utilize the all accumulated training data to retrain the hash functions and regenerate the hash codes. In addition, the experimental settings for all compared methods are chosen according to the suggestions of their original papers.

Evaluation Metrics: The quantitative performance is evaluated by the popular mean Average Precision (mAP) [19], precision-recall [17] and topK-precision [14]. The mAP@K scores are computed on the top K retrieved documents of each query. In the retrieval, data points which share at least one same label are considered as relevant.

Table 1. The mAP@100 scores on MIRFlickr and NUS-WIDE datasets

Method	MIRFlickr								NUS-WIDE							
	I to T				T to I				I to T				T to I			
	16	32	64	128	16	32	64	128	16	32	64	128	16	32	64	128
CCA	0.5625	0.5802	0.5798	0.5926	0.5826	0.5976	0.6129	0.6243	0.4826	0.4977	0.5114	0.5243	0.4526	0.4686	0.4787	0.4850
CMFH	0.5233	0.5299	0.5280	0.5297	0.5553	0.5573	0.5621	0.5659	0.3767	0.3828	0.3874	0.3905	0.3810	0.3880	0.3931	0.3995
IMH	0.6452	0.6427	0.6465	0.6370	0.7324	0.7412	0.7568	0.7636	0.4967	0.4776	0.4608	0.4476	0.5024	0.4891	0.4747	0.4581
FSH	0.6671	0.6599	0.6751	0.6791	0.7106	0.6957	0.7243	0.7380	0.5353	0.5607	0.5578	0.5637	0.5709	0.6467	0.6494	0.6640
SCM	0.6943	0.6953	0.6901	0.7000	0.7038	0.7042	0.7120	0.7263	0.5780	0.6126	0.6029	0.6332	0.5312	0.6251	0.6302	0.6401
SMFH	0.6913	0.6831	0.6830	0.6867	0.6576	0.6711	0.6755	0.6866	0.3831	0.3973	0.4070	0.4033	0.3780	0.3876	0.3853	0.4142
SePH	0.7406	0.7545	0.7606	0.7656	0.8467	0.8574	0.8661	0.8743	0.5595	0.5729	0.5838	0.5853	0.7159	0.7431	0.7648	0.7616
GSePH	0.7374	0.7388	0.7551	0.7563	0.8598	0.8649	0.8745	0.8823	0.5583	0.5724	0.5819	0.5890	0.7335	0.7467	0.7613	0.7703
DCH	0.7476	0.7546	0.7825	0.7632	0.9025	**0.9117**	0.9078	0.9070	0.6128	0.6088	0.6091	0.6453	0.8090	0.8172	0.8101	0.8239
OCMH	0.5746	0.5749	0.5602	0.5889	0.5796	0.5792	0.6001	0.6021	0.4784	0.4733	0.4178	0.4334	0.4920	0.5144	0.4331	0.4704
OCMFH	0.6386	0.6382	0.6287	0.6291	0.7025	0.7247	0.7559	0.7745	0.4088	0.4353	0.4496	0.4426	0.5141	0.5482	0.5568	0.5712
OLSH	0.7973	0.8136	0.7882	0.7981	0.7890	0.8587	0.8693	0.8521	0.6799	0.6897	0.6857	0.7011	0.8282	0.8312	0.8556	0.8465
ODSPH-m	0.8038	0.8173	0.8249	0.8102	0.8547	0.8636	0.8671	0.8701	0.7346	0.7507	0.7834	0.7893	0.8426	0.8661	0.8808	0.8892
ODSPH	**0.8127**	**0.8284**	**0.8305**	**0.8211**	**0.9042**	0.9078	**0.9082**	**0.9097**	**0.7725**	**0.7946**	**0.7960**	**0.7991**	**0.8586**	**0.8733**	**0.8817**	**0.8996**

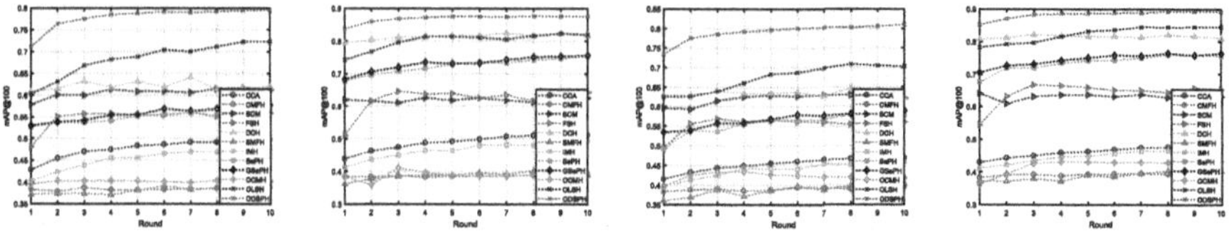

(a) 32 bits (I → T)   (b) 32 bits (T → I)   (c) 64 bits (I → T)   (d) 64 bits (T → I)

Fig. 2. The mAP@100 scores tested on NUS-WIDE at each round.

4.3   Experimental Result and Analysis

We analyze the experimental results of ODSPH in following three aspects, to demonstrate the efficiency of the proposed ODSPH method.

1) *Results of Retrieval Tasks:* Table 1 shows the mAP@100 scores of all compared methods. In general, online methods should lose retrieval accuracy in comparison with batch based methods, for reason that the online methods often selected limited data for training. However, as shown in Table 1, it can be observed that the proposed ODSPH method yields the best results. The main reason is that the correlation is well preserved through the label regression method. Compared with the two online learning methods, i.e., OCMH, OCMFH, and OLSH, the proposed ODSPH method also shows higher mAP@100 scores. The reason is that OCMH and OCMFH ignore the use of label information. Meanwhile, ODSPH also outperforms OLSH in all cases, because the designed online framework make the relevance of the old and new data well preserved, and can obtain more discriminant binary hash codes. Besides, ODSPH takes into account the loss of updating the hash function at each round and adopts the adaptive strategy of momentum updating to improve its performance.

Moreover, in order to prove the advantages of ODSPH in streaming data, we show the mAP@100 scores tested on NUS-WIDE at each round in Fig. 2. Remarkably, our proposed ODSPH method obtains the highest scores at each round of mAP@100. Although occasionally DCH shows competitive results, it is less stable and efficient than the online learning methods. Besides, it can be

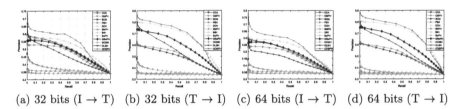

(a) 32 bits (I → T)   (b) 32 bits (T → I)   (c) 64 bits (I → T)   (d) 64 bits (T → I)

Fig. 3. The precision-recall curves obtained on NUS-WIDE.

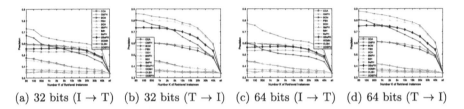

(a) 32 bits (I → T)   (b) 32 bits (T → I)   (c) 64 bits (I → T)   (d) 64 bits (T → I)

Fig. 4. The representative topK-precision curves tested on NUS-WIDE

found that most batch based methods are inefficient in this online scenario, which means that batch based methods are not suitable for streaming data.

Further, Table 2 records the mAP@*all* scores to demonstrate the effectiveness of our method, and ODSPH also performs well from this perspective. The precision-recall curves and the representative topK-precision curves tested on NUS-WIDE dataset are also reported in Fig. 3 and Fig. 4, respectively. It can be observed that the smaller of recall or topK values, the better retrieval performances are achieved. It indicates that our proposed ODSPH method can search more similar samples at the beginning, which is significantly important for a practical retrieval system.

2) *Results of ablation studies*: The method ODSPH-m reported on Table 1 represents the proposed ODSPH method without utilizing momentum updating. Compared with ODSPH, it can be observed that ODSPH-m degrades its performance with lower mAP@100 score, which prove that the strategy of using momentum updating is beneficial to the retrieval performance. Specifically, for the large-scale data sets, i.e., MIRFlickr and NUS-WIDE, the proposed ODSPH method outperforms the ODSPH-m in all different hash lengths. That is, the proposed momentum updating scheme is able to well obtain the mapping functions for hash code learning, which is particularly suitable for online hash learning.

Meanwhile, according to the mAP@100 scores tested on NUS-WIDE at each round in Fig. 2, it can be found that the curves of most competitive methods have fluctuated to some degree. Comparatively speaking, the proposed ODSPH approach not only yields higher mAP values in different retrieval tasks, but also generates more stable curves than other competing methods.

3) *Results of Training Time*: Figure 5 shows the training times on NUS-WIDE dataset at each round. It can be clearly observed that the batch based methods often need larger training time in comparison with online learning methods. For

Table 2. The mAP@all scores on MIRFlickr and NUS-WIDE datasets

Task	Method	MIRFlickr		NUS-WIDE		Task	Method	MIRFlickr		NUS-WIDE	
		32	64	32	64			32	64	32	64
I to T	GSePH	**0.7879**	0.8002	0.5481	0.5582	T to I	GSePH	0.7440	0.7557	0.5481	0.5582
	DCH	0.7710	0.7919	0.6219	0.6398		DCH	0.7746	0.7946	0.6219	0.6398
	OCMH	0.5554	0.5562	0.3404	0.3442		OCMH	0.5547	0.5555	0.3415	0.3435
	OCMFH	0.5554	0.5598	0.3695	0.3713		OCMFH	0.5551	0.5576	0.4104	0.4235
	OLSH	0.6459	0.6564	0.5229	0.5295		OLSH	0.6521	0.6641	0.6321	0.6348
	ODSPH	0.7844	**0.8096**	**0.6315**	**0.6514**		ODSPH	**0.7762**	**0.8086**	**0.6537**	**0.6692**

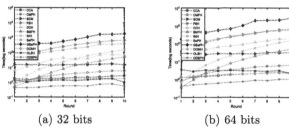

(a) 32 bits   (b) 64 bits

Fig. 5. The training time on NUS-WIDE at each round.

instance, GSePH often needs long time to learn the hash codes from the training process. Although the online OCMH and OLSH methods are able to reduce the training time, they often involve larger matrix computations or learn the hash codes bit by bit. The proposed ODSPH method requires the smallest training time to achieve different retrieval tasks due to its simple and effective online framework. That is, the proposed ODSPH method not only has the advantages of producing high retrieval performance, but also shows the strong ability to exhibit the less training time.

5 Conclusion

In this paper, we propose an efficient online discriminative semantic-preserving hashing method for cross-modal retrieval, particular for streaming media data. The proposed method aims to update the hash function online with the new data, while giving a very simple yet effective online regression method to generate the hash code for new data. Meanwhile, the proposed learning framework designs a novel momentum updating method to adaptively update the hash function, which can produce discriminative hash code for different retrieval tasks. The extensive experiments have shown its outstanding performances.

References

1. Cao, Y., Long, M., Wang, J., Zhu, H.: Correlation autoencoder hashing for supervised cross-modal search. In: Proceedings of the ACM on International Conference on Multimedia Retrieval, pp. 197–204 (2016)

2. Shen, H.T., et al.: Exploiting subspace relation in semantic labels for cross-modal hashing. IEEE Transactions on Knowledge and Data Engineering (2020)
3. Ma, X., Zhang, T., Xu, C.: Multi-level correlation adversarial hashing for cross-modal retrieval. IEEE Trans. Multimed. **22**(12), 3101–3114 (2020)
4. Rastegari, M., Choi, J., Fakhraei, S., Hal, D., Davis, L.: Predictable dual-view hashing. In: Proceedings of the International Conference on Machine Learning, pp. 1328–1336 (2013)
5. Wei, Y., Song, Y., Zhen, Y., Liu, B., Yang, Q.: Heterogeneous translated hashing: a scalable solution towards multi-modal similarity search. ACM Trans. Knowl. Discov. Data **10**(4), 36 (2016)
6. Zhang, L., Zhang, Y., Hong, R., Tian, Q.: Full-space local topology extraction for cross-modal retrieval. IEEE Trans. Image Process. **24**(7), 2212–2224 (2015)
7. Bronstein, M.M., Bronstein, A.M., Michel, F., Paragios, N.: Data fusion through cross-modality metric learning using similarity-sensitive hashing. In: Proceedings of the IEEE Computer Society Conference on Computer Vision and Pattern Recognition, pp. 3594–3601 (2010)
8. Jiang, Q.Y., Li, W.J.: Deep cross-modal hashing. In: Proceedings of the IEEE Conference on Computer Vision and Pattern Recognition, pp. 3232–3240 (2017)
9. Yan, T.K., Xu, X.S., Guo, S., Huang, Z., Wang, X.L.: Supervised robust discrete multimodal hashing for cross-media retrieval. In: Proceedings of the ACM International on Conference on Information and Knowledge Management, pp. 1271–1280 (2016)
10. Zhang, D., Li, W.J.: Large-scale supervised multimodal hashing with semantic correlation maximization. In: Proceedings of the AAAI Conference on Artificial Intelligence, pp. 2177–2183 (2014)
11. Lin, Z., Ding, G., Hu, M., Wang, J.: Semantics-preserving hashing for cross-view retrieval. In: Proceedings of the IEEE Conference on Computer Vision and Pattern Recognition, pp. 3864–3872 (2015)
12. Mandal, D., Chaudhury, K.N., Biswas, S.: Generalized semantic preserving hashing for n-label cross-modal retrieval. In: Proceedings of the IEEE Conference on Computer Vision and Pattern Recognition, pp. 4076–4084 (2017)
13. Liu, H., Ji, R., Wu, Y., Huang, F., Zhang, B.: Cross-modality binary code learning via fusion similarity hashing. In: Proceedings of the IEEE Conference on Computer Vision and Pattern Recognition, pp. 7380–7388 (2017)
14. Xu, X., Shen, F., Yang, Y., Shen, H.T., Li, X.: Learning discriminative binary codes for large-scale cross-modal retrieval. IEEE Trans. Image Process. **26**(5), 2494–2507 (2017)
15. Liu, X., Hu, Z., Ling, H., Cheung, Y.: Mtfh: a matrix tri-factorization hashing framework for efficient cross-modal retrieval. IEEE Trans. Pattern Anal. Mach. Intell. **43**(3), 964–981 (2021)
16. Xie, L., Shen, J., Zhu, L.: Online cross-modal hashing for web image retrieval. In: Proceedings of the AAAI Conference on Artificial Intelligence, pp. 294–300 (2016)
17. Yao, T., Wang, G., Yan, L., Kong, X., Su, Q., Zhang, C., Tian, Q.: Online latent semantic hashing for cross-media retrieval. Pattern Recogn. **89**, 1–11 (2019)
18. Ding, G., Guo, Y., Zhou, J.: Collective matrix factorization hashing for multimodal data. In: Proceedings of the IEEE Conference on Computer Vision and Pattern Recognition, pp. 2075–2082 (2014)
19. Song, J.K., Yang, Y., Yang, Y., Huang, Z., Shen, H.T.: Inter-media hashing for large-scale retrieval from heterogeneous data sources. In: Proceedings of the ACM SIGMOD International Conference on Management of Data, pp. 785–796 (2013)

20. Tang, J., Wang, K., Shao, L.: Supervised matrix factorization hashing for cross-modal retrieval. IEEE Trans. Image Process. **25**(7), 3157–3166 (2016)
21. Wang, T., Zhu, L., Cheng, Z., Li, J., Gao, Z.: Unsupervised deep cross-modal hashing with virtual label regression. Neurocomputing **386**, 84–96 (2020)
22. Lin, Q., Cao, W., He, Z., He, Z.: Semantic deep cross-modal hashing. Neurocomputing **390**, 113–122 (2020)
23. Huang, L.K., Yang, Q., Zheng, W.S.: Online hashing. In: Proceedings of the International Joint Conference on Artificial Intelligence, pp. 1422–1428 (2013)
24. Jain, P., Kulis, B., Dhillon, I.S., Grauman, K.: Online metric learning and fast similarity search. In: Proceedings of the Advances in Neural Information Processing Systems, pp. 761–768 (2009)
25. Leng, C., Wu, J., Cheng, J., Bai, X., Lu, H.: Online sketching hashing. In: Proceedings of the IEEE Conference on Computer Vision and Pattern Recognition, pp. 2503–2511 (2015)
26. Cakir, F., He, K., Adel Bargal, S., Sclaroff, S.: Mihash: online hashing with mutual information. In: Proceedings of the IEEE International Conference on Computer Vision, pp. 437–445 (2017)
27. Wang, D., Wang, Q., An, Y.Q., Gao, X.B., Tian, Y.M.: Online collective matrix factorization hashing for large-scale cross-media retrieval. In: Proceedings of the International ACM SIGIR Conference on Research and Development in Information Retrieval, pp. 1409–1418 (2020)
28. Gui, J., Liu, T., Sun, Z., Tao, D., Tan, T.: Fast supervised discrete hashing. IEEE Trans. Pattern Anal. Mach. Intell. **40**(2), 490–496 (2018)
29. Huiskes, M.J., Lew, M.S.: The mir flickr retrieval evaluation. In: Proceedings of ACM International Conference on Multimedia Information Retrieval, pp. 39–43 (2008)
30. Chua, T., Tang, J.H., Hong, R.C., Li, H.J., Luo, Z.P., Tao, Z.Y.: Nus-wide: a real-world web image database from national university of singapore. In: Proceedings of ACM International Conference on Image and Video Retrieval, pp. 1–9 (2009)
31. Rasiwasia, N., Costa Pereira, J., Coviello, E., Doyle, G., Lanckriet, G.R., Levy, R., Vasconcelos, N.: A new approach to cross-modal multimedia retrieval. In: Proceedings of the ACM International Conference on Multimedia, pp. 251–260 (2010)

Empirical Study on the Impact of Different Sets of Parameters of Gradient Boosting Algorithms for Time-Series Forecasting with LightGBM

Filipa S. Barros[1]([✉]), Vitor Cerqueira[2], and Carlos Soares[3]

[1] Faculty of Engineering, University of Porto, Porto, Portugal
f.barros@fe.up.pt
[2] Dalhousie University, Halifax, Canada
[3] INESC TEC, Porto, Portugal

Abstract. LightGBM has proven to be an effective forecasting algorithm by winning the M5 forecasting competition. However, given the sensitivity of LightGBM to hyperparameters, it is likely that their default values are not optimal. This work aims to answer whether it is essential to tune the hyperparameters of LightGBM to obtain better accuracy in time series forecasting and whether it can be done efficiently. Our experiments consisted of the collection and processing of data as well as hyperparameters generation and finally testing. We observed that on the 58 time series tested, the mean squared error is reduced by a maximum of 17.45% when using randomly generated configurations in contrast to using the default one. Additionally, the study of the individual hyperparameters' performance was done. Based on the results obtained, we propose an alternative set of default LightGBM hyperparameter values to be used whilst using time series data for forecasting.

Keywords: Gradient boosting · Forecasting · Time series · Hyperparameter tuning

1 Introduction

A time series is a collection of observations made sequentially through time [8]. Forecasting the value of future observations of time series is vital in many scientific and industrial activities. Moreover, forecasting using time series data is particularly relevant in applications such as sales and model evaluation.

Many algorithms have been developed for forecasting. However, traditional regression algorithms can be used, after a simple data transformation is done. In particular, gradient boosting has gained interest in the forecasting community after the LightGBM algorithm [18] won the M5 forecasting competition [17].

LightGBM is sensitive to different hyperparameters [15]. However, there are only a few works that focus on the tuning of hyperparameters for time series

© Springer Nature Switzerland AG 2021
D. N. Pham et al. (Eds.): PRICAI 2021, LNAI 13031, pp. 454–465, 2021.
https://doi.org/10.1007/978-3-030-89188-6_34

data, and these are domain specific [25,29]. Thus this project aims to understand which hyperparameters are the most important and which values are the most promising when dealing with time series data. This subset of hyperparameters can serve to warm-start an optimization process. As such, we have the primary goal of understanding and answering whether it is essential to tune LightGBM's hyperparameters to obtain better accuracy in time series forecasting and whether it can be done efficiently.

After data collection, experimentation, and testing of 58 dataframes, we conclude that the use of randomly generated configurations outperforms the use of the default one by a maximum of 17.45% mean squared error reduction. We also studied the individual hyperparameters' performance and, based on the results obtained, proposed an alternative set of hyperparameters values to be used when dealing with forecasting problems using time series data.

This paper is organized as follows. We start with a literature review emphasizing forecasting, LightGBM for forecasting, and the importance of hyperparameters tuning in Sect. 2. Afterwards, the methodology of the work is presented in Sect. 3. Section 4 presents the experimental setup, hyperparameters' generation, and search processes and results. Finally, conclusions are discussed in Sect. 5.

2   Literature Review

This section is subdivided into forecasting, LightGBM for Forecasting and Hyperparameter Tuning.

2.1   Forecasting

As stated before, forecasting is an important activity that attempts to predict future values of time series. A good example is the forecasting of the demand for stock-keeping units (SKU). Daily SKU predictions are particularly challenging, for they tend to be characterized by intermittency and erraticness [24]. Some machine learning algorithms have been shown to have significantly better performance than previously used statistical ones both in terms of accuracy and bias [24].

Since forecasting can be too demanding, many techniques have been applied to it. Some simple forecasting methods consist of applying statistical measures such as average, Naive, seasonal Naive, and drift [13]. Another option when no historical data exists can be to apply judgemental forecasting [16]. However, when a more complex mathematical relation may be found, non-linear regression can also be used [22].

To be able to detect the various patterns time series can exhibit, it is often helpful to divide a time series into several parts, based on some underlying metric or specification (example: diving time series representing a day in daytime and nighttime). Such methodology is called time series decomposition, and many algorithms such as moving averages, X11, SEATS [10], and STL [9] have proven to give reasonably good results in such cases. Exponential smoothing is another forecasting method proposed in [5]. Exponential smoothing-based methods use weights having the most recent observations, weighing the most. It achieves reliable forecasts expeditiously and for a wide range of time series [11].

Auto-regressive Integrated Moving Average models (ARIMA) aim to describe the auto-correlations in data and provide another approach to time series forecasting. These models are mainly used in cases where data show evidence of non-stationarity (relating to mean). To make it stationary, in a unified ARIMA, the data is differenced (further analyzed in Sect. 3). Most economical and market data present trends, so differencing aims to eliminate every tendency and seasonal structures [4].

In more complex problems, advanced forecasting methods such as neural networks [14], bootstrapping and bagging [2] and vector auto-regressions [1] (creating lag variables) are used. Given the described importance of forecasting and the plethora of available algorithms, forecasting competitions have become popular in recent years, given their objectivity in evaluating existing forecasting methods, adding brand-new ones, and defining how to improve forecasting theory.

One of the most recognized competitions is the M competition which in 2020 had its fifth instance (M5). That year, the competition focused on a retail sales forecasting application, specifically Walmart's time-series data. The goal was to produce the most accurate point forecasts for 42,840-time series representing the largest retail company's hierarchical unit sales in the world, Walmart. The forecasting application accurately predicts retail companies' daily unit sales across various locations and product categories [17]. The winner of the 2020 competition was the LightGBM algorithm gaining its recent popularity through such a win.

2.2 LightGBM for Forecasting

The LightGBM algorithm takes its roots in the Gradient Boosting Decision Tree, also recognized as GBDT, a widely used machine learning algorithm that is valuable in many implementations. GBDT uses regression trees as weak classifiers. The weak learners measure the error observed in each node splitting the node using a test function, with a threshold and return values. The identifying triplet then obtains the optimal split (threshold and values) [23]. The authors in [15] have, however, proposed a lighter GBDT implementation, also known as Light-GBDM, that tackles the known issues GBDT faces with efficiency and scalability when the feature dimension is large, and the data size is extensive. They attribute this problem to the need to scan all the data instances for each feature to estimate the information gain of all possible split points, which is very time-consuming. They propose using two new techniques: Gradient-based One-Side Sampling (GOSS) and Exclusive Feature Bundling (EFB). GOSS 's primary purpose is to reject a notable proportion of data occurrences with small gradients and solely use the remainder to estimate the information gain. With this, it is determined that since the data instances with more substantial gradients play a more critical role in the computation of information gain, GOSS can obtain quite an accurate estimate of the information gain with much meagerer data size. With EFB, they bundle ordinarily exclusive features to lessen the number of features. It is then proven that optimal bundling of exclusive features is NP-hard, but a greedy algorithm can accomplish a good approximation ratio. LightGBM is shown to speed up the training process of conventional GBDT by up to over 20 times while reaching around the same accuracy.

2.3   Methods

The authors in [19] propose an automated method for obtaining weighted forecast combinations using time series features. The suggested process involves two stages. First, a time series gathering is used to train a meta-model for attributing weights to various possible forecasting methods. The inputs to the meta-model are features that are extracted from each series. Then, in the second phase, they forecast a new series using a weighted forecast combination, where the weights are obtained from our previously trained meta-model. Such a method outperforms a simple forecast combination and all of the most popular individual techniques in the time series forecasting literature. The approach even achieved the second position in the M4 competition.

2.4   Hyperparameter Tuning

Several methods have been proposed to improve the accuracy of Machine Learning Models such as the tuning of algorithms' hyperparameters. A straightforward way of selecting a configuration is to use default settings, often proposed, and publish and implement a new algorithm. Those default values are usually chosen in an ad-hoc manner to work well enough on many datasets.

The importance of hyperparameter settings across datasets has been thoroughly explored and credited by the literature [20,26,28]. The results confirm that the hyperparameters selected are indeed essential and that the obtained priors (the probability distribution expressing one's beliefs about a quantity before evidence is taken into account) also lead to statistically significant improvements in hyperparameter optimisation [26]. This principled approach usually improves performance but adds additional algorithmic complexity and computational costs to the training procedure. Given this complexity, the authors in [20] propose learning a set of complementary default values from an extensive database of prior empirical results. Selecting an appropriate configuration on a new dataset requires only a simple parallel search over this set. This approach is demonstrated to be more effective and efficient in comparison to random search and Bayesian Optimisation.

The authors in [28] introduce a collaborative filtering method for hyperparameter tuning. The method forms a matrix of the cross-validated errors of many supervised learning models on a large number of datasets. The experiments demonstrate that the model delivers a performance faster than competing approaches.

3   Methodology

In this section, the methodology used during our work is described. The text is divided into the data used for forecasting and random hyperparameters' search.

3.1   Data for Forecasting

This work followed the methodology described in [6] to transform a univariate time series, representing a temporal sequence of values, in a data frame later used for forecasting the next iteration value. Shortly, the time series was reconstructed as a geometric object by applying a time delay embedding using the Takens theorem to frame the predictive task as a multiple regression problem [21]. We constructed a set of observations of the form (X, y). In each observation, the value of y is modeled based on the past p values before it. Conclusively, the time series is transformed into the data set D(X; y). The learning goal is to produce a regression model approximating an unknown function $f : X!Y$. The principle behind this method is to model the conditional distribution of the i-th value of the time-series given its p past values: $f(y_i \rightarrow X_i)$.

3.2   Random Hyperparameters' Search

Despite grid and manual search being the most used strategies for hyperparameter optimization, randomly chosen trials are more efficient than trials on a grid. In contrast to grid search, chosen parameters are not equally spaced and are searched randomly, providing a broader scope of cases than grid search [3]. In this work, we follow such a methodology for hyperparameters' search.

4   Experiments

The experiments' performed in this work are described in this section and are divided into case study description, hyperparameters' experiment description and finally, tests and results.

4.1   Case Study

The data was collected from the Time Series Data Library (TSDL) database [12] and consisted of fifty-eight time-series dataframes. From that database, all univariate time series with at least 1000 observations were selected. This condition regarding the minimum of observations is justified since the methods need a reasonable amount of data to build a good predictive model. This query to the database returned the referred fifty-eight data sets.

From there, we limited the maximum number of observations to 10,000 for the computation process to become faster. Besides, differencing was applied to account for a trend component that can be found in time series. Differentiation consists of the process of subtracting the current value of the time series with the previous value: [7]

$$y_i' = y_i - y_{i-1} \qquad (1)$$

In Eq. 1, y_i' corresponds to the i-th transformed value of the time series.

Our Target variable was t-1 representing the next iteration of the time series from the generated matrices.

4.2   Hyperparameters

To establish the hyperparameters worth being used in the specific case of LightGBM, we consulted the LightGBM documentation. In the documentation, it is referred that the parameters that should be tuned for better accuracy were the maximum number of bins, which should be large; the reduction of the learning rate using a large number of iterations; the enlargement of the number of leaves; and the possible use of the DART algorithm. An important parameter to avoid over-fitting is the use of a maximum depth.

It should be noted that the use of a large number of bins could cause the computation to slow down and that a large number of leaves may cause overfitting. Regarding the components themselves, a short description of each follows. The number of bins sometimes called a class interval, is a way of sorting data. Its principle is very similar to putting data into categories; The learning rate is a hyperparameter that controls how much to change the model in acknowledging the predicted error each time the model weights are renewed. Choosing the learning rate is daring as a value too minute may issue a lengthy training process that could become stuck in a local optimum. In contrast, a value too large may ensue in learning a sub-optimal assortment of weights unreasonably fast or an unstable training process. An iteration indicates the number of times the algorithm's parameters are updated. A tree leaf is labeled with a class or a probability distribution over the classes. As such, the tree has classified the data set into either a specific category or into a particular probability distribution. Finally, the DART algorithm consists of an algorithm that drops trees to solve the over-fitting [27].

Table 1. LightGBM hyperparameters for better accuracy.

Hyperparameters	Definition	Default	Range
max_bin	Max number of bins that feature values will be bucketed in	255	>1
learning_rate	The rate at which the algorithm learns	0.1	>0.0
num_iterations	Number of boosting iterations	100	≥ 0
num_leaves	Max number of leaves in one tree	31	$1 < num\_leaves \leq 131072$
boosting	Boosting algorithm to be used	gbdt	gbdt,rf,dart,goss

In Table 1 one finds the used hyperparameters, definitions, default values, and possible range. To generate the hyperparameters, a table containing all combinations possible within a reasonable range was generated. For the maximum number of bins, a list ranging from 100 to 500 with a step of 11 was created. The learning rate values tested were 0.01, 0.1,0.2 and 0.5. The number of iterations values consisted of a fixed amount of 1000 iterations. The maximum depth consisted of a list of values being these −1,3,5 and 10. The number of leaves consisted of a list comprised of the values 16, 31, 50, 100, and finally, the boosting algorithm could either be gbdt, the default algorithm, or dart. As stated before, these parameters were combined using a mesh grid of all possible values and stored for later use.

4.3   Tests and Results

There were two primary concerns and goals in our work. The first consisted of having a general overview of the impact of random hyper-parameterization as a whole for forecasting time series in LightGBM. The second consisted of understanding which of the hyperparameters had the most significant impact/importance in reducing the Mean Squared Error (MSE).

Overview of Hyper-Parameterization. To understand the impact of random search applied to hyperparameters, we randomly chose 251 random configurations of the previously generated table of hyperparameters. Next, we applied these configurations as hyperparameters of LightGBM with each of the fifty-eight available data frames. To measure each configuration's impact, we applied the default configuration as the hyperparameter vector with each of the data frames. When obtaining the predictions from LightGBM we calculated the Mean Squared Error (MSE). MSE measures the average of the squares of the errors calculated as shown in Eq. 2.

$$MSE = \left(\frac{1}{n}\right) \sum_{i=1}^{n} \left(Y_i - \hat{Y}_i\right)^2 \tag{2}$$

After having the MSE for both the default and the 500 randomly selected configurations, we normalized the error using:

$$MSE_{i,j} = \frac{(mse_j - mse_{i,j})}{mse_j} * 100 \tag{3}$$

where j represents the 58 datasets, i represents the 251 configurations, mse_j represents the MSE of j using the default configuration and $mse_{i,j}$ represents the MSE measured in dataset j using hyperparameter configuration i out of the 251 randomly chosen ones.

Table 2. Metrics for MSE error for top configurations for all datasets

Mean(%)	Minimum(%)	Maximum(%)	Standard Deviation(%)
3.28	0.11	17.45	3.43

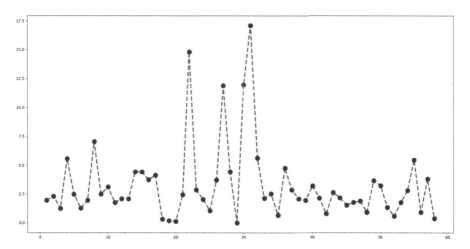

Fig. 1. Dataset *vs* percentage of improvement in MSE value using the best random configuration found.

Using the default configuration as a benchmark, we compared all the random configurations and found that most of the random ones performed better to reduce the measured MSE.

In Table 2 we represent the top performing absolute normalized scores in the percentage of MSE for the random configurations for each dataset by showing the mean, minimum, maximum, and standard deviation of these values. We can also observe that our range of reduction varies up to 17.45% in more significant default MSEs. Complementary, in Fig. 1, we can observe all of the top configuration performance regarding MSE percentage improvement for each dataset.

Individual Study of Hyperparameters. To study each of the hyperparameters' individual performance and impact, we took the previously-stored results and analyzed the effect of each possible different category. We performed the median value of the MSEs for configurations containing each of the possible hyperparameter values for each dataset, storing the result. As such, we obtained fifty-eight median values for each possible category of the hyperparameter and calculated the median of the list. Then, we compared the final median values of each of the categories and concluded that the results were as described in the following paragraph for each of the different hyperparameters.

The boosting algorithm that minimizes MSE is `DART` with a reduction of the MSE value of approximately −2.62 on average. The number of leaves that minimizes MSE is 50, reducing the MSE value by approximately −0.89 on average. The learning rate that minimizes MSE is 0.1 with a reduction of the MSE value of approximately −2.63 on average, corresponding to the default configuration. The maximum number of bins that minimizes MSE is 400, reducing the MSE value by approximately −0.9 on average. The maximum depth that minimizes MSE is: −1 T with a reduction of the MSE value of approximately −1.7 on average, corresponding to the default configuration.

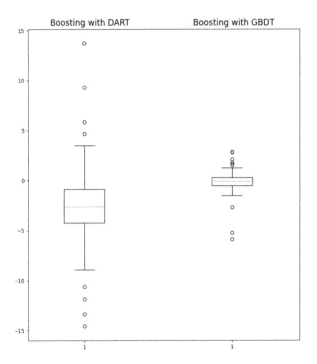

Fig. 2. Boosting algorithms MSEs' comparison.

We further analyzed the impact of using different categories of each of the values to see the difference made by using one configuration or the other. Such analysis was majorly executed using box plots. We analyze the impact of the boosting algorithm in Fig. 2. On average, the DART algorithm proves to be a better choice than the default gbdt algorithm.

The analysis of the impact of the number of leaves is shown in Fig. 3a. As discussed before, on average, the number of leaves that minimizes the MSE in our range of used categories is 50 proving to give better accuracy than the default 31 number of leaves.

In Fig. 3b we analyze the impact of the number of bins used. It can be seen that 400 gives a better accuracy than the default 255. Finally we concluded that the default configurations prove to have the best results out of our selection of values for both the maximum depth and learning rate hyperparameters.

Despite some parameters showing better accuracy, one should be aware of over-fitting when augmenting the value of the maximum number of bins, the number of leaves and maximum depth. With that in mind, we propose that an alternative for better accuracy in a time series forecasting problem using LightGBM by using the hyperparameters shown in Table 3

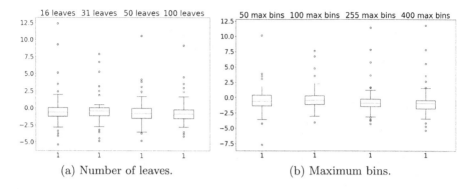

(a) Number of leaves.   (b) Maximum bins.

Fig. 3. Comparison of MSEs' in terms of number of leaves and maximum bins.

Table 3. LightGBM's suggested hyperparameters for time series forecasting problems

max_bin	learning_rate	num_iterations	num_leaves	boosting	max_depth
400	0.1	1000	50	dart	−1

5   Conclusions

Our work consisted of exploring the importance of hyperparameter tuning in LightGBM for forecasting time series. We started by establishing hyperparameters that could be tuned for better accuracy for LightGBM. We then applied 251 randomly selected for each one of the 58 time-series data frames available using LightGBM and calculated the MSE error of each of the configurations. Using the default configuration as benchmarks in a broader scope, we concluded that randomly selecting configurations can lower the MSE up to 17.45%. We then studied the individual performance and impact of each of the hyperparameters and suggested an alternative beginning configuration for LightGBM when faced with a time series forecasting problem.

As future work, we would like to test the DART boosting algorithm to further enhance our solution especially given the impact of DART in lowering the MSEs in our case study. We would like to study the impact of the suggested configuration on multivariate times series datasets.

References

1. Athanasopoulos, G., Poskitt, D.S., Vahid, F.: Two canonical varma forms: scalar component models vis-à-vis the echelon form. Econ. Rev. **31**(1), 60–83 (2012)
2. Bergmeir, C., Hyndman, R.J., Benítez, J.M.: Bagging exponential smoothing methods using STL decomposition and box-cox transformation. Int. J. Forecast. **32**(2), 303–312 (2016)
3. Bergstra, J., Bengio, Y.: Random search for hyper-parameter optimization. J. Mach. Learn. Res. **13**(1), 281–305 (2012)

4. Box, G.E., Jenkins, G.M., Reinsel, G.C., Ljung, G.M.: Time Series Analysis: Forecasting and Control. John Wiley & Sons, Hoboken (2015)
5. Brown, R.G.: Statistical Forecasting for Inventory Control. McGraw/Hill, New York (1959)
6. Cerqueira, V., Moniz, N., Soares, C.: Vest: automatic feature engineering for forecasting. arXiv preprint arXiv:2010.07137 (2020)
7. Cerqueira, V.M.A.: Emsembles for Time Series Forescating. Ph.D. thesis, Faculty of Engineering of the University of Porto, s/n, Rua Doutor Roberto Frias, 4200–465 Porto (7 2019)
8. Chatfield, C.: Time-Series Forecasting. CRC Press, Boca Raton (2000)
9. Cleveland, R.B., Cleveland, W.S., McRae, J.E., Terpenning, I.: STL: a seasonal-trend decomposition. J. Official Stat. **6**(1), 3–73 (1990)
10. Bee Dagum, E., Bianconcini, S.: Seasonal Adjustment Methods and Real Time Trend-Cycle Estimation. SSBS, Springer, Cham (2016). https://doi.org/10.1007/978-3-319-31822-6
11. Gardner, E.S., Jr.: Exponential smoothing: the state of the art–part ii. Int. J. Forecast. **22**(4), 637–666 (2006)
12. Hyndman, R.: TSDL: Time series data library (2021). https://pkg.yangzhuoranyang.com/tsdl/
13. Hyndman, R.J., Athanasopoulos, G.: Forecasting: Principles and Practice. OTexts (2018)
14. Kaastra, I., Boyd, M.: Designing a neural network for forecasting financial. Neurocomputing **10**, 215–236 (1996)
15. Ke, G., et al.: LightGBM: a highly efficient gradient boosting decision tree. In: Advances in Neural Information Processing Systems, pp. 3146–3154 (2017)
16. Lawrence, M., Goodwin, P., O'Connor, M., Önkal, D.: Judgmental forecasting: a review of progress over the last 25 years. Int. J. Forecast. **22**(3), 493–518 (2006)
17. Makridakis, S., Spiliotis, E., Assimakopoulos, V.: The m5 accuracy competition: results, findings and conclusions. Int. J. Forecast. (2020)
18. Microsoft: Lightgbm documentation (2021). https://lightgbm.readthedocs.io/en/latest/
19. Montero-Manso, P., Athanasopoulos, G., Hyndman, R.J., Talagala, T.S.: Fforma: feature-based forecast model averaging. Int. J. Forecast. **36**(1), 86–92 (2020)
20. Pfisterer, F., van Rijn, J.N., Probst, P., Müller, A., Bischl, B.: Learning multiple defaults for machine learning algorithms. arXiv preprint arXiv:1811.09409 (2018)
21. Rand, D., Young, L.-S. (eds.): Dynamical Systems and Turbulence, Warwick 1980. LNM, vol. 898. Springer, Heidelberg (1981). https://doi.org/10.1007/BFb0091903
22. Sheather, S.: A Modern Approach to Regression with R. Springer, New York (2009). https://doi.org/10.1007/978-0-387-09608-7
23. Son, J., Jung, I., Park, K., Han, B.: Tracking-by-segmentation with online gradient boosting decision tree. In: Proceedings of the IEEE International Conference on Computer Vision (ICCV) (2015)
24. Spiliotis, E., Makridakis, S., Semenoglou, A.A., Assimakopoulos, V.: Comparison of statistical and machine learning methods for daily SKU demand forecasting. Oper. Res., 1–25 (2020)
25. Sun, X., Liu, M., Sima, Z.: A novel cryptocurrency price trend forecasting model based on lightGBM. Finan. Res. Lett. **32**, 101084 (2020). https://doi.org/10.1016/j.frl.2018.12.032
26. Van Rijn, J.N., Hutter, F.: Hyperparameter importance across datasets. In: Proceedings of the 24th ACM SIGKDD International Conference on Knowledge Discovery & Data Mining, pp. 2367–2376 (2018)

27. Vinayak, R.K., Gilad-Bachrach, R.: Dart: dropouts meet multiple additive regression trees. In: Artificial Intelligence and Statistics, pp. 489–497. PMLR (2015)
28. Yang, C., Akimoto, Y., Kim, D.W., Udell, M.: Oboe: collaborative filtering for automl model selection. In: Proceedings of the 25th ACM SIGKDD International Conference on Knowledge Discovery & Data Mining, pp. 1173–1183 (2019)
29. Zhang, Y.: LightGBM-based model for metro passenger volume forecasting. IET Intell. Transp. Syst. **14**, 1815–1823(8) (2020). https://digital-library.theiet.org/content/journals/10.1049/iet-its.2020.0396

Evolutionary
Computation/Optimisation

A Two-Stage Efficient Evolutionary Neural Architecture Search Method for Image Classification

Gonglin Yuan[(✉)], Bing Xue, and Mengjie Zhang

School of Engineering and Computer Science, Victoria University of Wellington,
PO Box 600, Wellington 6140, New Zealand
{gonglin.yuan,bing.xue,mengjie.zhang}@ecs.vuw.ac.nz

Abstract. Deep convolutional neural networks (DCNNs) have achieved promising performance in different computer vision tasks in recent years. Conventionally, deep learning experts are needed to design convolutional neural network's (CNN's) architectures when facing new tasks. Neural architecture search (NAS) is to automatically find suitable architectures; however, NAS suffers from the tremendous computational cost. This paper employs a genetic algorithm (GA) and a grid search (GS) strategy to search for the micro-architecture and adjust the macro-architecture efficiently and effectively, named TSCNN. We propose two mutation operations to explore the search space comprehensively. Furthermore, the micro-architecture searched on one dataset is transferred to another dataset to verify its transferability. The proposed algorithm is evaluated on two widely used datasets. The experimental results show that TSCNN achieves very competitive accuracy. On the CIFAR10 dataset, the computational cost is reduced from hundreds or even thousands to only 2.5 GPU-days, and the number of parameters is reduced from thirty more million to only 1.25 M.

Keywords: Convolutional neural network · Genetic algorithm · Grid search · Neural architecture search

1 Introduction

Deep convolutional neural networks (DCNNs) have attracted significant attention in recent years and have been applied to many fields of computer vision [24], such as image classification, semantic segmentation, and object recognition. Some DCNNs outperform most traditional human-designed image processing techniques, achieving state-of-the-art performance, mainly due to their superior automatic feature extraction ability, such as VGG [19], GooLeNet [23], ResNet [8], and DenseNet [9]. Nevertheless, the architecture of the convolutional neural network (CNN) needs to be delicately designed to solve different problems on various datasets, as the same CNN may perform differently on different datasets.

Because of the reasons mentioned above, deep learning experts are needed when encountering a new task, so it is inconvenient for people who do not know

© Springer Nature Switzerland AG 2021
D. N. Pham et al. (Eds.): PRICAI 2021, LNAI 13031, pp. 469–484, 2021.
https://doi.org/10.1007/978-3-030-89188-6_35

much about deep learning to enjoy DCNNs' superiority. As a result, there is a surge of interest in automatically searching the architecture, which is named neural architecture search (NAS) [14,26].

Some NAS methods search for the whole architecture from scratches, such as CNN-GA [22], NAS [30], Large-scale Evolution [17], DAGCNN [28], and IPPSO [25]. The main limitation of these methods is the search space is very big, usually consuming a lot of computational resources and searching time. For example, NAS [30] spends 28 days using 800 Graphics Processing Units (GPUs) to find the promising architecture on the CIFAR10 dataset; Large-scale Evolution [17] consumes 2,750 GPU-days for the same dataset.

Inspired by the repeated blocks in manually designed architectures, some NAS approaches search for the micro-architecture, i.e., the structure of the cells, and stack the cells to form the final CNN, such as Hierarchical Evolution [13], NASNet [31], Block-QNN [29], and AmoebaNet [16]. These methods are much more preferred than searching for the whole architecture because of the much smaller search space. Nevertheless, there are two main limitations of these approaches: the first one is that the macro-architecture, which refers to the system-level organization of multiple micro-architectures into a CNN architecture, is usually in a predefined manner, which reduces the degree of automation, i.e., human experts are still needed to decide the number of searched cells and how to connect them. Another limitation is that the efficiency is still not promising—NASNet [31] consumes 2,000 GPU-days, and Hierarchical Evolution [13] spends 300 GPU-days for CIFAR10. In fact, many individual users or even university research teams do not have sufficiently powerful GPUs to support such a tremendous computation amount. Therefore, in this paper, an efficient NAS algorithm with a self-adjustable macro-architecture search strategy will be proposed.

The overall goal of this paper is to design an efficient approach to automatically constructing promising CNN architectures, which could adjust the macro-architecture dynamically. The goals are specified as follows:

1) Propose a two-stage efficient search strategy to speed up the searching process. The first stage is employing a genetic algorithm (GA) [5] to search for the micro-architecture while limiting the network's width to a small range and fixing the depth to a small number. In this case, the scales of the searched CNNs are strictly restricted to a relatively small space, which could speed up both the offspring generating process and the fitness evaluation process. The second stage uses the grid search (GS) [11] to explore the proper depth and width of the macro-architecture, since GS is suitable when there are a small number of parameters.

2) Design two mutation operators to cope with the graph-based variable-length encoding strategy. The node-level mutation adds, removes, or modifies a whole layer, and the parameter-level mutation changes the layer's number of kernels and which layers to be the preceding ones. Because the encoding information is complicated, performing two different mutations could help explore the search space more comprehensively.

3) Explore the transferability of the searched micro-architecture. As there are similarities among different datasets, the network architecture learned from one dataset may be used on others to reduce the tedious searching process. The micro-architecture searched on one dataset is transferred to another different dataset. The whole network's width and depth are further adjusted by the GS stage in order to fit the new dataset.

2 Background

2.1 CNN Architectures

CNNs are composed of a number of layers that are of different types. Various layers have various functions: convolutional layers are to extract the features from images or feature maps, and the kernel size and the number of kernels are two main parameters of convolutional layers; pooling layers filter the features and reduce the size of feature maps; fully-connected layers are usually used for mapping the learned feature representation to the label space.

Some variants of convolutions are designed to reduce the number of parameters and the computational cost: depthwise-separable convolutions [4] are composed of depthwise convolution and pointwise convolution; dilated convolutions [27] enlarge the receptive field with pixel skipping; spatially separable convolutions divide a kernel into two smaller kernels across their spatial axes.

2.2 Genetic Algorithms

Genetic algorithms [1,5] search for the optimal solution by simulating the natural evolutionary process. Specifically, the solutions are encoded into chromosomes, and the evaluation criterion is the fitness of individuals. Generally, the main steps of GAs are as follows:

Step 1: Initialize the initial population according to the encoding strategy.
Step 2: Evaluate the individuals with the fitness evaluation function.
Step 3: Select the promising individuals according to their fitness.
Step 4: Perform crossover and mutation operations, and select individuals to generate the offspring.
Step 5: Evaluate the new offspring, and perform environmental selection to generate the next generation.
Step 6: Go to step 3 if the termination criterion is not met. Otherwise, select the best individual to be the optimal solution.

Commonly, the termination criterion is a predefined maximal number of generations. The crossover and mutation operators need to be designed corresponding to the encoding strategy.

2.3   Grid Search Algorithms

Grid Search [11] is an exhaustive optimization algorithm. Therefore it is mainly implemented when there are a small number of parameters, and each with a small and limited search range. The Cartesian product of the parameters leads to particular combinations. GS is commonly used to search for the optimal combination of parameter values in training a machine learning model, where it employs each parameter variety to train the model. The ones leading to the best performance on the validation set are picked as the final parameter combination.

3   The Proposed Algorithm

3.1   Algorithm Overview

We name the proposed algorithm as TSCNN (Two-Stage CNN). Figure 1 shows the procedure of TSCNN, which mainly involves two stages: GA searches for the best cell structure, and GS explores the appropriate number of cells and number of feature maps of the convolutional layers. The upper part of Fig. 1 exhibits the flowchart of the GA stage, which follows the standard GA procedure introduced in Sect. 2.2. The whole network is stacked by several dense blocks, and each dense block is composed of some cells, and the cells in the same block are connected by dense connections [9]. Please note that all the cells share the same micro-architecture.

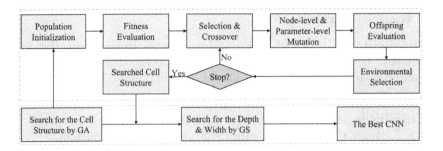

Fig. 1. The flowchart of TSCNN.

3.2   Individual Representation and Population Initialization

In TSCNN, the first stage is using the GA to search for the micro-architecture. The micro-architecture is represented by a directed acyclic graph (DAG), which is composed of some nodes and directed connections. A node represents a layer, and a directed connection represents the data flow between layers. We mainly employ some kinds of convolutional operations and an *identity* operation. The *identity* operation just connects its preceding layer to its output layer without processing the feature maps, increasing the flexibility of the architecture. There are nine types of candidate operations:

- Type 1: 3×3 depthwise-separable convolution
- Type 2: 5×5 depthwise-separable convolution
- Type 3: 7×7 depthwise-separable convolution
- Type 4: 3×3 convolution
- Type 5: 1×5 then 5×1 convolution
- Type 6: 1×7 then 7×1 convolution
- Type 7: 3×3 dilated convolution
- Type 8: 5×5 dilated convolution
- Type 9: identity

We employ a variable-length encoding strategy to represent DAGs with different numbers of nodes, making the represented architectures more flexible. A five-integer vector is employed to represent a node, and the integers are the node index, the operation type, the corresponding parameter, and two preceding nodes' indexes. For the convolution operation, the parameter is the number of kernels, and there is no parameter for the *identity* layer, represented by 0. Please note that the input layer's index is set to 0. If the preceding node's index is -1, the node has no corresponding predecessor. If two indexes of the predecessors are neither negative, the feature maps of them are concatenated together and then inputted to the corresponding layer.

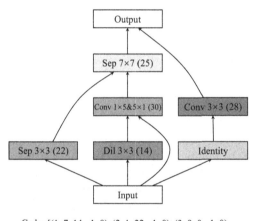

Code=[(1, 7, 14, -1, 0), (2, 1, 22, -1, 0), (3, 9, 0, -1, 0),
(4, 5, 30, 0 ,1), (5, 4, 28, -1, 3), (6, 3, 25, 2, 4)]

Fig. 2. An example of the encoding strategy.

Figure 2 illustrates an example of the encoding strategy. Each rectangle represents a specific layer, and the types of the layers are displayed. The numbers in brackets are the number of kernels of the convolution layers. All the layers that do not connect to other layers are concatenated together to form the output.

Algorithm 1: Population Initialization

Input: The population size N, the minimal number of nodes N_{min}, the maximal number of nodes N_{max}.

Output: Initialized population P_0.

1 $P_0 \leftarrow \emptyset$;
2 **for** $i = 1; i \leq N; i \leftarrow i + 1$ **do**
3      $ind \leftarrow \emptyset$;
4      $n_{node} \leftarrow$ Randomly generate an integer between $[N_{min}, N_{max}]$;
5   **for** $j = 1; j \leq n_{node}; j \leftarrow j + 1$ **do**
6          $node \leftarrow \emptyset$;
7          $n_{type} \leftarrow$ Randomly generate an integer between $[1, 9]$;
8   **if** $n_{type} \leq 8$ **then**
9              $n_{para} \leftarrow$ Randomly select the number of kernels;
10             $pre_1, pre_2 \leftarrow$ Randomly generate two integers between $[-1, j-1]$;
11   **else**
12             $n_{para} \leftarrow 0$;
13             $pre_1 \leftarrow -1$;
14             $pre_2 \leftarrow$ Randomly choose an integers between $[0, j-1]$;
15   **end**
16         $node \leftarrow j \cup n_{type} \cup n_{para} \cup pre_1 \cup pre_2$;
17         $ind \leftarrow ind \cup node$;
18   **end**
19     $P_0 \leftarrow P_0 \cup ind$;
20 **end**
21 **Return** P_0.

Algorithm 1 shows the pseudo-code of the population initialization process. Briefly, the range of the number of nodes in the DAG needs to be predefined considering the effectiveness of the represented architecture and the computational resources. The individuals are generated separately until reaching the predefined population size N (lines 2–20). For each individual, the number of nodes n_{node} is randomly determined within the predefined range (line 4), and each node is generated according to the encoding strategy (lines 5–18). Specifically, the operation of the node is randomly selected from 9 types of operations (line 7). If the operation is convolution-related, the number of kernels is determined randomly (line 9), and the two predecessors are chosen from no predecessor (represented by -1), the original input future maps (represented by 0), and the preceding nodes $[1, j-1]$. Otherwise, if the node's type is *identity*, the parameter of the node is set to 0 (line 12), and only one predecessor is chosen (lines 12–13) from the original input feature maps and the preceding nodes (line 14). Afterward, the node's index j, the node type n_{type}, the corresponding parameter n_{para}, and the predecessors' indexes pre_1 and pre_2 are integrated into a vector to represent the node (line 16). All the node vectors are connected to form the individual (line 17). Finally, all individuals build the population (line 19).

3.3   Fitness Evaluation

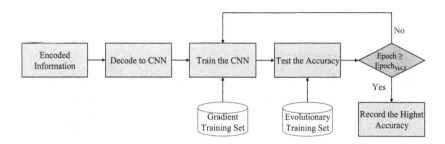

Fig. 3. The process of the fitness evaluation in the GA search.

Fitness evaluation is a crucial part of GAs, which evaluates the individuals quantitatively, indicating suitable individuals being parents to produce offspring with potentially better performance.

Figure 3 indicates the fitness evaluation procedure in the GA search. To evaluate individuals' fitness, the encoded information of the individuals needs to be decoded to the corresponding CNN architectures first. Specifically, the encoded information is decoded according to the representation policy, and all the convolution-related layers are followed by batch-normalized layers and rectified linear unit layers. After converting the encoded information to the corresponding micro-architecture, the cells that share the same micro-architecture in the same block are densely connected, as shown in Fig. 4. Average pooling layers are employed to connect two adjacent blocks, and a global average pooling layer followed by a fully-connected layer is added at the end of the network.

Fig. 4. The framework of the whole CNN.

The whole dataset is divided into two separate parts: the training set and the test set, and only the training set is used during the whole NAS process, and it is further divided into the evolutionary training set and the gradient training set, respectively. The evolutionary training set is used for training the weights of the networks, and the gradient training set is used to evaluate the networks' fitness during the search process.

Next, the decoded whole network is trained by the gradient training set and tested by the evolutionary training set for a predefined small number of epochs. Only a small number of epochs are used here with the goal of reducing the computational cost. Although this reduces the fidelity of the fitness evaluation, it is expected to not significantly reduce the overall performance since the relative performance of individuals can be roughly indicated, which is sufficient for performing the genetic operators to generate new offspring. Finally, the best testing accuracy is recorded as the fitness of the individual.

3.4   Offspring Generation

In TSCNN, two parent individuals are selected from the current population by a binary tournament selection method. Next, the crossover operation is performed on them. Then, a node-level mutation operation and a parameter-level operation are proposed to perform mutation on the offspring. In the end, new offspring is generated.

A random number between 0 and 1 is generated, and if it is smaller than the predefined crossover probability, the crossover operation is carried out: two different positions are randomly chosen from the shorter parent, and the nodes between them are switched with the nodes of the same parts on the longer one. At last, two offspring are generated.

As the encoded information is composed of several nodes, and a node is represented by a five-bit vector, two mutation operators are designed to change the vectors in the individual and the bits in the vector, respectively. The proposed node-level mutation operation is performed on the offspring first. There is a predefined probability to decide whether to perform the mutation operation. If the mutation is to be performed, a node is randomly chosen, and a mutation type is randomly selected from *adding*, *removing*, and *modifying*. If the type is *adding*, a new node is randomly generated according to the encoding strategy and is added behind the chosen node. Accordingly, for the nodes on the right side of the inserted one, the indexes and corresponding predecessors may also change. If the type is *removing*, the chosen node is deleted; also, other nodes' encoded information would change to keep consistency with the initial intention. Otherwise, the chosen node is replaced by a newly generated node.

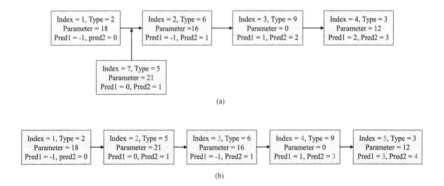

Fig. 5. An example of the *adding* mutation.

To better understand the node-level mutation process, an example of the *adding* mutation is presented in Fig. 5. Before mutation, the individual is composed of four nodes: $[(1, 2, 18, -1, 0), (2, 6, 16, -1, 1), (3, 9, 0, 1, 2), (4, 3, 12, 2, 3)]$, and the first node is chosen. A new node is then randomly generated according to the encoding strategy, and the predecessors are determined based on the node's position in the individual. Next, the new node is added next to the first node. Please note that the following nodes' indexes and the predecessors' indexes are also changed accordingly. All the changed information is displayed in red color in Fig. 5.

Algorithm 2: Parameter-level Mutation Operation of TSCNN

Input: The offspring individual o_1, parameter-level mutation propability p_{pm}.
Output: The mutated offspring.

1   **for** *node* in o_1 **do**
2     $r_{pm} \leftarrow$ Randomly generate a number between $[0, 1]$;
3   **if** $r_{pm} < p_{pm}$ **then**
4   **if** *node's type* is not *identity* **then**
5         $r \leftarrow$ Randomly generate a number between $[0, 1]$;
6   **if** $r < 0.5$ **then**
7   generate a new number to replace the *parameter* of o_1
8   **else**
9   generate new predecessors to replace pre_1 and pre_2 of o_1
10   **end**
11   **else**
12   generate a new predecessor to replace pre_2 of o_1 ;
13   **end**
14   **end**
15 **end**
16 **Return** o_1.

As the node-level mutation alters a whole node instead of changing a node's specific parameter, a parameter-level mutation is proposed to complement the node-level mutation for a better exploration performance. Algorithm 2 exhibits the details of the parameter-level mutation operation. Generally, there is a probability of modifying the parameter or the predecessors for each node in the offspring. Suppose the node's type is convolution-related (line 4), there is a tossing coin probability of modifying the parameter in the predefined range (lines 6–7) or generating two new predecessors' indexes for the node according to the corresponding principle mentioned before (line 9). Otherwise, if the node's type is *identity*, only one predecessor is changed, for there is no parameter for the *identity* node, as well as it only has one predecessor.

3.5   Environmental Selection

Environmental selection is used to select some individuals of the current population to survive to the next generation. Conventionally, a good population should have both convergence and diversity to promise the effectiveness of the evolution and prevent the premature convergence problem.

In TSCNN, a binary tournament selection operator is employed to select individuals from the current population to form the next generation. Specifically, two individuals are randomly selected and compared, and the better one is passed on to the next generation. Besides, an elitist strategy is utilized to promise the current best individual could survive.

3.6   Grid Search

GS is used to explore the appropriate depth and width of the macro-architecture. The depth is controlled by the number of cells in each dense block, and a multiplication factor controls the width. The final number of feature maps in a layer is the product of the one searched by GA and the multiplication factor.

Specifically, the number of cells in each dense block and the multiplication factor are traversed together. The CNN is generated according to the decoding strategy illustrated in Sect. 3.3 with the candidate depth and width, and is then trained on the gradient training set. Then, the CNN is tested on the evolutionary training set. The process will repeat until all the candidate depths and widths are tested. The depth and width leading to the best performance on the evolutionary training set are selected as the final macro-architecture's depth and width.

The micro-architecture searched by the GA on one dataset could be adjusted by the GS stage on another dataset to explore the transferability of the micro-architecture since different datasets may share some common features. Finally, the searched CNN is fully trained on the training set, and the performance is estimated on the test set.

4   Experiment Design

4.1   Benchmark Datasets

To verify the effectiveness and efficiency of the proposed algorithm, the CIFAR10 and CIFAR100 datasets are chosen as the benchmark datasets. Many peer competitors are trained and tested on them, and the scale is suitable for our available computational resources. Please note that the data augmentation technique is not employed during the NAS process but is performed for the post-search training process. The augmentation method is similar to other peer competitors: padding and flipping, without the *cutout* [6] technique.

4.2 Peer Competitors

For the purpose of verifying the effectiveness and efficiency of the proposed algorithm, some state-of-the-art approaches are selected to be compared with TSCNN. These peer competitors could be divided into two categories according to whether the CNN is designed manually. The first category is the human-designed CNNs. They are FractalNet [10], Maxout [7], ResNet [8], DenseNet [9], Highway Network [20], and VGG [19]. These competitors are all trained and tested on both CIFAR10 and CIFAR100.

Another category belongs to NAS, such as CGP-CNN [21], NAS [30], Large-scale Evolution [17], Block-QNN [29], MetaQNN [2], EIGEN [18], CNN-GA [22], PNASNet [12], and AmoebaNet [16].

4.3 Parameter Settings

The parameter settings follow the convention of the evolutionary algorithm and deep learning, as well as considering the computational capability of the resources available. Particularly, Table 1 exhibits the parameter settings.

In the micro search process, the Adam optimizer is used to train the network for 10 epochs; and a standard stochastic gradient descent (SGD) optimizer is employed to train each network for 50 epochs in the macro search process.

Table 1. Parameter settings.

Parameters	Value	Parameters	Value
GA		# kernels in convolutional layers	[8, 36]
population size	30	# cells in each dense block	4
# generations	10	GS	
crossover rate	0.8	# cells in each dense block	[4, 7]
node-level mutation rate	0.2	multiplication factors of # kernels	0.8, 1.0, 1.5
parameter-level mutation rate	0.1	fitness evaluation for macro search	
micro-architecture		initial learning rate	0.1
# layers	[5, 10]	momentum	0.9

In the post-search training process, similar to [3] and [15], an auxiliary classifier [23] is appended to about 2/3 depth, and its loss is weighted by 0.4 to improve the training performance. In addition, the learning rate is set to 0.1 initially and is decayed with a cosine restart schedule for 600 epochs.

The experiments are implemented on one *Quadro RTX 6000* GPU card.

5 Experiment Results

5.1 Overall Performance

The proposed TSCNN method is compared with the manually designed approaches from two aspects: the number of parameters and the classification error rate, since the number of parameters affects the deployment of the CNN, and a network with a large number of parameters usually has a complex architecture, which is more likely to lead to a lower classification error rate. When compared with other NAS methods, the GPU-days is also taken into account, which indicates the search process costs how many days using a single GPU card, implying the algorithm's computational cost.

The search is repeated for five times, and the median run measured by the classification error rate is reported. Table 2 exhibits the experimental results of TSCNN and the competitors on CIFAR10 and CIFAR100. On the CIFAR10 dataset, TSCNN achieves an error rate of 4.89%, and 5 peer competitors outperform it. However, their numbers of parameters are much larger than TSCNN. As for the computational cost, TSCNN only costs 2.5 GPU-days, ranking second over the search algorithms. EIGEN [18] only needs 2 GPU-days, but its error

Table 2. The comparisons between TSCNN, TSCNN(Transfer), and state-of-the-art peer competitors in terms of the number of parameters, error rate, and computational cost on CIFAR10 and CIFAR100 datasets.

Model	#Parameters	CIFAR10	CIFAR100	GPU-Days
FractalNet [10]	38.6M	5.22%	22.3%	–
Maxout [7]	–	9.3%	38.6%	–
ResNet-101 [8]	1.7M	6.43%	25.16%	–
DenseNet (k = 40) [9]	25.6M	3.5%	17.2%	–
Highway Network [20]	–	7.72%	32.39%	–
VGG [19]	20.04M	6.66%	28.05%	–
CGP-CNN [21]	2.64M	5.98%	–	27
NAS [30]	2.5M	6.01%	–	22,400
Large-scale Evolution [17]	5.4M	5.4%	–	2750
Large-scale Evolution [17]	40.4M	–	23%	>2730
Block-QNN-S [29]	6.1M	4.38%	20.65%	90
MetaQNN [2]	–	6.92%	–	100
MetaQNN [2]	–	–	27.14%	100
EIGEN [18]	2.6M	5.4%	—	2
EIGEN [18]	11.8M	–	21.9%	5
CNN-GA [22]	2.9M	4.78%	–	35
CNN-GA [22]	4.1M	–	20.03%	40
PNASNet-5 [12]	3.2M	3.41%	–	150
AmoebaNet-B [16]	34.9M	2.98%	–	3150
TSCNN	1.25M	4.89%	–	2.5
TSCNN	4.31M	–	21.38%	5.5
TSCNN(Transfer)	4.09M	–	22.03%	3

rate is 0.51% higher than TSCNN's, and the model scale is 2.08 times of TSCNN. Other competitors' computational costs are much larger than TSCNN.

As for CIFAR100, TSCNN's error rate ranks fourth among the 11 peer competitors, and only ResNet-101 [8] and CNN-GA's [22] network scales are smaller than TSCNN. Nevertheless, ResNet-101's classification accuracy is 3.78% worse than TSCNN, and CNN-GA's computational cost is 7.27 times of TSCNN. Only EIGEN's [18] computational cost is 9.1% lower than TSCNN, while its error rate is 0.52% higher than TSCNN, and the network scale is 2.74 times of TSCNN. So we can say TSCNN is a very competitive algorithm considering the model scale, classification error rate, and computational cost.

5.2 Transferability Justification

To justify the transferability of the micro-architecture, the cell structure searched on CIFAR10 is transferred to the GS process, and the GS is performed on CIFAR100 to search for the final depth and width of the network. The experimental result is exhibited in Table 2, denoted as 'TSCNN (Transfer)'. The error rate of TSCNN (Transfer) is 22.03%, and it is only 0.65% higher than directly using CIFAR100 to search for the micro-architecture, but the model size becomes smaller, and the computational cost is the lowest among all the competitors. Please note that the computational cost contains both the micro-architecture search process on the CIFAR10 dataset and the GS phase on CIFAR100. To conclude, the result achieved by transfer learning is also competitive, which demonstrates the excellent transferability of the searched cell structure.

5.3 Searched Cell Structures

Figure 6 presents the cell structures searched by the GA in the first stage of TSCNN on CIFAR10 and CIFAR100, respectively. The architecture obtained on CIFAR100 contains more layers and is more sophisticated compared with the

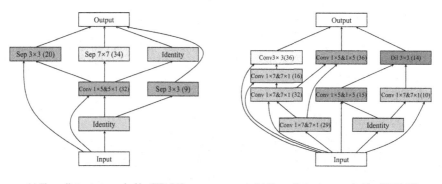

(a) The cell structure searched by CIFAR10   (b) The cell structure searched by CIFAR100

Fig. 6. The cell structures searched on different datasets.

architecture searched on CIFAR10. The reason is probably that the classification task of CIFAR100 is much more challenging, as the categories of objectives are 10 times that of CIFAR10, but the number of images of each class is only one-tenth of that of CIFAR10.

The cell structures are based on DAG, and there are multi-branch connections and skip connections in the searched motifs, which could help to improve the feature extraction ability.

6   Conclusions

In conclusion, this paper aimed to design an efficient NAS algorithm to automatically search for the micro-architecture and adjust the macro-architecture to improve the classification performance. This objective has been successfully achieved by employing GA to search for the cell structure and using GS to explore the appropriate depth and width of the macro-architecture. Besides, two mutation operators are applied to improve the exploration performance of GA. The proposed algorithm is implemented on two popular benchmark datasets and is compared with 15 state-of-the-art peer competitors. For the CIFAR10 dataset, the experimental results show TSCNN's error rate ranks 6th, but the model size and the computational cost are much smaller than the first 5 algorithms. On CIFAR100, TSCNN's classification accuracy ranks 4th with small number of parameters, and consume much less time and computational resources. Besides, the micro-architecture searched on CIFAR10 is transferred to CIFAR100, and the results show its error rate is only a little worse than TSCNN without transfer learning, but with a smaller network size, and the computational cost is less than all the competitors. All these prove the searched cell's good transferability.

References

1. Al-Sahaf, H., et al.: A survey on evolutionary machine learning. J. Roy. Soc. New Zealand **49**(2), 205–228 (2019)
2. Baker, B., Gupta, O., Naik, N., Raskar, R.: Designing neural network architectures using reinforcement learning. arXiv preprint arXiv:1611.02167 (2016)
3. Chen, Y., et al.: Renas: Reinforced evolutionary neural architecture search. In: Proceedings of the IEEE Conference on Computer Vision and Pattern Recognition, pp. 4787–4796 (2019)
4. Chollet, F.: Xception: deep learning with depthwise separable convolutions. In: Proceedings of the IEEE Conference on Computer Vision and Pattern Recognition, pp. 1251–1258 (2017)
5. Davis, L.: Handbook of genetic algorithms (1991)
6. DeVries, T., Taylor, G.W.: Improved regularization of convolutional neural networks with cutout. arXiv preprint arXiv:1708.04552 (2017)
7. Goodfellow, I., Warde-Farley, D., Mirza, M., Courville, A., Bengio, Y.: Maxout networks. In: International Conference on Machine Learning, pp. 1319–1327. PMLR (2013)

8. He, K., Zhang, X., Ren, S., Sun, J.: Deep residual learning for image recognition. In: Proceedings of the IEEE Conference on Computer Vision and Pattern Recognition, pp. 770–778 (2016)
9. Huang, G., Liu, Z., Van Der Maaten, L., Weinberger, K.Q.: Densely connected convolutional networks. In: Proceedings of the IEEE Conference on Computer Vision and Pattern Recognition, pp. 4700–4708 (2017)
10. Larsson, G., Maire, M., Shakhnarovich, G.: Fractalnet: ultra-deep neural networks without residuals. arXiv preprint arXiv:1605.07648 (2016)
11. LaValle, S.M., Branicky, M.S., Lindemann, S.R.: On the relationship between classical grid search and probabilistic roadmaps. Int. J. Rob. Res. **23**(7–8), 673–692 (2004)
12. Liu, C., et al.: Progressive neural architecture search. In: Proceedings of the European Conference on Computer Vision (ECCV), pp. 19–34 (2018)
13. Liu, H., Simonyan, K., Vinyals, O., Fernando, C., Kavukcuoglu, K.: Hierarchical representations for efficient architecture search. arXiv preprint arXiv:1711.00436 (2017)
14. Liu, Y., Sun, Y., Xue, B., Zhang, M., Yen, G.G., Tan, K.C.: A survey on evolutionary neural architecture search. IEEE Trans. Neural Netw. Learn. Syst. (2021)
15. Lu, Z., et al.: Multi-objective evolutionary design of deep convolutional neural networks for image classification. IEEE Trans. Evol. Comput. **25**, 277–291 (2020)
16. Real, E., Aggarwal, A., Huang, Y., Le, Q.V.: Regularized evolution for image classifier architecture search. In: Proceedings of the AAAI Conference on Artificial Intelligence, vol. 33, pp. 4780–4789 (2019)
17. Real, E., et al.: Large-scale evolution of image classifiers. In: Proceedings of the 34th International Conference on Machine Learning, vol. 70, pp. 2902–2911 (2017)
18. Ren, J., Li, Z., Yang, J., Xu, N., Yang, T., Foran, D.J.: Eigen: ecologically-inspired genetic approach for neural network structure searching from scratch. In: Proceedings of the IEEE Conference on Computer Vision and Pattern Recognition, pp. 9059–9068 (2019)
19. Simonyan, K., Zisserman, A.: Very deep convolutional networks for large-scale image recognition. arXiv preprint arXiv:1409.1556 (2014)
20. Srivastava, R.K., Greff, K., Schmidhuber, J.: Highway networks. arXiv preprint arXiv:1505.00387 (2015)
21. Suganuma, M., Shirakawa, S., Nagao, T.: A genetic programming approach to designing convolutional neural network architectures. In: Proceedings of the Genetic and Evolutionary Computation Conference, pp. 497–504 (2017)
22. Sun, Y., Xue, B., Zhang, M., Yen, G.G., Lv, J.: Automatically designing CNN architectures using the genetic algorithm for image classification. IEEE Trans. Cybern. **50**, 3840–3854 (2020)
23. Szegedy, C., et al.: Going deeper with convolutions. In: Proceedings of the IEEE Conference on Computer Vision and Pattern Recognition, pp. 1–9 (2015)
24. Ulhaq, A., Born, J., Khan, A., Gomes, D.P.S., Chakraborty, S., Paul, M.: Covid-19 control by computer vision approaches: a survey. IEEE Access **8**, 179437–179456 (2020)
25. Wang, B., Sun, Y., Xue, B., Zhang, M.: Evolving deep convolutional neural networks by variable-length particle swarm optimization for image classification. In: 2018 IEEE Congress on Evolutionary Computation (CEC), pp. 1–8. IEEE (2018)
26. Wang, D., Li, M., Gong, C., Chandra, V.: Attentivenas: improving neural architecture search via attentive sampling. In: Proceedings of the IEEE/CVF Conference on Computer Vision and Pattern Recognition, pp. 6418–6427 (2021)

27. Yu, F., Koltun, V.: Multi-scale context aggregation by dilated convolutions. arXiv preprint arXiv:1511.07122 (2015)
28. Yuan, G., Xue, B., Zhang, M.: A graph-based approach to automatic convolutional neural network construction for image classification. In: 2020 35th International Conference on Image and Vision Computing New Zealand (IVCNZ), pp. 1–6. IEEE (2020)
29. Zhong, Z., Yan, J., Wu, W., Shao, J., Liu, C.L.: Practical block-wise neural network architecture generation. In: Proceedings of the IEEE Conference on Computer Vision and Pattern Recognition, pp. 2423–2432 (2018)
30. Zoph, B., Le, Q.V.: Neural architecture search with reinforcement learning. arXiv preprint arXiv:1611.01578 (2016)
31. Zoph, B., Vasudevan, V., Shlens, J., Le, Q.V.: Learning transferable architectures for scalable image recognition. In: Proceedings of the IEEE Conference on Computer Vision and Pattern Recognition, pp. 8697–8710 (2018)

Adaptive Relaxations for Multistage Robust Optimization

Michael Hartisch$^{(\boxtimes)}$

University of Siegen, 57072 Siegen, Germany
`michael.hartisch@uni-siegen.de`

Abstract. Multistage robust optimization problems can be interpreted as two-person zero-sum games between two players. We exploit this game-like nature and utilize a game tree search in order to solve quantified integer programs (QIPs). In this algorithmic environment relaxations are repeatedly called to asses the quality of a branching variable and for the generation of bounds. A useful relaxation, however, must be well balanced with regard to its quality and its computing time. We present two relaxations that incorporate scenarios from the uncertainty set, whereby the considered set of scenarios is continuously adapted according to the latest information gathered during the search process. Using selection, assignment, and runway scheduling problems as a testbed, we show the impact of our findings.

Keywords: Multistage robust optimization · Game tree search · Relaxations · Quantified integer programming

1 Introduction

Most aspects of decision making are highly affected by uncertainty. In order to take such uncertainty into account different methodologies have been developed, such as stochastic programming [25] or robust optimization [4]. In this setting, multistage models can be used to obtain an even more realistic description of the underlying problem. While there are several real multistage stochastic approaches (e.g. [23,30]), extensions to robust optimization with more than two stages only recently gained more attention (e.g. [5,11]). Due to their PSPACE-complete nature [32], tackling multistage robust problems is a very complicated task and for the human mind even comprehending a solution is rather challenging. Solution approaches include approximation techniques [6], dynamic programming [36], and solving the deterministic equivalent problem (DEP), also referred to as robust counterpart [4], often using decomposition techniques (e.g. [38]). We, on the other hand, exploit the similarity of multistage robust problems with two-person zero-sum games and apply a game tree search to solve quantified

This research was partially funded by the Deutsche Forschungsgemeinschaft (DFG, German Research Foundation) - 399489083.

D. N. Pham et al. (Eds.): PRICAI 2021, LNAI 13031, pp. 485–499, 2021.
https://doi.org/10.1007/978-3-030-89188-6_36

integer programs (QIPs) [14,37]. QIPs are integer linear programs with ordered variables that are either existentially or universally quantified, and provide a convenient framework for multistage robust optimization, allowing polyhedral or even decision-dependent uncertainty sets [21]. The very intuitive approach of applying a game tree search in order to solve the very compact QIP formulation paves the way for large multistage problems: a recent computational study showed that solving robust discrete problems with multiple stages is well within the reach of current computational prowess [17].

As in any tree search algorithm, a rapid but high-quality assessment of the potential of different subtrees is crucial for the search process. This can be done by relaxing some problem conditions in order to obtain a bound on the optimal value of a (sub)problem. In mixed integer linear programming (MIP), variants of the linear programming (LP)-relaxation of a problem are employed [3]. Equivalently for QIPs, the quantified linear programming (QLP)-relaxation can be used. But its DEP's size remains exponentially large, even when tackled with decomposition techniques [28]. By further relaxing the variables' quantification the LP-relaxation of a QIP arises, which, however, completely neglects the problem's multistage and uncertain nature. In order to restore the robust nature of the problem, we exploit that a solution must cope with *any* uncertain scenario: fixing (originally) universally quantified variables in this LP-relaxation yields a very powerful tool in our tree search algorithm. Furthermore, we show that if only a small subset of the uncertainty set is considered in the QLP-relaxation, the correseponding DEP remains small enough to yield an effective relaxation. This local approximation, which has similarites to sampling techniques [18], is utilized to eventually obtain the optimal solution for a multistage robust optimization problem.

For both enhanced relaxations the selection of incorporated scenarios crucially affects their effectiveness, i.e. having reasonable knowledge of which universal variable assignments are particularly vicious can massively boost the search process. We partially rely on existing heuristics, developed to analyze and find such promising assignments in a game tree search environment [2,35] as well as for solving SAT problems [31]. As these heuristic evaluations change over time, the relaxations adapt based on newly gathered information.

In Sect. 2 we introduce the basics of quantified programming and outline the used game tree search. In Sect. 3 we present the utilized relaxations and we illustrate the strength of our approach in a computational study in Sect. 4, before we conclude in Sect. 5.

2 Quantified Programming

In the following, we formally introduce quantified integer programming. [19] can be consulted for a more detailed discussion.

2.1 Basics of Quantified Integer Programming

A QIP can be interpreted as a two-person zero-sum game between an *existential player* setting the existentially quantified variables and a *universal player* setting the universally quantified variables. The variables are set in consecutive order according to the variable sequence $x_1, \ldots, x_n$. For each variable x_j its domain is given by $\mathcal{L}_j = \{y \in \mathbb{Z} \mid l_j \leq y \leq u_j\} \neq \emptyset$ and the domain of the entire variable vector is $\mathcal{L} = \{\boldsymbol{y} \in \mathbb{Z}^n \mid \forall j \in \{1, \ldots, n\} : y_j \in \mathcal{L}_j\}$. In the following, vectors are always written in bold font and the transpose sign for the scalar product between vectors is dropped for ease of notation. Let $\boldsymbol{Q} \in \{\exists, \forall\}^n$ denote the vector of quantifiers. We call each maximal consecutive subsequence in $\boldsymbol{Q}$ consisting of identical quantifiers a *block*. The quantifier corresponding to the i-th quantifier block is given by $Q^{(i)} \in \{\exists, \forall\}$. Let $\beta \in \{1, \ldots, n\}$ denote the number of variable blocks. With $\mathcal{L}^{(i)}$ we denote the corresponding domain of the i-th variable block as in $\mathcal{L}$. At each move $\boldsymbol{x}^{(i)} \in \mathcal{L}^{(i)}$, the corresponding player knows the settings of $\boldsymbol{x}^{(1)}, \ldots, \boldsymbol{x}^{(i-1)}$ before taking her decision. Each fixed vector $\boldsymbol{x} \in \mathcal{L}$, that is, when the existential player has fixed the existentially quantified variables and the universal player has fixed the universally quantified variables, is called *a play*. If $\boldsymbol{x}$ satisfies the *existential constraint system* $A^\exists \boldsymbol{x} \leq \boldsymbol{b}^\exists$, the existential player pays $\boldsymbol{cx}$ to the universal player. If $\boldsymbol{x}$ does not satisfy $A^\exists \boldsymbol{x} \leq \boldsymbol{b}^\exists$, we say *the existential player loses* and the payoff is $+\infty$. Therefore, it is the existential player's primary goal to ensure the fulfillment of the existential constraint system, while the universal player tries to violate some constraints. If the existential player is able to ensure that all constraints are fulfilled he tries to minimize $\boldsymbol{cx}$, whereas the universal player tries to maximize her payoff.

We consider QIPs with polyhedral uncertainty [19,20] where a *universal constraint system* $A^\forall \boldsymbol{x} \leq \boldsymbol{b}^\forall$ is used. The main goal of the universal player becomes satisfying this universal constraint system and therefore the universally quantified variables are restricted to a polytope. Here, in contrast to a decision-dependent uncertainty set [21], the submatrix of $A^\forall$ corresponding to existentially quantified variables is zero. Therefore, the system $A^\forall \boldsymbol{x} \leq \boldsymbol{b}^\forall$ restricts universally quantified variables in such way that their range only depends on previous universal variables. In particular, a universal variable assignment must not make it impossible to satisfy the system $A^\forall \boldsymbol{x} \leq \boldsymbol{b}^\forall$.

Definition 1 (QIP with Polyhedral Uncertainty). *Let $\mathcal{L}$ and $\boldsymbol{Q}$ be given with $Q^{(1)} = Q^{(\beta)} = \exists$. Let $\boldsymbol{c} \in \mathbb{Q}^n$ be the vector of objective coefficients, for which $\boldsymbol{c}^{(i)}$ denotes the vector of coefficients belonging to block i. Let $\mathcal{D} = \{\boldsymbol{x} \in \mathcal{L} \mid A^\forall \boldsymbol{x} \leq \boldsymbol{b}^\forall\} \neq \emptyset$ where all entries of $A^\forall$ that correspond to existentially quantified variables are zero. The term $\boldsymbol{Q} \circ \boldsymbol{x} \in \mathcal{D}$ with the component-wise binding operator $\circ$ denotes the* quantification sequence $Q^{(1)}\boldsymbol{x}^{(1)} \in \mathcal{D}^{(1)} \ Q^{(2)}\boldsymbol{x}^{(2)} \in \mathcal{D}^{(2)}(\boldsymbol{x}^{(1)}) \ \ldots \ Q^{(\beta)}\boldsymbol{x}^{(\beta)} \in \mathcal{D}^{(\beta)}(\boldsymbol{x}^{(1)}, \ldots, \boldsymbol{x}^{(\beta-1)})$ *such that every quantifier $Q^{(i)}$ binds the variables $\boldsymbol{x}^{(i)}$ of block i ranging in their domain $\mathcal{D}^{(i)}(\boldsymbol{x}^{(1)}, \ldots, \boldsymbol{x}^{(i-1)})$, with $\mathcal{D}^{(i)}(\tilde{\boldsymbol{x}}^{(1)}, \ldots, \tilde{\boldsymbol{x}}^{(i-1)}) =$*

$$
\begin{cases}
\mathcal{L}^{(i)} & \text{if } Q^{(i)} = \exists \\
\{\boldsymbol{y} \in \mathcal{L}^{(i)} \mid \exists \boldsymbol{x} = (\tilde{\boldsymbol{x}}^{(1)}, \ldots, \tilde{\boldsymbol{x}}^{(i-1)}, \boldsymbol{y}, \boldsymbol{x}^{(i+1)}, \ldots, \boldsymbol{x}^{(\beta)}) \in \mathcal{D}\} & \text{if } Q^{(i)} = \forall.
\end{cases}
$$

We call

$$\min_{\boldsymbol{x}^{(1)} \in \mathcal{D}^{(1)}} \left(\boldsymbol{c}^{(1)}\boldsymbol{x}^{(1)} + \max_{\boldsymbol{x}^{(2)} \in \mathcal{D}^{(2)}} \left(\boldsymbol{c}^{(2)}\boldsymbol{x}^{(2)} + \min_{\boldsymbol{x}^{(3)} \in \mathcal{D}^{(3)}} \left(\boldsymbol{c}^{(3)}\boldsymbol{x}^{(3)} + \ldots \min_{\boldsymbol{x}^{(\beta)} \in \mathcal{D}^{(\beta)}} \boldsymbol{c}^{(\beta)}\boldsymbol{x}^{(\beta)} \right) \right) \right)$$

$$s.t.\ \boldsymbol{Q} \circ \boldsymbol{x} \in \mathcal{D} : A^{\exists}\boldsymbol{x} \leq \boldsymbol{b}^{\exists}$$

a QIP with polyhedral uncertainty given by the tuple $(A^{\exists}, A^{\forall}, \boldsymbol{b}^{\exists}, \boldsymbol{b}^{\forall}, \boldsymbol{c}, \mathcal{L}, \boldsymbol{Q})$.

Note that the domains $\mathcal{D}^{(i)}(\boldsymbol{x}^{(1)}, \ldots, \boldsymbol{x}^{(i-1)})$ in the quantification sequence force the universally quantified variables to fulfill $A^{\forall}\boldsymbol{x} \leq \boldsymbol{b}^{\forall}$. We use $\mathcal{L}_{\exists}$ to describe the domain of the existentially quantified variables, given by their variables bounds as in $\mathcal{L}$. $\mathcal{L}_{\forall} \neq \emptyset$ is the domain of universally quantified variables, i.e. the uncertainty set, given by their domain and the universal constraint system. $\boldsymbol{x}_{\exists}$ and $\boldsymbol{x}_{\forall}$ denote the vectors only containing the existentially and universally quantified variables of game $\boldsymbol{x} \in \mathcal{D}$, respectively. We call $\boldsymbol{x}_{\forall} \in \mathcal{L}_{\forall}$ a *scenario* and refer to a partially filled universal variable vector as a *subscenario*. Additionally, we use $\mathcal{L}_{relax}$ to describe the domain given by $\mathcal{L}$ without the integrality condition.

Example 2. *We consider an instance with* $n = 6$ *binary variables, i.e.* $\mathcal{L} = \{0, 1\}^6$. *Let* $Q = (\exists, \forall, \exists, \forall, \exists, \exists)$ *and thus* $\beta = 5$ *with the second and fourth variable being universally quantified. The universal constraint system contains the single constraint* $x_2 + x_4 \geq 1$. *The objective function, the quantification sequence as well as the existential constraint system are given as follows (the min/max alternation in the objective and the domains in the quantification sequence are omitted):*

$$\min \quad 2x_1 + 2x_2 - 2x_3 - 2x_4 + 3x_5 + x_6$$
$$s.t. \quad \exists x_1\ \forall x_2\ \exists x_3\ \forall x_4\ \exists x_5\ \exists x_6 :$$
$$x_1 + x_2 + x_5 \geq 1$$
$$x_3 + x_4 + x_6 \geq 1$$

The optimal first stage solution is $x_1 = 0$ *and the optimal play, i.e. the assignment of the variables if both players play optimally, is given by* $\tilde{\boldsymbol{x}} = (0, 1, 1, 0, 0, 0)$. *Hence the optimal worst-case objective value is* 0 *and therefore the existential player has a strategy that ensures an objective value less than or equal to* 0. *Note that for the instance without the universal constraint* $x_2 + x_4 \geq 1$, *even though* $x_1 = 0$ *remains the optimal first stage solution, the optimal strategy can only ensure an objective value of* 1.

2.2 Solving QIP via Game Tree Search

A game tree can be used to represent the chronological order of all possible moves, given by the quantification sequence $\boldsymbol{Q} \circ \boldsymbol{x} \in \mathcal{D}$. The nodes in the game tree represent a partially assigned variable vector and branches correspond to assignments of variables according to their variable domain. A solution of a QIP is a so-called winning (existential) strategy, that defines how to react to each legal move by the universal player, in order to ensure $A^\exists x \leq b^\exists$. Hence, a solution is a subtree of the game tree with an exponential number of leaves with respect to the number of universal variables. If no such strategy exists the QIP is *infeasible*. If there is more than one solution, the objective function aims for a certain (the "best") one, whereat the value of a strategy is defined via the worst-case payoff at its leaves (see Stockman's Theorem [34]). The play $\tilde{x}$ resulting in this leaf is called the *principal variation* [8], which is the sequence of variable assignments being chosen during optimal play by both players.

The heart of our search-based solver for 0/1-QIPs [13] is an arithmetic linear constraint database together with an alpha-beta algorithm, which has been successfully used in gaming programs, e.g. chess programs for many years [12,26]. The solver proceeds in two phases in order to find an optimal solution:

- feasibility phase: It is checked whether the instance has any solution. The solver acts like a quantified boolean formula (QBF) solver [7,27] with some extra abilities. Technically it performs a null window search [33].
- optimization phase: The solution space is explored via alpha-beta algorithm in order to find the provable optimal solution.

The alpha-beta algorithm is enhanced by non-chronological backtracking and backward implication [10,15]: when a contradiction is detected a reason in form of a clause is added to the constraint database and the search returns to the node where the found contradiction is no longer imminent. The solver deals with constraint learning on the so-called primal side as known from SAT- and QBF-solving (e.g. [16,29]), as well as with constraint learning on the dual side known from MIP (e.g. [9]). Several other techniques are implemented, e.g. restart strategies [24], branching heuristics [1], and pruning mechanisms [22]. Furthermore, relaxations are heavily used during the optimization phase: at every search node a relaxation is called in order to asses the quality of a branching decision, the satisfiability of the existential constraint system or for the generation of bounds.

3 Enhanced Relaxations

3.1 Relaxations for QIPs

In case of a quantified program, besides relaxing the integrality of variables, the quantification sequence can be altered by changing the order or quantification of the variables. An LP-relaxation of a QIP can be built by dropping the integrality and also dropping universal quantification, i.e. each variable is considered to be an existential variable with continuous domain. One major drawback of this LP-relaxation is that the worst-case perspective is lost by freeing the constraint system from having to be satisfied for any assignment of the universally quantified variables: transferring the responsibility of universal variables to the existential player and solving the single-player game has nothing to do with the worst-case outcome in most cases. In order to strengthen this relaxation we use that for *any* assignment of the universally quantified variables the constraint system must be fulfilled. Hence, fixing universally quantified variables according to some element of $\mathcal{L}_\forall$ still yields a valid relaxation. This can be interpreted as knowing the opponent moves beforehand and adapting one's own moves for this special play.

Definition 3 (LP-Relaxation with Fixed Scenario). *Let* $P = (A^\exists, A^\forall, b^\exists, b^\forall, c, \mathcal{L}, \mathcal{Q})$ *and let* $\hat{x}_\forall \in \mathcal{L}_\forall$ *be a fixed scenario. The LP*

$$\min \left\{ cx \mid x \in \mathcal{L}_{relax} \wedge x_\forall = \hat{x}_\forall \wedge A^\exists x \leq b^\exists \right\}$$

is called the LP-relaxation with fixed scenario $\hat{x}_\forall$ *of* P.

Proposition 4. *Let* $P = (A^\exists, A^\forall, b^\exists, b^\forall, c, \mathcal{L}, \mathcal{Q})$ *and let* R *be the corresponding LP-relaxation with fixed scenario* $\hat{x}_\forall \in \mathcal{L}_\forall$. *Then the following holds:*

a) *If* R *is infeasible, then also* P *is infeasible.*
b) *If* R *is feasible with optimal value* z_R, *then either* P *is infeasible or* P *is feasible with optimal value* $z_P \geq z_R$, *i.e.* z_R *constitutes a lower bound.*

Proof.

a) Let $A_\exists^\exists$ and $A_\forall^\exists$ be the submatrices of $A^\exists$ consisting of the columns corresponding to the existentially and universally quantified variables, respectively. If R is infeasible then

$$\nexists x_\exists \in \mathcal{L}_\exists : \ A_\exists^\exists x_\exists \leq b^\exists - A_\forall^\exists \hat{x}_\forall \,,$$

and since $\hat{x}_\forall \in \mathcal{L}_\forall$ there cannot exist a winning strategy for P. As a gaming argument we can interpret this the following way: If there is some move sequence of the opponent we cannot react to in a victorious way—even if we know the sequence beforehand—the game is lost for sure.

b) Let $z_R = c\hat{x}$ be the optimal value of R, and let $\hat{x}_\exists$ be the corresponding fixation of the existential variables. It is

$$\hat{x}_\exists = \arg\min_{x_\exists \in \mathcal{L}_\exists} \left\{ c_\exists x_\exists \mid A_\exists^\exists x_\exists \leq b^\exists - A_\forall^\exists \hat{x}_\forall \right\} . \tag{1}$$

If P is feasible, scenario $\hat{x}_\forall$ must also be present in the corresponding winning strategy. Let $\tilde{x}$ be the corresponding play, i.e. $\tilde{x}_\forall = \hat{x}_\forall$. With Eq. (1) obviously $z_R = c\hat{x} \leq c\tilde{x}$ and thus with Stockman's Theorem [34] $z_R \leq z_P$.

As we will show in Sect. 4 adding a scenario to the LP-relaxation already massively speeds up the search process compared to the use of the standard LP-relaxation. However, partially incorporating the multistage nature into a relaxation should yield even better bounds. Therefore, we reintroduce the original order of the variables while only taking a subset of scenarios $S \subseteq \mathcal{L}_\forall$ into account.

Definition 5 (S-Relaxation). *Given* $P = (A^\exists, A^\forall, b^\exists, b^\forall, c, \mathcal{L}, Q)$. *Let* $S \subseteq \mathcal{L}_\forall$ *and let* $\mathcal{L}_S = \{x \in \mathcal{L}_{relax} \mid x_\forall \in S\}$. *We call*

$$\min_{x^{(1)} \in \mathcal{L}_S^{(1)}} \left(c^{(1)} x^{(1)} + \max_{x^{(2)} \in \mathcal{L}_S^{(2)}} \left(c^{(2)} x^{(2)} + \min_{x^{(3)} \in \mathcal{L}_S^{(3)}} \left(c^{(3)} x^{(3)} + \ldots \min_{x^{(\beta)} \in \mathcal{L}_S^{(\beta)}} c^{(\beta)} x^{(\beta)} \right) \right) \right)$$

$$\text{s.t. } Q \circ x \in \mathcal{L}_S : \; A^\exists x \le b^\exists \tag{2}$$

the S-relaxation of P.

Proposition 6. *Let* $P = (A^\exists, A^\forall, b^\exists, b^\forall, c, \mathcal{L}, Q)$ *be feasible and let* R *be the S-relaxation with* $\emptyset \neq S \subseteq \mathcal{L}_\forall$ *and optimal value* $\tilde{z}_R$. *Then* $\tilde{z}_R$ *is a lower bound on the optimal value* $\tilde{z}_P$ *of P, i.e.* $\tilde{z}_R \le \tilde{z}_P$.

Proof. Again we use a gaming argument: with $S \subseteq \mathcal{L}_\forall$ the universal player is restricted to a subset of her moves in problem R, while the existential player is no longer restricted to use integer values. Furthermore, any strategy for P can be mapped to a strategy for the restricted game R. Hence, the optimal strategy for R is either part of a strategy for P or it is an even better strategy, as the existential player does not have to cope with the entire variety of the universal player's moves. Therefore, $\tilde{z}_R \le \tilde{z}_P$.

In general, $\mathcal{L}_\forall$ has exponential size with respect to the number of universally quantified variables. Therefore, the main idea is to keep S a rather small subset of $\mathcal{L}_\forall$. This way the DEP of the S-relaxation—which is a standard LP— remains easy to handle for standard LP solvers.

Example 7. *Consider the following binary QIP (The min/max alternation in the objective is omitted for clarity):*

$$\min -2x_1 + x_2 - x_3 - x_4$$
$$\text{s.t. } \exists x_1 \, \forall x_2 \, \exists x_3 \, \forall x_4 \in \{0,1\}^4 :$$
$$x_1 + x_2 + x_3 + x_4 \le 3$$
$$-x_2 - x_3 + x_4 \le 0$$

The optimal first-stage solution is $\tilde{x}_1 = 1$, *the principal variation is* $(1,1,0,0)$ *and hence the optimal value is* -1. *Let* $S = \{(1,0),(1,1)\}$ *be a set of scenarios.*

Table 1. Solutions of the single LP-relaxations with fixed scenarios.

Scenario	$x_2 = 1, x_4 = 0$	$x_2 = 1, x_4 = 1$
	$\min -2x_1 - x_3 + 1$	$\min -2x_1 - x_3 + 0$
Relaxation	s.t. $\quad x_1 + x_3 \le 2$	s.t. $\quad x_1 + x_3 \le 1$
	$\quad -x_3 \le 1$	$\quad -x_3 \le 0$
Solution	$x_1 = 1, x_3 = 1$	$x_1 = 1, x_3 = 0$
Objective	-2	-2

*The two LP-relaxations with fixed scenario accoring to the two scenarios in S
are shown in Table 1. Both yield the optimal first stage solution of setting x_1 to
one. Now consider the DEP of the S-relaxation in which $x_{3(\tilde{x}_2)}$ represents the
assignment of x_3 after x_2 is set to $\tilde{x}_2$:*

$$
\begin{aligned}
&\min\ k\\
&\text{s.t.} \left.\begin{array}{r}
-2x_1 -x_{3(1)} +1 \le k\\
x_1 +x_{3(1)}\quad\ \le 2\\
-x_{3(1)}\quad\ \le 1
\end{array}\right\} \text{Scenario } (1,0)\\
&\left.\begin{array}{r}
-2x_1 -x_{3(1)} +0 \le k\\
x_1 +x_{3(1)}\quad\ \le 1\\
-x_{3(1)}\quad\ \le 0
\end{array}\right\} \text{Scenario } (1,1)\\
&\quad\ x_1,\ x_{3(1)} \in [0,1]
\end{aligned}
$$

*In the S-relaxation it is ensured that variables following equal sub-scenarios are
set to the same value. As x_2 is set to 1 in each considered scenario in S, x_3
must be set to the same value in both cases. The solution of the DEP is $x_1 = 1$,
$x_{3(1)} = 0$ and $k =\ 1$. Thus, the S-relaxation yields the lower bound -1 for the
original QIP. This is not only a better bound than the one obtained by the two
LP-relaxations with individually fixed scenarios but it also happens to be a tight
bound.*

3.2   Scenario Selection

Both for the LP-relaxation with fixed scenario as well as the S-relaxation the
selection of scenarios is crucial. For the S-relaxation additionally the size of
the scenario set S affects its performance, in particular if too many scenarios
are chosen, solving the relaxation might consume too much time. We use three
heuristics to collect information on universal variables during the search:

VSIDS Heuristic [31]. Each variable in each polarity has a counter, initialized
to 0. When a clause is added, due to a found conflict, the counter associated with
each literal is incremented. Periodically, all counters are divided by a constant.

Killer Heuristic [2]. When a conflict is found during the search the current
assignment of universal variables—and thus the (sub)scenario leading to this
conflict—is stored in the `killer` vector. This is a short-term information and is
overwritten as soon as a new conflict is found.

Scenario Frequency. For each scenario and subscenario the frequency of their
occurrence during the search is stored.

The LP-relaxation with fixed scenario is implemented as follows: before calling the LP solver in a decision node, all variable bounds must be updated according to the current node anyway. When doing so (yet unassigned) universally
quantified variables are set as in Algorithm 1. Hence, the considered scenario is
adapted in every decision node based on the latest heuristic information.

Algorithm 1. Building a scenario

1: **for** each universal variable block $i \in \{1, \ldots, \beta \mid Q^{(\beta)} = \forall\}$ **do**
2:     **for** each unassigned variable x_j in block i, in random order **do**
3:         **if** killer[j] $\not/$ undefined then Value $-$ killer[j]
4:         **else** Value $= \arg\max_{p \in \{0,1\}}$ VSIDS$[j][p]$
5:         **if** setting x_j to Value is legal according to $\mathcal{D}^{(i)}$ **then** $x_j =$ Value
6:         **else** $x_j = 1 -$ Value

The S-relaxation is adapted at each restart. The scenario set S is rebuilt by considering the $\bar{S} \in \mathbb{N}$ most frequently used (sub)scenarios. Subscenarios are extended to a full scenario according to Algorithm 1. Even though starting with $\bar{S}$ (sub)scenarios, S often contains fewer unique scenarios, as extending a subscenario may result in a scenario already contained in S.

Furthermore, our implementation merges the LP-relaxation with fixed scenario into the S-relaxation: the final relaxation takes all scenarios in the scenario set S, as well as one additional scenario that can be updated at each decision node into account. Hence, the used relaxation in fact reflects $|S| + 1$ scenarios and in case of $S = \emptyset$ the LP-relaxation with fixed scenario remains. The DEP of this final relaxation is built and solved with an external LP solver.

The S-relaxation is currently only used while the search is in the very first variable block, i.e. as soon as all variables of the first block are assigned, only the LP-relaxation with fixed scenario is used. The reason why this relaxation is no longer used in later variable blocks is that then universally quantified variables are already fixed according to the current search node. Hence, some scenarios in S are no longer relevant as they refer to other parts of the search tree. Therefore, in order to use the S-relaxation in higher blocks it needs to be rebuilt each time a universal variable block is bypassed.

4 Experiments

4.1 Problem Descriptions

We conduct experiments on three different QIPs with polyhedral uncertainty. For a more detailed discussion on the problem formulations we refer to [19].

Multistage Robust Selection. The goal is to select p out of n items with minimal costs. In an initial (existential) decision stage a set of items can be selected for fixed costs. Then, in a universal decision stage, one of $N \in \mathbb{N}$ cost scenario is disclosed. In the subsequent existential decision stage further items can be selected for the revealed costs. The latter two stages are repeated iteratively $T \in \mathbb{N}$ times. Hence, there are $2T + 1$ variable blocks.

Multistage Robust Assignment. The goal is to find a perfect matching for a bipartite graph $G = (V, E)$, $V = A \cup B$, $n = |A| = |B|$, with minimal costs. In an initial (existential) decision stage a set of edges can be selected for fixed costs. Then, in a universal decision stage, one of $N \in \mathbb{N}$ cost scenario is disclosed. In the subsequent existential decision stage further edges can be selected for the revealed costs. Those two stages are repeated iteratively $T \in \mathbb{N}$ times. Both for the selection and the assignment problem, a universal constraint system is used to force the universally quantified variables to reveal exactly one scenario per period.

Multistage Robust Runway Scheduling. Each airplane $i \in A$ has to be assigned to exactly one time slot $j \in S$ and at most $b \in \mathbb{N}$ airplanes can be assigned to one time slot (as there are only b runways). As soon as the (uncertain) time window in which the airplane can land is disclosed by universally quantified variables, the initial plan has to be adapted. The goal is to find an initial schedule that can be adapted according to the later disclosed time windows with optimal worst-case costs, as for each slot that the airplane is moved away from its originally planned time slot, a cost is incurred. The time window disclosure occurs in $T \in \mathbb{N}$ periods: the airplanes are partitioned into T groups and after the initial schedule is fixed the time windows are disclosed for one group after the other. After each disclosure the schedule for the current group of airplanes has to be fixed right away, before knowing the time windows for the subsequent groups. The universal constraint system contains a single constraint, demanding that the disclosed time windows are comprised of 3 time slots on average.

4.2   Computational Results

Our solver utilizes CPLEX (12.6.1) as its black-box LP solver to solve the relaxations and all experiments were run with AMD Ryzen 9 5900X processors.

First we provide details on the benefit of utilizing the LP-relaxation with fixed scenario as given in Definition 3 compared to the standard LP at each decision node. Therefore, we consider the following testset:

- 350 selection instances with $n = 10$ items, $N = 4$ scenarios per period and $T \in \{1, \ldots, 7\}$ periods
- 1350 assignment instances with $n \in \{4, 5, 6\}$, $N \in \{2^1, 2^2, 2^3\}$ scenarios per period and $T \in \{1, \ldots, 3\}$ periods
- 270 runway scheduling instances with $A \in \{4, 5, 6\}$ planes, $b = 3$ runways, $S \in \{5, \ldots, 10\}$ time slot and $T \in \{1, \ldots, 3\}$ periods

In Table 2, as one of our major results, the overall runtimes when using the basic LP-relaxation and the LP-relaxation with fixed scenario are displayed. In each case, explicitly setting the universally quantified variables to a fixed scenario results in a massive speedup that is most impressive for the selection instances. This emphasizes, that partially incorporating the worst-case nature of the underlying problem into the basic LP-relaxation is clearly beneficial and does not have any negative side effects: the bounds of the variables in the LP-relaxation have to be updated at each search node anyway and fixing the universally quantified variables even decreases the number of free variables in the resulting LP.

Table 2. Overall runtime (in seconds) when only using the standard LP-relaxation vs. the LP-relaxation with fixed scenario.

Used relaxation	Selection	Assignment	Runway
LP	29 501	7 152	12 902
LP with fixed scenario	348	837	4 520

We now investigate how the use of the more sophisticated S-relaxation in the first variable block changes the solver's behavior. Therefore, the scenario set S is built from $\bar{S} = 2^i$ (sub)scenarios, with $i \in \{0, \ldots, 6\}$. In case of $\bar{S} = 0$ only the LP-relaxation with fixed scenario is utilized in the first variable block. The used testset consists of the following instances

- 1050 selection instances with $n \in \{10, 20, 30\}$ items, $N = 4$ scenarios per period and $T \in \{1, \ldots, 7\}$ periods
- 450 assignment instances with $n \in \{7\}$, $N \in \{2^1, 2^2, 2^3\}$ scenarios per period and $T \in \{1, \ldots, 3\}$ periods
- 360 runway scheduling instances with $A \in \{4, 5, 6, 7\}$ planes, $b = 3$ runways, $S \in \{5, \ldots, 10\}$ time slot and $T \in \{1, \ldots, 3\}$ periods

As one indicator we consider the number of decision nodes visited during the optimization phase of the search. We denote $N(i, \bar{S})$ the number of visited decision nodes when solving instance i with $\bar{S}$ scenarios used to build the corresponding S-relaxation. We compare each run with $\bar{S} = 2^i$ to the basic run with $\bar{S} = 0$ by considering the relative difference $D_r(i) = \frac{N(i,\bar{S})-N(i,0)}{\max(N(i,\bar{S}),N(i,0))}$. If $N(i, \bar{S}) - N(i, 0) < 0$, i.e. if fewer decision nodes were visited while using the S-relaxation, $D_r(i)$ is negative, with its absolute value indicating the percentage savings. Similarly, if $N(i, \bar{S}) - N(i, 0) > 0$, $D_r(i)$ is positive. The data on all instances is cumulated in Fig. 1 showing the corresponding box plots . It can be seen that the median of the relative difference values is always negative and tends to decrease when more scenarios are considered in S, i.e. the larger the scenario set the fewer decision nodes have to be visited during the search. Note that compared to the box plots for the selection and runway instances, for the assignment instances the upper whisker remains at a rather high level. But does a decreasing

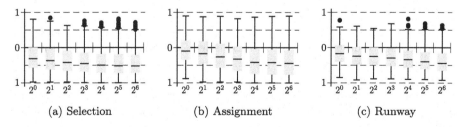

(a) Selection   (b) Assignment   (c) Runway

Fig. 1. Boxplots of the D_r values for all three testset and $\bar{S} \in \{2^0, \ldots, 2^6\}$

number of visited decision nodes also result in a lower runtime? For now consider
the columns of Table 3 representing the heuristic scenario selection as presented
in Sect. 3.2. Both for the selection and the runway scheduling problem the overall
runtimes tend to decrease when $\bar{S}$ increases. Compared to only using the LP-
relaxation with fixed scenario ($\bar{S} = 0$), the runtimes decreased up to about 30%
and 35% for the selection and runway scheduling instances, respectively. The
slightly increased runtime for $\bar{S} = 64$ indicates that the solution time of such a
large relaxation can no longer be compensated by fewer visited decision nodes.
For the assignment instances, however, the overall runtime increases, up to a
factor of four times the runtime when solely using the LP-relaxation with fixed
scenario. Hence, even though fewer nodes are visited, the time it takes to process
and generate information at these nodes increases considerably for this type of
problem.

Table 3. Overall runtime (in seconds) when using the S-relaxation with heuristic and
random scenario selection

$\bar{S}$	Selection instances		Assignment instances		Runway instances	
	Heuristic	Random	Heuristic	Random	Heuristic	Random
0	12 561	53 348	2 091	1 853	33 335	32 401
2^0	11 324	35 316	2 111	1 865	29 313	30 418
2^1	9 900	30 970	2 022	2 046	25 876	26 412
2^2	9 700	31 158	2 210	2 232	25 876	26 101
2^3	9 394	29 087	2 220	2 708	23 915	24 795
2^4	9 030	27 503	2 931	3 718	23 958	24 860
2^5	8 843	26 857	4 223	7 300	21 788	26 777
2^6	9 149	26 590	8 632	17 400	23 073	30 292

In Table 3 we additionally provide information on how well our scenario building routine performs on the considered testset. Therefore, instead of extending
the $\bar{S}$ most frequently visited (sub)scenarios via Algorithm 1, the scenario set
S now contains $\bar{S}$ random scenarios. Similiarly, for the LP-relaxation with fixed
scenario, we replace the heuristic Value selection in lines 3 and 4 of Algorithm 1
by randomly assigning the value 0 or 1. Note, however, that even though the
killer and VSIDS information is neglected while building the relaxation, it is still
utilized in other situations during the search. The overall runtimes are shown in
the according columns of Table 3. For the selection problem, randomly selecting
the scenario results in a runtime about three times longer compared to using the
heuristic selection process. For the runway instances, our heuristic also slightly
outperforms the use of random scenarios. For the assignment instances the random scenario selection tends to be more favorable when only few scenarios are
involved.

5   Conclusion and Outlook

We investigated how adaptive relaxations influence our search-based solution algorithm for multistage robust optimization problems. Our experimental results show that incorporating a single scenario in the standard LP-relaxation significantly speeds up the search process and clearly dominates the basic LP-relaxation. Furthermore, the use of the S-relaxation which incorporates a subset of scenarios in a slim DEP, considerably decreases the number of visited nodes, even if only utilized in the very first variable block. While this smaller search space also resulted in a faster solution time for multistage selection and runway scheduling problems, the solution time tended to increase for multistage assignment instances. Additionally, we showed that our scenario selection heuristic outperforms a random scenario selection.

Several research questions arise from the presented experimental results. Is it possible to improve the heuristic scenario selection? Currently our heuristic focuses on including seemingly harmful scenarios but does not consider the diversity of the scenario set S, which might be one reason why using random scenarios already works quite well on specific problems. In contrast to our currently implemented search-information-based scenario selection heuristic, we find it interesting to deploy AI methods in order to classify scenarios as relevant and irrelevant for general QIP. Additionally, relevant characteristics of instances have to be found, in order to dynamically adjust the size of the used scenario set S. Furthermore, deploying the S-relaxation in all—not only the very first—variable blocks is a very promising yet challenging task, as the implementation of such a frequently modified S-relaxation must be done carefully. In this case having the ability to update all considered scenarios in each decision node is also of interest, in particular as our results showed that having few scenarios in the relaxation is already very beneficial.

References

1. Achterberg, T., Koch, T., Martin, A.: Branching rules revisited. Oper. Res. Lett. **33**(1), 42–54 (2005)
2. Akl, S., Newborn, M.: The principal continuation and the killer heuristic. In: Proceedings of the 1977 annual conference, ACM 1977, pp. 466–473. Seattle, Washington, USA (1977)
3. Balas, E.: Projection and lifting in combinatorial optimization. In: Jünger, M., Naddef, D. (eds.) Computational Combinatorial Optimization. LNCS, vol. 2241, pp. 26–56. Springer, Heidelberg (2001). https://doi.org/10.1007/3-540-45586-8_2
4. Ben-Tal, A., Ghaoui, L.E., Nemirovski, A.: Robust Optimization. Princeton University Press, Princeton (2009)
5. Bertsimas, D., Dunning, I.: Multistage robust mixed-integer optimization with adaptive partitions. Oper. Res. **64**(4), 980–998 (2016)
6. Bertsimas, D., Georghiou, A.: Design of near optimal decision rules in multistage adaptive mixed-integer optimization. Oper. Res. **63**(3), 610–627 (2015)

7. Cadoli, M., Schaerf, M., Giovanardi, A., Giovanardi, M.: An algorithm to evaluate quantified boolean formulae and its experimental evaluation. J. Autom. Reasoning **28**(2), 101–142 (2002)

8. Campbell, M., Marsland, T.: A comparison of minimax tree search algorithms. Artif. Intell. **20**(4), 347–367 (1983)

9. Ceria, S., Cordier, C., Marchand, H., Wolsey, L.A.: Cutting planes for integer programs with general integer variables. Math. Program. **81**(2), 201–214 (1998)

10. Chen, X., Van Beek, P.: Conflict-directed backjumping revisited. J. Artif. Intell. Res. **14**, 53–81 (2001)

11. Delage, E., Iancu, D.A.: Robust multistage decision making. In: The operations research revolution, pp. 20–46. INFORMS (2015)

12. Donninger, C., Lorenz, U.: The chess monster hydra. In: Becker, J., Platzner, M., Vernalde, S. (eds.) FPL 2004. LNCS, vol. 3203, pp. 927–932. Springer, Heidelberg (2004). https://doi.org/10.1007/978-3-540-30117-2_101

13. Ederer, T., Hartisch, M., Lorenz, U., Opfer, T., Wolf, J.: Yasol: an open source solver for quantified mixed integer programs. In: Winands, M.H.M., van den Herik, H.J., Kosters, W.A. (eds.) ACG 2017. LNCS, vol. 10664, pp. 224–233. Springer, Cham (2017). https://doi.org/10.1007/978-3-319-71649-7_19

14. Ederer, T., Lorenz, U., Martin, A., Wolf, J.: Quantified linear programs: a computational study. In: Demetrescu, C., Halldórsson, M.M. (eds.) ESA 2011. LNCS, vol. 6942, pp. 203–214. Springer, Heidelberg (2011). https://doi.org/10.1007/978-3-642-23719-5_18

15. Giunchiglia, E., Narizzano, M., Tacchella, A.: Backjumping for quantified boolean logic satisfiability. Artif. Intell. **145**(1), 99–120 (2003)

16. Giunchiglia, E., Narizzano, M., Tacchella, A., et al.: Learning for quantified boolean logic satisfiability. In: Proceedings of the AAAI Conference on Artificial Intelligence, pp. 649–654 (2002)

17. Goerigk, M., Hartisch, M.: Multistage robust discrete optimization via quantified integer programming. Comput. Oper. Res. **135**, 105434 (2021)

18. Gupta, A., Pál, M., Ravi, R., Sinha, A.: Boosted sampling: approximation algorithms for stochastic optimization. In: Proceedings of the Thirty-sixth Annual ACM Symposium on Theory of Computing, STOC 2004, pp. 417–426 (2004)

19. Hartisch, M.: Quantified Integer Programming with Polyhedral and Decision-Dependent Uncertainty. Ph.D. thesis, University of Siegen, Germany (2020). https://doi.org/10.25819/ubsi/4841

20. Hartisch, M., Ederer, T., Lorenz, U., Wolf, J.: Quantified integer programs with polyhedral uncertainty set. In: Plaat, A., Kosters, W., van den Herik, J. (eds.) CG 2016. LNCS, vol. 10068, pp. 156–166. Springer, Cham (2016). https://doi.org/10.1007/978-3-319-50935-8_15

21. Hartisch, M., Lorenz, U.: Mastering uncertainty: towards robust multistage optimization with decision dependent uncertainty. In: Nayak, A.C., Sharma, A. (eds.) PRICAI 2019. LNCS (LNAI), vol. 11670, pp. 446–458. Springer, Cham (2019). https://doi.org/10.1007/978-3-030-29908-8_36

22. Hartisch, M., Lorenz, U.: A novel application for game tree search - exploiting pruning mechanisms for quantified integer programs. In: Cazenave, T., van den Herik, J., Saffidine, A., Wu, I.C. (eds.) Advances in Computer Games. ACG 2019. Lecture Notes in Computer Science, vol. 12516, pp. 66–78. Springer, Cham (2020). https://doi.org/10.1007/978-3-030-65883-0_6

23. Hemmi, D., Tack, G., Wallace, M.: A recursive scenario decomposition algorithm for combinatorial multistage stochastic optimisation problems. In: Proceedings of the AAAI Conference on Artificial Intelligence, vol. 32 (2018)

24. Huang, J., et al.: The effect of restarts on the efficiency of clause learning. In: IJCAI, vol. 7, pp. 2318–2323 (2007)
25. Kall, P., Mayer, J.: Stochastic Linear Programming. Models, Theory and Computation. Springer, Boston (2005). https://doi.org/10.1007/b105472
26. Knuth, D., Moore, R.: An analysis of alpha-beta pruning. Artif. Intell. **6**(4), 293–326 (1975)
27. Lonsing, F., Biere, A.: DepQBF: a dependency-aware QBF solver. J. Satisfiability Boolean Model. Comput. **7**(2–3), 71–76 (2010)
28. Lorenz, U., Wolf, J.: Solving multistage quantified linear optimization problems with the alpha-beta nested benders decomposition. EURO J. Comput. Optim. **3**(4), 349–370 (2015)
29. Marques-Silva, J., Lynce, I., Malik, S.: Conflict-driven clause learning SAT solvers. In: Handbook of Satisfiability, pp. 131–153. IOS Press (2009)
30. Mercier, L., Van Hentenryck, P.: Performance analysis of online anticipatory algorithms for large multistage stochastic integer programs. In: IJCAI, pp. 1979–1984 (2007)
31. Moskewicz, M.W., Madigan, C.F., Zhao, Y., Zhang, L., Malik, S.: Chaff: Engineering an efficient sat solver. In: Proceedings of the 38th Annual Design Automation Conference, pp. 530–535 (2001)
32. Papadimitriou, C.: Games against nature. J. Comput. Syst. Sci. **31**(2), 288–301 (1985)
33. Pearl, J.: Scout: A simple game-searching algorithm with proven optimal properties. In: Proceedings of the First AAAI Conference on Artificial Intelligence, AAAI 1980, pp. 143–145. AAAI Press (1980)
34. Pijls, W., de Bruin, A.: Game tree algorithms and solution trees. Theor. Comput. Sci. **252**(1), 197–215 (2001)
35. Schaeffer, J.: The history heuristic and alpha-beta search enhancements in practice. IEEE Trans. Pattern Anal. Mach. Intell. **11**(11), 1203–1212 (1989)
36. Shapiro, A.: A dynamic programming approach to adjustable robust optimization. Oper. Res. Lett. **39**(2), 83–87 (2011)
37. Subramani, K.: Analyzing selected quantified integer programs. In: Basin, D., Rusinowitch, M. (eds.) IJCAR 2004. LNCS (LNAI), vol. 3097, pp. 342–356. Springer, Heidelberg (2004). https://doi.org/10.1007/978-3-540-25984-8_26
38. Takriti, S., Ahmed, S.: On robust optimization of two-stage systems. Math. Program. **99**(1), 109–126 (2004)

ALGNN: Auto-Designed Lightweight Graph Neural Network

Rongshen Cai[1], Qian Tao[1(✉)], Yufei Tang[2], and Min Shi[3]

[1] School of Software, South China University of Technology, Guangzhou, China
msthemocker@mail.scut.edu.cn, taoqian@scut.edu.cn
[2] Department of Computer and Electrical Engineering and Computer Science,
Florida Atlantic University, Boca Raton, USA
tangy@fau.edu
[3] Institute for Informatics, Washington University School of Medicine in St. Louis,
St. Louis, USA
mins@wustl.edu

Abstract. Graph neural networks (GNNs) are widely used on graph-structured data, and its research has made substantial progress in recent years. However, given the various number of choices and combinations of components such as aggregator and activation function, designing GNNs for specific tasks is very heavy manual work. Recently, neural architecture search (NAS) was proposed with the aim of automating the GNN design process and generating task-dependent architectures. While existing approaches have achieved competitive performance, they are not well suited to practical application scenarios where the computational budget is limited. In this paper, we propose an auto-designed lightweight graph neural network (ALGNN) method to automatically design lightweight, task-dependent GNN architectures. ALGNN uses multi-objective optimization to optimize the architecture constrained by the computation cost and complexity of the model. We define, for the first time, an evaluation standard for consumption cost with the analysis of the message passing process in GNNs. Experiments on real-world datasets demonstrate that ALGNN can generate a lightweight GNN model that has much fewer parameters and GPU hours, meanwhile has comparable performance with state-of-the-art approaches.

Keywords: Graph neural network · Nerual architecture search · Particle swarm optimization · Multi-objective optimization · AutoML

1 Introduction

Graph neural networks (GNNs) are currently widely used on non-Euclidean data, e.g., computational biology [12], social network [8], and knowledge graph [22]. GNN follows a message passing scheme to gradually spread the information of neighboring nodes in each layer. With the increase of GNN layers and the expansion of graph data, the selection and combination of functions such as message

© Springer Nature Switzerland AG 2021
D. N. Pham et al. (Eds.): PRICAI 2021, LNAI 13031, pp. 500–512, 2021.
https://doi.org/10.1007/978-3-030-89188-6_37

aggregation and activation have a great influence on the model performance. It is usually heavy manual work to design an effective GNN for a specific task and dataset. Moreover, unlike typical neural networks, the GNN message passing process is much more computationally expensive. Many practical applications, however, require GNN models to be both effective and computationally efficient, e.g., have low power consumption in mobile applications and low latency in internet-of-things applications.

Neural architecture search (NAS) has a great impact by automating neural network architecture design. The architecture is optimized for accuracy and efficiency (i.e., computational cost) under the constraints (e.g., FLOPs, latency, memory). NAS has shown promising results in automatically designing architectures for CNN and RNN and has demonstrated success in various deep learning tasks, such as image classification, detection, and segmentation. NAS methods based on reinforcement learning (RL) and evolutionary computation (EC) [17,23] have recently gained much attention. Generally, NAS searches for architectures with maximal predictive performance. However, in real applications, additional objectives such as inference time and computational consumption must be considered. Multi-objective NAS methods [15,19] are further proposed to search for high performance under computation resource constraints.

There are preliminary studies [7,25] of GNNs architecture search with RL. However, those methods have low search efficiency with limited consideration of the computational cost. In this paper, we propose a novel auto-designed lightweight GNN (ALGNN) architecture search method based on multi-objective optimization. We stratify and expand the search space of GNN, to be more specific, we divide the search space into message passing search space and hyperparameter search space to find the hyperparameters that are more suitable for the current model combination. ALGNN regards the computation cost of the GNN message passing process as one of the objectives in the architecture search, meanwhile takes into account the GNN parameters. To aid the evaluation of the generated lightweight model, we further define a novel standard $MCost$ with the analysis of message passing process in GNNs.

We adopt the multi-objective particle swarm optimization (MOPSO) as our NAS search algorithm and evaluate the generated model using the accuracy, parameters, and computational consumption as multiple objectives. Experimental results show that ALGNN can generate a lightweight GNN model with performance comparable to the best architecture of previous graph NAS work but with a much lower computational cost. Moreover, the experimental results show that, compared with the RL-based graph NAS methods, our proposed ALGNN has a better searching efficiency. In short, we make the following contributions in this paper:

- We propose a novel graph NAS framework ALGNN to search for a lightweight GNN model. The proposed approach uses the MOPSO as the search algorithm and expands the search space in previous work.
- With the analysis of the computational complexity of the message passing process, we define a novel GNN evaluation standard $MCost$ as one of the

objectives to assist the searching process for generating a portable GNN. To the best of our knowledge, this is the first work to consider the computational consumption constraints in the graph neural architecture search.
- Experimental results show that ALGNN can generate a lightweight GNN that is comparable in performance to the best architecture of the previous graph NAS work and has the lowest computational cost in terms of model parameters and GPU hours.

2   Related Work

2.1   Graph Neural Networks

GNNs integrate neural networks with graph-structured data and are widely used [12]. Graph propagation is the core operation in GNN, in which information is propagated from each node to its neighborhood through some certain rules [22]. In general, the graph propagation rules can be divided into spectral-based convolutions [3] and spatial-based convolutions [8]. Recently, improved methods [7,16,20] have been proposed on the message passing architecture. Determining the suitable GNN structure for a specific problem normally necessitates tremendous expert knowledge and laborious trials. With the expansion of graph data and the demand for mobile applications, the size of GNN models needs to be optimized [21]. To improve training efficiency on large graphs, FastGCN [1] and HAGs [9] have been proposed. Our paper solves the conflict of automatically optimizing GNN efficiency while maintaining model performance accuracy using the multi-objective neural architecture search method.

2.2   Neural Architecture Search

NAS is a hot research topic in AutoML and has shown promising results in designing architectures for deep learning models. RL [14] and EA [17,18,23] are the two main methods used in NAS. However, RL-based methods have steep computational requirement for the search process [14]. Moreover, they are not readily applicable for multi-objective NAS. On the other hand, EA-based methods do not need to train the controller and the search process only depends on the model training time. EA-based methods firstly initialize a population of architectures and evolve with mutation and crossover. The architectures with competitive performance will be retained during the search progress. Recently, graph NAS has made preliminary progress [7,24,25], exclusively based on RL-based methods. In this paper, we use an EA-based method (i.e., MOPSO) for GNN architecture search.

2.3   Multi-Objective NAS

Multi-objective NAS is currently a hot research branch in the field of NAS, where the goal is not only optimizing the model accuracy for a given task but also considering resource consumption. NEMO [11] is one of the earliest evolutionary multi-objective approaches to evolve CNN architectures. NSGA-Net [15] adopts the classic non-dominated search algorithm (NSGAII) to handle trade-off among multiple objectives. LEMONADE [5] utilizes Lamarckian inheritance mechanism which generates children with performance warm-started by their parents. MnasNet [19] uses a customized weighted product method to approximate Pareto optimal solutions. Our proposed ALGNN uses MOPSO to find the Pareto approximate optimal solution, which is the first work of multi-objective graph neural architecture search.

3   Methods

3.1   Problem Statement

We consider a method that will maximize a GNN model performance, constrained by the computation cost and model complexity. In this work, the search algorithm implies a multi-objective bi-level optimization problem [2,4], shown in the following:

$$\min_{m \in \mathcal{M}} \boldsymbol{F}(\boldsymbol{m}) = (f_1\left(\boldsymbol{m}; \boldsymbol{w}^*(\boldsymbol{m})\right), f_2(\boldsymbol{m}))$$
$$\text{s.t.} \quad \boldsymbol{w}^*(\boldsymbol{m}) \in \operatorname{argmin} \mathcal{L}(\boldsymbol{w}; \boldsymbol{m}) \tag{1}$$

where $\mathcal{M}$ is the message passing search space, $\boldsymbol{m}$ is a candidate architecture, and $\boldsymbol{w}$ represents the model parameters weight. $\boldsymbol{F}(\boldsymbol{m})$ comprises of the model error f_1 on the validation data $\mathcal{D}_{val}$, and the complexity f_2 of the GNN model architecture. The objective $\mathcal{L}(\boldsymbol{w}; \boldsymbol{m})$ is the cross-entropy loss on the training data $\mathcal{D}_{tra}$.

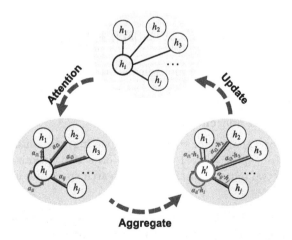

Fig. 1. An illustration of message passing process. Given an input graph that node h_i is connected with $h_1, h_2, ..., h_j$. Attention mechanism is to measure the relation between neighbor nodes and calculate the attention weight α_{ij}. Aggregator integrates the information between neighbor nodes with the attention weights α_{ij}.

3.2 GNN Message Passing Computation

The message passing process of GNN requires a lot of computational consumption. The aggregation of the message passing process and the update process all need to extract and integrate the information of the entire input graph. Assume the input graph $G = (V, E)$ has node V and edge $\mathcal{E}$. For each node, $\mathcal{N}(v)$ represents the neighbor set of v and h_v represents the input node characteristics. A GNN iteratively learns the representation of each node on the entire graph through multiple layers. Figure 1 illustrates the message passing process in a typical GNN that contains attention mechanism and aggregate function.

The attention mechanism helps to focus on the most relevant neighbors to improve the representative learning of node embedding. According to GAT [20], the attention of the edge e_{ij} from node i to j is as follows:

$$e_{ij} = Att_{\mathcal{M}}(W_{h_i}, W_{h_j})$$

$$\alpha_{ij} = \text{softmax}\,(e_{ij}) = \frac{\exp\,(e_{ij})}{\sum_{k \in \mathcal{N}(i)} \exp\,(e_{ik})}$$

in which, the computation cost of the edge weight a_{ij} is related to the number of edges in the graph. In addition, the calculations of a_{ij} are attention functions dependent. We need to consider the selection of attention function in the calculation of message passing.

Aggregate function is to capture neighborhood structure for learning node representation. For node v with neighbor $\mathcal{N}(v)$, the k-th layer aggregation function is as follows:

$$h_i^{(k)} = Agg_{\mathcal{M}}(\alpha_{ij}^{(k-1)} h_j^{(k-1)} | j \in \mathcal{N}(i))$$

With the analysis of the two components, we define the computation cost $MCost$ for GNN message passing layer as:

$$MCost(\mathcal{M}, G) = K \times Att_{\mathcal{M}}(|\mathcal{E_G}|) + \sum_{v \in V} Agg_{\mathcal{M}}(|\mathcal{N}(v)|) \qquad (2)$$

where K represents the heads in multi-heads attention, and $\mathcal{E_G}$ is the number of edges of the input graph G.

3.3 Multi-faceted Search Space

Based on the above analysis of the message passing mechanism, we propose a multi-faceted search space to deal with multi-objective optimization. We divide search space into two parts: message passing search space and hyper-parameters search space.

Message Passing Search Space (or Macro Search Space): The message passing process in GNN requires multiple steps to complete, including the design of aggregation, attention, activation, and dropout. We refer to previous work [7,25]. For a fair comparison, we use the same search space in aggregate function, attention function, and activation function. Table 1 shows the search space of the message passing layer.

Table 1. Macro search space.

Type	Search space
Attention function	*const, gcn, gat, sym-gat, cos, linear, gene-linear*
Attention head	1, 2, 4, 8, 12, 16
Aggregation function	*sum, mean pooling, max pooling, MLP*
Activation function	*sigmoid, tanh, relu, identity, softplus, leaky relu, relu6, elu*
Hidden unit	2, 4, 8, 16, 32, 64, 128
Dropout	False, 0.1, 0.3, 0.5, 0.7

Table 2. Hyper-parameters search space.

Type	Search space
Layer connectivity	*stack, skip-sum, skip-cat*
Message passing layers	2, 3, 4
Learning rate	5e-4, 1e-3, 5e-3, 1e-2
L2 regularization strength	0, 1e-3, 1e-4, 1e-5, 5e-5, 5e-4
Decay rate	5e-4, 8e-4, 1e-3, 4e-3

Hyper-Parameters Search Space: Only optimizing message passing layer structures may lead to a suboptimal searched model since the change of learning parameters could severely degrade the fine-tuned GNN structure. The training configuration includes decay rate, learning rate, optimizer parameters, etc., which all have a great impact on the performance of the model. Therefore, we design the message passing layer and the hyperparameters iteratively. With the increase of GNN layers, skip connections began to be used in GNN research. We add skip connections to the hyperparameter search target to find the most suitable skip connections method. Table 2 shows the set of hyper-parameters.

3.4   Search Algorithm

Multi-Objective PSO: The problem in Eq. (1) poses two main computational bottlenecks for GNN bi-level optimization methods. To attack it, we use the MOPSO algorithm. PSO is a population-based algorithm, motivated by the social behaviour of fish schooling or bird flocking [10], commonly used for solving optimization problems without rich domain knowledge. In PSO, each particle represents a potential solution to a problem, and particles fly in the search space to find the best solution by updating velocity and position vector according to Eqs. (3) and (4), respectively:

$$v_{ij}(t+1) = c_1 \cdot r_1 \cdot (Pbest_{ij}(t) - x_{ij}(t)) + c_2 \cdot r_2 \, (Gbest_j(t) - x_{ij}(t)) \tag{3}$$

$$x_{ij}(t+1) = x_{ij}(t) + v_{ij}(t+1) \tag{4}$$

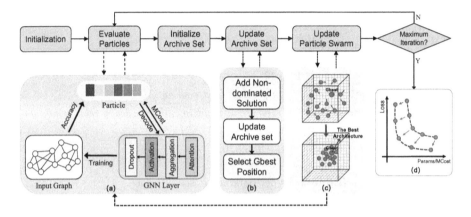

Fig. 2. Overview of the proposed ALGNN. (a) The particles are decoded into a GNN model and then evaluated by training input graph data to obtain the classification accuracy and the cost $MCost$. (b) In MOPSO, $Archive$ set is to keep a historical record of the nondominated particles found along the search process. The best GNN architecture $Gbest$ is then selected in the current generation. (c) Update each particle velocity and position vector according to Eqs. (3) and (4). (d) Find the Pareto optimal solution within the maximum number of iterations.

Algorithm 1. Search Algorithm of ALGNN

Input: target graph $\mathcal{G}$; training set $\mathcal{D}_{tra}$; validation set $\mathcal{D}_{val}$; message passing search Space $\mathcal{M}$; hyperparameters search space $\mathcal{P}$; archive set $\mathcal{A}$.
Parameter: $\mathcal{N}_p$: population size;
K_m: the number of message passing searching iterations;
K_p: the number of hyperparameters searching iterations.
Output: optimal message passing structure $^*m$ and hyperparameters $^*p$.

1: Initialize the *Particles* and *Archive*.
2: **for** i ⟵ 1 to K_m **do**
3:    Evaluate *Particles* (training *GNN* model).
4:    **if** Premature convergence appears **then**
5:       Perturb and update *Pbest* and *Gbest*.
6:    **end if**
7:    Update *Archive* and select the *Gbest* in the *Archive*.
8:    Update the particles.
9: **end for**
10: **for** i ⟵ 1 to K_p **do**
11:    Evaluate *Particles*(training *GNN* model).
12:    **if** Premature convergence appears **then**
13:       perturb and update *PBest* and *Gbest*.
14:    **end if**
15:    Update *Archive* and select the *Gbest* in the *Archive*.
16: **end for**
17: **return** $^*m$ and $^*p$

Table 3. Node classification performance and model parameters comparison for different architectures (including human experts, random search, the optimal ones found by GraphNAS and our proposed ALGNN) on the Cora, Pubmed, and Citeseer datasets.

Search methods	Architectures	Cora		Pubmed		Citeseer	
		#Params	Accuracy	#Params	Accuracy	#Params	Accuracy
Human experts	GCN	0.05M	81.5%	0.02M	79.0%	0.12M	70.3%
	GAT	0.09M	83.0 ± 0.7%	0.03M	79.0 ± 0.3%	0.23M	72.5 ± 0.7%
	LGCN	0.06M	83.3 ± 0.5%	0.05M	79.5 ± 0.2%	0.05M	73.0 ± 0.6%
	Graph U-Net	0.07M	84.4 ± 0.6%	0.04M	79.6 ± 0.2%	0.16M	73.2 ± 0.5%
	APPNP	0.18M	83.8 ± 0.3%	0.06M	79.7 ± 0.3%	0.23M	71.6 ± 0.5%
Random	Random	2.95M	82.3 ± 0.5%	0.13M	77.9 ± 0.4%	0.95M	71.9 ± 1.2%
RL	GraphNAS-R	0.14M	83.3 ± 0.4%	0.07M	79.6 ± 0.4%	3.80M	73.4 ± 0.4%
	GraphNAS	0.37M	83.7 ± 0.4%	0.20M	80.5 ± 0.3%	1.92M	73.5 ± 0.3%
PSO	**ALGNN-S**	**0.12M**	**84.3 ± 0.5%**	**0.13M**	**81.2 ± 0.3%**	**0.09M**	**74.6 ± 0.4%**
	ALGNN	**0.04M**	**84.2 ± 0.4%**	**0.02M**	**80.9 ± 0.4%**	**0.03M**	**74.3 ± 0.3%**

where v_{ij} represents the velocity of the particle i in the j-th dimension, x_{ij} represents the position of particle i in the j-th dimension, $Pbest_{ij}$ and $Gbest_j$ are the local best and the global best in the j-th dimension, r_1, r_2 are random numbers between 0 and 1, c_1 and c_2 are PSO parameters used to tweak the performance.

MOPSO adds the *Archive* set and calculate the set from particles with the principle of Pareto dominance. The best particle *Gbest* is randomly selected in the *Archive* set. To overcome local optimal solution, we propose a variant of MOPSO in this paper. When the distance between particles falls below a specific threshold, we double perturb *Pbest* and *Gbest* to avoid particles trapped into local optimum. Algorithm 1 shows the pseudocode and corresponding steps from a sample run of ALGNN. Figure 2 shows the whole framework of our proposed method.

We search for the two types of search space hierarchically. In the message passing layer search process, we use the multi-objective PSO algorithm, and the optimization objectives are the accuracy of the model and the computational consumption of the model. The definitions of these two conflict objective functions in the message passing layer search process are described as follow:

$$f_1 = 1 - Acc(GraphNet(w^*(x_m)), D_{val}) \tag{5}$$
$$f_2 = \lambda MCost(x_m) + (1 - \lambda)Parameters(x_m) \tag{6}$$

where x_m represents the solution to message passing layer, w^* denotes the associated weights, *Acc* represents the accuracy of the model *GraphNet* in the validation set D_{val}, and λ controls the proportion between *MCost* and *Parameters*.

Next, the model hyperparameters are optimized through the general PSO algorithm. The optimization goal of this process is focused on the model accuracy. Since we have determined the message passing layer to design M, the *MCost* and *Parameters* are also fixed. The definition of fitness function in the hyperparameter search process is described as follow:

Table 4. Search efficiency comparison with NAS methods on Pubmed datasets.

Architectures	Search methods	Params (M)	Accuracy (%)	GPU Hours
GraphNAS-R	RL	0.85	79.0 ± 0.4	10
GraphNAS-S	RL	0.07	79.6 ± 0.3	8
GraphNAS	RL	0.20	80.5 ± 0.3	7
ALGNN-S	**PSO**	**0.32**	**81.2 ± 0.3**	**2**
ALGNN	**PSO**	**0.03**	**80.9 ± 0.5**	**1.5**

$$f_h = Acc(GraphNet(w^*(x_p(M)), D_{val}) \tag{7}$$

where x_p represents the solution to hyperparameter layer search and w^* denotes the associated weights.

4   Experiments

Datasets Details. The datasets are divided into two categories: transductive learning tasks and inductive learning tasks. For the transductive learning tasks, we use the datasets Cora, Citeseer, and Pubmed obtained from semi-GCN [12] to ensure a consistent comparison. We follow the same setting used in semi-GCN that allows 20 nodes per class for training, 500 nodes for validation and 1,000 nodes for testing. In inductive learning tasks, the experiment dataset is the protein-protein interaction (PPI) [8].

Implementation Details. We implemented ALGNN using PyTorch, and completed the implementation of the GNN message passing layer in PyTorch Geometric [1]. In the search process, with repeated experiments, the hyperparameters of our MOPSO algorithm are set as follows. We set the number of MOPSO particles to 15, and the dimensions of the particles change according to the number of message passing layers. The number of iterations K_m of the message passing layer is set to 50, and the number of iterations K_p of the hyperparameter search is set to 30. The hyperparameters c_1, c_2 of the particle velocity update are both set to 1.8, and w is set to 0.8.

To ensure a consistent comparison with the state-of-the-art GNN NAS methods, we set the number of GNN layers to 2 in transductive learning tasks and 3 in inductive learning tasks. The training epoch is 300. In the message passing layer search, We apply the L_2 regularization with $\lambda = 0.0005$, dropout probability dp = 0.6, and learning rate $lr = 0.005$ as the default parameters. For all searches and training, we used a single NVIDIA GeForce RTX 2080Ti.

---

[1] https://github.com/rusty1s/pytorch_geometric.

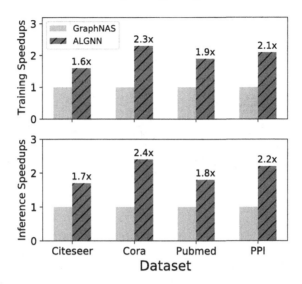

Fig. 3. Per-epoch training time and inference latency comparison between GraphNAS and ALGNN on two tasks and four datasets. The performance numbers are normalized by the GraphNAS. GNN architectures designed by ALGNN provide significant speedups.

4.1 Classification Performance and Efficiency

Table 3 summarizes the performance of ALGNN and the baselines on the three transductive learning datasets. From Table 3, we observe the GNN model designed by our method achieves better performance compared with baselines (including human experts [6,13], random, and other NAS methods) across all datasets. Without computation cost constraints, ALGNN-S can get a slightly better performance model, but the scale of the network in terms of parameter size is not competitive. With the addition of multi-objective search conditions, a model with slightly better performance and extremely low parameter and computational consumption can be obtained.

In terms of search efficiency, since the MOPSO algorithm does not need to train the controller, the MOPSO search process only related to the computation cost for training the model. Without parameter sharing, the search efficiency (i.e., GPU time) of MOPSO and the state-of-the-art RL-based GraphNAS is shown in Table 4. ALGNN achieves comparable performance to both the GraphNAS generated architectures with 0.2× search cost and 6× less number of parameters respectively.

4.2 Effectiveness Validation of Multiple Objective

We further study the effectiveness of the ALGNN multi-objective search algorithm. In ALGNN, we set the second target as the computational cost of the GNN model to constrain the parameters and computational complexity. Figure 3

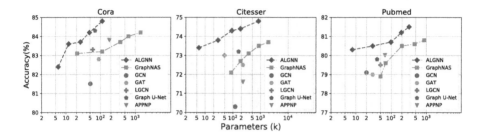

Fig. 4. Node classification accuracy vs. model parameters comparison on transductive learning task. On all three datasets, ALGNN could find more accurate solutions with fewer parameters.

compares our models with other methods in terms of both accuracy performance and parameters. In the three transductive learning datasets, the top-5 accuracy model designed by ALGNN is competitive in terms of parameter quantity and accuracy performance. Meanwhile, Fig. 4 compares the per-epoch training time and inference latency between the Top-1 GraphNAS and ALGNN model across all the four datasets. Compared to GraphNAS, ALGNN can improve the training and inference performance by up to 2.3× and 2.4×, respectively.

4.3   Ablation Studies

Here, we verify the disturbance effect of the MOPSO algorithm. In Sect. 3.4, we mentioned that when the particle swarm is too crowded and the search algorithm trapped into the local optimum, we perturb and update Pbest and Gbest. From Fig. 5, we can observe that adding perturbation helps the swarm to avoid local optima during iteration to search for a better position. It is worth mentioning that the double perturbation is more efficient than the single perturbation in the iteration.

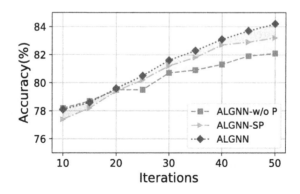

Fig. 5. ALGNN without perturbation, with single perturbation, and with double perturbation during 50 iterations.

5 Conclusions

We proposed a neural architecture search method ALGNN for designing lightweight graph neural networks. ALGNN uses a multi-objective optimization algorithm to restrict the network scale and computation cost of graph neural networks. With the analysis of the message passing process in GNN, we defined an evaluation standard $MCost$ for GNN consumption cost. We enlarged the search space and added hyperparameters that affect model performance. Experiment results showed that ALGNN can generate a lightweight GNN model that has comparable performance with state-of-the-art Graph NAS methods. The study also revealed that the search process of ALGNN is more efficient than the current Graph NAS methods.

Acknowledgments. This work is supported in part by the Guangdong province Natural Science Foundation under Grant No. 2018A030313396 and in part by the National Key RD Program of China No. 2019YFC1510400.

References

1. Chen, J., Ma, T., Xiao, C.: Fastgcn: fast learning with graph convolutional networks via importance sampling. In: International Conference on Learning Representations (2018)
2. Coello, C.A.C., Pulido, G.T., Lechuga, M.S.: Handling multiple objectives with particle swarm optimization. IEEE Trans. Evol. Comput **8**(3), 256–279 (2004). https://doi.org/10.1109/TEVC.2004.826067
3. Defferrard, M., Bresson, X., Vandergheynst, P.: Convolutional neural networks on graphs with fast localized spectral filtering. Adv. Neural Inf. Process. Syst. **29**, 3844–3852 (2016)
4. Eichfelder, G.: Multiobjective bilevel optimization. Math. Program. **123**(2), 419–449 (2010)
5. Elsken, T., Metzen, J.H., Hutter, F.: Efficient multi-objective neural architecture search via lamarckian evolution. In: International Conference on Learning Representations (2019). https://openreview.net/forum?id=ByME42AqK7
6. Gao, H., Ji, S.: Graph u-nets. In: Proceedings of the 36th International Conference on Machine Learning (2019)
7. Gao, Y., Yang, H., Zhang, P., Zhou, C., Hu, Y.: Graph neural architecture search. In: IJCAI, vol. 20, pp. 1403–1409 (2020)
8. Hamilton, W., Ying, Z., Leskovec, J.: Inductive representation learning on large graphs. In: Advances in Neural Information Processing Systems, pp. 1024–1034 (2017)
9. Jia, Z., Lin, S., Ying, R., You, J., Leskovec, J., Aiken, A.: Redundancy-free computation for graph neural networks. In: Proceedings of the 26th ACM SIGKDD International Conference on Knowledge Discovery & Data Mining, pp. 997–1005 (2020)
10. Kennedy, J., Eberhart, R.: Particle swarm optimization. In: Proceedings of ICNN'95-International Conference on Neural Networks, vol. 4, pp. 1942–1948. IEEE (1995)

11. Kim, Y.H., Reddy, B., Yun, S., Seo, C.: Nemo: neuro-evolution with multiobjective optimization of deep neural network for speed and accuracy. In: ICML 2017 AutoML Workshop (2017)

12. Kipf, T.N., Welling, M.: Semi-supervised classification with graph convolutional networks. In: 5th International Conference on Learning Representations, ICLR (2017). https://openreview.net/forum?id=SJU4ayYgl

13. Klicpera, J., Bojchevski, A., Günnemann, S.: Combining neural networks with personalized pagerank for classification on graphs. In: International Conference on Learning Representations (2019)

14. Liu, H., Simonyan, K., Yang, Y.: DARTS: differentiable architecture search. In: International Conference on Learning Representations (2019). https://openreview.net/forum?id=S1eYHoC5FX

15. Lu, Z., Deb, K., Goodman, E., Banzhaf, W., Boddeti, V.N.: NSGANetV2: evolutionary multi-objective surrogate-assisted neural architecture search. In: Vedaldi, A., Bischof, H., Brox, T., Frahm, J.-M. (eds.) ECCV 2020. LNCS, vol. 12346, pp. 35–51. Springer, Cham (2020). https://doi.org/10.1007/978-3-030-58452-8_3

16. Qu, M., Bengio, Y., Tang, J.: GMNN: graph Markov neural networks. In: International Conference on Machine Learning, pp. 5241–5250 (2019)

17. Real, E., Aggarwal, A., Huang, Y., Le, Q.V.: Regularized evolution for image classifier architecture search. In: Proceedings of the AAAI Conference on Artificial Intelligence, vol. 33, pp. 4780–4789 (2019)

18. Sun, Y., Xue, B., Zhang, M., Yen, G.G., Lv, J.: Automatically designing CNN architectures using the genetic algorithm for image classification. IEEE Trans. Cybern. 50, 3840–3854 (2020)

19. Tan, M., et al.: Mnasnet: platform-aware neural architecture search for mobile. In: Proceedings of the IEEE Conference on Computer Vision and Pattern Recognition, pp. 2820–2828 (2019)

20. Veličković, P., Cucurull, G., Casanova, A., Romero, A., Liò, P., Bengio, Y.: Graph attention networks. In: International Conference on Learning Representations (2018)

21. Wu, F., Souza, A., Zhang, T., Fifty, C., Yu, T., Weinberger, K.: Simplifying graph convolutional networks. In: International Conference on Machine Learning, pp. 6861–6871 (2019)

22. Wu, Z., Pan, S., Chen, F., Long, G., Zhang, C., Philip, S.Y.: A comprehensive survey on graph neural networks. IEEE Trans. Neural Netw. Learn. Syst. 32, 4–24 (2020)

23. Xie, L., Yuille, A.: Genetic cnn. In: Proceedings of the IEEE International Conference on Computer Vision, pp. 1379–1388 (2017)

24. You, J., Ying, Z., Leskovec, J.: Design space for graph neural networks. In: Advances in Neural Information Processing Systems, vol. 33 (2020)

25. Zhou, K., Song, Q., Huang, X., Hu, X.: Auto-GNN: neural architecture search of graph neural networks. arXiv preprint arXiv:1909.03184 (2019)

Automatic Graph Learning with Evolutionary Algorithms: An Experimental Study

Chenyang Bu, Yi Lu, and Fei Liu[✉]

School of Computer Science and Information Engineering,
Hefei University of Technology, Hefei, China
chenyangbu@hfut.edu.cn, {luyi,feiliu}@mail.hfut.edu.cn

Abstract. In recent years, automated machine learning (AutoML) has received widespread attention from academia and industry owing to its ability to significantly reduce the threshold and labor cost of machine learning. It has demonstrated its powerful functions in hyperparameter optimization, model selection, neural network search, and feature engineering. Most AutoML frameworks are not specifically designed to process graph data. That is, in most AutoML tools, only traditional neural networks are integrated without using a graph neural network (GNN). Although traditional neural networks have achieved great success, GNNs have more advantages in processing non-Euclidean data (e.g., graph data) and have gained popularity in recent years. However, to the best of our knowledge, there is currently only one open-source AutoML framework for graph learning, i.e., AutoGL. For the AutoGL framework, traditional AutoML optimization algorithms such as grid search, random search, and Bayesian optimization are used to optimize the hyperparameters. Because each type of traditional optimization algorithm has its own advantages and disadvantages, more options are required. This study analyzes the performance of different evolutionary algorithms (EAs) on AutoGL through experiments. The experimental results show that EAs could be an effective alternative to the hyperparameter optimization of GNN.

Keywords: Automatic graph learning · Evolutionary algorithms · AutoML

1 Introduction

Automated machine learning (AutoML) [1–3] refers to the automation of the entire machine learning process from model construction to application. Compared with traditional machine learning, AutoML can achieve results equivalent

C. Bu—Was partly supported by the National Natural Science Foundation of China (No. 61806065 and No. 91746209), the Fundamental Research Funds for the Central Universities (No. JZ2020HGQA0186), and the Project funded by the China Postdoctoral Science Foundation (No. 2018M630704).

© Springer Nature Switzerland AG 2021
D. N. Pham et al. (Eds.): PRICAI 2021, LNAI 13031, pp. 513–526, 2021.
https://doi.org/10.1007/978-3-030-89188-6_38

to or better than human experts with no or few human interventions. Therefore, AutoML can lower the threshold of algorithm learning and use; thus, it can be helpful for applications in machine learning algorithms in real scenarios.

Most of the existing AutoML research and frameworks do not consider the particularity of graph data, therefore they cannot be directly applied to graph machine learning models [4]. Many research problems in different fields can be naturally modeled into graph machine learning, such as social media analysis [5], recommendation systems [6], and protein modeling. Although traditional deep learning methods have achieved great success, their performance in processing non-Euclidean spatial data may be unsatisfactory [7,8]. For example, in e-commerce, a graph-based learning system can use the interaction between users and products to make very accurate recommendations, but the complexity of graphs makes existing deep learning algorithms face huge challenges [6]. This is because the graph is irregular; that is, each graph has an unordered node with a variable size, and each node in the graph has a different number of adjacent nodes. The characteristics of graph data lead to some important operations (such as convolution) that are easy to calculate in image processing no longer suitable for direct use in graph data [7]. In addition, a core assumption of existing deep learning algorithms is that data samples are independent of each other [7]. For graphs, this is not the case. That is, each data sample (i.e., a node) in the graph has edges related to the other nodes. This information can be used to capture the interdependence between instances [7]. Therefore, graph neural networks (GNNs) [9] have been proposed to specifically process graph data. Compared with traditional neural networks, GNNs have better reported experimental results in processing graph data. Thus, this research line has received widespread attention recently [10]. Typical GNNs include graph convolution networks (GCNs) [11] and graph attention networks (GAT) [12].

Automatic graph learning (AutoGL) refers to AutoML for graph data. According to [4], AutoGL is the first open-source automatic graph learning toolkit[1] that was released on December 21, 2020 [4]. This tool supports fully automatic machine learning on graph data, implements typical GNNs including GCN and GAT, and supports the two most common tasks in graph machine learning, that is, node classification and graph classification. Hyperparameter optimization (HPO) algorithms mainly include grid search, random search, simulated annealing, and Bayesian optimization methods. However, each HPO algorithm adopted in AutoGL has its own disadvantages. For example, grid search is not efficient, because it tries every possible combination of hyperparameters. Random search generally performs better than grid search in previously reported results; however, the obtained results may still not be good in the case of limited computing resources. Simulated annealing uses a single individual for optimization, leading to the final solution having a certain dependence on the initial solution. Gradient descent requires gradient information, which typically cannot be obtained for the model training process because only the input and output of

---

[1] https://github.com/THUMNLab/AutoGL.

the models are available during the tuning process. Therefore, we require more HPO options for the AutoGL.

In this study, we attempted to apply evolutionary algorithms (EAs) to AutoGL, as a class of nature-inspired population-based stochastic search algorithms. Because searching is based on a population of candidate solutions, instead of a single one, EAs have good adaptability and robustness [13]. Moreover, no or few restrictions are required for cost functions, therefore EAs are suitable for solving complex problems that cannot be solved well by traditional methods [14,15]. Therefore, EAs have been widely used to solve various optimization problems in practical applications [16–19].

Researchers may be concerned about two research questions concerning the application of EAs in automatic graph learning. The first question is whether EAs perform better than other traditional HPOs for AutoGL. Second, EAs are so diverse that researchers may find it difficult to choose which EA to apply in their own experiments, or they may need to spend an unexpected time to compare.

This study focuses on analyzing the above two research questions through experiments. Both the topology and learning parameters of GNNs were encoded into chromosomes for simultaneous optimization using different EAs. Several EAs have been applied, and a number of experiments on two real-world datasets have been performed. To the best of our knowledge, this is the first study to compare the experimental performance of various EAs for AutoGL. The experimental results show that EAs could be an effective alternative to the HPO of AutoGL.

In summary, the contributions of this study are as follows:

1. To the best of our knowledge, this is the first study to apply EAs to the AutoGL framework, where AutoGL is the first open-source AutoML framework for graph learning.
2. An experimental analysis was conducted of the performance of different EAs for AutoGL through extensive experiments. This study may have reference value for researchers attempting EAs in this field.

The rest of this paper is organized as follows. Details of the algorithm is given in Sect. 2. The experiments are discussed in Sect. 3, and Sect. 4 concludes the paper.

2   Approach

In this section, we introduce the motivation of this study and the specific operation process of the method mentioned.

2.1   Motivation

The open-source toolkit AutoGL [4] shares various HPO algorithms for GNNs, such as grid search, random search, simulated annealing, and Bayesian optimization methods. However, there are disadvantages detailed in Fig. 1. Therefore, we

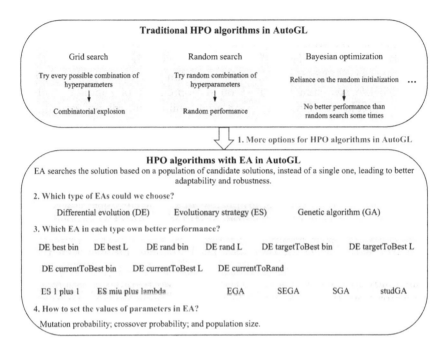

Fig. 1. The motivation of this study to present an experimental study of AutoGL with EA. The main task of the study is to solve the four points.

attempt to show more options for HPO algorithms for GNNs, i.e., AutoGL with EA algorithms.

EA has been widely used to solve various optimization problems [20,21]. In this study, EA is applied to HPO for GNNs to attempt to address the above disadvantages of the existing HPO algorithms, as reflected in the following aspects.

– Because some existing HPO algorithms (e.g., simulated annealing and Bayesian optimization methods) use a single individual for optimization, the final solution has a certain dependence on the initial solution. EA is introduced into HPO algorithms because it searches the solution based on a population of candidate solutions, instead of a single one, owing to its good adaptability and robustness [13,14].
– Some existing HPO algorithms (e.g., grid search and random search) are not efficient when computing resources are limited. HPO algorithms using EA obtain high-quality individuals through population evolution based on heuristic information.

To facilitate researchers to choose AutoGL with EA in applications, the following research points are analyzed in the experimental study, as shown in Fig. 1: 1) More options for the HPO algorithm are displayed. 2) Various types of EAs are compared. 3) EAs in each type are compared. 4) Different values of parameters in EA are set to analyze the performance.

Table 1. Search space of discrete parameters

Parameter name	Type	Min	Max	Scaling type
Learning Rate $\mathcal{P}_1$	float	0.01	0.05	Log
Weight Decay Rate $\mathcal{P}_2$	float	0.0001	0.001	Log
Dropout Rate $\mathcal{P}_3$	float	0.2	0.8	Linear

Table 2. Search space of continuous parameters

Parameter name	Searching space
Number of Hidden Units $\mathcal{H}_1$	{4, 5,..., 16}
Number of Attention Heads $\mathcal{H}_2$	{6, 8, 10, 12}
Activation Function $\mathcal{P}_4$	{leaky relu, relu, elu, tanh}
Max Epoch $\mathcal{P}_5$	{100, 101,..., 300}
Early Stopping Round $\mathcal{P}_6$	{10, 11,..., 30}

In this section, AutoGL with EA is modeled (corresponding to point 1). Then, the experimental results are analyzed from the aspects of the abovementioned points 2 to 4.

2.2 Optimized Parameters

In this subsection, AutoGL with EA is used to optimize the hyperparameters of two typical GNN models, i.e., GCN and GAT.

In GCN, the number of layers in the convolution structure was fixed, and only the number of units in the hidden layer ($\mathcal{H}_1$) was adjusted. It is because when the number of layers is above two, the effect is not greatly improved, and when the number of layers is too high, the training effect is significantly reduced [11]. In GAT, the number of nodes in the hidden layer ($\mathcal{H}_1$) of the model and the number of multi-head-attentions ($\mathcal{H}_2$) in the GAT model participated in the optimization of the model, and the same number of hidden layers was fixed.

In addition to the abovementioned hyperparameters, the common hyperparameters of GCN and GAT are the learning rate ($\mathcal{P}_1$), weight decay rate ($\mathcal{P}_2$), dropout rate ($\mathcal{P}_3$), activation function ($\mathcal{P}_4$), maximum epoch ($\mathcal{P}_5$) and early stopping round ($\mathcal{P}_6$).

The parameters involved in the optimization are discrete and continuous, and information such as the range of values for continuous parameters is presented in Table 1. The range of the discrete parameters is listed in Table 2.

2.3 Encoding

The encoding methods of the hyperparameters in GCN and GAT are given in this subsection.

The encoding process contains the following two parts: the encoding of the topological structure of the network and the encoding of the hyperparameters

Fig. 2. An example encode of solution

in the training process, where the former is embodied in the coding of the number of hidden units and attention heads. To better participate in the search in the EA, the data types of each parameter were re-coded and the upper and lower limits were set; discrete parameters, such as categories and integers, were re-coded as floating-point numbers to facilitate the operation of the EA, and some parameters were logged before they participated in the optimization of the EA. At each evaluation, it was converted from the floating-point number to the original data type through a certain decoder and within the valid range.

For GCN model, chromosome is represented as Eq. (1).

$$f = \{\mathcal{H}_1^*, \mathcal{P}_1^*, \mathcal{P}_2^*, \mathcal{P}_3, \mathcal{P}_4, \mathcal{P}_5, \mathcal{P}_6\}. \tag{1}$$

For GAN model, chromosome is represented as Eq. (2).

$$f = \{\mathcal{H}_1^*, \mathcal{H}_2^*, \mathcal{P}_1^*, \mathcal{P}_2^*, \mathcal{P}_3, \mathcal{P}_4, \mathcal{P}_5, \mathcal{P}_6\}, \tag{2}$$

where $\mathcal{H}_1^*$ represents the number of hidden units $\mathcal{H}_1$ transformed as $\ln \mathcal{H}_1$. $\mathcal{H}_2^*$ represents the mapping of the value $\mathcal{H}_2$ in the discrete value space to the represented ordinal number. $\mathcal{P}_1^*$ represents the number of units $\mathcal{P}_1$ transformed as $\ln \mathcal{P}_1$. $\mathcal{P}_2^*$ represents the number of unit $\mathcal{P}_2$ been transformed as $\ln \mathcal{P}_2$. $\mathcal{P}_4^*$ represents the mapping of the value $\mathcal{P}_4$ in the discrete value space to the represented ordinal number. f represents the individuals of this set of hyperparameters.

For example, a set of hyperparameters are as follows, the number of hidden units: 12, the number of attention heads: 8, learning rate: 0.015, weight decay rate: 0.005, dropout rate: 0.5, activation function: relu, max epoch: 250, and early stopping round: 24. They are encoded as (2.484906, 1.00000, −4.199705, −5.298317, 0.500000, 1.000000, 250.000000, 24.000000), for a more intuitive view, referred to Fig. 2.

2.4   Parameter Evolution

The objective of HPO algorithms is to optimize the individual fitness, where the individual represents the encoded chromosome regarding the hyperparameters. The following equations are used to evaluate the fitness of individual as shown in Eq. (3).

$$fitness(I_i) = loss(Model_{opt}(i)), \tag{3}$$

Table 3. Dataset statistics [22]

Dataset	Classes	Nodes	Edges	Features
Cora	7	2708	5429	1433
Citeseer	6	3327	4732	3703

where I_i denotes the individual. $fitness(I_i)$ denotes the fitness function of individual I_i. $loss()$ denotes the loss function, e.g., accuracy and logloss. $Model_{opt}(i)$ is shown in Eq. (4).

$$Model_{opt}(i) = model.train(decode(f_i)), \tag{4}$$

where $Model_{opt}(i)$ denotes the optimized model after the training process using the hyperparameter setting I_i. f_i denotes the encoded chromosome according to Eq. (2). $decode(f_i)$ denotes the reverse process of encoding, reversing all the values in the gene nodes into the original format to facilitate the construction of the model.

3   Experiment

In this section, the performance of HPO with EAs is experimentally investigated in the following aspects. 1) The performance between the HPO with EA and the traditional HPO algorithm is compared (Sect. 3.2) on different tasks, i.e., GCN and GAT. 2) The performance comparison between the HPO with various EAs is analyzed (Sect. 3.3). 3) The effects of different parameter settings in the EAs on the results are shown, including the mutation probability, the crossover probability, and the population size (Sect. 3.4).

All experiments were performed on a PC with an Intel(R) Xeon(R) Gold 6151 CPU, 32 GB memory, and a GeForce RTX 2080 TI GPU. The implementation of genetic algorithms relies on the open-source library[2].

3.1   Setup

The setup is detailed in the subsection, including datasets, baselines, and metrics.

Datasets. In the experiment, two famous datasets, i.e., Cora and Citeseer are used, where the dataset statistics [22] are presented in Table 3.

Baselines. The HPO models using various EAs were compared with the traditional HPO models with the same number of evaluations. And the parameter setting in the experiment for EAs is shown in Table 4. The parameters are not finely turned.

The baselines are the traditional HPO methods, shown as follows.

---

[2] https://github.com/geatpy-dev/geatpy.

Table 4. Parameter setting

Table 4. Parameter setting

Population size	Mutation rate	Crossover rate	Evaluation rounds
100	0.2	0.7	10000

- GCN-Random search. Random search which conducted on the GCN task.
- GAT-Random search. Random search which conducted on the GAT task.
- GCN-Bayesian optimization. Bayesian optimization which conducted on the GCN task.
- GCN-Bayesian optimization. Bayesian optimization which conducted on the GAT task.
- GCN-Simulated annealing. Simulated annealing (SA) which conducted on the GCN task.
- GCN-Simulated annealing. SA which conducted on the GAT task.

The HPO with EAs applied three types of EAs, i.e., the differential evolution (DE) algorithms, the evolutionary strategy (ES) algorithms, and the genetic algorithms (GA). For a more comprehensive comparison, various algorithms are chosen in each type of EAs, listed as follows. The same as the baselines, these EAs are also conducted on the GCN and GAT tasks.

- DE: DE best bin [23], DE best L [23], DE rand bin [23], DE rand L [24], DE targetToBest bin [25], DE targetToBest L [25], DE currentToBest bin [26], DE currentToBest L [26], and DE currentToRand [26].
- EA: ES 1 plus 1 [27] and ES miu plus lambda [27].
- GA: EGA, SGA, SEGA [28], and studGA [29].

Metrics. The accuracy is used to quantify the performance from the classification perspective, shown as follows. Larger values indicate a better performance.

$$accuracy = \frac{TP + TN}{TP + TN + FP + FN}, \tag{5}$$

where TP, FP, TN, FN denote the numbers of true positives, false positives, true negatives, and false negatives, respectively.

3.2   Comparison Between HPO with EA and Traditional HPO

Different types of EAs share the same parameter setting (detailed in Table 4) to conduct the GCN and GAT tasks. Note that the results are the average values from 10 independent tests to avoid accidental results.

As shown in Fig. 3, they have different performances for the tasks, however, the performance of HPO with EA is better than those of the traditional HPO methods in most cases. It demonstrated that the HPO with EA is a good option for AutoGL. The detailed results are displayed in Table 5. It can be found

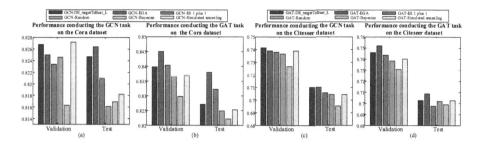

Fig. 3. Performance comparison between HPO with EA and traditional HPO conducting the GCN and GAT tasks on the Core and Citeseer datasets. The ordinate of each subgraph is the accuracy (the higher, the better). It demonstrated that the HPO with EA is a good option for AutoGL.

Table 5. Accuracy performance results among the various types of EAs

Method	Cora		Cora	
	Average (validation)	Standard deviation (validation)	Average (test)	Standard deviation (test)
GCN-DE_targetToBest_1_L	0.8268	0.0022	0.8247	0.0086
GCN-EGA	**0.825**	0.0037	**0.8264**	0.0093
GCN-ES_1_PLUS_1	0.8234	**0.0020**	0.8209	**0.0053**
GCN-Random (baseline)	0.8246	0.0027	0.8161	0.0058
GCN-Bayes (baseline)	0.8163	0.0042	0.8169	0.0086
GCN-Anneal (baseline)	0.8272	0.0027	0.8182	0.0083
GAT-DE_targetToBest_1_L	0.8398	**0.0017**	0.8271	**0.0058**
GAT-EGA	**0.845**	0.0033	**0.838**	0.0071
GAT-ES_1_PLUS_1	0.8404	0.0020	0.8322	0.0068
GAT-Random (baseline)	0.8366	0.0027	0.8249	0.0091
GAT-Bayes (baseline)	0.8298	0.0026	0.8222	0.0083
GAT-Anneal (baseline)	0.837	0.0018	0.8253	0.0090
Method	Citeseer		Citeseer	
	Average (validation)	Standard deviation (validation)	Average (test)	Standard deviation (test)
GCN-DE_targetToBest_1_L	**0.7414**	**0.0020**	**0.7102**	0.0036
GCN-EGA	0.739	0.0031	0.7101	**0.0029**
GCN-ES_1_PLUS_1	0.738	0.0033	0.7057	0.0090
GCN-Random (baseline)	0.7366	0.0039	0.7045	0.0099
GCN-Bayes (baseline)	0.7267	0.0033	0.6953	0.0069
GCN-Anneal (baseline)	0.739	0.0034	0.7045	0.0074
GAT-DE_targetToBest_1_L	0.746	0.0037	0.7026	0.0138
GAT-EGA	**0.752**	0.0042	**0.7086**	0.0070
GAT-ES_1_PLUS_1	0.7436	0.0041	0.6975	**0.0039**
GAT-Random (baseline)	0.7384	**0.0034**	0.7019	0.0107
GAT-Bayes (baseline)	0.7308	0.0084	0.699	0.0109
GAT-Anneal (baseline)	0.7402	0.0050	0.7026	0.0100

that the HPO with EA perform the better average values and standard deviations of accuracy than the traditional HPO algorithms. Furthermore, under the

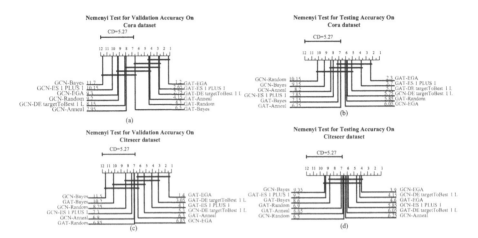

Fig. 4. Nemenyi test results for the validation and testing accuracy on the GCN and GAT tasks. The average rank of each algorithm is marked along the axis (lower ranks to the right). The models on the same horizontal line have a similar prediction performance. The average ranks of the HPO with EA in the validation and testing accuracy outperform those of the traditional HPO methods.

parameter settings and experimental task in this paper, the type of GA owns the excellent performance in the tasks, comparing with DE and ES.

To provide a comprehensive performance comparison between the HPO with EA and traditional HPO, the Friedman and Nemenyi tests [30] were conducted in the experiments, which are widely used to statistically compare different algorithms over multiple datasets. As shown in Fig. 4, the average ranks of the HPO with EA in the validation and testing accuracy outperform those of the traditional HPO methods.

In the Nemenyi tests, it is considered that a significant difference exists if the average ranks of two models differ by at least one critical difference (CD), which is calculated using a 5% significance level. The CD diagrams for the validation and testing accuracy are plotted in Fig. 4, where the average rank of each algorithm is marked along the axis (lower ranks to the right). In Fig. 4, the models on the same horizontal line have similar prediction performance.

3.3   Comparison Among Various Types of EAs

This subsection is to show the performance of various EAs in DE, ES, and GA types, and therefore to provide some options for tasks in AutoGL. They are compared on the GCN and GAT tasks.

Table 6 shows that, for the tested GCN tasks, DE rand bin performs better than other tested DE variants, and ES miu plus lambda performs the best for the tested ES variants. For the GAT tasks, DE best L and ES miu plus lambda performs better than other tested DE and ES variants, respectively. Note that

Table 6. Accuracy performance comparison among the various types of EAs

Method	GCN		GAT	
	Cora	Citeseer	Cora	Citeseer
DE best bin	0.823	0.703	0.843	0.712
DE best L	0.828	0.697	**0.849**	**0.714**
DE rand bin	**0.832**	**0.722**	0.838	0.712
DE rand L	0.823	0.702	0.820	0.709
DE targetToBest bin	0.826	0.703	0.832	0.718
DE targetToBest L	0.826	0.705	0.839	0.713
DE currentToBest bin	0.826	0.705	0.838	0.729
DE currentToBest L	0.827	0.709	0.823	0.706
DE currentToRand	0.827	0.703	0.825	0.720
ES plus	0.814	0.704	0.823	0.706
ES miu plus lambda	**0.816**	**0.719**	**0.828**	**0.721**
EGA	**0.825**	0.721	0.845	0.709
SEGA	0.817	0.717	**0.847**	0.710
SGA	0.818	0.710	0.838	**0.714**
studGA	0.810	**0.722**	0.832	0.710

these are under the specific parameter settings and experimental tasks in this paper.

In addition, the effect of EA parameters on the tested tasks is shown in Fig. 5. The adjusted parameters are population size, crossover rate, and mutation rate.

3.4 Findings

To summary, several findings are concluded as follows. It should be pointed out that the analysis and the findings are under the experimental settings in this paper. The comparison results may be different in different experimental settings or tasks.

1. When the classification accuracy on the verification set is considered as the target to be optimized, most HPO methods using EAs perform better than the optimal method among traditional HPO methods.
2. When considering the type of EAs in the HPO of GNNs for good performance, GA is a good choice based on the experiments under the specific parameter setting in this paper.
3. According to our experiments, DE rand bin, DE best L, and ES miu plus lambda might be good options for optimizing the GCN and GAT. And the experimental results of genetic algorithm are relatively stable for the tested cases.

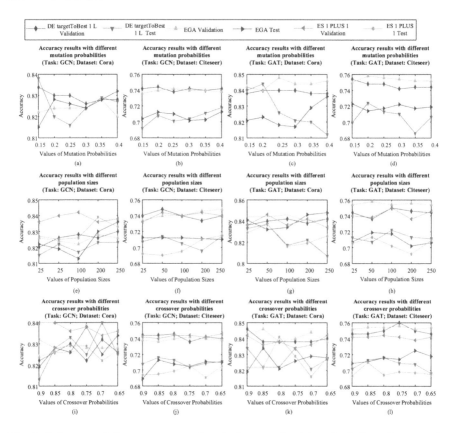

Fig. 5. Influence of the parameters of evolutionary algorithm, including the mutation probability, the population size, and the crossover probability. Three algorithms, i.e., DE targetToBest 1 L, EGA, and ES 1 Plus 1, are conducted on the GCN and GAT tasks on the validation and testing data of Cora and Citeseer datasets.

4   Conclusion

In this study, we aim to demonstrate the validity of EAs in the HPO work of automatic graph neural network learning. We have performed many experiments to test the performance differences of different EAs. The experiments are conducted on the Cora and Citeseer datasets. The experimental results show that the EAs could be an effective alternative to the hyperparameter optimization of GNN, which could provide a reference for later researchers interested in this field.

References

1. Elshawi, R., Maher, M., Sakr, S.: Automated machine learning: State-of-the-art and open challenges, pp. 1–23 (2019). arXiv preprint arXiv:1906.02287

2. Hutter, F., Kotthoff, L., Vanschoren, J. (eds.): Automated Machine Learning. TSS-CML, Springer, Cham (2019). https://doi.org/10.1007/978-3-030-05318-5

3. He, X., Zhao, K., Chu, X.: Automl: a survey of the state-of-the-art. Knowl.-Based Syst. **212**(106622), 1–27 (2021)

4. Guan, C., et al.: Autogl: a library for automated graph learning, pp. 1–8 (2021). arXiv preprint arXiv:2104.04987

5. Liu, Y., Zeng, K., Wang, H., Song, X., Zhou, B.: Content matters: a GNN-based model combined with text semantics for social network cascade prediction. In: Karlapalem, K. (ed.) PAKDD 2021. LNCS (LNAI), vol. 12712, pp. 728–740. Springer, Cham (2021). https://doi.org/10.1007/978-3-030-75762-5_57

6. Fan, W., et al.: Graph neural networks for social recommendation. In: Proceedings of The World Wide Web Conference, pp. 417–426. ACM (2019)

7. Wu, Z., Pan, S., Chen, F., Long, G., Zhang, C., Philip, S.Y.: A comprehensive survey on graph neural networks. IEEE Trans. Neural Netw. Learn. Syst. **32**(1), 4–24 (2020)

8. Liu, M., Gao, H., Ji, S.: Towards deeper graph neural networks. In: Proceedings of the 26th ACM SIGKDD International Conference on Knowledge Discovery & Data Mining, pp. 338–348. ACM (2020)

9. Gori, M., Monfardini, G., Scarselli, F.: A new model for learning in graph domains. In: Proceedings of 2005 IEEE International Joint Conference on Neural Networks, 2005, vol. 2, pp. 729–734. IEEE (2005)

10. Zhou, J., et al.: Graph neural networks: a review of methods and applications. AI Open **1**(1), 57–81 (2020)

11. Kipf, T.N., Welling, M.: Semi-supervised classification with graph convolutional networks, pp. 1–14 (2016). arXiv preprint arXiv:1609.02907

12. Veličković, P., Cucurull, G., Casanova, A., Romero, A., Lio, P., Bengio, Y.: Graph attention networks, pp. 1–12 (2017). arXiv preprint arXiv:1710.10903

13. Bu, C., Luo, W., Yue, L.: Continuous dynamic constrained optimization with ensemble of locating and tracking feasible regions strategies. IEEE Trans. Evol. Comput **21**(1), 14–33 (2017)

14. Dang, D., Jansen, T., Lehre, P.K.: Populations can be essential in tracking dynamic optima. Algorithmica **78**(2), 660–680 (2017)

15. Zhou, Z., Yu, Y., Qian, C.: Evolutionary Learning: Advances in Theories and Algorithms. Springer, Heidelberg (2019). https://doi.org/10.1007/978-981-13-5956-9

16. Eiben, A.E., Smith, J.: From evolutionary computation to the evolution of things. Nature **521**(7553), 476–482 (2015)

17. Bu, C., Luo, W., Zhu, T., Yue, L.: Solving online dynamic time-linkage problems under unreliable prediction. Appl. Soft Comput. **56**, 702–716 (2017)

18. Zhu, T., Luo, W., Bu, C., Yue, L.: Accelerate population-based stochastic search algorithms with memory for optima tracking on dynamic power systems. IEEE Trans. Power Syst. **25**, 268–277 (2015)

19. Yi, R., Luo, W., Bu, C., Lin, X.: A hybrid genetic algorithm for vehicle routing problems with dynamic requests. In: 2017 IEEE Symposium Series on Computational Intelligence, SSCI 2017, Honolulu, HI, USA, 27 November–1 December 2017, pp. 1–8. IEEE (2017)

20. Real, E., Moore, S., Selle, A., Saxena, S., Suematsu, Y.L., Tan, J., Le, Q.V., Kurakin, A.: Large-scale evolution of image classifiers. In: Precup, D., Teh, Y.W. (eds.) Proceedings of the 34th International Conference on Machine Learning, ICML 2017, Sydney, NSW, Australia, 6–11 August 2017. Proceedings of Machine Learning Research, vol. 70, pp. 2902–2911. PMLR (2017)

21. Bu, C., Luo, W., Zhu, T., Yi, R., Yang, B.: Species and memory enhanced differential evolution for optimal power flow under double-sided uncertainties. IEEE Trans. Sustain. Comput. **5**(3), 403–415 (2020)
22. Yang, Z., Cohen, W., Salakhudinov, R.: Revisiting semi-supervised learning with graph embeddings. In: Proceedings of The 33rd International Conference on Machine Learning, pp. 40–48. PMLR (2016)
23. Storn, R.: On the usage of differential evolution for function optimization. In: Proceedings of North American Fuzzy Information Processing, pp. 519–523. IEEE (1996)
24. Opara, K.R., Arabas, J.: Differential evolution: a survey of theoretical analyses. Swarm Evol. Comput. **44**(1), 546–558 (2019)
25. Price, K.V., Storn, R.M., Lampinen, J.A.: Differential Evolution: A Practical Approach to Global Optimization. NCS, Springer, Heidelberg (2005). https://doi.org/10.1007/3-540-31306-0
26. Das, S., Suganthan, P.N.: Differential evolution: a survey of the state-of-the-art. IEEE Trans. Evol. Comput. **15**(1), 4–31 (2010)
27. Beyer, H.G., Schwefel, H.P.: Evolution strategies-a comprehensive introduction. Nat. Comput. **1**(1), 3–52 (2002)
28. Holland, J.H., et al.: Adaptation in Natural and Artificial Systems: An Introductory Analysis with Applications to Biology, Control, and Artificial Intelligence. MIT press, Cambridge (1992)
29. Khatib, W., Fleming, P.J.: The stud GA: a mini revolution? In: Eiben, A.E., Bäck, T., Schoenauer, M., Schwefel, H.-P. (eds.) PPSN 1998. LNCS, vol. 1498, pp. 683–691. Springer, Heidelberg (1998). https://doi.org/10.1007/BFb0056910
30. Demšar, J.: Statistical comparisons of classifiers over multiple data sets. J. Mach. Learn. Res. **7**(1), 1–30 (2006)

Dendritic Cell Algorithm with Group Particle Swarm Optimization for Input Signal Generation

Dan Zhang$^{(\boxtimes)}$ ⓘ and Yiwen Liang

School of Computer Science, Wuhan University, Wuhan, China
{zhangxiaobei125,ywliang}@whu.edu.cn

Abstract. Dendritic cell algorithm (DCA) is a classification algorithm that simulates the behavior of dendritic cells in the tissue environment. Selecting the most valuable attributes and assigning them a suitable signal categorization are crucial for DCA to generate input signals on the data pre-processing and initialization phase. Several methods were employed (e.g., Correlation Coefficient and Rough Set Theory). Those studies preferred to measure the importance of features based on the degree of relevance with the class and determined a mapping relationship between important features and signal categories of DCA based on expert knowledge. Generally, those researches ignore the effect of unimportant features, and the mapping relationship determined by expertise may not produce an optimal classification result. Thus, a hybrid model, GPSO-DCA, is proposed to accomplish feature selection and signal categorization based on Grouping Particle Swarm Optimization (GPSO) without any expertise. This study transforms feature selection and signal categorization into a grouping task (i.e., the selected features are divided into different signal groups) by redefining the data coding and velocity updating equations. The GPSO-DCA searches the optimal feature grouping scheme automatically instead of performing feature selection and signal categorization. The proposed approach is verified by employing the UCI Machine Learning Repository with significant performance improvement.

Keywords: Dendritic cell algorithm · Grouping particle swarm optimization · Input signal generation.

1 Instruction

DCA is a binary classification algorithm inspired by the functioning of the dendritic cells in the natural immune system [1,2]. DCA classifies the data items into two classes, class 1: normal; or class 2: anomalous. DCA is designed for low-dimensional space, and a pre-processing and initialization phase generally is required to generate suitable input signals with three signals for DCA. The input of DCA contains three signals: pathogen-associated molecular patterns (PAMP),

© Springer Nature Switzerland AG 2021
D. N. Pham et al. (Eds.): PRICAI 2021, LNAI 13031, pp. 527–539, 2021.
https://doi.org/10.1007/978-3-030-89188-6_39

danger signals (DS), and safe signals (SS) [2]. The work of this phase includes two components: feature selection/extraction and signal categorization [3], and is crucial for DCA to obtain reliable results. The aim of those works is to appropriately map a given problem domain to the input space of DCA. Feature extraction projects the original high-dimensional features to a new feature space with low dimensionality, and feature selection, on the other hand, directly selects a subset of relevant features for model construction [4]. After feature selection/extraction, each selected/extracted feature is assigned to a specific signal category, either PAMP, DS, or SS.

Several researchers select useful features from the original data set to make up a feature subset. Some other researchers use the feature extraction method to generate new feature space with low dimensionality. In the pre-processing and initialization phase of DCA, Gu et al. [5] applied Principal Component Analysis(PCA), a feature extraction technique, to project the original data onto a new feature subspace with low dimensionality. Due to destroying the implied meaning of features in the original data set, feature extraction techniques have received criticism for performing DCA pre-processing work. Feature selection is another dimensionality reduction technique, and various selection methods are researched such as Correlation Coefficient (CC) [5], null Linear Discriminant Analysis (LDA) [6] and Rough Set Theory(RST) [7–9]. Alok Sharma et al. [6] used the null LDA method to arrange the full features in descending order, and then the r highest-ranked features were selected in turn to form a feature subset. They used null LDA method and nearest neighbor classifier to compute the classification accuracy of this feature subset. They proposed that those works with different r perform repeatedly, and the feature subset with optimum r maintained good classification ability without significant loss of discriminant information. Due to the good performance of feature selection technology in machine learning, Gu et al. [5] attempted to apply the CC method to perform the pre-processing work of DCA. They measured the relevance between attributes and the class as the importance of attributes. The features whose importance degree exceeded a certain threshold were selected to make up a feature subset. Chelly et al. [7–9] proposed RST-DCA, RC-DCA, and QR-DCA by hybridizing the Rough Set Theory and DCA to select features for DCA using RST. RST-DCA and RC-DCA measured the importance degree of a feature by computing the difference between the positive region of an original data set and the positive region of the data set without this feature. Based on the importance degree of features, a family of feature reducts and a core of these reducts were achieved for feature selection. Due to the expensive costs for calculating reducts and core, QR-DCA adopted the QuickReduct algorithm to generate only one reduct. For DCA, those approaches [5,7–9] based on the CC method and RST filter weakly important or unimportant features and select the most important features with their data-intrinsic methods. For signal categorization of DCA, each selected feature is assigned to a particular signal category based on the ranks of features and signal categories, or just by users. Features in the original feature set are ranked according to their relevance/importance degree of the classification. A rank of input signals of the DCA is achieved based on their significance in the algorithm's classification stage. For example, Gu et al. [5] proposed that values of the PAMP or Danger signal are positively correlated to class anomalous, and the value of the safe signal is positively correlated to class normal, according to the semantics of the DCA's signal categories. In [5], features, highly positively correlated or highly negatively correlated to the class, were assigned to a specific signal based on their importance. The ranks of feature and input signals are derived from the intuitions, similar to the principle used in manual methods with expert knowledge. RST-DCA [7] assigned only one attribute randomly from a reduct to both PAMP and SS based on specialist knowledge, as well as combined the rest features of this reduct to represent DS. RC-DCA [8] and QR-DCA [9] assigned attributes of the core to PAMP/SS based on expert knowledge, as well as combined the rest of a reduct to represent DS. However, it is essential to realize that relevance/importance according to those definitions does not imply membership in the optimal feature subset, and the irrelevance does not imply that a feature cannot be in the optimal feature subset [4]. Hence, due to ignoring the effects of those filtered features, those approaches may not generate the optimal feature subset. For signal categorization of DCA, expert knowledge or artificial experience used in the research mentioned before may not assign features to the most appropriate signal. Thus, the process of feature selection and signal categorization based on CC method and RST may lead unsatisfied classification results.

Aiming to overcome those problems, this study proposes a novel method, GPSO-DCA, to perform the feature selection and signal categorization in a coherent procedure automatically without any artificial experience. This study transforms the tasks of feature selection and signal categorization into a job of feature grouping. Divide features of original data set into four groups: PAMP, DS, SS, and UN. The group of UN contains all the features unselected. The PAMP group includes all the attributes assigned to the signal PAMP, and so do DS, SS. The GPSO-DCA, hybridizing GPSO and DCA, automatically gives each feature in the original data set to a group, either PAMP, DS, SS, or UN. A search space is composed of all possible grouping schemes. DCA is considered a black box (i.e., no knowledge of DCA is needed, just the interface) to evaluate schemes' performance. The GPSO is the search engine to find an optimal scheme that wraps around the DCA. The classification results of the mentioned techniques (e.g., DCA base CC, RST-DCA, RC-DCA, QR-DCA) are discussed and compared with GPSO-DCA on the UCI Machine Learning Repository. This study also compares GPSO-DCA with the K-Nearest Neighbor (KNN) [10] and the Decision Tree (DT) [11], the potent tools for classification in Machine Learning. Through the experiments, the GPSO-DCA performs better than them and is found successful enough to obtain good classification results.

The remaining paper is organized as follows: Sect. 2 reviews the brief introduction related to the DCA and the GPSO. The novel model, GPSO-DCA, is proposed in Sect. 3. The experiments, the preparation of the investigation, the result, and the analysis are elaborated in Sect. 4. Finally, the conclusion and future work are reported in Sect. 5.

2   Related Work

This section provides a brief introduction to Dendritic Cell Algorithm and Group Particle Swarm Optimization.

2.1   Dendritic Cell Algorithm

The behavior of dendritic cells depends on the concentration of the immuno-logical signals in a tissue environment, namely pathogen-associated molecular patterns (PAMP), danger signals (DS), safe signals (SS) [3]. Inspired by the behavior and mechanism of dendritic cells, GreenSmith [2] proposed a binary classification algorithm, DCA. In the algorithm, the input signals of DCA correspond to those immunological signals respectively. Each data item is denoted as an antigen to be processed by detectors. The algorithm contains four main phases: the pre-processing and initialization phase, the detection phase, the context assessment phase, and the classification phase [3]. In the pre-processing and initialization phase, the appropriate features should be chosen from the original data sets and assigned a specific signal category, either as PAMP, DS, or SS. After that, combine the signal categories and antigens to achieve a signal database. Each row in the signal database represents an antigen, with three attributes: PAMP, DS, and SS, to be classified. A weighted sum equation and a weight matrix are utilized to compute the input signals mentioned previously throughout the detection phase. When a DC detects an antigen, the input signals are transformed into three interim signals, known as the costimulatory molecule signal value (CSM), the semi-mature signal value (SEMI), and the mature signal value (MAT) [3]. The three interim signals of a DC are continuously accumulated during the process of antigen processing. Equation (1) shows the weighted sum equation. The weights of PAMP, DS, and SS used for generating CSM respectively are [2,1,2], the weights for SEMI are [0,2,–1], and the weights for MAT is [2,1,–2].

$$(CSM, SEMI, MAT) = \sum_{n=1}^{T} \frac{W_{PAMP} \times C_{PAMP}}{|W_{PAMP}| + |W_{SS}| + |W_{DS}|}$$
$$+ \sum_{n=1}^{T} \frac{W_{DS} \times C_{DS}}{|W_{PAMP}| + |W_{SS}| + |W_{DS}|} \qquad (1)$$
$$+ \sum_{n=1}^{T} \frac{W_{SS} \times C_{SS}}{|W_{PAMP}| + |W_{SS}| + |W_{DS}|},$$

where the C_{PAMP} represents the value of input signal $PAMP$, the C_{SS} represents the value of input signal SS, the C_{DS} represents the value of input signal DS, the W_{PAMP} is the weight for C_{PAMP}, the W_{DS} is the weight for C_{DS}, the W_{SS} is the weight for C_{SS}, T is the number of antigens detected by a DC.

In the context assessment phase, the three cumulative interim values are used to assess the state of the context around a DC. The CSM measures the concentration of antigens around a DC, and a migration threshold is incorporated into the DCA. As soon as the cumulative CSM of a DC exceeds the migration threshold, the DC ceases to detect new antigens and its context is assessed. If the cumulative SEMI of the DC is more than its cumulative MAT, the antigens around the DC are considered as normal, and vice versa.

In the algorithm, a DC can detect many antigens, and an antigen can also be detected by many DCs. Therefore, the class of an antigen is determined by analyzing and computing the decisions of DCs that have detected this antigen. In the last phase, the Mature Context Antigen Value (MCAV) is incorporated into the DCA, shown as Eq. (2). In general, there is a threshold value of MCAV to represent the probability that an antigen is anomalous. If the MCAV of an antigen exceeds the threshold value mentioned before, the antigen is labeled as anomalous, and vice versa.

$$MCAV = \frac{DC_{mature}}{DC_{semi} + DC_{mature}}, \tag{2}$$

where DC_{mature} is the number of DCs that label the antigen as anomalous; and DC_{semi} is the number of DCs that label the antigen as normal.

2.2 Grouping Particle Swarm Optimization

Grouping Particle Swarm Optimization (GPSO) is an extension of the traditional Particle Swarm Optimization to solving grouping problems. The PSO. [12], first proposed by Kennedy and Eberhart, is inspired by observing the bird flocking and fish schooling where the synchrony of flocking behavior is through maintaining optimal distances between individuals and their neighbors. PSO preserves a swarm of particles that fly through a virtual search space and communicate with each other to find the global optimum. Each position visited by particles represents a potential solution to the problem. The search of each particle (whose position represents a possible solution to the problem) is simultaneously guided by two positions, the personal best position and the global best position found by the whole swarm. The main components of PSO are the grouping scheme representation and velocity updating equations. Compared with PSO, GPSO uses a special encoding scheme (group encoding) to take into account the structure of grouping problems and redefines the velocity updating equations.

Due to the excellent grouping capacity, Ali Husseinzadeh Kashan et al. [13] applied GPSO to the single batch machine scheduling problem and bin packing problem, and results were compared with the results reported by GGA. Computational results testified that GPSO was efficient and could be regarded as a new solver for the wide class of grouping problems. Xiaorong Zhao et al. [14] constructed an elite swarm to replace the worst one in every iteration for improving the performance of GPSO. In addition, they applied a simple mutation operator to the best solution so as to help it escape from local optima. Their GPSO was compared with several variants of PSO and some state-of-the-art evolutionary algorithms on CEC15 benchmark functions. As demonstrated by the experimental results, their proposed GPSO outperformed its competitors in most cases.

Experimental results show that GPSO is promising to solve the grouping problem. In this paper, GPSO is firstly applied to perform the feature selection and signal categorization synchronously for DCA.

3 Proposed Method

As showing in Fig. 1, a novel method named GPSO-DCA is presented that hybridizes the DCA with GPSO. GPSO-DCA is a framework that contains three components, search space, search method (GPSO), and evaluation method (DCA).

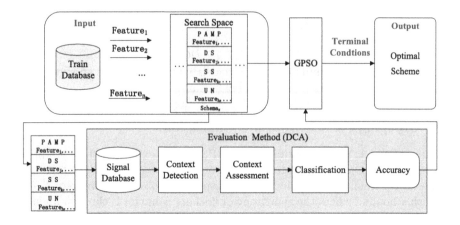

Fig. 1. The model of GPSO-DCA.

This study transforms the tasks of feature selection and signals categorization into a procedure of feature grouping. A feature grouping scheme is a solution for generating the input signal of DCA. After that, a search space is constructed which contains all the possible grouping schemes. Aiming to find an optimal grouping scheme, DCA is a part of the performance evaluation function, and GPSO is a search method wrapping around DCA to find the optimal grouping scheme. The three components, search space, search method (GPSO), and evaluation method (DCA), are described in detail in the following sections.

3.1 Search Space

As shown in Fig. 2, the work of feature selection is to select independent features from the original data set to construct a feature subset. The work of signal categorization is to establish a mapping relationship between selected features and signal categories, shown as Eq. (3).

$$f : (Feature_i, Feature_j, Feature_k, ...) \rightarrow (PAMP, DS, SS) \qquad (3)$$

Establishing a mapping relation can be considered as grouping the attributes into four groups, either PAMP, SS, DS, or UN. The features in PAMP, SS, DS groups are the selected features, and the groups represent the special signal categorization assigned for those features. Thus, grouping schemes of the features represent solutions of feature selection and the possible signal categories of selected features. Thus, the aim of the data pre-processing is to search for a suitable feature grouping scheme.

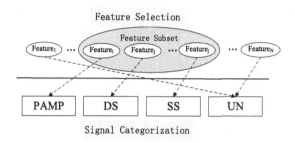

Fig. 2. Steps of feature selection and signal categorization.

In the search space, each state represents a grouping scheme of features. A scheme is denoted as { $subset_{PAMP}$ ($Feature_i$ ...), $subset_{DS}$ ($Feature_j$ ...), $subset_{SS}$ ($Feature_k$ ...), $subset_{UN}$ ($Feature_h$ ...) }. The group order is unique, and { $Feature_i$, $Feature_j$, $Feature_k$, $Feature_h$, ...} are independent features in the original data set. The $subset_{PAMP}$ ($Feature_i$ ...) represents that the features $\in$ { $Feature_i$ ... } are assigned to signal PAMP, the $subset_{DS}$ ($Feature_j$ ...) represents that the features $\in$ { $Feature_j$ ... } are assigned to signal DS, the $subset_{SS}$ ($Feature_k$ ...) represents that the features $\in$ { $Feature_k$ ... } are assigned to signal SS, and the $subset_{UN}$ ($Feature_h$ ...) represents that the features $\in$ { $Feature_h$ ... } are not assigned to any signals. Transform a state to another by new velocity updating equations.

3.2 Evaluation Method

The evaluation method is utilized to evaluate each state in the search space. This study adopts the classification accuracy of DCA to evaluate the performance of states. To estimate the accuracy of DCA, this study performs classification multiple times for 10-fold cross-validation with a particular signal database contributed by a state. The average accuracy of 10 times experiments is calculated as the performance of a state.

3.3 Search Method: GPSO

Step1: Data Encoding. In GPSO, the position of each particle represents a state in the search space. GPSO maintains a particle swarm where the personal best position and the best position found by swarm guide them to update their position. Through updating positions, GPSO searches globally for as many schemes as possible to find the optimal. This study uses real number $\{1, 2, 3, ..., N\}$ to represent features in the original data set (N is the amount of the total features). This study determines a 4-dimensional vector $V = \{ (i\ ..), (j\ ...), (k...), (h...) \}$, shown in Fig. 3, as a position of particles ($\{0 \leq i, j, k, h \leq N, i \neq j \neq k \neq h\}$, i, j, k and h are the real number to represent independent features from the original data set). The vectors with different orders represent different positions, e.g., $\{ (i...), (j...), (k...), (h...) \} \neq \{ (j...), (i...), (k...), (h...) \}$ (i, j, k, h are the real number to represent independent features of the original data set).

Feature$_i$, ...	Feature$_j$, ...	Feature$_k$, ...	Feature$_h$, ...
PAMP	DS	SS	UN

Fig. 3. Data encoding scheme of GPSO: a 4-dimensional vector V.

Step 2: Fitness Function. This study adopts the classification accuracy of DCA to evaluate the performance of a position described in Sect. 3.2.

$$fitness(V) = 10 - foldCrossValidation(Accuracy(DCA(V))), \qquad (4)$$

where V is a postion of particles, $fitness(V)$ is the fitness value of postion V. $Accuracy(DCA(V))$ is the classification accuracy of DCA running on the signal database based on the postion of particles V. This study uses 10-fold cross-validation to estimate the classification accuracy of DCA.

Step 3: Velocity Updating Equations. After computing the fitness for each particles' position in the current swarm, the velocity updating equations are utilized to update the positions of the whole swarm. Generally, the velocity updating equations contain two-part: Eq. (5) and Eq. (6).

$$v_{id}^{t+1} = w v_{id}^t + c_1 r_1 (p_{id}^t - x_{id}^t) + c_2 r_2 (p_{gd}^t - x_{id}^t) \qquad (5)$$

$$v_{id}^{t+1} = x_{id}^{t+1} - x_{id}^t \qquad (6)$$

where d is the dimensionality of grouping for the positions and velocities, and this study set d to be 4; $i = 1, ..., NP$, NP is the size of swarm; t represents the number of iterations; x_{id}^{t+1} is the d_{th} group of position at the i_{th} particle for the $(t+1)_{th}$ iteration; p_{id} is the currently optimal position of the i_{th} particle at the d_{th} group in the t_{th} iteration; p_{gd} is the currently optimal position of the sarm at the d_{th} group in the t_{th} iteration; v_{id}^{t+1} is the velocity of i_{th} particle at the d_{th} group for the $(t+1)_{th}$ iteration; w is the inertia weight; c_1 and c_2 are private and population acceleration coefficients respectively; r_1 and r_2 are random numbers between 0 and 1.

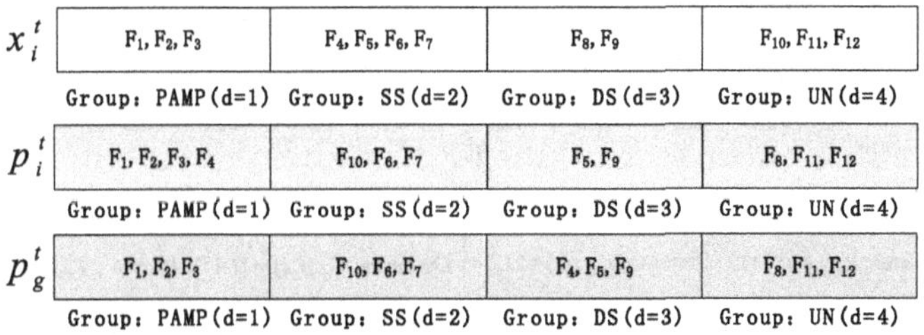

x_i^t	F_1, F_2, F_3	F_4, F_5, F_6, F_7	F_8, F_9	F_{10}, F_{11}, F_{12}
	Group: PAMP (d=1)	Group: SS (d=2)	Group: DS (d=3)	Group: UN (d=4)
p_i^t	F_1, F_2, F_3, F_4	F_{10}, F_6, F_7	F_5, F_9	F_8, F_{11}, F_{12}
	Group: PAMP (d=1)	Group: SS (d=2)	Group: DS (d=3)	Group: UN (d=4)
p_g^t	F_1, F_2, F_3	F_{10}, F_6, F_7	F_4, F_5, F_9	F_8, F_{11}, F_{12}
	Group: PAMP (d=1)	Group: SS (d=2)	Group: DS (d=3)	Group: UN (d=4)

Fig. 4. An example about three position.

In particular, this study substitutes operator "$-$" with a group dissimilarity measure denoted as $Distance()$.

$$Distance(G, G') = 1 - \frac{Num(|G \cap G'|)}{Num(|G \cup G'|)} \tag{7}$$

The G and G' are two groups; the measure $Distance(G, G')$ is 0 to 1; if $G = G'$, the measure is equal to 0; if $G \cap G' = \emptyset$, the measure is equal to 0. Substituting "$-$" in Eq. (5) and Eq. (6) with the $Distance$, the updating equations in GPSO are introduced as follows:

$$v_{id}^{t+1} = wv_{id}^t + c_1 r_1 Distance(p_{id}, x_{id}^t) + c_2 r_2 Distance(p_{gd}, x_{id}^t) \tag{8}$$

$$v_{id}^{t+1} = Distance(x_{id}^t, x_{id}^{t+1}) = 1 - \frac{Num(|x_{id}^t \cap x_{id}^{t+1}|)}{Num(|x_{id}^t \cup x_{id}^{t+1}|)} \tag{9}$$

$Distance(p_{id}, x_{id}^t)$ represents the number of different features between two groups of p_{id} and x_{id}^t; $Distance(p_{gd}, x_{id}^t)$ represents the number of different features between two groups of p_{gd} and x_{id}^t; $Num(|x_{id}^t \cap x_{id}^{t+1}|)$ is the number of identical features between two groups of x_{id}^t and x_{id}^{t+1}; $Num(|x_{id}^t \cup x_{id}^{t+1}|)$ is the number of all the unique features between two groups of x_{id}^t and x_{id}^{t+1}.

The shared features between two groups of x_{id}^t and x_{id}^{t+1} are one of the parts. The x_{id}^{t+1} can inherit the shared features of x_{id}^t. The number of shared feature is as follow:

$$Num(|x_{id}^t \cap x_{id}^{t+1}|) = (1 - v_{id}^{t+1})Num(|x_{id}^t \cup x_{id}^{t+1}|) \tag{10}$$

Stripping out the shared features, this study assigns the remaining features to special groups by some rules. Hence, this study concerns more about the percentage of shared features in x_{id}^t. This study defines that the n_{id}^{t+1} is close to Eq. (11).

$$Num(|x_{id}^t \cap x_{id}^{t+1}|) \approx (1 - v_{id}^{t+1})x_{id}^t \tag{11}$$

For exsample, the x_i^t, p_i and p_g are shown in Fig. 4. The $Distance()$ between the four groups of x_i^t, p_i^t and p_g^t is shown in Fig. 5. Suppose that $c_1 r_1 = 0.2$; $c_2 r_2 = 0.4$; $v_{i1}^t = 0.1$; $v_{i2}^t = 0.2$; $v_{i3}^t = 0.3$; $v_{i4}^t = 0.4$; $w = 0.5$. After computing

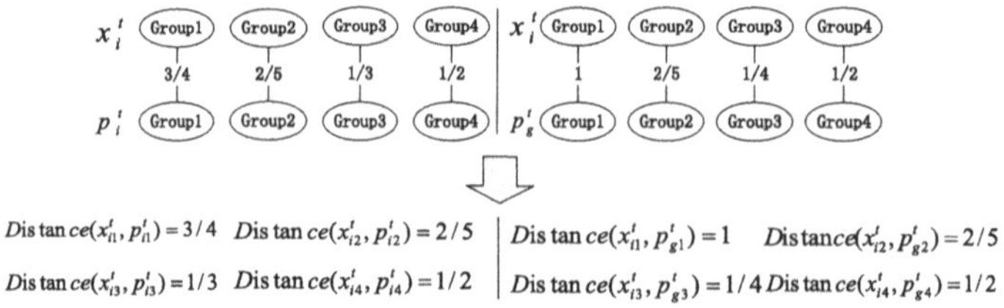

Fig. 5. The computing of $Distance()$.

the $Distance()$ of four groups, the four velocities of the i_{th} particle is achieved as follows:

$$\begin{cases} v_{i1}^{t+1} = 0.5 * 0.1 + 0.2 * 3/4 + 0.4 * 1 = 0.24, \\ v_{i2}^{t+1} = 0.5 * 0.2 + 0.2 * 2/5 + 0.4 * 2/5 = 0.34, \\ v_{i3}^{t+1} = 0.5 * 0.3 + 0.2 * 1/3 + 0.4 * 1/4 = 0.32, \\ v_{i3}^{t+1} = 0.5 * 0.4 + 0.2 * 1/2 + 0.4 * 1/2 = 0.5 \end{cases} \quad (12)$$

Based on the four velocities achieved before, the share features of four groups between x_i^t, p_i and p_g is achieved as follows:

$$\begin{cases} Num(|x_{i1}^t \cap x_{i1}^{t+1}|) = \lfloor (1 - 0.24) \times 3 \rfloor = 2, \\ Num(|x_{i2}^t \cap x_{i2}^{t+1}|) = \lfloor (1 - 0.34) \times 4 \rfloor = 2, \\ Num(|x_{i3}^t \cap x_{i3}^{t+1}|) = \lfloor (1 - 0.32) \times 2 \rfloor = 1, \\ Num(|x_{i4}^t \cap x_{i4}^{t+1}|) = \lfloor (1 - 0.5) \times 3 \rfloor = 1 \end{cases} \quad (13)$$

The shared features of four groups are randomly selected from the four corresponding groups of x_i^t. The missing features are assigned a special signal categorization first according to its group in p_g, and secondly according to p_i.

Step 4: Termination Conditions. The search process is running iteratively until satisfying one of the two conditions. The first condition is when the fitness value of a position is larger than a threshold. The second condition is when the number of iterations executes up to a certain number $MaxIterations$.

4   Experimentation

In this section, four data sets, (e.g., Spambase(SP), Sonar and Cancer), are applied to validate the proposed approach from UCI Machine Learning Repository [15]. In this work, non-numerical features are transformed into numerical features.

4.1   Experiment Setup

To study the feasibility and superiority of the proposed approach, two experiments are performed. In the first experiment, GPSO-DCA, RST-DCA, RC-DCA, QR-DCA, and the DCA based on the CC perform classification tasks on the three

Table 1. Quantitative comparison results on the test sequences from four datasets: SP, Sonar and Cancer. The arrow each after each metric indicates that the higher (↑) or lower (↓) value is better. Best in bold.

Dataset	Method	Metric	
		Accuracy %(↑)	F-Measure% (↑)
SP	**GPSO-DCA (Ours)**	**94.7**	**93.6**
	RST-DCA	89.32	88.03
	RC-DCA	93.35	92.21
	QR-DCA	93.17	92.01
	DCA based CC	93.48	92.35
Sonar	**GPSO-DCA (Ours)**	**99**	**98**
	RST-DCA	92.9	92.41
	RC-DCA	89.67	89.04
	QR-DCA	88.38	88.16
	DCA based CC	85.16	80.67
Cancer	**GPSO-DCA (Ours)**	**99**	**99**
	RST-DCA	94.28	95.83
	RC-DCA	92.71	94.68
	QR-DCA	92.28	94.45
	DCA based CC	90.86	93.36

data sets. Furthermore, the classification performance of the well-known classifiers, the KNN and the DT, are also compared with the proposed approach. This study utilizes 5-fold cross-valication to estimate the classification performance of each algorithm. The stratified sampling method divides each data set into two disjoint sets: training and testing. The sizes commonly used for those sets are 80% of the data for the training and 20% for testing. To evaluate the performance of the above approaches, the accuracy and F-measure are calculated. Those algorithms train their model on the train data, and the results obtained from the above experiments are generated across many trials.

4.2 Parameters Description

In this work, the size of the DC poll is set as 100, and each antigen is sampled by up to 10 DCs. The migration threshold is the combination of the weight values and the max signal values by using Eq. (1). The threshold of MCAV is set to 0.6. The $MaxIterations$ of GPSO-DCA is 10 in each experiment. The acceleration coefficients c_1 and c_2 are 0.49 and 0.51 respectively. The inertia weight w is 0.5.

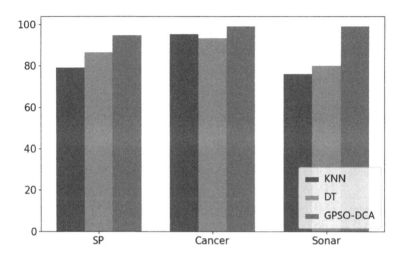

Fig. 6. Comparison of classifiers average accuracy on the 3 binary data sets.

4.3   Results Analysis and Comparison

Table 1 shows the classification performance of the proposed approaches on the UCI Machine Learning Repository. The GPSO-DCA performs classification on the SP data set and achieves the best accuracy/f-measure (94.7%, 93.6%) compared with RST-DCA (89.32%, 88.03%), RC-DCA (93.35%, 92.21%), QR-DCA (93.17%, 92.35%), and DCA based CC (93.48%). Compared with those approaches, GPSO-DCA also performs better on the other data sets with the highest accuracy and F-measure.

This study also compares the performance of GPSO-DCA to other popular classifiers including KNN and DT in terms of the accuracy on the three data sets. The classification process of KNN and DT are shown in [10] and [11] respectively. As shown in Fig. 6, when applying those approaches to the SP data set, Cancer data set and Sonar data set, GPSO-DCA outperforms the other two approaches in terms of accuracy.

In summary, GPSO-DCA is a feasible classification technique that accomplishes feature selection and signal categorization synchronously and automatically without any expert knowledge. This study shows that grouping suitable feature to signal categories is crucial. Those promising results are achieved by the appropriate application of the GPSO in the DCA data pre-processing phase.

5   Conclusion

This study firstly transforms the works of feature selection and signal categorization into a grouping work of features. To accomplish those works synchronously and automatically, a novel hybrid DCA based on GPSO is proposed. This study redefined the data coding of particles and velocity updating equations in GPSO to find the optimal feature grouping scheme globally without any expertise. The future works include two parts: on the one hand, the search method with less running time in GPSO-DCA will be explored; on the other hand, an optimization method of weight matrix for GPSO-DCA should be researched to let GPSO-DCA preserve good classification results on more challenging data sets.

References

1. Zhou, W., Liang, Y.: A new version of the deterministic dendritic cell algorithm based on numerical differential and immune response. Appl. Soft Comput. **102**, 107055 (2021). https://doi.org/10.1016/j.asoc.2020.107055
2. Greensmith, J., Aickelin, U.: The dendritic cell algorithm. Technical Report (2007)
3. Chelly, Z., Elouedi, Z.: A survey of the dendritic cell algorithm. Knowl. Inf. Syst. **48**(3), 505–535 (2015). https://doi.org/10.1007/s10115-015-0891-y
4. Li, J., et al.: Feature selection: a data perspective. ACM Comput. Surv. **50**(6) (December 2017). https://doi.org/10.1145/3136625
5. Gu, F.: Theoretical and Empirical Extensions of the Dendritic Cell Algorithm. Ph.D. thesis (11 2011). https://doi.org/10.13140/RG.2.1.5155.1848
6. Sharma, A., Imoto, S., Miyano, S., Sharma, V.: Null space based feature selection method for gene expression data. Int. J. Mach. Learn. Cybern. **3**(4), 269–276 (2012)
7. Chelly, Z., Elouedi, Z.: RST-DCA: a dendritic cell algorithm based on rough set theory. In: Huang, T., Zeng, Z., Li, C., Leung, C.S. (eds.) ICONIP 2012. LNCS, vol. 7665, pp. 480–487. Springer, Heidelberg (2012). https://doi.org/10.1007/978-3-642-34487-9_58
8. Chelly, Z., Elouedi, Z.: RC-DCA: a new feature selection and signal categorization technique for the dendritic cell algorithm based on rough set theory. In: Coello Coello, C.A., Greensmith, J., Krasnogor, N., Liò, P., Nicosia, G., Pavone, M. (eds.) ICARIS 2012. LNCS, vol. 7597, pp. 152–165. Springer, Heidelberg (2012). https://doi.org/10.1007/978-3-642-33757-4_12
9. Chelly, Z., Elouedi, Z.: QR-DCA: a new rough data pre-processing approach for the dendritic cell algorithm. In: Tomassini, M., Antonioni, A., Daolio, F., Buesser, P. (eds.) ICANNGA 2013. LNCS, vol. 7824, pp. 140–150. Springer, Heidelberg (2013). https://doi.org/10.1007/978-3-642-37213-1_15
10. Erturul, O.F., Taluk, M.E.: A novel version of k nearest neighbor: dependent nearest neighbor. Appl. Soft Comput. J. **55**, 480–490 (2017)
11. Blanquero, R., Carrizosa, E., Molero-Rio, C., Romero Morales, D.: Optimal randomized classification trees. Comput. Oper. Res. **132**, 105281 (2021)
12. Kennedy, J., Eberhart, R.: Particle swarm optimization, vol. 4, pp. 1942–1948. Perth, Aust (1995)
13. Husseinzadeh Kashan, A., Husseinzadeh Kashan, M., Karimiyan, S.: A particle swarm optimizer for grouping problems. Inf. Sci. **252**, 81–95 (2013)
14. Zhao, X., Zhou, Y., Xiang, Y.: A grouping particle swarm optimizer. Appl. Intell. **49**(8), 2862–2873 (2019). https://doi.org/10.1007/s10489-019-01409-4
15. Asuncion, A., Newman, D.: Uci machine learning repository (2007)

Knowledge Representation
and Reasoning

Building Trust for Belief Revision

Aaron Hunter$^{(\boxtimes)}$

British Columbia Institute of Technology, Burnaby, Canada
aaron_hunter@bcit.ca

Abstract. Trust plays a role in the process of belief revision. When information is reported by another agent, it should only be believed if the reporting agent is trusted as an authority over some relevant domain. In practice, an agent will be trusted on a particular topic if they have provided accurate information on that topic in the past. In this paper, we demonstrate how an agent can construct a model of knowledge-based trust based on the accuracy of past reports. We then show how this model of trust can be used in conjunction with Ordinal Conditional Functions to define two approaches to trust-influenced belief revision. In the first approach, strength of trust and strength of belief are assumed to be incomparable as they are on different scales. In the second approach, they are aggregated in a natural manner.

Keywords: Belief revision · Trust · Knowledge representation

1 Introduction

Belief revision is concerned with the manner in which an agent incorporates new information that may be inconsistent with their current beliefs. In general, the belief revision literature assumes that new information is more reliable than the initial beliefs; in this case, new information must always be believed following belief revision. However, in many practical situations this is not a reasonable assumption. In practice, we need to take into account the extent to which the source of the new information is *trusted*. In this paper, we demonstrate how an agent can actually build trust in a source, based on past reports.

Suppose that an agent believes ϕ to be true, and they are being told by an agent R that ϕ is not true. In this kind of situation, we will use *ranking functions* to represent both the initial strength of belief in ϕ as well as the level of trust in R. Significantly, however, the trust in R is not uniform over all formulas. Each information source is trusted to different degrees on different topics. The extent to which R is trusted on a particular topic is determined by how frequently they have made accurate reports on that topic in the past.

In the rest of the paper, we proceed as follows. In the next section, we give a motivating example that will be used throughout the paper. We then review formal preliminaries related to belief revision and trust. We then introduce *trust graphs*, our formal model of trust. We define a simple approach for building a

© Springer Nature Switzerland AG 2021
D. N. Pham et al. (Eds.): PRICAI 2021, LNAI 13031, pp. 543–555, 2021.
https://doi.org/10.1007/978-3-030-89188-6_40

trust graph from past revisions, and prove some basic results. We then demonstrate how trust rankings can influence belief revision in two different ways. First, we consider the naive case, where the strength of trust is independent of the strength of belief. Second, we consider the more complex case, where strength of trust is aggregated with strength of belief.

2   Preliminaries

2.1   Motivating Example

Consider a situation where there are two rooms A and B located inside a building. There are two agents, which we call *Absent* and *Present*. Informally, *Absent* is not in the building whereas *Present* is in the building. These agents communicate about the status of the lights in each room. For simplicity, we say that A is true when the light is on in room A and we say B is true when the light is on in room B.

We focus on the beliefs of *Absent*, who initially thinks that the light in room A is on and the light in room B is off. Now suppose that *Present* sends a message that asserts the light is off in A and the light is on in room B. If *Present* is completely trusted, this is not a problem; the report simply leads *Absent* to believe they were incorrect about the lights.

But suppose that *Present* has given incorrect reports in the past. We can collect these reports, and check to see when they have been correct and when they have been incorrect. For example, suppose that *Present* is always correct about the light status in room A, whereas they are often incorrect about the light status in room B. We might draw the conclusion that they are normally physically in the room A, and that they are too lazy to walk to a another room to check the lights.

Formally, *Absent* does not need a plausible story to explain the mistakes in the reports; they need some mechanism for modelling trust over different propositions. By looking at the accuracy of reports on different topics, they build a model of trust that allows information reported from *Present* to be incorporated appropriately. In this paper, we develop formal machinery that is suitable for capturing all facets of this seemingly simple example.

2.2   Belief Revision

We assume an underlying set $\mathbf{V}$ of propositional variables. A *formula* is a propositional combination of elements of $\mathbf{V}$, using the usual connectives $\rightarrow, \wedge, \vee, \neg$. We will assume that $\mathbf{V}$ is finite in this paper, though that need not be the case in general. A *state* is a propositional interpretation over $\mathbf{V}$, which assigns boolean values to all variables. We will normally specify a state by giving the set of variables that are true. A *belief state* is a set of states, informally representing the set of states that an agent considers possible. We let $|\phi|$ denote the set of states where the formula ϕ is true.

The dominant approach to belief revision is the AGM approach. A revision operator is a function $*$ that maps a belief state K and a formula ϕ to a new belief state $K * \phi$. An AGM revision operator is a revision operator that satisfies the so-called AGM postulates. We refer the reader to [1] for a complete introduction to the AGM theory of belief revision.

Although we are concerned with AGM revision at times, in this paper we actually define the beliefs of an agent in terms of Ordinal Conditional Functions (OCFs) [13], which are also called *ranking functions*. An OCF is a function κ that maps every state s to an ordinal $\kappa(s)$. Informally, if $\kappa(s_1) < \kappa(s_2)$, this is understood to mean that the agent considers it more likely that s_1 is the actual state, as opposed to s_2. Note that κ defines a belief state $Bel(\kappa)$ as follows:

$$Bel(\kappa) = \{s \mid \kappa(s) \text{ is minimal }\}.$$

We can also define a revision operator $*$ associated with κ as follows:

$$Bel(\kappa) * \phi = \min_{\kappa}(|\phi|).$$

The operator on belief states specified in this manner defines an AGM belief revision operator, for any underlying OCF.

2.3   Trust

The notion of trust plays an important role in many applications, including security [5,10] and multi-agent systems [9,12]. In this paper, we are concerned primarily with *knowledge-based* trust. That is, we are concerned with the extent to which one agent trusts another to have the knowledge required to be trusted on particular statements. This is distinct from trust related to honesty or deception.

We refer occasionally to *trust-sensitive* belief revision operators [4]. Trust-sensitive belief revision operators are defined with respect to a trust-partition over states. The equivalence classes of a trust partition Π consist of states that can not be distinguished by a particular reporting agent. In our motivating example, we might define a trust partition for *Present* that consists of two equivalence classes: one that includes all states where the light is on in room A, and one that includes all states where the light is off in room A. In this case, *Present* is informally trusted to be able to tell if the light in room A is on or off. However, *Present* is not trusted to be able to tell if the light in room B is on or off.

A trust-sensitive revision operator $*_\Pi$ is defined with respect to a given AGM revision operator $*$ and a trust partition Π. The operator $*_\Pi$ operates in two steps when an agent is given a report ϕ. First, we find the set $\Pi(\phi)$ of all states that are related by Π to a model of ϕ. Then we perform regular AGM revision with this expanded set of states as input. Hence, the model of trust is essentially used to pre-process the formula for revision, by expanding it to ignore distinctions that we do not trust the reporter to be able to make.

2.4   Trust Rankings

We can also define trust in terms of a distance function between states. The notion of distance required is generally an ultrametric.

Definition 1. *An* ultrametric *is a binary function d over a set X, such that for all* $x, y, z \in X$*:*

- $d(x, y) \geq 0$.
- $d(x, y) = 0$ *if and only if* $x = y$.
- $d(x, y) = d(y, x)$.
- $d(x, z) \leq \max\{d(x, y), d(y, z)\}$.

If we remove condition 2, then d is a pseudo-ultrametric.

The following definition of a trust ranking is given in [8].

Definition 2. *For any propositional vocabulary, a* trust ranking *is a pseudo-ultrametric over the set S of all states.*

A trust ranking is intended to capture the degree to which an agent is trusted to distinguish between states in a graph. If $d(s_1, s_2)$ is large, this means the agent can be trusted to distinguish the states s_1 and s_2. However, if the distance is small, they can not be trusted to draw this distinction.

3   Building Trust

3.1   Trust Graphs

We now turn to our main problem: building a notion of trust from data. We assume throughout this paper a fixed, finite vocabulary **V**. All states, belief states, and formulas will be defined with respect to this underlying vocabulary.

Definition 3. *Let S be the set of states over* **V**. *A* trust graph *over S is a pair* $\langle S, w \rangle$, *where* $w : S \times S \to \mathbf{N}$.

Hence, a trust graph is just a complete weighted graph along with a distance between states. Informally, a trust graph represents the trust held in another agent. The weight on the edge between two states s_1 and s_2 is an indication of how strongly the agent is trusted to *directly* distinguish between those states.

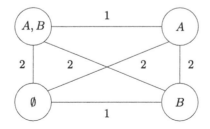

Fig. 1. A trust graph

Example 1. Consider the motivating example, in the case where *Absent* trusts *Present* more strongly to check if the light in room *A* is on as opposed to room *B*. This could be captured by the trust graph in Fig. 1, by having a higher weight on edges that connect states that differ on the value of *A*. Note that the minimax distance *d* can easily be calculated from this graph.

The edge weights represent how strongly a reporting agent is trusted to distinguish between a pair of states. If the weight is high, we interpret this to mean that the agent is strongly trusted to distinguish between the states. If the weight is low, then the reporting agent is not trusted to distinguish the states.

In order to build a notion of trust in an agent, we need to have a history of the past reports that agent has provided. Our basic approach is to assume that we start with a set of statements that a reporting agent has made in the past, along with an indication of whether the reports were correct or not.

Definition 4. *A report is a pair (ϕ, i), where ϕ is a formula and $i \in \{0, 1\}$. A report history is a multi-set of reports.*

We let Φ, possibly with subscripts, range over report histories. A report history Φ represents all of the claims that an agent has truthfully or falsely claimed in the past. Informally, if $(\phi, 1) \in \Phi$ then the agent in question has reported ϕ in the past in a situation where ϕ was shown to be true. On the other hand, $(\phi, 0) \in \Phi$ means that ϕ has been reported in a situation where it was false.

3.2 Construction from Reports

Suppose we start with a trust graph in which the reporting agent is essentially trusted to be able to distinguish all states, with a default confidence level. For each true report in the history, we strengthen our trust in the reporting agent's ability to distinguish certain states. For each false report, we weaken our trust.

Definition 5. *For any $n > 0$, the initial trust graph $T_n = \langle S, w \rangle$ where S is the set of states, and w is defined such that $w(s, t) = 0$ if $s = t$ and $w(s, t) = n$ otherwise.*

The idea of the initial trust graph is that the reporting agent is trusted to distinguish between all states equally well.

We are now interested in giving a procedure that takes a report history, and returns a trust graph; this is presented in Algorithm 1. The algorithm looks at each report in the history R, and it increases the weight on edges where there have been true reports and decreases the weight on edges where there have been false reports.

Proposition 1. *Given a report history R, the weighted graph returned by Algorithm 1 is a trust graph.*

This result relies on the fact that w only returns non-negative values; this is guaranteed by the choice of n for the initial trust graph.

Algorithm 1. Construct_from(R)
___
Input R, a report history.
$n \leftarrow$ size of R.
$T = \langle S, w \rangle$ is the initial trust graph for n.
while $R \neq \emptyset$ **do**
   Get some $(\phi, i) \in R$
   if $i = 0$ **then**
      $w(s_1, s_2) \leftarrow w(s_1, s_2) - 1$ for all s_1, s_2 such that $s_1 \models \phi$ and $s_2 \not\models \phi$
   else
      $w(s_1, s_2) \leftarrow w(s_1, s_2) + 1$ for all s_1, s_2 such that $s_1 \models \phi$ and $s_2 \not\models \phi$
   end if
   $R = R - (\phi, i)$.
end while
Return $\langle S, w \rangle$.
___

Example 2. We return to our running example. Suppose that we have no initial assumptions about the trust held in *Present*, and that the report history R consists of the following reports:

$$\langle A, 1 \rangle, \langle A, 1 \rangle, \langle B, 0 \rangle, \langle A \wedge B, 1 \rangle$$

Since our report history has size 4, the initial trust graph would look like Fig. 1, except that all edge weights would be 4. After the first report, the edge weights would be increased on the following edges:

$$(\{A, B\}, \emptyset), (\{A, B\}, \{B\}), (\{A\}, \emptyset), (\{A\}, \{B\}).$$

The same thing would happen after the second report. On the third report, we would subtract one from the following edges:

$$(\{A, B\}, \emptyset), (\{A, B\}, \{A\}), (\{B\}, \emptyset), (\{A\}, \{B\}).$$

Finally, the fourth report would add one to the following edges:

$$(\{A, B\}, \emptyset), (\{A, B\}, \{A\}), (\{A, B\}, \{B\}).$$

The final trust graph is given in Fig. 2. Based on this graph, *Present* is least trusted to distinguish the states $\{B\}$ and $\emptyset$. This is because the positive reports were all related to the truth of A, and the only false report was a report about the trust of B. Hence, the graph is intuitively plausible.

3.3   Basic Results

We have defined an approach to building trust graphs from reports. We remark that the edge weights will not be used directly when it comes to belief revision. For belief revision, what we need is a single *trust ranking* that is derived from

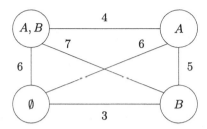

Fig. 2. Graph construction

the trust graph. However, constructing the graph allows us to define the ranking function as sort of a consequence of the reports. In this section, we show the construction satisfies some desirable properties.

First, we define the trust ranking associated with a trust graph.

Definition 6. *For any trust graph $T = \langle S, w \rangle$, let d_T denote the minimax distance between states.*

The distance d_T captures an overall trust ranking that can be used to inform belief revision. Informally, even if an agent is not trusted to distinguish two states directly, they may be trusted to distinguish them based on a path in the graph. The important feature of such a path is the minimax weight. The following is a basic result about the notion of distance defined by a trust graph.

Proposition 2. *For any trust graph $T = \langle S, w \rangle$, the function d_T is a pseudo-ultrametric on S.*

Recall from Sect. 2 that a pseudo-ultrametric over states can be used to define a ranking that is suitable for reasoning about trust. We remark that, in fact, every ultrametric over a finite set is actually equivalent up to isomorphism to an ultrametric defined by the minimax distance over some weighted graph. This means that every trust ranking can be defined by a trust graph.

The next result shows that there is nothing particularly special about the trust graphs constructed by our algorithm.

Proposition 3. *Every weighted graph over S is the trust graph obtained from some report history R.*

This can be proven by a simple construction where each report only modifies a single edge weight.

In the next results, we adopt some simplifying notation. If R is a report history and r is a report, we let $R \cdot r$ denote the multiset obtained by adding r to R. Also, if R is a report history, we let $T(R)$ denote the trust graph obtained from R and we let d_R denote the distance d defined by $T(R)$.

As stated, Algorithm 1 can only construct a trust graph starting from scratch. However, the following proposition states that we can iteratively modify a trust graph as we get new reports.

Proposition 4. *Let R be a report history and let r be a report. Then $T(R \cdot r)$ is identical to the trust graph obtained by modifying $T(R)$ as follows:*

- *Increment weights between states that disagree on ϕ, if r is a positive report.*
- *Decrement weights between states that disagree on ϕ, if r is a negative report.*
- *Defining a new minimax distance d in accordance with the new edge weights.*

Hence, rather than viewing trust graphs as something created with no a priori knowledge, we can think of trust graphs as a simple model of trust together with an operation that tweeks the weights to respond to a new report.

One desirable feature of our construction is that a report of $(\phi, 0)$ should make the reporting agent less trustworthy with regards to reports about the trust of ϕ. The next proposition shows that this is indeed the case.

Proposition 5. *Let R be a report history, let s_1 and s_2 be states such that $s_1 \models \phi$ and $s_2 \not\models \phi$. Then*

$$d_R(s_1, s_2) \geq d_{R \cdot (\phi, 0)}(s_1, s_2).$$

We have a similar result for positive reports.

Proposition 6. *Let R be a report history, let s_1 and s_2 be states such that $s_1 \models \phi$ and $s_2 \not\models \phi$. Then*

$$d_R(s_1, s_2) \leq d_{R \cdot (\phi, 1)}(s_1, s_2).$$

Taken together, these results indicate that negative (resp. positive) reports of ϕ make the reporting agent less (resp. more) trusted with respect to ϕ. We remark that the inequalities in the previous theorems would be strict if we were considering actual edge weights; but they are not strict for d_R, since there may be multiple paths between states.

We have seen that trust graphs define a distance over states that represents a general notion of trust that is implicit in the graph. Significantly, trust graphs can be constructed in a straightforward way by looking at past reports; the implicitly defined trust ranking is based on the accuracy of these reports. In the next section, we consider how the notion of trust defined by a trust graph can be used to construct different approaches to revision.

4   Using Trust Graphs

4.1   Example Revisited

Consider again our example involving reports about the lights in a building. We previously pointed out that *Absent* might not actually trust the reports from *Present*, and we gave an approach to construct a trust graph.

Informally, when talking about trust, we might make assertions of the following form:

1. *Present* is not trusted to know which room they are in.
2. *Present* is not trusted to check two rooms at once.

These kind of assertions give us a hint about how belief revision might occur. For example, in the first case, *Absent* would interpret a report to mean that *exactly one* of the rooms is lit.

Note, however, that a trust graph does not simply give a binary notion of trust; it defines a distance function that indicates strength of trust in various distinctions. Similarly, the beliefs of an agent might be held with different levels of strength. So, even if we have a trust graph, there are still problems with incorporating reports related to comparing *strength of belief* with *strength of trust*.

In our example, if *Absent* just left the building, they might believe *very strongly* that the light in room A must be off. They might believe this so strongly that they disregard *Present*'s report entirely. But disregarding reports is not the only option. It might be the case that the exact strength of *Absent*'s beliefs needs to be considered. Suppose *Absent* believes the light in room A is off with a *medium* degree of strength. In that case, a report from a weakly trusted agent will not change their beliefs, whereas a report from a strongly trusted agent would be more convincing. Moreover, *Absent* also needs to have a strength ranking over possible alternatives. Hence, this is not simply a binary comparison between strength of degree and strength of trust. In order to model interaction between belief and trust, we need a precise formal account that permits a comparison of the two. We also need to account for the way that *Present* develops a reputation, either for laziness or inaccuracy.

4.2   Naive Revision with Trust Graphs

In the remainder of this paper, we assume that the beliefs of an agent are represented by an OCF. We show how a trust graph allows us to capture an approach to belief revision that takes trust into account. In fact, the approach in this section depends only on a pseudo-ultrametric d_T defined by a trust graph.

For any pseudo-ultrametric d, we define a family of revision operators $*_n$.

Definition 7. *Let κ be an OCF and let d be a pseudo-ultrametric over S. For each n, the operator $*_n$ is defined such that $Bel(\kappa) *_n \phi$ is equal to:*

$$\min_{\kappa}\{s \mid there\ exists\ t\ such\ that\ d(t, s) \leq n\ and\ t \models \phi\}$$

From the theory of metric spaces, we have the following.

Proposition 7. *For any pseudo-ultrametric d over a set X, if $n \in \mathbf{N}$ then the collection of sets $Y_x = \{y \mid d(x, y) \leq n\}$ is a partition of X.*

The next result relates these revision operators to trust-sensitive revision operators. A parallel result is proved in [8], although the result here is stated in terms of OCFs rather than AGM revision.

Proposition 8. *Let κ be an OCF and let T be a trust graph. For any formula ϕ and any n:*

$$Bel(\kappa) *_n \phi = Bel(\kappa) *^\Pi \phi$$

where Π is the partition defined by (d_T, n) and $*^\Pi$ is the trust-senstive revision operator associated with Π.

Hence κ and d_T define a set of trust-sensitive revision operators. The parameter n specifies how close two states must be to be considered indistinguishable in the partition.

We refer to the operators $*_n$ as *naive* trust-sensitive revision operators in this paper. These operators are naive in the sense that they do not allow us to take into account the relative magnitudes of the values in κ and the distances given by d_T. In other words, the scales of κ and d_T are not compared; it doesn't matter if the initial strength of belief is high or low. This makes sense in applications where the magnitudes in κ and d_T are seen as independent.

Example 3. We refer back to our motivating example. Suppose that the initial beliefs of *Absent* are given by κ such that:

$$\kappa(\{A\}) = 0, \qquad \kappa(\{B\}) = 1, \qquad \kappa(\{A, B\}) = 1, \qquad \kappa(\emptyset) = 2$$

Hence the initial belief set for *Absent* is $\{A\}$. Now suppose that *Present* passes a message that asserts $\neg A \wedge B$; in other words, the light is off in A while it is on in B. If this information was given to *Absent* as infallible sensory data, then the result could be determined easily with regular AGM revision. But this is not sensory data; this is a report, and trust can play a role in how it is incorporated.

To make this concrete, suppose that *Absent* thinks that *Present* is generally lazy and unaware of the room that they are in. It is unlikely therefore, that *Present* would run quickly from one room to another to verify the status of the light in both. So perhaps the trust graph T constructed from past reports defines the distance function d_T from $\{B\}$ as follows:

$$d_T(\{B\}, \{A\}) = 1$$
$$d_T(\{B\}, \{B\}) = 0$$
$$d_T(\{B\}, \{A, B\}) = 10$$
$$d_T(\{B\}, \emptyset) = 5$$

This distance function does indeed encode the fact that *Present* is not strongly trusted to distinguish $\{A\}$ and $\{B\}$; this is because they do not always know where they are.

We have supposed that *Present* reports $\neg A \wedge B$. So, what should *Absent* believe? It depends on the threshold n. If we set $n = 3$, then by Proposition 6, $*_3$ is the trust-sensitive revision operator defined by the partition with cells $\{\{A\}, \{B\}\}$ and $\{\{A, B\}, \emptyset\}$. Since $\{A\}$ and $\{B\}$ are in the same cell, it follows that revision by B is equivalent to revision by $A \vee B$. Hence:

$$Bel(\kappa) *_3 B = \{\{A\}\}.$$

This is a belief state containing just one state; so *Absent* believes that the most plausible state is the unique state where only the light in room A is on. Hence, if *Present* reports that the light in room B is on, it will not change the beliefs of A at all.

For naive operators, it does not matter how strongly *Absent* believes the light in room A is on. It only matters whether or not the reporting agent can distinguish between particular states.

4.3 General Revision with Trust Graphs

In the previous section, we considered the case where strength of belief and strength of trust are incomparable; the magnitudes of the values are not on the same scale. In this case, we can not meaningfully combine the numeric values assigned by κ with the numeric distances given by a trust graph; we essentially have two orderings that have to be merged in some way. This is the general setting of AGM revision, and trust-sensitive revision.

However, there is an alternative way to define revision that actually takes the numeric ranks into account. First, we define a new OCF, given some initial beliefs and a trust distance function.

Definition 8. *Let κ be an OCF and let d be a pseudo-ultrametric. For any $s \in S$:*

$$\kappa_d^\phi(s) = \kappa(s) \cdot \min\{d(s,t) \mid t \models \phi\}.$$

The OCF $\kappa_d^\phi(s)$ combines the a priori belief in the *likelihood* of s along with a measure indicating how easily s can be distinguished from a model of ϕ. Essentially, this definition uses d to construct a ranking function over states centered on $|\phi|$. This ranking is aggregated with κ, by adding the two ranking functions together.

Given this definition, we can define a new revision operator.

Definition 9. *Let κ be an OCF and let d be a pseudo-ultrametric. For any formula ϕ, define $\circ_d$ such that*

$$Bel(\kappa) \circ_d \phi = \{s \mid \kappa_d^\phi(s) \text{ is minimal}\}.$$

This new definition lets the initial strength of belief be traded off with perceived expertise. We return to our example.

Example 4. Consider the light-reporting example again, with the initial belief state κ and the distance function d_T specified in Example 3. Now suppose again that *Present* reports $\phi = \neg A \wedge B$, i.e. that only the light in room B is on. We calculate $\kappa_d^\phi(s)$ for all states s in the following table.

Since the first two rows both have minimal values, it follows that

$$Bel(\kappa) \circ_d * \neg A \wedge B = \{\{A\}, \{B\}\}.$$

Following revision, *Absent* believes exactly one light is on.

s	$\kappa(s)$	$d(\{B\}, s)$	$\kappa_d^{\phi}(s)$
$\{A\}$	0	1	1
$\{B\}$	1	0	1
$\{A, B\}$	1	10	11
$\emptyset$	2	5	7

This example demonstrates how the strength of belief and the strength of trust can interact. The given result occurs because the strength of belief in $\{A\}$ is identical to the strength of trust in the report of $\{B\}$. Increasing or decreasing either measure of strength will cause the result to be different. Note also that this approach gives a full OCF as a result, so we have a ranking of alternative states as well.

5   Related Work

This work fits in the general tradition of formalisms that address notions of trust and credibility for belief revision. There are alternative approaches, based on *non-prioritized* and *credibility-limited* revision as well [2,3,7]. The notion of trust has been explored in the setting of Dynamic Epistemic Logic (DEL), by adding an explicit measure of trust to formulas [11].

But fundamentally, this work is really about building trust in a source based on the knowledge demonstrated in past reports; our goal is to develop a formal model of knowledge-based trust. To the best of our knowledge, this problem has not been explored previously in the context of formal belief change operators. However, it has been explored in some practical settings, such as the formulation of search engine results [6].

6   Conclusion

In this paper, we have addressed the problem of building trust from past reports. We demonstrated that, in the context of OCFs, trust can be interpreted in two ways. First, if the scale used for the the strength of belief is deemed to be independent of the distance metric, then we can use a trust ranking to define a family of *naive* revision operators for trust-sensitive revision. On the other hand, if strength of trust and strength of belief are considered to be comparable on the same scale, then we have shown how the two can be aggregated to define a new approach to trust-influenced belief revision.

There are many directions for future research. Beyond expanding the formal theory, we are primarily interested in practical applications of this work. Natural candidate problems include modelling trust and belief change for Internet search results, or for improving the safety and reliability of drone controllers.

References

1. Alchourrón, C.E., Gärdenfors, P., Makinson, D.: On the logic of theory change: partial meet functions for contraction and revision. J. Symb. Logic **50**(2), 510–530 (1985)
2. Bonanno, G.: Credible information, allowable information and belief revision - extended abstract. In: Moss, L.S. (ed.) Proceedings Seventeenth Conference on Theoretical Aspects of Rationality and Knowledge, TARK 2019, Toulouse, France, 17–19 July 2019, EPTCS, vol. 297, pp. 82–90 (2019)
3. Booth, R., Fermé, E., Konieczny, S., Pérez, R.P.: Credibility-limited revision operators in propositional logic. In: Brewka, G., Eiter, T., McIlraith, S.A. (eds.) Principles of Knowledge Representation and Reasoning: Proceedings of the Thirteenth International Conference, KR 2012, Rome, Italy, 10–14 June 2012. AAAI Press (2012)
4. Booth, R., Hunter, A.: Trust as a precursor to belief revision. J. Artif. Intell. Res. **61**, 699–722 (2018)
5. Carbone, M., Nielsen, M., Sassone, V.: A formal model for trust in dynamic networks. In: International Conference on Software Engineering and Formal Methods, pp. 54–61 (2003)
6. Dong, X., et al.: Knowledge-based trust: Estimating the trustworthiness of web sources. In: Proceedings of the VLDB Endowment, vol. 8 (2015). https://doi.org/10.14778/2777598.2777603
7. Hansson, S.O., Fermé, E.L., Cantwell, J., Falappa, M.A.: Credibility limited revision. J. Symb. Log. **66**(4), 1581–1596 (2001)
8. Hunter, A., Booth, R.: Trust-sensitive belief revision. In: Yang, Q., Wooldridge, M.J. (eds.) Proceedings of the Twenty-Fourth International Joint Conference on Artificial Intelligence, IJCAI 2015, Buenos Aires, Argentina, 25–31 July 2015, pp. 3062–3068. AAAI Press (2015)
9. Huynh, T.D., Jennings, N.R., Shadbolt, N.R.: An integrated trust and reputation model for open multi-agent systems. Auton. Agents Multi-Agent Syst. **13**(2), 119–154 (2006)
10. Krukow, K., Nielsen, M.: Trust structures. Int. J. Inf. Secur. **6**(2–3), 153–181 (2007)
11. Liu, F., Lorini, E.: Reasoning about belief, evidence and trust in a multi-agent setting. In: An, B., Bazzan, A., Leite, J., Villata, S., van der Torre, L. (eds.) PRIMA 2017. LNCS (LNAI), vol. 10621, pp. 71–89. Springer, Cham (2017). https://doi.org/10.1007/978-3-319-69131-2_5
12. Salehi-Abari, A., White, T.: Towards con-resistant trust models for distributed agent systems. In: Proceedings of the 21st International Joint Conference on Artificial Intelligence (IJCAI), pp. 272–277 (2009)
13. Spohn, W.: Ordinal conditional functions: a dynamic theory of epistemic states. In: Harper, W., Skyrms, B. (eds.) Causation in Decision, Belief Change, and Statistics, vol. II, pp. 105–134. Kluwer Academic Publishers (1988)

Correcting Large Knowledge Bases Using Guided Inductive Logic Learning Rules

Yan Wu, Zili Zhang$^{(\boxtimes)}$, and Guodong Wang

College of Computer and Information Science, Southwest University,
Chongqing 400715, China
zhangzl@swu.edu.cn

Abstract. Domain-oriented knowledge bases (KBs) such as DBpedia and YAGO are largely constructed by applying a set of predefined extraction rules to the semi-structured contents of Wikipedia articles. Although both of these large-scale KBs achieve very high average precision values (above 95% for DBpedia (The estimated precision of those statements is 95% in the Data Set 3.9 of DBpedia) and YAGO), subtle mistakes in a few of the underlying extraction rules may still impose a substantial amount of mistakes derived from specific relations. By applying the same regular expressions to detect mistakes of range constraint of relation, some special features of negative statements are erased while mining the rules. For traditional rule-learning approaches based on Inductive Logic Programming (ILP), it is very difficult to correct these extraction mistakes from the Wikipedia, since they usually occur only in a relatively small subdomain of the relations' arguments. In this paper, we thus propose a GILLearn, a Guided Inductive Logic Learning model, which iteratively asks for small amounts of feedback automatically over a given KB to learn a set of knowledge correction rules. The GILLearn introduces the guided information to rule augmentation and provides the respective metrics for the validation of corrected triples. Our experimental evaluation demonstrates that the proposed framework achieves the significant performance on the large knowledge bases.

Keywords: Negative statements · Rule learning · Knowledge correction

1 Introduction

Recent advances in knowledge correction have motivated the automatic construction of large domain-oriented knowledge bases. The KBs are always noisy and incomplete. There are a number of recent approaches that specifically tackle the problem of learning error detection from a given KB (or from a fixed training subset of the KB) for data-cleaning purposes [7,19]. However, few of scholars focus on the main issues of error correction or find the missing facts in the KB. The errors of knowledge base are derived in the knowledge acquisition process, or in the source data. In the KBs, constraint-based approaches detect erroneous

© Springer Nature Switzerland AG 2021
D. N. Pham et al. (Eds.): PRICAI 2021, LNAI 13031, pp. 556–571, 2021.
https://doi.org/10.1007/978-3-030-89188-6_42

values that violate the constraint and most data items receive a high confidence according to the traditional rule-mining metrics [36]. Items violating the constraints are marked as incorrect by the data-cleaning framework. Specifically, Wikidata [31], DBpedia [3], YAGO [30], and the Google Knowledge Graph [28] originated from the Wikipedia wipe out the invalid items in the process of data cleaning. There are 2.8% error rates estimated in the core of knowledge source of DBpedia from Wikipedia [32]. For example, by applying the same regular expressions to extract person nationality, DBpedia erroneously swaps most of entities regarding the type of ethnic group as nationality. For these entities with the *ethnic group*, they have erroneous nationality relied on range constraint of relation. For human understanding, we can ascertain the nationality with the attribute values. However, these special features of negative statements are erased while mining the rules. For general error correction systems [16], they contain majority fault values in the tables and leverage the correction values as the sample repairs. Conversely, these systems are not available for the knowledge base with inferior inaccuracy. Here, a rule correction system is established for the KB with few and special errors. As an illustration, it is an obvious false truth that everyone has more than one birthplace. Additionally, some people regard single or multiple nationalities as a notable classification feature. Perhaps one of birthplaces is false, or both of nationalities are correct in terms of ethnic attributes. In some semantic scenarios, some facts are captured in the sentence: *"Albert Einstein was a German − born."* Like this, Albert Einstein's nationality is Germany. Checking the messages in the DBpedia, the head entity (*Einstein*) ignores the items of nationality. Also, the DBpedia catches the *German* as the inaccurate tail in the triple, which holds the nationality as the relation. In the semantic KBs, it is usually hard to guarantee its quality and completion without external information. For this purpose, systematic users need to keep the triple quality in the process of knowledge extraction. Some researchers do this work using integrity constraints [12], statistics [17], or machine learning [35], etc. In the knowledge base completion (KBC) [29], rule learning can mine the logic relations to deduce the missing facts. Piyawat et al. [14] correct the range violation errors in the DBpedia for the completion. Fortunately, the state-of-art rule learning algorithm is observed to refine the KB, i.e., AMIE3 [13]. Other rule learning algorithms [18] based on Inductive Logic Programming [21] are also leveraged to improve the KB. In the AMIE3 rule learning algorithm, they mine the first-order rules [33] to infer the logic constraints of entities in the KB. Few facts are the critical deficiency in the search space, which trigger the rules to fall into a local optimal solution. At the same time, the logic rules can't be generated with insufficient samples in the rule learning models. In recent years, some scholars design RuDiK [23], a system for the discovery of declarative rules over KBs. Especially, the inequality rules are detected with entities features, such as, time, length, weight, etc. In the embedding model [14], the implicit information is fetched by the internal relations of instances. For example, the classical TransE model is utilized to correct the error triples in the KBs. Furthermore, the Statistical Distributions [25] can be extended to filter out the faulty statements and all distribution of entities are in the closed word assumption. In the [6], the incorrect facts are detached by the embedding models with the Word2vec method in the Knowledge base. Also, some mistaken tails of the triples are recognized by wrong links between different KBs and each link is embedded into a feature vector in the learning model [24]. After that, the researchers [1] propose the correction tower with the embedding method of the error recognition for knowledge graph correction. Here, we only explore the triple outliers without numeric values to refine and correct the KBs. Viewing as the errors extracted from the KB's sources, some sparse errors have unknown knowledge that is worth of exploration. One instance, the entity *"England"* has the type of *Country*, but the *England* is the part of United Kingdom since the extracted news is not rigorous in KB. If the KBs only consider the simple range violation errors, many negative statements are ignored in the range type of relation property.

In this paper, the GILP [34] model is updated to correct the wrong items by correction rules. Further, we correct these errors exploiting the co-occurring similar entities [10] in the publicly available knowledge graphs, like Wikidata or DBpedia. First, the negative and positive feedback are adopted by the conflict-with constraint[1]. Then, we choose the heuristic method to evaluate the feedback and rewrite the rule queries to extract the correction rules. For solving these errors in the KB, we propose a reasonable rule-based correcting and learning model, **Guided Inductive Logic Learning model (GILLearn model)**, to correct the KB in our system. And more features are learned in depth to refine the knowledge base by small samples. In this paper, the proposed system are leveraged to visualize the meaningful rewriting queries and pick the appropriate repair as the final correction by the cross similarity measures. The ability of GILLearn is to annotate error tail of triple in specified relation environment and the logic links are illustrated in the KB.

The rest of this paper is organized as follows. In the Sect. 2, preliminaries are exhibited. Section 3 introduces the proposed framework of Guided Inductive Logic Learning model and Sect. 4 shows experimental results and analysis. Finally, the conclusion remarks are presented in Sect. 5.

2   Preliminaries

In this section, we introduce the basic notation that is used through the rest of the paper.

Triple: Let ξ be a set of entities, R be a set of predicates(relations), defining a 3-tuple that stand for the relation r between subject s and object o, where s, t $\in$ ξ and r $\in$ R, refer to triples as <subject/head, predicate/relation, object/tail>. Let K be a set of triples of $\{< s, p, o > |s, o \in \xi, p \in R\}$. We define a knowledge base by the 3-tuple (ξ, R, K). We denote a knowledge base as KB. We focus on RDF formulation [9] to encode the triples which represent the facts. For example,

---

[1] https://www.wikidata.org/wiki/Help:Property_constraints_portal.

the sentence *(Yao Ming was born in Shanghai)* is translated to new formulation, $< Yao\_Ming,\ wasBornIn,\ Shanghai>$.

First-order Logic Definitions: Learn the first-order logic definitions [27] from an input knowledge base and training examples. Training examples E are usually tuples of a single target relation, mainly, positive(E^+) or negative(E^-) examples. The given knowledge base is also called background knowledge. The *hypothesis space* is the set of all possible first-order logic definitions probed in the learning algorithm. A hypothesis is each member of the hypothesis space. Clause C covers an entity e if the instance I $\wedge C \models e$, where $\models$ is the entailment operator, i.e., we can know e is positive while I and C are correct. Also, Definition H covers an entity e if at least one clauses covers e. Horn clauses are also called Datalog rules (without negation) or conjunctive queries. Also, we call the first-order horn clause as the first-order logic rule.

Problem Statement: At this point, the paper concentrates on correcting ABox property assertions $<s, p, o>$ where o is an *entity assertion* that has the mistaken type. Stating a relation assertion, some triples with erroneous tail *(wrong object)* are captured in the models. Notably, some simple canonicalizations are obtained in the former case, e.g., the property assertion $< dbr:Hiro\_Arikawa,\ dbo:nationality,\ dbr:Japanese\_people>$[2] should be amended to $< dbr:Hiro\_Arikawa,\ dbo:nationality,\ dbr:Japan>$.

The incorrect tail assertions can be detected automatically by the new GILP model. It is significant to mention that the KB is an OWL ontology and the set of object properties connecting two items should be disjoint. In practice, the DBpedia often do not respect this constraint. A set of entities are regarded as faulty by the analysis of the object type. For each assertion $<s, p, o>$ in the set, the proposed correction framework aims at observing an entity from K as an object substitution, such that e is semantically related to o and the new triple $<s, p, e>$ is true. Or the new target replacing one old entity exists in the real world and not in the K. For example, the fact *formerTeam(Alan_Ricard,Buffalo_Bill)* is an erroneous fact, where the correct tail should be the NFL team Buffalo_Bills instead of the character Buffalo_Bill. The CoCKG (Correction of Confusions in Knowledge Graphs) [19] model is utilized to do the correction by exploiting disambiguation links (*dbo:wikiPageDisambiguates* relation in DBpedia) and approximate string matching for this situation.

Inspired by the rudik model [23], we follow the type features to recognize the negative triples. This way can avert some false negative entities. Besides, the PaTyBRED [20] method incorporates type and path features into local relation classifiers for the detection of relation assertion errors in KB. In our model, the plugins of rule discovery are exploited to grasp the strict negative statements without false negative instances in the search space.

---

[2] dbr: http://dbpedia.org/resource; dbo: http://dbpedia.org/ontology.

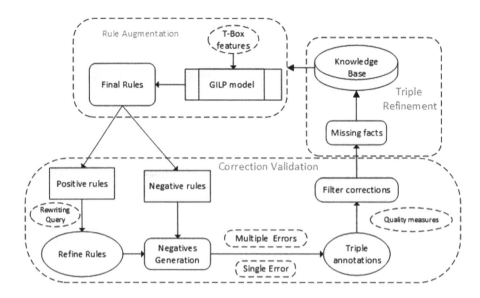

Fig. 1. Correction Architecture in the GILLearn workflow

3   GILLearn Model

In this section, we formally define our correction model. Our goal is to do the rule corrections by learning consistency constraints iteratively over a relational representation of KBs. We also provide a unifying approach to denote relations and constraints as first-order literals or rules that capture both positive and negative feedback, respectively. we outline our GILLearn Model, which implements the correction rules to refine the large knowledge base and pulls some missing facts for KB completion, depicted by the framework of Fig. 1. In the model, the logic rules with high quality are realized automatically by the random initial feedback. And a guidance of the repair process is offered to correct the KB. The GILLearn model has three modules, namely, Rule Augmentation, Correction Validation, Triple Refinement. Especially, we illustrate how to initialize our framework to generate seed rules in the rule augmentation. Next, the refinement operators are defined in the module of correction validation and the plugin gathers the overall set of candidate rules to seize the repairs from the seed rules. Also, the quality measures are submitted to accept or reject these candidate repair rules. Finally, some corrected facts existed in real-world are learned in the model and the KB are enriched by new facts. Overall, the rule augmentation component explores rule patterns in the KBs. The correction validation module provides the best triple patterns and the items annotations interacting with other KBs. And this part comments the triples by the rules for the repairs in the KB. It also generates possible repairs for the erroneous triples in the negative rules. The triple refinement section detects some missing facts to mend the KB.

3.1   Rule Augmentation

Given small initial feedback in KB, the template interprets the semantics of rules w.r.t. the given KB and identifies correct or wrong triples in batches. The module computes and identifies top-k optimal rules, which are visualized to the users via a simple graph representation. Since it's complex to realize the system's automatic selection of the best rule, the models leverage the semantic KB's special feature (*TBox*) to catch the associated rules. If a false triple contains an error object whose type is right, we do the second feedback from the co-occurring similar entities with other KB. In the DBpedia, we filter the positive/negative feedback by the *TBox* property of fixed relations. For instance, the *TBox* property of *nationality* contains *type, subclassof, equivalentClass*, etc. Compared with the expert knowledge, the generation time of rules in the AMIE3 model [13] are reduced by the *TBox* property. Here, we employ the wordNet property of YAGO to take the false positive feedback and the algorithm has the faster computation than the PRA method [15]. The Rule Augmentation module utilizes the types of the entities and the relationships between facts in the DBpedia since types hold the unique marks. One positive/negative rule pattern is represented as a labeled graph where the body of rule shows attributes or its associated type. A recycle rule represents the associated relationships in the targeted relation. The Sparql queries are issued to supply the initial feedback by the fundamental and super types of the given relation. If there is only one partial match from feedback to rules, either the rule is incomplete or the tuple is simply erroneous in the rule.

Algorithm 1: Rule Augmentation

$\Phi_{acc} := \emptyset;\ \mathcal{T} := \emptyset;\ \Phi := \Phi_0;\ \mathcal{F} := \mathcal{F}_0;$

$\Phi_0 := \text{generateSeedRules}(\mathcal{F}_0);$

while $\Phi \neq \emptyset$ *or* $\mathcal{T}$ *changed* **do**

  $\Phi_i :=$ all rules in Φ which are accepted based on $\mathcal{P}$ in TBox or linked KB's property;

  $\Phi_{acc} :=$ top-k optimal rules from Φ_i;

  $\mathcal{T} :=$ facts predicted by Φ_{acc};

  $\Phi := \Phi \cup \text{ILP}(\mathcal{F}, \mathcal{K});$

  $\mathcal{F} := \mathcal{F} \cup \text{pullFeedback}(\mathcal{T});$

end

return $\Phi_{acc};$

Algorithm 1 illustrates our basic model of Rule Augmentation. Inspired by the algorithm GILP [34], we update the model of rule generation. We generate the set of *seed rules* Φ_0 from the *initial user feedback* $\mathcal{F}_0$. The sets of *accepted rules* Φ_{acc} and *predicted facts* $\mathcal{T}$ (which will be based on all rules in Φ_{acc}) are initially set to be empty. Similarly, we initialize the iteratively merged sets of overall rules Φ and feedback facts $\mathcal{F}$ to Φ_0 and $\mathcal{F}_0$, respectively. At each GILP iteration, all rules in Φ which are accepted based on the schema axioms in *TBox* or linked KB's property. Next, the set of accepted rules Φ_{acc} is selected from the current Φ based on the top-k rules we collected so far. Here, we leverage the rank of confidence to find the optimal rules. Next, we utilize the mean quantity of generated rules between each iterations to decide k value. Similarly, $\mathcal{T}$ is expanded by the facts predicted by Φ_{acc} at the current iteration. Next, we expand the set of all rules Φ by using any general ILP subroutine which supports the refinement operations for the kinds of constraints we wish to learn based on the current set of feedback facts $\mathcal{F}$ over the knowledge base $\mathcal{K}$. Finally, pullFeedback($\mathcal{T}$) collects the next round of user feedback as a randomly chosen subset of the currently predicted facts $\mathcal{T}$. We terminate the GILP iterations either when no rules in Φ could initially be generated, or when $\mathcal{T}$ remains unchanged among two iterations.

We attach the TBox or linked KB's property to do the feedback iteratively. Then, the GILP model is updated to learn the final rules automatically while the property of type is used to replace the expert knowledge in the part of feedback generation. For the KB, the search space is explored in the RDF3X engine by RDF sparql query in YAGO, DBpedia or wikidata. In the process of feedback generation, the characteristics of KB are reflected on the TBox property of DBpedia or wordNet property of YAGO. Both of the two KBs, there are over one type for each relation property. Here, the domain or range of relation are only taken into consideration in the search space. First, the feedback is randomly selected by the TBox property, i.e., the type of *nationality* range is *dbo:Country*. The triples including the same type of range are regarded as the positive feedback, others considered as the negative feedback while they have the same relation and the type of domain. Similarly, the relation of *isCitizenOf* in YAGO are leveraged to select the feedback by the type of *wordnet_country*. In this way, the feedback is picked up automatically in this module. For other semantic KBs, the type of property can be replaced with other specific background, e.g., the expert knowledge, special rules, internal characteristics, contextual news, etc.

3.2   Correction Validation

To design a complete set of error corrector model, the system leverages all triple feedback comprising negative and positive statements. In principle, to fix a set of error triples in a given negative rule, we can apply two error contexts: Range of erroneous tail of triple and Error information in associated KBs.

In the module of Correction Validation, the most appropriate query patterns are selected to explain the semantics of correction rules by rewriting the negative rules with the positive rules. Once the pattern is chosen, the GILLearn model scans all the tuples from each new query in the revised negative rules. It marks the tuples as positive if the new rules of the KB covers all tuples of the feedback. Otherwise, an ambiguity is raised about whether this is caused by the incompleteness of the KB or the query is simple wrong. To resolve such ambiguity, the GILLearn model connects auxiliary KB to validate the correction by the fusion features. In the measure of similarity, the GILLearn model can get more accurately annotated triples.

For human validation, the system encounters some tails(alike, the attribute values in the table) with erroneous property of specified type. For instance, *Germans* has the incorrect type of *Country*. Like that, some initial positive feedback picked are respected as false positive items and the specifics are ignored by general correction algorithms. The errors extracted from the source of DBpedia are pondered and top-k most meaningful candidates are created to fix the KB in the framework of correction. The basic assumption is that the targets predicated by the single-value correction model with higher scores tend to contain the correct entity in the tail of triple. The feedback can't be fully overlaid by the correction query in each iteration. We can't induce repairs for rule's remedy, in case of the positive triples without the property of (*wikidata:Q6256*). Two possible reasons stated, the KB is incomplete with exact triples and the tuple itself contains property errors. Such ambiguity is tackled by utilizing the extra KB(*wikidata*) since the *wikidata* is more completion than the DBpedia and it has a connection to the DBpedia by the property *sameAs*. Compared to the human validation, the algorithm saves computing time and has high fidelity for the automatic type validation without expert knowledge. The GILLearn will further disclose the similarity results from the collections of the annotated triples with property sparsity. The Single-value Correction Architecture exhibits how to bridge KBs and achieve reliable triple correction by the co-occurring knowledge base, such as, the wikidata.

Algorithm 2: Rule Correction algorithm

$(\phi_n^+, \phi_n^-) := \mathrm{GILP}(\mathcal{F}_0, \mathcal{K})$;
$\mathcal{T}^- :=$ facts predicted by ϕ_n^-;
$[\gamma(x)] := \phi^-(x,y) -> \xi(x,y,z)$;
$Refine := (\phi^+(x,y), \phi^-(x,y)) -> \phi_{refine}$;
$Corr_0 := \emptyset$;
while $\xi(x,y,z) \neq \emptyset$ **do**
  $\quad \mathcal{T} :=$ all predictions in ϕ_{refine} which are accepted based on $\mathcal{P}$ in T-Box;
  $\quad Corr_i := pullCorrections(filterRepairs(\mathcal{T}))$;
  $\quad \xi(x,y,z)$ remove $\mathcal{T}^-$;
end
return $Corr_n$;

The rules are mined with Algorithm 2, which is an adaption of correction rule mining [26]. Here, the relation of nationality in the DBpedia is appeared as the example. Our algorithm is introduced to mine positive/negative rules from the KB with two versions(one is in 2016, another is in 2020). Then, we apply the algorithm to correct the negative rules. The (ϕ_n^+, ϕ_n^-) shows the final pairs of positive and negative rules. $\emptyset$ is the empty. The function of $filterRepairs$ is presented in the Subsect. 3.4.

For instance, the entity's (*Moshe_Safdie*) relation (*nationality*) has two tails (*United_States, Canadians*). The violation is ⟨ *Moshe_Safdie, nationality,*

Canadians⟩ and constraint instance: Γ_0*(Canadians)*. The previous algorithm has given us a list of relevant past corrections based on fixed relations. To find available correction seeds, the first step of the algorithm pre-computes for each constraint a set of atomic modification patterns matching the possible correction seeds. In the instance, there is only one pattern: the deletion pattern *(_, <?, nationality, ?>)*. And the symbol of _ can be anything except that the instance has the type of person. Simultaneously, it matches both the deletion of *<?, nationality, ?>* and its replacements. The algorithm only respects past corrections involving assertions, desires them to be relevant for the current *TBox*, and computes the correction seed patterns by the conjunctive queries in the body $b(x)$ and the head $h(x)$. Each atom occurs in the rewriting of a constraint corresponds to a deletion pattern in the negative rule's body and a completeness constraint corresponding to an addition pattern in the positive rule's body. We converge the patterns for the constraint Γ in the set Patterns (Γ). The second step of the algorithm verifies whether it works out some constraint violation for each correction seed in the past (DBpedia's version in 2016).

The approach relies on error detection methods automatically based on type predictors. It leverages string similarity algorithms [11] to detect the target similarity, e.g., Levenshtein Distance, Cosine similarity, Jaccard index, and so on. The entities with similar IRIs or wikidata pages (if available) are searched to meet candidate instances with the type property of same target for correcting the facts in the DBpedia. Next, we detail our instantiation of the rule correction. In this module, the system generates top-k possible repairs for the wrong triples. The system applies properly property of *sameAs* without the unique name assumption to verify the errors. Last, the GILLearn model breeds the rewriting query to generate a set of possible repairs for the tuples in negative rules. Generally, the number of possible repairs for one of error items can be large. Most automatic correction algorithms use minimality as a guidance to pick possible values conforming to the patterns [8]. Here, we renovate the cross-similarity [22] containing string similarity methods to filter the optimal correction.

3.3   Triple Refinement

Query Rewriting. [2,4] represents one of the most promising algorithmic approaches to search engine or query answering. We redecorate the query rewriting algorithmic approach combining the positive or negative features. The approach consists of a rewriting step where the input query (a negative conjunctive query) is transformed into a new query (adding positive query, called a rewriting) in the KB. The rewriting query encodes the relevant information from the knowledge base and it is evaluated over the data using positive query followed by a second step. The positive rewriting query is utilized to correct the negative query. Thus, we leverage the rewriting query to correct the knowledge base with special property. Particularly, we only reckon with the rewriting query transformed from the first-order rules. Consider the Horn Description Logics (DLs) [5], the following query $q1$ is shown below. The $q1$ is a rewriting query w.r.t. property of nationality. We evaluate the preceding query over the knowledge base and gain the correction item (*Germany*) to replace the error target (*German_people*) in the relation of *nationality*, as expected.

q1: *relative(?a, ?b), stateOfOrigin(?b, German_people), nationality(?a, German_people)* ∩ *birthPlace (?a, ?c), country(?c, ?d)* ⇒ *nationality*(?a, ?d)*.

3.4 Quality Measures

Repairs Similarity. For computing similarity from the rule corrections, we rely on a weighted similarity function in the entities extracted from the Wikipedia. And the function considers two entities (error entity and any repair) as similar parameters while the weight is the number of the shared types and their mixed similarity distances. We utilize the frequency of items shared in the *wikiPageWikiLink* as one part of similarity. The d_L represents string similarity distance. Subsequently, we calculate a custom similarity measure $s(e_0, e_i)$ between an error entity e_0 and a candidate item e_i. The first element is the probability of (d_L) distance of two entities' all match tokens. And the second component estimates the number of matched attribute values in special property(P_{e_i}, *wikiPageWikiLink*) to capture the shared information of the linked source, shown in the Function 1(a). The measure is also shown in the Eq. 1(b).

$$a : sim\_outer(e_0, e_i) = \frac{|P_{e_0}| \cap |P_{e_i}|}{|P_{e_0}|}$$
$$b : s(e_0, e_i) = 1 - \frac{d_L(e_0, e_i)}{max(|e_0|, |e_i|)} + sim\_outer(e_0, e_i) \tag{1}$$

Similarity Harmonic Average Ratio. We design a new function f_{sim}, which is the harmonic means of *sim_inner* and *sim_outer*, in order to balance the inner and outer correction levels. Our ultimate goal is to find out which repair can represent the optimal correction in the candidate triples.

$$f_{sim} = \frac{2 \times sim\_inner(e_0, e_i) \times sim\_outer(e_0, e_i)}{sim\_inner(e_0, e_i) + sim\_outer(e_0, e_i)} \tag{2}$$

In the function 2, the part of $sim\_inner(e_0, e_i)$ reflects the best similarity of two entities. Here, some similarity algorithms are chosen to detect the best suitable methods, solely indicating their own features, e.g., *the Levenshtein_distance*, *Cosine_similarity*, *Sorensen_Dice*, *Jaro_Winkler*, etc. The link entities shared in the original source are applied to Analys the outer similarity of two entities. Here, the outer similarity leverages the property of *wikiPageWikiLink*, since they are extracted from the Wikipedia in the DBpedia.

4 Experiments

4.1 Setup and Datasets

In the experiments, we exploit KBs including two versions of DBpedia(2016, 2020)[3], the wikidata[4] and the YAGO[5]. Also, we pick up two openly and available

---

[3] texthttps://wiki.dbpedia.org/develop/datasets.
[4] https://query.wikidata.org/.
[5] https://www.mpi-inf.mpg.de/departments/databases-and-information-systems/research/yago-naga/.

query editors (DBpedia[6] and wikidata[7]) to search the triples online. All models and framework are implemented in Java 1.8.0. The experiments are run on a notebook with an Intel i7 CPU @1.80 GHz and 16 GB memory.

A strength of our GILLearn framework is that it relies on very few tuning parameters only. First, The size of initial and further feedback sets is **40**. Second, the maximum rule length (and depth of expansion sets) is **3**. Last, the accuracy threshold to either accept or reject candidate rules is defined as **0.9**. Additional AMIE3 parameters, such as the minimum head coverage (HC min) and the minimum standard confidence (STD min) are both kept at their default value of 0.01 in the rule learning model, AMIE3(openly available). Then we evaluate our model using a filtering similarity function and their harmonic mean measure, as shown in Eq. 2.

4.2   Results and Discussions

In our experiments, the classic rule learning algorithm, i.e., AMIE+, is modified to filter rules automatically through the auxiliary details in the case of DBpedia. Here, the search space is pruned with hierarchical classification. Combining the positive and negative rules, the new logical queries are created to correct the false statements. One negative rule randomly is selected to find negative triples in batches. Then, the similar statistics is to filter special features in positive rules. By the unique attributes, the best match positive rules are adopted to construct the logical queries. Analysing the search space of the negative rule, the positive rule is leveraged to build the logical query for correction. Finally, the new refined query and one example are shown in the below:

The negative rule:

$birthPlace(a, f) \wedge populationPlace(b, f) \rightarrow nationality^-(a, b).$

the positive rule:

$birthPlace(a, d) \wedge rdfType(d, Country) \rightarrow nationality^+(a, d).$

The revised rule($\phi\_Revised$):

$birthPlace(a, f) \wedge populationPlace(b, f) \wedge nationality(a, b) \wedge rdfType(f, Country) \rightarrow nationality^*(a, f).$

The entities in the variable f are regarded as the repairs from the refined query. Generally, the corrected targets of *nationality* have multi-values. So the similarity is applied to filter the top-k repairs as the final corrections. We randomly select the triples based on the relation of *nationality*, we can get over 92% accuracy feedback for the correction. Compared with the correct facts in the wikidata, we acquire the figure of the precision shown in Fig. 2. The more erroneous triples existed and the external knowledge base utilized (wikidata), more time is spent to do the corrections while matching the error triples. Then the correction tail of triple can be caught to replace the old entity. The algorithm is easy and quick in the small sample of KBs. For large KBs, the model provides plenty of rules and errors with special semantics like the example. The single rule offers two associated relations to the targets of triple. Here, the top-k rules are leveraged to refine queries in the KB. Finally, the top-k refined logic rules are regarded

---

[6] https://dbpedia.org/sparql.
[7] https://query.wikidata.org/.

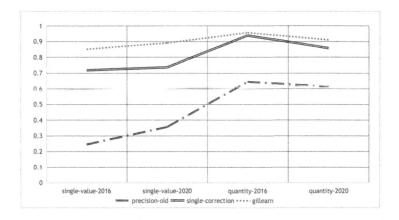

Fig. 2. Precision of type and quantities

as the correction rules. In short, the model exploits the positive rules ϕ_i^+ to correct the false statements. Give one error fact: <Jeroen_Willems, nationality, Dutch_people> and extract features in the ϕ^+: <Jeroen_Willems, birthPlace, Netherlands>, <Netherlands, type, Country> → <Jeroen_Willems, nationality, Netherlands>. Last, the corrected fact is attained: <Jeroen_Willems, nationality, Netherlands>.

In the closed world assumption, two methods are taken to correct the negative statements in the DBpedia with two versions since it's convenient to filter the wrong triples with the TBox property. In Fig. 2, there are obvious improvements in the single-value condition. The GILLearn model and single-value correction have the closed performance in the same KB. Both of two algorithms have near 0.9 precision after refining the whole KB. The results display that the GILLearn model has better significant effects and the proposed logic rules are full of nice explanation.

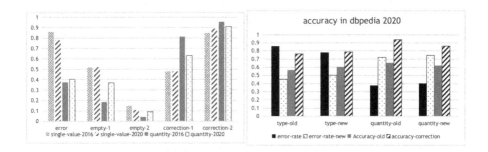

Fig. 3. Error and correction rates in DBpedia

In Fig. 3, we count the empty and correction rates with original error rate in the experiment. Four situations of DBpedia have the correction rate over 80% and there is empty rate below 15% in the GILLearn model. Here, the single-value method consider the whole KB in the closed world assumption. Especially, the GILLearn model also can be practiced in the open world assumption. They receive the correction rates

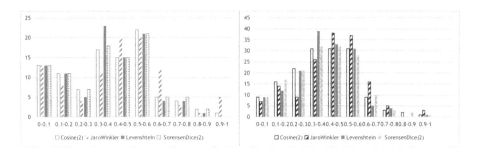

Fig. 4. Similarity harmonic average ratio

based on all entities in the final rules containing nearly over 80% entities in the given relations of DBpedia. Through the final results, the GILLearn algorithm is suitable for the correction of the large KB. In addition, the single-value error correction is proper correct method in the small samples. Also, the accuracy of correction has little effect on the type and quantity of errors.

The results of one random rule correction test are shown in Fig. 4. Here, we only discuss the error targets of triples and ignore their quantity. For each error sample, we calculate the maximum ratio interval of harmonic average similarity for all pairs of repairs and basic objects in the triple. Since all entities exist in real world and have some interconnections, the model only reflects internal associations (literal similarity) and external alliances (extracted source). Here, the system holds the maximum similarity harmonic average ratio to do the selection of correction. And the precision of final correction is centralized on the interval of [0.3, 0.6], since the great majority of error targets have small search space to do the correction. In the expert validation, we deduce that the final correction has the better effect while the selection measure reaches exceeding 0.5. Here, we can correct over 80% errors from the negative rules in the GILLearn model. At the same time, we can detect some semantic details in the negative rules. For instance, the facts with ethnic group have close ties with the nationality. These negative statements give us an new guidance to extend new views in the answer question systems. As mentioned above, the system can serve users with a negative perspective to refine the large KBs.

5   Conclusions

In this paper, the framework aims to correct errors extracted automatically from the Wikipedia. Logical queries are utilized to detect targets of triples existed in the KB to replace the errors in batches. Based on rule learning, repairs of range errors are a significant issue for knowledge base completion. A rule correction and refinement framework was proposed to leverage the rewriting sparql query from semantic KBs. Furthermore, we explored the challenge of learning rules directly from the perspective of interesting negative statements. The ontological knowledge of range constraints is adopted for knowledge cleaning and the learning model is updated to mine logic rules for knowledge base correction. Our empirical results showed that our proposed model is efficient and effective over large knowledge bases. In the future, we will investigate the conflicting feedback and expand the search space with co-occurring similar entities to refine the KBs, such as, the contextual information and schema axioms. Moreover, the inductive correction algorithm will be combined with the markov logic network and graph neural network for knowledge base correction and knowledge base completion.

References

1. Abedini, F., Keyvanpour, M.R., Menhaj, M.B.: Correction tower: a general embedding method of the error recognition for the knowledge graph correction. Int. J. Pattern Recogn. Artif. Intell $34(10)$, 2059034 (2020)
2. Andresel, M., Ortiz, M., Simkus, M.: Query rewriting for ontology-mediated conditional answers. In: Proceedings of the AAAI Conference on Artificial Intelligence, vol. 34, pp. 2734–2741 (2020)
3. Auer, S., Bizer, C., Kobilarov, G., Lehmann, J., Cyganiak, R., Ives, Z.: DBpedia: a nucleus for a web of open data. In: Aberer, K., et al. (eds.) ASWC/ISWC -2007. LNCS, vol. 4825, pp. 722–735. Springer, Heidelberg (2007). https://doi.org/10.1007/978-3-540-76298-0_52
4. Bienvenu, M.: Ontology-mediated query answering: harnessing knowledge to get more from data. In: IJCAI: International Joint Conference on Artificial Intelligence (2016)
5. Bienvenu, M., Hansen, P., Lutz, C., Wolter, F.: First order-rewritability and containment of conjunctive queries in horn description logics. arXiv preprint arXiv:2011.09836 (2020)
6. Chen, J., Chen, X., Horrocks, I., B. Myklebust, E., Jimenez-Ruiz, E.: Correcting knowledge base assertions. In: Proceedings of The Web Conference 2020, pp. 1537–1547 (2020)
7. Chu, X., Ilyas, I.F., Krishnan, S., Wang, J.: Data cleaning: overview and emerging challenges. In: Proceedings of the 2016 International Conference on Management of Data, pp. 2201–2206 (2016)
8. Chu, X., et al.: Katara: reliable data cleaning with knowledge bases and crowdsourcing. Proc. VLDB Endow. $8(12)$, 1952–1955 (2015)
9. Galárraga, L.A., Teflioudi, C., Hose, K., Suchanek, F.: Amie: association rule mining under incomplete evidence in ontological knowledge bases. In: Proceedings of the 22nd International Conference on World Wide Web, pp. 413–422 (2013)
10. Heist, N., Paulheim, H.: Information extraction from co-occurring similar entities. arXiv preprint arXiv:2102.05444 (2021)
11. Islam, A., Inkpen, D.: Semantic text similarity using corpus-based word similarity and string similarity. ACM Trans. Knowl. Disc. Data (TKDD) $2(2)$, 1–25 (2008)
12. Khayyat, Z., et al.: Bigdansing: a system for big data cleansing. In: Proceedings of the 2015 ACM SIGMOD International Conference on Management of Data, pp. 1215–1230 (2015)
13. Lajus, J., Galárraga, L., Suchanek, F.: Fast and exact rule mining with AMIE 3. In: Harth, A., et al. (eds.) ESWC 2020. LNCS, vol. 12123, pp. 36–52. Springer, Cham (2020). https://doi.org/10.1007/978-3-030-49461-2_3
14. Lertvittayakumjorn, P., Kertkeidkachorn, N., Ichise, R.: Correcting range violation errors in dbpedia. In: International Semantic Web Conference (Posters, Demos & Industry Tracks) (2017)

15. Lin, X., Liang, Y., Wang, L., Wang, X., Yang, M.Q., Guan, R.: A knowledge base completion model based on path feature learning. Int. J. Comput. Commun. Control **13**(1), 71–82 (2018)

16. Mahdavi, M., Abedjan, Z.: Baran: effective error correction via a unified context representation and transfer learning. Proc. VLDB Endow. **13**(12), 1948–1961 (2020)

17. Mayfield, C., Neville, J., Prabhakar, S.: Eracer: a database approach for statistical inference and data cleaning. In: Proceedings of the 2010 ACM SIGMOD International Conference on Management of Data, pp. 75–86 (2010)

18. Meilicke, C., Chekol, M.W., Fink, M., Stuckenschmidt, H.: Reinforced anytime bottom up rule learning for knowledge graph completion. arXiv preprint arXiv:2004.04412 (2020)

19. Melo, A., Paulheim, H.: An approach to correction of erroneous links in knowledge graphs. In: CEUR Workshop Proceedings, vol. 2065, pp. 54–57. RWTH (2017)

20. Melo, A., Paulheim, H.: Detection of relation assertion errors in knowledge graphs. In: Proceedings of the Knowledge Capture Conference, pp. 1–8 (2017)

21. Muggleton, S., De Raedt, L.: Inductive logic programming: theory and methods. J. Logic Program. **19**, 629–679 (1994)

22. Nguyen, P.T., Di Rocco, J., Rubei, R., Di Ruscio, D.: An automated approach to assess the similarity of github repositories. Softw. Qual. J **28**, 1–37 (2020)

23. Ortona, S., Meduri, V.V., Papotti, P.: Robust discovery of positive and negative rules in knowledge bases. In: 2018 IEEE 34th International Conference on Data Engineering (ICDE), pp. 1168–1179. IEEE (2018)

24. Paulheim, H.: Identifying wrong links between datasets by multi-dimensional outlier detection. In: WoDOOM, pp. 27–38 (2014)

25. Paulheim, H., Bizer, C.: Improving the quality of linked data using statistical distributions. Int. J. Semant. Web Inf. Syst (IJSWIS) **10**(2), 63–86 (2014)

26. Pellissier Tanon, T., Bourgaux, C., Suchanek, F.: Learning how to correct a knowledge base from the edit history. In: The World Wide Web Conference, pp. 1465–1475 (2019)

27. Picado, J., Davis, J., Termehchy, A., Lee, G.Y.: Learning over dirty data without cleaning. In: Proceedings of the 2020 ACM SIGMOD International Conference on Management of Data, pp. 1301–1316 (2020)

28. Singhal, A.: Introducing the knowledge graph: things, not strings. Official google blog 16 (2012)

29. Speranskaya, M., Schmitt, M., Roth, B.: Ranking vs. classifying: measuring knowledge base completion quality. arXiv preprint arXiv:2102.06145 (2021)

30. Suchanek, F.M., Kasneci, G., Weikum, G.: Yago: a core of semantic knowledge. In: Proceedings of the 16th International Conference on World Wide Web, pp. 697–706 (2007)

31. Vrandečić, D., Krötzsch, M.: Wikidata: a free collaborative knowledgebase. Commun. ACM **57**(10), 78–85 (2014)

32. Weaver, G., Strickland, B., Crane, G.: Quantifying the accuracy of relational statements in wikipedia: a methodology. In: JCDL, vol. 6, pp. 358–358. Citeseer (2006)

33. Wolter, U.: Logics of first-order constraints-a category independent approach. arXiv preprint arXiv:2101.01944 (2021)

34. Wu, Y., Chen, J., Haxhidauti, P., Venugopal, V.E., Theobald, M.: Guided inductive logic programming: cleaning knowledge bases with iterative user feedback. EPiC Ser. Comput. **72**, 92–106 (2020)

35. Yakout, M., Berti-Équille, L., Elmagarmid, A.K.: Don't be scared: use scalable automatic repairing with maximal likelihood and bounded changes. In: Proceedings of the 2013 ACM SIGMOD International Conference on Management of Data, pp. 553–564 (2013)
36. Yan, J.N., Schulte, O., Wang, J., Cheng, R.: Detecting data errors with statistical constraints. arXiv preprint arXiv:1902.09711 (2019)

High-Quality Noise Detection for Knowledge Graph Embedding with Rule-Based Triple Confidence

Yan Hong[1,2], Chenyang Bu[1,2(✉)], and Xindong Wu[1,2,3]

[1] Ministry of Education Key Laboratory of Knowledge Engineering with Big Data,
Hefei University of Technology, Hefei, China
{chenyangbu,xwu}@hfut.edu.cn
[2] School of Computer Science and Information Engineering, Hefei University of Technology,
Hefei, China
[3] Mininglamp Academy of Sciences, Mininglamp Technology, Beijing, China

Abstract. Knowledge representation learning is usually used in knowledge reasoning and other related fields. Its goal is to use low-dimensional vectors to represent the entities and relations in a knowledge graph. In the process of automatic knowledge graph construction, the complexity of unstructured text and the incorrect text may make automatic construction tools unable to accurately obtain the semantic information in the text. This leads to high-quality noise with matched entity types but semantic errors. Currently knowledge representation learning methods assume that the knowledge in knowledge graphs is completely correct, and ignore the noise data generated in the process of automatic construction of knowledge graphs, resulting in errors in the vector representation of entities and relations. In order to reduce the negative impact of noise data on the construction of a representation learning model, in this study, a high-quality noise detection method with rule information is proposed. Based on the semantic association between triples in the same rule, we propose the concept of rule-based triple confidence. The calculation strategy of triple confidence is designed inspired by probabilistic soft logic (PSL). The influence of high-quality noise data in the training process of the model can be weakened by this confidence. Experiments show the effectiveness of the proposed method in dealing with high-quality noise.

Keywords: Knowledge representation · Knowledge graph · Noise detection

1 Introduction

In recent years, in the background of big data and big knowledge [1], knowledge graph [2] is widely used to describe concepts in the world. In the knowledge graph, in order to transform knowledge into a structured knowledge system, knowledge is generally stored in the form of triple as (head entity, relation, tail entity), where nodes represent entities and the line segments between nodes represent relations. Freebase [3], DBpedia [4], YAGO [5] and other large-scale general knowledge graph have been widely used in

© Springer Nature Switzerland AG 2021
D. N. Pham et al. (Eds.): PRICAI 2021, LNAI 13031, pp. 572–585, 2021.
https://doi.org/10.1007/978-3-030-89188-6_43

question answering system [6, 7], entity disambiguation [8], entity alignment [9], entity linking [10], and other fields.

There are several problems in symbolic representation of the knowledge graph such as difficulty in operation, hard to calculate, sparse data distribution and so on. In order to solve these disadvantages, a new research direction, Knowledge Representation Learning (KRL) [11], has been proposed and rapidly attracted widespread attention. The main idea of knowledge representation learning is to project entities and relations into low-dimensional vector space through model training. Knowledge representation learning can effectively circumvent the disadvantages of symbolic computation.

At present, the construction of knowledge graph by manual annotation is no longer suitable for the updating and increasing speed of knowledge graph, so a large number of automatic construction technologies of knowledge graph have emerged. However, in the process of automatic construction of knowledge graph, some noise and conflict triples are usually introduced due to inaccurate data in real corpus and complex language logic in unstructured text data. For example, (LiBai, IsmarriedTo, DuFu) is a high-quality noise of entity type matching but semantic error. Most traditional knowledge representation learning methods assume that the knowledge in the existing knowledge graph is completely correct, ignoring a large number of noises in real life [12]. Therefore, how to find possible errors from the knowledge graph with noise or conflict has become an urgent problem.

The work in this paper focuses on detecting high-quality noise in the knowledge graph, considering the approximate relationship between rule-constrained triples to assist noise detection. A novel concept of rule-based triple confidence is proposed, which is applied to the representation learning model based on translation method. RCKRL (Rule Confidence-Aware KRL Framework) method for high quality noise detection based on Rule information is proposed. Through the RCKRL model, the confidence of the high-quality noise triple is reduced, the influence of noise data on the model training process is weakened, and the quality of model embedding representation is improved.

The main contributions of this paper are threefold: (1) Combining the representation learning method with the symbolic method, a novel concept of rule-based triple confidence is proposed; (2) The rule-based triple confidence is used to improve the triple confidence function of CKRL model and enhance the noise detection ability of knowledge graph representation.; (3) RCKRL can effectively reduce the influence of high-quality noise in the process of model training, and has achieved a relatively significant effect in the experimental part.

The rest of this paper is organized as follows: Sect. 2 describes the background, including the concepts of KG embedding and KG noise detection. Section 3 introduces the preliminary. Section 4 presents the framework of our method and the proposed algorithms. Experimental results and analysis are presented in Sect. 5, followed by the final section summarizes our main conclusion and future work.

2 Background

In this section, we discuss the background including knowledge graph (KG) embedding and knowledge graph noise detection.

KG Embedding. Knowledge graphs is usually represented by symbol, but the symbol representation has several problems, such as difficult to operate, hard to calculate, and sparse data distribution. To tackle these issues, knowledge representation learning has been proposed and widely applied in many areas of KGs. KG embedding is mainly to embed entities and relations in knowledge graph in vector space. At present, the models can be divided into three categories: models based on translation [13, 14], models based on tensor decomposition [15] and models based on neural network [16].

KG Noise Detection. Noise detection of knowledge graph is to detect and eliminate the noise generated in the process of knowledge graph construction. From the perspective of research, there are mainly two kinds of noise detection methods of knowledge graph. (1) Symbol-based approach. According to whether external knowledge is used, symbol-based noise detection methods can be divided into internal noise detection methods and external noise detection methods [17]. The internal approach [18] is designed to use the known information in a given knowledge graph to determine the wrong entity types, relationships, and so on. External methods [19] employ additional corpora or human knowledge to assist in judging noise or conflicts. (2) The method based on embedding [20–22]. In this method, the reliability of a triple is judged according to the distance between vectors. The concept of triple confidence is introduced to enhance the model training quality.

3 Preliminary

Probabilistic soft logic (PSL) is a framework for collective probabilistic reasoning in the relational domain [23]. It can use simple logic syntax to define the model, and perform operations through fast convex optimization. PSL has a wide range of applications in many fields such as natural language processing, social network analysis, knowledge graphs, recommendation systems, and computational biology. PSL uses the soft truth value between [0, 1] as the calculated value.

Each rule has an associated non-negative weight, and the relative importance of the rule can be captured by the weight, which is the confidence of the rule. The confidence can also be regarded as a soft truth value between [0, 1]. In order to determine the degree of satisfying the basic rules, PSL uses Lukasiewiczt paradigm and its corresponding co-paradigm as the relaxation of logical AND and OR. These relaxations are accurate in certain situations and can provide consistent logical mapping. In the application field of knowledge graph, given the triplet T_n, the truth value calculation formulas of logical conjunction ($\wedge$), disjunction ($\vee$) and negation ($\neg$) are defined as follows:

$$d(T_1 \wedge T_2) = \max\{0, f(T_1) + f(T_2) - 1\} \tag{1}$$

$$d(T_1 \vee T_2) = \min\{f(T_1) + f(T_2), 1\} \quad (2)$$

$$d(\neg T_1) = 1 - d(T_1) \quad (3)$$

The rules are represented by symbols and the length of the rule body is variable. If we want to use the rule to obtain the rule confidence of the triple, we need mathematically express the whole rule body. Using the PSL method, combined with the calculation of the triple scoring function, the overall score of the rule body can be obtained. For example, as shown in Fig. 1. Given a rule, the score of each part of the triple is calculated by the translation model. Using formula (1), the overall score of the rule body can be calculated as: $d(r_{body}) = max\{0, 1.9 - 1\} = 0.9$

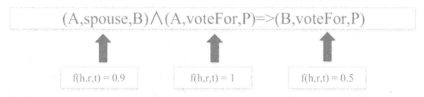

(A,spouse,B)$\wedge$(A,voteFor,P)=>(B,voteFor,P)

f(h,r,t) = 0.9   f(h,r,t) = 1   f(h,r,t) = 0.5

Fig. 1. Rules and their component triples score

4 Method

In this section, the motivation is introduced in Sect. 4.1 and an overview of our proposed model is presented in Sect. 4.2. Next, we introduce our method in detail in Sects. 4.3 and Sects. 4.4.

4.1 Motivation

High-quality Noise Problem In KGs. In our previous works [24, 25], the task of low-quality noise detection was considered to filter triples with the wrong entity type. For example, (Libai, IsmarriedTo, Shandong) is a low-quality noise, because the tail entity is expected to be a person, but not a province. However, "high-quality noise" with the same entity type but semantic misunderstanding should also be considered, which is more difficult to detect. For example, the noise triple (Nanjing, IscapitalOf, China) is extracted by a famous tool, where the correct triple should be (Beijing, IscapitalOf, China). Because "Nanjing" and "Beijing" share the same entity type, this kind of error is regarded as high-quality noise. The example of two noise types are shown in Fig. 2.

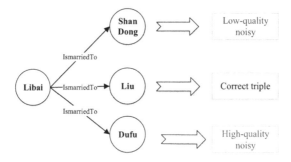

Fig. 2. The example of two noise types

Rules Contain Semantic Information. The rules contain rich semantic information, and the triples linked by the rules are highly correlated. Therefore, through making full use of semantic associations between triples contained in rules, high-quality noise errors can be found. Using the semantic connection between the triples connected by rules, if the head of the rule is error, then the rule tail is regarded as a possible noise. Adjust the embedding representation of entities and relations in the triples through this connection is necessary. For example, the rule "isMarriedTo$(x, y) \Rightarrow$ isMarriedTo(y, x) confidence $=$ 0.97" obtained by extracting rules from the YAGO37 dataset through the AMIE + tool. High-quality noisy triple (Kobe Bean Bryant, isMarriedTo, Tracy McGrady) is existed in the knowledge graph. After rule grounding, we can obtain the triple (Tracy McGrady, isMarriedTo, Kobe Bean Bryant). After dynamically adjusting the confidence of triples in the CKRL model, it can be seen that the confidence of (Kobe Bean Bryant, isMarriedTo, Tracy McGrady) is low, which represent this is possibly an error triple. So the other triple (Tracy McGrady, isMarriedTo, Kobe Bean Bryant) which connected by the rules, its confidence should be lower as well. Therefore, using the approximate relationship between the rule-constrained triples can more effectively reduce the confidence of the wrong triples, finally reduce the influence of noisy data on the model training process.

4.2 Overall Architecture

In this section, we first explain the assumption of the approximate relationship between the triples based on rule constraints, and use this assumption to initialize the rule confidence of the triples, the method described in Sect. 4.3. Then based on rule confidence, a high-quality noise detection method based on rule information is introduced. High-quality noise detection method is fully described in Sect. 4.4. From these two steps, our method RCKRL can effectively reduce the negative impact of high-quality noise on the training process of the representation learning model. In order to make our approach more intuitive, the details of the proposed model are summarized in Algorithm 1 below.

Algorithm 1. High-quality noise detection based on rules

Input: entity and relation vector after TransE pre-training, set of triples with high-quality noise $S = \{(h,r,t)\}$

1: $LT(h,r,t)=1$←Initialize the confidence of local triples

2: Initialize the confidence of the triple by using the approximate relation of the rule constraint $RC(h,r,t)$

3: **loop**

4:    $S_{batch} \in S$←Select mini batch of triples

5:    **for** $(h,r,t) \in S_{batch}$ do

6:       Generate high-quality negative sample sets

         $N_{batch} \leftarrow N_{batch} \cup \{(h,r,t),(h',r,t')\} \cup \{(h,r,t),(h,r',t)\}$

7:    **end for**

8:    Update vector representations of entities and relationships by formula (8)

9:    Update the rule-based confidence of the triple by formula (5)

10:   Update $C(h,r,t)$ by formula (7)

11: **end loop**

Output: Model with high-quality noise detection capability

4.3 Approximate Relations of Rule Constraints

The approximate relationship between rule-constrained triples means that a certain rule contains multiple sets of triples, the triples in the rule body and the triples in the rule header have similar semantics. For example, there is a rule "?b was born in ?a = > ?a nationality ?b". The rule contains two relations "place of birth" and "nationality". This rule states that a person born in a certain country is more likely to have nationality of the country. Each such relationship pair $\left(r_{body}, r_{head}\right)$ is associated with a weight ϕ, this weight is the confidence of the rule. The higher weight of the rule, the higher credibility of the rule. Therefore, the rule can be expressed as "$r_{body} => r_{head}\phi$". There is an assumption that if a rule is correct, then the rule header score should be higher or equal to the score of rule body. According to the above assumptions, the approximate implication relationship between r_{head} and r_{body} in the rule can be expressed as follow:

$$f(h, r_{head}, t) \geq \phi \cdot f\left(h, r_{body}, t\right) \tag{4}$$

Where $f(h,r,t)$ represents the score of each part of the triple in the rule, and ϕ is the confidence level of the rule. Using the approximate relationship guided by the rule, it can be known that if the rule body is a noise triple, there is a high probability that the rule head will become a noise triple. Therefore, the concept of rule-based triple confidence $RC(h,r,t)$ is proposed, which is defined as follow:

$$RC(h, r, t) = \left[\phi \cdot f(RBODY) - f(RHEAD)\right]_{+} \tag{5}$$

Since the vector representation of entities and relations changes dynamically during the training process, the scores of the triples also can be changed. Because the rule-based triple confidence uses the score of the translation model, the confidence will also change with the model training process. This change can better capture the status of entities and relationships in the current knowledge graph. When the rule length is 2, $f(RBODY)$ is the score of the triple in the rule body, and the rule-based confidence of the triple in the rule body can be initialized or updated directly. When the rule length is longer than 2, the rule body contains several triples, so the score cannot be calculated directly by the score function. In order to solve the calculation problem, the PSL method in Sect. 3 is used to transform the symbolic representation of the rule body into a mathematical representation. Then the confidence of each triple in the rule body can be updated with the process of the model training. The overall calculation method of the rule body is as follow:

$$f(RBODY) = f(T_1 \wedge T_2) = max\{0, f(h_1, r_1, t_1) + f(h_2, r_2, t_2) - 1\} \qquad (6)$$

After extracting the data through AMIE + [26], the rule "?b /film/film/written_by ?a $=>$?a /film/writer/film ?b 0.93" is obtained. This rule indicates that if B movie is written by A, the probability that A wrote B is 0.93. After rule grounding process through the training set, the rule body (Harry Potter, written_by, Jacob) and the rule header (Jacob, writer, Harry Potter) are obtained respectively. These two triples are both high-quality noise triple. According to the global path confidence of the CKRL model, the score of the rule body triple is low. According to the approximate relationship between the rule-constrained triples, the rule-based confidence score of the head triple should also be low. By introducing negative sample triples, the distance in the vector space between entities and relations in the noise triples is increased, thereby reducing the influence of noise data in model training process.

4.4   High-Quality Noise Detection

According to the assumption of the translation model, the vector in the same triple must satisfy $h + r\text{-}t = 0$ after training. Since the automatic construction of the knowledge graph introduces a large number of high-quality noise, it cannot be guaranteed that all triples can satifity the assumptions after training. According to translation assumptions, entities with similar semantics will form clusters in adjacent positions in the vector space. Due to the close distance between entities with similar semantics, high-quality noise is difficult to distinguish in the calculation process, which greatly affects the link prediction between entities and relations. Noisy or conflicting triples should have lower confidence. Use rule-guided approximation to punish triples that violate translation rules, reduce the impact of high-quality noise in the model training process.

It should be noted that the CKRL [20] model uses local and global structures and designs local triple confidence and global triple confidence respectively. In our study, referring to the NCKRL model, only the confidence of the local triple is considered. Combined with the method proposed in this paper, the overall triple confidence is updated to a combination of two confidences as shown below:

$$C(h, r, t) = \lambda_1 \cdot LT(h, r, t) + \lambda_2 \cdot RC(h, r, t) \qquad (7)$$

Among them, $\lambda 1$, $\lambda 2$ are hyperparameters, $LT(h, r, t)$ is the global path confidence of the triple, and $RC(h, r, t)$ is the rule confidence of the triple proposed in Sect. 4.3.

On the basis of the NCKRL model, the rule-guided triple confidence is added, and the confidence is used to assist model training. The objective function is defined as L:

$$L = \sum_{(h,r,t)\in S} \sum_{(h',r',t')\in S'} \left[\gamma + f(h, r, t) - f\left(h', r', t'\right) \right]_+ \cdot C(h, r, t) \qquad (8)$$

$f(h, r, t)$ is the score of the triple, $C(h, r, t)$ guides the model to pay more attention to the more convincing facts. S' represents the generated negative sample set expressed as:

$$S' = \left\{\left(h', r, t\right)|h' \in E\right\} \cup \left\{\left(h, r, t'\right)|t' \in E\right\} \cup \left\{\left(h, r', t\right)|r' \in R\right\}$$

5 Experiments

In this section, our method is evaluated in the link prediction task and noise detection task. If we could obtain a more accurate representation of entities and relations, this meant that a relatively higher quality of the learned model, which further shows that the model had capable of filtering noise and conflicts in KGs. We first introduce the datasets and experimental settings, then show the experimental results and corresponding discussions.

5.1 Datasets

The dataset FB15K used in this section is a standard knowledge graph dataset. However, the data in FB15K is completely correct, without considering the noise or conflicting data in real life. Xie et al. [20] based on the FB15K dataset, by simulating the high-quality noise generated by the automatic construction of knowledge graphs in real life, selecting the head entity or tail entity of the same entity type to replace the triples in the correct dataset. Through this method three datasets FB15K-1, FB15K-2 and FB15K-4 with different noise ratios (10%, 20% and 40%) are generated. The detailed data of the FB15K original dataset is shown in Table 1. The data information of different noise ratios is shown in Table 2.

Table 1. Statistics of FB15K

Dataset	#rel	#ent	#train	#valid	#test
FB15K	1,345	14,951	483,142	50,000	59,071

The AMIE + was adopted to extract logical rules for specific knowledge graph. Considering the validity of the rules, the length of the extracted rules should not exceed 2 and the PCA (partial completeness assumption) confidence should not be less than 0.8. Under the above restrictions, 628 rules are extracted, and some examples of rules are shown in Table 3.

Table 2. Different ratios of negatives on FB15K

Dataset	FB15K-1	FB15K-2	FB15K-4
*neg triples	46,408	93,782	187,925

Table 3. Rules extracted from FB15K

Rule	PCA
/location/people born here(x, y)⇒/people/place of birth(y, x)	1.00
/director/film(x, y)⇒/film/directed by(y, x)	0.99
/film/directed by(x, y)∧/person/language(y, z)⇒/film/language(x, z)	0.88

The grounding of the rule is to replace the variables in the rule with the specific triples in the training set. For example, there is a rule ∀x, y: /location/people born here(x, y) ⇒ /people/place of birth(y, x). After replacing the variables in the rules with the triples in the FB15K training set, the instantiated rules can be obtained as follow: (Emmanuel-Macron, /location/people born here, France) ⇒ (EmmanuelMacron, /people/place of birth, France). Through the above method, the three datasets with different noise ratios were instantiated, 207,379, 312,416, and 450292 pieces of grounding data were obtained.

5.2 Experiment Setup

Three state-of-the-art algorithms were used for comparison: TransE [13], CKRL(LT) [20], and NCKRL [22]. In this paper, only the confidence of local triple(LT) in the CKRL model is considered by referring to the NCKRL model. The proposed algorithm is called RCKRL. In addition, in order to consider the influence of the rule length on the model, experiments were performed on the length of 2, the length of 3, and the combination of the two lengths, denoted as RCKRL-2, RCKRL-3 and RCKRL.

In order to make a fair comparison, the parameter settings of the proposed algorithms are given as follows: the number of negative samples NG = 20, learning rate is 0.001 and $\gamma = 1.0$. The overall score function adopts the L1 paradigm, dimension d is 50. The experiment uses the "bern" strategy when generating negative samples. This strategy is defined during model training, replacing the head entity or tail entity with different probabilities to generate negative samples. Two hyperparameters that affect the proportion of the confidence of the two rules are $\lambda_1 = 1.5$, $\lambda_2 = 0.4$.

5.3 Link Prediction Task

Link Prediction is one of the important methods of knowledge graph completion, which aims to predict the missing edges in the knowledge graph. In this task, given two known elements, predict the missing entity or relation in the triple.

By convention, MR, MRR and Hits@10 were selected as our metrics, where MR is the average ranking of correct answers, MRR represents the average value of the reciprocal ranks of the results and Hits@10 represents the proportion of correct alignments in the first ten results. The larger the value of MRR and HIT@10, the better the model effect, and the smaller the value of MR, the results can be better. Follow NCKRL, we both consider raw and filter cases. The results of the entity prediction with different datasets are shown in Table 4.

Under the evaluation indicators of MRR and Hits@10, the RCKRL results are better than the other three comparison models. Under the MR evaluation, the value is lower than the CKRL model, however the result is better than the improved NCKRL model and the classic TransE model. Therefore, the result indicating that the algorithm in this paper can reduce the impact of high-quality noise data on the training process. At the same time, it can be seen from the experimental results that RCKRL has achieved good results in the case of different rule lengths. The model that combines two type rules is more accurate than the model that combines a single length rule, which further illustrates the ability of the semantic connection implied by the rules in noise detection. The rule length of 2 is better than the rule length of 3 in most cases, indicating that the smaller the rule length, the higher the credibility.

In addition to entity prediction, this paper also performed relation prediction on three datasets with different noise ratios. The experimental results are shown in Table 5. It can be seen from this table that although the algorithm results are poor under the MR index, the RCKRL algorithm has achieved better experimental results than NCKRL on Hits@1. When predicting relationships, the method in this chapter performs poorly in predicting the average ranking of all relationships, but the probability that the correct relationship ranks first is very high, indicating that RCKRL has the ability to accurately predict the position of the correct relationship, which further confirms the performance of our model.

5.4 Noise Detection Task

In order to verify the ability to detect noise and conflicts in the knowledge graph, a high-quality noise detection task of the knowledge graph is proposed. This task can intuitively express the model noise detection ability. The purpose of this task is to detect potential noise in the knowledge graph based on the scores of the triples. This experiment uses the TransE score function to calculate the score of the triple. The triple is ranked according to the score, and the triple with a higher score can be considered as noises. By matching the ranking of the triples with the high-quality noise dataset, the number of noises can be obtained. According to this method, the accuracy of the proposed method in noise detection can be verified.

By convention, Precision was selected as our metrics, where Precision is the ratio of the detected high-quality noise to the overall noise data is calculated. We conducted high-quality noise detection verification on the 20% and 40% noise ratio datasets, and the experimental results are shown in Table 6.

Table 4. Entity prediction on FB15K with different ratios of noise

FB15K-N1	MR		MRR		Hits@10 (%)	
	Raw	Filter	Raw	Filter	Raw	Filter
TransE	249	155	0.122	0.234	45.2	59.9
CKRL(LT)	**230**	**133**	0.136	0.278	45.9	62.5
NCKRL	278	178	0.138	0.334	47.9	68.3
RCKRL-2	256	155	0.25	0.49	49.9	71.4
RCKRL-3	283	181	0.25	0.48	48.6	69.7
RCKRL	258	157	**0.26**	**0.49**	**50.3**	**71.6**
FB15K-N2	MR		MRR		Hits@10 (%)	
	Raw	Filter	Raw	Filter	Raw	Filter
TransE	251	157	0.114	0.209	43.3	56.6
CKRL(LT)	**236**	**140**	0.128	0.255	44.7	60.4
NCKRL	287	188	0.133	0.305	46.8	65.9
RCKRL-2	267	165	0.25	0.45	48.1	68
RCKRL-3	287	184	0.24	0.47	47.5	67.8
RCKRL	271	170	**0.25**	**0.45**	**48.2**	**68.2**
FB15K-N3	MR		MRR		Hits@10 (%)	
	Raw	Filter	Raw	Filter	Raw	Filter
TransE	268	175	0.099	0.176	40.4	51.9
CKRL(LT)	**246**	**150**	0.119	0.232	43.1	57.4
NCKRL	304	206	0.127	0.281	45.6	63.1
RCKRL-2	288	183	0.23	0.42	46.0	64.6
RCKRL-3	312	205	**0.24**	0.42	46.1	**66.1**
RCKRL	290	185	**0.24**	**0.45**	**46.2**	64.5

From the results, it can be found that the algorithm proposed in this section performs better under the Precision evaluation, and RCKRL can detect a higher proportion of high-quality noise. The experimental results are better than the other two comparison models, so RCKRL not only improves the prediction effect of the representation learning model, but also better detect the high-quality noise in the knowledge graph, which further illustrates the noise detection ability of the improved model in this section.

Table 5. Relation prediction on FB15K with different ratios of noise

FB15K-N1	MR		Hits@1 (%)	
	Raw	Filter	Raw	Filter
NCKRL	**6.9182**	**6.5504**	62.76	79.72
RCKRL	6.7244	6.3598	**63.13**	**80.48**
FB15K-N2	MR		Hits@1 (%)	
	Raw	Filter	Raw	Filter
NCKRL	**6.9141**	**6.5520**	62.14	78.92
RCKRL	7.3495	6.9904	**62.72**	**79.83**
FB15K-N3	MR		Hits@1 (%)	
	Raw	Filter	Raw	Filter
NCKRL	**6.9107**	**6.5434**	61.87	78.80
RCKRL	7.8115	7.4545	**62.97**	**79.76**

Table 6. High-quality noise detection results on FB15K

	TransE		NCKRL		RCKRL	
Noisy rate	20	40	20	40	20	40
Precision	46.3%	43%	47.6%	44.6%	**49.9%**	**45.1%**

6 Conclusion and Future Work

In this study, we designed a RCKRL model for high-quality noise detection using semantic information contained in rules. By reducing the confidence of the noise triples during the training process, and quantifying the correctness of semantics and the truth of the facts, we can effectively improve the embedding quality of noise knowledge graphs. The experimental results demonstrated that our model achieved good performance in most cases. In the future, we will study how to introduce additional information, such as ontology and entity descriptions, into noise detection in knowledge graphs, so as to design a more effective noise detection strategy.

Acknowledgments. This work was partly supported by the National Natural Science Foundation of China (No. 61806065 and No. 91746209), the Fundamental Research Funds for the Central Universities (No. JZ2020HGQA0186), and the Project funded by the China Postdoctoral Science Foundation (No. 2018M630704).

References

1. Wu, X., Chen, H., Wu, G., Liu, J., Zheng, Q., He, X., et al.: Knowledge engineering with big data. IEEE Intell. Syst. **30**(5), 46–55 (2015)

2. Dong, X., Gabrilovich, E., Heitz, G., Horn, W., Lao, N., et al.: Knowledge vault: a web-scale approach to probabilistic knowledge fusion. In: Proceedings of the 20th ACM SIGKDD International Conference on Knowledge Discovery and Data Mining, pp. 601–610 (2014)
3. Bollacker, K., Evans, C., Paritosh, P., Sturge, T., Taylor, J.: Freebase: a collaboratively created graph database for structuring human knowledge. In: Proceedings of the 2008 ACM SIGMOD International Conference on Management of Data, pp. 1247–1250 (2008)
4. Lehmann, J., Isele, R., Jakob, M., et al.: DBpedia – a large-scale, multilingual knowledge base extracted from wikipedia. Semantic Web **6**(2), 167–195 (2015)
5. Suchanek, F.M., Kasneci, G., Weikum, G.: Yago: a core of semantic knowledge. In: Proceedings of the 16th international conference on World Wide Web, pp. 697–706 (2007)
6. Bordes, A., Weston, J., Usunier, N.: Open question answering with weakly supervised embedding models. In: Calders, T., Esposito, F., Hüllermeier, E., Meo, R. (eds.) ECML PKDD 2014. LNCS (LNAI), vol. 8724, pp. 165–180. Springer, Heidelberg (2014). https://doi.org/10.1007/978-3-662-44848-9_11
7. Saxena, A., Tripathi, A., Talukdar, P.: Improving multi-hop question answering over knowledge graphs using knowledge base embeddings. In: Proceedings of the 58th Annual Meeting of the Association for Computational Linguistics, pp. 4498–4507 (2020)
8. Zheng, Z., Si, X., Li, F., Chang, E. Y., Zhu, X.: Entity disambiguation with freebase. In: IEEE/WIC/ACM International Conferences on Web Intelligence and Intelligent Agent Technology, pp. 82–89 (2012)
9. Jiang, T., Bu, C., Zhu, Y., Wu, X.: Two-stage entity alignment: combining hybrid knowledge graph embedding with similarity-based relation alignment. In: The 16th Pacific Rim International Conference on Artificial Intelligence, pp. 162–175 (2019)
10. Li, J., Bu, C., Li, P., Wu, X.: A coarse-to-fine collective entity linking method for heterogeneous information networks. Knowl.-Based Syst. **288**(2), 107286 (2021)
11. Wang, Q., Mao, Z., Wang, B., Guo, L.: Knowledge graph embedding: a survey of approaches and applications. IEEE Trans. Knowl. Data Eng. **29**(12), 2724–2743 (2017)
12. Pujara, J., Augustine, E., Getoor, L.: Sparsity and noise: where knowledge graph embeddings fall short. In: Proceedings of the 2017 Conference on Empirical Methods in Natural Language Processing, pp. 1751–1756 (2017)
13. Bordes, A., Usunier, N., Garcia-Duran, A., Weston, J., Yakhnenko, O.: Translating embeddings for modeling multi-relational data. In: Advances in Neural Information Processing Systems, pp. 2787–2795 (2013)
14. Zhang, Z., Cai, J., Zhang, Y., Wang, J: Learning hierarchy-aware knowledge graph embeddings for link prediction. In: Proceedings of the AAAI Conference on Artificial Intelligence, pp. 3065–3072 (2020)
15. Lin, Y., Liu, Z., Sun, M., Liu, Y., Zhu, X.: Learning entity and relation embeddings for knowledge graph completion. In: Proceedings of the 29th AAAI Conference on Artificial Intelligence, pp. 2181–2187 (2015)
16. Xie, R., Liu, Z., Jia, J., Luan, H., Sun, M: Representation learning of knowledge graphs with entity descriptions. 30th AAAI Conf. Artif. Intell. **30**(1) (2016)
17. Paulheim, H.: Knowledge graph refinement: a survey of approaches and evaluation methods. Semantic Web **8**(3), 489–508 (2017)
18. Melo, A., Paulheim, H.: Detection of relation assertion errors in knowledge graphs. In: Proceedings of the Knowledge Capture Conference, pp. 22:1–22:8 (2017)
19. De Meo, P., Ferrara, E., Fiumara, G., Ricciardello, A.: A novel measure of edge centrality in social networks. Knowl.-Based Syst. **30**, 136–150 (2012)
20. Xie, R., Liu, Z., Lin, F., Lin, L.: Does William Shakespeare really write Hamlet? Knowledge representation learning with confidence. In: Proceedings of the 32nd AAAI Conference on Artificial Intelligence, pp. 4954–4961 (2018)

21. Jia, S., Xiang, Y., Chen, X., Wang, K.: Triple trustworthiness measurement for knowledge graph. In: The World Wide Web Conference, pp. 2865–2871 (2019)
22. Shan, Y., Bu, C., Liu, X., Ji, S., Li, L.: Confidence-aware negative sampling method for noisy knowledge graph embedding. In: 2018 IEEE International Conference on Big Knowledge, pp. 33–40 (2018)
23. Kimmig, A., Bach, S., Broecheler, M., Huang, B., Getoor, L.: A short introduction to probabilistic soft logic. In: NIPS Workshop on PPFA, pp.1–4 (2012)
24. Hong, Y., Bu, C., Jiang, T.: Rule-enhanced noisy knowledge graph embedding via low-quality error detection. In: IEEE International Conference on Knowledge Graph, pp. 544–551 (2020)
25. Bu, C., Yu, X, Hong, Y., Jiang, T.: Low-quality error detection for noisy knowledge graph. J. Database Manage. **32**(4), article 4
26. Galárraga, L., Teflioudi, C., Hose, K., Suchanek, F.M.: Fast rule mining in ontological knowledge bases with AMIE. VLDB J. **24**(6), 707–730 (2015)

Multi-agent Epistemic Planning with Inconsistent Beliefs, Trust and Lies

Francesco Fabiano[1]([✉]) [iD], Alessandro Burigana[2] [iD], Agostino Dovier[1] [iD],
Enrico Pontelli[3] [iD], and Tran Cao Son[3] [iD]

[1] University of Udine, Udine, Italy
{francesco.fabiano,agostino.dovier}@uniud.it
[2] Free University of Bozen-Bolzano, Bolzano, Italy
burigana@inf.unibz.it
[3] New Mexico State University, Las Cruces, NM, USA
{epontell,tson}@cs.nmsu.edu

Abstract. Developing autonomous agents that can reason about the perspective of their (human or artificial) peers is paramount to realistically model a variety of real-world domains. Being aware of the state of mind of others is a key aspect in different fields—*e.g., legal reasoning, business negotiations, ethical AI* and *explainable AI*. In particular, in the area of *Multi-Agent Epistemic Planning (MEP)*, agents must reach their goals by taking into account the *knowledge* and *beliefs* of other agents. Although the literature offers an ample spectrum of approaches for planning in this scenario, they often come with limitations. This paper expands previous formalization of MEP to enable representing and reasoning in presence of *inconsistent beliefs* of agents, *trust* relations and *lies*. The paper explores the syntax and semantics of the extended MEP framework, along with an implementation of the framework in the solver *Epistemic Forward Planner (EFP)*. The paper reports formal properties about the newly introduced epistemic states update that have been also empirically tested via an actual implementation of the solver.

Keywords: Epistemic planning · Multi-agent · Belief update · Knowledge representation

1 Introduction

The branch of AI interested in studying and modeling technologies in which agents reason about the activities required to achieve a desired goal is referred to as *automated planning*. In particular, *multi-agent planning* [1,6–9,18] provides a powerful tool to model and manage scenarios which include multiple agents that interact with each other. To maximize the potentials of such autonomous systems each agent should be able to reason on both *i)* her perspective of the "physical"

Partially supported by Indam GNCS grants, by Uniud PRID ENCASE and by NSF grants 1914635 and 1833630.

world; and *ii)* her beliefs of other agents' perspective of the environment—that is, their viewpoints of the "physical" world and of other agents' beliefs. In the literature, the planning problem in this setting is referred to as *multi-agent epistemic planning*. Existing epistemic action languages [3,4,9,19] are able to model several families of problems, but cannot comprehensively reason on aspects like trust, dishonesty, deception, and incomplete knowledge.

In this paper, we expand the language $m\mathcal{A}^{\rho}$ [9] with the concept of agents' *attitudes*. Our idea of attitudes stems from the concept of *dynamic attitudes* that *"represent the agent's assessment of the reliability of the source"* introduced by Rodenhäuser [20]. We define basic attitudes that capture how an agent reacts when another agent is informing her about something. In the real world, in fact, it is often the case that we associate an idea of reliability to an information source. This work captures this idea by having agents behave according to the following attitudes: *doubtful, impassive, trustful, mistrustful* or *stubborn* (the detailed description is given in Sect. 3). Specifically, we present, to the best of our knowledge, the first transition function that is able to update an *epistemic state—i.e.*, the knowledge/belief-graph of the agents—when considering: *i) inconsistent beliefs, i.e.*, discrepancies between the beliefs currently held by an agent and some new information that she acquires; *ii) trust* relations between agents; and *iii)* the possibility for an agent to *lie*.

2   Background

In this section, we introduce the core elements of *Multi-agent Epistemic Planning (MEP)* following the notation proposed by Baral *et al.* [3]. Let $\mathcal{AG} = \{1, 2, \ldots, n\}$ be a set of agents and $\mathcal{F}$ be a finite set of propositional atoms, called *fluents*. Fluents describe the properties of the world in which the agents operate; a *possible world* is represented by a subset of $\mathcal{F}$ (*i.e.*, those fluents that are *true* in that world). Agents often have incomplete knowledge/beliefs, thus requiring them to deal with a set of possible worlds. The incompleteness of information applies also to the agent's knowledge/beliefs about other agents' knowledge/beliefs. Agents can perform actions drawn from a finite set of possible actions $\mathcal{A}$. In MEP, each action can be performed by a set of agents $\alpha \subseteq \mathcal{AG}$. The effects of an action can either directly modify the state of the world (*ontic* action) or the knowledge or beliefs of some agents (*epistemic* action). Nevertheless, both action types can affect the agents' knowledge or beliefs.

To formally define concepts related to information change we make use of *Dynamic Epistemic Logic (DEL)* [21]. The language of well-formed DEL formulae with *common belief* $\mathcal{L}^{C}(\mathcal{F}, \mathcal{AG})$ is defined as follows:

$$\varphi ::= \mathtt{f} \mid \neg\varphi \mid \varphi \wedge \varphi \mid \mathbf{B}_{\mathtt{i}}\varphi \mid \mathbf{C}_{\alpha}\varphi,$$

where $\mathtt{f} \in \mathcal{F}$, $\mathtt{i} \in \mathcal{AG}$ and $\emptyset \neq \alpha \subseteq \mathcal{AG}$. A *fluent formula* is a DEL formula with no occurrences of modal operators. $\mathbf{B}$ captures the concept of $\mathbf{B}$*elief* and we read the formula $\mathbf{B}_{\mathtt{i}}\varphi$ as "i believes that φ." $\mathbf{C}_{\alpha}$ captures the $\mathbf{C}$*ommon belief* of the set of agents α.

DEL formulae semantics is traditionally expressed using *pointed Kripke structures* [16]. Instead, in this paper we make use of an alternative semantics based on the concept of *Possibilities* adopted by Fabiano *et al.* [9].

Definition 1 (Possibility [13]).
– *A possibility* $\mathtt{u}$ *is a function that assigns to each fluent* $\mathtt{f} \in \mathcal{F}$ *a truth value* $\mathtt{u}(\mathtt{f}) \in \{0, 1\}$ *and to each agent* $\mathtt{i} \in \mathcal{AG}$ *an information state* $\mathtt{u}(\mathtt{i}) = \sigma$*;*
– *An information state* σ *is a set of possibilities.*

We denote the set of *literals* that are "true" in a possibility $\mathtt{u}$ with $\mathtt{u}(\mathcal{F}) = \{\mathtt{f} \mid \mathtt{f} \in \mathcal{F} \wedge \mathtt{u}(\mathtt{f}) = 1\} \cup \{\neg\mathtt{f} \mid \mathtt{f} \in \mathcal{F} \wedge \mathtt{u}(\mathtt{f}) = 0\}$. Possibilities capture the concept of *epistemic state* (*e-state*) that consists of two components: *i)* information about the possible worlds (the interpretation of the fluents $\mathtt{u}(\mathcal{F})$); and *ii)* information about the agents' beliefs (represented by the set of possibilities $\mathtt{u}(\mathtt{i})$). The possible world that represents the real state of affairs is called *pointed possibility*. Due to space constraints, we refer the interested reader to [10,13] for the notion of entailment for possibilities and further details on this topic.

We now recall the concept of *domain*. An MEP domain contains the information needed to describe a planning problem in a multi-agent epistemic setting.

Definition 2 (MEP Domain). *A multi-agent epistemic planning domain is a tuple* $\mathcal{D} = \langle \mathcal{F}, \mathcal{AG}, \mathcal{A}, \varphi_{ini}, \varphi_{goal} \rangle$*, where* $\mathcal{F}$*,* $\mathcal{AG}$*,* $\mathcal{A}$ *are the sets of fluents, agents, actions of* $\mathcal{D}$*, respectively;* φ_{ini} *and* φ_{goal} *are DEL formulae that must be entailed by the* initial *and* goal *e-state, respectively. The former e-state describes the domain's initial configuration while the latter encodes the desired one.*

We refer to the elements of a domain $\mathcal{D}$ with the parenthesis operator; *e.g.*, the fluent set of $\mathcal{D}$ is denoted by $\mathcal{D}(\mathcal{F})$. An *action instance* $\mathtt{a}\langle\alpha\rangle \in \mathcal{D}(\mathcal{AI}) = \mathcal{D}(\mathcal{A}) \times 2^{\mathcal{D}(\mathcal{AG})}$ identifies the execution of action $\mathtt{a}$ by a set of agents α. Multiple executors are needed in sensing actions (introduced in detail in the next sections), since we consider as executors all the *attentive* agents. On the other hand, announcement actions only require one executor ($|\alpha| = 1$), *i.e.*, the *announcer*. Let $\mathcal{D}(\mathcal{S})$ be the set of all possible e-states of the domain. The *transition function* $\varPhi : \mathcal{D}(\mathcal{AI}) \times \mathcal{D}(\mathcal{S}) \rightarrow \mathcal{D}(\mathcal{S}) \cup \{\emptyset\}$ formalizes the semantics of action instances (the result is the empty set if the action instance is not executable).

Since we are interested in capturing the *beliefs* of agents (as opposed to their knowledge), we consider possibilities that satisfy the well-know axiom system $\mathbf{KD45}_n$ (see Chapter 3 of [11] for more details), where n denotes the presence of multiple agents. When an e-state is consistent with such axioms, we call it a $\mathbf{KD45}_n$-state.

The Action Language $m\mathcal{A}^\rho$**.** Our work builds on the action language $m\mathcal{A}^\rho$ [9], which has been used in the solver *Epistemic Forward Planner* (EFP) proposed by Fabiano *et al.* [9]. The language allows three different types of action: *i)* *ontic* actions, used to change the properties of the world (*i.e.*, the truth value of fluents); *ii) sensing* actions, used by a group of agents to refine their beliefs, and *iii) announcement* actions, performed by an agent to affect the beliefs of others.

The action language also captures agents' *observability relations* on action instances. Namely, an agent may be *fully observant* (aware of both the execution of the action instance and its effects), *partially observant* (aware of the action execution but not of the outcome), or *oblivious* (ignorant about the execution of the action) w.r.t. a given action instance.

Following previous approaches [9,17], actions' effects are assumed to be deterministic. Therefore, we assume the presence of a unique fluent literal that describes the effects of an epistemic action to further avoid non-determinism. In fact, the transition function of epistemic actions presented in this paper considers the negation of the effects that, if defined as conjunction, would generate a disjunctive form (*i.e.*, non-deterministic effects).

3   Inconsistent Beliefs and Attitudes

In real-world situations, it is often the case that we learn a fact that discords with our previous beliefs. When such a discrepancy arises we talk about *inconsistent belief*. Since we consider $\mathbf{KD45}_n$-states, inconsistencies are relative only to the beliefs of an agent (and not to the actual world). Let us assume that agent i believes that $\neg\varphi$ is the case in the e-state u (*i.e.*, $\mathbf{u} \models \mathbf{B_i}\neg\varphi$); in $m\mathcal{A}^\rho$ there are two main sources of inconsistencies: *i)* i observes the real world—performing a *sensing* action—and learns φ (the opposite of what she believed); *ii)* i learns φ as a result of an *announcement* performed by another agent j.

In both scenarios, we must account for the belief of i after the action. In particular, the resulting e-state u' must be consistent with axiom *D*. In the former case *i)*, we resolve the inconsistency by having i believe φ; *i.e.*, we make sure that $\mathbf{u}' \models \mathbf{B_i}\varphi$. This is a reasonable solution, as we assume that agents trust their senses when observing the world. In the latter *ii)*, we must take into account the *attitude* of the agent w.r.t. the announcer j. As in [20], *"we are not only interested in the acceptance of new information (based on trust), but also in its rejection (based on distrust)"*. For instance, the listener may be skeptical or credulous, and thus she would change her belief according to her attitude.

Let us notice that inconsistent belief is different from *false belief*. An agent has a false belief about a property φ if she believes φ to be true, but such property does not hold in the actual world. False beliefs are already allowed in $m\mathcal{A}^\rho$ as a result of the presence of oblivious agents in action instances.

Going back to the attitudes of agents, the notion of *trust* naturally arises. It is reasonable to have the listener i believe the announcer j if i trusts j. In this work, we consider three attitudes for fully observant agents that listen to an announcement: *trustful, mistrustful,* and *stubborn*. *Trustful* agents believe what the announcer tells them; *mistrustful* agents believe the opposite of what is announced; and *stubborn* agents do not modify their beliefs. Considering the case of *semi-private* announcements, we need to introduce the concept of attitude for partially observant agents as well. Specifically, we consider *impassive* and *doubtful* agents. *Impassive* agents keep their current beliefs, while *doubtful* agents do not believe neither what is being announced nor the opposite, regardless of their previous beliefs. Note that *stubborn* and *impassive* agents are different, as the former are aware of what is being announced—*i.e.*, the truth value of the property φ. Let us note that such attitudes are named to capture our personal idea of the behaviour they represent and they are not meant to wholly describe the nuances of complex social attitudes such as, for example, stubbornness.

When communicating with their peers, agents might announce something that is *false* relative to their own point of view. We call *lies* such announcements. Similar to the notion of inconsistent belief, the truthfulness of announcements depends on the point of view of the announcer i—*i.e.*, , i truthfully announces φ iff $\mathbf{u} \models \mathbf{B_i}\varphi$.

4   Enriched Semantics

In this section, we provide a formalization of the transition function of $m\mathcal{A}^\rho$ that captures the aspects that we previously discussed. When clear from the context, we use a to indicate the action instance $\mathsf{a}\langle\alpha\rangle$, with $\alpha \subseteq \mathcal{D}(\mathcal{AG})$.

Definition 3 (Frame of reference [3]). *The* frame of reference *of an action instance* $\mathsf{a}\langle\alpha\rangle$ *is a partition* $\rho_{\mathsf{a}\langle\alpha\rangle} = \langle \boldsymbol{F_a}, \boldsymbol{P_a}, \boldsymbol{O_a}\rangle$ *of the set* $\mathcal{D}(\mathcal{AG})$*, denoting the* **F***ully observant,* **P***artially observant and* **O***blivious agents of* $\mathsf{a}\langle\alpha\rangle$*, respectively.*

The concept of attitude is strictly related to announcements. Therefore, in what follows, $\mathsf{a}\langle\alpha\rangle$ is assumed to be an announcement action. We recall that announcement action instances are assumed to have a single executor ($|\alpha| = 1$), that we call the *announcer*. In this case, we make use of the short notation $\mathsf{a}\langle\mathsf{j}\rangle$ in place of $\mathsf{a}\langle\{\mathsf{j}\}\rangle$.

Definition 4 (Attitude). *The* attitude *of an agent determines how she updates her beliefs when new information is announced. Attitudes induce a refined partition of the frame of reference* $\rho_{\mathsf{a}\langle\mathsf{j}\rangle} = \langle \boldsymbol{F_a}, \boldsymbol{P_a}, \boldsymbol{O_a}\rangle$ *as follows:*

- $\boldsymbol{F_a} = \{\mathsf{j}\} \cup \boldsymbol{T_a} \cup \boldsymbol{M_a} \cup \boldsymbol{S_a}$*: fully observant agents may be the executor, Trustful, Mistrustful, or Stubborn;*
- $\boldsymbol{P_a} = \boldsymbol{I_a} \cup \boldsymbol{D_a}$*: partially observant agents may be Impassive or Doubtful.*

Attitudes are specified with $m\mathcal{A}^\rho$ statements of the form "**has_attitude i wrt j att if** φ" (where **att** is one of the attitudes of Definition 4) and they define the *trust relations* among agents. Such a statement asserts that i bears the attitude **att** towards j if the condition φ is met. We assume that the attitudes of the agents are publicly visible, *except for the attitude that the announcer has w.r.t. herself.* That is, the announcer knows whether she is being truthful, lying or announcing something that she is unaware of, while other agents do not. Instead, trustful and stubborn agents believe that the announcer is truthful (*i.e.*, they believe that the executor believes the announced property), whereas mistrustful agents believe the announcer to be lying (*i.e.*, they believe that the announcer believes the negation of such property). Finally, we assume that the announcer does not modify her own beliefs about the property being announced.

Definition 5 (MEP domain with attitudes). *A* MEP domain with attitudes *is a tuple* $\mathcal{D} = \langle \mathcal{F}, \mathcal{AG}, \mathcal{A}, \mathcal{T}, \varphi_{ini}, \varphi_{goal} \rangle$, *where the additional element* $\mathcal{T}$ *contains the attitudes relations of agents:*

$$\mathcal{T} = \{(\texttt{i}, \texttt{j}, \texttt{att}, \varphi) \mid [\textbf{has\_attitude i wrt j att if } \varphi]\}.$$

4.1   Transition Function

In the remainder of this section we define the $m\mathcal{A}^\rho$ transition function Φ. Let $\mathcal{D} = \langle \mathcal{F}, \mathcal{AG}, \mathcal{A}, \mathcal{T}, \varphi_{ini}, \varphi_{goal} \rangle$ be an MEP domain with attitudes, $\texttt{j} \in \mathcal{D}(\mathcal{AG})$, $\texttt{u} \in \mathcal{D}(\mathcal{S})$ and $\texttt{a} \in \mathcal{D}(\mathcal{AI})$. The frame of reference $\rho_\texttt{a}$ and the attitudes of the agents are determined by confronting the elements of the attitudes relation $\mathcal{T}$ with the possibility $\texttt{u}$. If $\texttt{a}$ is not executable in $\texttt{u}$, then $\Phi(\texttt{a}, \texttt{u}) = \emptyset$. Otherwise, we distinguish between ontic and epistemic actions.

Ontic Actions. Since ontic actions are not affected by the introduction of inconsistent beliefs, nor attitudes, the previous formalisation described by Fabiano *et al.* [9] is maintained, and it is omitted due to space constraints.

Epistemic Actions. Sensing and announcement actions modify the beliefs of agents. Since agents might acquire information that discords with previous beliefs, we must resolve the discrepancies. In the case of sensing actions, we consider all fully observant agents as executors. Since each agent trusts her senses, we have $\mathbf{F}_\texttt{a} = \mathbf{T}_\texttt{a}$. Similarly, we assume partially observant agents to keep their beliefs about the physical features of the world unchanged, *i.e.*, $\mathbf{P}_\texttt{a} = \mathbf{I}_\texttt{a}$. Hence, the refined frame of reference of sensing actions is $\rho_{\texttt{a}\langle \mathbf{T}_\texttt{a}\rangle} = \langle \mathbf{T}_\texttt{a}, \mathbf{I}_\texttt{a}, \mathbf{O}_\texttt{a}\rangle$.

In the case of announcement actions, it is necessary to state both the executor $\texttt{j} \in \mathcal{D}(\mathcal{AG})$ and the attitudes in order to resolve inconsistent beliefs. Therefore, the frame of reference of announcement actions is $\rho_{\texttt{a}\langle \texttt{j}\rangle} = \langle (\{\texttt{j}\}, \mathbf{T}_\texttt{a}, \mathbf{M}_\texttt{a}, \mathbf{S}_\texttt{a}), (\mathbf{I}_\texttt{a}, \mathbf{D}_\texttt{a}), \mathbf{O}_\texttt{a}\rangle$. During the computation of the update, the attitude of the announcer $\texttt{j}$ is set to match the perspective of the agent being currently handled by the transition function.

Let ℓ be the (unique) fluent literal such that $[\texttt{a } \textbf{senses/announces } \ell] \in \mathcal{D}$. With a slight abuse of notation, we define the *value* of ℓ in a possibility $\texttt{w}$ as $val(\texttt{a}, \texttt{w}) = \texttt{w}(\ell)$. The *effect* $e(\texttt{a})$ of action $\texttt{a}$ is equal to 1 if ℓ is a positive fluent literal ($e(\texttt{a}) = 0$, otherwise). We use the following simplifications: given a possibility $\texttt{p}$, *i)* $\texttt{p}'$ denotes the updated version of $\texttt{p}$; and *ii)* if not stated otherwise, we consider $\texttt{p}'(\mathcal{F}) = \texttt{p}(\mathcal{F})$. For clarity, we briefly describe each component of the transition function after its definition.

Definition 6 (Transition Function for Epistemic Actions). *Let* $\texttt{i}$ *be an agent (i.e.,* $\texttt{i} \in \mathcal{D}(\mathcal{AG})$*). Applying an epistemic action instance* $\texttt{a}$ *on the pointed possibility* $\texttt{u}$ *results in the updated pointed possibility* $\Phi(\texttt{a}, \texttt{u}) = \texttt{u}'$ *such that:*

$$u'(i) = \begin{cases} u(i) & \text{if } i \in \textbf{O}_a \\ P(a,u) & \text{if } i \in \textbf{P}_a \\ F(a,u,1) & \text{if } i \in \textbf{T}_a \\ F(a,u,0) & \text{if } i \in \textbf{M}_a \\ S(a,u,e(a),1) & \text{if } i \in \textbf{S}_a \\ S(a,u,e(a),0) & \text{if } i = j \end{cases}$$

where P, F, S are defined below.

Description: Φ modifies the beliefs of each agent on the announced fluent w.r.t. to her attitude. Each sub-function (P, F, S) updates the beliefs that the agents have of others' perspectives.

We first define the helper functions χ and $\bar{\chi}$. Let $w'_x = \chi(a, w, x)$ and $\bar{w}'_x = \bar{\chi}(a, w, \bar{x})$ with: i) w'_x and $\bar{w}'_x$ represent the possibility w updated with χ and $\bar{\chi}$, respectively; ii) x and $\bar{x}$ represent opposite boolean values s.t. $x = \neg\bar{x}$; and iii) let b be 1 and 0 when executing χ and $\bar{\chi}$, respectively. Then w'_x and $\bar{w}'_x$ are defined as follows:

$$w'_x(\ell) = \begin{cases} x & \text{if } \ell = f \\ u(\ell) & \text{otherwise} \end{cases} \qquad \bar{w}'_x(\ell) = \begin{cases} \bar{x} & \text{if } \ell = f \\ u(\ell) & \text{otherwise} \end{cases}$$

$$\left. \begin{array}{c} w'_x(i) \\ \\ \bar{w}'_x(i) \end{array} \right\} = \begin{cases} w(i) & \text{if } i \in \textbf{O}_a \\ P(a,w) & \text{if } i \in \textbf{P}_a \\ \bigcup_{v \in w(i)} \chi(a,v,x) & \text{if } i \in \textbf{T}_a \vee (i = j \wedge b = 1) \\ \bigcup_{v \in w(i)} \bar{\chi}(a,v,\bar{x}) & \text{if } i \in \textbf{M}_a \vee (i = j \wedge b = 0) \\ S(a,w,x,1) & \text{if } i \in \textbf{S}_a \end{cases}$$

Description: Functions χ and $\bar{\chi}$ recursively update the nested beliefs by specifying the correct value of x to guarantee that the higher-order beliefs are in line with the agents' point of view. These functions make us of two boolean variables: i) x to encode the truth value of ℓ believed by i; and ii) b: a flag that keeps track of whether i is trustful $(b = 1)$ or mistrustful $(b = 0)$ w.r.t. the announcer.

1) Let $w'_p = P(a, w)$. Then:

$$w'_p(i) = \begin{cases} w(i) & \text{if } i \in \textbf{O}_a \\ \bigcup_{v \in w(i)} P(a,v) & \text{if } i \in \textbf{I}_a \\ \bigcup_{v \in w(i)} \chi(a,v,0) \cup \chi(a,v,1) & \text{if } i \in \textbf{D}_a \\ \bigcup_{v \in w(i)} \chi(a,v,val(a,v)) & \text{if } i \in \textbf{T}_a \cup \textbf{M}_a \cup \{j\} \\ \bigcup_{v \in w(i)} S(a,v,val(a,v),1) & \text{if } i \in \textbf{S}_a \end{cases}$$

Description: *Function* P *updates the beliefs of partially observant agents. It updates their "direct beliefs" (i.e., that represent their point of view) on ℓ and the nested beliefs of fully observant agents (by calling χ with* $x = val(a, w)$). *This guarantees that agents in* P_a *believe that (mis)trustful agents are aware of the action's effect. For doubtful agents* χ *is executed with* $x = 0$ *and* $x = 1$, *forcing them to be ignorant about* ℓ.

2) *Let* $w'_f = F(a, w, b)$. *Then:*

$$
w'_f(i) = \begin{cases}
w(i) & \text{if } i \in O_a \\
P(a, w) & \text{if } i \in P_a \\
\displaystyle\bigcup_{v \in w(i)} \chi(a, v, e(a)) & \text{if } i \in T_a \vee (i = j \wedge b = 1) \\
\displaystyle\bigcup_{v \in w(i)} \bar{\chi}(a, v, \neg e(a)) & \text{if } i \in M_a \vee (i = j \wedge b = 0) \\
\displaystyle\bigcup_{v \in w(i)} S(a, v, e(a), 1) & \text{if } i \in S_a
\end{cases}
$$

Description: *Function* F *updates the point of views on* ℓ *of trustful and mistrustful agents, calling* χ *and* $\bar{\chi}$, *respectively. Moreover,* F *deals with the beliefs of other agents w.r.t. to (mis)trustful agents. The flag* b *keeps track of whether* F *is executed from the perspective of a trustful* ($b = 1$) *or a mistrustful* ($b = 0$) *agent allowing to update* i*'s perspective on the beliefs of the announcer.*

3) *Let* $w'_s = S(a, w, x, s)$. *Then:*

$$
w'_s(i) = \begin{cases}
w(i) & \text{if } i \in O_a \\
P(a, w) & \text{if } i \in P_a \\
\displaystyle\bigcup_{v \in w(i)} \chi(a, v, x) & \text{if } i \in T_a \vee (i = j \wedge s = 1) \\
\displaystyle\bigcup_{v \in w(i)} \bar{\chi}(a, v, \neg x) & \text{if } i \in M_a \\
\displaystyle\bigcup_{v \in w(i)} S(a, v, x, s) & \text{if } i \in S_a \vee (i = j \wedge s = 0)
\end{cases}
$$

Description: *Function* S *keeps the "direct" beliefs of the executor and stubborn agents unchanged and it updates their perspective on other agents' beliefs. Here, we make use of two boolean variables: i)* x *is defined as in* $\chi/\bar{\chi}$; *ii)* s *is used to identify whether the function has been called by a* s*tubborn agent* ($s = 1$) *or if it is updating the "direct" beliefs of the executor* ($s = 0$).

Let a be an announcement action (a sensing action can be thought of as a special case of an announcement). The point of view of oblivious agents remains untouched. Since a is an epistemic action, the fluents of the pointed world u' are unchanged w.r.t. its previous version u. On the other hand, trustful agents' points of view are changed to fit the announced property ℓ; mistrustful agents believe the opposite of what is announced; stubborn and impassive agents do not change their belief on ℓ. The perspective of doubtful agents is built by including also the opposite point of view w.r.t. ℓ. Higher-order beliefs are also correctly updated as stated in Proposition 1. Finally, the announcer considers herself stubborn, since the announcement does not intact her beliefs, while other agents derive the attitude of the announcer depending on their own. As mentioned before, trustful and stubborn agents consider the announcer to be truthful, while mistrustful agents consider the announcer to be lying. Notice that the announcer is aware of the other agents' perspective on her attitude.

Examples of actions' executions are presented in the *Supplementary Documentation* (available at http://clp.dimi.uniud.it/sw/) due to space constraints.

Desired Properties. Following Baral *et al.* [3] and Fabiano *et al.* [9], we list some properties concerning the effects of actions and attitudes in $m\mathcal{A}^\rho$. Complete proofs are available in the *Supplementary Documentation*.

Proposition 1 (Epistemic Actions Properties). *Let* $\mathsf{a}\langle\mathsf{j}\rangle$ *be an epistemic action instance such that* j **announces** ℓ *(where* ℓ *is either* f *or* $\neg\mathsf{f}$*). Let* u *be an e-state and let* u' *be its updated version, i.e.,* $\Phi(\mathsf{a},\mathsf{u}) = \mathsf{u}'$*, then it holds that:*

1. $\mathsf{u}' \models \mathbf{C}_{\boldsymbol{F}_\mathsf{a}}(\mathbf{C}_{\boldsymbol{T}_\mathsf{a}}(\ell \wedge \mathbf{B}_\mathsf{j}\ell))$ – **F**ully observant*s think that* **T**rustful*s believe that the announced property holds and that the announcer believes such property;*
2. $\mathsf{u}' \models \mathbf{C}_{\boldsymbol{F}_\mathsf{a}}(\mathbf{C}_{\boldsymbol{M}_\mathsf{a}}(\neg\ell \wedge \mathbf{B}_\mathsf{j}\neg\ell))$ – **F**ully observant*s think that* **M**istrustful*s believe that the announced property does not hold and that the announcer does not believe such property;*
3. $\forall \mathsf{i} \in (\boldsymbol{S}_\mathsf{a} \cup \{\mathsf{j}\})$, $\mathsf{u}' \models \varphi$ *if* $\mathsf{u} \models \varphi$ *with* $\varphi \in \{\mathbf{B}_\mathsf{i}\ell;\ \mathbf{B}_\mathsf{i}\neg\ell;\ (\neg\mathbf{B}_\mathsf{i}\ell \wedge \neg\mathbf{B}_\mathsf{i}\neg\ell)\}$ – **S**tubborn*s and the announcer do not modify their beliefs about the property;*
4. $\forall \mathsf{i} \in \boldsymbol{F}_\mathsf{a}$, $\mathsf{u}' \models \mathbf{C}_{\boldsymbol{P}_\mathsf{a}}(\mathbf{B}_\mathsf{i}\ell \vee \mathbf{B}_\mathsf{i}\neg\ell)$ – **P**artially observant*s believe that* **F**ully observant*s (including the announcer) are certain on the value of the property;*
5. $\forall \mathsf{i} \in \boldsymbol{D}_\mathsf{a}$, $\mathsf{u}' \models \mathbf{C}_{(\boldsymbol{F}_\mathsf{a} \cup \boldsymbol{P}_\mathsf{a})}(\neg\mathbf{B}_\mathsf{i}\ell \wedge \neg\mathbf{B}_\mathsf{i}\neg\ell)$ – *Non-***O**blivious *believe that* **D**oubtful*s are uncertain on the truth value of the announced property;*
6. *for every pair of agents* $\mathsf{i} \in \mathcal{D}(\mathcal{AG}), \mathsf{o} \in \boldsymbol{O}_\mathsf{a}$, *and a belief formula* φ, $\mathsf{u}' \models \mathbf{B}_\mathsf{i}(\mathbf{B}_\mathsf{o}\varphi)$ *if* $\mathsf{u} \models \mathbf{B}_\mathsf{i}(\mathbf{B}_\mathsf{o}\varphi)$ – *Every agent (even* **O**blivious*) believe that* **O**blivious *do not change their beliefs.*

5   Related Work

The enriched semantics of $m\mathcal{A}^\rho$ has been implemented in the C++ solver EFP (available upon request) that is now able to tackle families of problems that consider complex aspects such as doxastic reasoning, lying agents, faulty perception etc. Examples of execution can be found in the *Supplementary Documentation*.

To the best of our knowledge, in the literature only one other solver, RP-MEP [19], is able to tackle such domains. The solver firstly encodes an MEP problem into a classical planning problem and then handles the solving phase with a "classical" planner. The key difference between EFP and RP-MEP is that while RP-MEP grounds the agents' beliefs and reasons on them as if they were "static facts", EFP builds and interprets e-states, and it updates them using a full-fledged epistemic transition function. For this reason, the latter constitutes a more comprehensive framework. In fact, given the effects of an action instance (a single literal/conjunction of literals), the transition function of $m\mathcal{A}^\rho$ propagates the effects and updates the nested beliefs of agents automatically. Conversely, RP-MEP needs the *propagated* effects to be explicit.

Other theoretical approaches explore the idea of trust between agents [5,15,20]. For example, following [5], Herzig *et al.* [15] devised a logic to capture *"truster's belief about certain relevant properties of the trustee with respect to a given goal"*. While this logic elegantly captures the ideas of Castelfranchi and Falcone [5] it does not actively use the notion of trust to modify the outcome of an action's execution w.r.t. an agent's perspective, that is what we are trying to accomplish with our idea of attitudes. Conversely, Rodenhäuser [20] proposes a theoretical framework where agents make use of the reliability of the source (using the so-called *dynamic attitudes*) to correctly update their beliefs. While our idea of attitudes stems from such work, we only introduced attitudes that are intuitively derived from real-world scenarios without considering more complex ones. In the future we plan to expand our formalization and the planner with the attitudes presented in [20] along with the idea of *"plausibility"*.

Belief revision [2] in presence of inconsistent/false beliefs has been explored by Baral *et al.* [3] and Herzig *et al.* [14]. These works focus on the introduction of a theoretical framework for resolving inconsistencies. Baral *et al.* [3] mainly focuses on *false beliefs*, and while their solution correctly accounts for false beliefs, it is not sufficient to resolve inconsistent beliefs. On the other hand, Herzig *et al.* [14] propose a multi-agent extension of AGM-style belief revision [12]. While revising the agents' beliefs could be a viable solution we believe that having to decouple the belief revision from the e-state update for each action execution would generate an excessive overhead in the solving process.

6   Conclusions

This paper presented a novel MEP framework supporting inconsistent beliefs, trust relations and lies, in the presence of ontic, sensing and announcement actions with different degrees of observability. The framework, based on the logic $\mathcal{L}^C(\mathcal{F}, \mathcal{AG})$, is capable of reasoning in the presence of higher-order beliefs without limitations and thanks to attitudes, the updated transition function can handle inconsistent beliefs. E-states are updated in an homogeneous fashion that solely depends on agents' attitudes. This generates a flexible framework that can be expanded by simply defining attitudes that represents novel ideas.

Attitudes represent a first step towards building complex behavior of agents in an epistemic/doxastic setting. As future works, we plan to characterize more sophisticated attitudes. Moreover, we want to investigate attitudes and trust relations that can be affected by actions. We also plan to analyse *private* trust relations—*e.g.*, allow each agent to have her own belief about the attitudes of others.

References

1. Allen, M., Zilberstein, S.: Complexity of decentralized control: Special cases. In: 23rd Annual Conference on Neural Information Processing Systems 2009, 7–10 December, Vancouver, British Columbia, Canada, pp. 19–27. Curran Associates, Inc. (2009), https://proceedings.neurips.cc/paper/2009/hash/fec8d47d412bcbeece3d9128ae855a7a-Abstract.html
2. Baltag, A., Smets, S.: A qualitative theory of dynamic interactive belief revision. Logic Found. Game Decis. Theor. (LOFT 7) **3**, 9–58 (2008)
3. Baral, C., Gelfond, G., Pontelli, E., Son, T.C.: An action language for multi-agent domains: Foundations. CoRR abs/1511.01960 (2015). arXiv:1511.01960
4. Bolander, T., Andersen, M.B.: Epistemic planning for single-and multi-agent systems. J. Appl. Non-Class. Logics **21**(1), 9–34 (2011). https://doi.org/10.1016/0010-0277(83)90004-5
5. Castelfranchi, C., Falcone, R.: Principles of trust for mas: cognitive anatomy, social importance, and quantification. In: Proceedings International Conference on Multi Agent Systems (Cat. No. 98EX160), pp. 72–79. IEEE (1998)
6. De Weerdt, M., Clement, B.: Introduction to planning in multiagent systems. Multiagent Grid Syst. **5**(4), 345–355 (2009). https://doi.org/10.3233/MGS-2009-0133
7. Dovier, A., Formisano, A., Pontelli, E.: Autonomous agents coordination: action languages meet CLP() and Linda. Theor. Pract. Logic Program. **13**(2), 149–173 (2013). https://doi.org/10.1016/S0004-3702(00)00031-X
8. Durfee, E.H.: Distributed problem solving and planning. In: Luck, M., Mařík, V., Štěpánková, O., Trappl, R. (eds.) ACAI 2001. LNCS (LNAI), vol. 2086, pp. 118–149. Springer, Heidelberg (2001). https://doi.org/10.1007/3-540-47745-4_6
9. Fabiano, F., Burigana, A., Dovier, A., Pontelli, E.: EFP 2.0: a multi-agent epistemic solver with multiple e-state representations. In: Proceedings of the Thirtieth International Conference on Automated Planning and Scheduling, Nancy, France, 26–30 October 2020, pp. 101–109. AAAI Press (2020). https://aaai.org/ojs/index.php/ICAPS/article/view/6650
10. Fabiano, F., Riouak, I., Dovier, A., Pontelli, E.: Non-well-founded set based multi-agent epistemic action language. In: Proceedings of the 34th Italian Conference on Computational Logic, Trieste, Italy, 19–21 June 2019. CEUR Workshop Proceedings, vol. 2396, pp. 242–259. CEUR-WS.org (2019). http://ceur-ws.org/Vol-2396/paper38.pdf
11. Fagin, R., Halpern, J.Y.: Reasoning about knowledge and probability. J. ACM (JACM) **41**(2), 340–367 (1994). https://doi.org/10.1145/174652.174658
12. Gärdenfors, P., Makinson, D.: Revisions of knowledge systems using epistemic entrenchment. In: Vardi, M.Y. (ed.) Proceedings of the 2nd Conference on Theoretical Aspects of Reasoning about Knowledge, Pacific Grove, CA, USA, March 1988, pp. 83–95. Morgan Kaufmann (1988)
13. Gerbrandy, J., Groeneveld, W.: Reasoning about information change. J. Logic Lang. Inf. **6**(2), 147–169 (1997). https://doi.org/10.1023/A:1008222603071
14. Herzig, A., Lang, J., Marquis, P.: Action progression and revision in multiagent belief structures. In: Sixth Workshop on Nonmonotonic Reasoning, Action, and Change (NRAC 2005), Citeseer (2005)
15. Herzig, A., Lorini, E., Hübner, J.F., Vercouter, L.: A logic of trust and reputation. Logic J. IGPL **18**(1), 214–244 (2010)
16. Kripke, S.A.: Semantical analysis of modal logic i normal modal propositional calculi. Math. Logic Q. **9**(5–6), 67–96 (1963). https://doi.org/10.1002/malq.19630090502

17. Le, T., Fabiano, F., Son, T.C., Pontelli, E.: EFP and PG-EFP: epistemic forward search planners in multi-agent domains. In: Proceedings of the Twenty-Eighth International Conference on Automated Planning and Scheduling, pp. 161–170. AAAI Press, Delft, The Netherlands (24–29 June 2018). https://aaai.org/ocs/index.php/ICAPS/ICAPS18/paper/view/17733

18. Lipovetzky, N., Geffner, H.: Best-first width search: exploration and exploitation in classical planning. In: Proceedings of the Thirty-First AAAI Conference on Artificial Intelligence, pp. 3590–3596, San Francisco, California, USA (4–9 February 2017). http://aaai.org/ocs/index.php/AAAI/AAAI17/paper/view/14862

19. Muise, C.J., et al.: Planning over multi-agent epistemic states: a classical planning approach. In: Proceedings of the Twenty-Ninth AAAI Conference on Artificial Intelligence, 25–30 January 2015, Austin, Texas, USA, pp. 3327–3334. AAAI Press (2015). http://www.aaai.org/ocs/index.php/AAAI/AAAI15/paper/view/9974

20. Rodenhäuser, L.B., et al.: A matter of trust: Dynamic attitudes in epistemic logic. Universiteit van Amsterdam [Host] (2014)

21. Van Ditmarsch, H., van Der Hoek, W., Kooi, B.: Dynamic Epistemic Logic, vol. 337. Springer, Netherlands (2007). https://doi.org/10.1007/978-1-4020-5839-4

Correction to: Federated Learning for Non-IID Data: From Theory to Algorithm

Bojian Wei⬤, Jian Li⬤, Yong Liu⬤, and Weiping Wang⬤

Correction to:
Chapter "Federated Learning for Non-IID Data: From Theory to Algorithm" in: D. N. Pham et al. (Eds.): *PRICAI 2021: Trends in Artificial Intelligence*, **LNAI 13031, https://doi.org/10.1007/978-3-030-89188-6_3**

In the originally published version of chapter 3 the second affiliation of the author Bojian Wei was incorrect. The second affiliation of the author Bojian Wei has been corrected as "School of Cyber Security, University of Chinese Academy of Sciences, Beijing, China".

The updated version of this chapter can be found at
https://doi.org/10.1007/978-3-030-89188-6_3

D. N. Pham et al. (Eds.): PRICAI 2021, LNAI 13031, p. C1, 2022.
https://doi.org/10.1007/978-3-030-89188-6_45

Author Index

Printed in the United States
by Baker & Taylor Publisher Services